HISTORY OF BRITISH AVIATION
1908—1914

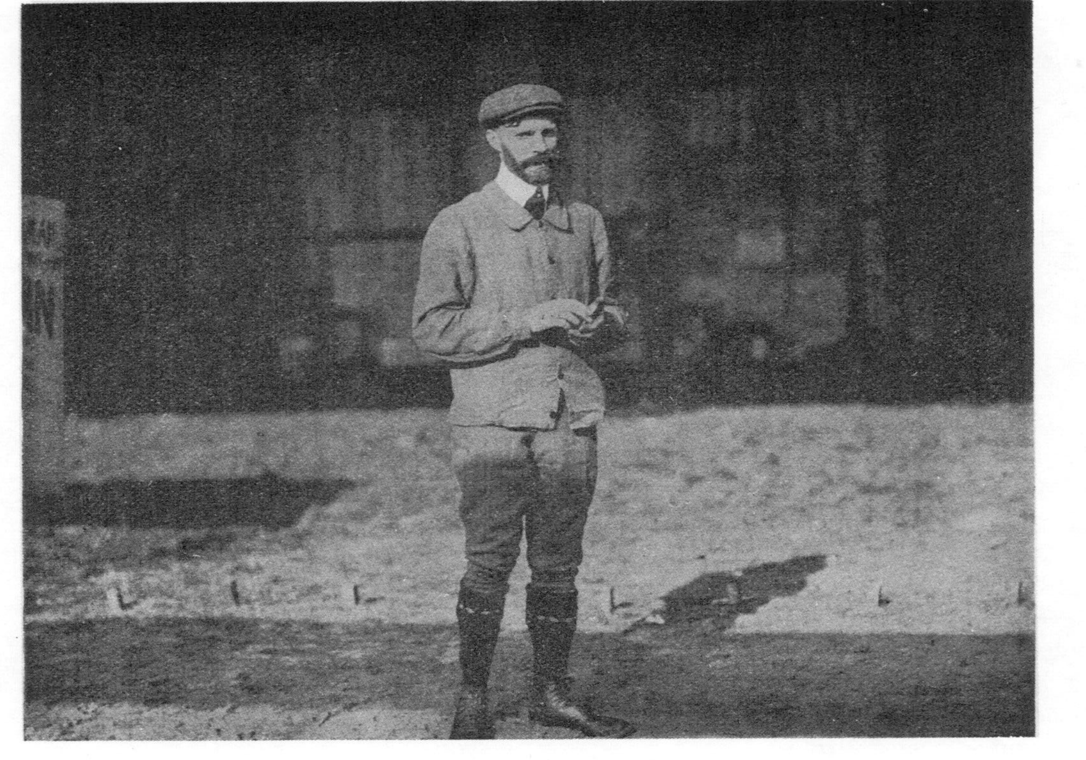

"Flight" photo

1.—Mr. Henry Farman, the Anglo-French designer, constructor and pilot, and the greatest of all the European pioneers.

Frontispiece

HISTORY OF BRITISH AVIATION 1908—1914

By

R. DALLAS BRETT
Late Honorary Secretary of the
Cinque Ports Flying Club, Lympne.

Volume I.

EIGHTIETH ANNIVERSARY
EDITION. COPY No. 337
OF 1,000

AIR RESEARCH PUBLICATIONS
in association with
KRISTALL PRODUCTIONS

First published as two
separate volumes, 1933.

This combined edition
published 1988 by
Air Research Publications
in association with Kristall
Productions Ltd, 71b Maple
Road, Surbiton, Surrey,
KT6 4AG, England

ISBN 0 904811 14 X

Printed and bound in Great
Britain by LR Printing Services Ltd,
Crawley, West Sussex, RH10 2QN

Dedicated to the Memory of the Men whose Names are recorded in The Roll of Honour contained in Volume II.

NOTE TO THIS EDITION

Volumes I and II of this work are combined in a single book for this edition. Each volume is indexed separately and an index follows each part of the work.

The publishers wish to acknowledge the kind co-operation of aviation historian John D. R. Rawlings whose original copies were used in the reproduction of this work.

FOREWORD TO ORIGINAL EDITION

By the Right Honourable SIR PHILIP SASSOON, Bart, G.B.E., C.M.G., M.P.

Under-Secretary of State for Air

MR. DALLAS BRETT is to be congratulated on having collected and put together in an attractive form this wealth of material connected with the history of British aviation from 1908–1914.

It is the epic story of the early days in this country of a science which is due to play an ever increasingly important part in world communications.

Mr. Dallas Brett has brought to bear on his task an obvious enthusiasm for his subject, and I hope that his work will prove deservedly successful.

Port Lympne,
Hythe,
Kent.

PHILIP SASSOON.

INTRODUCTION TO THIS EDITION

PERHAPS not surprisingly, one of the least recorded periods in British aviation history is the first six years leading up to the First World War from 1908. So often it has been stressed that the really great advances were made by the French, Germans and Americans, while Britain lagged behind. But this is nowhere near so true as superficial generalisations would lead us to believe. Here again objectivity has been clouded over by the partisan claims for and against the work of Cody, so if one wants to find out what really happened the task is not easy and much research has to be done.

During the early 1930s R. Dallas Brett, a leading figure in the Cinque Forts Flying Club at Lympne (now termed Ashford Airport), acquired a complete set of early *Flight* magazines and from these he began to set in order a comprehensive chronicle of the events in British aviation from 1908 to the outbreak of the First World War in August, 1914. Of course such a chronicle will be dependent on what was contained in the pages of *Flight* and, of course, the objectivity will to some extent be compromised by any particular bias that *Flight*'s editor would have wished to show, but on the whole Mr. Brett aimed to compile a factual record and did so. Towards the end of the 1930s this book came to be something of a standard work, for even then few people could find or acquire copies of *Flight* or *The Aero* for the period 1908–1914. This book provided a handy basic and generally accurate framework in which to gain a perspective of the beginnings of British aviation.

This book still does and its value is in no way diminished by the plethora of glossy histories of aviation which have appeared on the bookstalls in recent years and which, of necessity, treat the period in question more superficially, usually re-hashing the same somewhat limited range of facts. Dallas Brett has been out of print for over fifty years now and it would seem that, to make it available once again to the aeronautically minded will be of value to British aviation as a whole, and of interest all enthusiasts whose knowledge of the vital happenings which brought forth the great names and companies of the early days of British aviation may be less than comprehensive.

The original editor says in this preface, "In a book containing such a wealth of detail there are bound to be some mistakes." Inevitably this may be so but nowhere else is recorded so much factual detail about this important period, in chronological order, between the covers of one book. On this basis alone this important volume is commended to readers of today.

JOHN D. R. RAWLINGS

AUTHOR'S PREFACE

THIS book owes its conception to the "air-mindedness" of my aunt, Mrs. Cumberland-Lowndes, and of her husband, who was one of the earliest members of the Royal Aero Club. They were regular subscribers to *Flight* from its inception, and they very kindly presented their valuable set of back numbers to me.

When I took up flying as a sport in 1928, I began to study these volumes with some care, and became increasingly interested and astonished at the amazing feats which had been performed in the air before the War 1914–18.

It occurred to me that if this great wealth of detailed information could be sorted out and re-arranged into a coherent story, that story would make very interesting reading.

I approached the proprietors of *Flight* and they very kindly consented to my using the books in this manner, and have afforded me every facility, even to the extent of lending me their files for inspection and of providing the photographs and drawings which illustrate this book.

To them I offer my best thanks, and also to Commander H. E. Perrin, R.N., Secretary of the Royal Aero Club, who has given me valuable information from his Club's records.

It is generally considered that a historian should permit a period of at least fifty years to elapse between the happening of the events to be recorded and the compilation of his work. It is contended that a proper perspective is unattainable at a shorter range of time owing to the influence of current events, which tends to distort the historian's retrospective vision.

This argument, sound as it is in most cases, cannot be said to apply to that period in the history of aviation which I am about to describe, for it is a period self-contained, sundered from the record of the steady progress of mankind by a hard and fast line, drawn by the War of 1914–18.

There is, however, another cogent argument against premature histories. It is often more discreet for the author to wait until the last of the actors in his story is dead and buried. Dead men neither tell tales nor issue writs for damages for libel.

There is plenty of criticism and frank comment in this book, but nothing libellous. I must risk arousing the ire of some of the characters who appear in my story as persons of little enough importance, but who have since become famous and influential men. If I do so I shall be sorry, but I shall have the consolation of knowing that, in setting out the facts as I see them, I have been actuated by a conscious desire to be fair. At any rate, none of the early pilots can complain of being ignored completely for, even if he does not appear in the narrative, he will find his name in Appendix E.

In a book containing such a wealth of detail there are bound to be some mistakes. For these I apologize in advance, and I shall be duly grateful to any reader who will take the trouble to write to me and to point out any error which he or she may discover, so that in the event of a second edition of this book being required, I shall be able to correct it.

And now a word about the significance of the period with which I am concerned.

Many people think that the War of 1914–18 accelerated the development of the aeroplane to a marked degree.

That is entirely untrue.

The War deflected the progress of aviation from the broad road to success, along which it was sweeping with gathering velocity early in 1914, into a lane which led nowhere.

The War dealt practical aviation a blow which knocked it senseless for eleven years, and it was not until 1925 that consciousness returned, and people began to take up flying again, on aeroplanes which had much the same performance as those in use in 1914.

As early as 1913 we had a two-seater light aeroplane, the Sopwith Tabloid, which would cruise at 85 m.p.h. and land at 37 m.p.h., a better performance than that of the original de Havilland Moth, which was produced ten years afterwards. It is true that the Tabloid was not so comfortable, nor so reliable, nor so strong as the Moth, but its top speed was 95 m.p.h. and it could climb to 1,200 feet in 60 seconds.

Few people realize the extraordinary state of efficiency, the tremendous vital force, manifested in British aviation at the outbreak of war.

In 1908 there was no practical flying in this country at all, but during 1913 English people were flocking to learn to fly, and the combined British schools of flying were turning out one new pilot nearly every day.

This very advanced stage of development had been reached in the incredibly short space of five years.

It is the story of this astonishing period that I tell in this book.

It is the story of Great Britain's part in the initial conquest of a new element by the human race. In telling it, I have made no attempt to cloak the facts in a mantle of romance. The romance is there in plenty and the discerning reader will find it springing to his mind from the cold statements on the printed page.

The ideal situation in which to study this book would be a deck chair on the tarmac, soon after dawn on a summer's morning, with the queer fizzing sound of a Gnôme engine in one's ears and the whiff of burnt castor oil, the most exciting smell in the world, in one's nostrils.

Unfortunately that cannot be, for the Gnôme is gone and Lord Wakefield has taken the scent, if not the romance, out of castor oil.

I hope that the pictures in this book and the occasional stories which I am able to tell in the pilots' own words will help the reader to recapture the spirit of those strange and thrilling days.

R. DALLAS BRETT.
Romney Elm,
Hythe, Kent.

TABLE OF CONTENTS

LIST OF DIAGRAMS

FACING PAGE

LIST OF PLATES

CHAPTER I

1908–1909

1. PRACTICAL AVIATION BEGINS IN FRANCE :—HENRY FARMAN, LOUIS BLERIOT AND J. T. C. MOORE-BRABAZON

IN searching back for a suitable starting point from which to develop this History, it is satisfactory to find that the flight which signalized the beginning of practical flying in Europe was made by a man of English birth, although his sympathies lay more with France than with England, and he used a French aircraft.

On January 13th, 1908, Mr. Henry Farman succeeded in flying a circular course of one kilometre in his Voisin biplane, and thus won the Deutsch-Archdeacon prize of 50,000 francs.

This tremendous achievement has been overshadowed by the successes of the Wright Brothers who arrived in Europe nearly a year later, at a time when Farman was unable, owing to troubles with his engines, to put up any competitive show against them.

In that pre-Wright period there were two men, one English and the other French, working upon very different lines with outstanding success. The Englishman, Mr. Henry Farman, flew the products of the Voisin Frères, which were variations of the type which came to be known as the " boxkite." They were pusher biplanes with biplane tails, and a monoplane elevator protruding in front of the *nacelle* in which the pilot sat. The Frenchman, M. Louis Bleriot, held much more advanced ideas. From the beginning he displayed an eye for streamline and his aircraft were clean-looking tractor monoplanes with a very much higher stalling speed than the cumbersome Voisins.

Both men flew with magnificent dash and with no regard for the very real risks involved. M. Bleriot crashed machine after machine, and in course of time evolved the theory that it was impossible to save both aircraft and pilot, but that the latter need never be injured if he kept a cool head. His own plan was to throw himself upon one of the wings when he saw that a smash was inevitable, and he stated that, although this usually broke the wing, it seldom failed to save him from injury.

In those early times flights were measured in metres, and the idea of flying outside the boundaries of an aerodrome was regarded as too foolhardy for serious consideration by all except these two great sportsmen. On October 31st, 1908, they both got out their machines and took off almost simultaneously on the first two cross-country flights. Mr. Farman flew his Voisin from Chalons to Rheims, a distance of 27 kilometres, or 16½ miles, whilst M. Bleriot covered the 14 kilometres from Toury to Artenay in 11 minutes.

Thus before the advent of the Wrights in Europe, Henry Farman had established the first European records for duration round a closed circuit and for distance flown in a straight line, whilst another Englishman, Mr. J. T. C. Moore-Brabazon, had also acquired a Voisin boxkite and was teaching himself to fly it.

2. THE WRIGHTS ARRIVE IN FRANCE: THE 1908 MICHELIN CUP

The Wrights were very different temperamentally from the European pilots. Wilbur Wright set himself to fly his crazy contrivance with the cold reasoning courage of the research worker, the courage of Science which does not recognize bravery. He flew it with immense skill, precisely, and without dash. The atmosphere at Le Mans and later at Pau was that of a laboratory. There was a contempt for publicity. People could watch provided that they didn't interfere with the experiments; or they could stop away.

Throughout the closing months of the year 1908, Wilbur Wright continued to electrify Europe. His immediate goal was the Michelin Cup which was to be awarded for the longest duration flight round a closed circuit performed during that year. In September he made three flights of over fifty minutes under official observation, followed by two flights of over an hour, each with a passenger aboard, which were not officially observed.

The supreme effort was made on the afternoon of the last day of the contest. The machine took off from its catapult at 2 p.m. on December 31st, 1908, and flew round and round a circuit of 2·2 kilometres in circumference fifty-six times, landing at 4.20 p.m. just after sunset. This flight established a world's record for duration and for distance flown in a closed circuit, although the official figure for the latter record of 123·2 kilometres (76 miles) was obviously far short of the actual distance travelled owing to the absurdly small circuit used.

The state of European aviation at that time can be gauged by the fact that Wilbur Wright had only two serious competitors in this competition, although the Michelin Cup was worth 10,000 francs and carried with it a cash prize of no less than 20,000 francs. These competitors were the two Englishmen. Mr. Henry Farman, the more formidable of the two, made several unimportant flights before the Committee, but was dogged by misfortune, became disheartened and abandoned his attempt. The other was Mr. J. T. C. Moore-Brabazon, who was prevented from competing by an unfortunate accident in which his mechanic was injured when

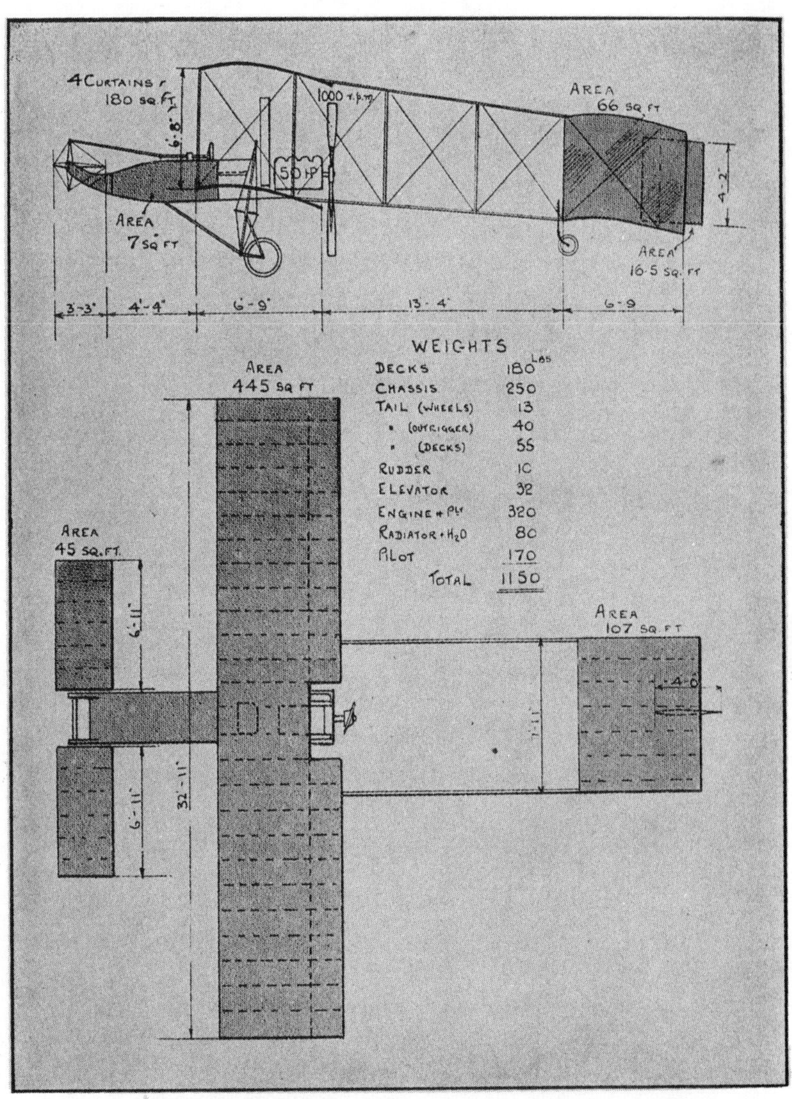

"*Flight*" *copyright*

1.—The Voisin Biplane (50 h.p. Vivinus) on which Mr. J. T. C. Moore-Brabazon learned to fly.

Facing page 22

"Flight" photo

2.—Mr. S. F. Cody on the British Army Aeroplane at Laffan's Plain.

the petrol tank of his Voisin (50 h.p. Vivinus) exploded. His chances must, in any case, have been small since he had not yet learned to turn in the air, and did not, in fact, accomplish this feat until January 18th of the following year. The glorious optimism he displayed was typical of the spirit of those times.

Faced with the accomplished fact of controlled flight over a respectable distance, the French experimenters aroused themselves and commenced with feverish energy to catch up with the Wrights. Fortunately the majority of them refrained from any attempt to mimic the faulty design and construction of the Wright aeroplane, and were content to apply themselves to the development of their own existing types, which were eventually to supersede the American ideas altogether.

3. PREPARATIONS FOR FLIGHT IN ENGLAND: FARMAN BECOMES A CONSTRUCTOR

In England, where few people had had the opportunity of witnessing the Wrights' efforts at first hand, profound scepticism reigned. Moore-Brabazon wrote a letter to *Flight* urging English experimenters to follow his example and emigrate to France in order to escape the ridicule which greeted all attempts at flight in England. Mr. Hubert Latham, the son of an Englishman, born in Paris and educated at Oxford, soon joined him at Chalons in February 1909, and was destined to make an international reputation for himself as a brilliant pilot.

It was about this time that Mr. Henry Farman, who had thitherto confined his activities to flying the Voisin aeroplanes, decided to set up as a designer and constructor on his own account, and it was not long before his pusher biplanes were universally adopted as the standard type of aeroplane for primary training all over the world. Farman demonstrated his confidence in his products by acting as his own test pilot.

At home in England Mr. Pemberton Billing, a far-sighted idealist who was already living years ahead of his time, had acquired a great natural aerodrome over 3,000 acres in extent amongst the marshes near Fambridge, Essex. He constructed thereon two enormous hangars of about the same size and shape as those that adorn the R.A.F. stations to-day, each containing lockups for housing private owners' aircraft. Twenty four-roomed bungalows were provided for resident pilots, each at a rental of three shillings per week. Those early aviators were poor people for the most part, and spent all their available cash on pieces of wire, bamboo, or linen for their aircraft. This model aerodrome was also equipped with a general stores, a post office, hotel and a club house, and represented an amazing piece of intelligent anticipation. Unfortunately there was no one ready to take advantage of the scheme.

4. THE FIRST PRACTICAL FLIGHTS IN ENGLAND: S. F. CODY

The only practical activity in this country was centred around the British Army Aeroplane which had been constructed by those indefatigable enthusiasts, Major Capper and the Balloon Section R.E. at Farnborough. This machine was an extraordinary medley of wires and bamboo poles which looked like an enlarged Wright with the addition of a tail. Mr. S. F. Cody, who was then an American citizen, made several short but precarious flights with it at Laffan's Plain, notably one of 400 yards at a height of twelve feet, in February 1909. Duringthis flight a speed of 10 to 12 m.p.h. was recorded against the wind. As a wind of more than 10 m.p.h. definitely ruled out flying for the day, this aeroplane was scarcely calculated to break records, except for stalling speed. Mr. Cody succeeded in turning it through 90° before it sagged to the ground, which was no mean feat considering all things.

During the early part of 1909 the Aero Club's aerodrome at Shellbeach, Sheppey, was being prepared. Messrs. Short Brothers were already established in a hangar where they engaged in the construction, under licence, of Wright aircraft to the order of various members of the club.

5. THE FIRST OLYMPIA SHOW: THE GNÔME ROTARY ENGINE

The first British Aero Show, which opened at Olympia on March 19th, 1909, attracted eleven full-scale exhibits made up of seven pusher biplanes, two monoplanes, and two freak machines described as "orthopters."

Of the biplanes only the two Voisins and the Delagrange, which was merely another Voisin from which the side curtains between the interplane struts had been removed, could be described as practical aeroplanes.

The Howard-Wright and Breguêt pusher biplanes were constructed of steel tubing throughout and the former had two concentric propellors designed to revolve in opposite directions and driven through a differential gear by a single Metallurgique engine of 50 h.p. The Breguêt was shown without an engine, and the Pischoff, which was a very large structure on Farman lines, had a diminutive 2-cylinder motor which was obviously no match for it. The other biplane was an unfinished skeleton, exhibited by the Short Brothers, which was clearly inspired by the Wright. None of these was in a fit state to fly.

Only one of the two monoplanes was of a practical nature. This was the R.E.P., designed by Mons. Esnault-Pelterie, who had carried out some controlled flights on it in France. The other monoplane exhibit was a power-driven version of the Weiss glider, which had not yet succeeded in lifting a man.

The show suffered from the absence of the latest Farman and

Bleriot designs, which would have given it a more practical atmosphere.

Neither Howard-Wright nor the Short Brothers would give any definite guarantee of performance, but Esnault-Pelterie and the Voisin Frères claimed that their models would fly for three miles.

Prices ranged from £1,400 for the R.E.P. to £500 for the Weiss, but it was obvious that the Voisin at £950 represented the best value for money.

If the aeroplane exhibits were unimpressive, the aero-engines afforded a most interesting study.

The English exhibitors were Green, N.E.C., Simms, E.N.V., International-Rotary and Wolseley ; whilst amongst the foreigners were such famous firms as Metallurgique, Gobron, Vivinus, R.E.P., Dutheil-Chalmers and Renault.

An exhibit which attracted little attention, and which was regarded by many as a freak, was the new Gnôme rotary engine designed by Mons. Seguin, which appeared for the first time in England.

It is impossible to exaggerate the importance of this remarkable invention, which contributed more than any other single factor to the rapid development of practical aviation.

The unreliability, coupled with the great weight, of contemporary engines drove the pioneers to despair. They were continually experimenting with larger and larger power units in a fruitless endeavour to find the power they needed whilst at the same time economizing in weight. Mons. Seguin produced the Gnôme much as a conjurer might produce a rabbit from a hat. At first the astonished audience seemed doubtful if it was real, but a trial soon convinced them that here was a reasonably reliable engine which would give an honest 50 h.p. for a weight of 165 lbs., which was extremely accessible, which took up a minimum of space, and which was easy to fit.

It was the answer to their prayer. There was only one serious disadvantage in its use, and that was the fact that it had to be run on castor oil, of which it consumed prodigious quantities ; but that was a small drawback when compared with a gain in performance of at least 50 per cent. over its nearest rivals.

Its immediate success was assured, and for the next four years the Gnôme reigned supreme as the aero engine *par excellence*, not only in Europe, but all over the world.

6. MOORE-BRABAZON AT SHELLBEACH : CODY AGAIN

It was not until May 1909 that anyone flew with any confidence and ability from English soil. Mr. Moore-Brabazon had brought his Voisin biplane, now fitted with an 8-cylinder E.N.V. motor in place of the ill-starred Vivinus, to England for exhibition at the Aero show. Subsequently it was dismantled and taken from Olympia to the Shellbeach aerodrome where Mr. Moore-Brabazon flew it successfully for a few hundred yards until the slipping of the steering drum, which was clamped but not keyed to its shaft, robbed him of lateral control at a crucial moment. Thus Messrs. Short Brothers acquired their first repair job.

The authorities had by this time practically given up all hope of making a success of the British Army Aeroplane. Mr. Cody, however, was a man of infinite patience and refused to be discouraged. On May 14th, 1909, he brought out the old machine and made a splendid flight of over a mile from Laffan's Plain to Danger Hill, where he landed without breaking anything, having set up the first British records for duration and for distance flown in a straight line. The former record was probably considerable but does not seem to have been recorded. In the afternoon, H.M. King George V, then Prince of Wales, arrived from Aldershot, having heard of the morning's triumph, and requested a repetition. Mr. Cody took off, but in endeavouring to turn to avoid some troops, he crashed gently into an embankment and demolished the tail.

7. THE ADVENT OF HUBERT LATHAM

Mr. Hubert Latham was still at Chalons teaching himself to fly the interesting Antoinette monoplane, which was the first practical aeroplane to use a thick wing section. In the last week of May he suddenly attained that splendid confidence which was to make him the hero of the aviation world for the next few months, and demonstrated his ability by flying for 37 minutes 37 seconds at a speed of 72 k.p.h. (45 m.p.h.) at a height of over 100 feet. The following week he established a duration record for European aircraft, which seriously challenged the Wrights, by maintaining his Antoinette in the air for 1 hr. 7 mins. 37 secs. During this flight he "calmly took his hands off the steering wheel, rolled a cigarette and lighted it, thus creating a new record. He undoubtedly is the first man who has had the audacity to light and smoke a cigarette while in full flight." As the Antoinette pilots sat *on*, rather than *in*, their exiguous fuselages in the full blast of the slipstream, this was certainly clever, and there must be very few modern pilots who can roll a cigarette anyway, even under the most favourable conditions!

Flight commenting upon his performance in its leader of June 19th, 1909, stated: "There is something Byronic in the methods of the latest Frenchman of English blood to leap prominently into the public view in connection with human flight. Of Mr. Latham it may be said that he awoke one morning to find that he had a motor that could work, so he set it going and it made his machine fly, and himself famous. Not for him the cautious

"Flight" photo

3.—THE 50 H.P. GNÔME ROTARY ENGINE, THE PRIMARY CAUSE OF THE RAPID DEVELOPMENT OF PRACTICAL AVIATION.

"Flight" photo

4.—All-British: Mr. A. V. Roe flying his Triplane (10 h.p. J.A.P.).

Facing page 27

system of increasing flights at the rate of ten minutes each day. As long as his machine would keep in the air, so long would he have it to stay there with himself aboard. . . . Now that the preliminary scientific work is at an end we are in need of such men, because their delight and their real bent is in demonstration. They revel in breaking 'the record' and reck not for risks run. Of course there must be the inevitable toll of accidents; but in view of the magnitude of such a thing as the achievement of enabling mankind to ride the air at will, we must expect to pay the usual price in human life. Meantime, it is extraordinary that so much has been achieved at numerically so small a cost."

8. AN AMERICAN ODYSSEY

Just such a man as *Flight* extolled was Mr. Ulysses Lorensen, the village blacksmith of Berwyn, U.S.A. He had designed and constructed an aeroplane and, rather than risk the ignominy attached to any failure to take off from the ground, he arranged for the preliminary trials to take place at an altitude of 3,500 feet! To this end he chartered a balloon which took him and his apparatus up to the desired height and duly cast the whole affair overboard. The aircraft was not so good as anticipated, but fortunately it stalled near the ground after rolling over and over in its fall. The fortunate Ulysses sustained nothing worse than a number of bruises and, on recovering consciousness half an hour later, gave an interview to the press. "I'm all right," said Ulysses, "and my aeroplane is all right, and, what's more, that blamed thing is going to fly, and solve the problem of flying. Just as soon as this soreness wears off, I'll begin work on another one. I have already ordered the material, and I'll be all right in a couple of days. You see, the rudder got jammed, and refused to keep the aeroplane in a horizontal position. We tipped forward, and then we turned over. After that we just kept on turning over until I thought we were spinning around like a top going sideways, I can't imagine how the rudder happened to jam. I am positive the thing will fly if given half a chance. Why didn't I fall out? I didn't have time to fall. That aeroplane was falling just as fast as I was, and, anyway, I was braced in. We went down like a streak of lightning, it seemed to me, and yet I was sure I was falling for at least a month. I didn't once think of being killed. In fact, I never thought what would happen when I hit the ground. All I thought was to get that lever and rudder working. Yes, I'm sore, but I'm more sore at that rudder than anything else. In my next machine I'll make no mistake, and it will fly all right." That was undoubtedly an "intrepid birdman."

9. SOME EARLY EXPERIMENTERS: COCKBURN, CODY, AND ROE

Mr. Cockburn was the next member of the Aero Club to take up the practical side of aviation. He bought a biplane from Mr. Henry Farman and proceeded to Chalons to teach himself to fly it. His initial effort was not very successful, for, after taking off and flying for 500 yards, he " pulled the wrong lever, or pulled it in the wrong direction." The result was a violent zoom which caused the top plane to break and the machine stalled and crashed, fortunately without injury to the pilot.

At home Mr. Cody had completed the repairs to the British Army Aeroplane and proceeded to demonstrate that he had at last found the knack of coaxing it round corners, by executing a circular flight of nearly two miles, landing close to his starting point. Observers noted that he pursued an undulating course, so that the aircraft seems to have been somewhat unstable fore and aft, although in a round robin addressed to his numerous critics, Mr. Cody emphatically denied this, and asserted that both the wavelike movement and the yawing from right to left were " mostly intentional," although space forbade him to state his reasons for such a course.

At the same time, Mr. A. V. Roe, a man destined to have tremendous influence on British aviation in the future, was experimenting with a small triplane of his own design and construction on Lea Marshes. This machine was driven by a tractor screw operated by a 10-h.p. J.A.P. motor-cycle engine, and seems to have been the first aircraft to fly with an air-cooled motor in this country. Mr. Roe was one of the first people to realize that the tail should be raised whilst gaining speed for the take off. Most pilots allowed their machines to stall off with their tails on or near the ground in those days. Mr. Roe was very incensed at the attitude of the authorities in forbidding the use of public commons and parks around London by experimenting pilots. He wrote a letter to *Flight* complaining of this unnecessary red tape, and pointing out that his own aerodrome was covered with stumps and that his machine had twice suffered damage through colliding with these obstructions.

10. PREPARING TO CONQUER THE CHANNEL

The *Daily Mail* newspaper had offered a prize of £1,000 for the first aeroplane flight across the Straits of Dover and many pilots had entered and were beginning to gather on the French side around Sangatte in preparation for an attempt.

Mr. Henry Farman appeared at Boulogne in the first week of July 1909, and investigated the lie of the land. Shortly afterwards Mr. Hubert Latham, who had already crossed from England to

France by air in a balloon, brought his Antoinette to Sangatte and commenced to erect it in the old Channel Tunnel workings there, whilst the Compte de Lambert leased a field at Wissant and ran up a shed to house his Wright biplane. Mr. Latham had adopted a suit composed of a fabric worn by fencers in *epée* competitions, which was designed to prevent the pilot from being punctured by splinters from the spars in a crash. He made a trial flight in the Antoinette, taking off after a quarter-mile run along the grass verge of the road adjoining the Channel Tunnel works, and damaged his undercarriage slightly through dropping heavily into a corn-field. Fortunately the crash-proof suit was not needed on this occasion.

11. COCKBURN AND CODY PROGRESS

Whilst all eyes were turned on the cliffs around Calais, news arrived from Chalons that Mr. Cockburn had made a successful flight in his Farman, culminating in a drop-wing landing which necessitated repairs to a lower wing-tip. At home, Mr. Cody had ruthlessly torn a number of the " supplementary surfaces " off the British Army Aeroplane and discovered that these had been responsible for a certain sluggishness of the controls. He celebrated the discovery by performing a number of short flights at Laffan's Plain, in which he manœuvred with unaccustomed freedom in the air.

12. FIRST CROSS-CHANNEL ATTEMPT: HUBERT LATHAM

On Monday, July 19th, 1909, Mr. Hubert Latham accomplished one of the splendid failures of history. The summer day was ideal for the attempt. The Channel presented an oily calm. There was no wind. A mist which sheathed the Dover cliffs at dawn dispersed with the rising sun. For the first time on record wireless telegraphy was used for the purpose of obtaining weather reports to assist a great flight. The first report was received from Sangatte at the Lord Warden Hotel, Dover at 4.30 a.m., and signals were interchanged until at 5.20 a.m. Dover reported visibility ten miles. At 6.16 a.m. M. Levavasseur, the official in charge aboard the French T.B.D. *Harpon*, was satisfied with the conditions, and ordered the firing of the three guns which gave the signal to start to those on the cliffs above. Six minutes later the Antoinette was ticking over in position for the take-off. At 6.42 Latham took off for England, gaining height in a wide sweeping climbing turn. At 1,000 feet he set his course and pushed out to sea. Below him he could see the *Harpon* tearing through the water, black smoke belching from her funnels as she strove desperately to keep the Antoinette in view. Latham nonchalantly picked up his camera and, leaning over the side of his fuselage, endeavoured to focus the destroyer below. As he did so his motor coughed, spluttered, and slowed up. Hastily stowing his camera away, Latham ran over all the electrical connections within his reach but was unable to find any fault. Then he concentrated on putting the aircraft down as gently as possible within easy reach of his escort. He made an excellent job of the landing, stalling on to the calm sea at about 30 m.p.h. He did not even get his feet wet, and was able to sit smoking quietly on the fuselage until the *Harpon* came and picked him up.

That night saw Latham in the Antoinette factory in Paris demanding another machine, and by the evening of the following day Antoinette VII was in the train for Calais.

13. THE SUCCESSFUL ATTACK: LOUIS BLERIOT

Latham proceeded feverishly with the erection and testing of his new mount, for the redoubtable Louis Bleriot had arrived at Les Baraques with his diminutive monoplane Bleriot XI (25 h.p. 3 cylinder Anzani). A week previously the French pilot had staggered the aviation camps in France by flying this same machine across country from Chicheny to Croix-Briquet-Cheville, a distance of 41·2 kilometres (25 miles) in 44 minutes, thereby proving most conclusively that the Channel was within his grasp.

The dashing Frenchman was not the man to let the grass grow under his feet and Sunday morning, July 25th, 1909, saw him taking a motor ride at 2.30 a.m. to blow the cobwebs away, whilst waiting for the wind to drop. This soon came to pass, and Bleriot immediately took off on a preliminary test flight to try the air. As everything went well he sent a message to the destroyer *Escopette*, which was to act as escort, and at 4.40 a.m. the monoplane took off once more and set out for England. The pilot had neither compass nor clock to help him, and soon overtook and lost sight of the *Escopette*. Thereafter for ten minutes Bleriot was out of sight of land or shipping and consequently in great danger. He confessed later to feeling very disturbed lest he should fail to keep approximately straight. As a matter of fact, he swerved to the right during this period and first sighted the Kent coast off Deal. He accordingly turned left and flew along the high cliffs towards Dover, until he saw a French newspaper correspondent who was signalling to him with a flag from the spot which had previously been selected as a landing place. Unfortunately M. Bleriot missed the chosen field and put his machine down on the precipitous slope of a nearby valley, thus breaking the airscrew and the engine bearers.

It was calculated that the actual length of the flight was about thirty-one miles and the time was approximately 40 minutes, which sets the average speed at about 45 m.p.h. This speed caused the utmost astonishment at the time. The Chief Coastguard at Dover said " the speed was almost incredible " and *Flight* in its résumé of the achievement stressed the figures, and pointed out that the monoplane must be regarded as "the racer of the air" and that few pilots would feel safe or comfortable at such a high rate of travel !

14. LATHAM'S SECOND FAILURE

M. Bleriot set the seal on his reputation for sportsmanship by sending a message back to Latham, offering to share the *Daily Mail* prize with him if he could get across that day. Unfortunately, the wind began to increase shortly after the victor's landing and, although Latham was willing and anxious to make an attempt, yet his co-directors, MM. Levavasseur and Gastambide, definitely forbade him to risk his new machine.

Two days later the weather cleared and, after a trial flight in which the undercarriage was damaged, the Antoinette took off from Cap Blanc Nez at 5.50 p.m. for Dover. The news of the start was flashed across the Channel and 40,000 people gathered on the cliffs above Dover to welcome the plucky pilot. Soon he came in sight and all the ships blew their sirens, while the crowd cheered itself hoarse. Suddenly, when within a mile of the shore, the new 100 h.p. 8-cylinder Antoinette motor cut out and once again Mr. Latham suffered a forced landing in the sea. This time the additional weight of the new motor caused the speed of impact to be much higher and the pilot's goggles were broken, and he had to receive medical attention.

Thus ended dramatically the race for the conquest of the Channel, and the Anglo-Frenchman deserves no less praise for his astonishing pertinacity and pluck in defeat than the Frenchman deserves for his brilliant success.

The effect of these flights was to awaken the whole world to the realization that aviation had arrived at last as a practical proposition. The sceptical British public was suddenly aroused to a perfect frenzy of enthusiasm. Mr. Gordon Selfridge, with his customary enterprise, had arranged for the exhibition of the triumphant Bleriot monoplane in his Oxford Street shop, and so great was the general interest that no less than 120,000 people filed past it in four days.

15. CODY FORGES AHEAD : HANDLEY PAGE, A. V. ROE, A. E. GEORGE, AND MORTIMER SINGER

Mr. Cody had at last succeeded in getting the British Army Aeroplane to behave itself and the combination made several excellent flights from Laffan's Plain with the aid of the 80 h.p. E.N.V. motor which had been installed. Colonel Capper flew in the machine as a passenger for a mile and a half, and immediately afterwards Mrs. Cody annexed the distinction of being the first lady to fly from English soil, Mr. Cody making several turnings and a figure of eight with her perched precariously behind him.

Shortly afterwards, he demonstrated his skill as a pilot and the practical nature of his machine, in a manner which confounded his many critics, by carrying out a series of four cross-country flights, culminating in a circuit of Aldershot at a height of 100 feet, during which he covered eight miles in nine minutes fifteen seconds. During the following week he joined the select band of first-class pilots by covering forty miles around Laffan's Plain in one hour three minutes, and reaching an altitude of 600 feet.

Messrs. Handley-Page, Ltd., portentous name, established an aerodrome at Barking and commenced experiments with a monoplane, a biplane with a Green engine, and a species of helicopter. Not far away, Mr. A. V. Roe was succeeding in making short hops on his triplane, one of which terminated in his being projected through the middle plane, necessitating protracted repairs.

Across the river, Mr. A. E. George, who had driven Argyll and Darracq racing cars in the I.O.M. races, was busy with Mr. Moore-Brabazon's Voisin which he had recently purchased. He took off from Shellbeach on an experimental flight, but landed suddenly on his nose. Mr. George was thrown out but immediately picked himself up and walked round the machine, only to pitch forward unconscious. He soon recovered, however.

Another Englishman to take up practical flying at this time was Mr. Mortimer Singer, who went to Chalons and began to teach himself to fly one of the early type Voisins.

16. THE FIRST RHEIMS MEETING

On August 22nd, 1909, the first great International Aviation Week opened at Rheims. The only English representatives were Mr. G. B. Cockburn, whose Farman biplane (50 h.p. Gnôme) was officially entered by the Aero Club, and Mr. Henry Farman, whose machine was fitted with a 50 h.p. Vivinus engine. Mr. Hubert Latham entered an Antoinette. There were thirty-eight aircraft engaged, consisting of seven Voisins, six Wrights, five Bleriots, four Farmans, four R.E.P.'s, three Antoinettes, two Curtiss, one Santos Dumont, one Breguêt, one Sanchis, and four nameless types. One of the Voisins and one of the Bleriots were equipped with the British-built and designed E.N.V. motor, an 8-cylinder V. engine of 50 h.p.

Mr. Cockburn had achieved a flight of eleven kilometres, followed by one of more than twenty minutes, whilst training at Chalons under the personal supervision of Mr. Henry Farman. The latter had an unfortunate accident a week before the meeting, when the radiator of his motor burst and a jet of steam caught his left cheek, inflicting a nasty scald.

Mr. Cockburn flew well in the competition, but without out-

"Flight" photo

5.—THE CONQUEROR OF THE CHANNEL: M. LOUIS BLERIOT.

Facing page 32

"Flight" photo

6.—Blackpool: Mr. Henry Farman and his Biplane

standing success. Mr. Latham, however, created an Anglo-French triumph by setting up a world's speed record for 100 kilometres (62 miles) by covering that distance in 1 hr. 28 mins. 17 secs. in his Antoinette (50 h.p. 8-cylinder Antoinette) at an average speed of 42 m.p.h. Mr. Henry Farman flew magnificently, in spite of his scalded face, and annexed no less than 63,000 francs of the prize money, after he had discarded his Vivinus motor and substituted one of the latest Gnômes. Amongst his successes were the world's records for duration and for distance flown in a closed circuit, which he captured during a great flight of 180 kilometres (112½ miles) in 3 hrs. 4 mins. 56⅗ secs. Mr. Latham was the second biggest prize winner with 42,000 francs.

There was no aircraft of British design or construction entered for this first great international contest, which resolved itself into a duel between the French and American types, the performance of which proved to be not greatly dissimilar, but it is some satisfaction to note that an English-born pilot put up the finest performance of the whole meeting, that an Anglo-Frenchman ran him a close second, and that our official representative, Mr. Cockburn, at least displayed practical ability as a pilot, although only about one-third of the thirty-eight aircraft entered for the contests actually succeeded in leaving the ground.

17. THE FIRST ENGLISH FLYING MEETINGS: BLACKPOOL

The next event of importance was the simultaneous promotion of the first two flying meetings to be held in this country at Blackpool and Doncaster respectively. A very great deal of bad feeling manifested itself between the organizers of these rival shows, of which that at Blackpool had the backing of the Aero Club and the municipal authorities, whilst the affair at Doncaster owed its conception to so many and diverse influences, that an application was made to the High Court, on the opening morning, for the appointment of a Receiver to safeguard the takings!

The field at Blackpool comprised three Voisins in the hands of Rougier, Fournier, and Mortimer Singer, a lone Henry Farman (50 Gnôme), which was flown alternately by its designer and Louis Paulhan, two Bleriots in charge of Leblanc and Parkinson, Latham's Antoinette, A. V. Roe's triplane (10 h.p. 2-cylinder J.A.P.), three anonymous monoplanes belonging to Messrs. Saunderson, Creese, and Neale, and a small biplane in the hands of Señor Fernandez. Thus there were a dozen aircraft assembled, of which five got off the ground during the week.

Mr. Roe was the first competitor to attempt to fly, but his 10 h.p. J.A.P. was wholly inadequate for its task, and he wisely retired into his hangar and proceeded with the fitting of the 24 h.p. motor which he had recently acquired. When this had been done, he succeeded in making one or two short hops with his little triplane.

The meeting was memorable on account of Mr. Hubert Latham's spectacular flight in a high wind. The anemometer recorded a mesne speed of 20 m.p.h., with frequent gusts up to 38 m.p.h., when the Antoinette took off and completed two laps of the course in just over ten minutes. This flight marked a new departure in aviation. For the first time a pilot had definitely defied the elements, by pitting his skill against a gusty wind. It was a very splendid achievement and marked the foundation of Mr. Hubert Latham's reputation as a bad-weather pilot.

Mr. Henry Farman once again annexed most of the premier awards, winning £2,400 in the aggregate, as compared with £820 won by M. Rougier, £530 won by M. Paulhan, and £400 won by Mr. Latham. Mr. Farman's best flight was made early in the week when he covered 47 miles 1,544 yds. in 1 hr. 32 mins. 16⅘ secs., at an average speed of 31 m.p.h.

18. DONCASTER

The rival meeting at Doncaster produced a field of nine aircraft, comprising five Bleriots in the hands of Delagrange, who had a Gnôme engine installed, the two French racing-car experts, MM. Molon and le Blon, M. Prevôt and Captain Lovelace, and a Farman flown by M. Sommer. Mr. Cody flew the British Army Aeroplane, Captain Maitland tried unsuccessfully to fly a Voisin to which "gyroscopes" had been fitted, whilst the comic element was safe in the hands of a Mr. Windham, who produced a monoplane of his own design and construction.

The meeting opened with a line up of the competing aircraft for photographic purposes. Mr. Windham posed himself gracefully on his machine, but he had gravely under-estimated its strength. As the cameras clicked, there was a loud cracking noise and the Windham monoplane collapsed, depositing its proud owner on the grass. He took it away and repaired it, but at its next appearance it came gently into contact with a stationary motor car and instantly disintegrated once more. Fortunately it never got into the air.

The meeting was not without thrills, as the Bleriot of M. Delagrange went very fast under the influence of the Gnôme, and his time of 1 min. 47⅕ secs. for a lap worked out at 49·9 m.p.h., which was announced, probably without justification, as a world's speed record. To add to the excitement, M. le Blon and Capt. Lovelace crashed their respective Bleriots in full view of the crowd in a most spectacular manner.

During a lull in the proceedings, Mr. Cody completed his naturalization as a British subject and immediately entered for the *Daily Mail* £1,000 prize for the first British pilot to complete a circular flight of one mile on an all-British aeroplane. He failed, however, to compete with the French aircraft present, as he had the misfortune to run into a patch of sand on the second day and nosed over, reopening a cut on his forehead which he had acquired during a heavy landing the previous week. Thereafter he contented himself with short straight hops up and down before the Grand Stand.

The best flight of the meeting was put up by Roger Sommer (Farman) who covered twenty laps, or practically thirty miles, in forty-five minutes. He also won the cup for the greatest aggregate distance flown throughout the meeting.

19. THE FIRST WOMAN PILOT

Towards the end of October 1909, there occurred an event of considerable significance. Mme. la Baronne de la Roche had for some time been undergoing instruction at Chalons from M. Chateau, the Voisin instructor. On Friday, October 22nd, 1909, she was sent solo and performed a " straight " of 300 yards, and followed this on the next day by a most creditable flight of two circuits of the parade ground in a strong gusty wind. The distance covered was about four miles, and observers stated that her turns were excellent. She thus achieved the unique distinction of becoming the first lady pilot.

20. " DAILY MAIL " £1,000 ALL-BRITISH FLIGHT: ACTIVITY AT SHELLBEACH

The following Saturday, October 30th, 1909, may be said to mark the inauguration of all-British aviation. The hero was Mr. J. T. C. Moore-Brabazon who for nearly a year past had devoted himself to the perfection of the aircraft which Messrs. Short Bros. were constructing to his order at Shellbeach. He had voluntarily abandoned his trusty Voisin with which he had performed so well in France, and set himself to produce and fly an all-British aeroplane and to win the *Daily Mail's* £1,000. The machine was not very good. It was a flagrant copy of the Wright, for the construction of which Messrs. Short Bros. held a licence. Moreover, it used the clumsy catapult device for starting which had already been discarded by the French Wright pilots. Moore-Brabazon's first trials resulted in disaster, and he experienced the utmost difficulty in obtaining a suitable motor of English design and construction. However, he stuck gamely to his self-imposed task, and eventually succeeded in capturing the prize with the aid of a 50–60 h.p. Green engine, and thus forestalled the newly naturalized Mr. Cody. In a way this was hard luck on the ex-American, for he had already eclipsed anything that the Short machine could do on his all-British Army Aeroplane.

Shellbeach began to wake up at last. Messrs. Short Bros. completed their first Wright aeroplane to the order of the Hon.

C. S. Rolls, who rapidly found his touch as a pilot of this tricky machine, and flew it for a mile and a half two days after Moore-Brabazon's success. A second British-built Wright aeroplane was delivered to Mr. A. Ogilvie who had been conducting numerous successful experiments with a Wright-type glider, and who established himself at Rye, using Camber Sands as an aerodrome.

21. BROOKLANDS BECOMES AN AERODROME

Mr. A. V. Roe had recently conducted experiments with his triplane on the concrete of the finishing straight at Brooklands, and whilst this activity was taking place at Sheppey, the Brooklands Automobile Racing Club had realized the possibilities of developing their property as an aerodrome, and had approached Monsieur L. Paulhan with a view to him giving exhibition flights there. This he consented to do, and the B.A.R.C. officials began to prepare the ground on the Byfleet side for his use, thus laying the foundations of an airport which has had a lasting effect upon British sporting and military aviation down to the present time. It is interesting to note that Capt. Duncan Davis, the present managing director of Brooklands Aviation, Ltd., was at this time intimately concerned with the activities of Mr. Cody at Laffan's Plain, a few miles away.

M. Paulhan made some splendid flights at Brooklands with his Farman biplane, attaining a height of 720 feet and covering 96 miles in 2 hrs. 49 mins. 20 secs. He then moved to Sandown Park racecourse and succeeded in breaking the world's altitude record by climbing to 977 feet.

22. VARIOUS DOINGS AT HOME AND ABROAD

In the meantime, Mr. Henry Farman had broken his own world's record for duration, by flying for 4 hrs. 17 mins. 53 secs. at Chalons, during which time he covered about 150 miles.

Both Mr. Moore-Brabazon and the Hon. C. S. Rolls continued their successes at Shellbeach, the former flying across country for about three and a half miles in his Short, accompanied by one small pig as passenger, just to prove the fallibility of old proverbs in modern times. Simultaneously, Mr. A. Rawlinson, who was connected with the distribution of Darracq cars in this country, appeared at Chalons with a Farman biplane powered by a 100 h.p. Darracq motor with which he flew half a mile at his first attempt, whilst Mr. McArdle began instruction at the Bleriot school there.

Mr. Cody had established himself on Aintree racecourse preparatory to an attack on the £1,000 prize which had been offered for a flight from Liverpool to Manchester. *Flight* records that "he went slightly off his course, and when trying to get back again found himself faced with a high hedge. He decided to come down immediately, but could not bring the machine to rest in time to avoid a collision with the hedge." The machine was somewhat damaged. There is no evidence to show whether or not the hedge in question was the redoubtable Becher's Brook.

Messrs. Short Bros. turned out another Wright aeroplane to the order of Mr. F. K. McClean, a member of the committee of the Aero Club, who succeeded in making a number of short flights with it, whilst Mr. G. W. Parkinson had purchased a Bleriot and succeeded in getting off the ground for 200 yards at Newcastle. Mr. Neale, who had appeared with a machine on the ground at the Blackpool Meeting, took a Bleriot to Brooklands and made some straight flights at a height of twenty feet, and Mr. Mortimer Singer made three splendid flights of between ten and fifteen minutes duration at Chalons with his Henry Farman.

At Pau, Mr. Claude Grahame-White was very busy. He had purchased a new type of Bleriot with an 80 h.p. 8-cylinder E.N.V. motor which attained a velocity of no less than 96 k.p.h., or just under 60 m.p.h., round a circular course on its first trials. This machine was a two-seater designed for instruction. Another one was on order, and Mr. Grahame-White already owned two 25 h.p. single-seater Bleriots, and was awaiting delivery of a Farman biplane with the new 7-cylinder 50 h.p. Gnôme. Already his schemes for the establishment of a school of flying near London were under way, and he had acquired the exclusive rights for the distribution of Farman aeroplanes in Central and South America. It was obvious that a new and powerful influence was coming to bear upon British aviation.

The Aero Club had established an auxiliary flying ground at Eastchurch, not far from Shellbeach, and some of the experimenters had removed their aeroplanes to the new site. The Hon. C. S. Rolls took a very practical view of aviation, and on taking delivery of his Wright at the Short Works at Leysdown, whither it had been sent for repairs, he decided to save everybody trouble by flying it back to Eastchurch, instead of adopting the usual form of transport by lorry. Accordingly he took off, circled over Shellbeach, where the Hon. Maurice Egerton was practising with his new Wright, and flew fifteen miles across country to his destination, landing just as the Dunne aeroplane was brought out for trials and adjustment.

On December 20th, 1909, the English pilot, Mortimer Singer, who had been steadily acquiring proficiency at Chalons, suddenly leapt into the front rank with a magnificent flight of 1 hr. 1 min. 6 secs., during which his Farman biplane covered forty-one miles. On the following day he attained an altitude of over 200 feet with a passenger and made a whole series of successful flights.

This brings us to the end of the chronological recital of the events of this momentous year 1909, and it is now opportune to look back and summarize the effect of those events upon British aviation.

23. 1909 REVIEWED

The dominating figure of those days, the Grand Old Man of European aviation, was the Anglo-Frenchman, Henry Farman.

During that hectic year he had flown a very great number of hours. He had designed and constructed the most efficient type of aeroplane as yet known to mankind. He had broken record after record, he had instructed a great number of pupils in the most brilliant manner, and he had won many thousands of pounds in prize money. At the close of 1909 he held the most important of the world's records, including that for duration with a flight lasting 4 hrs. 17 mins. 53 secs., when no other pilot in the world had succeeded in staying in the air for three consecutive hours. That was a just measure of his superiority over his competitors both as designer, constructor, and pilot.

The most spectacular and daring pilot of the year proved to be the other Anglo-Frenchman, Hubert Latham. His two attempts on the Channel, his superb flight in a gale of wind at Blackpool, and his series of successful attacks on the altitude record, combined to set him up as a universal hero.

Third place must be awarded to the Anglo-American, S. F. Cody, for his great patience, pertinacity, and skill in making a real flyer out of the unpromising material of the original British Army Aeroplane, and for the pluck with which he flew it. To him goes the honour of being the first man to fly an aeroplane of British design and construction across the English countryside.

Mr. Moore-Brabazon was the second Englishman, Mr. Henry Farman being the first, to become a pilot and he subsequently annexed the enviable distinction of becoming holder of the first aviator's certificate issued by the Aero Club. His work with the Short biplane was very valuable, and it may be claimed with some justification, that he and the Short Bros. between them founded the aircraft industry in Great Britain.

Mr. A. V. Roe was greatly handicapped in his experiments by lack of funds, which resulted in lack of power for his triplane. He exhibited as much patience in adversity as did Cody, with less compensation, and at that time there would have been few to prophecy that he was destined to become one of the most powerful influences in British aviation.

At the end of 1909, there were but two British-built aeroplanes which could really be said to have flown properly, Mr. Cody's and the Short, both of which were based upon the Wrights' design, and there was but a small band of English pilots who were even moderately safe in the air. They may be listed as follows in order of merit, together with the aircraft which they had flown :—

1. Henry Farman (Voisin, Farman), (Anglo-French).
2. Hubert Latham (Antoinette), (Anglo-French).
3. S. F. Cody (British Army Aeroplane), (Anglo-American)

4. Mortimer Singer (Voisin, Farman).
5. J. T. C. Moore-Brabazon (Voisin, Short).
6. G. B. Cockburn (Farman).
7. C. S. Rolls (Wright).
8. C. Grahame-White (Bleriot, Farman).
9. A. Ogilvie (Wright).
10. M. Egerton (Wright).

In addition to the above, there was a host of amateur pilots, constructors and designers hovering on the brink. One or two of them had purchased French aeroplanes, mostly Bleriots, which they did not understand and could not fly, even if they succeeded in rigging them correctly. Others had designed and constructed machines to their own ideas, which were often positively puerile in conception and execution. A handful of these experimenters was destined to follow A. V. Roe to success, but the vast majority fell back into obscurity, and the curious products of their labours worked out their destiny as fowl runs and tool sheds.

24. WORLD'S RECORDS AT END OF 1909

Below will be found a list of the principal records which had been set up at the end of the year 1909. The record for absolute speed in the air has been omitted because the timing methods then in vogue were conspicuous for their inaccuracy, and the current practice was to clock the machines over one lap of a small circular course, a system which obviously gave no real measure of the aircraft's capabilities, as everything depended upon the pilot's cornering. There can be little doubt that the fastest aeroplane in existence was either the two-seater Bleriot of Grahame-White, or the single seater Bleriot (50 Gnôme) of M. Delagrange. The official record was held by Capt. Ferber on a Voisin at 32 m.p.h.

WORLD'S RECORDS AT END OF 1909

Pilot	*Nationality*	*Aircraft*	*Nationality*	*Engine*	*Nationality*	*Time or Distance*	*Place*
			DURATION				
H. Farman	Anglo-French	Farman	French	50 Gnôme	French	4h. 17m. 53⅗s.	Chalons
			DISTANCE IN A CLOSED CIRCUIT				
H. Farman	Anglo-French	Farman	French	50 Gnôme	French	234·212 Km. (145 miles)	Chalons
			ALTITUDE				
H. Latham	Anglo-French	Antoinette	French	Antoinette	French	453 metres (1,485 feet)	Chalons

CHAPTER II

1910

I. MANUFACTURING DEVELOPMENTS IN ENGLAND: CAIRO AND LIVERPOOL—MANCHESTER

THE year 1910 was to witness the blossoming forth of British aviation in much the same manner as the previous year had seen the successful establishment of flying in France.

Already early in January significant developments were taking place on the manufacturing side. Mr. A. V. Roe set up in business as a constructor of monoplanes, biplanes, and triplanes, under the style of "A. V. Roe and Co.," whilst the great motor firm of Humber at Coventry began to build Bleriots under licence, equipping them with the Humber 30 h.p. 3-cylinder radial engines. The Humber company made every part of the aircraft and engine, including the airscrews, in their own shops, and also produced a 4-cylinder motor of 50 h.p. which, like the radial model, was equipped with dual ignition.

Two of these Humber-Bleriots were taken out to the flying meeting at Heliopolis by Mr. Ballin Hinde, where they were flown by Capt. Dawes and Mr. Neale. Both pilots suffered slight accidents in practice, damaged their machines, and failed to perform in the competitions. Mr. Mortimer Singer (Farman) was the official representative of Great Britain at this important meeting, but, unfortunately, he sustained a very nasty accident in practice and retired to hospital with a broken thigh.

Mr. Cody was still set upon winning the £1,000 Liverpool-Manchester prize, but on his latest attempt he flew into fog and found himself bunkered by some telegraph wires, which necessitated a sudden landing after ten miles had been covered. This was accomplished without damage to the aircraft, but eventually the time limit expired before he was ready for another attempt.

The New Engine Co., Ltd., produced a very advanced type of aero engine in 2, 4, and 6-cylinder models. This was nothing less than a supercharged two-stroke, which employed a series of Roots blowers to pack the charge into the cylinders and subsequently to clear away the exhaust gases. The 4-cylinder N.E.C. developed about 40 h.p. for a weight of 155 lbs., or 3·875 lbs. per h.p., which was exceedingly creditable.

2. FLYING IN IRELAND, FRANCE, AND AUSTRALIA

In Ireland several experimenters had been at work, and Mr. H. G. Ferguson of Belfast had attained some success with a monoplane built upon Bleriot lines, and powered with an 8-cylinder 35 h.p. air-cooled J.A.P. engine.

M. de Baeder had equipped his Voisin biplane with a 60 h.p. Wolseley engine and immediately achieved startling results by annexing four prizes in one day at Chalons, the tests involving a climb to 107 metres (350 feet). Unfortunately this pilot wrecked his machine immediately afterwards by colliding with a tree, an unfortunate example which was emulated a few days later by the Baronne de la Roche, the tail of whose aircraft became entangled in a lofty poplar. The Baroness was fortunate to escape with a broken collar-bone.

At the end of January 1910 news arrived in England of the first successful flights in Australia. Mr. Colin Defries, a well-known racing-car driver, had imported a Wright, fitted it with a wheeled undercarriage of his own design and flown it for a mile at a height of thirty-five feet above the racecourse at Sydney, N.S.W. On the following day he made a further short flight with a passenger.

Mr. Grahame-White was completing his arrangements for the transfer of his now flourishing School of Flying at Pau to England. He had secured possession of the site of Hendon Aerodrome and was only awaiting the completion of the sheds there before he brought his six Bleriots and two Henry Farmans across the Channel. Amongst his pupils at Pau were Miss Spencer Kavanagh, the first British lady to take up aviation, and Mr. Armstrong Drexel, who was destined to become an exceptionally brilliant pilot. Mr. Grahame-White himself had brought a Bleriot to Brooklands where a few short test flights were made.

3. SHELLBEACH AND BROOKLANDS: ROYAL RECOGNITION FOR AVIATION

Mr. Cecil Grace was a newcomer to Shellbeach where the Hon. C. S. Rolls and Mr. F. K. McClean were flying their Wrights with consistent success. Mr. Grace had purchased a Voisin with which he soon began to fly in a capable manner, and he also flew one of the Short-built Wright machines. The Hon. Maurice Egerton accomplished a flight of more than six miles on his Wright.

In France Mr. Maurice Farman, brother of the great Henry Farman, had been making some remarkably fine cross-country flights in stages. Mr. Maurice Farman was soon to take up construction, and eventually to surpass his brother in this branch of aviation. At Mourmelon, Capt. Bertram Dickson was under instruction at the Farman school and was showing considerable aptitude as a pilot, making a flight of thirty minutes on February 17th.

On February 15th, 1910, H.M. King Edward VII honoured the Aero Club by granting it permission to use the prefix "Royal" and thenceforth the club has been known as "The Royal Aero Club of the United Kingdom." His Majesty further bestowed his patronage upon the forthcoming Aero Show at Olympia, and this display of interest in high places undoubtedly did much to encourage the many experimenters in this country to face with a cheerful countenance the ridicule to which they were still subjected.

The little colony at Brooklands, which was destined to do so much to develcp aviation at home, was already gathering in the western corner of the track. Nine hangars were already completed and housed the interesting Lane monoplane, which had been fitted with a 4-cylinder N.E.C. supercharged two-stroke, Mr. C. A. Moreing's Voisin biplane, Mr. H. J. D. Astley's monoplane, one of Mr. Grahame-White's Bleriots and two machines belonging to Mr. Holt and Mr. Neale. These were joined shortly afterwards by Mr. A. V. Roe's triplane and the Avis monoplane, which had been built by the Scottish Aeroplane Syndicate. The latter followed Bleriot lines in its general arrangement, but the tail was a copy of that used by the eminent Brazilian, Santos Dumont. The motor was a standard 25/30 h.p. Anzani radial.

4. THE 1910 OLYMPIA SHOW

Interest was now centred on the show at Olympia where thirty full-sized aeroplanes and forty-five engines were on view. Of the aircraft the following were of British design and construction :— Monoplanes : the Avis, the Blackburn, the Handley Page, the Humber, two Lanes, the Mann and Overton of Santos Dumont type, the Mulliner, the Nicholson built by Holland and Holland, the Ornis, the Spencer Stirling, the Star, which was based on the Antoinette design, the Warwick Wright and a Zodiac, which was built by the now famous Bristol Company. Biplanes : the George and Jobling, the Short with which Moore-Brabazon had won the *Daily Mail* prize, the Twining, a very flimsy Humber, and a Zodiac. In addition, Mr. Roe's triplane was exhibited.

Nearly all of the monoplanes were shameless copies of the Bleriot, whilst the George and Jobling and the Zodiac biplanes were inspired by the Farman and the Short and Twining machines by the Wright. Those aeroplanes which displayed any originality of design or construction were, with few exceptions, freaks which never actually flew. At the same time, it was encouraging to note a great advance upon the show of the previous year, and it could truthfully be said that at least two of the British exhibits had flown with success.

The advertised prices of the machines on view ranged from £1 500 for the Short to £300 for a Santos Dumont Demoiselle. The engines fitted varied in nominal horse power from 60 to 20 and comprised the following makes:—Anzani, Green, Gregoire, Advance, Darracq, Humber, N.E.C., Lascelles, J.A.P., Clement, Dutheil-Chalmers, R.H., Star, Phoenix, and E.N.V.

5. THE NICE MEETING

Towards the end of April 1910, an important meeting took place at Nice at which Great Britain was ably represented by the Hon. C. S. Rolls on his Short-built Wright, and Mr. A. Rawlinson on his Henry Farman. The latter, after making some excellent and spectacular flights, suffered a disaster when Effimoff, flying another Henry Farman biplane, passed so close above him that the slip-stream blew his machine down on to the sea. The thoughtless Russian was severely reprimanded by the officials and fined 100 francs, which did little to console Rawlinson for his immersion and the loss of a new aircraft.

Rolls continued to fly well throughout the week, his best performance being a flight of 64 kilometres (40 miles) and he was eventually placed fourth in the final order of merit. Latham carried off the Tour de Piste prize and the altitude contest but could not do better than fifth place in the general category, which was won by Effimoff, who had covered 960 kilometres (600 miles approximately) during the meeting.

6. LONDON—MANCHESTER

On Saturday, April 23rd, 1910, Mr. Claude Grahame-White leaped into the limelight and established himself as the undoubted leader of British aviation.

The *Daily Mail* newspaper had offered £10,000 to the first pilot of any nationality who should fly from a point within five miles of their London offices to a point within five miles of their Manchester offices, or *vice versa*.

Two pilots, one English and the other French, had entered for the contest. Both were mounted on Henry Farman biplanes with 50 h.p. Gnôme rotary engines. Mr. Grahame-White erected his machine at Park Royal, whilst M. Louis Paulhan was awaiting the arrival of his at Hendon. It had not been received when Mr. Grahame-White took off at 5.15 a.m. on the Saturday morning and circled round Mr. Harold Perrin, then, as now, Secretary of the R.Ae.C., who was ensconced on the top of a gasometer at Wormwood Scrubs, armed with the starting flag.

All went well until Rugby was reached two hours five minutes later and it began to look as if the £10,000 would be won before M. Paulhan had a chance to start. Unfortunately, however, the wind began to increase and the English pilot was forced down near Lichfield to await better weather.

All Saturday night the pilot and his crew stood by in case the wind should abate, but a gale was brewing and conditions became steadily worse. The final misfortune occurred on Sunday afternoon, when a gust blew the aircraft over in the field and did very considerable damage.

Undaunted by this catastrophe, Mr. Grahame-White set about stripping the wrecked machine, which was rushed back to his depot for repair. He and his crew worked incessantly day and night until Wednesday morning when the aircraft was once more airworthy. The pilot thereupon retired to bed for a much needed rest, preparatory to making a fresh start early on the following morning.

At six a.m. on that Wednesday morning, Paulhan's machine had arrived at Hendon and he proceeded feverishly with its erection under the personal supervision of Henry Farman. The factory experts had it assembled ready for flight by 5 p.m., and at 5.21 p.m. it was in the air bound for Manchester.

Grahame-White was woken up and told of the Frenchman's departure at 6.10 p.m.

Within ten minutes the English pilot was out of bed, dressed, and in the air! At 6.29 p.m. he crossed the official starting line and flew steadily northward into the gathering dusk.

Paulhan landed at Lichfield at 8.10 p.m., 117 miles out from London, whilst his pursuer was forced down by darkness at Roade after sixty miles had been covered at 7.55 p.m. Thus the Frenchman, with only about fifty-six miles to go, held a lead of sixty-seven miles and had averaged 44 m.p.h. against Grahame-White's 42 m.p.h.

Such a desperate situation called for desperate measures and Grahame-White arose magnificently to the occasion. Assembling a multitude of cars around his field he utilized their head lamps as floodlights and essayed the incredible hazard of a night flight in order to overtake the Frenchman.

The attempt was nearly successful. Grahame-White took off safely at 2.50 a.m. and had reached a point only ten miles short of the spot where Paulhan was still preparing to resume his flight, when engine trouble brought him down at Polesworth, 107 miles from London, just before 4 a.m. About three minutes later Paulhan took off once more, completed the journey without mishap, and annexed the £10,000 prize.

Thus ended an epic sporting contest in which the honours, but not the spoils, were equally divided between victor and vanquished, and which bore a strange resemblance to the struggle for the Channel prize in the previous year. It would have been a more fitting result if fate had been kinder to the Englishman and allowed him to fight out that last stage in the air, within sight of his opponent.

In any case, the race had been well worth while. The magnitude of the stake, the practical nature of the contest, the splendid sportsmanship displayed by both pilots and the resultant spate of publicity did more than any number of flying meetings could have done to rouse the British public from their lethargy and awake them to the realization that flying was no longer a kind of vaudeville turn like trick cycling, but a serious method of transport.

7. A SPANISH ADVENTURE

Meanwhile, Mr. L. D. L. Gibbs, a Farman pilot trained at Mourmelon, who had been concerned in the secret experiments with the Dunne aeroplane at Blair Atholl, in 1908, was having a much more exciting time than Mr. Grahame-White.

He had contracted to appear at Durango, Spain, to give exhibition flights. Owing to delay in transit the Henry Farman only arrived at 11.30 p.m. on the evening preceding the meeting, and Mr. Gibbs and his mechanics began to erect it at 3.30 a.m.

They worked away steadily all the morning and afternoon whilst a sceptical crowd, estimated to exceed 30,000, were thronging into the enclosures. The people had come prepared to jeer and, when they found nothing to jeer at, they began to exhibit signs of impatience.

Mr. Gibbs described the subsequent developments as follows :—

" I was asked to bring the machine out of the shed to allow the crowd to see it, and to see the work being carried on.

" Directly we wheeled it out the spectators pressed round it, sat on it, leant on it, and treated it so callously that I thought it advisable to return it to the shed in order to continue the work in peace before any damage was done, owing to ignorance on the part of the sightseers.

" I took the opportunity of returning it to its shed while a Bleriot was brought out.

" The Bleriot ran along the ground but did not rise, owing to its elevator being broken (that's what we were told).

" Upon the return of the Bleriot the crowd began to throw stones, and at this juncture the mounted Civil Guards charged with drawn swords.

" Five minutes later, however, they returned more ferociously, hurling stones, etc., so that it was impossible to carry on any further work. My mechanic was disabled. Being unable to speak Spanish is a great drawback while the shed was being torn down. I tried to explain that we wanted a few more minutes to adjust the magneto. At one point in the shed they tore a large opening with a knife, through which came a volley of stones. I went up to the opening smiling, and trying to explain about the magneto. I was met by a dozen wild individuals with a long pole pointed, with which they were going to ram.

"I smiled, or rather forced a smile, and talked fast in French, whereupon one of them—in bad French—whipped out his knife, and said they were going to knife me, as flying was impossible, there being no such thing as aviation and they cried 'Down with Science, long live Religion!'

"Whereupon I opened my coat, and pointed to where my heart ought to be, and said, 'Fire away, to avenge the motor,' still forcing a smile. Thank God it struck him (the spokesman) in a humorous light, and he sheathed his knife, and babbled words to the effect that motors were bad things, and that he was sorry he could not hurt the motor.

"At this juncture I was advised to leave, under escort, with the rest, as the authorities said they would not be responsible for our lives if we stayed any longer, and possibly it might save the plane from being wrecked.

"This I thought was good advice, and went under escort back to the judge's house, being stoned and struck the whole way back.

"I was promised that the plane would be perfectly safe under protection of the Civil Guard. Half an hour later I was informed that everything had been burnt, lock, stock and barrel."

Such were the joys of aviation in priest-ridden Spain, just over twenty years ago.

It is evident that Mr. Gibbs' life and those of his associates were only saved by his own magnificent courage and presence of mind.

8. CAPT. DICKSON'S SUCCESS ABROAD: MANY ACTIVITIES AT HOME

At the beginning of May, Capt. Bertram Dickson (Henry Farman 50 h.p. Gnôme) easily won the first prize in general classification at the meeting at Tours, by covering 267 kilometres (166 miles) during the week. This was the first important prize to be snatched from the French by an English pilot. Capt. Dickson beat a formidable gathering of foreign aviators, including MM. Chavez, Molon, Metrot, Küller and Duray, and the Baronne de la Roche.

At home there was considerable activity. Brooklands was rapidly taking on the appearance of a large airport, and already sheltered a number of machines, amongst the more successful being the Avis monoplane, on which the Hon. Alan Boyle made a flight of more than five miles at an altitude of forty feet. The first of the Bristol boxkites, made by the British & Colonial Aeroplane Co., Ltd., was installed in a hangar next to Mr. Grahame-White's Farman.

The latter pilot created a sensation when he flew across country to Woking in order to attend the police court to answer a summons for driving a car at 40 m.p.h. Honour having been satisfied by a five-pound fine the delinquent took tea with one of the magistrates and subsequently flew back again to Brooklands.

Besides the collective activities at Brooklands, Shellbeach and

Eastchurch, a number of isolated experimenters were at work in various remote parts of the country and amongst these were several who were destined to leave indelible marks on British aviation.

Mr. Geoffrey de Havilland, now the world's foremost constructor of private aircraft, had suffered a set-back when his first machine broke up in the air on its initial test flight. Fortunately he was not dismayed, and towards the end of May 1910 he completed his second machine, and took it to Litchfield, Hants., for trials.

On the Marske Sands on the Yorkshire coast Mr. Robert Blackburn was conducting painstaking experiments with his first monoplane, whilst Mr. Compton Paterson was using Southport sands for the trials of his Curtiss-type biplane.

At Brockenhurst in the New Forest, Messrs. McArdle and Drexel had established a flourishing school equipped with no less than seven Bleriots. A hangar could be rented there for under a pound a week, and there was an efficient repair shop on the aerodrome.

Unfortunately the Brockenhurst enterprise was not destined to survive, but another aerodrome which was to exercise a lasting influence on British aviation and to develop a character all its own, was established at this time. Mr. H. H. Piffard had built a biplane which vaguely resembled a Wright, fitted it with a British 8-cylinder 40 h.p. E.N.V. motor, and installed it at Shoreham, Sussex.

Mr. James Radley had been gradually mastering his Bleriot and he made some successful flights with it from the polo ground at Bedford, and subsequently gave the first exhibition flights to be seen in Scotland at Pollok. Unfortunately the ground was unsuitable, and Mr. Radley smashed his machine in endeavouring to turn to avoid the crowd, which had got out of hand

9. THE HON. C. S. ROLLS ACHIEVES DOUBLE CHANNEL CROSSING

The Channel had been crossed from France to England for the second time in May by M. Jacque de Lesseps in a Bleriot, but no one had yet flown from England to France. In June 1910, the Hon. C. S. Rolls not only accomplished this feat but actually made the return flight without alighting. He took off from Dover in his Short-built Wright biplane at 6.30 p.m., dropped a letter addressed to the Aero Club of France near Sangatte at 7.15 p.m., then flew back to England and made a perfect landing alongside his starting rail at 8.6 p.m.

He thus annexed the distinctions of being the first English pilot to cross the Channel, the first man to cross from England to France, the first man to make the double crossing, and the first cross-Channel pilot to land at a prearranged spot without damage to the air-frame. Altogether this flight was a most memorable and praiseworthy achievement, carried out in a workmanlike manner without unnecessary fuss, and Mr. Rolls richly deserved the Gold Medal of the R.Ae.C. which was conferred upon him.

10. CAPT. DICKSON'S WORLD'S RECORD: THE NEW SHORT: HEIGHT RECORDS

In France Capt. Bertram Dickson continued to uphold British prestige in no uncertain manner. He entered his Henry Farman biplane for the four-day meeting at Anjou and secured two prizes on the opening day. Later he captured second place in the altitude contest, and on June 6th, he capped his performance by breaking the world's duration record for a passenger flight by staying in the air for exactly two hours, during which he covered 98·75 kilometres (61 miles). This was the first world's record to fall to an English pilot, if we except Mr. Henry Farman's brilliant achievements of 1909, which were officially credited to France. Unfortunately, it did not stand very long as M. Aubrun flew with a passenger in his Bleriot for 2 hrs. 9 mins. $7\frac{4}{5}$ secs. on July 9th.

From Anjou Capt. Dickson went to Rouen where he captured the prize for the longest single flight, by staying aloft for 2 hrs. 27 mins., during which he covered 140 kilometres (87 miles). He had a great struggle throughout the meeting with the Italian pilot Cattaneo for the prize for total distance flown, and eventually the Englishman won this coveted award as well.

Messrs. Short Brothers had produced a new biplane of their own design, and Mr. Cecil Grace was appointed its test pilot. He achieved an instantaneous success with a flight from Eastchurch over the hills to Sheerness, where he circled above the battleships *Victorious* and *Bulwark* in a manner which gave the Lords of Admiralty furiously to think. He landed by his shed at Eastchurch forty-five minutes after the take off, and reported that the new Short system of ailerons for lateral control was quite as effective as the Wright warping wing.

This machine marked the abandonment by Short Bros. of the American Wright system of design and construction, and the adoption of the principles of Farman, Voisin, and Sommer, and was a great advance upon anything which had been produced in England thitherto.

It was remarkably easy to fly, as was evidenced by the case of Mr. Colmore, who flew it about eleven miles at his first attempt, and brought off a forced landing successfully. On the following day this brilliant beginner was out again in a gusty wind and made several flights, culminating in another successful forced landing from 100 feet. His total previous experience of flying consisted of twenty minutes taxying practice immediately before his first solo!

Mr. Armstrong Drexel had put the British height record up to 1,070 feet at Beaulieu on his Bleriot, but this achievement only

"Flight" photo

7.—Fighting a gale: Mr. Hubert Latham on his Antoinette at Blackpool.

Facing page 48

"Flight" photo

8.—Shellbeach: Mr. Moore-Brabazon (Short—60 h.p. Green) starting on the first All-British circular flight of one mile.

Facing page 48

stood for a few hours, as Mr. Cecil Grace took the new Short up to 1,180 feet on the following day, cut his motor and glided the whole way back to earth.

11. THE WOLVERHAMPTON MEETING

The Midland Aero Club arranged the first British meeting of 1910 on the Dunstall Park racecourse at Wolverhampton, and a surprising number of British pilots appeared, although only two used British aircraft. The meeting was spoiled by bad weather, which prevented any outstanding performances. Mr. Grahame-White on his Henry Farman (50 h.p. Gnôme) captured the duration competition with a total of 1 hr. 15 mins. flying during the week. He also took second place in the lap speed contest and in the competition for shortest take-off.

The Hon. C. S. Rolls (Wright) won the lap speed contest by a substantial margin owing to his clever cornering, whilst Mr. Cecil Grace (Short) captured the altitude prize at 600 feet, Mr. Cockburn (Hy. Farman) winning the take-off competition with a run of 100 feet.

The most spectacular flight of the meeting was performed by Mr. Cecil Grace, who flew around outside the racecourse for about half an hour, performing various evolutions, culminating in an engine-off descent from 150 feet.

12. RHEIMS, 1910

None of the Continental experts appeared at Wolverhampton, as they were engaged at Rheims, where no less than forty-six aircraft, all of French construction, competed. The best performance was put up by M. Olieslagers on a Bleriot (Gnôme) monoplane, who broke Mr. Henry Farman's world's duration record with a magnificent flight of 5 hrs. 3 mins. 5⅕ secs., during which he covered 392·750 kilometres (245 miles) and won the Michelin Cup and 20,000 francs. Olieslagers put in 19 hrs. 11 mins. 45 secs. in the air during the meeting, covering 1,693 kilometres (1,051 miles), and his total prize money was no less than 42,000 francs.

Mr. Hubert Latham on his Antoinette raised the European altitude record to 1,384 metres (4,440 feet) and was ranked fifth in general order of merit.

13. THE BOURNEMOUTH WEEK: ROLLS KILLED

On July 10th, 1910, the great aviation week at Bournemouth opened. This was the first occasion upon which the British pilots and machines competed with representatives of the Continental pilots on level terms in this country.

Bleriot monoplanes were popular, the English exponents of this *marque* including McArdle, the local expert, and James Radley, whilst the ultimate winner of the competition was Mons. L. F. Morane, on a Bleriot powered with a 60 h.p. 7-cylinder Gnôme.

Other well-known English pilots were Grahame-White, Bertram Dickson, Robert Loraine the actor, Capt. Rawlinson, and L. D. L. Gibbs fresh from his excitements in Spain, all on Henry Farman biplanes with 60 h.p. 7-cylinder Gnôme motors.

There were two Short biplanes, one with a 65 h.p. 8-cylinder E.N.V. engine handled by Cecil Grace, and one with a 50 h.p. 4-cylinder Green, which was flown by Mr. G. C. Colmore. The Hon. C. S. Rolls had a French-built Wright, whilst Mr. Ogilvie used a Short-built one from Leysdown.

The principal foreign competition came from Morane's Bleriot, Christiaens on a Henry Farman, Louis Wagner on the new Hanriot monoplane with the 40 h.p. 4-cylinder Clergêt engine, and E. Audemars, who used a Bayard-Clement monoplane.

The proceedings opened with the arrival, on the evening preceding the competition, of Mr. McArdle in his partner's Bleriot. He had flown across the New Forest from Beaulieu with his luggage aboard. This splendid flight created a deep impression.

Honours on the first day went to Christiaens and Grahame-White (Henry Farmans) for distance flown, the former covering eighty-three miles in 2 hrs. 20 mins., and the latter eighty-nine miles in 2 hrs. 31 mins.

The promoters had arranged a prize for the slowest lap which attracted the attention of Rolls, who managed to stall his Wright round in 4 mins. 13 secs. at a speed of 25½ m.p.h. He then put his mount at the lap record and clocked 2 mins 39⅖ secs., which gave a lap speed of 40⅕ m.p.h., thus showing a very useful speed range.

The second day was marred by a tragedy. With almost incredible foolishness, the officials had set out the bull's-eye for the landing competition right under the shadow of the grand stand and immediately to windward of it. Several competitors attempted cross-wind landings on to the mark along the side of the stand, but naturally these efforts were not conspicuously successful. Mr. Rolls realized that in order to make a good showing, it was essential to approach and land into wind. He therefore decided to experiment, and flew out behind the grand stand. As he approached the enclosure he saw the landing mark close beneath him, and pushed forward his elevator to dive down over the roof of the stand. Apparently he realized that he would be unable to flatten out in time, and accordingly pulled the stick back violently. The strain was too great for the flimsy construction of the Wright and one or more of the tail booms gave way. Rolls was killed almost instantaneously—the first British power pilot to give his life to the cause of aviation, and one we could ill afford to lose.

This tragic affair was followed two days later by a serious

accident to Capt. Rawlinson, who was badly hurt when the undercarriage of his Farman collapsed in landing. On the following day another Farman collapsed and Christiaens joined Rawlinson in hospital—whilst on the Saturday the Hon. Alan Boyle wrecked his Avis monoplane and was carried off with concussion.

The best flying of the meeting was done by L. Morane, Armstrong Drexel, McArdle (who was not officially entered as a competitor), Grahame-White, Dickson, and the actor-pilot, Robert Loraine.

The best flights were made between Southbourne and the Needles, I.O.W., Morane and Drexel making the return trip on their Bleriots, whilst Loraine was forced to land his Farman on the Island in a rainstorm, after a plucky flight in very tricky weather. The only other machine to do the crossing was Grahame-White's Farman, which averaged only 27·44 m.p.h. One suspects faulty navigation as the cause.

Mons. L. F. Morane (Bleriot-Gnôme) was adjudged winner on general merit, with Messrs. Armstrong Drexel (Bleriot) and Grahame-White (Farman) equal second, and Capt. B. Dickson (Farman) third.

Notable feats were Morane's lap at 56 m.p.h. and his climb to 4,107 feet in just under seventeen minutes.

14. THRILLS FOR MCARDLE AND FERGUSON

Messrs. McArdle and Drexel each flew a Bleriot home to their New Forest school at the conclusion of the meeting, the latter taking a passenger with him in the two-seater, which the firm had purchased from M. Morane. The former, who flew the single-seater which he hȧd delivered for Drexel before the meeting, had a very exciting experience. He took off from Bournemouth at 6.15 p.m., eight minutes after Drexel's two-seater, and climbed steadily towards Hurst Castle, which he passed at 6.25 p.m.

Almost immediately afterwards he was sighted flying over his aerodrome at 1,000 feet, at the same moment as Drexel arrived below him, but he had not reckoned on a strong following wind which swept him past towards Southampton before he realized what had happened.

The Bleriot's motor was throwing out a lot of oil and this got into McArdle's eyes and caused curious tricks of vision.

He realized that he was lost, and came down low to try to get a bearing. For over an hour he twisted and turned, half blinded by oil, following the little New Forest roads about in the gathering haze, but failed to discover where he was. Eventually he gave up hope of finding his aerodrome and made a forced landing in a small oat field near Fordingbridge, damaging the airscrew slightly. He was 1 hr. 35 mins. out from Bournemouth, during which he must have flown over seventy miles, and had consumed ten gallons of petrol and *four and a half gallons* of oil.

At about this time another remarkable experience befell Mr. Ferguson, who was flying a monoplane of his own design and construction, off Magilligan Strand. The machine suddenly lost height whilst over Lough Foyle and actually touched the water. Mr. Ferguson, keeping the throttle wide open, managed to coax it back into the air again and eventually landed drenched in spray.

15. THE FIRST BRITISH WOMAN PILOT

I have previously mentioned Miss " Spencer Kavanagh " who was almost certainly the first British lady pilot to fly solo, and who flew Bleriots at the Grahame-White school at Pau early in 1910. This lady was a professional parachute jumper, who was well known under the name of " Viola Spencer." Towards the end of July 1910 she was fatally injured whilst making a jump from a balloon at Coventry, and at the inquest it was disclosed that her real name was Miss Edith Maud Cook.

16. THE SECOND BLACKPOOL MEETING

Grahame-White took his Farman down to the West Country and flew over the Fleet in Torbay, prior to dispatching it to Blackpool, where he was to take part in the second International Meeting to be held there under the auspices of the Lancashire Aero Club. He had two Bleriots at this meeting in addition to the trusty Farman.

Mr. A. V. Roe, still dogged by misfortune, had the heart-rending experience of having both his triplanes destroyed by fire in a goods train *en route* to Blackpool, and this occurred just after he had achieved some really encouraging flights with one of them at Brooklands. Mr. Roe was certainly the most unlucky of all our pioneers. Mr. Grace's Short biplane was in the next truck, but fortunately escaped undamaged.

The Blackpool Flying Carnival opened on July 28th, 1910, and lasted for three weeks.

After a quiet start, due to the usual unpreparedness of both officials and competitors, the thrills came thick and fast. Robert Loraine had given indications at Bournemouth of his dashing temperament, and now he proceeded to throw discretion to the winds and treat the crowds to some hair-raising aviation of a strictly practical nature. After a short flight in a high wind on the Saturday, when he was forced down in a field outside the aerodrome, Loraine brought out his racing Farman, which had a clipped bottom wing, and took off on Bank Holiday at 3.15 p.m. He did one circuit of the aerodrome and then struck off across country towards Lytham. At 4.15 p.m., someone telephoned from Liverpool that he was flying over the city and a few minutes later news came in that he was passing New Brighton. At 5.5 p.m. he made a forced landing on a sandbank at Fairhaven, six miles from the aerodrome, because he had discovered that the fabric covering his tail plane had become sodden with oil, and was bellying upwards and making the machine tail heavy. The fabric was soon riveted down again and the pilot resumed his journey at 6.45 p.m., landing on the aerodrome just before 7 p.m., after an adventure lasting nearly four hours.

For some reason this magnificent flight did not count for the duration prize, so the indefatigable pilot refuelled forthwith and proceeded to lap the aerodrome until dusk.

Messrs. McArdle and Drexel, who were the foremost Bleriot exponents resident in England at that time, were flying borrowed machines and entered as rivals for the altitude contest. McArdle was obviously uncomfortable in one of Grahame-White's Bleriots, and made a forced landing outside the aerodrome soon after taking off. Armstrong Drexel borrowed Cecil Grace's new and untried Bleriot, and took off for the height prize. He had a most alarming ride as the machine oscillated dangerously as soon as it got into the air, and seemed to the spectators to be out of control. Drexel stuck to it until he had reached 600 feet, when he lost height in a steep dive, flattened out and made a perfect landing. An examination disclosed that the fuselage bracing wires were slack, allowing the tail to twist relative to the main wing. Drexel was awarded the £100 " Daily Merit " prize for this flight.

Grahame-White had a happy knack of thinking of little touches to please the press and the spectators, and to spread abroad a belief in the practical worth of aeroplanes as vehicles of transport. He also had the skill and dash to carry them out neatly and efficiently. Blackpool provided him with several opportunities.

His first adventure was a flight to the Victoria Pier, where he landed on the sands and visited the Lancashire Aero Club's premises on the front opposite, afterwards returning and taking off from the beach whilst policemen held back the crowd.

On the following day he flew twelve miles to Southport, once again landing on the sands, and spent an hour in the town before returning to his machine and flying back to the aerodrome.

In the afternoon, Grahame-White annexed the " Daily Merit " £100 for that day by a masterly exhibition of figures of eight on the Farman. Having done this, he settled down to " joy-riding " for the rest of the evening, the majority of his passengers being ladies.

The next day produced a violent wind, and the only pilot to venture aloft was Grahame-White, who trusted himself to his Henry Farman and put in several laps of the course in spite of being severely buffeted by 30 m.p.h. gusts. He was timed to exceed 70 m.p.h. ground speed down-wind during this stirring flight.

A. V. Roe had succeeded in building another of his triplanes out of spare parts. He began this work on the Thursday morning, when he heard of the destruction of his other two machines, and on the following Monday afternoon it flew four laps—and crashed. Two days later Roe brought it out again, flew two laps and pancaked, damaging the undercarriage. This was repaired and Roe took off once more, only to crash heavily in trying to avoid a mark tower. The officials awarded him a special prize of £50 for his pertinacity.

Roe soon had his machine repaired once more and proceeded to do short flights throughout the ensuing week, until he attempted to land down a 20 m.p.h. wind, with the usual result. It was soon repaired again and was still flying, in between crashes, at the end of the meeting.

On August 10th, Robert Loraine and Grahame-White both performed spectacular cross-country flights in their Farmans from Blackpool. Loraine went to Southport and turned boldly out to sea, aiming for the Welsh coast, which he crossed at Rhos, where he landed on the golf links after covering sixty miles in an hour and a half.

Later he took off again and flew out to sea once more. Presently he came into touch with the coast of Anglesey and decided to land, as he had been two hours in the air since leaving Rhos, and his petrol was running short. He landed at Cemlyn, near Holyhead. In attempting to take off next morning, the undercarriage was damaged, thus terminating a very plucky flight.

Grahame-White flew to Fleetwood Barracks, where he landed, then crossed Morecambe Bay to Barrow, and thence flew back to Blackpool.

On the last day of the meeting, Grahame-White flew for seventeen minutes in a perfect gale of wind, thus proving that a cool and clever pilot, in a machine which was aerodynamically sound, could ride out any ordinary English weather in safety. This heroic flight netted him £400 in prize money and not one of his competitors grudged him a penny of it.

So ended the second Blackpool meeting, which resulted in a financial loss estimated at £20,000. The weather had been bad throughout, and the crowd had discovered that it was really unnecessary to pay to see the flying, as a perfect view could be obtained from the hills outside the aerodrome.

The only record which was broken at the meeting was the European altitude record, which was raised to 5,887 feet by the Peruvian pilot, Chavez, on a Bleriot.

The most consistent performers were Grahame-White and Robert Loraine on Farmans, Tetard on a Sommer, and Armstrong Drexel and Cecil Grace on Bleriots. These five pilots managed to keep up the interest and to make up for the absence of many of our best men at the rival meeting at Lanark.

17. THE MEETING AT LANARK

Competent observers stated that the organization of Scotland's first flying meeting at Lanark surpassed anything which had yet been done in Europe. The aerodrome chosen was Lanark race-course, which gave a smooth grass circuit of one and three-quarter miles to the lap.

At that time no one had yet grasped the fact that landings and take-offs should invariably be made into the wind, and it was pointed out that the position of the time-keeper's box at Lanark rendered it necessary for all pilots to take off down the prevailing wind, and for this reason it was not anticipated that any records for quick get-off would be broken !

It was just this astonishing lack of perception on the part of the officials and pilots alike which had resulted in the fatality at Bournemouth. These meetings were organized with both eyes on the turnstiles, and everything was subordinated to the object of giving the populace its money's-worth, quite regardless of the risks involved. Landing circles were placed, as at Bournemouth, a few feet in front of the most expensive seats in the grand stand, and competitors were compelled to take off and land up and down the front of the enclosures, whatever the direction of the wind.

There were twenty-two competitors, of whom half were English. The entry list included six English-built machines, comprising a Short-built Wright (40 h.p. E.N.V.), a Humber (40 h.p. Humber), two Shorts, one with a 50 h.p. Green and the other with a 60 h.p. E.N.V., and two Bristol biplanes fitted with a 60 h.p. Gnôme and an 80 h.p. E.N.V., respectively. In addition, our Anglo-American friend, S. F. Cody, turned up again with a new biplane of his own design and construction. The French aircraft included seven Bleriots, four Farmans, two Sommers, two Hanriots, a Voisin, a Tellier, an Antoinette, and a Demoiselle. The last-named had been flown at Bournemouth by the Swiss pilot, Audemars, where it was entered as a Bayard-Clement.

By a singular coincidence the Bleriot and Antoinette machines of Chavez and Küller had been damaged by fire on a goods train in transit, but fortunately Mr. L. D. L. Gibbs was able to lend the former a new Bleriot, whilst the Dutch pilot set about rebuilding his Antoinette with the pertinacity characteristic of his race.

The discovery of the meeting was James Radley, who had put a lot of power into his Bleriot's Gnôme, and proceeded to amaze the crowds with his speed and clever corner work.

McArdle made one of his courageous cross-country essays in an unpremeditated attempt to reach Edinburgh, and would probably have been successful if he had not run into a fog, which forced him to put his Bleriot down only one mile out of the capital.

The Wednesday of the week broke all gate records for a British flying meeting, with a crowd of 50,000, who saw some splendid sport. Young Marcel Hanriot, who was then under seventeen years of age, delighted them with an exhibition of polished flying on his father's monoplane, whilst the Italian Cattaneo broke the British distance and duration records in his Bleriot, by covering 141 miles 188 yards in 3 hrs. 11 mins. Radley began to show off the terrific speed of his Bleriot, and the thrills were provided by Champel, who dropped his Voisin on to a wood of fir trees.

On the following day a world's record was captured. Armstrong Drexel, McArdle's American partner, made a most determined attack on the altitude record. At 3,000 feet he entered a cloud bank and disappeared. No word was received from him until two and a half hours later, when he telegraphed from Cobbinshaw near Edinburgh. His sealed barograph recorded 6,750 feet, which was subsequently corrected to 6,621 feet, which was 440 feet better than the previous record held by Brookins (U.S.A.) on a Wright.

On the following day Küller stalled his rebuilt Antoinette on to Champel's Wood and this unfortunate example was followed by Colmore, who put his Short down amongst the trees near the same place. Altogether 270 trees had to be felled during the meeting, in order to retrieve various aeroplanes which had nested in them. It was miraculous that nobody was hurt.

Cody's new aircraft, which weighed one and a quarter tons empty, was grossly underpowered, and did little but taxi around the aerodrome.

The net result of a highly successful meeting was a triumph for the Bleriot-Gnôme combination. The most notable performances were Drexel's altitude record and Radley's speed records.

This was the first occasion in the world upon which aeroplanes had been accurately timed over a straight measured distance. The first world's records were set up over one mile and one kilometre. One flight served for both records, which were timed by Mr. A. V. Ebblewhite, and the competitors flew with a breeze of about 10 m.p.h. behind them. It is very interesting to note the result of this test. The figures for the kilometre were as follows :—

1. Radley (Bleriot) .. .. .. 77·67 m.p.h.
2. McArdle (Bleriot) .. .. .. 72·62 ,,
3. Cattaneo (Bleriot) .. .. .. 72·60 ,,
4. Grace (Farman) .. .. .. 55·92 ,,
5. Colmore (Short) .. .. .. 52·75 ,,

Thus it will be seen that Radley's tuning had given him 5 m.p.h. over his Bleriot rivals, and that the slowest Bleriot was 16 m.p.h. faster than the best of the other types.

Radley's Flying Mile record was 75·95 m.p.h., and the brilliance of his piloting was demonstrated by the fact that he covered five laps of a one and three-quarter mile course, at an average speed of 58·32 m.p.h., beating the Italian star by over 2 m.p.h.

By way of contrast Ogilvie won the prize for the slowest circuit,

"Flight" photo

9.—Brooklands: L to R: Mr. Astley's Lane Monoplane, Mr. Roe's Triplane and Mr. Moreing's Voisin Biplane.

Facing page 56

"Flight" photo

10.—London–Manchester: Mr. Grahame-White (Farman—50 h.p. Gnôme) ready to start on his first attempt.

by dawdling around on his Wright at 24·11 m.p.h. There must have been considerable temptation to swing out on the corners in these competitions and the figures should not be taken too seriously.

Cattaneo won the prize for aggregate distance flown by covering a few yards short of 400 miles during the week, whilst Mr. Cecil Grace on a Farman (Gnôme) headed the prize list with £1,950

18. EXCITING FLIGHTS IN IRELAND

It was not only in Spain that trouble arose on account of the inability of the crowds to realize that there were some conditions under which pilots could not fly. Mr. James Radley took his Bleriot to Belfast in order to give some exhibition flights, but a very high wind rendered it obviously unsafe for any attempt at aviation. The crowd soon became threatening, and tried to break up the monoplane, so Radley determined to give them something for their money, with a view to pacifying them. He had only just left the ground when a gust caught his machine and he collided with a tree, breaking the wings and airscrew.

Similar boisterous winds served to curtail the flying at the Dublin meeting at the end of August. Only three pilots had been engaged to appear at this two-day exhibition, and it was well for the promoters that all three were of the highest class. Cecil Grace and Bertram Dickson on Farmans put up really great demonstrations of bad-weather flying, whilst Armstrong Drexel took his Bleriot up to a satisfying height on the first day.

19. ACROSS THE IRISH SEA: ROBERT LORAINE

After the excitement of the big meetings at Bournemouth, Blackpool, and Lanark, there ensued a quiet period in this country, except for spasmodic activity at the new aerodrome at Wolverhampton, at Brooklands, and at Eastchurch, where Mr. Cecil Grace put in several hours on the Bleriot, with which first Morane and subsequently Drexel, had beaten the world's altitude record.

The calm was broken dramatically by one of the most sensational flights in history.

Robert Loraine, the actor, who had burst into prominence at Blackpool, had left his Farman near Holyhead, where he had crashed it at the termination of his grand flight from Blackpool to Anglesey. Evidently he had nursed the ambition to do the first crossing to Ireland for some considerable time.

A modern pilot with not more than ten hours solo to his credit, could not be blamed if he thought twice about tackling over sixty miles of ocean in a well-found Moth. Loraine apparently suffered no qualms. He arranged for no naval escort to accompany him, there were no elaborate preparations. He simply started up the

Gnôme, took off, climbed to 4,000 feet, and steered out to sea to the westward.

His ordeal began when it became evident that the machine had not been properly rigged after its crash, and before very long the wires began to snap here and there !

As if it was not enough to bear to have his aircraft breaking up under him, the pilot was brought face to face with death by drowning when his motor stopped dead, about twenty miles out from land.

It was a saving grace of the early rotary engine that it turned very easily in a glide, even if it was not firing, and there was always a chance that it would resume business of its own accord.

This happened to Loraine after he had lost 2,500 feet, and he immediately climbed back to 4,000 feet again and resumed the flight.

It was fortunate that he kept as high as he could, because there was an obstruction in his petrol feed, and the Gnôme stopped work *five* times more before he sighted land !

On each occasion he had to dive the machine towards the cold sea for hundreds of feet before the petrol worked through again and the motor picked up.

Every time he dived, another wire would snap. There were plenty of wires on those old Henry Farmans, but obviously it was only a question of time before the whole contrivance would fold up in the air.

Loraine, cither by luck or by brilliant navigation, happened to strike the Irish coast where Baily Lighthouse marks the promontory on the north side of Dublin Bay, and he decided to get down here on the first dry land he met, and abandon his intention of flying on to Dublin, and landing in Phœnix Park.

Just as he turned into wind to land by the lighthouse, the Gnôme dried up for the last time and immediately before the machine hit the water, another wire gave out !

Loraine swam the last seventy feet to the shore, having suffered a series of experiences unique in the annals of aviation.

No pioneer ever attempted a more dangerous task and none ever had so many successive escapes from death in so short a time.

20. GRAHAME-WHITE IN U.S.A. : GEOFFREY DE HAVILLAND

Claude Grahame-White had taken his Henry Farman to the United States and was having a great success at the Boston meeting, where he amazed the Americans with his finished flying and the reliability of his aircraft and engine.

On September 7th, 1910, he won a £2,000 prize offered by the *Boston Globe* newspaper, by covering a cross-country course of thirty-three miles in 40 mins. 1⅗ secs. In addition to this big triumph he scored four firsts and three seconds at the meeting, which brought his total prize money up to £6,420 for the week.

At home there was renewed activity at Brooklands, where Mr. D. Graham Gilmour was doing very well on a Bleriot, and at Laffan's Plain, where Mr. Cody had begun to achieve really good results from his large new biplane, after fitting one of the latest Green engines.

Down in the New Forest, the McArdle-Drexel Bleriot school housed no less than ten aeroplanes, and many pupils were under instruction, the most noteworthy being Mr. B. H. Barrington Kennett, of the Grenadier Guards, of whom much will be heard later in this history.

Mr. Geoffrey de Havilland's second machine had shown considerable promise in its early trials, getting off in a dead calm in less than forty yards with its de Havilland engine. This ancestor of the Gipsy-Moth resembled a Sommer in appearance.

21. A MEETING AT FOLKESTONE

At the end of September 1910, a small flying meeting was organized on the Folkestone racecourse within half a mile of the site of Lympne Airport. Only three pilots attended, but the spectators saw some first-class aviation by the American Moisant, who had recently made a plucky flight by stages from Paris to London with a passenger, in a Bleriot monoplane. Mr. Cecil Grace flew his record-breaking Bleriot, and gave a masterly exhibition of high flying, followed by long spiral glides. The meeting was marred by a serious accident to Mr. G. A. Barnes, who had trouble with the controls of his Humber-Bleriot, and jumped overboard from an altitude of quite thirty feet. Barnes fell very heavily, sustaining head injuries and a broken wrist, from which he subsequently recovered. The empty Bleriot leaped upwards, stalled itself and crashed to the ground upside down a few yards away.

M. Louis Bleriot was essentially a practical engineer, and he had designed his popular production model Bleriot XI with an eye on ease of handling. His system was so successful that when Mr. Cecil Grace's machine returned by road from Folkestone to Eastchurch, it was taken off the lorry, erected, and flown within ten minutes.

22. DONCASTER'S ALL-FRENCH MEETING

The Doncaster authorities, undeterred by the fiasco of the previous year, had organized another flying week, which took place at the same time as the Folkestone meeting. The entry list was entirely French, the pilots being Ladougne (Goupy), Paul de Lesseps and Mamet (Bleriots), Mme. Dutrieu, Beau, and Bruneau de Laborie (Farmans). The Goupy machine was a very advanced design of tractor biplane, with a biplane tail, both main and tail planes being staggered in the modern fashion. It was certainly the first tractor biplane to be seen in this country, and may justly claim to be the original precursor of the standard aeroplane of the present day. No outstanding flights were achieved at this meeting, which was spoiled by bad weather.

Most of the pilots and machines from Doncaster subsequently appeared at a meeting at Burton-on-Trent, where much better weather prevailed. Some excellent flying was done, notably by Mamet and Paul de Lesseps (Bleriots).

23. THE BRISTOL COMPANY AND THE WAR OFFICE

The Bristol Company had established a depot on Salisbury Plain in addition to their hangar at Brooklands, and had been busy developing their Farman type biplanes under the close supervision of the Military authorities.

It was arranged that the company should co-operate with the War Office in the Army manœuvres at the end of September, and Capt. Dickson and Mr. Robert Loraine were given a Bristol each, whilst Lieut. L. D. L. Gibbs flew his own clipped-wing racing Farman.

The experiments were a great success, and it is difficult to exaggerate their importance. One of the most interesting features of the trials was the attempt by Loraine to transmit wireless messages from his machine in flight to a portable wireless station at Lark Hill. One way communication was maintained up to a distance of a quarter of a mile.

At the close of the manœuvres on September 30th, 1910, Mr. Loraine continued these experiments and increased the range of transmission to over a mile.

The immediate result of the manœuvres was the appointment of Major Sir A. Bannerman to command the Balloon Section R.E. at Farnborough, *vice* Col. Capper, and the determination of the authorities to "enlarge the scope of the work hitherto carried out at the Balloon School . . . by affording opportunities for aeroplaning. . . ."

From this decision sprang the Royal Air Force.

24. BROOKLANDS DEVELOPMENTS

Brooklands was becoming very busy and there were almost daily additions to the band of enthusiasts who lived in the huts around the famous Blue Bird Café, which had recently been opened under the shadow of the Byfleet Banking. Among the machines which were being flown was the Neale VII biplane, which was an interesting design with twin rudders between the wing tips and a Green engine. This aircraft was expressly designed to avoid infringing the Wright patents, concerning which a great deal of expensive and fruitless litigation was taking place. The Neale was flown by its designer and Mr. Rippen.

Lieut. Maitland was in charge of the Bristol biplane and Messrs. Wickham and Spottiswoode were flying Avis monoplanes with J.A.P. motors. Mr. Keith Davis performed excellently on the Hanriot monoplane (E.N.V.), Mr. Watkins flew a Howard-Wright, whilst Mr. Graham Gilmour broke the Brooklands duration record with a flight of more than one hour on his J.A.P. engined Bleriot.

25. HENDON OPENED

On October 1st, 1910, M. Louis Bleriot opened Hendon Aerodrome to the public. This field which was to have a very great influence on British aviation, had for some time past been used by various pilots for experiments, and it had also been the scene of Paulhan's departure on his London–Manchester flight.

The Bleriot company erected eight hangars, three of which were leased to the Aeronautical Syndicate, Ltd., who had produced a strange tailless pusher monoplane known as the Valkyrie, which flew with some success, albeit dangerously.

Bleriot stocked the remainder of the sheds with cross-Channel Bleriot monoplanes (Gnômes), and installed M. Pierre Prier as chief pilot instructor. His first pupil was the celebrated balloonist, Mr. Frank Hedges Butler.

26. CAPT. DICKSON IN FIRST AIR COLLISION

The first collision in the air occurred at the Milan meeting, at the beginning of October 1910. Capt. Bertram Dickson had taken his Henry Farman out to Italy and had thrilled the crowds with his masterly gliding descents from high altitudes. It was during one of these exhibitions that M. Thomas, who was making a fast descent with engine on in his Antoinette monoplane, flew right down on to the top wing of the Farman. The machines became entangled with each other and fell together in the centre of the aerodrome. The French pilot escaped uninjured, but Capt. Dickson was badly hurt, spent several weeks in hospital, and eventually emerged crippled for life. He never flew again.

27. THE PARIS SALON

The annual Paris Salon followed upon the Milan meeting, but Great Britain was not represented.

The most notable advance was seen in the Voisin two-seat pusher biplane, which was shown with a *mitrailleuse* mounted in the *nacelle*. Voisin had abandoned the vertical side curtains between the interplane struts, which had always been a feature of the *marque* and had adopted aileron control.

28. T.O.M. SOPWITH

October 22nd, 1910, saw the *début* at Brooklands of another pioneer who was to leave his name written large across our flying history. Six years later our German friends were to have cause to curse the name of Sopwith as fervently as we were wont to consign the Dutchman Fokker to perdition. Mr. T. O. M. Sopwith first appeared at Brooklands with a Howard-Wright biplane (E.N.V.) which he had just purchased. It was characteristic of the man that he took the new machine for its first test flight without having been in the air himself before. The result was nearly disastrous, for after flying for some three hundred yards, he pulled the stick back sharply and the aircraft shot up to forty feet, stalled, and crashed, breaking the airscrew, undercarriage, and one wing. Sopwith was fortunate to escape unhurt. Had it been otherwise, the whole course of the late War might have been changed to a remarkable degree.

29. GRAHAME-WHITE WINS GORDON-BENNETT CONTEST

The teams for the important Gordon-Bennett Cup Race which was flown at the end of October 1910 at Belmont Park, New York, U.S.A., comprised the following pilots :—Great Britain : Messrs. Grahame-White, Radley, and Ogilvie. France : MM. Latham and Leblanc. U.S.A. : Messrs. Brookins, Moisant, and Drexel. There was no restriction on the nationality of the aircraft or engine used by any pilot, the Aero Club of each competing nation nominating three of its own nationals to fly any machine which they cared to choose for the purpose of the race.

Mr. Grahame-White had taken his trusty old Farman out with him, but he soon saw that he would stand little chance against some of the foreign competitors, who were mounted on fast monoplanes. He was, of course, familiar with the standard Bleriot machines, which he had flown at Pau, and accordingly he cabled to M. Bleriot, asking that the latest racing type of that *marque* should be dispatched to him at New York. A little clipped-wing single-seat racer, fitted with the latest 14-cylinder Gnôme rotary motor, arrived at Belmont Park thirty-six hours before the contest, and Mr. Grahame-White's mechanics immediately began the work of erecting it and testing the new engine.

Bad weather prevented any prolonged test flights, and our first string went to the line for the contest in a machine with which he was entirely unfamiliar, and which embodied some startling innovations in design.

The course was most unsuitable for racing purposes, and several of the pilots petitioned the committee to make alterations with a view to their own safety. The request was, however, ignored and the competitors were set to fly twenty laps of the five kilometres circuit, which had been marked out round the racecourse.

The contest was not a race in the proper sense of the term, as each pilot could choose when he should start, and the one who covered the distance in the shortest time was the winner.

Mr. Grahame-White made the first and successful attempt, completing his twenty laps in 1 hr. 1 min. 4·74 secs. at the remarkable average speed of just over 60 m.p.h.

The next competitor was M. Leblanc (Bleriot) who flew with great dash and was leading Grahame-White by five and a half minutes as he entered on his last lap, only to crash into a telegraph pole, wrecking his machine and suffering severe cuts and bruises. This was astonishingly hard luck on the sporting Frenchman, who had lapped the five kilometres course at over 70 m.p.h., and who thoroughly deserved to win.

Ogilvie (Britain) was the next to make the attempt on his Wright racer, but he suffered a stoppage of fifty-four minutes owing to a sparking plug blowing out of his engine, so that his elapsed time was 2 hrs. 6 mins. 36 secs. He was followed by Brookins (U.S.A.) on another Wright, which got out of control and crashed from 200 feet in front of the grand stand. Brookins had a miraculous escape from injury.

Latham (France) completed the course in 5 hrs. 48 mins. 53 secs. on his Antoinette after a protracted stop for repairs, and Moisant (U.S.A.), who was the only other pilot to finish, brought his Bleriot into second place at the end of the day in 1 hr. 59 mins. 44·85 secs. after an intermediate landing due to engine trouble.

The final result was very gratifying for the R.Ae.C. :—

Winner.—Grahame-White (Brit.), Bleriot (Gnôme).
Second.—Moisant (U.S.A.), Bleriot (Gnôme).
Third. — Ogilvie (Brit.), Wright (Wright).
Fourth.—H. Latham (Fr.), Antoinette (Antoinette).

30. GRAHAME-WHITE WINS STATUE OF LIBERTY PRIZE

On the following day there occurred one of those unpleasant incidents which are now of such frequent occurrence in sporting contests in the U.S.A.

Mr. Ryan had given a prize of £2,000 for the pilot who should make the fastest time on a flight from Belmont Park round the Statue of Liberty and back. This was an extremely hazardous enterprise, calling for no little courage and skill on the part of the pilot.

Under the rules, the prize was to remain open for competition until the end of the meeting, which was fixed for the Monday night, each pilot being able to make any number of attempts, the best time to count. Only pilots " who shall have remained in the air in one continuous flight one hour or more, during the previous contests in the International Aviation Tournament " being eligible to complete.

Mr. Grahame-White, having qualified to enter by his magnificent flight for the Gordon-Bennett Cup, notified the Stewards that he wished to make the attempt, and was informed that he must get off before 3.45 p.m., as that was the latest hour for starting this competition on the Sunday afternoon. Starting in good time, therefore, he took his racing Bleriot over the thirty-three mile course in 35 mins. 21·3 secs. Mons. J. de Lesseps followed in another Bleriot, but took 44 mins. 56·25 secs., and, in any case, he had not qualified to enter.

The only other aspirant was the American Moisant (Bleriot) who had also omitted to qualify by executing the necessary one hour flight earlier in the competition, and who was therefore entirely ineligible to compete.

Moisant was not ready to take off until 4 p.m. but the committee allowed him to start, contradicting their ruling to Grahame-White, and stating that the competition would be open until the close of the meeting, i.e., until the evening of the following day.

Moisant completed the course in 34 mins. 38·8 secs. thus beating Grahame-White's time by some 42 secs. The Englishman announced that he would make another attempt then and there, whereupon the American pilot went to the committee and protested, asking that the meeting should be declared officially closed immediately instead of on the following afternoon, as was indicated in the programme.

The committee assented to this amazing subterfuge, and, still ignoring the fact that their pilot was not qualified even to enter the competition, awarded him the prize of £2,000 !

This astonishing display of bad sportsmanship caused an uproar amongst the pilots, most of whom refused to attend the official dinner given in their honour and attended a rival function hastily arranged by that great American sportsman, Armstrong Drexel.

Drexel wrote a letter to the press, in which he said : " I wish to protest against the action of the Belmont Park Aviation Committee in refusing to allow Mr. Grahame-White, the Englishman, to fly a second time for the Statue of Liberty Prize. Their doing so is contrary to all traditions of sport, and as an American myself, familiar with the conditions of sport in Europe, I cannot allow the action of the committee to pass without protest. . . . As a general result, it will be freely said in Europe that the Liberty prize was juggled into an American's hands. This will only be the plain truth, according to the conditions of the contest as understood by the aviators. . . . My disgust at this betrayal is more, almost, than I can express. What is the feeling of the Englishmen and French-

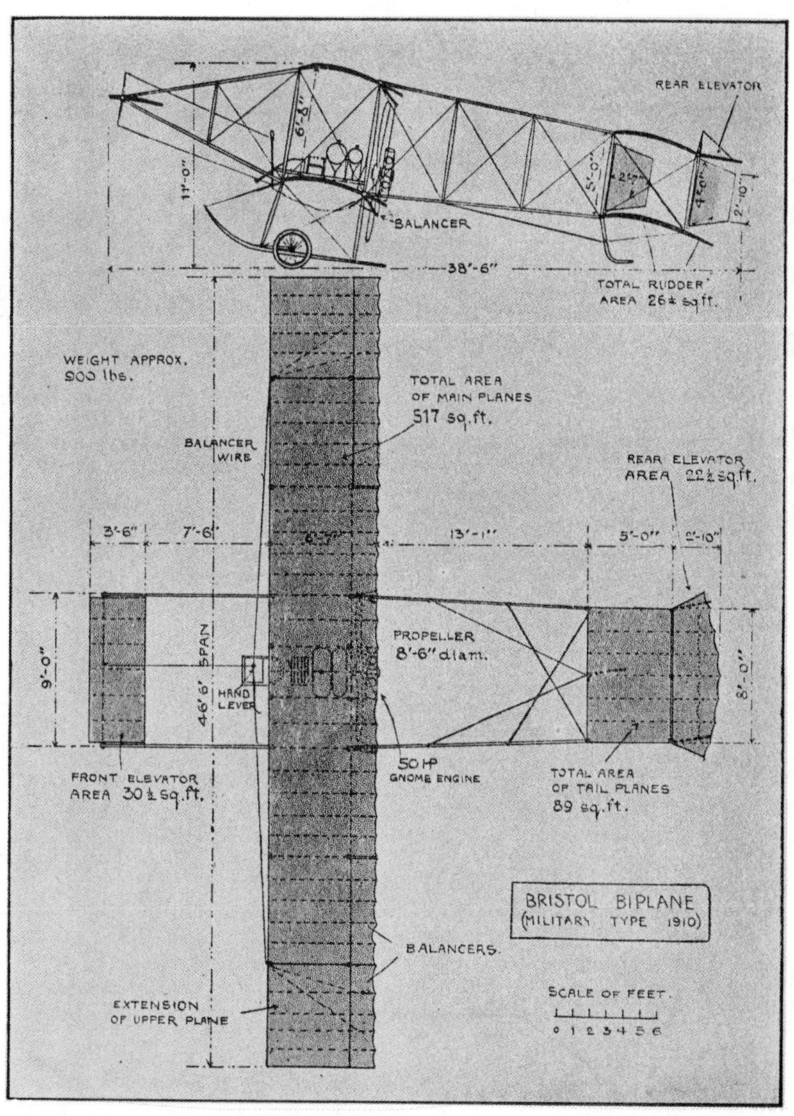

"Flight" copyright

2.—THE ORIGINAL BRISTOL BOXKITE (50 H.P. GNÔME), THE MOST SUCCESSFUL BRITISH TRAINING AEROPLANE.

Facing page 64

"Flight" photo

11.—THE FIRST BRITISH PILOT TO BREAK A WORLD'S RECORD:
CAPT. BERTRAM DICKSON (FARMAN—50 H.P. GNÔME).

men, could they be induced to speak their minds, I dare hardly imagine. Anyhow, it is my intention to resign immediately from the Aero Club of America. I hope all American sportsmen will follow my example."

Grahame-White lodged a protest with the R.Ae.C., who were backed by the Aero Clubs of France, Spain, Austria, and Holland in applying to the *Fédération Aéronautique Internationale* for an Extraordinary Conference to consider the protest. Two months later the Conference met in Paris and disqualified Mr. Moisant, who had been killed in an accident in the interim, holding that the American Committee's decision was unsupportable, and calling upon them to make a fresh award.

Grahame-White himself, with his customary good sportsmanship, went out of his way to find excuses for this lamentable affair, attributing the Committee's action to ignorance rather than to bias.

Unfortunately, any lingering doubts concerning the question of bias were removed when the Aero Club of America, evidently determined at all costs to keep the prize out of English hands, awarded it to M. Jacque de Lesseps, who was no better qualified to enter for the competition than Moisant had been. It was true that the Race Committee had allowed him to fly the course and that he had been officially timed, but Grahame-White had beaten his time by nearly ten minutes.

The Americans now alleged that the English pilot had fouled a pylon and disqualified him on this ground, although no such allegation had been made in the first place, nor had counsel representing the Aero Club of America made this suggestion at the hearing before the Federation in Paris.

The R.Ae.C. immediately entered a second protest and the *Fédération Aéronautique Internationale* met again in Rome more than a year after the contest and decided definitely that the £2,000 prize should be awarded to Mr. Grahame-White.

It was not until February 1912 that the Americans announced that they were prepared to pay it over to the rightful winner.

31. RADLEY IN U.S.A.

Mr. James Radley, a member of our official Gordon-Bennett team, remained in the U.S.A. after Mr. Grahame-White had returned to England and undertook a protracted tour of flying meetings. He had thoroughly mastered the secrets of tuning the 50 h.p. Gnôme which was fitted to his Bleriot, and he proceeded to astonish the Americans with the high speeds he attained. At Belmont Park he had beaten seventeen other 50 h.p. Bleriots, and at Los Angeles, where he delighted a huge crowd by making the first flight of forty miles over the waters of the Pacific, he captured first prize for speed each day. At San Francisco he flew out over the harbour, circling the U.S. Fleet at anchor there and created so much enthusiasm that a crowd of 200,000 people flocked to the aerodrome on the following day.

32. BRISTOL, AVRO, AND MARTIN-HANDASYDE DEVELOPMENTS

In the first week of November 1910 there was much activity at Brooklands. Bristol's had two biplanes there, one with a Gnôme engine, the other with a Gregoire. Mons. Edmond was the pilot in charge, but Lieut. Maitland, Capt. Wood and Mr. Low all flew the machines under his instruction.

Mr. Howard Pixton, who was destined to win a Schneider Trophy contest for England, was commencing instruction on the Avro triplane. Another portentous development was the appearance on the aerodrome of a fine monoplane, designed and built by Messrs. Martin and Handasyde, on which the former achieved some promising straight flights.

The Midland Aero Club had established an aerodrome at Dunstall Park where several unorthodox aircraft were being put through their paces. They included Mr. Holder's Humber-Bleriot, the Star monoplane made by the Star Car Co., of Wolverhampton, an interesting all-steel monoplane belonging to Mr. Mann and a freak biplane known as the Seddon. None of these craft was very successful.

The semi-military Bristol School near Stonehenge was very active and two of the pupils, Messrs. MacDonald and Hammond, were making first-class flights, going up to over 1,000 feet and cruising over the Plain for considerable distances.

33. CODY ATTACKS BRITISH MICHELIN CUP: GENERAL ACTIVITY

A British Empire Michelin Cup, value £500, had been presented for the longest distance flown in a closed circuit by a British pilot in a British aircraft during 1910. Mr. S. F. Cody stepped into the lead for this trophy with a very fine flight of 94½ miles in 2 hrs. 24 mins. at Laffan's Plain, on his new heavy biplane with the 60 h.p. Green engine. This flight set up new all-British records for distance and duration.

Things were quiet at Eastchurch except for the activities of Mr. Frank McClean, who was rapidly developing into a pilot of distinction on the Gnôme-engined Shorts, in which he had flown over 600 miles. He made a speciality of gliding descents, which were then known as *vols plané*, and became increasingly adept at this manœuvre.

The enterprising Bristol firm established their third aerodrome at Durdham Downs, just outside Bristol, where Lieut. Maitland and MM. Tetard and Jullerot made some excellent flights.

Mr. Geoffrey de Havilland had moved to Newbury where he

experienced some hazardous times dodging the local rabbit warrens and railway lines, whilst Mr. Cody failed to evade a telegraph wire which brought him down with a bump which did considerable damage to the machine.

Mr. Sopwith had discarded the Howard-Wright with which he had had his first adventures and had purchased a new model of the same make. He brought this out for the first time on November 21st, 1910. First of all he practised "rolling," as taxying was then called, next he did some straights, and, after lunch, some circuits. Later in the afternoon he qualified for his *brevet* and he completed his day's work by taking up his first passenger in the evening!

At the Freshfield aerodrome near Liverpool, five hangars had been erected to house a Curtiss biplane belonging to Mr. Paterson, two Bleriots owned by Messrs. Melly and Higginbotham respectively, a Henry Farman biplane and the biplane constructed by Planes Ltd., which was flown by Mr. Fenwick.

Capt. J. B. Fulton, after teaching himself to fly on a Bleriot monoplane at Salisbury, notified the R.Ae.C. that he wished to pass his tests for his *brevet*, but when the official observers arrived the Bleriot was *hors de combat*. Capt. Fulton was undismayed, borrowed a Farman biplane from Mr. Cockburn, and passed his tests in good style on that very different aircraft.

Already at this early stage the Yankee disciples of Ballyhoo were ready to exploit aviation for their own ends. Simultaneously with the arrival of the news that Ralph Johnstone had killed himself at Denver while performing a stunt flight, consisting of a series of short sharp dives, came the information that the World's First Aviation Circus comprising twenty aircraft and six pilots had opened for business at Richmond (Virginia). The programme set forth the modest announcement that "this circus has enrolled the greatest, grandest, and speediest aggregation of aerial chauffeurs in the world, and in death-defying, dare-devil races through the air they will give the public thrilling value for their money."

34. SOPWITH AGAIN: HOWARD PIXTON, F. P. RAYNHAM, AND OTHERS

To return to practical aviation. Mr. T. O. M. Sopwith was by no means content to rest upon his remarkable achievement of November 21st, more especially as he had his eye on the Michelin Cup, which carried with it a cash prize of £500. Accordingly he got out his Howard-Wright, which incidentally had no connection with the American Wright machines, but much more resembled a Farman, and proceeded to attack Mr. Cody's new records. The 60 h.p. E.N.V. ran perfectly, and Mr. Sopwith not only set up new all-British records of 107 miles for distance and 3 hrs. 12 mins. for duration, but also beat the British duration record for any type of aeroplane, British or foreign, and put himself in the lead for the

Michelin Cup. At the time when this record was made, Mr. Sopwith had certainly not more than ten hours solo to his credit !

Flight was pessimistic about Mr. Howard Pixton who had been flying the A. V. Roe triplane better than anyone else had ever done. They pointed out that while he was a very daring and pretty flyer, yet the sudden movements he made must have put a severe strain on the body work. Their Brooklands correspondent averred that "one dive and sudden righting appeared to actually bend the body" and doubted lugubriously whether Mr. Pixton would get through life unmaimed.

Another famous pilot appeared at Brooklands about this time. This was Mr. F. P. Raynham, who was experimenting with the Neale VI monoplane, and who was later to be associated with Messrs. Martin and Handasyde.

The British Government had placed an order for a Henry Farman and a Paulhan biplane for the use of the rapidly growing group of Army pilots, of whom the latest were Lieut. Cammell, R.E., who had made splendid flights with a Bleriot (E.N.V.) at Stonehenge, and Lieut. Snowden Smith, who had qualified under M. Blondeau on a Henry Farman at Brooklands. The latter performed a notable cross-country from Brooklands to Aldershot and back.

Capt. Burke and Mr. Holt Thomas went to Chalons to take delivery of the Henry Farman, which was tested by the designer in person. This aircraft had all its fittings nickel-plated and was the very latest thing in biplane design and construction.

It is interesting to note that while the Government found it necessary to go to France for aircraft for our Military needs, the well-known Continental pilot Christiaens came to England for two of the Bristol biplanes on which the majority of our Army pilots were being trained. These were the first two British-built aeroplanes to find a market abroad.

The first recorded auction sale of second-hand aircraft took place at Brooklands in December 1910, when the stock of the Scottish Aeroplane Syndicate went under the hammer. The Avis monoplane, on which the Hon. Alan Boyle had made some promising flights, was sold for £50, complete with 40 h.p. 8-cylinder J.A.P. motor.

Mr. Gordon England had fitted a tail and a 35 h.p. E.N.V. to the Weiss glider and he was also flying the Hanriot monoplane, which he deposited in the small pond behind the Bluebird Café. About a week later he stalled the Weiss on a turn and dropped it into the sewage farm.

Mr. A. V. Roe had produced a biplane with which Messrs. Howard Pixton and Gordon Bell were conducting experiments, and another famous pilot who commenced instruction at Brooklands at this time was Mr. Valentine, who was "rolling" with the Empress-Macfie monoplane. Mr. Graham Gilmour had mastered the Martin-Handasyde monoplane and flew it in a 30 m.p.h. wind

35. HENRY FARMAN'S BAD LUCK

In France Mr. Henry Farman had the most mortifying experience whilst making an attempt for the European Michelin Cup. He had flown round and round a small closed circuit for 8 hrs. 12 mins. and had covered 463 kilometres (288¾ miles) and had only to cover one more lap to beat the record of 465 kilometres set up by Maurice Tabuteau. Farman was ignorant of the distance he had covered as it was almost dark, and he was unable to read the signals of his lap counters. A large crowd was awaiting the consummation of the record flight and, as he wearily completed his penultimate lap, Farman heard a terrific burst of cheering. Thinking that he had beaten Tabuteau's figures he landed immediately, only to find that he was two kilometres short and that his great effort had been thrown away.

36. CODY WINS BRITISH EMPIRE MICHELIN CUP

Two fine flights were made for the British Michelin Cup in the last week of the year. Mr. S. F. Cody made an extremely perilous attempt in a 20 m.p.h. wind at Laffan's Plain, and succeeded in covering 115 miles in 2 hrs. 50 mins. before his aircraft was hurled to the ground by a gust of wind from a height of thirty-five feet. It speaks well for the undercarriage that nothing was broken or bent—although, of course, this involuntary landing put an end to the record attempt. The other competitor was Mr. Alec Ogilvie who covered 139¾ miles non-stop in 3 hrs. 55 mins. at Camber Sands near Rye. He used a Short-built Wright which had been fitted with one of the new N.E.C. two-cycle engines. He was eventually forced down by a leaking water tank. This fine flight placed Mr. Ogilvie in the lead for the British Michelin Cup with only three days to go before the close of the competition, and he must have felt that he had made his position fairly secure. However, two formidable competitors were standing by their machines in readiness for a last minute attempt. Mr. T. O. M. Sopwith was at Brooklands with his Howard-Wright and made a fine flight of two hours duration on the 29th in a gusty wind, which eventually forced him to give up after seventy miles had been covered. This procedure was repeated almost exactly on the following day and it seemed that Mr. Ogilvie had set an impossible task.

The last day of the year, however, saw Mr. Sopwith and the Howard-Wright lapping the track once more, and this time all went smoothly until the petrol tank ran dry 4 hrs. 7 mins. 17 secs. after the start, the distance covered being officially recorded at 150 miles 246 yards, or 8 miles 204 yards better than Mr. Ogilvie's figures.

Meanwhile the latter pilot was busily flying his Wright round and round the course at Camber in an endeavour to beat his own record and stave off the competition, but ignition trouble supervened and he was forced to land after covering 55 miles in 1 hr. 30 mins.

At the same time as Mr. Sopwith was circling round at Brooklands Mr. S. F. Cody was piling up the laps in the mist on Laffan's Plain. His British Green engine ran with great regularity and smoothness although the r.p.m. dropped off towards the end of the flight owing to the formation of a thick ice coating around the inlet pipes. Mr. Cody, in spite of the intense cold, a thick mist, and a gusty wind stuck to his task until the petrol tank was drained. He had remained aloft in a very low temperature entirely unprotected from the rush of air for 4 hrs. 47 mins., and had travelled 185·46 miles, thus winning the 1910 British Empire Michelin Cup and £500 by the substantial margin of 35 miles. Mr. Cody, who thoroughly deserved his win, set up new all-British records for duration and distance flown in a closed circuit.

37. SOPWITH WINS BARON DE FOREST'S £4,000 PRIZE

Exciting as this competition proved to be, it was surpassed by the contest for the Baron de Forest's £4,000 prize, which resulted in the destruction of four aircraft and the loss of one of our best pilots.

The prize had been offered to the British pilot who should, during 1910, fly an all-British aircraft from any point in England the farthest distance into the Continent of Europe measured in a straight line from his starting point.

Here was an idea which fired the imagination. The flight involved the Channel crossing, in itself a hazardous feat, followed by a long flight to the Eastward, unhampered by restrictions and limited only by the pilot's endurance and the tank capacity of his aircraft.

Towards the close of the year the machines began to gather in Kent ready for the attempt. Swingate Downs, Dover, attracted Messrs. Grahame-White (Bristol), Greswell (Bristol-built Farman), and Loraine (Bristol). The last two competitors were unfortunate, for the temporary hangars which housed their biplanes collapsed under the strain of a great gale of wind and the aircraft were very badly smashed. Mr. Grahame-White's hangar survived the storm but his machine was slightly damaged. Fate was against all those at Swingate Downs, however, for Mr. Grahame-White repaired his Bristol, only to crash heavily in attempting a low turn in a 30 m.p.h. wind. He was severely cut by the wires and fainted from loss of blood after extricating himself from the wreckage. He was taken to the Lord Warden Hotel and immediately ordered another machine from Bristol's, and this was dispatched to him within a few days. His doctor, however, refused to allow him to fly it in the competition.

Lieut. Watkins was established on the parade ground at Shorncliffe near Folkestone with Capt. Maitland's Howard-Wright. He made several practice flights there which culminated in a crash which caused extensive damage and put him out of the competition. Mr. Cody had announced his intention of starting from Farnborough, but he made no attempt on the prize.

Messrs. T. O. M. Sopwith (Howard-Wright E.N.V.), Frank McClean (Short-Green), and Cecil Grace (Short-built Farman) were at Eastchurch, tuning up and awaiting a spell of good weather. Mr. Sopwith's machine had been delivered by road from Brooklands and he had not yet attempted a cross-country flight, what little experience he had having been acquired doing circuits at Brooklands.

On Sunday, December 18th, 1910, the series of gales abated and Mr. Sopwith eagerly seized the opportunity. He took off down a gentle N.W. wind as the sun rose, and after a short practice flight, landed to fill his tanks. He discovered that the machine was sluggish off the ground when taking off downwind so when he taxied out for his competition attempt at 8.30 a.m. he headed upwind and the machine lifted well.

Sopwith spent a quarter of an hour in getting his height by circling the aerodrome, and then set off at 1,000 feet for Dover. He passed Canterbury and reached Dover thirty minutes after taking off, and twenty-two minutes later he crossed the French coast a few miles west of Cape Grisnez. A compass had been fitted to the machine but Sopwith found that it swung continually between N. and W., which was little help, and he decided to steer by the sun in the general direction of Chalons, where he hoped to land. Unfortunately the sun soon disappeared behind a bank of clouds and the pilot began, unconsciously, to swing to the left, or north of his course. Thus he traversed the N.E. of France, leaving Lille on his left and passing over Valenciennes. Presently he crossed the Belgian border and entered the hilly country, where he encountered ever-increasing bumps, one of which was sufficiently violent to throw him out of his seat on to the wing.

As the hills ahead appeared to be getting steeper and he could see no way around them, whilst the bumps became increasingly violent, Sopwith decided to land, which he did successfully after a thrilling flight of three hours and a half.

He discovered that he was at Thirimont, 169 miles in a direct line from Eastchurch, and that he had used less than half his petrol supply. As the machine was running perfectly, there was little doubt but that he could have penetrated much further into Europe, and yet it is possible that had he gone on, his left hand swing would have eventually brought him round nearer to Eastchurch than the spot at which he decided to land.

In any case, this splendid first cross-country flight by a mere beginner was more than good enough to win the Baron de Forest's £4,000, and no big prize has ever been more justly earned.

38. THE LOSS OF CECIL GRACE

Mr. Sopwith was closely followed out of Eastchurch by Mr. Cecil Grace who took off at noon. His Short-Farman averaged 60 m.p.h. to Dover, where the pilot found a thick mist over the Channel and a rising wind. He decided wisely to join the band of unfortunates on Swingate Downs and wait for better conditions. It was shortly after he landed that Mr. Grahame-White had his severe crash on the Bristol.

Four days later Mr. Grace left Swingate Downs at 9 a.m. and flew through mist and a head wind to Les Baraques where he landed, as he realized that the weather was too bad to allow him any chance of beating Sopwith.

The mist got steadily thicker, but Mr. Grace was anxious to get back to Dover so as to be in readiness for another attempt, as there were only nine days left before the closing day of the competition. He went down to the harbour and interviewed the Captain of the *S.S. Pas de Calais*, and arranged to take off just after the boat left and to use her smoke as his guide.

The boat was late in departing and Grace flew out into the fog unescorted. He was heard passing over the N. Goodwins Lightship and was sighted by a fishing boat near the E. Goodwins. His cap and goggles were picked up on the beach at Mariakerke, Belgium, a fortnight later and identified by his friend G. C. Colmore. That was the last that was ever seen or heard of a very gallant pilot, the second British aviator to give his life for the cause, and the first of a long list of victims of fog.

39. THE DUNNE EXPERIMENTS

I have previously mentioned the Dunne aeroplane, with which Mr. L. D. L. Gibbs had conducted a series of experiments for the War Office at Blair Atholl as far back as 1908.

This interesting machine was designed to be automatically stable in every direction, and its inventor had been working steadily upon it for several years, finally bringing his latest model to Eastchurch for submission to a practical test at the hands of the Aeronautical Society.

In order to demonstrate the chief claim for the machine, Mr. Dunne had provided the controls with locking levers designed to give a small number of set positions to correspond with turns, gliding, climbing, and the like.

The test was carried out on December 20th, 1910, at Eastchurch, the observers being Messrs. Griffith Brewer and Orville Wright, and the pilot being Mr. Dunne himself.

The pilot's own account of the trials is intensely interesting and I give it *verbatim* below :—

" As Mr. Orville Wright and Mr. Griffith Brewer were both pressed for time, I decided to make only short circular flights.

" Obviously, the first thing to do was to show that the machine could fly as well and as strongly as those of the ordinary T-shape, to exhibit the power of control and manœuvre given by the two little steering flaps, and above all to show that with this type of machine good turns, with the correct amount of banking, and no side-slipping, could be effected without recourse to the complicated 'three-rudder' system. I, therefore, contented myself with a closed circuit, allowing the machine to climb 100 feet on the turn, and as this was the first time I had turned at any height, I confined my attention to making a neat job of it, and made no particular attempt to show off the automatic stability of the machine, until it came to descending. It is a well-known rule of flying that, before throttling the engine, the machine's bow should be pointed slightly downwards to avoid the loss of speed that would otherwise ensue, and it is in the proper manipulation of the levers immediately afterwards, to maintain speed and keep the machine under control, that the trained aviator has to exercise his greatest skill. To throttle without first depressing the bow, and then leave the machine severely alone, is a stiff test of longitudinal automatic stability, though, of course, no test of lateral stability. So both in this flight and in the second, I first locked the levers in the central position in which they are left while flying, then throttled, and immediately threw up my arms and left the machine to come down from the flying tilt to the gliding tilt of its own accord, and thence find its way earthward. The steep slope of the ground at the point of landing rendered it unsafe to attempt the requisite flattening of the trajectory before touching earth by the use of the throttle alone, so at the last moment I utilized the flap-controls for this purpose.

" The next point was to prove the safety of the machine. As we have no place for passengers in the present apparatus I suggested that I should go round the same short circuit and carry out the writing test. I proposed this, as I know of nothing else which so thoroughly puts to the proof the aviator's real trust in his machine's fitness to look after itself, compelling, as it does absolute detachment of the mind. One may eat, drink, smoke, click a camera, take off one's coat, or do a hundred other things, and all the time keep one eye ahead to see what the machine is really doing, and be ready to snatch a lever if necessary. But when writing, sitting low in our big boat, one's attention is perforce completely withdrawn from one's surroundings. I ran down across the wind, hopped off, touched again, and then began to rise steadily. As soon as I saw that I would clear the bushes on the boundary dyke, I locked the levers, and felt for the paper and pencil given me by Mr. Griffith Brewer. The paper was in one pocket and the pencil in another ; by the time I had got them ready I must have flown a considerable way. I started to set down certain points I was anxious to observe and remember. First I counted the divisions on the revolution indicator, which has no figures between the 1,000 and 1,500 marks. When I began to set them down I found that, unfortunately, it was almost impossible to write on the thin paper with only the fingers and palm of my hand as a backing thereto, and that a certain amount of excitement rendered the task still more difficult. I then observed the positions of the levers relatively to their toothed racks and made a note of that, I next looked about inside the boat for something else to note, and while doing so became aware of the violent wind in my face, which curiously enough I had entirely failed to notice on the previous flight.

" As I had been anxious to ascertain how far the front screen shielded the aviator, I wrote this fact down. From the time I had first locked the levers, till now, I had not paid the smallest attention to what the machine was doing or where it was going. It had been left to follow its own fancy, and might by this time be anywhere or in any position for all I knew. However, looking up I saw that it was still level, but had drifted down-wind and was aiming to hit a wind-pump, so I decided to commence the turn.

" I separated the levers, holding them till the turn had started, noted its radius, which was shorter than I required, diminished the difference between the lever positions, locked them, waited a little time, hands off, until I was satisfied with the radius of the turn and with the rapidity with which the machine was mounting, got hold of my paper again and with some difficulty wrote ' turning now.' Looking over the port bow I saw a farm-house nearly beneath me, and realizing that the circle was now bigger than I had intended, and also that I was much higher than I had thought, I pushed each lever into the fourth notch, and, sitting with my hands in my lap, allowed the machine to swing itself sharply round. Then I locked the levers centrally and sat back, but did not continue writing as I was puzzled by a momentary failure to recognize the ground below me. I am not a balloonist and am unused to heights. After a moment I realized that a little dark green blob was the pond in the middle of the ground. So I turned the machine towards it, and then wrote ' straight again.' By the time I had got that down I saw that I should have to descend at once if I meant to get back to my starting point, so I moved the machine's nose a degree or two round aiming at the point in question, returned each lever carefully to its central notch, throttled the engine, and held up my arms. Instantly the machine's head dropped a little, and, without any abatement of forward speed, she began to sink towards the ground. I landed her as before described."

Mr. Dunne had had little previous air experience and his calm courage in making these test flights deserves recognition, although it was by no means an exceptional feat in those days.

40. 1910 REVIEWED: THE PILOTS

The most important achievement by a British pilot during 1910 was unquestionably the winning of the Gordon Bennett Contest in New York by Mr. Grahame-White. This was the first great international competition to be won for this country and the result was to raise the prestige of British aviation abroad to the level of France and America. It was regrettable that both the aircraft and engine used were of French design and construction, but that fact was generally overlooked, the main point being that Great Britain was officially credited with the victory, and that the R.Ae.C. had acquired the right to promote the next contest in England.

1910 was Grahame-White's year. Starting with his homeric contest with Paulhan, he went on from that splendid failure to score success after success. He did more than any other man to lift British aviation out of the ignominious position in which he found it at the end of 1909 and to make it a force to be respected all over the world. His flair for publicity, his calculated daring, his supreme skill as a pilot, and his unfailing good sportsmanship, stirred the interest of even the British public. His prize money totalled £10,280 and no one more richly deserved such a large reward.

Of the other pilots who appeared amongst the selected ten at the end of 1909, the two Anglo-Frenchmen were still doing well in France, and Mr. Cody, and Mr. A. Ogilvie remained in the first rank at home. Mr. Moore-Brabazon had given up practical flying after winning the first British Michelin Cup in March, the Hon. C. S. Rolls had given his life for the cause at Bournemouth, Mr. Mortimer Singer had been seriously injured at Cairo, and Messrs. Cockburn and Egerton were no longer very active.

Of the newcomers to the game, the outstanding personalities were Mr. R. Loraine and Mr. T. O. M. Sopwith.

The names of the best ten English pilots at the end of the year 1910 are tabulated below in order of merit, together with the machines which they had flown. As neither Henry Farman nor Hubert Latham had flown in England during the year, their names have been omitted, and the list becomes wholly English, Mr. Cody having become naturalized as a British subject.

1. C. Grahame-White (Bleriot, Farman, Bristol).
2. T. O. M. Sopwith (Howard-Wright).

3. S. F. Cody (Brit. Army Aeroplane, Cody).
4. R. Loraine (Farman).
5. A. Ogilvie (Wright).
6. B. Dickson (Farman).
7. W. D. McArdle (Bleriot).
8. L. D. L. Gibbs (Dunne, Farman).
9. J. Radley (Bleriot).
10. G. Gilmour (Bleriot, Martin and Handasyde).

Honourable mention should be made of Messrs. G. C. Colmore and F. McClean (Shorts), and Capt. Rawlinson, who flew a Henry Farman very successfully in France at the beginning of the season. But for their untimely deaths, Mr. Cecil Grace (Voisin, Short-Wright, and Bleriot) would have occupied a high place in the list, and the Hon. C. S. Rolls (Wright) would also have been included.

41. THE WORK OF THE SCHOOLS IN 1910

It was not until March 8th, 1910, that the R.Ae.C. began to issue its aviator's certificates in conjunction with the *Fédération Aéronautique Internationale.* On that date certificates numbers 1 and 2 were granted to Mr. J. T. C. Moore-Brabazon and the Hon. C. S. Rolls respectively.

By the end of the year forty-five certificates had been issued by the club, three of them to foreign subjects, but, in addition to these, fourteen British subjects had qualified in France, and had not bothered to apply for English certificates, as the French *brevet* was recognized in England. Thus it will be seen that fifty-six British pilots had qualified by the end of the year, of whom two had met their deaths in flying accidents.

The majority of these fifty-six pilots had learned at foreign schools or had taught themselves to fly; in fact, only eighteen of them had been trained in British schools of flying. There were six firms operating schools in England at the end of the year and their record was as follows:—

School.	*Aerodrome*		*No. of pupils trained up to the end of 1910.*
Bristol	Brooklands	4	6
	Salisbury Plain	2	
Bleriot	Hendon		5
McArdle and Drexel ..	Beaulieu (Hants)		2
Hewlett and Blondeau	Brooklands		2
Grahame-White ..	Pau (Fr.)	1	2
	Brooklands	1	
Hanriot	Brooklands		1
		Total	18

42. THE AEROPLANES OF 1910

On the construction side there was little progress to report. The Bristol Company and Mr. Howard Wright were turning out well finished variations of the Farman design, Messrs. Short Brothers continued to build Wright's under licence and also designed and made a few machines which owed a great deal to the ideas of either Farman or Wright. A.V. Roe continued to experiment and had abandoned the triplane in favour of a biplane, which, however, did not at first give very encouraging results. Geoffrey de Havilland, Martin and Handasyde, Blackburn and the other experimenters, dotted about the country, were having trouble in plenty with their machines. Only Cody had produced an aircraft which flew consistently well and this, the best of the all-British designed machines, could stand no comparison with the products of the French factories.

43. WORLD'S AND ALL-BRITISH RECORDS AT END OF 1910

Below are tabulated the principal world's records standing at the end of 1910, and it is illuminating to compare them with the figures for 1909 on p. 19, *supra*. It will be seen that the duration record, which was still held by Mr. Henry Farman, was practically doubled, the distance record was more than doubled, whilst the altitude record had gone up to more than seven times Mr. Latham's height of 1909.

The world's record for absolute speed is not given because no proper trials had taken place. A. Leblanc had done a lap of the Gordon-Bennett circuit (5 kilometres) at 71 m.p.h. and Mr. James Radley had covered a mile on another Bleriot at 75·95 m.p.h. with the assistance of a slight breeze. There seems little doubt but that Mons. A. Leblanc's Bleriot (100 h.p. Gnôme) was the fastest aeroplane in existence at the end of 1910, and it was probably capable of just over 80 m.p.h. in still air.

WORLD'S RECORDS AT THE END OF 1910

Pilot	*Nationality*	*Aircraft*	*Nationality*	*Engine*	*Nationality*	*Time or Distance*	*Place*
			DURATION				
H. Farman	Anglo-French	Henry Farman	French	100 Gnôme	French	8h. 12m. 47s.	Etampes
			DISTANCE IN A CLOSED CIRCUIT.				
M. Tabuteau	French	Maurice Farman	French	Renault	French	584·745 Km. (350 miles)	Buc.
			ALTITUDE				
G. Legagneux	French	Bleriot	French	Gnôme	French	3,200 m. (10,746 ft.)	Pau.

The above records may also be compared with the all-British

records set out below. The expression "all-British" means that the pilot was a British subject and the aircraft and engine were built in England.

ALL-BRITISH RECORDS AT THE END OF 1910

Pilot	*Aircraft*	*Engine*	*Time or Distance*	*Place*
		DURATION		
S. F. Cody	Cody	60 h.p. Green	4 hrs. 47 mins.	Laffan's Plain
		DISTANCE IN A CLOSED CIRCUIT		
S. F. Cody	Cody	60 h.p. Green	185·46 miles	Laffan's Plain
		DISTANCE IN A STRAIGHT LINE		
T. O. M. Sopwith	Howard-Wright	60 h.p. E.N.V.	169 miles	Eastchurch to Thirimont (Belgium)

No altitude or speed records had been established in the all-British category.

CHAPTER III

1911

1. THE ALEXANDER PRIZE: ARMY AERONAUTICS

EARLY in January 1911, the Advisory Committee for Aeronautics appointed by the Government issued its interim report for the year 1910–11, which included the result of the competition for the Alexander Prize, which had been conducted at the Government Flight Office, Bushey House, under the auspices of the Aerial League. Mr. Patrick Y. Alexander had offered £1,000 to the manufacturers of the British Aero Engine which should perform best under certain tests. The 4-cylinder in line watercooled Green Engine, with which Cody had won the British Empire Michelin Cup, proved the most successful, but the prize was withheld on the grounds that it had failed to maintain the stipulated output of 35 b.h.p. throughout the twenty-four hours endurance run, although it developed 36·4 b.h.p. at 1,390 r.p.m. for a short period. The average output during the endurance test was 31·5 b.h.p. at 1,213 r.p.m. for a weight of 219 lbs., or 6·952 lbs. per b.h.p. Its only competitors were a Wolseley and a Humber, neither of which succeeded in running non-stop for twenty-four hours.

The Balloon Factory at Farnborough now housed four aircraft, a Bleriot, a Wright, Mr. Geoffrey de Havilland's biplane and the new Henry Farman. The career of the last named was short and dramatic. Capt. Burke, who had taken his *brevet* at a French school, made a preliminary test flight of two miles at Laffan's Plain, and then took off again for a longer test. Before he had gone fifty yards, however, the biplane tilted up, dug her right wing into the ground and nosed over, smashing herself to pieces and severely injuring Capt. Burke.

2. THE SECOND BRITISH WOMAN PILOT: AN ATLANTIC PROJECT

The honour of being the second British woman to take up flying must be divided between Mrs. Hewlett, who was undergoing dual instruction at Brooklands on her own Henry Farman, which was flown by that capable pilot, M. Blondeau, and Miss Lilian Bland, who had designed and constructed her own biplane known as the Bland Mayfly, and who was teaching herself to fly it at Carnamony near Belfast. It seems to be a matter of doubt as to which of these ladies flew solo first.

Mr. H. J. D. Astley, who was one of the promising beginners at the Weybridge track, had an exciting experience whilst piloting Mr. Gibbs' Sommer biplane. He was following Mr. Conway Jenkins in a triplane when the latter landed abruptly just in front of him. Mr. Astley attempted to follow him down but found that he had insufficient room. He therefore opened up and flew his large biplane through the gap between the triplane and a telegraph pole, which left exactly two feet clearance at each side.

An American citizen, Mr. Harry Grahame Carter announced to all and sundry that he proposed to fly across the Atlantic in an aeroplane of his own design: He estimated that the passage would take fifty-four hours, and intended to build the machine of metal tubing which would be filled with petrol. The start was to take place from Sandy Hook early in March 1911. "We fancy he is wrong in his starting date," remarked *Flight* acidly ; and so he was. But few people would have guessed at that time that the feat was to be performed by an English pilot within nine years.

All the schools were busy in the middle of January, especially Brooklands, Hendon, and Salisbury Plain. At Hendon the curious Valkyrie pusher monoplanes of the Aeronautical Syndicate were almost continually in the air, but the Farmans of the Grahame-White establishment were working nearly as hard, whilst so great was the interest at Brooklands that Keith, Prowse & Co., Ltd. established a private wire to the aerodrome to facilitate the booking of passenger flights for their patrons in London.

3. HAMEL APPEARS : FARMAN TRIES WEIGHT LIFTING

Towards the end of the month, spectators at Hendon were thrilled by the first appearance of a bright new star in the British flying firmament. Mr. Gustav Hamel, who had learned to fly on the Continent, arrived at the Grahame-White school, borrowed a Bleriot (50 h.p. Gnôme) and proceeded to demonstrate his masterly touch. Mr. Gresswell, the chief instructor, had acquired a great reputation as a pilot on the G. W. Farmans and now turned his attention to the school Bleriots. On his first attempt he executed some perfectly judged " dead stick " landings from heights up to 600 feet. The all-British built E.N.V.-engined Farman, which had been damaged by the collapse of a tent at Dover, was still under repair, as the local souvenir hunters had stolen an aileron and the whole of the trailing edge of the bottom wing, as well as numerous smaller items.

The Bristol Company must have had some good engineers at Salisbury Plain, for when M. Vusepuy crashed one of their biplanes, breaking several struts, the skids and the propeller, the repairs were speedily effected *in situ* and the machine flew home in the kindly hands of M. Tetard.

The veteran Henry Farman continued to lead the way in

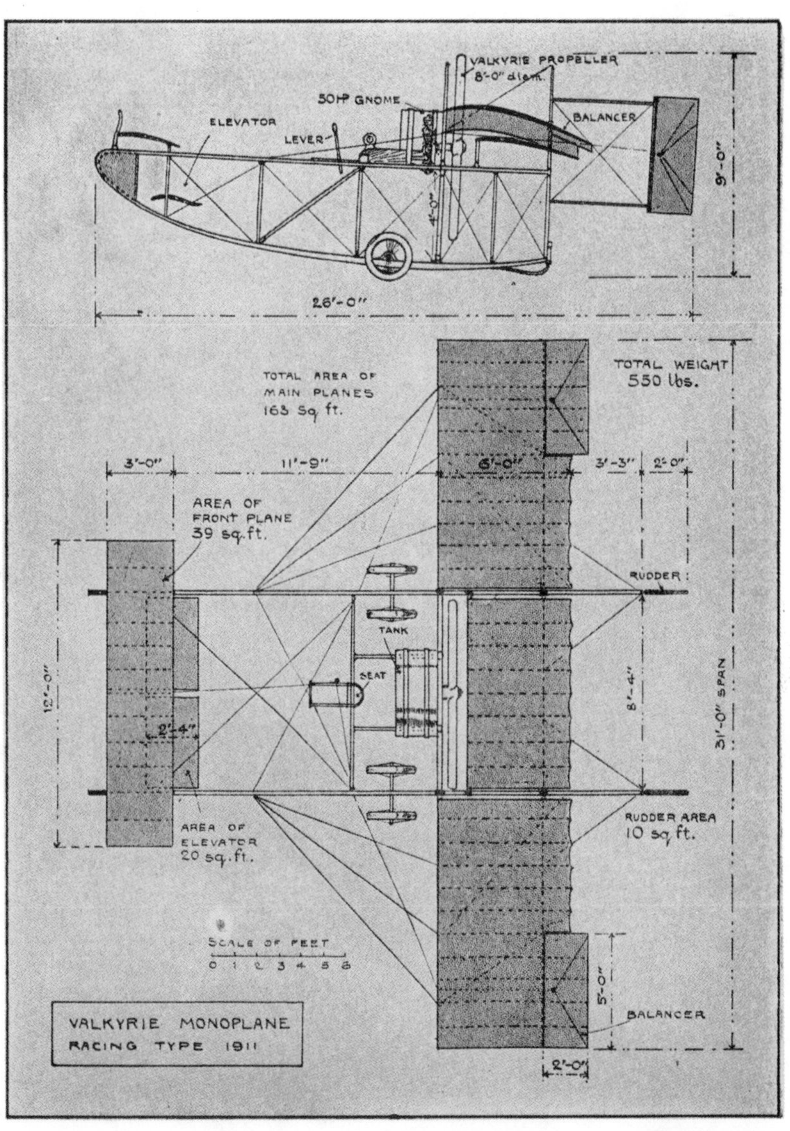

"Flight" copyright

3.—THE ONLY SUCCESSFUL PUSHER MONOPLANE EVER BUILT IN ENGLAND: MR. BARBER'S VALKYRIE (50 H.P. GNÔME).

Facing page 80

"Flight" photo

12.—Bournemouth: the Hon. C. S. Rolls flying his Wright just before his fatal smash.

France and once more broke fresh ground by carrying five passengers with him round the field at Bouy. Two of these brave but anonymous persons sat on the skids alongside the wheels a few inches from the ground with four large people and an engine piled up immediately above their heads. Their feelings as the aircraft came in to land must have been extremely harrowing. The total useful load carried was 420 kilogs (925 lbs.).

At Brooklands the brothers Pashley, who were later to become famous in connection with the Shoreham aerodrome, commenced instruction on Mr. Gibbs' Sommer biplane, and Mr. Gordon Bell, of the historic stutter, was experimenting unhappily with the Roe triplane.

4. SOME NEW PRIZES OFFERED

The Michelin Tyre Co. announced the award of a new British Empire Michelin Trophy which would carry with it a prize of £400 in 1911, £600 in 1912 and £800 in 1913. This contest was to be flown off round a cross-country circuit, the length of which would be increased annually, and the pilot making the fastest time over the course, non-stop, was to be the winner. The promoters very sensibly fixed the closing date on October 15th in each year instead of December 31st, thus ensuring that the final attempts of the contest should be flown in reasonable weather.

Mr. Mortimer Singer offered £500 each to the Army and Navy pilot, respectively, who should fly the greatest distance (non-stop) with a passenger before March 31st, 1912.

5. BRISTOLS IN AUSTRALIA AND INDIA

The Bristol Company, not content with using three aerodromes in England, had dispatched two of their biplanes to Australia in charge of the New Zealand pilot, Joseph Hammond, who had learned to fly at Salisbury Plain. On his first flight he crossed the harbour at Perth at an altitude of 2,000 feet. This was the real beginning of practical aviation in the Antipodes. Simultaneously, another Bristol touring company, under the command of M. Henri Jullerot, was operating in India, and achieved a success beyond the wildest hopes of the Company. The tour began at Calcutta and the first exhibition flight, on January 6th, 1910, attracted a crowd of nearly *three quarters of a million* people. I will quote M. Jullerot's own description of that first day. " As I flew some thousand feet in the air over this dense crowd, I could see them covering the ground and swarming in the trees, the only clear part being the green strip of the racecourse itself. I have never heard so strange a noise in all my life as the screaming and yelling and cheering with which these 700,000 people expressed their delight. It made the roar of the engine seem quite insignificant. I was using the

Bristol military biplane, and I flew from the racecourse over this ocean of heads to Fort William. . . . Passing over the fort I continued my flight . . . back to the grand stand of the racecourse, and after a few laps round the course, gave an exhibition of more tricky flying such as spiral *vol planés*, and the like, much to the delight of the crowd. It was the first absolutely successful flight they had ever seen. . . ."

Not only did the Bristol Company introduce aviation to India, but they introduced a very remarkable man to aviation.

Capt. Sefton Brancker was the officer detailed to accompany M. Jullerot on his flights from Aurungabad in connection with the cavalry manœuvres of the Indian Army, and later from Karghpur, whence they co-operated in the northern manœuvres.

At Aurungabad M. Jullerot stalled the Bristol in taking off owing to lack of power occasioned by bad petrol. There was a slight crash and, on looking round to see if his passenger was injured, the pilot observed Brancker " quizzing " him through his monocle, which had remained undisturbed in his eye. Those of us who had the privilege of knowing the late Air Vice-Marshal Sir Sefton Brancker, Director of Civil Aviation, will especially appreciate this characteristic incident.

Capt. Brancker had plenty of exciting flights at Karghpur, where the only possible place on which to land was an old polo ground, partly covered by bushes, which was used as the aerodrome.

No hangars or other form of protection were provided for the machines, and it says much for the early Bristol workmanship that, although continually exposed to temperatures up to 100°F. in the shade during a protracted tour, the aircraft gave no trouble of any sort.

6. THE KING AND MR. SOPWITH : MORISON AND J. V. MARTIN

An instance of H.M. the King's intense interest in aviation was afforded by his invitation to Mr. T. O. M. Sopwith to visit Windsor Castle. Mr. Sopwith left Brooklands in his Howard-Wright (E.N.V.) on February 1st in a thick mist and intense cold. So cold was it that his radiators froze as fast as they were filled. As soon as they were thawed out a mechanic nipped each tube above and below the burst with a pair of pliers, thus stopping the leak. After this primitive but effective solution, Mr. Sopwith took off and picked his way through the mist to Staines. At Staines he emerged into clear air, and climbing to 1,000 feet, he set out for Windsor. Unfortunately, several more radiator tubes had burst and he had to land at Datchet for further treatment with the pliers. Having executed the repair and had lunch, Mr. Sopwith took off once more, and finally landed below the east terrace, where he was received by His Majesty, who inspected the Howard-Wright closely, asking numerous questions about the controls.

Mr. Morison was rapidly coming to the front at Brooklands owing to the dashing manner in which he flew his Bleriot. He had an alarming experience on the day after Mr. Sopwith's reception at Windsor, when one of his main spars broke at 800 feet. The pilot immediately dived for the ground and succeeded in making a perfect landing. Four days later Mr. Morison was out again, having fitted a new pair of wings, and he proceeded to give the aircraft a searching test in a strong gusty wind.

Another daring pilot was an American pupil, named J. V. Martin, at the G. W. School at Hendon. After he had received three lessons as a passenger, Mr. Gresswell sent him solo on the E.N.V. Farman with instructions to do short, straight hops. Martin, with a regrettable, but none the less admirable, lack of discipline, took off and did two circuits round the aerodrome, but apparently found this a boring procedure and decided on a cross-country excursion. With an engine that was missing so badly that it barely kept the machine in the air, he staggered over the housetops of W. Hendon, turned, and just managed to get back into the aerodrome after threading his way between the trees. On the following day he passed all his tests for his R.Ae.C. certificate, and two days later he was doing trick flying, including sharp turns and steep *vols plané*. A fortnight afterwards he was acting as instructor to new pupils at the school.

7. BRISTOL PROGRESS: NAVAL OFFICERS AT EASTCHURCH

Some of the soundest flying in England was being accomplished unobtrusively at Salisbury Plain, where M. Tetard, Mr. A. R. Low, and Capt. H. F. Wood, flew the Bristols with splendid reliability. Mr. Conner of the R.F.A. was their most promising pupil, but M. Vusepuy wrecked another machine when he stalled it, following an engine stoppage. The Bristol Company, under the able direction of Sir George White, was already established in a big way of business. The working capital was £50,000 and the splendid works at Filton had turned out forty successful machines by the end of January 1911, and had reached an output of two aircraft per week. Eight biplanes were under construction for the Russian Government, to complete the first order ever placed with a British aircraft firm by a foreign power. Seven pilots had qualified on Bristol aeroplanes, including Mr. Herbert Thomas, aged eighteen, who was the youngest pilot in Great Britain at that time.

Mr. F. K. McClean, who had done such splendid work at Eastchurch with the Short machines, joined the Government expedition to the Fiji Islands to observe an eclipse of the sun, and placed his aircraft at the disposal of the Admiralty for the training of Naval officers as pilots. The offer was eagerly accepted and Mr. G. B. Cockburn volunteered to act as instructor to the three Naval officers and one Marine officer, detailed to take the six months course, whilst Messrs. Short Bros. arranged for their technical instruction in their factory at Leysdown. This patriotic action laid the foundation of the Royal Naval Air Service.

8. MORISON FLIES TO BRIGHTON: GRAHAM GILMOUR

The dashing Morison of Brooklands had long been considering the possibility of a spectacular cross-country flight, and by way of preliminary training he pushed the Brooklands altitude record up to 6,000 feet, and subsequently made a trip to Hampton Court and back at a height of 2,000 feet. On the following day he took off and steered for Brighton, rising to 3,000 feet as he approached the South Downs. He was drifting slightly to the westward and struck the coast at Worthing. Thence he followed the beach to Brighton and landed between the piers on what he thought was a patch of sand. Unfortunately, his wheels sank into soft shingle and he nosed over, damaging his undercarriage and airscrew. The Sussex Motor Yacht Club hurriedly organized a banquet in Mr. Morison's honour, at which he was presented with a gold cigarette case as a momento of the flight.

Mr. Morison's steep dives and abrupt take-offs were much appreciated by the Brooklands crowds, but he had a serious rival in Mr. Graham Gilmour, who was probably the greatest exponent of trick or spectacular flying in this country at that time. On one occasion, Mr. Gilmour took off in his two-seater Bleriot and a bowler hat, and on finding the latter unsuitable for aviation, he dived on his shed, flung the offending headgear at the bystanders, and instantly put the machine into a steep climbing turn. The Bristol firm was quick to recognize Mr. Gilmour's exceptional talent, and in the middle of February 1911 he joined their select band of expert pilots.

9. THE G.W. BABY AND THE BARNWELL MONOPLANE

At Hendon, Mr. Barber, the Valkyrie instructor, demonstrated the quick take-off of his mount by repeatedly charging at the crowd from a distance of fifty yards and pulling the machine off over their heads. The crowd apparently enjoyed this perilous performance.

Mr. Grahame-White had designed a new small pusher biplane with a front elevator and a boxkite tail. This machine, which was known as the G. W. Baby, incorporated features of the Farman and Curtiss designs. The little biplane proved to be fast and very handy.

Three Bristol pupils passed their tests for their aviators' certificates in one day; Mons. L. E. Maron and Mr. C. P. Pizey at Salisbury Plain, and Mr. Knight at Brooklands.

The first successful all-Scottish aeroplane was a handsome

"Flight" photo

13.—FIRST ACROSS THE IRISH SEA: MR. ROBERT LORAINE, THE ACTOR-PILOT, ON HIS FARMAN (50 H.P. GNÔME).

Facing page 84

"Flight" photo

14.—Mr. T. O. M. Sopwith, whose first cross-country set up an all-British record, which stood for four years.

Facing page 85

monoplane which resulted from the collaboration of Mr. R. H. Barnwell and the Grampian Motor Company. It was remarkable for its clean lines, fabric-covered fuselage, and the absence of external bracing wires. Mr. Barnwell won a £50 prize, offered by Mr. J. R. K. Law for a flight by a member of the Scottish Aeronautical Society, in this machine, which was fitted with a Grampian horizontally opposed twin-cylinder engine of 40 h.p.

Further south, Mr. C. C. Paterson continued to put in many hours in the air around the aerodrome at Freshfield, Liverpool. In February 1911, he flew his Henry Farman over to the Altcar Coursing meeting to the great delight of the large crowd assembled there. His landing somewhat disorganized the "sport" but, nevertheless, proved to be a very popular attraction.

10. B. C. HUCKS AT FILEY: THE FIRST AIR MAIL

On the Yorkshire coast at Filey Sands, Mr. Robert Blackburn continued his experiments with his monoplane. The trials were conducted by Mr. B. C. Hucks, of whom much will be heard later in this history. Hucks found difficulty in turning the machine owing to the negligible difference between its maximum and its stalling speed, which made any divergence from the straight and narrow path along the beach a perilous undertaking. Mr. Hucks had been associated with Mr. Grahame-White, whom he had accompanied on his American tour, for more than a year, and thus had obtained valuable practical experience, which had been denied to Mr. Blackburn.

The World's first official air mail service was successfully inaugurated at the end of February 1911. Capt. Windham and M. Pequet were the pilots, and the mail was flown in a Humber biplane (Humber engine) from the grounds of the exhibition at Allahabad, India, to the receiving post office at Naini, across the Jumna River. The Indian post office cut a special cancelling stamp for the service reading, "First Aerial Post, U.P. Exhibition, Allahabad 1911." The first batch of mail transmitted by this pioneer service arrived in England in the second week of March 1911, and the envelopes are very highly prized by collectors. Over 5,000 letters were carried in one day on the Humber.

11. THE AIR BATTALION: THE FIRST NAVAL PILOTS

A further step towards the establishment of the R.A.F. was taken in March 1911, when a special Army Order was issued by the War Office giving particulars of the new Air Battalion which was to supersede the existing Balloon School at Farnborough. The Air Battalion consisted of headquarters and two companies, and the personnel and equipment comprised a Major commanding, thirteen other officers, twenty-three N.C.O.'s, one hundred and fifty-three men of the Royal Engineers, two buglers, four riding horses, thirty-two draught horses, five experimental aeroplanes, including Wright, Farman, Paulhan, and de Havilland biplanes, and a Bleriot monoplane, and assorted airships, balloons, and kites. The War Office considered that desirable characteristics in officers applying for transfer to the Air Battalion from other units, comprised good eyesight, medical fitness, ability to read maps and make field sketches, an immunity from sea sickness and a knowledge of foreign languages. Special consideration was to be given to bachelors under 11 stone 7 lbs in weight, and thirty years of age. The Air Battalion came into existence on April 1st, 1911, under the command of Major Sir Alexander Bannerman, R.E., and the following officers were attached for duty :—Capt. Broke-Smith, R.E., Capt. J. B. Fulton, R.F.A., Capt. Burke, Royal Irish Regt., Capt. Maitland, Essex Regt., Capt. Carden, R.E., and Lieut. R. T. Snowden-Smith, A.S.C.

Exactly one month previously, on March 1st, 1911, the Naval contingent had commenced instruction under Mr. G. B. Cockburn at Eastchurch on the Short machines of Mr. Frank McClean. The officers detailed for this six months' course were Lieuts. R. Gregory, C. R. Samson and A. M. Longmore of the Royal Navy, and Lieut. G. V. W. Lushington of the Royal Marine Artillery.

12. FLYING AT BROOKLANDS AND SHOREHAM

Messrs. Keith Prowse & Co., Ltd., had acquired all booking rights at Hendon as well as at Brooklands, and issued a tariff of joy-rides. Short flights cost two guineas, while for three guineas one could do three circuits of the aerodrome terminating with "a *vol plané* landing."

Bad luck still dogged A. V. Roe, for just as Messrs. Howard Pixton, and Kemp had succeeded in obtaining really good results from the Avroplane, Mr. Beattie came along intending to fly it through the tests for his certificate. He stalled on a turn near the Paddock and severely damaged the machine. Mr. T. O. M. Sopwith tried the excellent Martin and Handasyde monoplane, and made some good long steady flights with it, until he landed with the tail too high and broke the skid and airscrew. In the meantime, Mr. Gustav Hamel had come over from Hendon and was flying Mr. Sopwith's Howard-Wright. The Avroplane was soon repaired and Mr. Roe and Mr. Pixton made some further flights in it until the latter essayed a sharp turn on the ground, when the fuselage broke in two, just aft of the pilot's seat. However, it was flying once more on the following day, when Mr. Pixton spent twenty-five minutes at 800 feet and Mr. Kemp was practising *vols plané*. A few days later Mr. Kemp went out for his certificate and had a very narrow escape when he stalled in attempting a climbing turn at 300 feet. Mr. Kemp fought the machine as it dived for the ground, and managed to flatten out just before she struck. The undercarriage and wings were wiped off, but the fuselage was untouched.

Mr. Morison had taken his Bleriot to Shoreham after the repairs necessitated by his landing on Brighton beach, and he flew over to Lancing College at the invitation of the headmaster, and landed on the cricket field. Unfortunately he struck a bank and broke his elevator so that he was unable to fly the machine back to the aerodrome. Mr. Morison spent a considerable time explaining the machine and demonstrating the controls to the boys, thus laying the foundation of the close connection with aviation since enjoyed by the well-known public school.

13. HAMEL WINS HENDON–BROOKLANDS CONTEST

The managements of Hendon and Brooklands had set up prizes for the fastest times achieved in a series of return flights between the two aerodromes. The initial contest took place in the second week of March 1911. The first to start was Mr. C. H. Gresswell from Hendon on a G.W. Bleriot (Gnôme). Unfortunately, he lost himself and landed at Ashford (Middlesex), fearing that he was short of petrol. The late starters also encountered a mist of varying density and had exciting experiences. Mr. J. V. Martin on the G.W. Baby biplane made a fast trip to Brooklands in 37 mins. 26 secs., but lost himself badly on the return journey, and eventually landed at St. Albans, whence he took off again and followed the Midland Railway back to Hendon. On this flight he met two other competing machines in the air. The first was a Farman, flown by M. Ducrocq, who was returning to Brooklands after an abortive attempt to get through to Hendon, and the second was a Bleriot flown by Gustav Hamel, who steered quite straight through the fog in both directions, and easily won the prize with a time of 58 mins. 38 secs. for the double journey.

14. THE AERO SHOW OF 1911

The Olympia Show of March 1911 was vastly more important than either of its predecessors. Foreign exhibits were scarce and some of the English experimenters were unrepresented, but the majority of the home products which were displayed showed a very real advance, both in design and construction.

The most noticeable feature was a dawning appreciation of the necessity for streamline. Seats were faired in by canvas coverings, struts were formed to a better shape, and wires were reduced in number, while two tractor biplanes of quite modern aspect made their *débuts*.

The extent of the general ignorance of the elementary principles of aerodynamics current even at this stage, can be judged from the remarks in the report on the show by *Flight*, the official organ of the R.Ae.C. Commenting on the prevalence of streamline struts, the writer stated that " as a matter of fact, moreover, this elaborate application of pure theory to practice is very apt to ignore practical considerations that are not taken into account in the theoretical hypothesis. For instance, aeroplanes nowadays no longer only fly in the calm. . . . If, therefore, the wind is not blowing in the line of flight, the axes of streamline forms on the machine *will be more or less athwart the relative wind*, and much of the advantage of the special shape will thus be set at nought."

Another writer in *Flight* seriously suggested that a lead plummet on a length of piano wire should be suspended to *windward* of the fore and aft line of the aircraft, and that its degree of divergence from that line would indicate the force and direction of the wind !

It took many years for even those in close daily association with aeroplanes to grasp the elementary fact that wind has no effect whatever upon an aircraft in the air, if the ground be left out of consideration. Some people, including a number of pilots, are still ignorant of this fundamental principle of mechanical flight.

There were twenty-one full-sized aeroplanes on view, of which seventeen were British built. Monoplanes and biplanes were almost equally divided, the former class including two French products, the Nieuport enclosed fuselage tractor with an horizontally opposed twin-cylinder motor and the latest edition of the Bleriot (Gnôme). The British monoplanes included two pushers, the Valkyrie and the Dunne, and seven tractors. The two most striking of the latter class, if we except the Cole tandem, which was a freak, were the all-enclosed Piggott, which possessed a beautifully-shaped fuselage, out of which pilot and passenger could catch glimpses of the surrounding atmosphere through minute portholes of solidified gelatine, and the Handley-Page, whose highly-polished *monocoque* body and gull-like wings made it a thing of real beauty. More stereotyped in design were the Bristol, Blackburn, Martin and Handasyde, and Mulliner-Kny monoplanes, each of which owed something to the Antoinette.

The two most interesting biplanes were the French Breguêt which was an all-steel tractor in which the passenger sat in front of the pilot, quite in the modern style, and the Bristol tractor, which had quite a good square-cut fuselage and an elaborate under-carriage. Both these machines had but one interplane strut each side of the centre section, and on the Bristol these struts were set perilously far back, almost in the centre of the chord of the wings. The idea of an enclosed fuselage tractor biplane had been originated by the Goupy machine in the spring of 1910, and A. V. Roe had applied the principle to his triplane still earlier, but Bristol and Breguêt deserve credit for being the first to follow the lead, although the results must have been extremely unairworthy.

Probably the most airworthy and efficient aircraft exhibited was the Maurice Farman (Renault), a pusher biplane with an enclosed *nacelle* for the pilot and passenger, a biplane tail and an elevator carried on an outrigger in front. This was the first of the famous " Longhorn " models on which the majority of pilots in the R.F.C. received their initial flying training up till the year 1916.

The other biplanes were merely improved versions of well-known types, including Wright, Bristol, the Humber air-mail machine, which was a copy of the Sommer, the G.W. Baby and the Sanders, which last was a variation of the Short.

The Bartelt ornithopter and the Cole tandem were the only freaks in the exhibition.

In the engine category the well-known Green 35 and 60 h.p. models, the E.N.V.'s of 35, 60 and 100 h.p., the N.E.C. 50 h.p. two-stroke, and the 60 and 120 h.p. Wolseleys appeared side by side with some interesting newcomers. The A.B.C. firm displayed 4, 8, and 12-cylinder models of 40, 80, and 120 h.p. respectively, whilst J.A.P., the well-known motor-cycle engine manufacturers, also staged three models rated at 20, 35, and 40 h.p. A complicated two-stroke rotary engine, the 100 h.p. Lamplough, was shown alongside two simple little flat twins in the 50 h.p. Alvaston and 15 h.p. Edwards. The most interesting newcomer, however, was the Isaacson radial engine as fitted to the Blackburn monoplane. Two models were exhibited, one of 50 h.p. with seven cylinders and a double edition with fourteen cylinders, rated at 100 h.p. The cruising speed of both models was only 800 r.p.m. and the smaller one gave 1 b.h.p. per 3·9 lbs weight, which was quite good, although the new 50 h.p. N.E.C. supercharged two-stroke was now giving 1 b.h.p. per 3 lbs. weight.

15. AVIATION AND THE BOAT RACE: A SAD COINCIDENCE

The Oxford *v.* Cambridge boat race seems to exercise considerable fascination for pilots. No less than six aeroplanes flew over the course during the 1911 contest. There were three Bleriots flown by Messrs. Gustav Hamel, C. H. Greswell, and P. Prier, and two Farmans, one flown by Mr. Grahame-White with Mr. C. C. Paterson as passenger, and the other by M. Hubert. All these machines came from Hendon and were met above the river by Mr. Graham Gilmour, who had come up from Brooklands on a Bristol biplane. The latter entertained the crowds, and annoyed the officials, by repeatedly zooming up, cutting off his engine and gliding down again above the crews. These proceedings were hurriedly terminated by a forced landing, due to lack of petrol, but Mr. Gilmour got down safely on the Chiswick Polytechnic cricket ground.

Mr. H. M. Maitland, brother of Capt. E. M. Maitland, had a very serious accident at Salisbury Plain while attempting a right-hand turn on the E.N.V.-engined Bristol biplane. The machine stalled and crashed to the ground from 100 feet. Mr. Maitland had both his legs broken and was removed to a London nursing home. An extraordinary feature of this accident was the fact that the biplane crashed at the identical spot on which Capt. E. M. Maitland fell in August 1910, and that the injuries sustained by the brothers in their respective smashes were also identical ! Coincidence could scarcely be carried further than this.

16. NOVEL NAVIGATION : FIRST FLIGHTS IN NEW ZEALAND

M. Tetard made an adventurous cross-country flight from Brooklands to Salisbury on another Bristol. The visibility was so bad that he lost himself repeatedly, and was forced to make frequent landings to discover his position. At each landing he took one of the natives on board as passenger, and was guided by his directions until the machine had passed out of the area covered by his local knowledge, when another descent was made to change guides. In this way, M. Tetard eventually arrived safely at Salisbury Plain, where he landed at the Bristol School in heavy rain and a boisterous wind.

Another Bristol instructor, M. Tabuteau, made a magnificent flight from Salisbury Plain to Filton on a Bristol biplane fitted with a 70 h.p. Gnôme engine. Four miles out from Salisbury the engine failed owing to a sticking valve, but a 50 h.p. Gnôme was sent out to him and fitted on the spot, and the flight was resumed immediately. The lower-powered motor brought M. Tabuteau safely to Bristol in good time.

Although Mr. Hammond was the first New Zealander to learn to fly, the actual pioneer of flying in that country was Mr. Leo Walsh, who had imported a Howard-Wright in which he flew before the Prime Minister of New Zealand at Papakura, on February 10th, 1911. A month later, Singapore was introduced to aviation by the Belgian pilot, Christiaens, who used a British Bristol biplane (Gnôme).

17. LONDON-PARIS : LONDON-BIRMINGHAM

British aviation received a great fillip by reason of the splendid flight from Hendon to Issy, which M. Pierre Prier accomplished in April 1911, on a Bleriot (Gnôme). M. Prier, who was the chief instructor at the Bleriot school at Hendon, made the trip on the spur of the moment as a result of a casual remark by M. Norbert Chereau. He steered north-about from Hendon, passing over Chatham, Canterbury, Dover, Calais, Boulogne, Abbeville, and Beauvais. He encountered bad visibility, except over the Channel, but in spite of the mist he kept his course accurately and covered 230 miles in 3 hrs. 56 mins., at an average speed of 62 m.p.h. This flight was not only the first non-stop passage by air between

London and Paris, but it also set up a world's record for distance flown in a straight line.

Two days previously, Mr. Grahame-White had flown his Farman (50 h.p. Gnôme) 115 miles to Birmingham from Hendon in four stages. He also was much bothered by bad visibility.

18. A WEEK-END TOUR

Messrs. Graham Gilmour and Gordon England set off from Salisbury Plain at 7.30 a.m. on April 12th, 1911, for an aerial tour in a Bristol biplane. Their immediate objective was Yeovil, but they followed the wrong railway from Salisbury and lost themselves. After about thirty miles Graham Gilmour landed in the grounds of a large house, which turned out to be Fryern Court, near Templecombe. Here they had breakfast, and took off later for Blandford, where they landed once more to call upon a friend of the pilot. Thence they flew to Eastbury Park and landed again to give joy-rides to friends. In the evening they left for Martock, but had not proceeded far before the wind freshened considerably and they were forced down at Henstridge Station. They put up for the night there and, on going out to the machine in the morning, found that the field in which they had landed was too small to permit of a take-off with two up. Gilmour accordingly flew the biplane out and landed in another field a mile away to pick up Gordon England. They reached Martock safely and stayed there all day giving exhibition flights. Earl Poulett invited them both to dinner at Hinton St. George, and the dashing Gilmour dispatched Gordon England by road, arranging to follow himself by air with a lady passenger. He had intended to land in the park, but when he arrived, he found too many trees and golf bunkers to make it attractive, so resolved to put the aircraft down on the lawn in front of the house. He accomplished this safely, but overran on the smooth turf and carried away one of his host's fences. The Bristol workmanship was proof against this, as the only damage was the breakage of a few wires and a dent in the lower member of the tail. This most interesting flight was abandoned at this stage. It was, undoubtedly, the first successful air tour undertaken in England, and was a fine demonstration of what one of those early biplanes could do in the hands of a skilful and determined pilot.

19. JOY-RIDING RESTRICTIONS: THE AVRO BIPLANE

At long last the R.Ae.C. took steps to protect an innocent public from some of the more dangerous pilots by enacting that any aviator who carried passengers, without having obtained an aviator's certificate, should have the subsequent granting of that certificate postponed for such period as the R.Ae.C. committee should determine.

Mr. A. V. Roe had produced a new Avro biplane, fitted with a 30 h.p. Green engine. This was a very great advance upon his previous machines, and was flown with considerable success by Messrs. Howard Pixton, Conway Jenkins, and Beattie. It must have been easy to handle because Lieut. Parke, R.N., beat all records for quick tuition on it, always excepting Mr. Sopwith's feat of the previous year, surpassing even Mr. J. V. Martin, whose exploits at Hendon I have already described. He began on April 11th, 1911, when Pixton helped him into an aeroplane for the first time and told him to taxi it about on the ground. Parke banged the throttle open, took off, and flew across to the paddock, where he turned round and flew back! On the following day, he essayed turns in a stiff wind, but stalled and crashed gently into the sewage farm. He then joined the Bristol school, and had one flight as a passenger, after which he was sent solo with instructions to do "straights." He took off and proceeded to do high circuits! On his next flight he did perfect figures-of-eight and landed out of a *vol plané*, and the same evening he gained his pilot's certificate, flying brilliantly in a strong wind.

Incidentally, Mr. J. V. Martin had taught his wife to fly, and boldly accompanied her as passenger in the G.W. Farman while she flew a couple of laps, terminating with an excellent landing.

Lieut. Dawes became entangled with some telegraph wires whilst flying a Humber monoplane near Bombay, and was forced down on the railway line. He accomplished the landing successfully, but was only just in time to jump out before the aircraft was run over by a goods train, only the motor escaping unharmed.

20. NAVAL AND MILITARY DEVELOPMENTS

The first two of the Naval officers, taking the course at Eastchurch under Mr. G. B. Cockburn, to pass their tests for the R.Ae.C. Certificate were Lieut. C. R. Samson, R.N., and Lieut. A. M. Longmore, R.N., who were quickly followed by Lieuts. Gregory, R.N., and Gerrard, R.M.L.I. These four Naval officers averaged only three solo flights each before taking their certificates, thus rivalling their *confrère* Parke at Brooklands.

Under increasing pressure from the press the War Office was beginning to take a wider interest in aviation. Col. Seely, the Under-Secretary for War, paid a semi-official visit to the Grahame-White School at Hendon. Although the weather was really unfit for flying, he prevailed upon Mr. Grahame-White to take him up in the G.W. Baby for a brief but exciting flight, from which he returned unshaken, but visibly impressed.

The great armament firm of Vickers, Ltd., was also turning its attention towards aeroplanes. Capt. Wood, a Farman pilot, had been appointed technical adviser, and in that capacity he visited Buc, where he set himself to master the R.E.P. monoplane,

"Flight" photo

15.—Three-quarter back view of the Dunne arrowhead Biplane.

Facing page 92

"*Flight*" *photo*

16.—Mr. Gustav Hamel (Bleriot—50 h.p. Gnôme), winner of the first race from London to Brighton.

designed by M. Esnault Pelterie, with considerable success. At a later date he visited La Brayelle with Mr. Low and tried out the Breguêt tractor biplane.

21. SOPWITH AND FISHER ON MONOPLANES

Mr. T. O. M. Sopwith was leaning towards the monoplane type—the Martin and Handasyde had given him his initial experience, and now he placed an order for one of the new 70 h.p. Gnôme-engined Bleriots, and went over to Pau with his friend Gustav Hamel to test its capabilities.

Mr. E. V. B. Fisher was rapidly coming to the fore at Brooklands by his consistent good flying on the Hanriot monoplane, which had now been fitted with a Clergêt rotary engine. He established a reputation for making the smallest and neatest figures of eight to be seen at Brooklands. Capt. Sykes, a Bristol pupil, and Mr. Fisher flew their tests for their certificates simultaneously, and there was nearly a terrible accident when the Hanriot overtook the biplane in the middle of a right-hand turn. The machines passed within a few feet of each other, and neither pilot saw the other. As a result of this incident, the R.Ae.C. instructed their observers that candidates were only to be sent for tests when the air was clear.

22. HAMEL WINS BROOKLANDS–BRIGHTON RACE: AVRO DEVELOPMENTS

On May 6th, 1911, the first handicap cross-country race was flown from Brooklands to Brighton, for a prize of £80. There were four competitors. First away was Mr. Graham Gilmour (Bristol biplane, Gnôme), who was followed four minutes later by Lieut. Snowden-Smith, on the Farman biplane (Gnôme) built by Hewlett and Blondeau at Brooklands. Mr. Howard Pixton on the Avro biplane (30 h.p. Green) should have started next, but he was busy trying to win the Manville prize at the time and did not leave for Brighton until twenty minutes after Mr. Gilmour's departure. Scratch man was Gustav Hamel (Bleriot monoplane, Gnôme) who took off twelve minutes, fifty seconds after the Bristol. All the competitors completed the course, and arrived safely at Shoreham. Mr. Hamel was an easy winner, his Bleriot taking only 57 mins. 10 secs. for the journey, which involved approaching Brighton down the Adur Valley and then flying up the coast eastwards, to the finishing line at the Palace Pier. The Farman overtook the Bristol within ten miles from the start, but Lieut. Snowden-Smith was disqualified for missing the Shoreham turn. His time was 1 hr. 21 mins. 6 secs. Gilmour took 1 hr. 37 mins. and Howard Pixton lost himself and landed on Plumpton racecourse to inquire the way and refuel. The competitors evidently had to face a head wind, as Mr. Hamel flew back from Shoreham to Brooklands after the race in the fast time of thirty-four minutes. Mr. Graham Gilmour stayed the week-end at Shoreham and then flew on to Portsmouth, where he bombed the submarine depôt at Fort Blockhouse with oranges and went on to land on the Haslar recreation ground.

The Avro school at Brooklands was making splendid progress on the new biplane and a Henry Farman was added to the fleet. This was flown by Lieuts. Watkins and Parke. Mr. F. P. Raynham, who was to become one of the greatest test-pilots in the world, took his certificate on the Avro machine, together with Messrs. Conway-Jenkins and Ronald Kemp.

23. THE POLITICAL DISPLAY AT HENDON

In the middle of May 1911 a most important flying meeting took place at Hendon. This was a demonstration of the military possibilities of aircraft, and was designed to impress members of Parliament, over 300 of whom attended by invitation. Amongst the guests were Mr. Asquith, Prime Minister, Mr. Balfour, who flew two circuits with Grahame-White, Mr. Lloyd George, Mr. Winston Churchill, Lord Roberts, Sir Herbert Samuel, Lord Haldane, Minister for War, Lord Northcliffe, and, of course, Col. Seely, together with hundreds of Naval and Military officers.

In ideal weather conditions the little band of pilots put up a show which left an indelible impression upon the spectators. Mr. Grahame-White demonstrated bomb-dropping from a Henry Farman, making deadly shooting with 100-lb. bags of sand suspended precariously from ropes below the wings. Messrs. Cody and Howard Pixton flew over from Brooklands and gave exhibition flights, but perhaps the most impressive event was Mr. Gustav Hamel's flights with dispatches to Aldershot and back. On the outward journey his Bleriot made the thirty-five miles passage in forty minutes, beating a telegram handed in at the moment of departure by fifteen minutes. The return trip was even faster, for Mr. Hamel landed at Hendon thirty minutes out from the Farnborough aerodrome, and this time the advisory telegram from Aldershot was not delivered until thirty minutes after his arrival. The Postmaster-General was amongst the spectators.

For some reason Mr. Barber was refused permission to demonstrate the Valkyrie machines, which was unfortunate. Another regrettable incident was Mr. Armstrong Drexel's crash, which was caused by a mechanic crossing the elevator controls of his Bleriot, with the result that, when he pulled the stick back to take off, the machine nosed over and was smashed. Fortunately Mr. Drexel was unhurt.

By arrangement with the War Office some troops had been posted under cover in the country between Hendon and St. Albans.

M. Hubert and Mr. C. C. Paterson flew two Army officers over the terrain at 3,000 feet, and the latter returned having correctly plotted the positions of the infantry and artillery on the maps provided.

These reconnaissance flights set the seal on a most successful and impressive demonstration.

24. BRISTOLS AT HOME AND ABROAD

Mr. Collyns Pizey of the Bristol Company had a thrilling experience on his first long cross-country flight. He had been instructed to deliver a new Bristol biplane to Mr. Morison at Shoreham, and soon after he took off from Salisbury Plain he flew into the midst of a terrific thunderstorm. Lightning played all around the machine and the rain was so dense that for some time the pilot could not see the ground, whilst the bumps were terrifying. The Bristol staggered through, however, and Mr. Pizey, safe but shaken, landed near Portsmouth for the night and delivered his charge to Shoreham on the following day. On the next day Messrs. O. C. Morison and Graham Gilmour held a match race on their Bristols from Shoreham to Black Rock, Brighton, Mr. Morison's new machine winning by ten seconds.

Bristols were without rivals in the Antipodean market. Following upon Mr. Hammond's success, Mr. Leslie MacDonald was making some splendid flights in N.S.W. He flew Gen. Gordon, commanding the military forces, over Sidney Harbour for thirty miles at 3,000 feet. Meanwhile Messrs. H. Busteed and E. Harrison of Melbourne had come to England for training at the Bristol headquarters on Salisbury Plain, where the brilliant Bleriot pilot, Pierre Prier, was now acting as an instructor.

By the end of May the Company had delivered nine machines to the Russian Government.

25. TWO NEW SCHOOLS: A FLYING GARDEN PARTY

A new school of flying was opened by Mr. W. H. Ewen on the ground which had been used for the Lanark meeting in the previous year. Mr. Ewen had a Bleriot monoplane there. Mr. Melly, who had been associated with the Freshfield Aerodrome, had also set up on his own at Waterloo, Liverpool, where he instructed Mr. Dukinfield-Jones on a two-seater Bleriot. There was also a single-seater provided for soloists.

Lord Northcliffe, whose generosity had already done so much for British aviation, gave a garden party at his house near Guildford, which was attended by a number of machines and pilots. Messrs. Grahame-White and Hamel came from Hendon, the latter running into a ditch and damaging his Bleriot. Mrs. Hewlett's Farman arrived from Brooklands accompanied by Lieut. Snowden-Smith

(Farman), Mr. Hewitt, and Mr. Astley. The last-named was baulked in landing by the crowd of aircraft on the ground, and was forced to approach across wind, with the result that his machine jumped a brook, knocked down three saplings, and finished up against a large oak tree. His aircraft escaped with crushed leading edges to the wings.

26. OGILVIE AT RYE: TWO FATALITIES: THE HANRIOT SCHOOL: SOPWITH IN U.S.A.

An instance of the amount of flying which was being done unobtrusively in out-of-the-way corners of the country, was provided by Mr. Alec Ogilvie, who had been using Camber Sands, near Rye, as his aerodrome for more than a year past. Mr. Ogilvie flew across country to Eastchurch on his Wright, with one stop at Ashford to rectify trouble in the oil feed of his two-stroke N.E.C. motor. The Eastchurch pilots were astounded to learn that Mr. Ogilvie had done no less than sixty hours in the previous three weeks. An average of twenty hours per week in the air is very seldom attained by amateur pilots to-day.

The first booked cross-country taxi flight took place on May 17th, 1911, when Mr. J. V. Martin flew a fare from Brooklands to Hendon on a G. W. Farman.

The third fatality to a British pilot occurred on May 25th, 1911, when Mr. B. G. Benson, a pupil at the Valkyrie School at Hendon, was killed in attempting his first *vol plané*, or gliding descent, from 200 feet. The glide was apparently "shaky" from the start, and it seems to be almost certain that he failed to maintain his speed, as the machine fell the last forty feet vertically, obviously as the result of a stall. His instructor, Mr. Barber, was exonerated from all blame, and it was evident that the aircraft and engine were in perfect order.

Two days later the fourth British power pilot was killed at St. Petersburg. He was Mr. Vladimir Smith, who was giving a demonstration flight on a Sommer biplane constructed at the Russo-Baltic works at Riga. It seems that Mr. Smith, who was not an experienced pilot, failed to pull out of a dive or steep glide in time, and flew into the ground at high speed.

The newly-established Hanriot School at Brooklands was attracting quite a following who wished for an opportunity of flying this advanced type of monoplane. The instructor, Mr. Fisher, was becoming an accomplished pilot and Señor Perojo, Mr. Gordon Bell, who had come over from the Avro school, Lieut. Manisty, and Mr. Jack Humphreys, were all making good progress. Mr. Hubert Oxley, after qualifying at Brooklands on the Hanriot, went to Filey and began to fly the Blackburn monoplane, on which Mr. B. C. Hucks had taken his certificate.

Mr. T. O. M. Sopwith had taken his Howard-Wright (60 h.p.

"Flight" photo

17.—Gordon-Bennett contest at Eastchurch: Mr. Gustav Hamel getting away in his clipped-wing Bleriot Racer (100 h.p. Gnôme), only to crash a moment later.

"*Flight*" *photo*

18.—Circuit of Britain: Vedrines (Morane-Borel-Gnôme) at Shoreham control.

E.N.V.) to the United States and, after a slight mishap at Mineola (Florida), he held a most successful one-man flying meeting at Philadelphia, circling round the City Hall at 1,200 feet to the immense delight of the crowd. Later he visited New York City and performed the remarkable feat of flying after the liner *Olympic* and dropping a parcel on to the deck, as she was passing Fort Hamilton, outward bound.

27. PANIC LEGISLATION: THE VALKYRIE RACER

At the beginning of June 1911 the provisions of the Air Navigation Bill, which provided very severe penalties for flying over towns or crowds of people, were being hotly debated in the House of Commons. An accident in Paris, which resulted in the death of the French War Minister, and the prospect of aircraft appearing above the impending Coronation procession, produced an unfavourable atmosphere for the calm discussion of the proposed legislation. The exploits of Mr. Graham Gilmour and others over the boat-race course were recalled, and the R.Ae.C. caused Mr. Gilmour to come before the Committee to be questioned concerning an incident when he flew over Salisbury and landed near the town. Mr. Melly was also questioned about an alleged flight over Liverpool. Mr. Gilmour's explanation was accepted, but he was advised to be careful in future. The rumours about Mr. Melly were discovered to be unfounded. The Bill broke all records for Parliamentary speed by passing through both Houses and receiving the Royal assent in less than seven days.

The new Valkyrie racing pusher monoplane was out on test at the beginning of June. Mr. Barber made a very fine flight from Hendon to Brooklands in twenty minutes dead, at a speed of 60 m.p.h. The weather was thick and he flew a compass course at 3,000 feet. He returned in thirty minutes, the extra time being accounted for by a head wind which had sprung up in the meantime. Mr. Barber landed within thirty yards of the enclosure, after a spiral descent from 4,000 feet with engine off. This flight was a very splendid performance on the part of both machine and pilot.

28. MORE NAVAL AND MILITARY PROGRESS

All the Naval pilots at Eastchurch had now attained the stage at which the actual flying of their machines had become automatic. Accordingly they initiated a series of experiments with compasses involving longer and longer cross-country courses to test their navigation. The passengers on these occasions were other Naval officers from the ships at Sheerness, and much valuable information was obtained by all concerned. Their Short aircraft continued to perform with great reliability. Lieut. Samson attempted the first cross-country from Eastchurch to Brooklands. Leaving Sheppey at 5 p.m. he landed at Horley for the night. Having slept beneath the wing of his aircraft, he resumed his journey, but lost himself and landed at Hawthorn Hill to inquire the way. Eventually he reached Brooklands, where his Short was much admired by the *habitués*. The machine was subsequently flown back to Eastchurch by Lieut. A. M. Longmore, R.N.

The Air Battalion officers at Salisbury Plain spent every possible moment in the air. A massed cross-country flight to Aldershot was undertaken early in June. Four machines were lined up on the aerodrome and took off at short intervals in the following order :—Capt. Burke (Henry Farman), Capt. J. B. Fulton (Bristol biplane), Lieut. Barrington-Kennett (Bristol biplane), and finally, Lieut. Cammell (Bleriot). The squadron landed safely at Farnborough, about 1 hr. 30 mins. after the first machine had left Amesbury.

So good were the Bristol military biplanes that M. Jullerot, the test pilot, was able to fly a brand new model, which he was testing at Bristol, direct to Amesbury on its initial flight. His time was 1 hr. 23 mins., and he climbed to 3,000 feet in under ten minutes, which was a startling performance in those days.

29. THE EUROPEAN CIRCUIT

By far the most important competition yet organized was the Circuit of Europe which started on June 18th, 1911. The contest was scheduled to last twelve days, the stages being as follows :—Paris (Vincennes) to Liège (via Rheims) ; Liège-Spa-Liège ; Liège–Utrecht (via Verloo) ; Utrecht–Brussels (via Breda) ; Brussels –Roubaix ; Roubaix–Calais ; Calais–London (via Dover and Shoreham) ; London–Calais (via Shoreham and Dover) ; and Calais–Paris (via Amiens).

The title accorded to the contest was somewhat exaggerated as the only countries visited were France, Belgium, Holland, and England, but the undertaking was a stupendous task for the aeroplanes and pilots of the time, involving, as it did, the double crossing of the Channel. There was plenty of incentive for the entrants as the prize money totalled £18,300.

It was an imposing array of forty-three aeroplanes that lined up in three rows at Vincennes, ready for the start at 6 a.m. Since midnight a vast crowd, estimated at more than half a million people, had waited in driving rain to see the departure. A guard of 6,000 soldiers and police had all their work cut out to keep control.

The field was extraordinarily representative, comprising as it did the following machines :—eight Moranes, seven Deperdussins, six Bleriots, three Sommers, three Caudrons, three Henry Farmans, two Maurice Farmans, two Bristols, two Voisins, two Astras, and one each of the following makes—Nieuport, Tellier, Antoinette,

Train, Bonnet-Lab, Danton, Barillon, Vinet, Pischoff, R.E.P., and van Meel. Some of these entrants failed to start, but the size and variety of the entry list is imposing, and in addition to the official civilian competitors, a dozen French military pilots set out to accompany the race by air.

England was represented by the two Bristols, which were entrusted to prominent French pilots, and by Mr. James Valentine of Brooklands, who was flying one of the French Deperdussin monoplanes.

The perilous nature of the contest was shown up in terrible fashion on the first day. Before the control at Rheims was reached, three pilots had been killed and another was badly injured. The fatal accidents occurred to Lemartin and Lieut. Princeteau (Bleriots) and Landron (Pischoff). The last two were burned to death, Lieut. Princeteau's Bleriot catching fire in the air, whilst Lemartin's Bleriot broke up in flight just after the start. The injured pilot was Lieut. Gaubert, whose Morane crashed at Soissons.

Maurice Tabuteau (Bristol) was first away, Tetard, on the second Bristol, following in fourth place, but the fast French monoplanes soon overtook the slow but reliable "boxkites." The leaders at Liège were:—1, Vidart (Deperdussin); 2, Vedrines (Morane); 3, Weymann (Nieuport); 4, "Beaumont" (Lieut. de Vaisseau Conneau), (Bleriot).

Only eight of the forty-three entrants reached Liège to schedule on the first day. The successful machines comprising the two Maurice Farmans, two of the Bleriots, the Nieuport, one of the Caudrons and a single Deperdussin. Tetard (Bristol) had disappeared early in the proceedings, but Tabuteau brought the second Bristol as far as Rheims and reached Liege on the following day. Valentine had landed his Deperdussin at Sainte Menehould, whence he proceeded to Rheims on the second day.

The short second stage from Liège to Spa and back had to be postponed on account of bad weather, until June 21st. Eighteen started on this flight and fifteen finished, the leaders at the end of the second stage being:—1, Vedrines (Morane); 2, Vidart (Deperdussin); and 3, "Beaumont" (Bleriot).

On the next day the competitors were set a cross-country to Utrecht, via Verloo. Ten machines arrived to schedule, including Tabuteau's Bristol. All the first three places changed hands on this leg of the course, the leaders at Utrecht being:—1, Gibert (R.E.P.), who had come up rapidly after being delayed between Paris and Rheims; 2, Garros (Bleriot), who had been seventh at Liège, and 3, Vidart (Deperdussin). The 23rd was a rest day, which enabled four more machines to reach Utrecht. These included Vedrines' Morane, which had been forced down shortly after leaving Liège.

Bad weather again delayed the race, and it was not until late on the 26th that the men were dispatched to Brussels. Tabuteau was in trouble on this section and landed near Breda. Garros (Bleriot) held his place, but "Beaumont" forced his Bleriot into the lead, whilst Vedrines (Morane) captured third position, owing to Vidart having crashed his fast Deperdussin at Louvain. Vidart motored into Brussels after his accident, bought a new machine, and resumed! The official placing at Brussels was:— 1, "Beaumont" (Bleriot); 2, Garros (Bleriot); and 3, Vedrines (Morane). On the corrected figures "Beaumont" led Garros by three hours and the Morane was seventeen hours behind the second Bleriot. A dozen competitors finished the stage to Brussels to schedule and Valentine, having cured the trouble with his Deperdussin, had cut across and proposed to complete the course *hors concours*.

On the 27th the leading dozen set off for Roubaix accompanied by Valentine. Fastest time on this leg was put up by Vedrines (Morane), followed by Kimmerling (Sommer), and Garros (Bleriot). Ten of the thirteen machines reached Roubaix to schedule.

There was a day's rest there, after which nine aircraft left for Calais, Prevost (Deperdussin) remaining at Roubaix. Seven competitors reached Calais according to plan, Valentine having dropped out fifteen kilometres from the start, and Train having damaged his machine in a forced landing at Renescure. The leaders at Calais were: Vedrines (Morane), Vidart on his new Deperdussin, and "Beaumont" (Bleriot).

The cross Channel stage was postponed until Monday, July 2nd, and this allowed several of the slower machines to catch up with the leaders. Train repaired his monoplane and proceeded, whilst Tabuteau brought the Bristol to Calais, and Valentine got through with his Deperdussin. The result was that eleven aircraft left Calais for Dover on the Monday morning.

All the machines crossed safely, the first to land at Dover being Vedrines (Morane), followed by Vidart (Deperdussin), and Gibert (R.E.P.)

After an hour's rest the field left for Shoreham, led by Vedrines. Barra (Maurice Farman) was delayed for an hour by engine trouble, but he got away eventually, only to be forced down at Heathfield, where he spent ten hours working on the machine. His team mate, Renaux, also suffered trouble with his Renault motor, and spent seven hours at work on it near Bodiam Castle. Train's misfortunes culminated at Newhaven, where he landed up the side of a steep hill intending to ask the way, and damaged his machine severely by running into a wire fence, backwards!

The others all reached Shoreham safely and left for Hendon after a short stop. Gibert (R.E.P.) lost himself and landed near Dorking. His monoplane was slightly damaged, but the pilot repaired it himself and continued. The times of the leading competitors over the whole journey from Calais to London (Hendon) were: 1, Vedrines (Morane) 2 hrs. 56 mins.; 2, Vidart (Deperdussin),

3 hrs. 27 mins; and 3, Kimmerling (Sommer), 3 hrs. 28 mins. Tabuteau (Bristol) lost his way between Shoreham and Hendon and took 5 hrs. 38 mins., but Valentine brought his Deperdussin through in the good time of 3 hrs. 44 mins., which placed him fifth on the day's racing.

After a day's holiday at Hendon the survivors left on their next journey, which had been shortened in order that the return flight across the Channel might be made a separate stage. Ten started for Shoreham, and all arrived except Valentine, who landed at Brooklands with his engine misfiring. Vedrines (Morane), who led at Shoreham, only stopped two minutes there and arrived at Dover a long way ahead of the field. He was followed by Vidart (Deperdussin) and "Beaumont" (Bleriot). Kimmerling (Sommer) landed at New Romney with engine trouble, and Renaux was again in difficulties and was forced to descend at Aldington, near Lympne. Both got through to Dover eventually.

On July 6th, nine machines crossed from Dover to Calais without incident. The fastest times were put up by Vedrines (Morane), 30 mins. 40 secs.; Gibert (R.E.P.), 33 mins. 28 secs.; and Kimmerling (Sommer) 34 mins. 23 secs. Tabuteau (Bristol) took 43 mins. 51 secs. Valentine had definitely abandoned at Brooklands.

The last stage was begun on July 7th, nineteen days after the start. The nine survivors all completed the course, although Kimmerling crashed, first at Calais, where he repaired the machine, and later at Amiens, where he took over a new Sommer which was waiting for him. Tabuteau had trouble with the Bristol at Claremont-sur-Oise where he spent the night, flying in to Paris the following day to complete the course. The first to arrive at Amiens were Vidart (Deperdussin), Gibert (R.E.P.), Garros (Bleriot), and Vedrines (Morane), who crashed on landing, and was forced to take another machine in to the finish.

The order of finishing at Vincennes was as follows:—1, Vidart (Deperdussin); 2, Gibert (R.E.P.); 3, Garros (Bleriot); and 4, "Beaumont" (Bleriot).

Gibert had put up an especially meritorious performance, as he was the only monoplane pilot who finished on the same machine with which he set out. There was nothing in the rules to prevent changing mounts in the course of the competition and nearly all the competitors had made the fullest use of this advantage.

The official placings in this great contest were as follows:—

1. "Beaumont" (Lieut. de Vaisseau Conneau), (Bleriot).
2. Garros (Bleriot).
3. Vidart (Deperdussin).
4. Vedrines (Morane).
5. Gibert (R.E.P.)
6. Kimmerling (Sommer).
7. Renaux (Maurice Farman).

Barra (Maurice Farman) and Tabuteau (Bristol) also arrived at Paris, but neither had completed the whole course to the satisfaction of the officials.

30. THE GORDON-BENNETT CONTEST

During the progress of the European Circuit the Gordon-Bennett International Contest was flown off at Eastchurch, in the presence of 10,000 people on July 1st, 1911.

Things were very badly mismanaged as regards the British entry. Although the rules still permitted the pilots representing the various competing nations to choose their own aircraft, it would be thought that the time had come when an effort should have been made to put up a team of British pilots in British machines.

Actually, the team selected by the Royal Aero Club consisted of Mr. Alec Ogilvie on his American Baby Wright machine with its British N.E.C. two-stroke engine, Mr. Gustav Hamel, who had succeeded M. Prier as chief pilot for Bleriots at Hendon, on an all-French Bleriot, and Mr. Graham Gilmour on a Bristol monoplane with a French Gnôme motor.

Messrs. J. Radley (Bleriot), O.C. Morison (Bristol-Gnôme) and James Valentine, who was busy flying his French Deperdussin in the circuit of Europe, were chosen as reserves. Mr. Graham Gilmour's mount was not ready in time, but none of these reserve pilots was ready either, so that Britain was left to face the formidable competition with a team consisting of two foreign aeroplanes, one of which could not exceed a mile a minute !

As at New York in the previous year, the competitors were allowed to pick their own time of starting and fly independently against the clock. First away was Gustav Hamel (G.B.) He was flying an extremely dangerous-looking Bleriot monoplane (100 h.p. Gnôme) which had had its wings clipped both in span and chord. The overall width of the machine was under seventeen feet. He started at a great speed, turned sharply at the first corner and flew straight into the ground with a terrific smash. Fortunately the pilot was only superficially hurt, although the aeroplane was rolled up into a small ball of twisted wreckage.

This left Great Britain with one very slow aeroplane to battle against three Nieuport monoplanes and another clipped-wing Bleriot racer.

M. Chevalier (Fr.) took off next in a Nieuport (28 h.p. Nieuport), and had completed eleven laps of the twenty-five-lap course in 50 mins. 53⅗ secs., when his motor failed and he broke his undercarriage in landing.

Next to start was Mr. C. Weymann (U.S.) on a racing Nieuport (100 h.p. Gnôme). He began to lap the six-kilometre course at over

75 m.p.h., and continued to increase his speed until he had completed the twenty-five laps (94 miles) in 1 hr. 11 mins. 36⅛ secs. at the astounding average speed of 78 m.p.h.

Before Weymann had completed the course, M. Chevalier mounted another Nieuport and made a second attempt, but this proved to be more unfortunate than the first, as the engine gave out before one lap had been covered.

About half an hour before the completion of Weymann's flight, Mr. Alec Ogilvie started on the Wright. He flew steadily and, of course, slowly. At the end of his twenty-second lap he stopped to refuel, thus losing about four minutes, but he was already so far behind the American entry that it would not have mattered if he had taken an hour over it. The Wright took thirty-eight minutes longer to complete the course than the Nieuport had done, and its average speed of 51·31 m.p.h. was 26·69 m.p.h. slower than that of the French machine.

M. Nieuport on another machine of his own design, fitted with a 70 h.p. Gnôme motor, took the air next and immediately began to lap really fast. Although the engine was rated at 30 h.p. less than that fitted to Weymann's aircraft, M. Nieuport succeeded in averaging 75·07 m.p.h. for the whole course.

Leblanc, who was the ace of French speed pilots at that time and the hero of the previous year's contest in New York, did not start until Weymann had nearly finished, so that he was aware that he had to go very fast indeed to win the cup for France. M. Bleriot had cut down the supporting surface of Leblanc's machine even more drastically than he had dealt with Hamel's, and everyone anticipated either terrific speed or a serious accident. But Leblanc, who had witnessed Hamel's smash, was not taking any undue risks and by cornering wide and cautiously, succeeded in finishing second. His time was 2 mins. 4 secs. longer than Weymann's.

Thus the American pilot's all-French machine beat the only American aircraft in the race, and won the blue riband of aviation for the U.S.A. !

Result :—

1. C. Weymann (U.S.A.) : Nieuport, 100 h.p. Gnôme, 78 m.p.h.
2. A. Leblanc (France) : Bleriot, 100 h.p. Gnôme, 75·83 m.p.h.
3. E. Nieuport (France) : Nieuport, 70 h.p. Gnôme, 75·07 m.p.h.
4. A. Ogilvie (G.B.) : Wright, 50 h.p. N.E.C., 51·31 m.p.h.

31. VALKYRIES AND THE GOVERNMENT : DUAL CONTROL

Mr. H. Barber, designer, manufacturer and test pilot of the Valkyrie pusher monoplanes at Hendon, who had been debarred from demonstrating his products at the display to which the politicians had been invited, heaped coals of fire on his detractors' heads, by announcing the generous gift of four Valkyrie aeroplanes to the Government. Two of these machines were two-seaters and two were single-seaters. The guaranteed maximum speeds of the various types ranged from 45 to 55 m.p.h. Mr. Barber, who also offered to act as designer, constructor, or pilot to the Government in his spare time, without remuneration, expressed the desire that two of the machines be handed over to the Navy to be fitted with floats and developed as seaplanes. The offer was gratefully accepted, and by way of emphasizing the value of his gift, Mr. Barber made a splendid flight on one of the machines from Shoreham to Hendon, carrying one of his women pupils, Miss Edith Meeze, as passenger.

Until the middle of 1911, it had been customary to instruct pupils by taking them up in two-seater machines and letting them lean over their instructor's shoulders and feel the stick in his hand. After one or two flights of this nature, the pupil was sent off alone with instructions to do "straights." When he had succeeded in getting the machine off and holding it up for a few yards, he was permitted to attempt half-circuits and so on. This method was obviously very dangerous, and it says much for the early pupils that so few fatalities occurred, especially as the likelihood of stalling on a turn and the probable results of a stall were not understood in those days. It was a great advance, therefore, when Mr. H. Barber fitted one of his school Valkyries with a primitive form of dual control early in July 1911.

32. MORISON'S MORANE: ANOTHER BRISTOL TOUR

Mr. Grahame-White initiated the Isle of Man to aviation, although he was seriously hampered by gusty winds, and about the same time, Mr. O. C. Morison made a grand flight from Paris to Shoreham, via Dieppe, Calais, and Dover, on his new Morane-Borel monoplane, whilst Mr. Gordon England flew a Bristol biplane from Shoreham to Shanklin, I.O.W., carrying the personal luggage of Messrs. Fleming and Collyns Pizey, who were touring on another Bristol. The latter machine went from Salisbury Plain to Brooklands, Rochester, Dover, Shoreham, Shanklin, and thence back to Amesbury, without any trouble.

Mr. O. C. Morison flew his Morane-Borel from Shoreham to Brooklands and thence to Hendon. On his return flight to Brooklands he had the advantage of a 30 m.p.h. wind at his back, and the monoplane covered the twenty miles in twelve minutes. Unfortunately, Mr. Morison was one of those who had still to learn that landings should always be made up-wind, and he attempted to alight down-wind at about 100 m.p.h. The undercarriage collapsed at the first touch and the machine nosed over. Fortunately, the pilot emerged unhurt, but the Morane was badly smashed.

33. ROUND BRITAIN FOR £10,000

The *Daily Mail* newspaper had offered another great prize of £10,000 for the winner of a race round Britain. The circuit chosen totalled 1,010 miles, with thirteen compulsory stops in controls, and the route was as follows:—1st day, Brooklands to Hendon (20 miles); 2nd day, Hendon to Edinburgh (343 miles) via Harrogate and Newcastle; 3rd day, Edinburgh to Bristol (383 miles) via Stirling, Glasgow, Carlisle, and Manchester; 4th day, Bristol to Brighton (224 miles) via Exeter and Salisbury Plain; 5th day, Brighton to Brooklands (40 miles).

On the face of it, this contest was not nearly so strenuous as the Circuit of Europe, but actually it was far more so. In the European race the competitors had been allowed to change their machines as often as they pleased, but the *Daily Mail's* rules not only forbade this practice, but also provided for the sealing of five parts of each airframe and five parts of each engine. At least two of each set of sealed parts had to remain in place throughout the race, but the promoters generously omitted undercarriages and airscrews from the list of irreplaceable components. This wise provision ensured that the contest should be a test of the aircraft rather than the pilot, and rendered the competition far more valuable than any which had been organized previously, either at home or abroad.

On Saturday, July 22nd, 1911, in the presence of an enormous concourse of people, whose cars, parked side by side, stretched in an unbroken line for nearly two miles around the track, twenty-one of the thirty entrants lined up at Brooklands for the first stage to Hendon.

Great Britain was represented by three monoplanes, two Blackburns, and a "Birdling," and six biplanes, viz., three Bristols, the new Cody, a Howard-Wright, and the Grahame-White "Baby."

Four English pilots chose to fly French monoplanes. They were Lieut. J. C. Porte, R.N., and Mr. James Valentine on Deperdussins, and Lieut. R. A. Cammel and Mr. Gustav Hamel on Bleriots.

The opposition was very strong, the French machines comprising two Breguêt all-steel tractor biplanes, a Bleriot, and a Morane-Borel monoplane. Another Bleriot was flown by the Swiss pilot, Audemars, a Henry Farman was entrusted to the Dutch expert, Wijnmalen, and the fast Nieuport monoplane was handled by the American winner of the Gordon-Bennett Cup, C. T. Weymann.

Austria was ably represented by Lieut. H. Bier on an Etrich monoplane.

The conditions at the start were very bad, as the concrete racing track lay under a burning sun, and each pilot had to face some tremendous bumps while taking off.

First away was "Beaumont" (Lieut. de Vaisseau Conneau) winner of the European Circuit, on his Bleriot (Gnôme), followed by H. J. D. Astley (Birdling). Then came a thrill when Lieut.

Porte, R.N., crashed his Deperdussin in taking off, right in front of the crowd. Compton Paterson (G.W. " Baby "), Jules Vedrines (Morane-Borel), Blanchet (Breguêt), Lieut. R. A. Cammell, and E. Audemars (Bleriots) and James Valentine (Deperdussin) followed each other away to time, and all got through to Hendon without incident except Lieut. Cammell, who was forced down on Hounslow Heath with engine trouble, but completed the stage later in the evening.

Then came a hitch, for Gordon England on the first of the Bristol team, was left at the post with serious loss of r.p.m. and was ultimately forced to abandon the competition on the starting line. His team mates, C. P. Pizey and Howard Pixton, got away to schedule, however, followed by S. F. Cody.

The next man, Conway Jenkins (Blackburn), was not ready to start and did not attempt to get off until after 6.30 p.m., when he had the misfortune to crash heavily, thus putting another British machine *hors de combat*. In the meantime, de Montalent (Breguêt) and Gustav Hamel (Bleriot) had made good starts. Lieut. Reynolds (Howard-Wright) and B. C. Hucks (Blackburn) were delayed until after 6 p.m., but both eventually arrived intact with the other starters at Hendon.

C. T. Weymann returned after travelling a short distance, as his map had broken adrift from its fastening. Having landed and secured it, he took off again and proceeded to average over 80 m.p.h. to Hendon, thus proving that he had the fastest machine in the race.

Wijnmalen was left at the post with his Henry Farman, whose Gnôme refused to operate, and he retired. Lieut. Bier brought the Etrich back after doing a circuit, and spent an hour and a half working on its engine before he left for Hendon.

The next day, being Sunday, no flying took place, much to the astonishment of the Continental pilots. On Monday, July 24th, it was planned to send the first competitor away on his long journey to Edinburgh, at 4 a.m. So great was the excitement occasioned by this race that nearly *half a million* people gave up their Sunday night's rest in order to see the start at Hendon, tens of thousands of them spending the night around camp fires in the neighbouring fields.

The competitors were dispatched in their order of precedence of arrival at each control. Vedrines (Morane-Borel) should thus have gone first but " Beaumont " (Bleriot) mistook the signal and got away before him, a few minutes before his proper time. Apparently the officials subsequently condoned this offence. Hamel (Bleriot) was third, followed by Valentine (Deperdussin). Audemars (Bleriot) was next, but was delayed by engine trouble. Eventually he got off, but soon returned and retired from the race. Howard Pixton (Bristol-Renault) suffered from misfiring and started late, whilst C. P. Pizey, on the other Bristol, had difficulty in clearing the crowd with a weak motor. Compton Paterson (G.W. "Baby"), retired for personal reasons at Hendon.

After Astley (Birdling), Blanchet (Breguêt) and Cody had got away, Lieut. Reynolds did about six trial circuits on his Howard-Wright, after which he descended to tinker with the E.N.V. motor. Lieut. Bier nearly smashed his Etrich (120 h.p. Austro-Daimler) in taking off over the crowd, but just managed to scrape clear. Hucks (Blackburn) left on schedule time, but Lieut. Cammell was delayed for some minutes on the line.

Lieut. Reynolds, having persuaded the E.N.V. to give more power, left at 6 a.m., followed at 8.15 a.m. by de Montalent (Breguêt). Weymann had amazingly hard luck as his airscrew caught in the door-runner when his Nieuport was being wheeled out of the hangar and was broken. It was not until 1 p.m. that he succeeded in obtaining a spare suitable for his 100 h.p. Gnôme. He then disappeared towards Harrogate at 90 m.p.h.

Fog caused much trouble on this first long stretch. Pixton smashed his Bristol in a forced landing at Spofforth, and the unfortunate Weymann abandoned after damaging his Nieuport in trying to avoid a crowd which had collected, when he landed near Leeds to inquire the way. Lieut. Cammell's Bleriot burst a cylinder at Wakefield, but de Montalent was another who lost himself, and the airscrew of his Breguêt was broken in the subsequent forced landing. Pizey (Bristol) had propeller trouble and landed at Melton Mowbray in order to fit his spare, but damaged his undercarriage in doing so.

Astley (Birdling) lost himself near Bedford and landed. Later he restarted, but the bumps made him sick and he came down again at Irthlingborough. Blanchet (Breguêt) nosed over in a cornfield at Streatley and broke his undercarriage, and Hucks (Blackburn) landed with engine trouble near Luton. The Austrian Etrich was wrecked at Hatfield and Lieut. Reynolds landed for the night at Doncaster.

So much for the nine unfortunates who failed to reach Harrogate. There was a crowd estimated at 150,000 people waiting at 7 a.m. for the arrival of the competitors at the first control. They were rewarded by sighting Vedrines (Morane-Borel) at 07·03 hours, hotly pursued by " Beaumont " (Bleriot) at 07·07 hours. Within an hour both had left for Newcastle. Valentine (Deperdussin) arrived thirty-six minutes behind the leader, and two hours later Cody appeared, followed, after a further two hours wait, by Hamel (Bleriot). No others got through to Harrogate that day. Cody had suffered a burst water tube at Rotherham and, subsequently, a petrol tank sprang a leak within twenty miles of Harrogate. Hamel's delay had been caused by a prolonged stop at Melton Mowbray for plug trouble.

Vedrines led at Newcastle with " Beaumont " pressing him hard, and both pilots continued to Edinburgh after only a short stop to refuel. Valentine mistook the landing ground at Newcastle and landed on some golf links, losing much valuable time thereby. However, he checked in eventually and left later for Edinburgh. Hamel arrived very late at Newcastle and rested there for the night.

Only Vedrines, "Beaumont," and Valentine completed the second stage in one day. Vedrines (Morane-Borel) led "Beaumont" (Bleriot) by 11 mins. 36 secs. and Valentine (Deperdussin) by 44 mins. 49 secs. All the British aircraft had gone out of the race except the Cody, the Birdling, and the Howard-Wright, which were far behind.

On the following day the course was from Edinburgh to Bristol. Vedrines and "Beaumont" continued their great struggle, the latter getting his Bleriot into the lead owing to the former missing the controls at Glasgow and Bristol, thereby losing 1 hr. 50 mins.

Valentine actually made fastest time as far as Stirling, but after leaving the control there, he lost himself in a rainstorm and landed to inquire the way. In doing so he broke his airscrew and rudder, which took a long time to repair. Eventually he struggled into the Glasgow control as dusk was falling, eleven hours out from Edinburgh.

Hamel suffered further engine trouble and took the whole day to get from Newcastle to Edinburgh. Cody had spent the night at Harrogate patching his leaking tank, and he attempted to push on to Newcastle but lost himself and smashed his undercarriage in landing at Langley Moor. Astley (Birdling) and Lieut. Reynolds (Howard-Wright) reached Harrogate and retired. "Beaumont" (Bleriot) led Vedrines (Morane-Borel) by 1 hr. 15 mins. 9 secs. at Bristol.

On Wednesday the two leaders decided to complete the course in one day, cutting out the night's rest at Shoreham. Vedrines made the most desperate efforts to pick up the time he had lost by his mistakes at Glasgow and Bristol, but "Beaumont's" Bleriot ran without a hitch, except for a slight adjustment in the Exeter control, and Vedrines could only succeed in gaining 6 mins. 10 secs. on the Naval officer, who finished at Brooklands with a lead of 1 hr. 8 mins. 59 secs., after one of the finest races in history. Lord Northcliffe presented Jules Vedrines with a consolation prize of £200 in recognition of his magnificent performance.

Valentine brought his Deperdussin as far as Carlisle, taking 4 hrs. 17 mins. for the eighty-six miles from Glasgow, and Hamel struggled across the difficult section from Edinburgh to Glasgow, and left for Carlisle, but his engine finally gave up at Dumfries, where he retired.

Valentine and Cody, who had repaired his undercarriage, stuck gamely to their task and both eventually finished the course, Valentine arriving at Brooklands on the Friday, two days after the leaders, and Cody on the Saturday, three days late.

The race proved the slight superiority of the Morane-Borel (70 h.p. Gnôme), which would undoubtedly have beaten the Bleriot (50 h.p. Gnôme) by about three-quarters of an hour, but for its pilot's mistakes at Glasgow and Bristol. It also proved that in James Valentine, Cody, and Gustav Hamel, we had three pilots who were fit to compete with the best in Europe, and it showed most conclusively that our aircraft were still far behind the Continental machines in performance and reliability, Cody's biplane being the sole British-built aircraft to complete the course.

34. VEDRINES' BENEFIT MEETING

Mr. Grahame-White conceived the happy idea of organizing a special "benefit" meeting at Hendon, in order to compensate Vedrines for his bitter disappointment at losing the £10,000 reward by so small a margin. Lieut. de Vaisseau Conneau, with true sportsmanship, eagerly agreed to collaborate with him and to take part in the flying.

Fifty thousand people paid for admission to see "Beaumont," Grahame-White, and Vedrines fly, and gave the latter a vociferous welcome when he arrived from Brooklands in his Morane-Borel monoplane.

The three pilots put up a very fine display in a thirty-mile-per-hour wind, and the crowd was well entertained.

The "gate," including a donation of £100 from the English pilot, Mortimer Singer, amounted to more than £800, and in addition, both Conneau and Vedrines were presented with magnificent silver trophies by the Hendon management. Mr. Elliman added a cheque for £1,000, and various other subscriptions were raised, so that eventually Jules Vedrines received upwards of £2,000 by way of consolation awards for his splendid flight in the Circuit of Britain.

35. MR. GRAHAM GILMOUR'S SUSPENSION

It was most unfortunate that the two racing monoplanes of new design, which had been specially prepared by the Bristol Company for the circuit of Britain, were unable to compete. One was crashed by M. Pierre Prier a few days before the start, and the other was to have been flown by Mr. Graham Gilmour. The latter's insatiable desire to perform above the Thames had once more brought him into trouble. It will be recalled that he first attracted unwelcome publicity by flying low over the University Boat Race in March, and that a few weeks later he was called before the committee of the R.Ae.C. to give an account of his flight over Salisbury. His next exploit was a flight low down along the river from Weybridge to Wapping and back, which occasioned a perfect spate of journalism in the London press.

Not content with this Mr. Gilmour visited Henley Regatta, where he proceeded to " shoot up " the crowded river in a highly dangerous manner. His exhibition concluded with a dive to the surface of the racing course where he ran his wheels in the water, afterwards pulling up over the crowd and landing in a field on the bank. This was too much for the R.Ae.C., who called him before the committee once more and suspended his certificate for one month.

The Bristol Company's directors were highly incensed at the suspension of their star monoplane pilot, which meant the elimination of their remaining machine from the race, as no other pilot could be found to fly it. Accordingly, they issued a writ against the R.Ae.C. for an injunction to restrain the Club from continuing to enforce the suspension. The injunction was refused, so the company took the matter to the Court of Appeal, which found that the R.Ae.Club's action was *ultra vires* and that the suspension had never in fact been effectual at all, as the Club had failed to comply with its own rules !

By this time the race was over and the Bristol Company had lost their chance of demonstrating their new machine for which they had paid an entrance fee of £100, and in addition, they had to pay their own costs in the action ; which was all quite unnecessary and most unsatisfactory.

36. TWO FATAL ACCIDENTS : THE VICKERS MONOPLANE

On August 1st, Mr. Gerald Napier, who had taken his R.Ae.C. certificate (No. 104) about three weeks previously, was killed at Brooklands in an accident to his Bristol biplane. After some practice flights during which he was seen to be flying very erratically, landing first with the right and then with the left wing down, Mr. Napier took off with a passenger.

He attempted a spiral descent and was caught by a gust which caused the machine to bank up too steeply and, before the pilot could recover, she had sideslipped into the ground.

Mr. Napier was struck by the engine and killed, but the passenger was thrown clear and escaped with shock and bruises.

The result of Capt. Wood's investigations in France on behalf of Vickers, Ltd., became apparent when that firm produced a well-finished version of the R.E.P. monoplane (60 h.p. 5-cylinder R.E.P. Semi-Radial engine) with a fuselage built up of steel tubing. This was a very handsome machine, although its lines were somewhat marred by the elaborate undercarriage with its four wheels and two large skids.

Another fatal accident occurred on August 18th, 1911. The victim was Lieut. Theodore Ridge, Assistant Superintendant of the Army Balloon Factory at Farnborough. Lieut. Ridge was primarily a dirigible pilot, and although he also held the R.Ae.C. aviator's certificate, his experience of heavier than air craft had been small. An experimental machine had been put through its initial tests by a mechanic when Lieut. Ridge decided to attempt to fly it, against the advice of Mr. de Havilland, the designer of the aircraft. He stalled on a gliding turn, dived into the ground and was trapped in the debris, receiving injuries from which he died the same night.

37. FIRST WORLD'S RECORD ON BRITISH AEROPLANE

On August 16th, Lieut. E. L. Gerrard, R.M.L.I., accompanied by Lieut. Wildman Lushington, R.M.A., set up British records for duration and distance flown with a passenger on Mr. Frank McClean's Short biplane No. 34 (Gnôme). Their time of 4 hrs. 13 mins. constituted a world's record for duration with a passenger, and the distance flown was officially recorded as 129 miles. The course was a ten-mile stretch between Leysdown Coastguard Station and H.M.S. *Actaeon,* which was lying off Sheerness.

This was the first world's record to be captured by a British pilot flying a British aircraft, and represented a very fine performance on the part of all concerned. The figures would have been better still if the pilot had not been compelled to land, owing to the failing light, at a time when he had plenty of petrol left and everything was going well.

Three days later Lieut. C. R. Samson, R.N., set up a new British duration record for pilot alone, in the other Short (No. 38), by remaining in the air above Eastchurch aerodrome for 4 hrs. 58 mins. 30 secs. Lieut. Samson was also forced to descend whilst his engine was running well with a good supply of petrol in the tanks, on account of the increasing bumpiness of the air, which threw the biplane about in a most alarming manner during the last hour and a half of the flight.

38. MRS. HEWLETT QUALIFIES

Miss Lilian Bland having given up her experiments in Ireland without making any attempt to obtain her certificate, and Miss "Spencer Kavanagh" having been killed in attempting a parachute descent from a captive balloon, it fell to Mrs. Maurice Hewlett to have the honour of becoming the first British woman to hold the R.Ae.Club's Licence (No. 122) to fly an aeroplane. Mrs. Hewlett had been receiving instruction at Brooklands from M. Blondeau on her Henry Farman biplane for many months, and her eventual success was thoroughly well deserved.

Immediately after Mrs. Hewlett's descent from her observed tests, Mr. J. L. Longstaffe took the machine off and a complete cylinder flew off the Gnôme engine in the air. The pupil made a safe landing, although he had not previously brought a machine down with engine off.

39. ARMY ACTIVITIES

No less than seventeen pupils were under instruction simultaneously at the Bristol headquarters on Salisbury Plain and M. Jullerot and Messrs. Fleming and Busteed worked all day instructing them.

The Army pilots on the aerodrome were also active and a massed flight of Bristols to Oxford was organized. Five machines, piloted by Captains Burke and Massy and Lieuts. Conner, Reynolds, and Barrington-Kennett, took off at short intervals. Unfortunately, Lieut. Conner was compelled to return and spend three days at work on his engine before he could complete the journey to Oxford, where he rejoined the others, all of whom had arrived safely.

On August 16th Brig.-Gen. David Henderson took his *brevet* at the Bristol school at Brooklands after only seven days tuition under Mr. C. Howard Pixton, who gave him about two hours air experience as a passenger, and thirty minutes taxying alone to get the feel of the controls. He then flew circuits alone for thirty-five minutes, and on his next flight he passed the tests. At that time General Henderson was Chief of Staff to Sir John French, and his example afforded no mean incentive to junior Army officers.

40. SOPWITH AND GRAHAME-WHITE IN U.S.A.

Mr. T. O. M. Sopwith was still in America and was having a most successful tour with his Bleriot and Howard-Wright machines. At the Chicago Meeting he broke an American record by flying for more than an hour with two passengers on the biplane and he obtained second prize in the speed races on the Bleriot. Later in the proceedings he won the fourteen-mile race across Lake Michigan, a Moisant monoplane and a Curtiss biplane being second and third. Sopwith collected 15,000 dollars in prize money at the Chicago meeting alone.

The next meeting was at Boston, where Sopwith met Grahame-White, who had acquired a Nieuport monoplane, about which he knew nothing whatever. The imperturbable Claude proceeded to annex the speed and altitude prizes on the first day, while Sopwith had to be content with first place in the quick take-off and bomb-dropping contests. No doubt his practice with the *Olympic* as a target stood him in good stead in the latter competition, in which he flew a Wright biplane which he had purchased in America. Sopwith annexed a further 6,000 dollars at Boston.

Both the English pilots appeared at the New York meeting, and Grahame-White won the cross-country race, with Sopwith second, and they also won the ten-mile relay race as a team. In addition, Sopwith secured second place in the passenger-carrying competition.

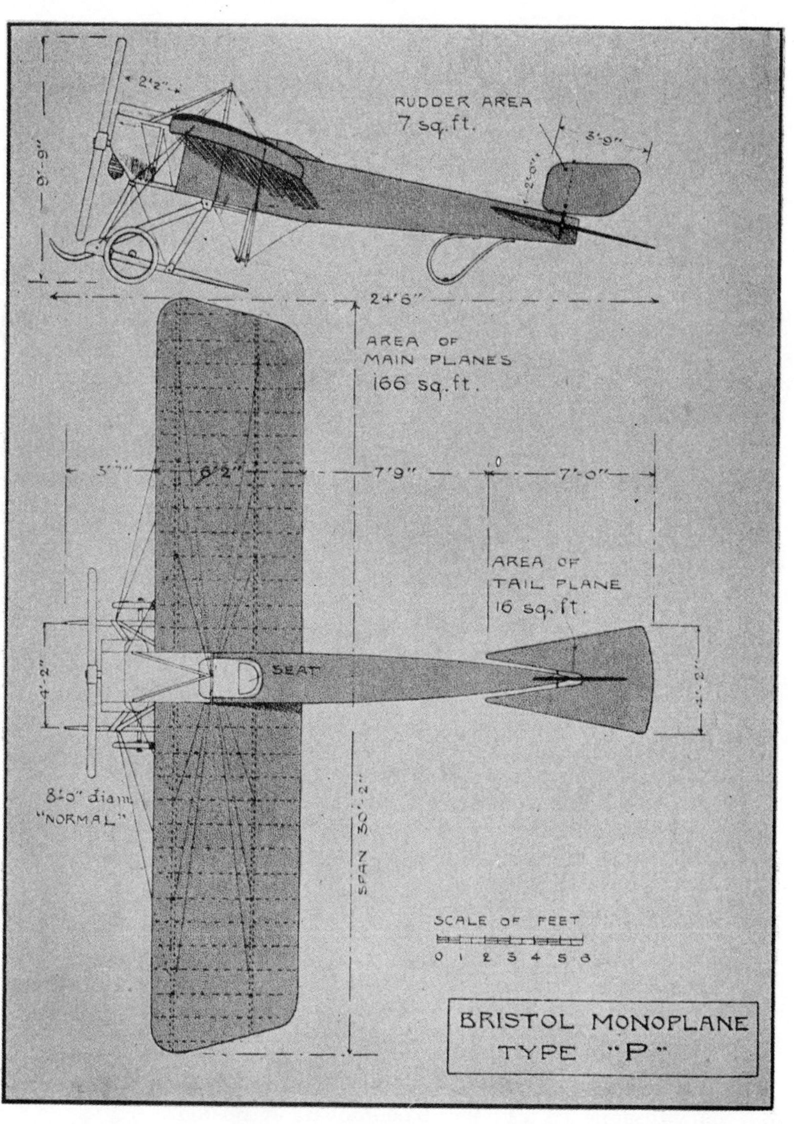

"Flight" copyright

4.—A sound design: the Bristol Monoplane (50 h.p. Gnôme) designed by M. Pierre Prier.

Facing page 112

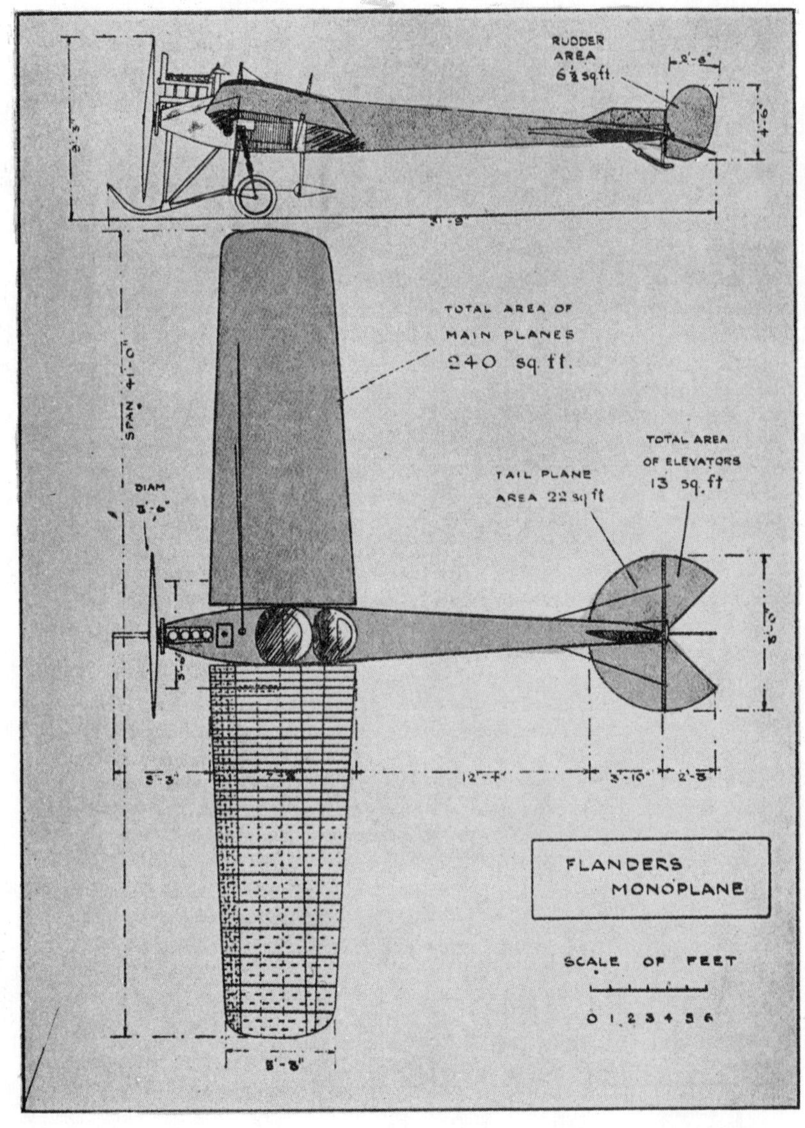

"*Flight*" *copyright*

5.—All-British: the Flanders Monoplane (60 h.p. Green) which was raced at Brooklands by Mr. E. V. B. Fisher.

Facing page 113

41. THE AMAZING ESCAPE OF CAPT. H. R. REYNOLDS: BRAKES AND CHOCKS

On the evening of August 19th, Capt. H. R. P. Reynolds was flying a Bristol "boxkite" biplane (50 h.p. Gnôme) at a height of 1,700 feet above Bletchley.

The weather was warm and fine and up to that point the air had been as smooth as silk, but a big black thunder cloud was approaching rapidly from the pilot's right front and, as it came nearer, the air became full of alarming bumps.

Capt. Reynolds wisely decided that it was time for him to land, more especially as he could see an excellent field just below him.

Here is his own description of what followed :—

"I began a glide, but, almost directly I had switched off, the tail of the machine was suddenly wrenched upwards as if it had been hit from below, and I saw the elevator" (which was carried on outriggers in front of the pilot) "go down perpendicularly below me. I was not strapped in, and I suppose I caught hold of the uprights at my side, for the next thing I realized was that I was lying in a heap on what ordinarily is the *under* surface of the top plane. The machine in fact was upside down. I stood up, held on and waited.

"The machine just floated about, gliding from side to side like a piece of paper falling. Then it over-swung itself, so to speak, and went down more or less vertically sideways, until it righted itself momentarily the right way up. Then it went down tail first, turned over upside down again, and restarted the old floating motion.

"We were still some way from the ground, and took what seemed like a long time in reaching it. I looked round somewhat hurriedly, the tail was still there, and I could see nothing wrong.

"As we got close to the ground the machine was doing long swings from side to side, and I made up my mind that the only thing to do was to try and jump clear of the wreckage before the crash.

"In the last swing we slid down, I think, about thirty feet, and hit the ground pretty hard. Fortunately I hung on practically to the end, and, according to those who were looking on, I did not jump until about ten feet from the ground. Something hit me on the head and scratched it very slightly, but what it was I did not know, for I was in too much of a hurry to get away from the machine to inquire at that time."

The biplane, which had landed on its back and rested on the top wing, had suffered surprisingly little damage.

Local residents reported that several small whirlwinds had visited the district at the time, one of which was sufficiently violent to strip all the leaves from a tree. It seems probable that one of these disturbances, which were strictly local in effect, had struck the tail of the machine and knocked it sharply upwards. Capt. Reynolds, having no belt to secure him to his exposed seat on the lower wing, was unable to reach the control column and pull it back before he was catapulted out, and it is obvious from the above graphic account, that the machine gave him no opportunity to get back to his seat after he had once left it.

The extreme folly of flying without a belt or harness has never been more vividly illustrated.

The extraordinary lack of perception of the elementary principles of aerodynamics to which I have previously alluded, continued to result in numberless accidents to aircraft, whose pilots would persist in taking off and landing down-wind.

Lieut. Cammell charged the doors of a hangar at Hendon at 30 m.p.h. after touching his Bleriot down more than 200 yards away. He was assisted by a strong following wind. Fortunately the doors gave way.

This accident gave rise to much discussion about brakes for aircraft. It was pointed out that tailskids did little or nothing to pull a machine up because " in most cases the tail does not drop to the ground until the machine has covered something in excess of a hundred yards after it has actually come to earth " ! Three-point landings were unheard of in those days, and it is no wonder that the life of an undercarriage was brief when almost every pilot attempted to execute wheel landings down-wind at full throttle !

A certain M. Garreau tried to solve the problem by means of a double rudder consisting of two plane surfaces hinged in such a manner that they could be opened out flat like a book athwart the slip-stream by way of an airbrake. It would seem that M. Garreau was not sufficiently foolish to try this device in actual flight, as I can find no evidence of his sudden death.

Another curious thing was the fact that chocks had still to be invented. Many machines were badly strained, and in some cases actually broken, by reason of the lack of chocks. It was customary for a number of hefty men to hold on to the fuselage, tail booms, wheels, or other convenient points, whilst the pilot ran up his motor. Very few of the engines then in use could be induced to run at small throttle openings, and the Gnôme rotary could only run all out. The result was that tremendous strains were thrown upon the points gripped by the men as the pilot " blipped " his switches, thus causing the engine to give recurrent bursts of full power.

42. THE FIRST AIR MAIL IN ENGLAND

Capt. W. G. Windham, who had been one of the pilots in the world's first Air Mail service at Allahabad (India) in February 1911, had returned to England and interested himself, with Mr. D.

Lewis Poole, in promoting an experimental Air Mail service from Hendon to Windsor, with the co-operation of the Postmaster-General.

Special envelopes and postcards, which were printed for the service and placed on sale at the big shops in London, met with a ready demand, the scheme having caught the public's imagination.

The care of the mails, for which the cautious Post Office assumed no liability, was entrusted to the staff pilots of the Bleriot and Grahame-White schools at Hendon.

Saturday, September 9th, which had been fixed for the inauguration of the service, provided a strong easterly wind and very bumpy conditions. This did not deter Gustav Hamel, who left Hendon on a Bleriot with the first bag at 4.58 p.m., and was wafted to Windsor in ten minutes at an average speed of just over 105 m.p.h.

On Sunday, there was no delivery scheduled, but on Monday the South African pilot, E. F. Driver, on a Farman, and Greswell and Hamel on Bleriots, carried eight bags of mail, and on the following day the same pilots took eleven bags, Driver making two journeys. M. Hubert was to have carried some of Monday's mail but, although he gallantly attempted to start on an exceedingly cranky old Farman, the high wind was too much for him and he crashed just after taking off, and broke both his legs.

On the Wednesday, the service was stopped by bad weather, but Gresswell and Hamel got through on the Thursday, only to be stopped once more by high winds on the next day. Gresswell took two bags on the Saturday, and Hamel made a double trip on the Monday. Gresswell also left Hendon with mail on that day, but was forced to abandon with engine trouble. Tuesday saw a high wind blowing, but Hamel managed to struggle across with two bags.

This concluded the experiment, which had proved very little beyond the fact that aircraft were still hazardous vehicles in rough weather, and extremely unreliable in the matter of timing.

Most of the journeys had taken about half an hour for the nineteen miles, but Hamel had done one trip in ten minutes, and Gresswell took 1 hr. 30 mins. on one occasion, when he lost himself in a slight mist and landed at Slough to inquire the way.

A few weeks later, Mr. G. Higginbotham, the principal of the Freshfield Flying School near Liverpool, started a private Air Mail service of his own between Freshfield and Southport. The mail was flown in his own pusher biplane (Gnôme), a curious machine which vaguely resembled an early Curtiss. On arrival at Southport, Mr. Higginbotham personally carried the bag to the Post Office, thus "doubling the act" of pilot and postman.

43. THE SHORT TWIN: THE BRISTOL AND FLANDERS MONOPLANES

The latest product of the Short Bros. was a remarkable machine, which had the distinction of being the first British-built twin-engined aeroplane. The airframe was no great departure from the usual Short practice, and consisted of a large biplane with a forward elevator carried on outriggers, and long tail-booms supporting a rear elevator and triple vertical rudders. On the bottom wing was a small *nacelle* to seat the pilot and passenger side by side.

At the back of this *nacelle* was a large propeller and *behind* and directly attached to this propeller was a 50 h.p. Gnôme engine. The front of the *nacelle* was sawn off short and carried another 50 h.p. Gnôme, secured on the flat face thus presented. Light chains, each more than twenty-four feet in length, ran out from the front engine to two slow speed airscrews mounted on each of the third interplane struts counting outwards from the *nacelle*.

This machine was flown by Mr. Frank McClean, who found that it would actually maintain height with either of the engines throttled down, which in the case of the Gnômes meant practically cut off. This was remarkable and the airframe must have been highly efficient, but the length of the chains obviously doomed the design to failure from the start.

The Short Bros. were not long in grasping this fact, and they set to work upon an improved version in which the two outboard tractor screws with their sprockets and chains were abolished, and a single airscrew coupled direct to the front engine was substituted for them. This second twin, which was fitted with full dual controls and which could actually climb on either engine, was tested at the end of October by Mr. McClean.

A more practical and equally interesting design was the new Bristol monoplane (50 h.p. Gnôme) which had been constructed under the supervision of M. Pierre Prier, and of which two had been entered for the Circuit of Britain. The wings were of Bleriot type, but the fuselage and undercarriage were original and of quite remarkable cleanness. The rudder and elevators were balanced, but the old-fashioned method of warping the wings for lateral control was retained. The flying wires were attached to various parts of the undercarriage, which must have led to difficulties in repairing the results of heavy landings.

Another admirable new aircraft was the Flanders monoplane, designed and constructed by Mr. Howard Flanders, and flown by Messrs. E. V. B. Fisher and Ronald Kemp at Brooklands. The fuselage, like that of the Bristol, was faired in with canvas and presented good clean lines. The undercarriage had a single central skid to protect the airscrew.

44. LIEUT. CAMMELL KILLED: SOME ACCIDENT FIGURES

The Army pilot who was detailed to take delivery of the first of the two Valkyrie pusher monoplanes, which had been presented to the War Office by Mr. Barber, was Lieut. R. A. Cammell.

No doubt he was chosen as he had had much more experience with monoplanes than any other officer.

He arrived at Hendon to execute his commission on September 17th, and it was arranged that he should have thirty minutes practice round Hendon aerodrome before he attempted to fly across country to Farnborough.

Apparently the pilot was over-confident, and, instead of waiting until he had become familiar with the peculiar controls of the Valkyrie, he began to execute steep turns, such as he was accustomed to perform on his own Bleriot, as soon as he had got it into the air.

After a few minutes of this, he was seen to cut off his engine and attempt a gliding turn. He over-banked and the machine side-slipped inwards to the ground.

Lieut. Cammell, who was thrown out on to his head and killed, had taken his R.Ae.C. certificate on December 31st, 1910, on a Bristol biplane. He was an accomplished Bleriot pilot and his death was a great loss to the Air Battalion.

The *Automobil-Welt* had compiled some statistics relating to fatal accidents which had occurred up to the end of October, 1911. According to these figures, which were only approximately accurate, the number of pilot's certificates issued by the leading countries of the world at that date was as follows :—

1. France	500
2. Germany	135
3. Great Britain	110
4. Russia	55
5. Italy	45
6. U.S.A.	35
Total	880

France had the best figure, not only as regards the overwhelming number of her pilots, but also as regards the percentage of fatal accidents which had overtaken them. Only 5·4 per cent. of the French pilots had been killed as against 8·2 per cent. of the Englishmen.

Of the small band of thirty-five American pilots, no less than twelve (or 34·3 per cent. of their number) had met their deaths in flying accidents. These terrible figures were accounted for partly by the inherent unsoundness of the design and construction of the Wright biplanes, with which most of the American aviators were equipped, and on which no fewer than eight pilots had crashed fatally, and partly by the craving of the American crowds for dangerous stunt exhibitions.

45. THE FIRST SPIN ?

Mr. F. P. Raynham had decided to make an attempt on the British Empire Michelin Cup No. 2, using a circuit starting and finishing at Hendon. Accordingly he set off from Brooklands in the Avro biplane, which was in a very bad state of repair, the fabric of the wings, which had been inadequately doped, having become so loose that the aircraft was unairworthy.

The standard of maintenance at the Avro school at Brooklands was rapidly becoming notorious. Wings had broken in the air, a fuselage had snapped in two on the ground, and the dirty and decrepit condition of the school's Farman was a standing joke on the aerodrome.

Raynham had not flown very far before he ran into a dense bank of fog. Instead of acknowledging defeat like a sensible man and returning to Brooklands, he determined to try to push through it.

He climbed to 1,500 feet by his altimeter so as to be clear of obstructions and set himself to fly a compass course.

Not unnaturally his compass soon began to behave queerly and he thought that something was wrong with it and stooped down to try to adjust it. The next thing he knew was that he was standing upright on the rudder pedals and whirling round. After two complete turns, he succeeded by some chance in pulling out and found himself down at 500 feet. Shortly afterwards he saw a clear patch and hastily landed.

There seems to be little doubt but that Raynham was the first British pilot, and possibly the first pilot in the world, to get a machine out of a spinning nose dive with engine-on, and that he had an extremely fortunate escape.

46. A FLOAT SEAPLANE : B. C. HUCKS ON TOUR : W. B. R.-MOORHOUSE

Various successful experiments had been made in the U.S.A. with Curtiss biplanes equipped with floats, but the first attempt in this country to adapt an aeroplane for rising from and alighting on the water, was made by Commander Schwann, R.N., at Barrow, in September 1911.

The aircraft used was an Avro biplane (Green), and the floats were invented by Commander Schwann himself and built by Naval personnel. The preliminary trials were not conspicuously successful, but this seems to have been due as much to Commander Schwann's almost complete ignorance of the art of flying as to any defect in his floats.

The Blackburn monoplane was now showing excellent results in the clever hands of Mr. B. C. Hucks, who had been touring in Somerset giving exhibition flights. Later he flew across the Bristol Channel and continued his one-man flying meetings in the neighbourhood of Cardiff and Newport, afterwards returning to Cheltenham and Gloucester, where he completed his tour after covering more than 1,000 miles without any sort of trouble.

The Huntingdon aerodrome at which James Radley had learned to fly, had been inactive for many months. One of the early pupils there, who had flown an old Anzani-Bleriot in 1910, was Mr. W. B. Rhodes-Moorhouse. He had purchased Mr. Morison's Bleriot (Gnôme) and it was delivered at the end of September 1911. Mr. Moorhouse started it up as soon as it was erected, took off in twenty yards, flew four circuits, and made a perfect landing. During the following week he made a series of magnificent cross-country flights from Huntingdon ranging as far as Northampton, Brooklands, and Hendon. Mr. Moorhouse was eventually to become one of the best pilots in the R.F.C., and to be the first officer of our Air Arm to win the Victoria Cross.

47. THE MANVILLE PRIZE

Mr. Manville had given a prize of £500 for the British pilot who should put in the longest aggregate time in the air with a passenger on nine specified days during the summer of 1911. The competition was limited to pilots flying all-British aircraft, and on October 4th, which was the last of the specified days, Mr. Howard Pixton was leading with 3 hrs. 7 mins., which had been done on the Avro biplane and a Bristol "boxkite." Mr. Cody, who stood second with 2 hrs. 36 mins. to his credit, managed to bring his total up to 3 hrs. 16 mins. on the last day. But Mr. Pixton was also busy at Brooklands and completed a total of 5 hrs. 16 mins. flying time, thus winning the prize comfortably by a margin of exactly two hours.

Pixton also headed the list for the biggest aggregate of hours flown throughout the season at Brooklands, for which he was awarded £150 in prize money.

48. THE BRITISH EMPIRE MICHELIN CUP NO. 2

The closing date of the first contest for the British Empire Michelin Cup No. 2 was fixed for October 15th and the rules required the competitors to complete a cross-country circuit of 125 miles. The entries were restricted to British subjects flying British-built aeroplanes, and the winner was to be the pilot who covered the circuit in the fastest time.

Although entries were received from F. P. Raynham (Avro), R. C. Kemp (Flanders), S. F. Cody (Cody), C. L. Pashley (Humber), H. J. D. Astley (Birdling), D. Graham Gilmour (Bristol monoplane), H. Pixton (Bristol biplane), and J. L. Longstaffe (Howard-Wright), only Cody succeeded in completing the course.

His flight was made on September 11th and occupied 3 hrs.

6½ mins., which gave an average speed of just over 40 m.p.h. A 60 h.p. Green engine was used.

Cody thus won his second Michelin Cup and a cash prize of £400.

49. THE BRITISH EMPIRE MICHELIN CUP NO. 1

The original British Michelin Cup was still open for competition contemporaneously with the new trophy mentioned above. It will be recalled that it had been won in the previous year by Mr. S. F. Cody with a distance of 185 miles, after an exciting contest with Messrs. Ogilvie and Sopwith.

This year it was necessary to cover no less than 250 miles non-stop in order to qualify for the competition.

All those pilots who had entered for the new cross-country Cup No. 2 had also entered for the original closed-circuit contest, with the sole exception of Mr. Astley.

The closing date was October 31st, and although Raynham (Avro), Kemp (Flanders), and Pashley (Humber), made several abortive attempts at Brooklands during the last few days, it became obvious that none of them had taken the matter sufficiently seriously, and that their engines were not in a fit condition to last for 250 miles.

Cody, however, had been preparing with his customary thoroughness for weeks previously, and after a false start on October 27th, he took off from Laffan's Plain two days later and put up a magnificent flight of 261½ miles round the seven-mile circuit there.

Once more his 60 h.p. Green engine ran without a falter for the five hours fifteen minutes which were occupied by the flight. Mr. Cody thus captured the Michelin Trophy for the second year in succession and another cash prize of £500. He also beat the British duration record set up in August by Lieut. C. R. Samson, R.N., by 16 mins. 30 secs.

50. MRS. DE BEAUVOIR STOCKS: A MOTHER INSTRUCTS HER SON

The second British woman pilot to secure her R.Ae.C. certificate was Mrs. C. de Beauvoir Stocks who had been under instruction at the Grahame-White school at Hendon for some months. Her certificate (No. 153) was gained on November 1st on a Henry Farman biplane (50 h.p. Gnôme).

On the conclusion of her tests, Mrs. Stocks celebrated the event by giving a joy-ride to her friend Mrs. Gates, the wife of the manager of the Grahame-White school.

On November 9th, Sub-Lieut. F. E. T. Hewlett, R.N., took his certificate at Brooklands on his mother's Henry Farman. M. Blondeau was his instructor, but Mrs. Hewlett had frequently taken him up during his training and had coached him on the ground. This instance of a mother teaching her son to fly is probably unique.

51. FOUR NEW BRITISH AIRCRAFT

Four interesting British aircraft were being put through their preliminary trials during November. One was the new Blackburn monoplane with 60 h.p. Renault engine, which took off in thirty yards, carrying a pilot, passenger, and petrol for four hours.

Another monoplane was the latest product of Messrs. Martin and Handasyde. This beautiful machine was notable for exquisite workmanship and the high-class finish which had been imparted to it by the Martinsyde mechanics. Mr. T. O. M. Sopwith, who had just returned from his American tour, undertook the test flights and was delighted with its performance ; subsequently it was flown by Mr. Graham Gilmour in very rough weather, and also by Mr. Gordon Bell.

Mr. Compton Paterson, who had built his first machine, a Curtiss-type biplane, at Freshfield in 1909, had produced a biplane which was especially designed with a view to ease of transport on the ground. The wings were in three sections, and the whole aircraft could be dismantled sufficiently to pass through a ten-foot gateway in five minutes.

The general lay-out of the machine followed accepted practice in so far as it was a biplane, having an elevator in front carried on an outrigger, and another elevator and a rudder supported by tail booms behind.

The *nacelle*, which provided accommodation for the pilot and two passengers, rested on the centre of the lower wing and the 50 h.p. Gnôme engine was behind the propeller, as in the Short twin. The designed speed with full load was 50 m.p.h.

Mr. Jezzi had long been established at Eastchurch, where he made careful experiments with a biplane of his own design. The latest version of this was an extremely neat tractor machine in which such details as the undercarriage struts were properly streamlined, and the fuselage tapered from the back of the pilot's head to the tail. The first tests were very encouraging and the biplane was little slower than the Bleriot monoplane which was now being flown by Lieut. Samson, R.N.

52. THE R.Ae.C. SUPERIOR CERTIFICATES

The R.Ae.C. had decided to introduce an advanced form of pilot's certificate, designed to carry more weight than the ordinary International *brevet*, which only required the barest evidence that the applicant could handle an aeroplane under ideal conditions.

The tests for this new testimonial involved a cross-country flight under official observation. The first candidate was Mr. S. F. Cody, who flew from Laffan's Plain to Salisbury and back.

Two days later, Mr. James Valentine and Capt. Fulton made their qualifying flights over the same course in the reverse direction.

Mr. Valentine flew one of the new Bristol monoplanes, which were now getting over their teething troubles, and showing that they were extremely satisfactory machines to fly in boisterous weather.

Incidentally, the Bristol Company extended their influence abroad by the sale of one of their biplanes to Lieut. Dahlbeck of the Swedish Army, and another to Mr. J. A. Weston, who flew it in South Africa.

The fourth pilot to qualify for the superior certificate was Mr. Geoffrey de Havilland, who flew his latest pusher biplane. This machine dispensed with the customary front elevator, and was designed and built throughout by Mr. de Havilland. Even the engine and propeller were constructed by him at Farnborough. The stalling speed was 32 m.p.h. and the maximum speed 41 m.p.h.

53. MORE SEAPLANE TRIALS: NIGHT FLYING: FATALITY AT FILEY

Following upon Commander Schwann's experiments at Barrow, the Avro firm built a Curtiss-type single-float hydro-aeroplane to the order of Capt. E. W. Wakefield. This machine was flown successfully from the surface of Lake Windermere by Mr. Stanley Adams. The engine used was a 50 h.p. Gnôme and the float was a three-step hydroplane constructed by Messrs. Borwich, and consisted of a mahogany framework over which canvas was stretched.

A daring experiment in night flying was conducted at the Nassau aerodrome, New York, by the two English pilots, Mr. G. M. Dyott and Capt. Patrick Hamilton, who had both qualified during August at the Bleriot school at Hendon. Dyott went to the Deperdussin factory in France and watched the construction of two monoplanes with which he and Capt. Hamilton proposed to tour the U.S.A. and Mexico, giving exhibition flights.

One of these machines had been fitted with a powerful searchlight, and Dyott flew it successfully on a pitch black night without any ground lighting of any kind. Capt. Hamilton accompanied him and operated the searchlight, picking up the aerodrome from a height of 300 feet, after a short flight across the surrounding countryside.

A terrible accident occurred at the Blackburn aerodrome at Filey on December 6th. Mr. Hubert Oxley, who had taken the place of Mr. B. C. Hucks as chief pilot at the Blackburn school, had for some time past been in the habit of diving the new large monoplane with the Renault engine and pulling up abruptly just prior to landing. Mr. Hunt, who had frequently ridden as a passenger with him, had personally been subjected to dives as steep as 65° and had warned the pilot that he was imposing undue strain upon the machine. The latter treated the matter lightly, and evidently did not appreciate the truth of Mr. Hunt's remarks.

On the day in question, Oxley took off with Mr. Robert J.

Weiss as passenger, with the object of flying over Leeds and giving an exhibition of stunting there.

Having reached a height of about 600 feet above the beach, he proceeded to dive over the top of the cliff towards the sea. He arrived within about fifty feet of the waves at a speed estimated at nearly 150 m.p.h. and then endeavoured to pull up sharply. Naturally enough the wings were torn off and both the occupants were killed.

Mr. Oxley, who was a very promising pilot, had learned to fly on the Hanriot monoplane at Brooklands. Mr. R. J. Weiss was one of the first pupils at the Blackburn school, and had recently been making good progress in solo straight flights.

54. BRITISH WORLD'S RECORD BEATEN: THE HUMPHREYS MONOPLANE

The world's duration record with one passenger, set up by Lieut. E. L. Gerrard, R.M.L.I., in August, was not allowed to stand for very long. It will be recalled that Lieut. Gerrard's Short biplane stayed aloft for 4 hrs. 13 mins. On December 8th, 114 days later, the German pilot, Suvelach, accompanied by a mechanic, kept his Etrich monoplane circling around the Johannisthal aerodrome for 4 hrs. 33 mins., thus beating Lieut. Gerrard's time by the small margin of twenty minutes.

Mr. Jack Humphreys had been experimenting with a large monoplane of his own design at Brooklands, but had wrecked it extensively in the early trials. This machine had now been rebuilt and was tested by Mr. Gordon Bell. The pilot only intended to do some taxying tests at first and, accordingly, proceeded to run across the aerodrome with the 60 h.p. Green at half-throttle, and with the stick well forward against the dashboard.

To the intense astonishment of everybody, including Gordon Bell, the monoplane proceeded to leave the ground at some 20 m.p.h. and climb steadily. Bell immediately stopped the engine and let her pancake gently to the ground. He then picked up a passenger and tried again to see if the extra weight would keep her down, but this apparently had no effect. Another substantial passenger was packed in, but still the Humphreys struggled off at half-throttle, in spite of all Bell's efforts to restrain her.

55. SHOREHAM GETS BUSY

Mr. M. Chanter had been established for some weeks in a hangar at Hendon, where he founded a small school, with two Bleriot monoplanes as a basis. At the same time he was experimenting with a delightful little single-seat monoplane of his own design. This machine, which was very small, was a miniature of the successful Nieuport monoplane and was driven by a 3-cylinder Anzani engine of 35 h.p. The pilot sat well forward in the nose and had an excellent view.

In the middle of November, Mr. Chanter moved his school to Shoreham, and several pupils were immediately attracted from Brighton.

The best flying at Shoreham at this period was done by Lieut. J. C. Porte, R.N., who had hired a hangar there for his two-seater Deperdussin monoplane. Lieut. Porte had entered into partnership with Mr. D. Lawrence Santoni, and they proposed to establish a factory for the production of Deperdussin aircraft in England.

The proceedings at Shoreham were further enlivened by the trials of the Collyer-England biplane, which was not, however, a very successful design.

56. THE GOVERNMENT AND AVIATION

Throughout the summer and autumn a tremendous press campaign had been waged with the object of compelling the Government to take some active steps to further the progress of British aviation.

The situation was indeed humiliating.

From the start, the Government had adopted the attitude of waiting to see whether or not the aeroplane was going to prove a success before committing itself to the expenditure of the taxpayers' money. Such caution was all very well in reason, but it began to appear that the Government would never be convinced that flying had come to stay.

The French authorities, who were naturally gifted with more imagination than our own politicians, had grasped the potentialities of aircraft very early in their development, and had spent large sums of money by way of prizes and subsidies in order to encourage their experimenters. The results had exceeded their expectations, and the French pilots and constructors were far ahead of the rest of the world in every branch of aviation.

At home our men were struggling along behind, spending their private fortunes on their experiments, which were strictly limited by the extent of those funds.

Machines were built or repaired at Brooklands with wood stripped from old packing cases. There were instances of constructors covering their wing surfaces with stout paper because they could not afford to buy canvas or linen.

Meanwhile the politicians sat back and waited for these men to produce an aircraft which would beat the world's best.

It is true that the Admiralty, which was pouring the taxpayers' gold, million by million, into the coffers of the Armament Trust in return for battleships, which were subsequently proved at Jutland to be thoroughly unsound, was graciously pleased to permit four of its officers to learn to fly on aeroplanes provided by a private citizen.

It is also true that the War Office, less hidebound but less wealthy than the Admiralty, had established the Air Battalion and equipped it with seventeen aeroplanes of eleven different types, most of them useless. It had also been announced that Army officers were free to have themselves trained as pilots at civilian schools at their own expense, and that after each had obtained his R.Ae.C. certificate he would be granted £75 and posted to the Air Battalion.

At Farnborough, Mr. Geoffrey de Havilland was still working at the Balloon Factory endeavouring to produce a satisfactory aeroplane for the Army with insufficient funds.

That was the limit set to the support and encouragement of British aviation by the politicians in control of the world's wealthiest Power, and this at a time when Germany was proposing to allocate £1,500,000 per annum to the development of heavier than air craft, and when France had spent £320,000 in subsidies to constructors in her last financial year, and had voted three-quarters of a million sterling for 1912.

The French Government had been taking stock of the fruit of its expenditure by means of an exhaustive test of aircraft designed for military purposes at Rheims.

The results were staggering. Twenty-nine different types of aeroplane were entered, comprising eight monoplanes, nineteen biplanes, and two triplanes ; all made in France to French designs and with French engines. The winner was the Nieuport firm, whose machine had been ably flown by Mr. Weymann. The French Government awarded them £11,200 as a prize and purchased the winning aircraft and ten replicas of it for £20,000. The Breguêt firm was second, their prize being £4,200 and a contract for six machines at £9,600. Deperdussin were third and received £2,320 and an order for four machines at £6,400.

This contest had been observed by a Commission from the Air Battalion consisting of Capts. Fulton and Sykes, and Lieut. Barrington-Kennett. They returned considerably impressed.

In November, the British constructors held a meeting and appointed a deputation to wait upon Col. Seely at the War Office and plead for Government support.

As a result of these occurrences, the War Office was at last persuaded that the time had come when some action must be taken. It was announced that the Government had decided to train 100 officers as pilots, and to order a sufficient number of aeroplanes for their use. Further, it was proposed to hold a series of trials on Salisbury Plain during the following year, in order to select the machines required.

The rules for this competition were published just before Christmas. In the main they were intelligently devised and afforded scope for no little ingenuity on the part of the designers. Important points were an insistence on dual control and easy means of communication between pilot and observer. Each machine was required to carry fuel for four and a half hours and to climb to

1,000 feet in five minutes. Probably the most severe provision was that which required each competitor to fly his aeroplane fully loaded at 4,500 feet for one hour. These rules will be considered in greater detail when the progress of the actual competition is described in the next chapter.

The matter which caused the utmost bad feeling amongst the British manufacturers was the niggardly nature of the sums which were offered as prizes. The aggregate prize money was only £11,000 and it was provided that no single competitor should win more than £5,000 of that sum.

Odious comparisons were made in plenty between the generosity of our politicians and those of France. It was recalled that the aggregate prizes in the French competition had totalled £53,000, and it was remarked that the wealthiest nation in the world was not so open-handed to its own subjects as Lord Northcliffe had been to two Frenchmen.

Just as these accusations were, it was universally agreed that, at any rate, the Government's action marked a step, albeit a belated and hesitant step, in the right direction, and the British manufacturers set themselves to build their machines for the competition, with renewed hope in the future.

57. THE PARIS SALON

The opening of the annual Paris Salon on December 16th disclosed a tremendous advance upon the exhibition of the previous year. The prevailing tendency was to adopt a tractor airscrew in place of the propeller, and this had led to a general abandonment of the tail booms and outriggers which had previously disfigured the biplanes, and the substitution of a fuselage therefor.

Many firms had gone over completely from the biplane to the monoplane type. Altogether there were twenty-nine monoplanes and fourteen biplanes on view, and of the latter class only four were pushers. The faithful few were Voisin, Sommer, and the brothers Farman, although Henry Farman and Roger Sommer exhibited monoplanes in addition to their biplanes.

Great Britain was represented, for the first time, by one of the two-seater Bristol monoplanes (50 h.p. Gnôme) which was guaranteed to achieve 65 m.p.h., and sold at £950. Considerable interest in this exhibit was aroused by a daring flight over Paris, which was carried out by Mr. James Valentine in an identical model a day or two before the show opened. The Bristol stood up to the criticism of the French experts very well and it was freely acknowledged to be one of the best machines in the exhibition.

An aeroplane which was to have a considerable effect upon British aviation made its *début* at this Salon. This was the little Caudron biplane (35 h.p. Anzani). It was remarkable for the fact that although the lay-out of the airframe was of the familiar pusher type, the tail being supported on long booms and the pilot and passengers being seated in a *nacelle* on the lower wing, the engine was attached to the front of the *nacelle* and drove a tractor airscrew direct. This machine, which sold at £320, with a guaranteed speed of 55 m.p.h., was obviously ideal for school work, and was to prove immensely popular for this purpose.

Mons. L. Morane had severed his connection with M. Borel and had gone into partnership with M. Saulnier. This combination had produced by far the most advanced design which had yet appeared. It was immeasurably superior to any other aircraft exhibited at the Salon, its only near competitors being the Bleriot and Nieuport monoplanes. Three models were shown, ranging in price from £680 to £960, and the racing model, which was to prove so popular at Hendon, was guaranteed to attain 75 m.p.h. with a 50 h.p. Gnôme.

58. 1911 REVIEWED: THE PILOTS

In reviewing the events of 1911, the name of James Valentine stands out before all others in British aviation. For a newcomer to flying the feats that he performed were prodigious, and his gameness in the face of the most disheartening adversity and his irrepressible good humour and sportsmanship, entitle him to be acknowledged as the greatest British pilot of the year.

In both the Circuit of Europe and the Circuit of Britain, he upheld British prestige in no uncertain manner. His decision to try to complete the course in the European contest, after a series of troubles sufficient to make any ordinary person abandon flying for good, was nothing short of heroic, and he and Cody displayed the same indomitable determination in the *Daily Mail* competition a month later.

I must give Cody the honour of second place. His thoroughness in preparation and his dogged perseverance in action entirely justified his considerable financial successes in winning both of the Michelin trophies, and the fame he achieved by establishing new British records for duration and distance flown. But Cody's best performance was his great struggle round Britain, when he finished fourth in a field of twenty-one on the only British aircraft which flew more than a quarter of the way round the course.

Of the remainder of the ten pilots whom I picked as the best at the end of 1910, Messrs. Sopwith and Grahame-White had set England's reputation very high in the U.S.A. by their brilliant flying against the pick of the American pilots, and Mr. Graham Gilmour had more than fulfilled his early promise. Mr. Ogilvie had done a great number of hours on his Wright and had performed meritoriously to the best of his machine's ability in the Gordon-Bennett fiasco.

Messrs. Dickson, McArdle, Gibbs, and Radley had faded into the background.

Most prominent amongst the newcomers were Gustav Hamel, O. C. Morison, B. C. Hucks, H. Barber, C. H. Gresswell, C. C. Paterson, F. P. Raynham, Rhodes-Moorhouse, E. V. B. Fisher and the Bristol experts, Collyns Pizey, H. R. Fleming, and Howard Pixton.

The Army and Navy pilots were nearly all good. The best of the former were Lieut. Barrington-Kennett, who was now flying a Nieuport, Capt. J. B. Fulton, and Lieut. Conner. Lieut. C. R. Samson, R.N., and Lieut E. L. Gerrard, R.M.L.I., led the small Naval contingent at Eastchurch. A certain amount of official secrecy clouded the movements of these pilots, and I propose to omit their names from the list, which will be confined to civilians.

In selecting the best ten for 1911, I have given preference to those who had had a considerable amount of cross-country experience, and also to those who had handled a number of different types, as these men were obviously of more practical value to aviation than those, such as Ogilvie, who confined their activities mostly to aerodrome flights on a single type.

My selection is as follows:—

1. James Valentine (Deperdussin and Bristol monoplanes).
2. S. F. Cody (British Army Aeroplane and Cody biplane).
3. T. O. M. Sopwith (Howard-Wright and Wright biplanes, and Bleriot and Martin-Handasyde monoplanes).
4. C. Grahame-White (Henry Farman, Bristol and G.W. "Baby" biplanes, and Bleriot and Nieuport monoplanes).
5. O. C. Morison (Bristol biplane and Bleriot and Morane-Borel monoplanes).
6. G. Hamel (Bleriot monoplane and Howard-Wright biplane).
7. Graham Gilmour (Bleriot, Bristol and Martin-Handasyde monoplanes and Bristol biplane).
8. Howard Pixton (Avro and Bristol biplanes).
9. C. H. Gresswell (Henry Farman and G.W. biplanes, and Bleriot monoplane).
10. H. Barber (Valkyrie monoplane).

59. ACCIDENTS IN 1911

Seven British pilots had been killed in accidents during 1911. Five of them had had very little experience, two, indeed, being pupils under instruction who had not yet taken their certificates, and, of these five, one met his death whilst flying as a passenger, two stalled on gliding turns, one side-slipped into the ground, and the remaining one misjudged a dive and hit the earth before he could pull out. Of the two experienced pilots, one side-slipped into the ground through taking liberties with a machine to which he was unaccustomed, and the other broke an aircraft in the air by violent handling.

"*Flight*" *photo*

19.—The Stormy Petrel: Mr. Graham Gilmour, whose dashing flying gave rise to much litigation.

Facing page 128

"*Flight*" *photo*

20.—The first British woman to qualify as a pilot: Mrs. Maurice Hewlett in winter flying kit.

Facing page 129

60. THE WORK OF THE FLYING SCHOOLS IN 1911

The industry of training pilots had leaped forward in the most astonishing manner during the year. At the end of 1910 the six schools in operation in England had trained only eighteen pilots between them. By the end of 1911 there were twelve commercial firms or private individuals operating schools and one semi-official training centre for Naval officers, and these thirteen organizations had produced a total of 109 new pilots in twelve months. This total included eleven foreign subjects, but thirteen English pilots had taught themselves to fly and four more had been trained in France, so that the list of British pilots received a net increase during the year of 115, bringing the grand total of British subjects who had qualified as pilots as at December 31st, 1911, up to 171, of whom seven had been killed in flying accidents.

The record of the British schools for 1911 was as follows :—

School	*Aerodrome*	*No. of pupils trained in* 1911
Bristol	Salisbury Plain 35 Brooklands 18	53
Grahame-White	Hendon	11
Hewlett and Blondeau	Brooklands	10
Avro	Brooklands	8
Bleriot	Hendon	8
Hanriot	Brooklands	6
Naval School	Eastchurch	4
Aeronautical Syndicate, Ltd.	Hendon	3
McArdle and Drexel	Beaulieu (Hants.)	2
Blackburn	Filey (Yorks.)	1
Melly	Freshfield (Lancs.)	1
Spencer	Brooklands	1
Deperdussin	Brooklands	1
	Total	109

The extraordinary efficiency of the Bristol organization will be noted. The output of their two schools had risen to more than one pilot every week and they had trained almost as many pupils as all the other twelve schools put together. This was a most remarkable feat considering the difficulties with which they had to cope, and the fact that there was no dual control in those days.

61. BRITISH AEROPLANES OF 1911

The greatest advance on the construction side during the year had been achieved by the Bristol Company. Their new monoplane was good and although their first tractor biplane proved to be a failure, yet its production demonstrated that the advantages of this type were recognized by the firm's design staff.

Blackburn had at last obtained encouraging results with his monoplanes. The performance of Hucks with the Gnôme-engined model was extremely praiseworthy. The Flanders and Martin-Handasyde monoplanes were better than anything which had been built at Brooklands before, and the latter set an example in workmanship and finish to the whole industry.

Of the biplanes the Jezzi tractor was the most interesting and the most advanced design, but it was doomed to fade into obscurity. The G.W. "Baby" and the Paterson were successful variations on the "boxkite" theme. Cody and A. V. Roe had both improved their designs by detail refinements and the Bristol pusher biplanes continued to uphold their reputation for reliability and sound construction.

The outstanding events of the year were the introduction of the Bristol monoplane and the development of the Short twin-engined biplane. The latter was the first attempt to obviate the necessity for frequent forced landings due to engine failure, and thus to obtain increased safety in the air. The experiment achieved more success than might have been expected in view of the difficulties involved, and undoubtedly it started a train of thought which was eventually to have a considerable effect upon design.

The British constructors were still a very long way behind the French, but during 1911 it became apparent that some of our experimenters were no longer content to make slavish copies of their competitors' machines, but rather were anxious to strike out a line for themselves. In this respect, the Bristol Company, the Short Bros., Robert Blackburn, Howard Flanders, and Messrs. Martin and Handasyde showed promise.

62. WORLD'S AND ALL-BRITISH RECORDS AT END OF 1911

To the records comprised in the list of those standing at the end of 1910 given on page 57 *supra*, I have been able to add the unofficial world's record for distance flown in a straight line. It is odd that no definite official attempt had as yet been made upon this obviously attractive and very important record. Long distances had been flown in stages on the continent, but generally speaking, the stages were comparatively short and no attention had been directed to their length. Great distances had been covered non-stop, but these had always been flown around a small closed circuit for convenience of observation.

In the same way no attempts had been made for the absolute speed record over a straight course in both directions. The record speeds for various distances round closed circuits of a few kilometres in circumference were obviously dependant as much upon the cornering skill of the pilot, as upon the capabilities of the machine, and were really valueless.

Probably the Nieuport monoplane (100 h.p. Gnôme) was the fastest aeroplane in the world at the end of 1911, although considerable speeds had been achieved with the latest Deperdussin monoplane. The greatest speed attained by the Nieuport in still air was in the neighbourhood of 90 m.p.h.

WORLD'S RECORDS AT THE END OF 1911

Pilot	*Nationality*	*Aircraft*	*Nationality*	*Engine*	*Nationality*	*Time or Distance*	*Place*
			DURATION				
Fourny	French	M. Farman	French	Renault	French	11h.1m.29·5s.	Buc.
			DISTANCE IN A CLOSED CIRCUIT				
Gobe	French	Nieuport	French	Gnôme	French	740·255 Km. (460 miles)	Buc.
			DISTANCE IN A STRAIGHT LINE (Unofficial)				
Pierre Prier	French	Bleriot	French	Gnôme	French	210 miles (approx.)	London to Paris
			ALTITUDE				
R. Garros	French	Bleriot	French	Gnôme	French	4,250 m. (13,943 ft.)	St. Malo

It will be observed that France still held all the principal records and that the Gnôme engine was responsible for three of them.

The duration record had been increased by nearly three hours, the distance in a closed circuit by over 100 miles, and the altitude by 3,000 feet.

All the record-breaking pilots of 1910 have disappeared from the list and Henry Farman's name is missing for the first time since the beginning of aviation in Europe.

No altitude or speed records had been established in the all-British category and the three principal records were still held by Messrs. Cody and Sopwith, although the former had increased his duration record by twenty-eight minutes and the distance in a closed circuit by seventy-six miles. No one had attempted to beat Sopwith's record for distance flown in a straight line.

ALL-BRITISH RECORDS AT THE END OF 1911

Pilot	*Aircraft*	*Engine*	*Time or Distance*	*Place*
		DURATION		
S. F. Cody	Cody	60 h.p. Green	5 hrs. 15 m.	Laffan's Plain
		DISTANCE IN A CLOSED CIRCUIT		
S. F. Cody	Cody	60 h.p. Green	261·5 miles	Laffan's Plain
		DISTANCE IN A STRAIGHT LINE		
T. O. M. Sopwith	Howard-Wright	60 h.p. E.N.V.	169 miles	Eastchurch to Thirimont (Belgium)

CHAPTER IV

1912

I. SPEED RANGE: DECK FLYING.

EARLY in January 1912, some interesting calculations and performance figures were published by Mr. Mervyn O'Gorman, who had been acting as Superintendant of the Army Aircraft Factory at Farnborough, where Mr. Geoffrey de Havilland had been flying a reconstructed Voisin with a silenced motor.

Some experiments had been conducted with certain types of aircraft with a view to determining their speed-ranges. Mr. O'Gorman showed that a Deperdussin monoplane gave the best results with a range of 45–55 m.p.h. whilst a Bleriot also stalled at 45 m.p.h. but could not exceed 54 m.p.h. in still air. A Breguêt tractor biplane had a range of only 7 m.p.h., as its minimum speed was 46 m.p.h. and its maximum 53 m.p.h.

These figures were probably somewhat unflattering to the types selected, as it is difficult to believe that the two monoplanes could not have exceeded 60 m.p.h. if their engines had been in perfect tune. All the same, it is remarkable to compare Mr. O'Gorman's results with the figures for the 1932 Fairey Firefly or Hawker Fury (*née* Hornet) both of which have a speed *range* exceeding 150 m.p.h.

On January 10th, a notable feat was performed by Lieut. C. R. Samson, R.N., who flew one of the Short biplanes from a staging erected above the forepart of H.M.S. *Africa*. The flight commenced at Eastchurch whence Lieut. Samson flew across the Medway to Cockleshell Hard where he landed. Naval personnel then placed the machine on a lighter which was towed out to the battleship. The biplane was hoisted out of the lighter on to the improvised flight deck by means of the ship's derrick, and two hours twenty minutes after leaving Eastchurch she ran down the staging and took off for Sheerness.

An American pilot had previously succeeded in landing a Curtiss biplane onto a battleship at sea, but this was the first successful take-off from a vessel and H.M.S. *Africa* may be credited with the distinction of being the first aircraft carrier in the Royal Navy and Lieut. Samson with the honour of being the first British deck-flying pilot.

2. SOME FAMOUS PUPILS: A NEW BIPLANE

Several pilots who were destined to make names for themselves in British aviation began to come into the limelight at this stage. At Brooklands Mr. Sydney V. Sippe passed his tests on the Avro biplane and Lieut. Spencer Grey, R.N., was doing some splendid flying on the Gnôme-engined Blackburn in company with Mr. B. C. Hucks. Mr. Sippe demonstrated his courage, and his lack of discretion, by attempting a flight from Brooklands to Oxford for his superior certificate a few days after obtaining his *brevet*. There was a dense fog and he was compelled to fly low down along the surface of the Thames for fear of getting lost. Eventually he gave up and landed at Abingdon. He had succeeded in keeping his Avro biplane level when out of sight of the ground, solely by keeping the r.p.m. of his Viale engine constant, by the careful use of his elevator.

At Hendon Mr. H. C. Biard, who was to have the privilege of winning a Schneider Trophy Contest for Great Britain, was making rapid progress on one of the G. W. school's Farmans. Mr. Lewis Turner, who had been acting as chief pilot to the Kennedy Aviation Company at St. Petersburg, had returned from Russia, and accepted a post as Instructor at the G. W. school, at which he had learned to fly originally.

Mr. Gordon Bell had been honoured by an invitation from the R.E.P. Company to become their chief demonstration pilot at their headquarters at Buc. He accepted the post and thus became the first English pilot to be employed by a foreign manufacturer. This was no mean distinction in view of the immense superiority of the French in all branches of aviation. Mr. Bell combined tuition with demonstration and test flying and one of his pupils at Buc was none other than Mr. E. B. C. Scholefield, who was only seventeen years of age at that time.

Mr. H. Barber of the Valkyrie School at Hendon had designed and built a biplane known as the Viking. This machine was a tractor with a single 50 h.p. Gnôme engine mounted in the nose of the fuselage, which drove two outboard airscrews situate near the centre of each wing by means of long thin chains. This arrangement was not very practical but the biplane flew satisfactorily on test. The most interesting feature of the aircraft was the provision of large ailerons set midway between the two main planes.

3. BRISTOL'S EXPANSION

The Bristol Company had doubled their working capital and now had £100,000 available. They had turned out over 100 machines during 1911, and as a direct result of the exhibition of the new monoplane at the Paris Salon, several orders were received from European governments. Early in January they dispatched another foreign expedition, this time to Spain. Messrs. Howard Pixton and Busteed were the pilots, and they flew both the monoplane and biplane types from an aerodrome just outside Madrid. The King of Spain and a number of staff officers were greatly impressed by the flights. Howard Pixton gave demonstrations of landing on to and taking off from freshly ploughed fields, by way of displaying the robust methods of construction employed.

Mr. Busteed won the Avia Cup for the first crossing of the City of Madrid by air with a splendid flight on the monoplane, at an altitude of nearly 5,000 feet.

This enterprise resulted in a large order from the Spanish Government for both monoplanes and biplanes.

On leaving Spain, Mr. Howard Pixton took the 2-seater monoplane to Berlin and demonstrated it at the Johannisthal aerodrome before the staff officers of the German Aviation Corps, several of whom were taken for flights in the machine.

Mr. W. E. Hart, who was the first Australian to pass the tests for his R.Ae.C. certificate in Australia, used a Bristol biplane for the purpose, and subsequently carried out a very fine cross country flight on it from Penrith to Sydney, a distance of about fifty miles. During this flight Mr. Hart attained a height of more than 6,000 feet.

4. PROGRESS AT LAFFAN'S PLAIN: DE HAVILLAND SUCCEEDS

Mr. Geoffrey de Havilland had been working steadily at the old Balloon Factory, now rechristened the Army Aircraft Factory, at Farnborough, in spite of innumerable set-backs and disappointments. His first two aeroplanes had disintegrated in the air and another had been smashed to pieces by Lieut. Ridge. In addition, he suffered continual trouble with his motors, which he designed and built himself.

Fortunately he refused to be discouraged or to admit defeat, even in face of the death of Lieut. Ridge, and at last, in January 1912, he produced a tractor biplane, which was not only an immense advance upon all previous biplane designs produced in England, but was also to be the prototype of a long series of highly successful aeroplanes and the common ancestor of the BE., R.E., and S.E. types, and eventually of the D.H. Moth, the world's most popular aircraft.

A close study of the accompanying photograph of this important aeroplane will disclose many features which are now common practice, but which were then decided novelties. Attention may be drawn especially to the form of the bottom wings, which might be those of a Gipsy Moth of to-day, except for the absence of ailerons, to the general arrangement of the fuselage, and to the streamlining of the interplane struts.

For some months past the French pilots had been conducting experiments in passenger-carrying, and their biplanes had staggered through the air with quite remarkable numbers of human beings perched precariously all over them.

The first English pilot to attempt a similar feat was Mr. Cody, who had already flown with two passengers standing on the wings. On January 27th, 1912, he improved on this feat and set up a British record by flying round Laffan's Plain for seven miles, at an altitude of about 100 feet, with no less than four passengers besides himself. The useful load, which was disposed in two tiers immediately behind and above the pilot, was 738 lbs. Mr. Cody had installed an 120 h.p. Austro-Daimler engine for this flight, and during a subsequent test it was found that the "Cathedral" was now faster than Mr. Sopwith's new Bleriot 2-seater, which exceeded 65 m.p.h.

5. PATERSON AND DRIVER AT CAPETOWN

Messrs. Compton Paterson and E. F. Driver had taken the former's new biplane and a Bleriot to South Africa on an exhibition tour. The proceedings opened badly, for Paterson had a very nasty smash at the Green Point Racecourse on one of his first flights. This accident was due to bad maintenance. The dopes then in use were not very efficient, and the little biplane had been exposed to the atmosphere for a long period without attention. On the day of the crash Paterson had flown through several rainstorms and very hot sunshine alternately, with the result that the fabric of the tail plane split at the leading edge.

When the machine took off, the air blew the tail plane open like a bag and forced the tail downwards. The result was that the biplane performed the first part of a loop off the ground, stalled on its back at 60 feet, and fell upside down with the pilot suspended from the joy stick. Paterson was lucky to escape with a fortnight in hospital, followed by two weeks on crutches.

Driver was more fortunate with the Bleriot, and succeeded in putting up some splendid flights in spite of the tricky conditions caused by down draughts from Table Mountain. After Paterson's smash he flew the first South African Air Mail, which had been organized by Capt. Guy Livingston, between Kenilworth and Muizenberg.

6. THE ALEXANDER PRIZE: MR. HOLT THOMAS

It will be recalled that the £1,000 prize for the best British aero engine, offered by Mr. Patrick Y. Alexander, had been withheld after the previous year's tests on the ground that even the Green, which was the most successful engine submitted, had failed to achieve the requisite standard of reliability.

The Green Engine Company had submitted one of their latest models for a further test and this time they succeeded in winning the prize. The successful engine had four separate cylinders mounted in line, and was water cooled and developed an average of 61 b.h.p., at 1,150 r.p.m., throughout two successive non-stop runs of twelve hours each. The power-weight ratio showed one b.h.p. for every 5·77 lbs. weight, which was not very satisfactory even in those days.

Mr. Holt Thomas had for some time past been interesting himself in the commercial aspects of aviation, and eventually he decided to take up the British rights for the products of Henry and Maurice Farman. There were no modern machines of either make in England at that time, although almost every aerodrome boasted at least one early model Henry Farman. Mr. Holt Thomas visited the Maurice Farman grounds at Buc and made a series of long cross-country test flights, piloted by the famous designer himself. Later he went on to Chalons and tested both the monoplane and biplane types manufactured by Henry Farman there.

7. ANOTHER WORLD'S RECORD CAPTURED

The closing date of the contest for Mr. Mortimer Singer's two prizes of £500 each for Army and Navy pilots was approaching, and several attempts had been made, but Capt. E. L. Gerrard's flight of 129 miles, which had established Britain's second claim to a world's record in August 1911, was still unbeaten by either a Naval or Military pilot.

For some months past, Lieut. B. H. Barrington-Kennett, who was easily the best of the Air Battalion pilots, had been flying a Nieuport monoplane (Gnôme), which had been purchased for his use by the War Office, and on January 29th, 1912, he put up a flight of 111 miles non-stop for the Army's share of the prize.

About a fortnight later, on February 14th, this officer made another attempt on the same machine with Cpl. Ridd, R.E., as passenger, and on this occasion he not only almost doubled Capt. Gerrard's distance, but he also set up a new British record for duration with one passenger by remaining in the air for 4 hr. 32 mins. and captured the world's distance record in a closed circuit with one passenger, with a total distance of 249 miles 840 yards. In addition. Lieut. Barrington-Kennett succeeded in his original object of winning the Army's section of the Mortimer Singer prize. This magnificent flight was made round a small circuit marked out on Salisbury Plain and the average speed works out at 55 m.p.h. It was unfortunate that both the aircraft and engine concerned were designed and built in France.

8. THE DEATH OF GRAHAM GILMOUR

On February 17th, British aviation suffered a great loss by reason of a fatal accident to Mr. Graham Gilmour. It was ironical that

Mr. Gilmour, whose exploits as a "contour-chaser" had received so much attention and publicity, should meet his death whilst flying peacefully above Richmond Park at an altitude of 400 feet. The air was exceptionally bumpy on the day in question, and Mr. Ewen on a Deperdussin at Hendon, Lieut. Lawrence on a Blackburn at Shoreham, and Lieut. Longmore, R.N., on a Short at Eastchurch all reported alarming experiences in the air, and conditions became so uncomfortable at Brooklands that all flying was suspended.

It was in these circumstances that Gilmour took off from Brooklands in the old Martin-Handasyde monoplane, which closely resembled an Antoinette and was fitted with an engine of that make.

Observers stated that the left wing broke up in the air, but an examination of the wreckage disclosed that the bracing wires were intact. A new pair of wings had been fitted three days previously. Whatever may have been the cause, there is no doubt but that the machine, which was cruising steadily along at 400 feet, suddenly dived to the ground and was smashed to pieces, the pilot being killed instantaneously.

Considering all the circumstances, it seems probable that a violent bump was encountered which put too much strain on the old monoplane, and thus caused some vital part to collapse in the air and rendered the machine uncontrollable.

Mr. Graham Gilmour, who had learned to fly on a Bleriot monoplane, was one of the Bristol Company's group of expert pilots, and was one of the ten best British pilots at the time of his death.

9. TWO NEW SHORTS

The Short Brothers produced two new models at Eastchurch during the early part of 1912. The first was a tractor biplane which had been designed in the summer of 1910 for Mr. Cecil Grace. The plans had been put aside after his death until they were shown to Mr. Frank McClean in the autumn of 1911. Mr. McClean was impressed with the design and placed an order for one machine immediately.

This aircraft was not exactly handsome, but it had its good points. The rectangular fuselage was set midway between the two wings, and the top wing was longer than the bottom one and carried large ailerons. The fuselage was exceptionally long and only the front portion, in which the pilot and observer sat, was covered in, the tail part being left in skeleton form, *à la Bleriot.* The machine did 56 m.p.h., when it was tested by Commander Samson, R.N., and Capt. Gerrard, R.M.L.I.

The other aircraft was a copy of the Bleriot single-seater monoplane. The Short Bros. introduced a few detail alterations of their own, but in general arrangement it differed scarcely at all from the original Bleriot design. This machine had a speed of just over 60 m.p.h.

Lieut. Spencer Grey, R.N., Lieut. L'Estrange Malone, R.N., Capt. Gordon, R.M.L.I., and Eng.-Lieut. Randell, R.N., had been posted to Eastchurch for training, and the first-named had brought his own Blackburn monoplane with him.

Several members of the Territorial Balloon Company were also learning to fly on Mr. McClean's Short biplanes at Eastchurch under the tuition of Mr. J. L. Travers. The first Territorial to pass his tests for the R.Ae.C. certificate was Sergt. H. D. Cutler, who was closely followed by Lieut. V. A. Barrington-Kennett and Sergt. C. W. Meredith.

10. DE HAVILLAND ON UNDERCARRIAGES

The extent to which Mr. Geoffrey de Havilland had progressed towards a full and complete understanding of the requirements of practical aviation and the art of air pilotage, was displayed in a paper which he prepared on the subject of aeroplane undercarriages.

In the course of his treatise he gave full instructions for the execution of three point landings, emphasized the necessity for taking off and alighting up-wind, and gave the excellent advice that cross-country flights should be carried out at an altitude exceeding 1,000 feet.

At that time many pilots were obsessed with the erroneous idea that they were safer if they careered through the air just above the tree tops. This delusion was probably assisted by the fact that only a minority of pilots were capable of executing a gliding turn safely, and there was thus a very real danger that in the event of a forced landing from a height, due to engine failure, the machine would stall and crash out of control.

Mr. de Havilland also stressed the risk of attempting to glide a machine too slowly.

All this excellent advice sounds very elementary to the pilots of to-day, but at that time it was revolutionary, and occasioned far more argument than did Mr. de Havilland's plea for efficient brakes for aircraft and for a greater degree of controllability on the ground; correlated problems of a far more difficult nature. It is only now, more than twenty years later, that efficient wheel brakes are coming into general use on aeroplanes.

11. HENRI SALMET'S FIRST CROSS-COUNTRY

Henri Salmet had taken over the post of chief pilot to the Bleriot Company's School at Hendon, in succession to Pierre Prier and Gustav Hamel. It will be recalled that M. Prier, who had taught Salmet to fly, had made the first non-stop flight from London to Paris. M. Salmet determined to go one better than his instructor and to perform the double journey in one day. This was a somewhat ambitious project for a pilot of little experience, who had never made a cross-country flight. However, he started on March 7th.

I set out below an extract from Henri Salmet's own account of his attempt. It is an epic in its way, and demonstrates, much more admirably than I could do, the unconquerable spirit of those pioneer pilots.

" For some time past I have wanted to fly to Paris and back in one day, and also as I should like to see M. Bleriot in Paris about business matters. I think, it being fine, on Thursday the 7th, I will go. The night before I paint on the wings of my Bleriot some varnish that keep the fabric tight and make it waterproof, and later I telegraph to the coastguard at Eastbourne to telephone me in the morning if the weather is good. Next morning early the message arrive. The coastguard say the Channel is clear of fog, so I get ready. The fuselage of my Bleriot had already been covered in with fabric and waterproof so as to make a float that keep me up if my engine fail and I go in the water. Round me I put an inner tyre from one of the school machines which I blow up. I run my engine and it go very well, so I wave my hand and I am away.

" When I left here it was exactly 7.45, with little wind behind me. The wind increased, and after about a quarter of an hour the wind was much more stronger, and my speed was about half as much again. At Eastbourne I was 1,200 metres " [about 4,000 feet] " high and about two miles over the sea, but the wind was too gusty. I came back, and I took 3,000 feet more high, and that took me thirteen minutes. After that, I started again on my way to Paris, and I flew for 1 hr. 40 mins. without seeing anything other than the clouds. The sight at that height was most marvellous—I think absolutely the best something I have seen in my life. At that height the clouds were more like big snowy mountains and flying through them was the most curious experience that could happen to anyone. A glance behind showed my wake in a swirl of fog disturbed by the propeller and the passage of the machine. So cold was it in the clouds, that I had constantly to increase my high so that I could get above them. This brought me to a height of between 6,000 and 7,000 ft., and as I could not see the sea, steering had to be entirely done by compass. This was hard to do, for the wind, although fairly steady, set the monoplane rolling slowly, and the compass needle kept swinging continually about ten degrees each side of the true line. This had to be accounted for. From points that I had recognized over English soil, I calculated that my speed was something over 130 kiloms. an hour " (80 m.p.h.), " and from the time I get my last glimpse of the earth, I flew for 1 hr. 40 mins., and then from my speed calculated just about where I ought to find myself. Here I thought I ought to descend, as I wanted to make sure that my compass was guiding me correctly, and that I was on my right way.

"For a long time I see nothing but the wings of my machine. I come down to 200 metres" [650 feet], "in order to distinguish points that I wanted to find. Then I flew round in big circles for 17 minutes, at last recognizing a castle that I had marked on my map. Picking up the adjacent railway line I reached Gisors. Here it was clearer, and I gradually elevated to 2,000 metres" [6,500 feet]. "Although it was possible to distinguish land marks, I did not look down once as I was so occupied in fighting the gusty wind that I did not trouble to do so, knowing full well my compass was steering me correctly. I saw the Eiffel Tower after a long struggle, and the sight gave me very big pleasure because it is the first cross-country flight I have make. I see Issy from 1,500 metres," [4,900 feet], "and commenced my *vol plané*.

"To battle against the *remous* caused by the big houses, I have to descend very steep to keep up my speed. Gusts rapidly struck me from below, and had I not gripped the *cabane* with all my might, I should have been thrown out several times. Issy was absolutely deserted because I arrived before my telegram. On landing I took from my machine the little can of paraffin I always carry, and washed over the engine—my good engine, which had brought me all the way from London without any trouble. All the more pleasure because I myself look after the engine, no one else touch it. Then I go to find someone, and I find a guardian of the aerodrome with a mechanic from the Astra Company, and I asked him, 'Where are the Bleriot hangars?' and he say 'Opposite there.' As I turned to go to the sheds he say to me, 'Can you tell me any news of the English aviator who should fly from London to Paris?' and I say 'The English aviator is me.' Then we shake hands. Then he say 'If you are the English aviator you speak French very well indeed. What is your name?' and I said 'Henri Salmet of the Bleriot school in England.' Then I go to the Bleriot sheds and get the mechanics to fetch my machine and put it safe in the hangar. I ask for M. Bleriot's telephone number to ring him up and tell him I arrived. I telephone and he speak himself and he say, 'Why do you not send a telegram?' At that moment the telegraph boy must have come into his office, for he say 'the telegram has just arrived now.' I say, 'When can I see you M. Bleriot?' and he say 'I see you about three or four,' but I reply 'I shall be far off by then.' He say, 'Why?' I say, 'Because I want to get back to London to-day.' Then he come down to Issy in a car with M. Leblanc,[1] and some reporters.

"M. Bleriot seem very please. He say '*Bon jour, Salmet. Toutes mes felicitations! Par où avez passé?*' I say that I had come by the way I had chosen, and that I had tell him some time before. He is very happy that I do cross the channel at the wide

[1] The Bleriot firm's racing pilot.

part, from Eastbourne to Dieppe—thing that had not been done since aviation existed. In his great joy he grasp my both hands, and squeeze so hard that he hurt much. And M. Leblanc also. Then we have lunch at the Café Syndicat des Aviateurs. They say to me, there is too much wind, and you cannot return. But I did not pay attention to that, as no matter what the struggle I had big confidence in my Bleriot, my Gnôme, and my wonderful Levasseur propeller, which give so much pull and runs so smoothly. It is the best I have try. With my three faithful friends, my machine, my motor, my propeller, the wind have no fear for me. So at 2.15 with the *anemometre* at 34 kilometres," [21 miles] "to the hour, I start once more. The start is not alone, because the ground is used by the soldiers, but I go to ask the Commandant to let me start. He say, 'Yes, with pleasure,' and he took his soldiers in a good place to give me plenty of room, and I go. I start straight on my line, but the ground is not much large and when I am over the houses I am very low, and the wind put me sometime in very bad situation. I am very long to take my high, because sometime I am up 200 metres" [650 feet] "up, and then I come down again with the wind.

"After I have crossed the Seine I have less *remous*, and I go more high. Since this time the wind is much more regular, but so strong that I take nearly four hours to make 220 kiloms." [136 miles—an average of 34 m.p.h.] "I am very cross against the weather, because I am obliged to land at Berck Plage with my petrol tank nearly empty.

"As soon after my landing I start to find petrol. That take me too long time, and after that it is too late to start. I had wanted very much to sleep on English ground that night. A friend help me find petrol and oil, and after filling the tanks, I go to take something to eat with him. As he knew I wanted to start early next morning, he locked me in my bedroom that night, so that I should not go without him seeing me. At five o'clock he come in my room and give me a good cup coffee. I took it, and soon after I go with him to where the machine is tied up. I give a little exhibition fly, and land on the shore. Then before they let me go I have to sign many postcards, and many people take photographs of the machine.

"Starting again just before ten, the wind was blowing about 32 kiloms" [20 m.p.h] "and was a little foggy. I fly for two miles, and my engine start missing. My magneto is wrong. I put it right, and I start again at 10.12. Then I go across the Channel from Cap Grisnez to Folkestone very fast indeed. I am across the other side in fifteen minutes," [this gives a speed of about 85 m.p.h.] "and there the wind come more badly. Having no map, and as the compass rock very badly, I keep over the main road. The wind and rain beat very hard in my face. I don't like to land because I like to put my machine in my shed at Hendon before landing anywhere. But the wind and rain coming always more strong, I think it more wise to land than to continue. It take me a quarter of an hour to go four miles." [16 m.p.h. It must have been a 40 m.p.h. gale.] "Then, seeing a good landing ground on my left, I come down, and find I am at Chatham. If I am very cross against the weather I meet there the best people I have ever met. All people is ready to help me for anything. They all want to give me something to eat. I go with Mr. Sills, who has a room where I can be quiet, for I am very tired after the struggle. The schoolmaster there makes a meeting in my honour, and I go there in the evening, and they give me a big tri-colour bouquet, and after much shouting I have to sign many postcards.

"The next morning I start at 6.15 in a very bad wind towards London. My *cloche* is always moving; but all is well until I fly into some fog. Near Maidstone I have to land in a *champ laboré*, and I break a piece off my propeller. My good friends from Hendon soon bring me another one, and we put it on. The weather is not favourable to start, but I am so hurry to come to Hendon that I look with a bad eye at those who say the weather is too bad. I go on again; but soon after my motor stopped, and I have to descend in a football field near Beckton gasworks. I land very deep from 800 metres" [2,600 feet] "because ground is small. I see I am going to hit a goal-post, so I pull back my *cloche* to clear it. My speed slackens as I rise, and a gust comes and blows me right over. I am sad, for it is the first smash I have ever had since I started to learn to fly. To me the smash itself was nothing, but to think that it should happen after those days of struggling grieved me much. However, the smash was done properly and so disgusted was I at not being able to get to Hendon, that I walked away without looking to see my machine. There I found friends who were very amiable to me, principally William Marsh, whom I shall not forget. The smash did not hurt me, for here I am, with only a little cut on my knuckle. Then—*Mais c'est tout! Voilà la fin de mon pauvre et triste voyage!*"

As M. Salmet landed at Saumont la Potterie (Seine Inf.) to inquire his way after his blind crossing of the Channel, M. Prier retained his record for the first and only non-stop flight from London to Paris.

12. M. BLERIOT AND MONOPLANE WING LOADINGS.

Something in the nature of a bombshell was thrown into aviation circles by the publication of Mons. L. Bleriot's report to the French Government on his investigations into the causes of the disasters which had resulted in the deaths of MM. Chavez, Blanchard, Lantheaume, Ducorneau, and Sevelle.

In each of these cases, the wings of the monoplane concerned had collapsed at the moment when the pilot had pushed his stick forward, in order to commence a steep glide or dive to earth.

M. Bleriot had discovered that considerable strains, thitherto unsuspected, were thrown upon the *top* surface of the wings by this manœuvre and that the landing wires, which were designed merely to support the wings at rest on the ground, were unable to bear the load, and broke forthwith. The collapse of the wings followed as a matter of course.

M. Bleriot was the largest manufacturer of monoplanes in the world at that time and the principal contractor to the French Government. His frank exposure of the inherent weakness of his own products was an act calling for considerable moral courage. He faced ruin at that moment, and accepted the risk calmly and courageously for the sake of his brother pilots who were flying his machines.

The French Government acted promptly and firmly. The edict went forth that no monoplane of any design was to go into the air from the French Army aerodromes until they had all been rebuilt according to the modifications proposed by M. Bleriot. The Government had no power to exercise similar control over civil aircraft.

13. THE AVRO MILITARY BIPLANE

The Government had announced its decision to purchase a considerable number of aircraft for the use of the Army pilots, without awaiting the result of the competitions which were to be held in the summer. Three of these machines were to be two-seater biplanes, fitted with 50 h.p. Gnôme engines, and an order for them had been placed with A. V. Roe and Co., of Manchester. As a preliminary to work on this order, the Avro firm produced an experimental model fitted with a 60 h.p. E.N.V. motor.

This machine was brought to Brooklands for test by Lieut. W. Parke, R.N., and it was at once observed that a most notable advance in design and construction had been achieved. The principal features were the general cleanness of the lines and the depth of the fuselage, which allowed the occupants to sit protected from the slip-stream with only their heads projecting. The passenger must have had a warm time as the engine was immediately in front of him, and large flat radiators formed both sides of the cockpit. Dual control was fitted, and the machine could be flown from the back seat, either with or without a passenger, as the latter was disposed over the centre of gravity.

14. LONDON-PARIS WITH A PASSENGER: THE END OF A.S.L.

The first flight by a British pilot between the British and French capitals was made on April 2nd. Gustav Hamel left Hendon on a two-seater Bleriot (70 h.p. Gnôme) at 9.38 a.m., with Miss

Trehawke Davies in the passenger's seat. To Miss Davies he entrusted the maintenance of air pressure in the petrol tank, but she failed to work the hand pump properly, and very nearly let the machine down in the Straits of Dover. Fortunately Hamel was at 7,000 feet when his motor dried up, and he was able to make a safe gliding descent and land near Ambleteuse. After a visit to M. Bleriot at Hardelot, the couple continued to Paris, where a landing was made at Issy-les-Molineux at 5.55 p.m.

At the beginning of April, Mr. H. Barber, chief pilot of the Aeronautical Syndicate Ltd., of Hendon, decided reluctantly to give up his active interest in aviation on account of the increasing cost of keeping pace with the latest developments.

Mr. Barber, who was one of the ten best British pilots, had taught himself to fly on a machine of his own design, when he was the solitary experimenter on the wastes of Salisbury Plain, in the year 1909. During his brief but exciting career, he had built over twenty machines, including all the various models of the well-known Valkyrie pusher monoplanes. During 1911 he had flown nearly 7,000 miles, and must have put in about 200 hours in the air. He had carried 151 passengers during the year without any accident.

Deprived of Mr. Barber's support, the A.S.L. firm was forced to close down. It had always been very much of a " one man " affair, as the only other pilot of any ability who had flown their Valkyrie machines was Mr. Ridley-Prentice. The whole of the aircraft, stock of spares and tools were purchased by Handley-Page Ltd.

The loss of this school was balanced by the great success of Mr. W. H. Ewen's establishment, which had been transferred to Hendon from Lanark. Mr. Ewen, who was a pilot of great courage and ability, provided a variety of different types for his pupils. He himself preferred the Deperdussin, but Bleriots and Nieuports were also available. Amongst his pupils was Mr. E. H. (Bill) Lawford, now a popular figure at Croydon Airport.

The New Forest School at Beaulieu had faded into obscurity, after producing one outstanding pilot in Lieut. B. H. Barrington-Kennett, but a new aerodrome had been established at Eastbourne, where Mr. Fowler was instructing on Bleriots.

15. THE MORTIMER SINGER PRIZES

In spite of a gallant attempt on the part of Lieut. Bowers on a Bristol monoplane, who flew for 66 miles round Salisbury Plain in a strong wind accompanied by rain and hail, no one had succeeded in beating Lieut. Barrington-Kennett's world's record flight of 249½ miles, and he was duly awarded the Army's share of the Mortimer Singer prize.

The Navy's share of the £1,000 went to Lieut. Longmore, R.N., who had succeeded in keeping the new Short tractor biplane (Gnôme) in the air above Eastchurch for exactly four hours, with

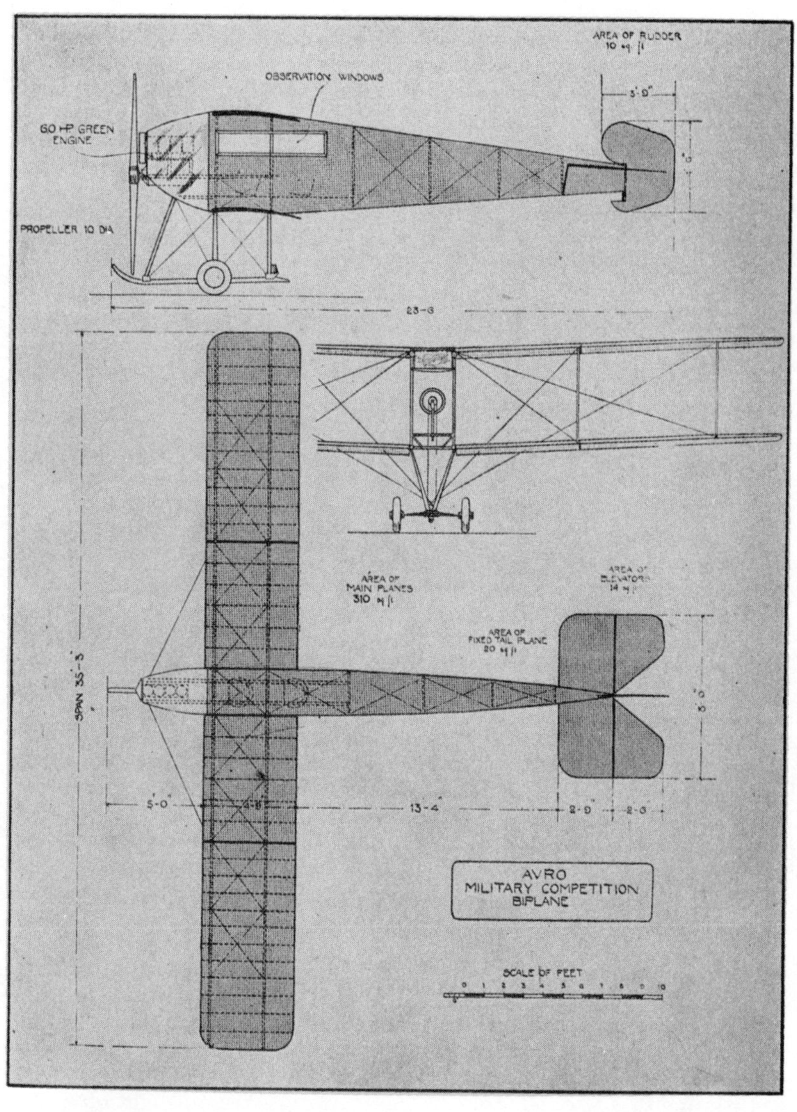

"*Flight*" *Copyright*

6.—THE FIRST SUCCESSFUL BRITISH CABIN AEROPLANE: THE AVRO BIPLANE (60 H.P. GREEN) FLOWN IN THE MILITARY TRIALS BY LIEUT. W. PARKE, R.N.

Facing page 144

"*Flight*" photo

21.—The second British woman Pilot: Mrs. de Beauvoir Stocks

E. R. A. O'Connor in the passenger's seat. During this flight, which was terminated by engine trouble when fuel for 2½ hours remained in the tank, Lieut. Longmore covered 172 miles at an average speed of 43 m.p.h.

16. EASTER AT HENDON

A four-day flying meeting was organized at Hendon during the Easter holidays, at which various races and competitions were to be held. Unfortunately, the weather was so bad that all the competitive events had to be cancelled with the exception of the altitude contest, for which Gustav Hamel (Bleriot) was the sole entrant. This event took place on Good Friday in a wind which was blowing at nearly 30 m.p.h. on the ground. After a preliminary test flight, during which the Bleriot's ground speed approached 100 m.p.h. down wind, Hamel took off and climbed steadily up and up until 6,000 feet was reached. At that height the wind was so powerful that his aircraft, which was capable of 65 m.p.h. in still air, was blown slowly backwards away from the aerodrome. Hamel landed after a long steep dive, having been in the air for twenty-five minutes.

The only other pilots to fly that day were Grahame-White and Lewis Turner, each of whom put in a few circuits on the old G. W. school Farman.

On Saturday, the wind was still unpleasantly strong and only short flights were attempted. Hamel was again the most conspicuous pilot, and he gave some clever demonstrations of sharp turns and gliding descents on his Bleriot. Ewen made a straight flight across the aerodrome on his Deperdussin (28 h.p. Anzani), and Grahame-White did a few circuits on his fast Nieuport (70 Gnôme), which had just arrived from the U.S.A.

Sunday was a better day. The proceedings were opened by Herr Prensiell, who flew his Bleriot (35 h.p. Anzani) straight into one of the substantial wooden pylons which had been erected to mark the turning points for the races. He succeeded in knocking the obstruction down without damaging himself.

The Blackburn pilot, B. C. Hucks, appeared on a Bleriot (Gnôme) and proceeded to demonstrate how good he was by taking the machine, with which he was unfamiliar, through two layers of clouds to 2,500 feet, and descending thence in a spiral glide.

Lewis Turner startled the crowd by lapping the racing course on an old Farman, banking steeply round the pylons and switchbacking along the straights, and Ewen was flying his Deperdussin. F. P. Raynham arrived from Brooklands on Sopwith's Burgess-Wright biplane, and handed it over to its owner, who made a number of passenger flights. Allen and Hamel flew Bleriots and Mrs. de Beauvoir Stocks a Farman, whilst Grahame-White completed five laps of the course on his Nieuport at 65 m.p.h. In the evening Raynham flew the Burgess-Wright back to Brooklands with a passenger against a very strong head wind. The journey of 20 miles occupied 52 mins., an average speed of 23 m.p.h.!

The big thrill of the meeting occurred on Bank Holiday. So strong was the wind that a tent hangar on the aerodrome had its roof ripped off, spectators' hats were blowing about the enclosures, and one of the great wooden pylons was blown down. The anemometer recorded gusts between 35 and 50 m.p.h.

All the spectators had been warned that flying was impossible, but 8,000 had paid for admission. Grahame-White was determined not to disappoint them and decided to "parade" his oldest Henry Farman, a veteran which had flown hundreds of hours since its first appearance at the Wolverhampton meeting in 1910.

The old biplane was brought out with Grahame-White in the pilot's seat and two mechanics at each wing tip and one at each skid. With engine full-on the machine progressed into the wind at a jog trot, with the six men straining every nerve to hold her down. After parading thus before the enclosures, Grahame-White stationed his chief ground engineers, Carr and Law, on the skids and flew for 200 yards at a height of ten feet. It took him about one minute to cover this distance, which gives a speed of 7 m.p.h. He repeated this perilous performance three times, until an exceptionally heavy landing resulted in a broken shock absorber. Whilst this was being repaired, it was found that the pilot had smashed up his cane seat and bent his rudder bar, in his struggles with the controls.

Grahame-White decided to attempt a longer flight and taxied out to the far corner of the aerodrome, with Lewis Turner and Carr seated on either side of him on the bottom wing. Just after the take off, a gust caught the machine under one wing tip and the controls were too sluggish to correct the tilt before the opposite wing tip dug into the ground. Grahame-White and Lewis Turner jumped for it and the biplane was blown over their heads, but Carr hung on and performed a ground loop with the machine. Fortunately no fire occurred and he crawled out smiling and unhurt.

Needless to say no other pilot attempted to emulate Grahame-White's splendid but foolhardy performance.

17. TWO FINE FLIGHTS

In accordance with the Government's new policy of securing specimens of the best Continental types, with a view to determining the requirements of the Naval and Military Air Services, an order had been placed for one of the latest two-seater Deperdussin monoplanes for the use of the Naval pilots at Eastchurch.

Lieut. Longmore, R.N., had visited the works in Paris on April 11th to observe the final stress tests, when the wings were loaded with sand to 2,500 lbs. On the following day, the machine made two test flights at Issy Les Molineux and, on the day after that, it was delivered by air to Eastchurch.

M. Prevost, chief test pilot of the Deperdussin firm, took off at 7 a.m., with Mr. Lawrence Santoni, who, with Lieut. J. C. Porte, R.N., represented the firm in England, in the passenger's seat. Two and three-quarter hours later a forced landing was made at Arrhes, ten miles short of Calais, to change a plug. After one hour on the ground, the journey was resumed to Calais, which was reached in fifteen minutes. Here the crew had breakfast and discussed the question of whether they should risk the Channel crossing, in view of the mist which shrouded the water. Eventually, they decided to trust their Monodep compass and took off again at noon.

A landfall was made at Deal and the monoplane landed at Eastchurch at 12.45 p.m., after being 3 hrs. 45 mins. in the air.

This was the first long distance delivery of an aircraft from the factory to the customer by air. Lieut. Longmore, R.N., who had had no previous experience of the Deperdussin, immediately put it through a series of test flights.

Miss Harriet Quimby, who was acknowledged to be the best woman pilot in the U.S.A., where she flew the Moisant monoplane, had arrived in England and had placed an order for a Bleriot (50 h.p. Gnôme). The machine was delivered to her at Deal and was tested by Gustav Hamel there.

On April 16th, Miss Quimby took off at 5.38 a.m. and flew to Dover, whence she set a compass course for Grisnez and landed at the Bleriot Aerodrome at Equihen near Boulogne about an hour later. She was thus the first woman pilot to fly across the Straits of Dover, although Miss Trehawke Davies had crossed as a passenger with Hamel, as I have already mentioned.

18. THE CREATION OF THE ROYAL FLYING CORPS

Details of the Government's proposals for developing Military and Naval aviation began to leak out during March, and the debate on the Army Estimates in the House of Commons disclosed that the sum of £320,000 had been allotted to the War Office for this purpose. No less than £90,000 was to be spent on laying out a new aerodrome on Salisbury Plain. It also appeared that thirty-six new aircraft, of which eighteen were British, had been ordered to supplement the sixteen machines already owned by the Army.

Mr. Churchill, on behalf of the Navy, was much more reticent, and no precise details were given as to the amount to be expended or the manner in which it was to be utilized.

On April 12th, a White Paper was published giving full details of the whole scheme, which had been worked out under the supervision of Col. Seely, whose practical experience of aviators and aviation had been of immense value to the Government.

In theory it was quite a good scheme.

It provided for the inclusion of the whole British Aeronautical Service, both Military and Naval, in one organization which, by special permission of H.M. The King, granted " in consideration of the specially difficult and arduous nature of the flying service," was to be known as " The Royal Flying Corps."

The Royal Flying Corps was to be divided into the following sections, namely :—1. The Central Flying School at Salisbury Plain. 2. The Military Wing. 3. The Naval Wing. 4. The Reserve, and 5. The Army Aircraft Factory at Farnborough, which was to be known thenceforth as " The Royal Aircraft Factory."

Reviewing these various divisions in order, we start with the most important, the C.F.S.

It was obvious that the prime necessity was pilots, and that these pilots must be properly trained and not merely persons who had just managed to pass for their *brevets*, and who had never flown outside an aerodrome.

At the same time it was desired to encourage the many civilian schools of flying about the country and not to deprive them of paying pupils. Accordingly, it was arranged that Military or Naval officers or civilians, wishing to take commissions in the R.F.C., should first learn the rudiments of the art at a civilian establishment, take their R.Ae.C. certificates there, and then join the C.F.S. for the necessary advanced training. If they were accepted at the C.F.S., each was to be awarded £75 towards the cost of his tuition at the civil school.

The old Army Air Battalion on Salisbury Plain was absorbed into the R.F.C., and its staff and equipment formed the nucleus around which the C.F.S. was built up.

The organization of the C.F.S. provided for three courses per annum, each of four months' duration, and instruction was to be given in the maintenance of aircraft and engines, meteorology, navigation, photography, and signalling in addition to the actual flying training.

Provision was made for ninety-one Military, forty Naval, and fifteen civilian pilots to pass through the school every year, and one-half of the Army and Navy pilots were to be of non-commissioned rank.

The Government had placed an initial order for twenty-five aeroplanes for the use of the C.F.S., and had arranged for the establishment of a Meteorological Section there under the control of Dr. Shaw of the Meteorological Office.

Thus was founded the Central Flying School of the British Air Arm, now universally recognized as the fount of all knowledge relating to practical flying, whither pilots from all over the world come to be taught the latest thing about their art, and where instructors are taught to instruct.

Next in importance was the Military Wing of the R.F.C. Obviously it would be impossible to set this up on a proper basis until the C.F.S. had got to work and manufactured the requisite number of pilots. The scheme provided however for the early establishment of seven squadrons of twelve aeroplanes each. Every officer was to be a qualified pilot, and each squadron was to have thirteen officers and the same number of non-commissioned pilots on its strength. It will be seen that eighty-four aeroplanes were required to equip the squadrons, without allowing for spare machines.

No details were given as to the organization of the Naval Wing. The Admiralty was anxiously awaiting the results of Mr. Sippe's experiments at Barrow with the Avro seaplane fitted with Com. Schwann's floats, and the memorandum merely stated that the existing establishment at Eastchurch would be maintained as an elementary flying training school, pending the production of some Naval pilots at the C.F.S. Later, the Eastchurch station was to be used for experimental purposes.

The Reserve of the Royal Flying Corps was divided into two parts. Officers of the First Reserve were to be either civilian pilots, or officers serving in the Army or Navy who kept their own aircraft or flew School machines. Evidence was to be produced at the end of each quarter that each officer had completed at least nine hours in the air, including a cross-country flight of more than one hour, in the preceding three months. Officers of the Second Reserve were to be pilots who were not under any obligation to keep up their flying, but who were to be instantly available in case of war. Pilots of the First Reserve were to be paid a retaining fee and to receive flying pay, but the Second Reserve was on a voluntary basis.

The Royal Aircraft Factory at Farnborough was deputed to train air mechanics, rebuild aeroplanes, repair the equipment of the Military and Naval Wings, and undertake the testing of new aircraft and engines, whether British or foreign.

It was emphasized that this programme was not to be extended so as to include the construction of aircraft in competition with the civil manufacturers. Unfortunately, that is exactly what did occur at a later date, by which time the civil servants in charge of the factory had established a very close *entente* with the political bosses concerned.

The Government had made arrangements for the use of private aerodromes by pilots of the R.F.C. engaged on cross-country flights, and had also made plans for the improvement of the aerodrome at Farnborough.

It will be seen that the whole scheme had been intelligently considered in detail, and that it was, on the whole, quite admirable.

But there was a most important provision to the effect that all Naval personnel in the Royal Flying Corps should be administered and paid by the Admiralty. This was the snag which was to upset the boat.

It seems almost incredible that anyone, even a politician,

could have been so obtuse as to fail to realize that a scheme which involved the joint command and administration of a force by the War Office and the Admiralty was doomed to failure. No intelligent person could anticipate for one moment that the arrogant bureaucrats at the Admiralty would be content to take the inferior position demanded of them by this project and to submit to accepting orders from their fellow civil servants at the War Office. Nor was it probable that the Admiralty would consent to contribute towards the maintenance of the C.F.S. so long as its administration remained in the hands of the " junior " Ministry.

If only the promoters had had the foresight to insist on undivided control for the new arm, the scheme would have been well nigh perfect.

19. RACING AT BROOKLANDS AND HENDON

In the middle of April some of the Brooklands pilots began to organize impromptu races amongst themselves. Mr. Handasyde undertook the handicapping with immense success. The first race, which was over a six-miles course to Chertsey Bridge and back, attracted five starters, who finished in the following order :—1, Collyns Pizey on a Bristol biplane (50 h.p. Gnôme), handicap 4 mins. 55 secs. ; 2, T. O. M. Sopwith on a Bleriot (70 h.p. Gnôme), scratch ; 3, E. V. B. Fisher on the Flanders (60 h.p. Green), 39 secs. ; 4, F. P. Raynham on a Wright biplane (50 h.p. Gnôme), 2 mins. 28 secs., and 5, H. Spencer on the reconstructed Macfie Farman type biplane (50 h.p. Gnôme), 3 mins. 12 secs. The race was won by thirty-five yards, and five seconds covered the first four !

On the following day another race was flown over a distance of about nine miles. The same machines participated except that Lieut. Lawrence (Bristol biplane, 50 h.p. Gnôme) deputized for Spencer. Sopwith won this time, with Fisher thirty-five seconds behind, and Pizey a good third.

Mr. Richard Gates, Grahame-White's enterprising manager at Hendon, had decided to popularize the aerodrome by holding regular week-end flying meetings, at which the principal attraction was to be racing round pylons erected in the aerodrome.

This form of contest is obviously of little practical use to aviation as a means of advancing the design of aircraft, but it served a useful purpose at that time by affording practice in turning for the pilots, and by getting the public accustomed to aeroplanes.

Pylon racing may be compared with dirt track racing, but cross-country racing is comparable with the Tourist Trophy contests as a valuable means of " improving the breed " of aircraft and motor-cycles respectively.

The first of the Hendon meetings took place on Saturday and Sunday, April 20th and 21st, and 22,000 people paid for admission on the two days. The most important event was a demonstration by M. Réné Caudron of the first Caudron tractor biplane (35 h.p. Anzani) to be delivered in England. This machine, which amazed everyone by its handiness and stability, was later flown by the purchaser, Mr. W. H. Ewen, in the competitions.

There were three starters in the pylon race, Hamel (Bleriot) being scratch and allowing Valentine (Bristol monoplane) 37 secs. and Hucks (Bleriot) 65 secs. Valentine finished first, but was disqualified for overtaking Hucks on the inside, so that the latter was awarded the race. Hamel was eleven seconds behind.

A cross-country race from Hendon round Harrow Church and back, was also won by Hucks from Valentine and Hamel. Lewis Turner (Farman) and W. H. Ewen (Caudron) also flew in this event, but neither finished.

20. ACCIDENT TO CODY: EWEN ON THE CAUDRON

S. F. Cody was to have competed at Hendon, but a few days previously he had met with a serious accident whilst flying as a passenger on his own machine under the care of his pupil, Lieut. Fletcher, who flew into some trees. Cody received severe injuries to his head and legs. By a cruel coincidence his son Frank, whilst cycling home to break the news to Mrs. Cody, ran over a dog and was badly hurt in the resultant smash. Father and son were brought home together unconscious.

The haphazard methods of the early pilots were well exemplified by Ewen's flights on the new Caudron. After it had been tested by its designer, Ewen flew it around the aerodrome in order to accustom himself to the controls. He then landed and decided to attempt a cross-country flight to Harrow. Soon after he had left the aerodrome he lost himself and flew about for half an hour without being able to pick up his bearings. He decided to land and ask the way, but the two rustics of whom he inquired pointed in quite different directions, so he took off again and flew on. After another thirty minutes in the air he was more thoroughly lost than ever, so he put down again on a golf course. None of the players knew the direction of Harrow or Hendon, but one of them suggested that he should follow a neighbouring railway line. He did this, and presently found himself at Harrow, but, just as he was turning on to the course for Hendon, his petrol gave out and he was forced down into a small field. By the time his mechanics arrived with supplies, it was nearly dark, but instead of leaving the machine in the field under guard for the night, Ewen determined to try to find his aerodrome. He stationed a mechanic at the far end of the field with instructions to strike matches as fast as he could to indicate the height of the hedge, whilst at Hendon flares had been lighted and rockets were sent up at intervals to guide him home. Ewen took off with the aid of the matches, followed the rockets, and made a perfect landing in pitch darkness at 8.30 p.m.

21. THE GNOSSPELIUS SEAPLANE: THREE ATTEMPTS TO FLY TO IRELAND

Mr. Gnosspelius had designed an interesting monoplane with an open lattice work fuselage of triangular cross-section, and fitted it with a large single-stepped float attached to an elaborate under-carriage. The wings were of Bleriot type but the rest of the air-craft was quite original. This was the first British seaplane to employ auxiliary wing-tip floats as an aid to stability on the water. It was flown successfully from the surface of Lake Windermere by the Avro pilot, Ronald Kemp.

Two private-owner pupils of the Bleriot school at Hendon, Messrs. Corbett-Wilson and D. L. Allen, decided to attempt a flight in company to Dublin. They left Hendon together, each in a Bleriot monoplane (50 h.p. Gnôme), on the afternoon of April 17th, but they soon became separated, Allen pursuing a much more northerly course than his friend. Corbett-Wilson landed at Almeley, a few miles north of Hereford and stayed there for the night, but Allen pushed on to Chester, after a landing at Crewe to inquire the way. The next morning he took off again and was sighted above Holyhead an hour later, steering out to sea on the course for Dublin. That was the last that was ever seen or heard of him and, no doubt, his engine let him down into the sea. He had not troubled to equip himself with a life-saving jacket. He was the tenth British pilot to pay the extreme penalty.

On the day of Allen's death, Corbett-Wilson flew on a few miles to Colva, where he was delayed for three nights, after which he proceeded as far as Fishguard. On the morning of his sixth day out from Hendon, he left Fishguard and flew across the St. George's Channel in 1 hr. 40 mins. and landed at Crane, about two miles from Enniscorthy. This was the second crossing from England to Ireland, the pioneer being Mr. Robert Loraine, who had made the passage, all except the last few yards, in 1910.

Mr. Vivian Hewitt, who had been flying his Bleriot (50 h.p. Gnôme) from a field at Rhyl with considerable success, began an attempt to fly to Dublin on the same day on which Corbett-Wilson reached Fishguard.

Hewitt had an extremely rough trip as far as Plas in Anglesey, where he was forced to land owing to the bumps making him ill. On the next day, whilst Corbett-Wilson was crossing, he reached Holyhead but was unable to continue on account of gales and fog lasting for four days. On April 26th, Hewitt took off and flew from Holyhead to Phœnix Park, Dublin, in 1 hr. 15 mins.

The distances flown by Corbett-Wilson and Vivian Hewitt on their actual sea-crossings were each about sixty-two miles, and the machines used were similar models of the same make, so that it may be presumed that Corbett-Wilson had to contend with a head wind, which would account for the substantial difference of twenty-five minutes between the times.

22. THREE CROSS-CHANNEL FLIGHTS

Gustav Hamel had resumed his aerial tour with Miss Trehawke Davies. Their Bleriot left Issy on April 25th for London *via* Brussels, but more trouble developed with the petrol feed and a forced landing was made at Compiègne. On the following morning it was decided to omit Brussels from the itinerary, and a start was made at 6 a.m. for London. Three hours later the machine landed at Hardelot to refuel and continued in the afternoon across the Channel to Canterbury, where another forced landing was made on account of a strong head wind.

Hamel left the machine at Canterbury and went to Hendon, where he won the cross-country handicap on another Bleriot from Valentine (Bristol monoplane) and Hucks (Bleriot). His victory was due much more to clever and daring cornering than to any superiority in speed, although he covered a ten-mile course out and home in 11 mins. 39 secs. from a standing start.

On April 29th, Hamel returned to Canterbury with Miss Davies and they took off again for France at 5.30 p.m. Aided by a following wind the Channel was crossed in 12 mins. 30 secs. and the Bleriot landed at Hardelot forty-two minutes out from Canterbury. On the following day they set off for Biarritz, but were forced to abandon the attempt at Antony, a short distance south-west from Paris, owing to the high wind. Three weeks later, on May 21st, Mr. Hamel and Miss Davies flew back in the same machine from Issy to Eastchurch in four stages.

M. René Caudron had produced a delightful little single seat monoplane with a 45 h.p. Anzani radial engine. The span was only 25 ft. 6 ins., and the overall length was 20 ft. 3 ins. The chord of the wings, which had the characteristic Caudron flexible trailing edge, was four feet. The fuselage was nicely streamlined and the pilot sat deep in the cockpit, with only the top of his head protruding through the padded opening.

W. H. Ewen had ordered one of these machines for use in his school at Hendon and decided to go over and fetch it back himself. After two days practice at Crotoy he left at 9.32 a.m. on May 2nd for Calais. Passing Boulogne he flew into low cloud and broke through a 300 feet ceiling into very bumpy air above Cap Gris Nez. Here he landed at 10.5 a.m., having covered almost exactly fifty miles in thirty-three minutes, at an average speed of approximately 90 m.p.h.

At 5.30 p.m. he left for Hendon, setting a course for Dover at 3,500 feet. In mid-Channel he flew into cloud and his compass began to swing. He was in great danger then, but fortunately he got a sight of the sun and found it directly behind him instead of broad on his left hand. By good fortune he picked up the English coast two miles east of Dover, where he stopped for the night. Just before he landed he hit a violent bump and his map, which he was holding in his hand, was blown overboard. After he had landed in a field, he sat in his seat watching some people running towards him, when his eye caught something fluttering on the grass ten yards away. He got out and picked it up. It was his map !

On the following day he flew to Chatham, where he encountered a black fog, rain, and a high wind. This combination was too much for him, so he wisely landed and sent the little monoplane on by train.

23. THE COVENTRY ORDNANCE BIPLANE : TAKE-OFF COMPETITIONS AT BROOKLANDS

At the end of April an interesting new machine arrived at Brooklands. This was a tractor biplane designed by Mr. W. O. Manning and built by Mr. Howard Wright. It boasted a number of new features, including an airscrew 11 ft. 6 ins. in diameter, driven by a 100 h.p. Gnôme through a 2·1 reduction gear at a normal rate of 600 r.p.m. No springs were provided for the wheels, reliance being placed on large squashy tyres similar to the modern "dough-nut." The fuselage had been carefully streamlined, but it was very wide and provided side-by-side seating for pilot and passenger. The wings were of equal chord, but the span of the top one was almost twice that of the bottom one. Twin rudders, horn-balanced both top and bottom, and horn-balanced elevators were fitted. Lateral control was by warp. Detail refinements were the provision of sliding aluminium inspection panels in the wing surfaces and the encasing of control pulleys within small streamline fairings. It was evident that a great deal of intelligent thought and much careful workmanship had been put into the production of this machine, which was known as the Coventry Ordnance.

It was tested at Brooklands by Mr. Sopwith, and proceeded to climb easily with two additional passengers seated on the bottom wing, one at each side of the fuselage.

The Brooklands pilots were amusing themselves by organizing impromptu quick starting competitions in addition to races. The first of these attracted ten entries and was won by Fleming (Bristol biplane), who came "unstuck" in 5½ secs. Eight competitors flew in the next contest which resulted in a win for Mrs. Maurice Hewlett (Farman biplane) from Sabelli on the racing Deperdussin. This was the first open event in aviation to be won by an English woman pilot. On the same day there was an exciting cross-country race to Chertsey and back. Sopwith (Bleriot) came up from scratch to catch Pizey (Bristol biplane) on the line and win by one length.

24. FLYING AT THE NAVAL REVIEW

Early in May H.M. the King held a great Naval Review at Portland, and it was decided that the Naval wing of the R.F.C. should play a prominent part in the proceedings.

One of the old pusher Shorts and the Short tractor biplane had been fitted with floats at the works at Leysdown and they were taken to Weymouth and housed in a canvas hangar with a slipway, down which they could be launched.

In addition, the old battleship *Hibernia* had been equipped with a sloping runway or platform, extending forward from her bridge and projecting beyond her stem, as it was intended that Com. Samson should give a demonstration of taking off from a ship at sea.

A Nieuport monoplane and a Deperdussin were also taken to Portland, although these were not fitted with floats. The pilots accompanying Com. Samson were Capt. Gerrard, R.M.L.I., and Lieuts. Spencer Grey and Longmore, R.N. All these pilots flew over the fleet and were joined in the air, unofficially of course, by Grahame-White (Nieuport) and B. C. Hucks (Bleriot), who had come down especially from Hendon.

Com. Samson flew both the Shorts on and off the water, and was launched successfully from the *Hibernia's* flight deck in the old pusher biplane whilst the ship was steaming at 15 knots. Earlier in the proceedings he had alighted on the water near the royal yacht and delivered a letter to the King, afterwards taking off and flying back to his slipway. Com. Samson was one of the Naval officers commanded to dine with His Majesty in the *Victoria and Albert* at the conclusion of the Review.

The Naval aircraft were brought back to Sheerness in the *Hibernia* and Com. Samson took off from the improvised flight deck on one of the Short seaplanes whilst the ship was steaming past Dover. He intended to fly to Eastchurch but engine trouble forced him down on the sea near Westgate. The destroyer *Recruit* took him in tow, and he retained his seat until Sheerness harbour had been reached safely. This Short was fitted with wheels as well as floats, and was the first British amphibian aircraft.

The latest pilot to qualify at the Eastchurch station was Capt. Godfrey Paine, R.N., of *H.M.S. Actaeon*. This senior officer received only four days tuition before passing his tests.

25. THE PUBLIC SAFETY COMMITTEE OF THE R.Ae.C.

The R.Ae.C. had established a sub-committee charged with the duty, now performed by the Accidents Branch of the Air Ministry, of carrying out investigations into the causes of all serious accidents to aviators. Persons with expert knowledge of aviation, not necessarily members of the Club, were appointed to inquire into and report upon all accidents occurring in the area under their charge. Mr. W. O. Manning was the Club's representative at Brooklands, and to him fell the unhappy task of carrying out the first investigation.

Mr. E. V. B. Fisher, the brilliant Hanriot pilot, and his passenger, an American financier named Mason, were killed on May 13th at Brooklands, whilst flying in the Flanders monoplane.

The Committee found that Mr. Fisher had attempted a left-hand turn at about 100 feet whilst flying tail down, and that the machine began a sideslip which had developed into a vertical dive before it struck the ground. It is obvious that actually the pilot stalled on a climbing turn, without sufficient height to recover.

It was thought that Mr. Fisher, who either fell or jumped out before the aircraft hit the ground, may have been thrown forward on to the control column, and, indeed, this may have been the case. In any event, the occurrence emphasized the necessity for safety belts.

Mr. Fisher, who was intimately concerned in Mr. A. V. Roe's earliest experiments, had been granted his certificate (No. 77) on May 2nd, 1911, and had a considerable number of hours to his credit. He had worked with Howard Flanders in the first permanent hangar to be erected at Brooklands, on the construction of the latter's first monoplane, and had been secretary of the original Shed-holders' Committee and the Founder of the first Brooklands Aero Club. He had learned to fly on the Hanriot monoplane, and had also flown the Vickers-R.E.P., on which he had a serious crash, and had then once more joined forces with his old friend, Howard Flanders, on whose latest machine he met his death. This accident resulted in a very serious loss to British aviation. Fisher was a man who could ill be spared and the aircraft, which was destroyed by the fire which followed the smash, was a most promising machine.

26. REVIEW OF THE MILITARY WING, R.F.C.

Following on the Naval Review H.M. King George V visited Farnborough and inspected the Military Wing of the R.F.C. He was received by Maj. F. H. Sykes of the 15th Hussars, who had been appointed to command the Military Wing, and witnessed flights by Capts. Burke and Loraine, and Lieuts. Fox, Reynolds, and Barrington-Kennett. The aircraft flown before His Majesty were three examples of the B.E. type, built at the Royal Aircraft Factory, a Nieuport and a Deperdussin. The new Avro biplane, which had been built to a War Office order, was paraded but not flown.

Mr. Geoffrey de Havilland flew the latest edition of his B.E. biplane and dived it from 2,500 ft. to 100 ft. in order to demonstrate its strength. This machine differed from his first two models in having staggered wings, a longer fuselage, and a four-bladed airscrew which was driven by a 50 h.p. Gnôme engine.

It was announced that a Naval officer, Capt. Godfrey M. Paine, R.N., had been appointed to the command of the C.F.S., and that Com. C. R. Samson, R.N. was to command the Naval Wing of the R.F.C. No one could quarrel with the latter choice, but common-sense should have dictated the appointment of an Army officer to control the sole source of the supply of pilots for the Military Wing, R.F.C.

27. WHITSUN RACING

The Whitsun meeting at Hendon produced some excitement. Mr. Cody flew over from Farnborough in the "Cathedral" to participate, but withdrew from the main event, a cross-country race over forty-four miles, as he was dissatisfied with his allotted handicap. This race was won by Valentine on his Bristol monoplane, in 52 mins. 20 secs., at an average speed of 53 m.p.h., with Hucks (Bleriot) just over a minute behind.

Valentine also won another cross-country race over the short course to Elstree and back, and the first of the pylon races.

The second pylon race was abandoned as the result of a serious accident to Ewen, who was caught by a bump whilst cornering steeply, low down. The lower wing tip of his Caudron biplane touched the ground and the whole machine performed a ground loop, the pilot being catapulted bodily through the top wing.

Fortunately, no bones were broken, but Ewen was carried off on a stretcher with extensive cuts and bruises, whilst the little biplane was reduced to firewood.

A more serious smash befell Prensiell, whose Bleriot monoplane (35 h.p. Anzani) suddenly dived into the ground from fifty feet, no doubt as the result of a flick stall. Prensiell suffered a broken right leg.

There was brisk competition at Brooklands also during Whitsun. Gordon Bell had returned from Buc, and was flying a Bleriot in great style. A quick take-off contest was won by Raynham from Sopwith by one-fifth sec., both competitors using the same machine, M. Blondeau's Farman, for this event.

A landing competition was the next item and this was won easily by Sopwith, who put his Bleriot down within two feet of the mark. Raynham on the Farman was second, and Hotchkiss, one of the Bristol instructors, took third place on Mr. Morison's Bristol monoplane.

A relay race with teams of two was won by Sopwith and Spencer from Rhodes-Moorhouse, who had moved his quarters from Huntingdon to Brooklands, and Hotchkiss.

So many entries were received for the cross-country race to Chertsey and back that it had to be run in two heats and a final.

The eventual winner was F. P. Raynham (Burgess-Wright), with Collyns Pizey (Bristol biplane) and L. Macdonald on the Vickers R.E.P. monoplane (60 h.p. Vickers) second and third respectively.

28. THE FIRST AERIAL DERBY

The *Daily Mail* newspaper had come forward once more to aid in popularizing aviation. This time it sponsored a race round London for a hundred-guinea trophy and cash prizes totalling £460. Messrs. Grahame-White and Harold Barlow were responsible for the organization.

The race, which was christened "The Aerial Derby," started and finished at Hendon, and passed round a circuit eighty-one miles in length, with turning points at Kempton Park, Esher, Purley, Purfleet, Epping, and High Barnet.

An intensive campaign by the *Daily Mail* whipped up enormous public interest in the event, and pouring rain in the morning, followed by a dull afternoon, did not prevent 45,000 people from paying for admission at Hendon on June 8th. This was but a small section of the multitude which witnessed the race, for the whole course of eighty-one miles was thronged with spectators, who clustered in tens of thousands at each turning point. The racing pilots were unable to recognize Esher Common as a landmark, as it was literally blackened by the swarming crowd. It was estimated that no less than *three million people* saw the contest.

The race brought out three interesting machines not hitherto seen in public in England. One of these was the latest model of the Hanriot monoplane, entered by Mr. S. V. Sippe. Mr. Sippe had spent some weeks at the Hanriot headquarters at Rheims, after the abandonment of the Avro-Schwann seaplane trials at Barrow. He had become an exceedingly skilful monoplane pilot in a short space of time, had flown every machine that was available at the factory, and had obtained the post of chief pilot to the newly-established English branch of the Hanriot firm.

Another important newcomer was the latest Maurice Farman biplane (70 h.p. Renault), which was the first machine to be delivered in England to Mr. Holt Thomas, managing director of the Aircraft Co., Ltd., and sole *concessionaire* for the products of the Farman brothers in this country. This imposing biplane was flown in the race by M. Pierre Verrier.

Quite the most attractive, and incidentally the second fastest, entry in the race was the little single-seat Caudron monoplane (45 h.p. Anzani radial engine), on which Ewen had made his great flight from Crotoy to Chatham, and which was handled in the race by M. Maurice Guillaux, who had flown over from Issy in a two-seater Caudron biplane, which he had to deliver to Mr. Ewen. The journey was made in four stages, via Crotoy, Walmer, and Eastchurch, and Mr. A. M. Ramsay came over in the passenger's seat.

The competitors took off singly at intervals of one minute in the following order: 1, S. V. Sippe (Hanriot monoplane); 2, T. O. M. Sopwith (Bleriot two-seater monoplane); 3, G. Hamel (Bleriot two-seater monoplane); 4, P. Verrier (Maurice-Farman two-seater biplane); 5, Rhodes-Moorhouse (Radley-Moorhouse Bleriot-type monoplane); 6, M. Guillaux (Caudron single-seat monoplane); and 7, J. Valentine (Bristol two-seater monoplane).

Sippe was soon in trouble as his engine let him down at Hounslow, but after a few minutes tinkering he got back into the air and passed the first turn in third place. He missed the next turn, and while he was trying to locate it, he was forced down a second time at Merstham where he abandoned.

Verrier had his map strapped to his back and was carrying a journalist in the passenger's seat, whose duty it was to look after the navigation. The plan was singularly unsatisfactory, more especially as the pilot insisted on flying amongst clouds at 2,000 feet. This machine almost reached Brighton and did not find its way back to Hendon until it was nearly dark, after three hours twenty minutes continuous flying, and one forced landing to ask the way.

Rhodes-Moorhouse also lost his way and did not discover his error until he was over Sevenoaks, but he regained the course without having to alight to make inquiries. Not so Valentine, who lost himself near Epsom and landed in a field where there was a man. This individual was too overcome by the sight of the Bristol to do anything but gape, so Valentine left him gaping and hopped over the hedge into another field where he had observed some more intelligent spectators, from whom he discovered his whereabouts.

The race resolved itself into a thrilling three-cornered contest between Sopwith, Guillaux, and Hamel. Sopwith's Bleriot was the fastest machine and he soon passed Sippe and began to draw away from the others. The diminutive Caudron was very little slower, and from sixth position it tore through the field in pursuit of Sopwith and overtook Hamel's Bleriot, which had started three minutes before it, on the leg to the south of the river.

Sopwith finished first but was disqualified for turning inside the mark at Purley, which was very hard luck as, being unable to see the Russell School which formed the actual mark, he had made an extra wide sweep for good measure. His Bleriot was the same model as Hamel's, but he had obtained several extra m.p.h. by covering in the back part of the fuselage with canvas.

Sopwith's disqualification seemed to leave Guillaux (Caudron) with the race in his hand, and he came into view of the crowd at Hendon ten minutes after Sopwith had crossed the line. Just as he approached the aerodrome, his engine spluttered and stopped, and he brought off a skilful forced landing within a mile of the finish. He had run out of petrol!

Gustav Hamel brought his Bleriot home, with Miss Trehawke Davies in her accustomed place in the passenger's seat, six minutes after Guillaux had been forced down, and was proclaimed the winner. It would have been a lucky win, but Hamel had flown a reasonably good course and, moreover, he was handicapped by carrying a passenger, so no one could have grudged him the trophy and the £250 first prize. Sopwith, however, was justly dissatisfied with his disqualification and lodged an appeal. Five months later the stewards of the R.Ae.C. reversed the decision of the race committee and declared him the winner, thus relegating Hamel to second place. Sopwith's time was 1 hr. 23 mins. 8⅖ secs., and his average speed 58·5 m.p.h.

Rhodes-Moorhouse returned from his excursion to Sevenoaks twenty-one minutes after Hamel had landed, but in time to secure third place, and Valentine also finished the course, more than three-quarters of an hour after the winner.

After the race, Mr. Grahame-White gave a thrilling exhibition of night flying. A large acetylene searchlight had been fitted to his old Farman biplane and others were arranged to act as floodlights, shining down from the top of one of the pylons and from the judge's box. As there were numerous unlighted pylons dotted about the aerodrome and the acetylene lamps provided were not very efficient, the experiment was highly spectacular and thoroughly dangerous. Fortunately, Mr. Grahame-White's skill was equal to the risks involved.

Three days after the first Aerial Derby, Gustav Hamel had the honour of giving a demonstration before H.M. the King at Ranelagh. Capt. Mark Kerr, R.N., accompanied him as passenger in his Bleriot, and Hamel negotiated the difficult approach to and landing on the small polo ground with consummate skill. His subsequent exhibition flight was one of the most spectacular displays yet seen in England, and His Majesty was intensely interested and had a long talk with the pilot as soon as he had landed.

29. B. C. HUCKS: FIRST N.C.O. PILOTS IN R.F.C.

Mr. B. C. Hucks had agreed to transfer his allegiance from the Grahame-White Company to Mr. Harold Barlow, who had paid a fee of £1,000 for his release from his contract. Mr. Barlow had ordered several modern machines for exhibition and passenger-carrying purposes, and he took Hucks across to Paris to fetch his first investment, a two-seater Bleriot monoplane (70 h.p. Gnôme).

After a preliminary test, during which he attempted to circle the Eiffel Tower but flew into cloud and very nearly collided with it instead, Hucks left Issy on June 17th for Hendon via Hardelot, with his new employer in the passenger's seat. There was little wind at the start, but conditions deteriorated as they

"Flight" photo

22.—The Ancestor of the Moth: Mr. Geoffrey de Havilland's B.E. Tractor Biplane (70 h.p. Renault).

Facing page 160

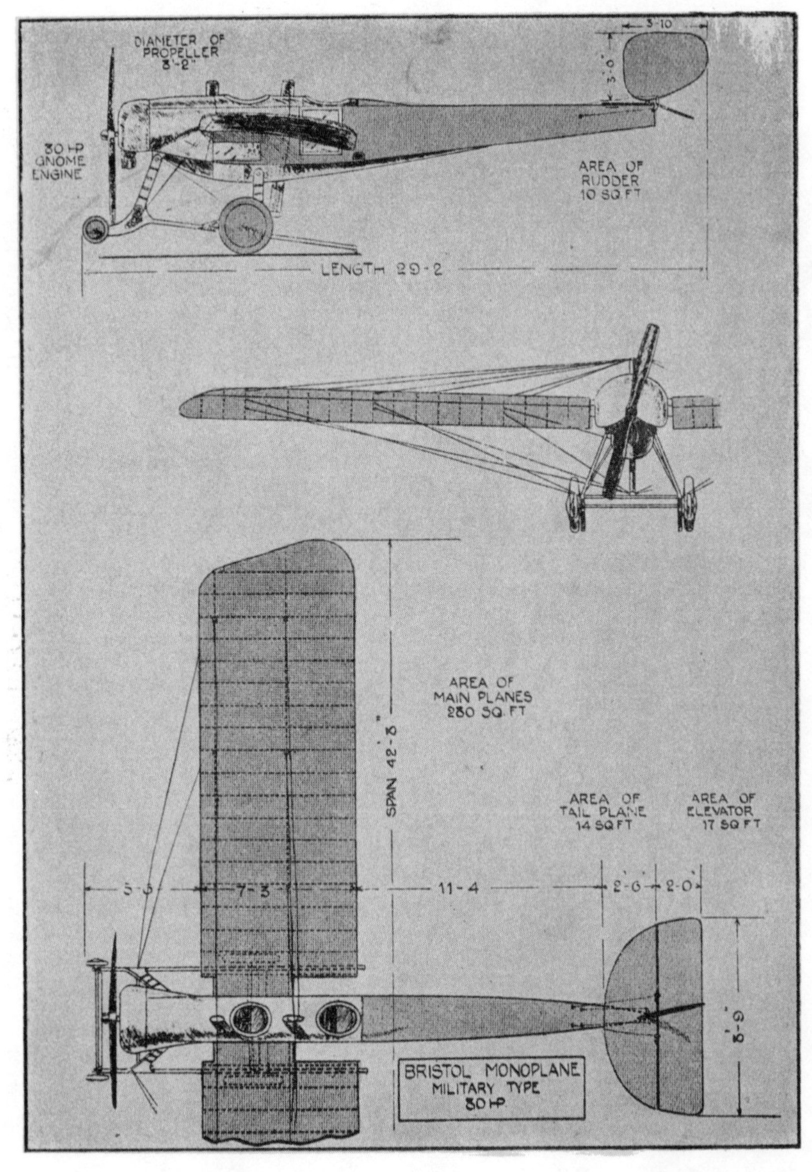

7.—The Bristol Monoplane (80 h.p. Gnôme) designed by Mons. Coanda for the Military Trials.

Facing page 161

approached the coast, and the bumps became so severe that it was difficult to operate the hand petrol pump. Hucks stuck to it, however, and finally arrived above Hardelot in a 40 m.p.h. gale. His first attempt to land on the beach was almost disastrous, as a savage gust of wind lifted him thirty feet at the crucial moment. Fortunately, he had the presence of mind to switch on his engine and make another approach, which was entirely successful. The Bleriot had covered 168 miles non-stop in 2 hrs. 25 mins., at an average speed of 69 m.p.h.

Two days later Hucks left for Hendon, and after a quick Channel crossing the engine stopped within gliding distance of Eastchurch aerodrome. The mechanics there diagnosed four broken inlet valve springs, which were replaced, and the Bleriot took off once more and arrived at Hendon without further incident, thus completing a grand flight in most difficult circumstances.

Corporal Frank Kidd, who had accompanied Lieut. B. H. Barrington-Kennett on his world's record flight for the Mortimer Singer prize, was the first N.C.O. of the R.F.C. to secure his *brevet* (No. 228), and he was followed a few days later by Staff-Sergt. R. H. V. Wilson. Both men received their instruction on Bristol biplanes from the officer pilots of the C.F.S. at Salisbury Plain.

30. THE "DAILY MAIL" TOUR: THE AE.C.F. GRAND PRIX

The *Daily Mail* newspaper had commissioned that fine pilot M. Salmet to tour the more out-of-the-way parts of England on his Bleriot, with a view to affording the country people an opportunity to witness some first-class flying. The tour was an immense success. Salmet worked very hard and flew very well. In the first four weeks there were twenty-four days on which flying was possible and eighteen of these saw his Bleriot in the air. The route lay through the difficult country of Devon and Cornwall, and called for dozens of landings in fields near remote villages, but the Bleriot stood up splendidly to this exacting test.

Following on this success the *Daily Mail* engaged Grahame-White, Gustav Hamel, W. H. Ewen, Lieut. Parke, R.N., and MM. Hubert and Fischer to fly aeroplanes and seaplanes in various parts of the country.

The race for the Grand Prix of the *Aero Club de France* was flown off on June 16th and 17th, and the course was over seven laps of a circuit starting and finishing at Angers. The total distance was 1,100 kilometres (683 miles).

This race attracted most of the best French pilots, and England was represented by Gustav Hamel, who took Mr. E. V. Sassoon as passenger in his two-seater Bleriot. No British aircraft competed.

The conditions on the first day were terrible, the course being swept by heavy rainstorms, driven before a gusty wind. Espanet

(Nieuport) led on the first lap, with Hamel seventeen minutes behind in second place, and Roland Garros (Bleriot), who had suffered a forced landing for an engine adjustment, third.

Hamel gave up on the second lap as the terrible bumping he had received had made him ill, and Espanet went out in the third round. By the end of the first day only Roland Garros remained in the contest and he succeeded in completing the course, thereby collecting 75,000 francs (£3,000) in prize money.

Mr. H. J. D. Astley appeared at Angers during the meeting and gave exhibition flights on an R.E.P. monoplane.

31. GRAHAME-WHITE'S WEDDING: DOUBLE FATALITY AT C.F.S.

On June 29th, Mr. Grahame-White was married to Miss Dorothy Taylor of New York City at Widford. The occasion was seized upon as a means of attracting further attention to the practical uses of aviation. It was arranged that the reception should take place at Sir Daniel Gooch's magnificent mansion, "Hylands," which boasts a smooth lawn several acres in extent, forming a convenient aerodrome.

The bridegroom flew to "Hylands" for the wedding on his old Howard-Wright, and landed on the lawn. On the morning of the wedding, M. Pierre Verrier (Maurice Farman) and Mr. B. C. Hucks (Bleriot) also arrived by air from Hendon, and the latter flew over to the church and landed in an adjacent field. As the couple emerged after the ceremony, he took off and sprinkled all and sundry with copious showers of confetti. During the reception exhibitions were given by Hucks and Verrier for the entertainment of the guests, amongst whom were eight well-known pilots, including Mrs. de Beauvoir Stocks.

A double tragedy occurred at the C.F.S. Salisbury Plain on July 5th. Capt. E. B. Loraine, who was one of the most capable and experienced pilots of the R.F.C., and who had learned to fly on a Valkyrie monoplane at Hendon, was flying a Nieuport monoplane (Gnôme) with Staff-Sergt. Wilson in the passenger's seat. Soon after taking off the pilot attempted a sharp turn, but the machine sideslipped inwards, and then the nose dropped and she dived vertically into the ground from 400 feet. Both the occupants were killed.

Evidence was given at the inquest by Cpl. Ridd to the effect that he had flown as passenger with Capt. Loraine on a flight immediately preceding the fatal one and a similar incident had then occurred, the machine slipping out of a steep turn and diving towards the ground. On that occasion the turn was begun at 1,000 feet and the pilot had managed to pull out of the dive with height to spare.

It is obvious that Capt. Loraine was suffering severely from over-confidence, and it is difficult to justify his action in repeating a manœuvre which he knew from such recent experience to be dangerous, without first attaining a safe height. This accident once more emphasized in no uncertain manner the vital necessity for gaining plenty of height when about to attempt unusual evolutions.

32. LONG DISTANCE SEAPLANE FLIGHTS: MR. F. P. RAYNHAM

It had been arranged for the Naval Wing of the R.F.C. to conduct certain experiments in conjunction with the Fleet at Portsmouth, and accordingly it was decided that two of the Short tractor biplanes (70 h.p. Gnômes) fitted with floats should be flown there from Eastchurch.

These machines were amphibious and Lieut. L'Estrange Malone, R.N., flew one of them from Eastchurch and alighted on the water at Sheerness beside *H.M.S. London*, which took the biplane and its pilot on board and set out for Portsmouth. When steaming at fifteen knots, at a distance of nineteen miles from the dockyard, Lieut. L'Estrange Malone took off from the battleship's flight deck and flew on ahead to the shore. He was thus the second pilot to perform this feat.

On July 4th, Com. Samson with Lieut. Trewin, and Lieut. Spencer Grey with Lieut. Sheppard, on two similar Shorts set out to make the journey of 196 miles round the coastline from Eastchurch to Portsmouth. Lieut. Grey had a forced landing at Newhaven for engine adjustments, but soon resumed and finished the course on the same day, but Com. Samson flew right through without landing, in a little over three hours. This splendid flight was the longest non-stop point-to-point cross-country trip yet made by a British pilot.

At the conclusion of the manœuvres Com. Samson flew the same machine from Portsmouth to Harwich, with one stop at Dover for the night. The total distance of this journey was 250 miles. These brilliant achievements finally dispelled any lingering doubts about the efficiency of the Short Bros.' latest product, and emphasized once more Com. Samson's outstanding ability as a pilot.

Mr. T. O. M. Sopwith had started a school of flying at Brooklands where several pupils had been turned out on Howard-Wright, Burgess-Wright and Farman machines, amongst them being Capt. T. Ince Webb-Bowen. Mr. Sopwith was too busy to do much instructing himself and the pupils had been left in the capable hands of Mr. F. P. Raynham, who acted as manager of the school.

Raynham had been offered the post of chief pilot to Mr. Howard Flanders, in place of the unfortunate E. V. B. Fisher, and he accepted this position. The new Flanders monoplane, of which a batch of four had been built to a War Office order, was a beautiful machine fitted with a 70 h.p. Renault engine.

Sopwith himself had produced a curious hybrid in the form of a tractor biplane with the wings of a Wright, a Farman undercarriage, and a 70 h.p. Gnôme motor.

33. GRAHAME-WHITE AND VALENTINE CROSS THE CHANNEL

Grahame-White had purchased the very latest edition of the Henry Farman (Gnôme). He went over to Paris and flew the machine back by stages with his chief engineer, Carr, as passenger. This magnificent pusher biplane was a most imposing aircraft, built up largely of steel tubing and having a span of fifty-seven feet, and was sold with a float undercarriage which could be changed for the wheel landing gear in ninety minutes by skilled mechanics.

Grahame-White adopted the practical course of flying it as a land machine as far as Boulogne, where he fitted his floats and flew to Folkestone. His land undercarriage followed in his yacht and was fitted once more for the remainder of the journey to London.

The machine had a very flat glide, so much so, that when Grahame-White and Carr arrived at Hendon they had to make five complete circuits of the aerodrome in gliding down from 900 feet. It must have had an excellent take-off too, for Grahame-White had succeeded in getting it off with Carr aboard from the soft shingle beach near Folkestone Harbour.

James Valentine temporarily discarded his Bristol monoplane and returned to his old Deperdussin for his ambitious project of making three crossings of the Straits of Dover in two days. He put up a splendid performance.

Leaving Dover on July 4th, he flew across the water to Wissant in thirty-five minutes, and subsequently took off again and flew non-stop back to Hendon. On the next day, he flew from Hendon to Abbeville, where he stayed the night, continuing to Paris on the following morning.

34. BRISTOL SCHOOL'S RECORD: A FATAL CRASH

At the end of July the Bristol Company was temporarily evicted from the Salisbury Plain depôt on account of their hangar accommodation there being required for the aircraft which were gathering to compete in the Military trials. Only a few of the monoplanes and two of the tractor biplanes were permitted to remain, the school machines being sent over to Brooklands together with the pupils.

The Brooklands branch was then in charge of Messrs. Hotchkiss and Merriam, and they took over all the Salisbury machines and pupils as well as their own, as M. Jullerot and Messrs. Gordon England, Howard Pixton, and Busteed, remained at the Plain to look after the Company's competition aircraft.

Hotchkiss and Merriam set out to show Brooklands what the Bristol Company could do, and their fleet of eight machines was up and down continually all day long with more than twenty pupils. In seven days over 300 separate flights were made, totalling nearly forty hours in the air, and one *brevet* was captured each day. The successful pupils were Maj. J. F. A. Higgins, Capts. C. P. Nicholas and A. M. Macdonell, Lieuts. F. F. Waldron and K. P. Atkinson, and Messrs. Sydney Pickles and R. G. Holyoake.

The two instructors retired to bed for a day and a night at the conclusion of this strenuous week, which was not surprising since the flying day started at 4 a.m. and continued till darkness fell. It was the practice at some schools for the instructor to fly over his pupils' houses at dawn in order to get them out of bed.

The jubilation felt by the pilots and pupils of the Bristol school at the splendid results which were being achieved was abruptly cut off by a fatal accident to Mr. Lindsay Campbell, who had qualified on May 19th, his forty-ninth birthday, on a Bristol biplane. He had been commissioned by the Australian Government to take a course of aviation preparatory to organizing an Australian Flying Corps.

Mr. Campbell set off on the morning of August 3rd, with the object of putting in some practice circuits of the Brooklands aerodrome on one of the 50 h.p. Bristol monoplanes. He was flying at 300 feet when the engine stopped, and it appeared to the onlookers that he had switched off. Instead of going into a glide Mr. Campbell held the nose up and the machine stalled and dropped a wing, afterwards going into a dive. The engine then came on for a few revolutions and the pilot pulled out of the dive, but the engine immediately stopped again and once more the nose was held up until a second stall occurred and the machine dived into the ground. The aircraft was not very badly damaged but Mr. Campbell was flung against the padded front edge of the cockpit with such force that he suffered injuries which proved fatal.

It is probable that had he been strapped into his seat, he would have escaped injury. It was his second flight on the monoplane.

35. RHODES-MOORHOUSE ON A BREGUÊT: PROGRESS OF THE "DAILY MAIL" TOURS

Mr. Rhodes-Moorhouse, who had learned to fly on a Bleriot and had had no experience of biplanes, went to Douai to collect a Breguêt tractor biplane and bring it over to England to compete in the Military trials. Accompanied by his wife and a friend he took off from Douai at 6.30 a.m. on August 4th, and set a course for Boulogne via Arras and Montreuil. He crossed the Channel between Boulogne and Dungeness in bad weather conditions and passed through two heavy rainstorms *en route*. Very bumpy air was encountered above Romney Marsh and Moorhouse decided to land at Bethersden near Ashford. Unfortunately he collided with a tree in doing so and damaged the Breguêt considerably, though without hurting himself or his crew. This was the first crossing of the Channel by a pilot with two passengers.

The *Daily Mail's* pilots were spreading the gospel of aviation far and wide about the countryside. M. Salmet visited Northampton, Colchester, Brightlingsea, Clacton, Frinton, Walton on the Naze, and Southend, whilst the Henry Farman seaplane was flown alternately by MM. Fischer and Hubert at Southsea, Bournemouth, Weymouth, Teignmouth, and Torquay. Another Henry Farman seaplane gave passenger flights from the beach at Eastbourne, Bexhill, Hastings, Brighton, and Cowes, I.O.W. This machine was handled by Mr. J. L. Travers of the G.W. school at Hendon, and Mr. Grahame-White himself supported him on a Paulhan-Curtiss seaplane. Mr. Ewen had trouble with his Caudron during his journey north, but Mr. Hucks put in some good work at Lincoln, Yarmouth, and Lowestoft, whilst Mr. Hamel, after giving some exhibitions at Sunderland and Newcastle on his Bleriot, crossed to the Isle of Man by steamer and commenced a tour of the island.

36. THE SOPWITH SCHOOL: BRITISH ALTITUDE RECORD

Mr. Perry had taken over the post of pilot-instructor to the Sopwith school at Brooklands in lieu of Mr. Raynham. He was conspicuously successful and his flying of the Burgess-Wright (Gnôme) in the races was a revelation to the less experienced competitors. Mr. Perry was the first to appreciate the fact that maximum speeds were attainable close to the ground, and he flew his races amongst the tree tops with great dash, easily beating faster machines whose pilots adopted the more cautious system of climbing up to a safe height before setting off round the course. Amongst his pupils was Maj. Hugh Montague Trenchard, who was destined to become the first Marshal of the Royal Air Force, and who took his R.Ae.C. Certificate (No. 270) on the school's old Henry Farman biplane (Gnôme) on July 31st.

Mr. Geoffrey de Havilland made a magnificent performance in the B.E.2 tractor biplane of his own design, which had been built by the Royal Aircraft Factory at Farnborough, and which was fitted with a Renault engine of 70 h.p. At 5 a.m. on August 12th, he took off from Salisbury Plain with Maj. F. H. Sykes, Commandant of the Military Wing, R.F.C., in the passenger's seat, on an attempt to break the British height record.

The machine weighed 1,274 lbs., to which must be added fuel and oil for three hours and 315 lbs. for the pilot and passenger. The 1,000 foot mark was passed in 2 mins. 55 secs., and 7,000 feet was reached in thirty-five minutes. About forty minutes later, Mr. de Havilland gave up trying to force the machine any higher as he had been stationary at 10,560 feet for half an hour. During the climb the aeroplane had passed through two layers of cloud and both the occupants were lost. On descending they noticed a railway station and flew past it low down in order to read the name "Hermitage" on the signboard. They followed this line to Newbury, branched off to Andover and landed at Amesbury at 8 a.m.

There could have been no more convincing demonstration of the efficiency of Mr. de Havilland's design than this great flight to 10,560 feet with a nominal 70 h.p. and a useful load in excess of 450 lbs.

The altitude was officially accepted by the R.Ae.C. as a British record whether with or without a passenger.

37. THAMES FLIGHT BY F. K. McCLEAN: OPENING OF THE C.F.S.

Mr. F. K. McClean had a Short pusher biplane equipped with floats housed at Harty Ferry, and he thought it would be a good idea to use it for the purpose of a business trip to London. Accordingly he started off and followed the course of the Thames. He passed between the upper and lower spans of the Tower Bridge and then proceeded to fly *underneath* all the remaining bridges to Westminster, where he alighted. The police made him taxi all the way back to Shadwell Basin and he damaged one of his floats, through striking a barge which was moored there, whilst taking off.

The R.Ae.C. issued an edict forbidding all flights above the Thames pending a joint conference with the Army, Navy, and Police authorities with a view to formulating some regulations to control such flights.

On August 17th, the Central Flying School of the R.F.C. at Upavon on Salisbury Plain was formally opened, when seventeen pupils commenced the first course. The Commandant was Capt. Godfrey Paine, R.N., and his Assistant Commandant was Lieut.-Col. Cook, R.G.A. The four instructors were Capt. Fulton, R.A., Capt. Gerrard, R.M.L.I., Capt. Broke-Smith, R.E., and Lieut. Longmore, R.N., and they had seven aeroplanes at their disposal. This instructional fleet was composed entirely of biplanes, and comprised two Avros, two Shorts, one Maurice Farman, one Henry Farman, and a Bristol.

38. THE MILITARY TRIALS

(*a*) The Entrants, (*b*) The Officials, (*c*) Constructional Requirements, (*d*) Quick Assembly Tests, (*e*) The Three Hours Test, (*f*) Climbing Tests, (*g*) Gliding Tests, (*h*) Consumption Tests, (*i*) Calculated Range, (*j*) Speed Tests, (*k*) Speed Range, (*l*) Landing Competition, (*m*) Quick Take-Off Tests, (*n*) Rough Weather Trial, (*o*) Summary of Results, (*p*) The Awards, (*q*) The Awards Criticized, (*r*) The B.E.2, (*s*) General Remarks, (*t*) A Fatal Accident, (*u*) An Observed Spin, (*v*) Flying without an Elevator.

(a) *The Entrants.*

Throughout the month of August the competitions for military aeroplanes, which had been so eagerly awaited by both British and foreign aircraft constructors, were flown off at Salisbury Plain.

As this trial was the most searching test to which flying machines had ever been subjected in Great Britain, or indeed anywhere in the world, I propose to describe it in considerable detail, and will endeavour to present the results in the neatest manner by means of tables.

Thirty-one different aeroplanes were entered and they are tabulated below together with the names of the pilots originally nominated to fly them :—

Aircraft	*Type*	*Engine*	*Pilot*
(*a*) *All-British Aircraft.*			
1. Avro ...	Tractor biplane	60 Green	Lieut. W. Parke, R.N.
2. Avro ...	Tractor biplane	60–80 A.B.C.	R. L. Charteris
3. Flanders ...	Tractor biplane	100 A.B.C.	F. P. Raynham
4. Harper ...	Tractor monoplane	60 Green	——
5. Mersey ...	Pusher monoplane	45 Isaacson	R. C. Fenwick

Note.—Of these machines Nos. 2 and 4 took no part in the competition. Nos. 2 and 3 were unable to fly because their A.B.C. engines were not completed in time, but No. 3 passed through the ground tests without its engine. The most interesting aircraft in this section was the Avro, which was the first successful all-enclosed aeroplane constructed in England. Pilot and passenger sat in tandem, in a narrow cabin protected by celluloid windows, and the fuselage, which was very narrow, filled the whole of the gap between the wings. This was the only cabin aircraft in the competition.

Aircraft	*Type*	*Engine*	*Pilot*
(*b*) *Aircraft designed and built in Great Britain fitted with foreign engines*			
6. Bristol ...	Tractor biplane	100 Gnôme	C. H. Pixton
7. Bristol ...	Tractor biplane	70 Daimler Mercedes	E. C. Gordon England
8. Coventry Ordnance ...	Tractor biplane	100 Gnôme	T. O. M. Sopwith
9. Coventry Ordnance ...	Tractor biplane	110 Chenu	T. O. M. Sopwith
10. Piggott ...	Tractor biplane	35 Anzani	Parr
11. Cody ...	Pusher biplane	120 Austro-Daimler	S. F. Cody
12. Bristol ...	Tractor monoplane	80 Gnôme	H. Busteed
13. Bristol ...	Tractor monoplane	80 Gnôme	J. Valentine
14. Vickers ...	Tractor monoplane	70 Viale	L. F. McDonald
15. Martin Handasyde ...	Tractor monoplane	75 Chenu	Gordon Bell
16. Handley-Page	Tractor monoplane	70 Gnôme	H. Petre
17. Cody ...	Pusher monoplane	120 Austro-Daimler	S. F. Cody
18. Aerial Wheel	Pusher monoplane	——	——

Note.—Of these machines Nos. 9, 10, 17, and 18, took no part in the proceedings. Both the Coventry Ordnance (No. 9), and the Martin Handasyde (No. 15), were detained on the ground most of the time by reason of a serious defect in the magneto drive of their Chenu engines. The Cody monoplane was a freak and Cody was wise to leave it behind, whilst the Piggott, which was obviously too small to lift two people, was damaged in taxying, and never got into the air, even with one up. The mysterious Aerial Wheel did not emerge from its shed.

Aircraft	*Type*	*Engine*	*Pilot*
(*c*) *Foreign Aeroplanes built in England*			
19. Deperdussin	Tractor monoplane	100 Gnôme	Jules Vedrines
20. Deperdussin	Tractor monoplane	100 Anzani	Lieut. J. C. Porte, R.N.
(*d*). *Foreign Aeroplanes*			
21. Hanriot ...	Tractor monoplane	100 Gnôme	Bielovucic
22. Hanriot ...	Tractor monoplane	100 Gnôme	S. V. Sippe
23. Bleriot ...	Tractor monoplane	70 Gnôme	Perreyon
24. Bleriot ...	Tractor monoplane	70 Gnôme	G. Hamel
25. Deperdussin	Tractor monoplane	100 Gnôme	Prevost
26. Borel ...	Tractor monoplane	80 Gnôme	Chambenois
27. Kny ...	Tractor monoplane	100 Mercedes	Lieut. Bier
28. Lohner ...	Tractor biplane	120 Austro-Daimler	Lieut. von Blaschke
29. Breguêt ...	Tractor biplane	110 Canton Unné	Moineau
30. Breguêt ...	Tractor biplane	110 Canton Unné	Rhodes-Moorhouse
31. M. Farman	Pusher biplane	70 Renault	Verrier

Note.—Of this last batch the Breguêt, No. 30, had been crashed by Rhodes-Moorhouse on its way to England, as already recorded, and the Kny, Lohner, and Borel machines failed to put in an appearance.

Allowing for withdrawals on account of the various causes indicated above, the competition resolved itself into a contest between nineteen machines comprising two all-British aircraft, the Avro and the Mersey, eight British aeroplanes with foreign engines, including the four Bristols, one of the Coventry Ordnance biplanes, Cody's "Cathedral" and the Vickers and Handley-Page monoplanes, and nine foreign machines consisting of three Deperdussins (two of which were British built), two Hanriots, two Bleriots, the Maurice Farman, and a Breguêt.

Altogether it was a formidable collection of aircraft and was fairly representative of the best efforts of both the British and foreign manufacturers. The majority of the machines were to a great extent experimental, and formed a most interesting study both from the point of view of design and construction.

Amongst the active competitors were four tractor biplanes, of which three were British, eleven tractor monoplanes, two pusher biplanes, and one pusher monoplane. The Bristol team was especially interesting as representing two quite distinct lines of thought. The monoplanes were designed by Mons. Coanda whilst the tractor biplanes, which were not so successful as the monoplanes, were built to the ideas of Mr. Gordon England. Both types were examples of the excellence of Bristol workmanship. All the Deperdussins were designed by Heer Koolhoven in collaboration with M. Bechereau, but the French-built machine was noticeably superior in construction and finish to the two British-made models, and was also much lighter.

(b). *The Officials.*

In a highly technical competition of this kind it is important that the judges be very carefully selected. In this case the

Government displayed unwonted acumen in picking its officials, bearing in mind the fact that these aeroplanes were being tested for the use of the R.F.C. Three of the four judges were certificated pilots and the other was in charge of the repair depot of the R.F.C. The names were as follows:—

1. Brig.-Gen. David Henderson, Director of Military Training.
2. Capt. Godfrey M. Paine, R.N., Commandant of the C.F.S.
3. Maj. F. H. Sykes, Officer commanding the Military Wing, R.F.C.
4. Mr. Mervyn O'Gorman, Superintendant of the Royal Aircraft Factory.

Each of these men was vitally concerned in the success of the trials and each was familiar with the difficulties and dangers of aviation. Probably there has never been an important international competition which occasioned less friction than did these trials. The competitors grumbled at their engines, which were dreadfully unreliable, and at the weather, which was appalling throughout, but no complaint was raised during the meeting against these four officials, who displayed the utmost tact and amiability.

It was regrettable that their ultimate judgment fell so far short of their organizing ability.

(c). *Constructional Requirements.*

And now for a detailed description of the contest.

First it is necessary to understand clearly the nature of the tests and their proper sequence, which latter had an important bearing on the results obtained.

There were certain initial requirements relating solely to the form of construction of the aircraft without reference to its performance. I have set these out below in the order of importance which the judges themselves attached to them.

1. Accommodation was to be provided for at least one passenger in addition to the pilot, and both occupants were to be afforded the best possible view of the ground in a forward arc.
2. The aircraft should stand still on the ground with the engine running without being held back and the engine should be capable of being started easily, preferably from the pilot's seat.
3. Dual controls were to be provided.
4. The occupants were to be sheltered from the wind and able to communicate with each other.
5. All parts of the airframe were to be strictly interchangeable, like parts with each other and also with sample parts picked from stock.
6. The operation of the machine should not throw an undue strain upon the pilot.
7. Each aircraft had to be capable of being dismantled and transported by road, either by trolley or on its own wheels, and

the width when packed for road travel was not to exceed ten feet.

8. Each aircraft was to be presented in a packing case suitable for rail transport, which could be taken to pieces easily and stored in a small space.

9. The engine should be silenced effectively.

The above may be referred to as the constructional requirements, and before proceeding to give an account of the flying tests it will be convenient to describe how each aircraft complied with these preliminary essentials.

The actual marks awarded by the Judges in connection with the constructional requirements were never published, but it is clear from their report that certain aircraft scored heavily on these tests.

The judges invented a practical way of testing the view afforded. Each machine was propped up in flying position on a floor marked in squares and the observer then seated himself in the machine and crossed off the " dead " area on a score sheet ruled with squares corresponding to those on the floor. The Cody and Maurice Farman pusher biplanes gave outstanding views to both pilot and observer, whilst the Deperdussin, Bleriot (both tandem and side-by-side seaters) and Bristol monoplanes were fairly good. The view from the cabin of the Avro tractor biplane and from the Hanriot monoplanes attracted adverse comment.

The Cody scored many marks in section 2 on the strength of its hand-starter and the fact that its big Austro-Daimler engine would tick over quite gently when throttled back. All machines with Gnôme engines lost marks heavily in this section.

Every machine was duly fitted with dual controls.

In section 4 the Avro gave the best results as its totally enclosed body protected the occupants from rain and draughts and enabled them to converse easily. The Bristol monoplanes gave good protection, but the pilot and passengers on the Cody were completely exposed to the elements, whilst the Hanriots earned bad marks for their draughty cockpits.

In section 6 full marks went to the Maurice Farman for its extraordinary ease of control, which was singled out for comment in the judge's report.

The competitors were unanimous in ignoring the stipulation that engines should be effectively silenced. None of them had any horse-power to waste on such refinements.

(d). *Quick Assembly Tests.*

The test devised by the judges to bring out the points covered by sections 5 and 8 of the constructional requirements was simple and practical. Each aeroplane was brought out in its packing case and the word to go was given. Its crew had to remove it from the case and erect it and its pilot was then required to fly it round the aerodrome, just to prove that nothing had been left undone. The time was taken up to the moment of leaving the ground in flight, an allowance being made for the time occupied in starting the engine.

The results of this test were as follow :—

Aircraft.	*Crew (No. of Men)*	*Time* *hrs.*	*mins.*	*secs.*
1. Avro biplane	6		14	30
2. Hanriot monoplane	5		14	43
3. Bristol monoplane ...	5		17	52
4. Hanriot monoplane ...	5		22	58
5. Bristol monoplane ...	4		23	35
6. Flanders biplane ...	6		40	—
7. Vickers monoplane ...	6		53	30
8. Bristol biplane ...	4		54	5
9. Bleriot monoplane ...	4		59	57
10. Bleriot monoplane ...	4	1	27	—
11. Bristol biplane ...	4	1	32	—
12. Martin-Handasyde monoplane	—	1	33	—
13. Cody biplane	6	1	35	—
14. Coventry Ordnance biplane...	5	1	51	45
15. Deperdussin monoplane	4	1	56	—
16. Deperdussin monoplane	5	2	—	55
17. Mersey monoplane ...	3	4	25	—
18. Deperdussin monoplane	5	7	15	—
19. Maurice Farman biplane	5	9	29	—

It is a heartbreaking picture that is conjured up of the five stalwart, and no doubt blasphemous, mechanics grappling with the Maurice Farman for nine and a half hours, what time the patient officials stood over them with watches in their hands.

At the end of the flying tests each machine had to be dismantled again, folded up, driven a few miles along the road, re-erected and flown once more in order to comply with section 7. As this test was taken at the end of the trials only a handful of survivors passed through it. The results were as follow :—

Aircraft	*Crew (No of men)*	*Dismantle* *hrs.*	*mins.*	*Reassemble* *hrs.*	*mins.*	*Total* *hrs.*	*mins.*
1. Avro biplane ...	6	–	12	–	11	–	23
2. Hanriot monoplane	5	–	13	–	18	–	31
3. Bleriot monoplane ...	4	–	17	–	27	–	44
4. Cody biplane ...	6	–	21	–	30	–	51
5. Bleriot monoplane ...	3	–	28	–	50	1	18
6. Deperdussin monoplane	4	–	53	–	51	1	44
7. Deperdussin monoplane	4	1	—	–	54	1	54
8. Maurice Farman bip'ne	4	1	18	1	48	3	6

It will be noticed that every competitor except the Hanriot had improved on the time taken in the first assembly test. This was no doubt due to the fact that the crews had had plenty of practice during the competition in stripping their machines in order to carry out repairs.

So much for the constructional requirements, in which Cody in regard to view and starting, Avro and Hanriot for quick assembly, and Avro again for comfort, had scored points victories.

(e). *The Three Hours Test.*

We can now turn to the actual flying tests.

The judges had decided wisely to modify the original rule that each machine was to remain for 1 hour at 4,500 feet. The modified test, which was an essential preliminary to obtaining any award in the competition, consisted of a flight of not less than three hours duration during which the machine had to carry a live load (two people) of 350 lbs., the usual instruments and fuel and oil for four and a half hours. At some time during this flight each machine had to attain an altitude of 4,500 feet and to remain at a height exceeding 1,500 feet for one hour.

That was a sufficiently stiff test for both the aircraft and the pilots of 1912, and it was surprising that eleven machines out of nineteen active competitors succeeded in passing it.

The first to attempt this three hours' trial was Perreyon, who piloted the tandem-seater Bleriot monoplane through the test at the head of the field. He was followed on the next day by Cody and Sippe (Hanriot). Bielovucic on the other Hanriot had the bad luck to break a valve-spring after two and three-quarter hours in the air.

Valentine was guilty of a piece of bad flying when he stretched a glide on his Bristol monoplane to the stalling point, in an attempt to clear a fence, and dived into the ground on his left wing and nose from a small height. The machine was badly damaged and to make matters worse, Gordon England of the same team broke up the undercarriage of the Gnôme-engined tractor biplane in a heavy landing.

Wilfred Parke smashed up the Avro cabin biplane, in attempting to land down-wind, to such an extent that it had to be taken back to Manchester in two pieces and completely rebuilt. A. V. Roe and Company, who were quite accustomed to this sort of thing, had the machine back at Salisbury within a week.

Following on these disasters, Valentine dropped out of the competition and Howard Pixton was appointed to take over his monoplane as soon as the repairs had been completed.

The Breguêt was suffering from an obscure trouble in its Canton

Unné motor, which refused to give sufficient power to take it off the ground and the Viale engine in the Vickers also proved refractory.

Gordon Bell put in some splendid flights on the Martin-Handasyde during the intervals of repairing the magneto drive of its Chenu, but he could not induce the engine to continue running for three hours, so eventually he abandoned the machine and took over one of the British-built Deperdussin monoplanes which should have been flown by Jules Vedrines, who had returned to France after some preliminary tests.

The other British Deperdussin suffered incessant trouble with its Anzani engine. The Chenu-engined Coventry Ordnance was in similar straits and its sister machine was fitted with an airscrew which was quite unsuitable for its 100 h.p. Gnôme. Hamel did not turn up to take over his Bleriot, so Perreyon had to put both the tandem seater and the side-by-side, or "sociable," model through all the tests, which he did very efficiently.

Eventually the following aeroplanes passed the three hours' test.

Aircraft	*Engine*	*Pilot*
1. Bleriot monoplane ...	70 Gnôme	Perreyon
2. Bleriot monoplane ...	70 Gnôme	Perreyon
3. Deperdussin monoplane	100 Gnôme	Prevost
4. Deperdussin monoplane	100 Gnôme	Gordon Bell
5. Hanriot monoplane ...	100 Gnôme	Bielovucic
6. Hanriot monoplane ...	100 Gnôme	Sippe
7. Bristol monoplane ...	80 Gnôme	Busteed
8. Bristol monoplane ...	80 Gnôme	Pixton
9. Maurice Farman biplane	70 Renault	Verrier
10. Cody biplane	120 Austro-Daimler	Cody
11. Avro biplane	60 Green	Parke

Thus eight monoplanes and three biplanes, comprising seven French aircraft, two British aeroplanes with French engines, one British aeroplane with an Austrian engine, and one all-British machine, became qualified to compete for the awards.

(f). *Climbing Tests*

During the three hours' test the judges took the opportunity of testing the climbing ability of the machines. The rules called for a climb to 1,000 feet at a minimum rate of 200 feet per minute with full load as set out above.

This test caused a great deal of trouble to the pilots with their underpowered machines and some of them had to make several attempts before they passed it. The Avro biplane failed completely in lamentable fashion. The results were as follow :—

Aircraft	*Engine*	*Pilot*	*Rate of climb Ft./min.*
1. Hanriot monoplane	100 Gnôme	Bielovucic	364
2. {Hanriot monoplane / Deperdussin m'plane}	100 Gnôme / 100 Gnôme	Sippe / Prevost	333
3. Cody biplane ...	120 Austro-Daimler	Cody	288
4. Deperdussin monoplane	100 Gnôme	Gordon Bell	267
5. Bleriot monoplane (tandem)	70 Gnôme	Perreyon	250
6. Bleriot monoplane (sociable) ...	70 Gnôme	Perreyon	235
7. Bristol monoplane	80 Gnôme	Pixton	218
8. Deperdussin monoplane	100 Anzani	Porte	210
9. Maurice Farman biplane	70 Renault	Verrier	207
10. Bristol monoplane	80 Gnôme	Busteed	200
11. Avro biplane ...	60 Green	Parke	105

(g). *Gliding Tests.*

Mr. F. Short of the Royal Aircraft Factory had invented an ingenious instrument for measuring the angle of glide of the competing machines. Briefly it consisted of a pitot tube which measured the forward speed through the air, coupled to a barograph. These two instruments recorded their results by means of glass gauges containing liquid, behind which a strip of photographic paper was wound over a drum by an electric motor at a constant speed. A clockwork device recorded the time on the photographic paper by means of a pencil. The resultant chart gave two sides of a right-angled triangle, the vertical side representing the height lost during the test, and the base showing the horizontal distance travelled during the glide. The hypotenuse would then correspond to the average slope of the path of gliding descent. This instrument was, of course, carried in the machine. The conditions of the trial stipulated for a minimum gliding angle of 1 in 6 and of the ten aircraft which submitted to the test only six passed successfully. The results were as follow :—

Aircraft	*Pilot*	*Gliding Speed m.p.h.*	*Gradient one in :*
(*a*) *Passed :*			
1. Maurice Farman biplane	Verrier	38	6·8
2. Hanriot monoplane ...	Bielovucic	61	6·6
3. Avro biplane	Parke	52	6·5
3. Bristol monoplane ...	Busteed	64·3	6·5
4. Cody biplane... ...	Cody	59	6·2
4. Deperdussin monoplane	Gordon Bell	—	6·2
(*b*) *Failed :*			
5. Hanriot monoplane ...	Sippe	68	5·9
6. Bleriot monoplane (tandem)	Perreyon	—	5·6
7. Deperdussin monoplane	Prevost	62	5·4
8. Bleriot monoplane (sociable)	Perreyon	52	5·3

The variation of gliding speeds is very interesting. It will be noticed that Bielovucic gained 1 in 0·7 over his team mate Sippe, by gliding his Hanriot 7 m.p.h. slower.

(h). *Consumption Tests.*

Petrol consumption was also carefully checked and the extremely wasteful characteristics of these low-powered engines were brought out into the limelight, as follows :—

Engine	*Aircraft*	*Petrol consumption (Gals. per hour)*
1. 60 Green	Avro biplane	4
2. 70 Gnôme	Bleriot monoplane (tandem)	5·4
3. 70 Gnôme	Bleriot monoplane (sociable)	6·3
4. 80 Gnôme	Bristol monoplane	7
4. 70 Renault ...	M. Farman biplane	7
5. 80 Gnôme	Bristol monoplane	8
5. 100 Gnôme ...	Hanriot monoplane	8
6. 100 Gnôme... ...	Deperdussin monoplane	8·4
7. 100 Gnôme... ...	Hanriot monoplane	8·6
8. 120 Austro-Daimler	Cody biplane	9
9. 100 Gnôme... ...	Deperdussin monoplane	9·8

It was notorious that the 100 h.p. Gnôme was considerably overrated, and it is doubtful if it gave more than 80 b.h.p. in the air. The average consumption of the four engines of this type tested works out at 8·7 gals. per hr., or twice as much as one would expect a modern Cirrus II engine of the same power to use.

If the petrol figures were bad, those for oil consumption were simply staggering. The Gnôme engines took the oil and flung it

"Flight" photo

23.—A World's Record Breaker: Lieut. B. H. Barrington-Kennett, the first Adjutant of the R.F.C.

Facing page 176

"Flight" photo

24.—M. Henri Salmet, the great Bleriot Pilot, at Hendon.

Facing page 177

all over the aeroplane and the surrounding landscape. Here are the results of the tests :—

Engine	*Aircraft*	*Oil consumption (Gals. per hour)*
1. 120 Austro-Daimler	Cody biplane	·42
2. 60 Green	Avro biplane	·5
3. 70 Renault ...	M. Farman biplane	·73
4. 100 Gnôme ...	Deperdussin monoplane	1·3
5. 80 Gnôme	Bristol monoplane	1·5
6. 80 Gnôme ...	Bristol monoplane	1·7
70 Gnôme ...	Bleriot monoplane	
70 Gnôme ...	Bleriot monoplane	
7. 100 Gnôme ...	Deperdussin monoplane	1·8
8. 100 Gnôme ...	Hanriot monoplane	2·1
9. 100 Gnôme ...	Hanriot monoplane	2·4

At their cruising speed of some 68 m.p.h. the Hanriot monoplanes would have covered about seven miles on a gallon of petrol, and six miles on a pint of oil, so that they were scarcely suitable mounts for an impecunious private owner, more especially as the Gnôme engines would only run with a special and costly type of oil.

(i). *Calculated Range.*

On the above figures the range of the competing machines in still air was calculated to be as follows :—

Aircraft	*Engine*	*Pilot*	*Range in miles*
1. Bristol monoplane	80 Gnôme	Pixton	420
2. Hanriot monoplane	100 Gnôme	Bielovucic	400
3. Hanriot monoplane	100 Gnôme	Sippe	361
4. Avro biplane ...	60 Green	Parke	345
5. Cody biplane ...	120 Austro-Daimler	Cody	336
6. Bristol monoplane	80 Gnôme	Busteed	328
7. Deperdussin monoplane	100 Gnôme	Gordon Bell	320
8. Deperdussin monoplane	100 Gnôme	Prevost	315
9. Bleriot monoplane (tandem) ...	70 Gnôme	Perreyon	295
10. M. Farman biplane	70 Renault	Verrier	266
11. Bleriot monoplane (sociable) ...	70 Gnôme	Perreyon	252

It was notable that in many cases the designers had provided such inadequate oil reservoirs that the lubricant was bound to run out, and the engine break up in consequence, long before the petrol supply was exhausted. The worst offenders in this respect were Coanda (Bristol) and Maurice Farman.

(j). *Speed Tests.*

The authorities had stipulated that each competitor should attain a speed of not less than 55 m.p.h. loaded as for the three hours test, and stressed the importance of flexibility of speed "to allow of landings and observations being made at slow speeds if required, while reserving a high acceleration for work in strong winds."

It is interesting to note that the organizers regarded speed range as of special importance, not so much from the point of view of safety, as from the curious idea that it was necessary to slow down in order to observe objects accurately from the sky.

In any case, the great thing was that speed range did in fact receive the eminent importance it deserved, and, in consequence, the arrangements provided for the most accurate tests of fast and slow speeds which had yet been carried out anywhere in the world. A distance of 3,000 yards had been marked out by permanent white lines and each competitor flew over this course four times, twice in each direction, first as fast as possible and then as slowly as possible. The times were checked by ground observers with stop watches and the mesne figure of each pair of runs was taken. The entry of a competitor into the timed section was signalled by means of flags. This method seems primitive when compared with modern electric photographic timing devices, but it is surprising what a degree of accuracy can be obtained by experts in the use of stop watches when dealing with comparatively low speeds over a long course.

Eleven competitors passed through the speed trials as follows :—

Aircraft	*Engine*	*Pilot*	*Speed m.p.h.*
(*a*) *Maximum Speeds*			
1. Hanriot monoplane	100 Gnôme	Sippe	75·4
2. Hanriot monoplane	100 Gnôme	Bielovucic	75·2
3. Bristol monoplane	80 Gnôme	Pixton	72·9
4. Cody biplane ...	120 Austro-Daimler	Cody	72·4
5. Bristol monoplane	80 Gnôme	Busteed	70·5
6. Deperdussin monoplane	100 Gnôme	Prevost	69·1
7. Deperdussin monoplane	100 Gnôme	Gordon Bell	68·2
8. Avro biplane ...	60 Green	Parke	61·8
9. Bleriot monoplane (tandem)	70 Gnôme	Perreyon	60·8
10. Bleriot monoplane (sociable) ...	70 Gnôme	Perreyon	58·9
11. M. Farman biplane	70 Renault	Verrier	55·2

Aircraft	*Engine*	*Pilot*	*Speed m.p.h.*
(*b*) *Minimum Speeds*			
1. M. Farman biplane ...	70 Renault	Verrier	37·4
2. Bleriot monoplane ... (sociable) ...	70 Gnôme	Perreyon	40·0
3. Cody biplane ...	120 Austro-Daimler	Cody	48·5
4. Avro biplane ...	60 Green	Parke	49·3
5. Bleriot monoplane (tandem)	70 Gnôme	Perreyon	51·0
6. Deperdussin monoplane	100 Gnôme	Gordon Bell	54·6
7. Bristol monoplane ...	80 Gnôme	Pixton	58·1
8. Deperdussin monoplane	100 Gnôme	Prevost	59·0
9. Hanriot monoplane ...	100 Gnôme	Bielovucic	59·9
10. Hanriot monoplane ...	100 Gnôme	Sippe	66·6
11. Bristol monoplane ...	80 Gnôme	Busteed	68·3

The slow speed test was naturally affected to a considerable extent by the varying ability of the pilots. This was notable in the case of the two Hanriots, which were identical models and which were within one-fifth m.p.h. of each other in the high speed trial, and yet Bielovucic flew his machine 6·7 m.p.h. slower than his English team mate Sippe. Similarly Busteed's slow speed was only 2·2 m.p.h. below his maximum, although Pixton kept his similar model down to more than 10 m.p.h. below Busteed's figure.

(k). *Speed Range.*

While studying the vitally important figures which follow, it would, therefore, be wise to ignore those relating to the Hanriot flown by Sippe and Busteed's Bristol, and to assume that the figures given for Bielovucic's and Pixton's machines more accurately represent the capabilities of the respective types.

Aircraft	*Engine*	*Pilot*	*Difference between max. and min. speeds m.p.h.*
Speed Range			
1. Cody biplane ...	120 Austro-Daimler	Cody	23·9
2. Bleriot monoplane (sociable) ...	70 Gnôme	Perreyon	18·9
3. M. Farman biplane ...	70 Renault	Verrier	17·8
4. Hanriot monoplane ...	100 Gnôme	Bielovucic	15·3
5. Bristol monoplane ...	80 Gnôme	Pixton	14·8
6. Deperdussin monoplane	100 Gnôme	Gordon Bell	13·6
7. Avro biplane ...	60 Green	Parke	12·5
8. Deperdussin monoplane	100 Gnôme	Prevost	10·1
9. Bleriot monoplane ... (Tandem) ...	70 Gnôme	Perreyon	9·8
10. Hanriot monoplane ...	100 Gnôme	Sippe	8·8
11. Bristol monoplane ...	80 Gnôme	Busteed	2·2

(l). *Landing Competition*:

The machines were further tested in regard to the distance required to come to rest after landing on a smooth and, alternatively, on a ploughed field.

These tests were so dependent on the personal ability of the pilots, that it is scarcely worth while to deal with them in detail here beyond stating that only seven machines succeeded in stopping within the seventy-five yards permitted on grass. These included the two Bleriots, the Avro, Busteed's Bristol, the M. Farman, Prevost's Deperdussin, and the Cody, the last-named being fitted with a primitive brake consisting of a chain looped round the skid, which could be drawn up by the pilot before taking off.

(m). *Quick Take-off Test.*

Another important competition was the test for quick take-off, which was flown from a harrowed field. Considering the low power of the machines and the fact that they were compelled to rise with full load, the results were surprisingly good, although only six of the competitors succeeded in passing this test. The figures were as follow :—

Aircraft	*Engine*	*Pilot*	*Yards run before lifting*
1. Deperdussin monoplane	100 Gnôme	Prevost	132
2. M. Farman biplane ...	70 Renault	Verrier	140
3. Deperdussin monoplane	100 Gnôme	Gordon Bell	200
4. Hanriot monoplane	100 Gnôme	Bielovucic	206
5. Bleriot monoplane (tandem) ...	70 Gnôme	Perreyon	250
6. Cody biplane ...	120 Austro-Daimler	Cody	320

(n). *Rough Weather Trial.*

One of the conditions of the trials required each competitor to demonstrate before the judges that his aircraft was stable in flight, and capable of flying in a wind *averaging* 25 m.p.h. without undue risk to the pilot. Eleven machines flew in *gusts* above the minimum, but in only five cases was the *average* wind velocity above 25 m.p.h. throughout the flight.

A splendid feat was performed by Howard Pixton in connection with this test. The wind had been rising steadily for an hour and was becoming more and more squally when, to the amazement of the other competitors, he brought out his Bristol monoplane for the

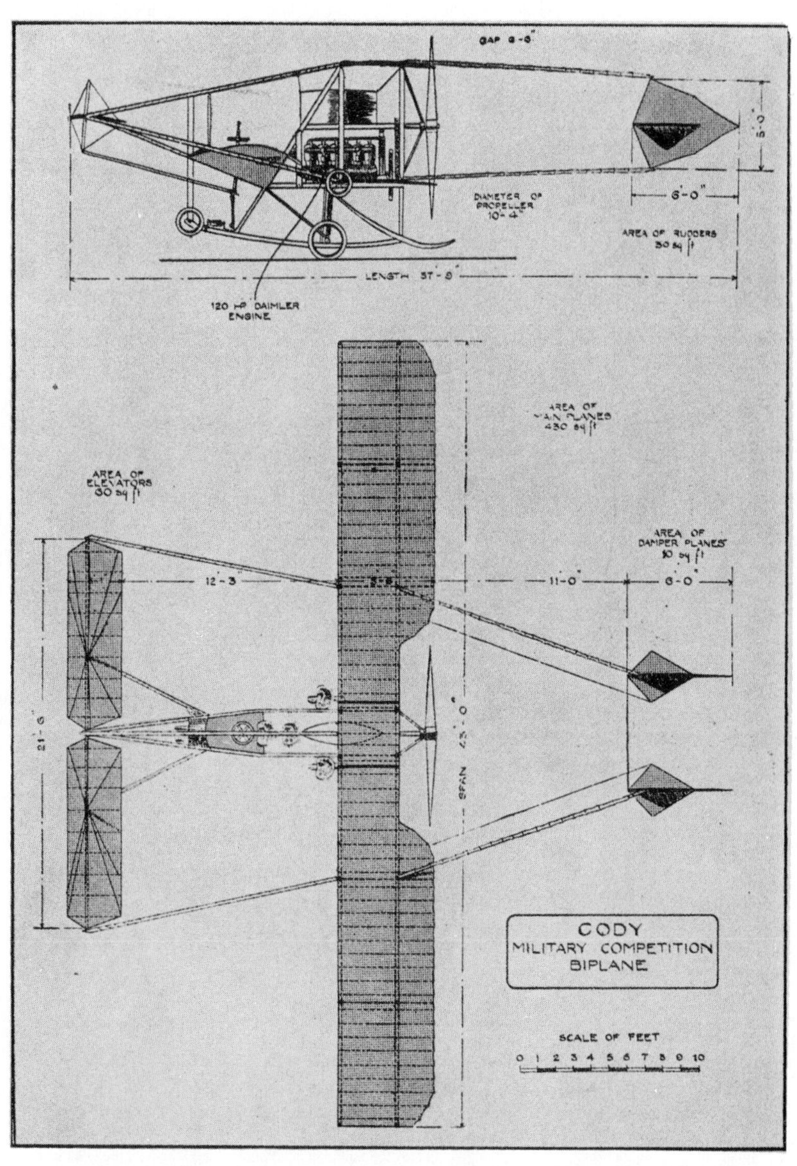

"Flight" copyright

8.—THE OFFICIAL WINNER OF THE MILITARY TRIALS: MR. S. F. CODY'S CATHEDRAL (120 H.P. AUSTRO-DAIMLER).

Facing page 180

"Flight" photo

25.—The Avro Biplane (60 h.p. E.N.V.) at Brooklands.

required demonstration. Capt. Patrick Hamilton, R.F.C., bravely volunteered to fly with him as observer.

Pixton fought the gusts, which varied between 17 and 44 m.p.h. for fifteen minutes, whilst the little monoplane was tossed violently about the sky. On many occasions during this grand flight the control column was jerked forcibly out of the pilot's hand.

The five machines which passed through the rough weather trial according to the conditions were as follow :—

Aircraft	*Engine*	*Pilot*	*Wind velocity in m.p.h.* Max.	Min.	Average
1. Bristol monoplane ...	80 Gnôme	Pixton	44	17	30·5
2. Hanriot monoplane ...	100 Gnôme	Sippe	31	25	28
3. Bleriot monoplane (sociable)	70 Gnôme	Perreyon	30	26	28
4. Hanriot monoplane ...	100 Gnôme	Bielovucic	31	21	26
5. Martin-Handasyde monoplane	75 Chenu	Gordon Bell	34	16	25

(o). *Summary of Results.*

I have now described all the important tests to which these aeroplanes were subjected with so much care and with such commendable thoroughness and before I divulge the judge's decision it will be interesting to summarize the results.

Below I set out the first three aeroplanes in each separate competition, the events themselves being arranged in order or importance.

Aircraft	*Engine*	*Pilot*	*Result*
a. Speed Range.			
1. Cody biplane	120 Austro-Daimler	Cody	23·9 m.p.h.
2. Bleriot monoplane (sociable)...	70 Gnôme	Perreyon	18·9 ,,
3. M. Farman biplane	70 Renault	Verrier	17·8 ,,
b. Maximum Speed			
1. Hanriot monoplane ...	100 Gnôme	Sippe	75·4 ,,
2. Hanriot monoplane	100 Gnôme	Bielovucic	75·2 ,,
3. Bristol monoplane	80 Gnôme	Pixton	72·9 ,,
c. Climb			
1. Hanriot monoplane	100 Gnôme	Bielovucic	364 ft./min.
2. { Hanriot monoplane	100 Gnôme	Sippe }	333 ,,
2. { Deperdussin monoplane ...	100 Gnôme	Prevost }	333 ,,
3. Cody biplane	120 Austro-Daimler	Cody	288 ,,
d. Range.			
1. Bristol monoplane	80 Gnôme	Pixton	420 miles
2. Hanriot monoplane	100 Gnôme	Bielovucic	400 ,,
3. Hanriot monoplane	100 Gnôme	Sippe	361 ,,
e. Take-off from harrow.			
1. Deperdussin monoplane ...	100 Gnôme	Prevost	132 yards
2. M. Farman biplane	70 Renault	Verrier	140 ,,
3. Deperdussin monoplane ...	100 Gnôme	Gordon Bell	200 ,,

Aircraft	*Engine*	*Pilot*	*Result*
f. Slow Speed.			
1. M. Farman biplane	70 Renault	Verrier	37·4 m.p.h.
2. Bleriot monoplane (sociable)	70 Gnôme	Perreyon	40 ,,
3. Cody biplane	120 Austro-Daimler	Cody	48·5 ,,
g. Glide.			one in :
1. M. Farman biplane	70 Renault	Verrier	6·8
2. Hanriot monoplane ...	100 Gnôme	Bielovucic	6·6
3. { Bristol monoplane ...	80 Gnôme	Busteed }	6·5
Avro biplane	60 Green	Parke }	
h. Quick dismantling and Re-assembly :—			
1. Avro biplane	60 Green	—	23 mins.
2. Hanriot monoplane ...	100 Gnôme	—	31 ,,
3. Bleriot monoplane	70 Gnôme	—	44 ,,
i. Stopping distance on grass :			
1. Cody biplane	120 Austro-Daimler	Cody	30 yards
2. Bleriot monoplane (sociable)	70 Gnôme	Perreyon	45 ,,
3. Avro biplane	60 Green	Parke	47 ,,

Now I propose to analyse these results and to adopt an elementary system of marking by awarding three marks for a first place, two marks for a second place, and one mark for a third place.

It will be seen that seven different makes of aircraft comprising seven tractor monoplanes, two pusher biplanes and one tractor biplane, and four different makes of engine figure in our prize list as follows :—

Aircraft	*Engine*	*Pilot*	*First*	*Second*	*Third*	*Marks*
1. Hanriot monoplane	100 Gnôme	Bielovucic	1	4	—	11
2. M. Farman biplane	70 Renault	Verrier	2	1	1	9
3. Cody biplane ...	120 Austro-Daimler	Cody	2	—	2	8
4. Bleriot monoplane (sociable) ...	70 Gnôme	Perreyon	—	3	1	7
5. Hanriot monoplane	100 Gnôme	Sippe	1	1	1	6
6. { Avro biplane	60 Green	Parke	1	—	2 }	5
Deperdussin monoplane ...	100 Gnôme	Prevost	1	1	— }	
7. Bristol monoplane	80 Gnôme	Pixton	1	—	1	4
8. { Bristol monoplane ...	80 Gnôme	Busteed	—	—	1 }	1
Deperdussin monoplane...	100 Gnôme	Gordon Bell	—	—	1 }	

It is perfectly obvious from the above table that the two Hanriot monoplanes, which had between them collected no less than seventeen marks, were by far the best aeroplanes in the competition and that Bielovucic's Hanriot was an easy individual winner. It is also plain that Verrier's Maurice Farman was a good second.

(p). *The Awards.*

Unfortunately the judges, unduly influenced no doubt by supposed military requirements, were unanimous in disregarding the

Hanriot's indisputable claim to the premier award. They placed the competing machines in the following order of merit :—

Aircraft	Engine	Pilot
1. Cody biplane	120 Austro-Daimler	Cody
2. Deperdussin monoplane	100 Gnôme	Prevost
3. { Hanriot monoplane ...	100 Gnôme	Bielovucic
3. { M. Farman biplane ...	70 Renault	Verrier
5. { Bleriot monoplane (tandem)	70 Gnôme	Perreyon
5. { Hanriot monoplane ...	100 Gnôme	Sippe
7. { Deperdussin monoplane	100 Gnôme	Gordon Bell
7. { Bristol monoplane ...	80 Gnôme	Busteed
7. { Bristol monoplane ...	80 Gnôme	Pixton
10. Bleriot monoplane (sociable)	70 Gnôme	Perreyon

The prizes were awarded as follows :—

a. *Prizes open to the World.*

1. S. F. Cody, £4,000 .
2. A. Deperdussin, £2,000.

b. *Prizes restricted to British subjects for aeroplanes manufactured wholly (except the engine) in the United Kingdom.*

1. S. F. Cody, £1,000.
2. Withdrawn, as no other British-built aeroplane passed through every test.
3. { British Deperdussin Co., Ltd., £500.
   British & Colonial Co., Ltd., (Bristol), £500.
   British & Colonial Co., Ltd., (Bristol), £500.

c. *Consolation Prizes.*

To the entrant of each of the following, for having submitted to all the tests—£100.

1. Hanriot monoplane.
2. Hanriot monoplane.
3. M. Farman biplane.
4. Bleriot monoplane (sociable)
5. Bleriot monoplane (tandem)
6. Avro biplane.

(q). *The Awards Criticized.*

The judges displayed an astonishing lack of intelligent criticism in making these awards, which undoubtedly did grave injustice to some of the competitors, while grossly flattering others.

There is no doubt that an exaggerated importance was attached to minor details which were supposed to be of special value for military purposes, such as the view from the observer's seat, the ability to dispense with chocks for starting, short run after landing, and ease of handling on the ground.

Had the judges concentrated solely upon selecting the two best flying machines, and left their subsequent adaptation to military uses to the practical intelligence of the R.F.C., they would have done much better, and they would have been compelled to choose the Hanriot tractor monoplane and the Maurice Farman pusher biplane. They could not have made a sounder choice.

Comparing the official order of precedence with my prize list we find that the big prize went to the third machine on my list, which had failed to fly in a wind of the average velocity demanded by the rules, which was a most complicated structure, built largely of bamboo and obviously unsuited to production in quantity for service requirements, and which afforded no protection of any sort for pilot or passenger.

The magnificent Austro-Daimler engine won this competition for Cody. It was by far the most powerful motor in the trials and it pushed the clumsy old "Cathedral" through the air at a satisfying speed, whilst the gentleness of its tick-over earned many marks. Cody's braking device and his hand starter were also in a great measure responsible for his victory, too much weight being given to these unimportant details. It must be remembered, however, that Cody won the competition for speed range, which was the most important of all the tests.

Second prize went to a machine which is placed no better than equal sixth in my list and which had definitely failed in the gliding test. It had a good climb and quick take-off, but in other respects had not distinguished itself and, although its pilot was one of the greatest French experts, it had not been flown in the 25 m.p.h. wind called for by the regulations.

In the all-British category the two Bristol monoplanes which received third prizes were seventh and eighth in my list, and one of them had only obtained a single mark in respect of a tie for third place in the gliding contest. The other third prize was given to a machine which merely scored one mark for third place in the take-off competition. The Avro biplane beat all three of them easily according to my marking, but although the judges gave it a consolation prize it was evidently not considered good enough even to be mentioned in their list of placings. By my scoring the Avro biplane was the equal of the Deperdussin which won the £2,000 prize in the open class.

The judges ranked the tandem-seater Bleriot, which never got so much as a third place in any of the competitions, equal fifth, and placed the sociable model, which had won three second places and one third place, at the bottom of the table.

The Hanriot and Avro firms had every reason to feel that they had been the victims of the gravest injustice.

(r). *The B.E.2.*

The outstanding feature of the trials was the astonishing performance of the B.E.2 which was flown *hors concours* by its designer, Mr. Geoffrey de Havilland.

This magnificent tractor biplane with its 70 h.p. Renault engine was the same machine with which Mr. de Havilland set up the British altitude record of 10,560 feet as previously recorded. It was used throughout the competitions as a quick means of transport for the officials, who flew about in it from point to point across the Plain as their duties demanded. In addition it was permitted to perform some of the official tests as a means of obtaining valuable comparative data, although it was not eligible to compete, having been built at the Royal Aircraft Factory.

The B.E.2 was submitted to the climbing, gliding, and speed tests.

It beat all the competition aircraft with a climb to 1000 feet at 365 ft/min., and it glided at a gradient of 1 in 6·25, which was bettered by only four of the other machines.

In the high speed trial it took sixth place, unofficially, with a top speed of 70 m.p.h., and in the slow speed test it beat everything but the Maurice Farman by getting down to 40 m.p.h. This wonderful feat gave it the outstanding speed range of 30 m.p.h., which was 6 m.p.h. better than Cody's winning figure.

In the face of these results it was quite obvious that Mr. Geoffrey de Havilland's B.E.2 was easily the best all-round aircraft present at the trials, and it must have been one of the best aeroplanes in the world at that time.

(s). *General Remarks.*

Engine troubles prevented many promising aircraft from showing their paces before the judges. Notable in this class of unfortunates were the Vickers monoplane (Viale), which flew excellently whenever its motor would go, the interesting Flanders tractor biplane (A.B.C.), which never received its engine at all; one of the Coventry Ordnance tractor biplanes, and the Martin-Handasyde monoplane, which were both afflicted with Chenu power plants, and the Breguêt, whose Canton Unné would not permit it to leave the ground. All the above were really good aeroplanes, especially the Breguêt.

The trials had provided a mass of data which was to prove of great value to designers and constructors. Never before had such a varied collection of aeroplanes been subjected to such searching tests. The results afford a splendid panoramic view of the state of European aviation at that date.

If we summarize them, and include the figures set up by the B.E.2, we find that if the best points of all the competing machines could have been combined in one ideal aeroplane, it would have had the following performance with a useful load, including fuel, of about 750 lbs.

Maximum speed	75·4 m.p.h.
Slow Speed	37·4 m.p.h.
Speed Range	38·0 m.p.h.
Climb	365 ft./min.
Ceiling	10,000 ft.
Range	420 miles.

Of course, none of the individual machines attained anything like this "ideal" performance, although the B.E.2 was not very far short of it. It is interesting to note that the original de Havilland Moth (Cirrus Mk. I), which was produced thirteen years later, gave performance figures very closely approximating to the ideal of 1912, with an engine of similar power to that installed in its ancestor, the B.E.2. As a matter of fact the Cirrus Mk I engine was composed largely of surplus parts taken from obsolete Renault engines similar to the original design.

(t). *A Fatal Accident.*

On Tuesday, August 13th, Mr. R. C. Fenwick, took out the all-British Mersey pusher monoplane (45 h.p. Isaacson) for a trial flight. This curious machine carried the motor in the normal position in the nose, but the propeller was behind the wing and was driven by a shaft which passed aft from the back of the engine between the pilot's and passenger's seats, which were set side by side in a small *nacelle* in the centre section of the wing. The tail was supported solely by two tubular steel booms braced by single piano wires, top and bottom, to the undercarriage and cabane respectively. This arrangement was obviously of a very precarious nature and it was said that Mr. Fenwick, who had designed and built the machine himself at Liverpool, was doubtful of its strength.

The aircraft had reached a point about a mile and a half from the sheds when it was seen to dive, recover for a moment, and then drop into an over-the-vertical dive in which it hit the ground. Mr. R. C. Fenwick was killed instantaneously.

It was shown at the R.Ae.C. inquiry that the aircraft was notoriously unstable fore and aft, and that the controls were found intact after the accident. It seems probable that the insecure bracing of the tail allowed that member to flex downwards under the strain of a bump to such an extent that the elevator was rendered inoperative.

Mr. Fenwick, who held R.Ae.C. certificate No. 35, issued to him on November 29th, 1910, was a man of original ideas and a very sound pilot. His death was a great loss to aviation in the north of England.

(u). *An Observed Spin.*

An incident which nearly ended tragically, but which actually served to provide very useful data, occurred to Lieut. Wilfred Parke, R.N., and his observer, Lieut. Le Breton, R.F.C., on August 25th.

Lieut. Parke had just completed his three hours qualifying flight on the Avro cabin tractor biplane (60 h.p. Green), and was approaching the aerodrome up-wind at a height of between 600 and 700 feet, preparatory to landing. He put the machine into a spiral glide in order to lose height, but soon found that the nose had dropped too much and that he was also slipping outwards on the turn owing to insufficient bank. He therefore pulled the stick back and to the left, and the machine instantly began to spin.

Parke kept his head and opened up his engine in the hope that this would pull his nose up, at the same time pulling the stick hard back against his chest in the central position and applying full rudder in the direction of the spin. Naturally enough this manœuvre merely served to tighten the spin.

Parke braced himself in his seat by pressing with one hand against the cabin wall, and thought rapidly. He noted that the rotating movement was the dominant sensation and this drew his attention to the rudder. As a last resource, and when within 50 *feet* of the tarmac in front of the sheds, he applied full opposite rudder against the direction of the spin and, although the elevator was still hard up, the machine came out instantly, and Parke was able to fly round one circuit and land.

Parke deserves the greatest credit for his calmness in face of an unexpected situation which would have caused the majority of pilots to lose their heads. There can be no doubt but that both he and his observer owed their lives to his quick yet orderly thinking, and the fact that his memory remained clear afterwards and enabled him to record a detailed description of the occurrence, and to describe the effect of each movement of the controls throughout the spin was of inestimable value to aviation.

Parke was the second British pilot to recover from a spin, the first having been F. P. Raynham, who got into a spin whilst flying through cloud on the old type Avro biplane as already recorded.

(v). *Flying without an Elevator.*

Another extraordinary escape from disaster was vouchsafed to Mr. E. C. Gordon England during the Military trials. The two Bristol tractor biplanes of his design had been officially withdrawn from the competition because they were found to be so underpowered that they had no prospect of winning any of the awards, but this did not prevent their designer from flying them for his own amusement.

One of these machines had been in the hangar for repairs and a mechanic had lashed the elevator wires together immovably, while he made an adjustment. The repair finished, the biplane was brought out and started up and Gordon England stepped in, opened the throttle of the 100 h.p. Gnôme and took off.

He flew it for nearly an hour and a half in a gusty wind and never discovered that his elevator was out of action until he tried to flatten out on landing !

Apparently he had been controlling the machine on his throttle, and the amazing natural stability of the type had ensured that alterations of fore and aft trim on account of bumps had been corrected automatically. When the machine failed to flatten out to land, the pilot pulled the nose up by opening the throttle for a moment and thus "arranged the impact" without breaking anything.

This story emphasizes the casual disregard for ordinary common sense precautions which characterized the pioneers of flight. There must be few pilots to-day who do not check over their controls before taking off, especially if the machine has just come out of the workshops, and in these enlightened times such a precaution is far less necessary than it was in those days, when ground engineers were just plain mechanics.

As a matter of fact, Gordon England was notoriously reckless of his own skin, for it was he who had volunteered to act in the capacity of live load for José Weiss, when the latter was conducting his experiments with gliders. England's part was to sit in the glider whilst it was shot forward over a precipice. No controls were provided, so that he could do nothing to influence events subsequent to the launch ; his but to reason why, and to make notes of the machine's behaviour and his own sensations, until such time as the apparatus returned to earth of its own volition, and in its own manner. He was a very brave man.

39. H. J. D. ASTLEY AND THE POMMERY CUP: DUBLIN-BELFAST RACE

Mr. H. J. D. Astley had designs on the *Coupe Pommery* which had been offered as a reward for the pilot covering the greatest distance in a straight line in one day, starting from French soil. The rules allowed as many intermediate landings for refuelling as might be required.

This competition fired the imagination of the French pilots and many splendid attempts had been made, notably by Audemars, who flew a Bleriot monoplane from Paris to Bochum in Westphalia, and continued to Berlin on the following morning. This was the first flight from the French to the German capital. This performance had subsequently been beaten by Bathiat, who flew from Calais to Contis les Bains near Biarritz, a distance of 820 kilometres (509 miles), in one day, on his Sommer monoplane (Gnôme).

"Flight" photo

26.—A GREAT CROSS-COUNTRY PILOT: MR. W. B. RHODES-MOORHOUSE.

Facing page 188

"*Flight*" *photo*

27.—THE MILITARY TRIALS: ONE OF THE TWO BRISTOL MONOPLANES (80 H.P. GNÔME).

Mr. Astley, who left Hendon at 7.45 a.m. on August 28th in Mr. Sopwith's new Bleriot two-seater monoplane (70 h.p. Gnôme), with Miss Trehawke Davies as passenger, flew across the Channel and landed at Hardelot at 9.30 a.m. Restarting at 12.45 p.m., he reached Issy-les-Molineux at 4.45 p.m.

At 5.29 a.m. on September 3rd, the Bleriot took off for Berlin and was next reported from Mezières at 11.20 a.m., where it was delayed for some hours. At 1.45 p.m. it left for Bonn, which was reached at 7 p.m.

This flight was a very good performance, even though it fell far short of previous attempts on the Cup.

Whilst returning from Bonn, Mr. Astley and Miss Davies had a very narrow escape from death. Above Lille the pilot's heel became wedged in a hole in the floorboard and he was unable to use his rudder. The machine side-slipped into the ground from 200 feet on to its right wing and was completely wrecked. Both occupants walked out unhurt.

A race had been organized by the Irish Aero Club from Dublin to Belfast and back for a prize of £300, and this event had attracted sixteen entries, including four Bleriot monoplanes flown by Messrs. G. Hamel, H. J. D. Astley, R. B. Slack, and Corbett Wilson, two Bristol monoplanes flown by Messrs. D. Arthur and H. Busteed, a Bristol biplane in the hands of Mons. H. Jullerot, two of the little Caudron monoplanes to be handled by Messrs. W. H. Ewen and E. Obré, Mr. S. V. Sippe's Hanriot monoplane, and Lieut. J. C. Porte's Deperdussin from the Military trials, Mr. James Valentine's old 50 h.p. Deperdussin, an Avro biplane flown by Mr. H. R. Simms, the Vickers and Handley-Page monoplanes, and the Twining biplane.

With such a field a good race was anticipated but, unfortunately, the weather was so bad that no single competitor could complete the outward stage to Belfast, and only four of the entrants started at all. H. J. D. Astley (Bleriot) and J. Valentine (Deperdussin monoplane) struggled as far as Newry, sixty miles from the start, where they landed and abandoned. The first prize was therefore divided equally between them, and Lieut. J. C. Porte, R.N. (Deperdussin), who returned to Dublin after travelling only three miles, won a second prize of £50, whilst the only other starter, Desmond Arthur (Bristol monoplane), who merely took off and landed immediately without flying outside the aerodrome, was lucky enough to capture the third prize of £25.

40. CRASHES AT THE AUTUMN MANOEUVRES

Each of the opposing forces in the Army's autumn manœuvres was provided with one squadron of aeroplanes (eight machines) of which twelve aircraft were supplied by the Military and four by the Naval Wing of the R.F.C.

The Naval contingent comprised Com. C. R. Samson, R.N., Capt. Gordon, R.M.L.I., and Lieuts. Wilfred Parke, Spencer Grey, Longmore, and L'Estrange Malone, R.N. Mr. S. F. Cody, who had been awarded the honorary rank of Colonel by the King, also attended the manœuvres with his "Cathedral."

The results obtained by the R.F.C. were kept secret, but it is known that in spite of very bad weather a number of magnificent flights were made, notably by Com. Samson, Capt. Raleigh, and Lieuts. Fox and Mackworth.

The weather and engine troubles caused innumerable forced landings and the R.F.C. paid a terrible price for its first official co-operation with the Army.

On Friday, September 6th, Capt. Patrick Hamilton, accompanied by Lieut Wyness-Stuart, was on reconnaissance in a Deperdussin monoplane (Gnôme) at a height of 2,500 feet above Graveley, near Hitchin. Witnesses saw the machine wobble violently following a loud report, and then the whole aircraft collapsed and broke into several pieces. Both officers were killed instantaneously.

Heer Fritz Koolhoven, the designer of the machine, gave evidence at the inquest to the effect that the probable cause of the disaster was that some part of the rotary engine had come off, burst through the cowling and cut one of the flying wires. This theory was corroborated by Major Brooke-Popham, who had been flying in company with the Deperdussin just prior to the accident. The Accidents Committee of the R.Ae.C. came to the conclusion that the airscrew had burst and the consequent vibration had caused the engine, which was not supported by the extra front bearing recommended by the makers, to foul the cowling. This would have broken the *cabane* to which the landing wires were attached.

Capt. Patrick Hamilton was a pilot of great experience who had learned to fly at the Bleriot school at Hendon, and had subsequently toured the United States and Mexico in company with Mr. G. M. Dyott. He was the most accomplished Deperdussin pilot in the R.F.C. Lieut. Wyness-Stuart was a pupil of the Bristol school.

Four days later, on September 10th, another double fatality occurred. This time the victims were Lieut. E. Hotchkiss, who was noted as the Bristol Company's brilliant chief instructor at their Brooklands school, and Lieut. C. Bettington.

Lieut. Hotchkiss was flying a Bristol monoplane (80 h.p. Gnôme) from Larkhill, Salisbury Plain, to Cambridge, with Lieut. Bettington as observer. The machine was one of the two which had competed in the Military trials.

The aircraft was seen at 2,000 feet above Port Meadow, Oxford, and it began to glide down as if the pilot had decided to land. It descended normally to 500 feet but at that point it began to dive steeply. At 200 feet the fabric tore off the right wing and the aircraft crashed vertically into the ground. Both the occupants were killed instantaneously. Lieut. Hotchkiss was the first officer of the R.F.C. Reserve to meet his death while engaged on Military duties.

The R.Ae.C. inquiry established beyond reasonable doubt that a quick-release catch, which was secured to a perforated steel strap screwed to the bottom of the fuselage, had opened. The flying wires were anchored to the ends of this strap, which had been torn from its fastenings by the heavy strain thrown upon them by the opening of the catch. A piece of flying metal had evidently punctured the wing and the fabric had ripped and torn off.

41. MONOPLANES BANNED

Faced with the break-up of two monoplanes of different types whilst flying normally in reasonable weather conditions, Col. Seely, Secretary of State for War, issued an edict banning the flying of all monoplanes by pilots of the Military Wing of the R.F.C.

This ill-considered decision was not followed by Mr. Winston Churchill, First Lord of the Admiralty, so that the peculiar position arose of officers in the same Corps working under quite different conditions. The spectacle of pilots owing allegiance to the Navy happily flying their fast monoplanes, whilst they themselves were confined to the slower biplane types, infuriated the Military officers of the R.F.C., and this unfortunate affair hastened the inevitable split between the two sections of the Service.

The ban was also a deadly blow at the more enterprising manufacturers, and was responsible in large measure for the unfair facilities which were accorded to the Royal Aircraft Factory to enter into direct subsidized competition with private constructors.

This official stupidity was to continue for five months, the ban not being finally removed until February 1913.

42. THE I.C.S. TOUR: THE GORDON-BENNETT CONTEST

The Imperial Correspondence Schools had engaged Mr. R. B. Slack to fly a Bleriot monoplane around the country giving demonstration flights. Their confidence was not misplaced, for Mr. Slack flew magnificently and covered a great area in the Midlands prior to coming south and giving exhibition flights along the coast. Following the example of Mons. H. Salmet, Mr. Slack made it a point of honour to fulfil his engagements regardless of weather conditions, and in carrying out his arduous programme he flew in winds up to 50 m.p.h. This enterprising institution put up a prize of £100 for the first of their pupils to fly one mile. This was won by Mr. J. H. James on a Caudron biplane (35 h.p. Anzani) on the same day on which he passed the tests for his *brevet*. Mr. James was a pupil of the Ewen School at Hendon.

After the previous year's fiasco, the R.Ae.C. made no effort to send a team to fetch the Gordon-Bennett Cup back from the U.S.A., beyond nominating Messrs. C. Grahame-White and Gustav Hamel as our representatives. As neither of them was able to afford the time to cross the Atlantic, and as no suitable machine was available in this country, this gesture served no useful purpose.

France, oddly enough, had never been awarded the Cup, although twice out of three times it had been won by a French aeroplane, and it was therefore decided to make a great effort this year. Accordingly, the Aero Club de France dispatched Jules Vedrines and Prevost with Deperdussin racing monoplanes (140 h.p. Gnômes) and Frey with an Hanriot monoplane to Chicago for the meeting.

On seeing this formidable trio in action, the Americans abandoned all hope of retaining the trophy and retired from the contest. Frey suffered engine trouble and failed to complete the course, but the two Deperdussins smashed all records, by covering 200 kilometres (125 miles) in 1 hr. 10 mins. 56 secs., and 1 hr. 15 mins. 25 secs. respectively. Vedrines' average speed was 105 m.p.h. and Prevost was only 1·4 m.p.h. slower. When it is considered that the race was flown round a small circular course, the prodigous effort made by both machines and pilots can be appreciated.

43. H. G. HAWKER: H. J. D. ASTLEY KILLED

On September 17th, the R.Ae.C. awarded aviator's certificate (No. 297) to Harry George Hawker, who had passed his tests at Brooklands on a Farman biplane, as a pupil of the Sopwith school there. Mr. H. G. Hawker was destined to become one of the finest pilots this or any other country has ever produced, and those of us who were fortunate enough to see him fly Sopwith Camels during the War 1914–18, will never forget his peerless exhibition flights, in which he displayed a mastery over that difficult machine which was never equalled by any other pilot.

On September 21st, Mr. H. J. D. Astley, who had taken his R.Ae.C. certificate (No. 48) on January 24th, 1911, was killed at Belfast. He had been commissioned, together with Mr. Valentine, to give exhibition flights from the Balmoral grounds, which were exceedingly narrow and, indeed, unsuitable for use as an aerodrome. The spectators' enclosures encircled the alighting area, and it was evident that Mr. Astley was bent upon placing his exhibition so that all who had paid for admission would have a good view. To this end he attempted to fly his Bleriot (70 h.p. Gnôme) round the narrow ground within the limits of the enclosures. This necessitated very sharp turns, and it is clear that he omitted to pull back sufficiently on the stick whilst steeply banked and side-slipped into the ground from about forty feet.

Mr. Astley, who died from his injuries some two hours after the smash, originally flew the Birdling monoplane and was a cross-country pilot of great ability.

44. IRISH SEA CROSSED AGAIN : THE KENNEDY IN RUSSIA : NIGHT FLYING AT HENDON

On September 19th, Mr. Corbett-Wilson, who had made the second crossing of the Irish Sea, as already recorded, left Farnborough on his Bleriot monoplane to fly to his home in Ireland. He reached Chepstow on that day and proceeded in the morning to Goodwick near Fishguard where he landed in the same field that he had used on his previous journey. On the following day he crossed the water and made a forced landing on the other side at Gorey, owing to engine trouble. This last stage of fifty-five miles had been covered in forty-five minutes, at an average speed of over 70 m.p.h.

It will be recalled that Mr. Lewis Turner had thrown up his post with the Kennedy Aviation Company of St. Petersburg, in order to become chief instructor at the Grahame-White school at Hendon. News arrived during September, that a biplane which had been produced by this Anglo-Russian firm, had been declared to be the best photographic, bombing, and reconnaissance machine submitted for testing at the trials of military aircraft, promoted by the Russian Government.

A form of entertainment which would be a considerable attraction nowadays was staged at Hendon on September 26th. This took the form of an exhibition of night flying by illuminated aeroplanes. Amongst the pilots who performed were Lewis Turner, J. L. Travers, Grahame-White, Richard Gates, and Louis Noel on Farmans, Marcel Desoutter on a Bleriot monoplane and Jules Nardini on a Deperdussin monoplane. The standard of flying was very high and there were no untoward incidents. The entertainment concluded with a firework display.

45. SCHOOL CHANGES : TWO NEW SEAPLANE STATIONS : BRISTOLS IN BALKAN WAR

Several important changes took place at the various schools during the early autumn. The Avro depot was moved from Brooklands to Shoreham, where permanent hangars and a fine new club-house had been built, and Mr. Simms was appointed chief instructor. Mr. H. Blackburn had established a school at Hendon and the well-known Bristol pilot, Hammond, had gone down to take charge of the inefficient aerodrome at Eastbourne, and soon succeeded in producing results with the aid of a Bristol "boxkite." Another Bristol pupil, Sydney Pickles, had taken the post of assistant instructor to Mr. Ewen at his Hendon school, where he flew the Caudron biplanes and monoplane very effectively. Mr. F. Warren Merriam had taken over the Bristol Company's depot at Brooklands in place of Mr. E. Hotchkiss, and Mr. W. Bendall was engaged as his assistant.

Robert Barnwell, having undergone a Bristol course of advanced instruction at Salisbury Plain, was posted as assistant to Mr. Macdonald at the Vickers school at Brooklands, and proceeded to fly the difficult Vickers monoplanes better than they had ever been flown before. Mr. Edward Petre, who had previously been associated with Mr. Handley-Page, took over the Martin Handasyde monoplanes at Brooklands, whilst Mr. Handley-Page moved his works from his aerodrome near Barking to Cricklewood, and engaged the Avro pilot, Lieut. Wilfred Parke, R.N., to fly his monoplane at Hendon. Messrs. Jameson and Temple opened a new school at Hendon, where instruction was given on Bleriot monoplanes. Mr. G. L. Temple was a well-known racing motor cyclist. Mr. W. L. Brock was appointed instructor at the Deperdussin school at Hendon, and Sopwith's instructor, Mr. Copland Perry, was retained by Mr. A. V. Roe to carry out test flights at Lisbon on an Avro biplane (50 h.p. Gnôme), which had been sold to the Portuguese Government. A little later Mr. Lewis Turner left the Grahame-White school and joined forces with Mr. W. H. Ewen, who was contemplating re-opening his old establishment at Lanark. M. Louis Noel was accordingly promoted to take charge of the Grahame-White school with Mr. Marcus Manton as his assistant.

A new seaplane station had been established at Carlingnose on the Firth of Forth and equipped with a Short tractor biplane (100 h.p. Gnôme) and one Short, and one Henry Farman pusher biplane, each equipped with floats. The first flights were made by Com. C. R. Samson, R.N., Capt. Gordon, R.M.L.I., and Lieut. Hewlett, R.N. Plans were also being made for the establishment of another seaplane station at Cleethorpes.

Howard Pixton had been dispatched to Bucharest, where he impressed the Staff officers of the Roumanian Army by his brilliant handling of the Bristol monoplane, which resulted in an order being placed for a batch of similar models. Meanwhile, Lieut. Loultchieff of the Bulgarian Army returned to Sofia, after taking a course of instruction at the Bristol school at Brooklands, to take over a similar machine, which had been supplied to his Government. These two nations were just about to declare war against each other so that the Bristol Company were well in with both sides, and were also reaping the benefit of training a number of Turkish officers at Salisbury Plain. In addition to this, the Italian Government had completed arrangements with the Company for the immediate construction in Italy under licence of twenty-eight Bristol two-seater monoplanes (80 h.p. Gnôme). This was the first instance of British aeroplanes being manufactured abroad. Lieut. Loultchieff wrote from Sofia inviting his instructor, Mr. Warren Merriam, and Messrs. Sabelli (Hanriot), Knight (Vickers), and Hedley (Sopwith), to journey to the front and help to organize the Bulgarian Air Force for the war. Messrs.

Hedley and Sabelli accepted, and left on October 31st, and a little later, Mr. H. Barber, of Valkyrie fame, set off on a mysterious mission to Constantinople.

46. THE OFFICERS OF THE R.F.C. IN OCTOBER 1912

The first appearance of the R.F.C. as a separate unit in the Army List was in October 1912, and I have set out below the names of the flying officers appointed as at the end of that month.

1. **The Central Flying School** (*Upavon*) **:**

Commandant : Capt. Godfrey M. Paine, M.V.O., R.N.
Instructor in Theory and Construction : Col. H. R. Cook.
Flying Instructors : (*a*) Maj. E. L. Gerrard, R.M.
(*b*) Maj. H. M. Trenchard, D.S.O.
(*c*) Capt. J. D. B. Fulton.
(*d*) Capt. P. W. L. Broke-Smith.
Inspector of Engines : Eng.-Lieut. C. R. J. Randall, R.N.

2. **The Military Wing :**

Commandant : Maj. F. H. Sykes.
Adjutant : Lieut. B. H. Barrington-Kennett.
No. 2 Squadron :
Squadron Commander : Maj. C. J. Burke.
Flight Commanders : Capt. G. H. Raleigh.
Capt. H. R. P. Reynolds.
Flying Officers : (1) Capt. G. W. P. Dawes.
(2) Lieut. C. A. H. Longcroft.
(3) Lieut. G. B. Haynes.
(4) Lieut. G. T. Porter.
(5) Lieut. C. T. Carfrae.
No. 3 Squadron :
Squadron Commander : Maj. H. R. M. Brooke-Popham.
Flight Commanders : Capt. C. R. W. Allen.
Capt. B. R. W. Beor.
Capt. D. G. Conner.
Flying Officer : Lieut. A. G. Fox.

3. **The Naval Wing :**

Officer Commanding : Com. C. R. Samson, R.N.
Flying Officers : (1) Capt. R. Gordon, R.M.
(2) Lieut. J. W. Seddon, R.N.
(3) Lieut. W. Parke, R.N.
(4) Lieut. C. J. L'Estrange Malone, R.N.
(5) Sub-Lieut. F. E. T. Hewlett, R.N.

4. **Reserve :**

Commandant : Brig.-Gen. D. C. B. Henderson, D.S.O., C.B.
Flying Officer : Lieut. O. Gordon Bell.

Both Nos. 2 and 3 Squadrons were officially based on Salisbury

Plain, but actually they operated from Farnborough. The Naval Wing was stationed at Eastchurch. No. 1 Squadron dealt only with airships and kites.

47. BRITISH EMPIRE MICHELIN TROPHIES

The rules of the competition for the British Empire Michelin Trophy No. 2 for the year 1912, called for a flight by a British pilot, in an all-British aeroplane, round an approved cross-country circuit of 186 miles in length. The pilot making the fastest time for the course was to be the winner.

The closing date was October 15th, and on October 12th, Mr. S. F. Cody flew his "Cathedral," which had been fitted with the new 100 h.p. 6-cylinder in line all-British Green engine, from Laffan's Plain round a circuit with turning points at Larkhill (Salisbury Plain), Newhaven, and Brooklands. He took off at 11.50 a.m., and completed the course without alighting by 3.16 p.m., which gives an average speed of only 45 m.p.h. The reason for this was that he lost his way after passing the Larkhill turn, and struck the coast at Southampton instead of Newhaven, so that, actually, he must have covered at least 220 miles. No one contested this performance, so Cody was declared the winner for the third year in succession, and awarded the trophy and £600 prize money.

Mr. H. G. Hawker, although still in the novice stage, wasted no time in making his presence felt. Awarded his certificate on September 17th, he immediately began a series of attacks on the British Empire Michelin Trophy No. 1, which was to be awarded to the British pilot who should have remained the longest time in the air on an all-British aeroplane in one flight, without touching the ground, between sunrise and one hour after sunset. A minimum of five hours was required in order to qualify for the prize.

Hawker obtained permission to fly the Sopwith Wright-type biplane, which had been fitted with one of the new 40-50 h.p. A.B.C. engines for the purpose.

On October 16th he made his first attempt, but was forced down after 3 hrs. 31 mins. Five days later he stayed up for 2 hrs. 40 mins., and on the following day he kept in the air for 3½ hrs. He carried out this last-mentioned flight simultaneously with F. P. Raynham, who was competing against him on an Avro cabin biplane, and who put in 3 hrs. 48 mins. before he too was compelled to land. Thus began a friendly rivalry between these great pilots, which was to continue for more than ten years.

The competition was due to close on October 31st, and both pilots resumed their attempts on the 24th. Raynham took off at dawn, and Hawker joined him in the air over Brooklands a few hours later. The oil was exhausted in the Green engine of Raynham's Avro after 7 hrs. 31½ mins., and he had to land, having

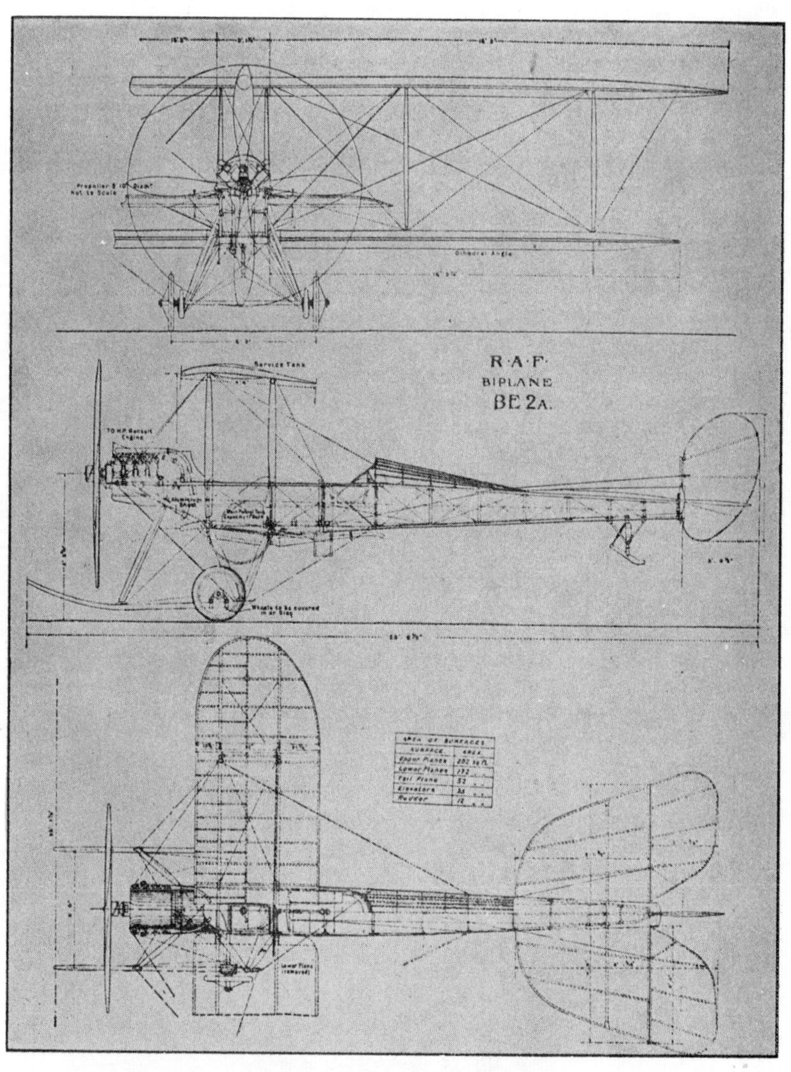

"Flight" copyright

9.—THE ANCESTOR OF THE MOTH: MR. GEOFFREY DE HAVILLAND'S BRILLIANT DESIGN, THE B.E.2A (70 H.P. RENAULT).

Facing page 196

"*Flight*" *photo*

28.—THE MILITARY TRIALS: THE REAL WINNER OF THE COMPETITION: THE HANRIOT MONOPLANE (100 H.P. GNÔME) FLOWN BY MONS. BIELOVUCIC.

broken the British duration record by a handsome margin—but still Hawker kept circling round.

It was not until darkness fell that the Sopwith pilot made a voluntary descent after a flight of 8 hrs. 23 mins., by which he not only captured the Michelin Trophy and a cash prize of £500, but also set up a new all-British record for duration.

Thus did Harry Hawker's pertinacity carry him from the position of an unknown pupil to the rank of record-breaker in the space of seven weeks. It was obvious that he was a force to be reckoned with in British aviation.

48. THE PARIS SALON

The Aero Show which opened in Paris on October 26th, was remarkable more on account of a general cleaning up of existing designs than for any revolutionary new types. This was a healthy sign. The great age of unfettered experiment was giving place to a steady development of the now-established theories, and to a persistent attention to detail improvements.

The tractor type built up around a fuselage in which the crew were housed in comfort, had won the day against the exponents of the " boxkite " school of thought.

In 1911 there had been forty-three aeroplanes exhibited, but this year there were seventy-seven machines on view, including twenty-seven belonging to the French Air Service. Of the total number, nine were float seaplanes, and there were two flying boats. One of the latter was the interesting little Donnet-Levêque, a specimen of which had been acquired by the Admiralty for the use of the Naval Wing of the R.F.C. at Eastchurch.

Of the sixty-six land machines no less than forty-six were monoplanes.

Great Britain was represented once more by the enterprising Bristol firm, who showed one of M. Coanda's two-seat monoplanes, of the type which did so well in the Military trials, fitted with a 50 h.p. Gnôme engine. This machine attracted a great deal of attention on account of the excellence of the Bristol workmanship. The English branch of the Breguêt firm showed a tractor biplane of the type already in use in the R.F.C.

The most interesting exhibit was the beautiful Deperdussin racer (140 h.p. Gnôme), with which Vedrines had won the Gordon-Bennett Cup, and which had a *monocoque* fuselage built up of innumerable small pieces of plywood glued together on a mould. This little machine was only twenty-two feet in span with an average chord to the wings of four feet. It was the first machine to be fitted with a conical spinner over the boss of the airscrew, and a streamline fairing for the top of its pilot's head.

Another outstanding design was the Nieuport racer (50 h.p.

Gnôme), which was a little monoplane of twenty-three feet span and beautifully clean lines. It was spoiled by an impractical undercarriage.

The *clou* of the salon was the Hanriot monoplane, which was shown in skeleton form in order to display M. Pagny's clever design and the exquisite workmanship. This aircraft fairly bristled with novel ideas, including devices for folding the wings and the tail plane without upsetting the rigging and facilities for removing the Gnôme engine complete in sixty seconds. The machine was of exactly the same type as those flown with such outstanding success by Bielovucic and Sippe at Salisbury Plain, but many detail refinements had been added, and the view had been improved.

49. FLYING IN THE NORTH AND IN THE ARGENTINE: JOHN ALCOCK QUALIFIES

Two pupils at Mr. Melly's school at Waterloo, near Liverpool, had at last begun to make real progress, and were handling the Bleriot monoplanes with confident ability. Towards the end of November, Messrs. Hardman and Birch made some excellent cross-country flights at heights up to 4,000 feet, and the latter pilot also attempted some cloud flying. Apart from Mr. Vivian Hewitt's fine performances at Rhyl and the efforts of visiting pilots from the south, this was the first indication of any real talent for practical flying in the northern counties.

Mr. George Newberry, an English resident in Buenos Aires, had learned to fly a Bleriot monoplane under the instruction of Cattaneo, and he made a successful attempt on the Argentine altitude record, during which he attained a height of 2,480 metres (8,134 feet). He was given a dinner by the Argentine Aero Club, of which he was President, in recognition of this fine flight. A few weeks later this pilot made a flight of 150 kilometres between the Argentine and Uruguay, crossing the Rio del Plata *en route*.

On November 16th Mr. John Alcock completed his tests tor his R.Ae.C. certificate (No. 368) at the Ducrocq school at Brooklands. After performing the requisite figures of eight, he put his Farman biplane down exactly on top of the observers' landing mark. Two days later Alcock made two short cross-country flights, on one of which he took a passenger. The next two days were devoted to more extended journeys outside the aerodrome, and to practising gliding descents from heights above 1,000 feet.

Seven days after taking his *brevet*, this brilliant pupil entered for his first race, and won it on handicap, beating such pilots as T. O. M. Sopwith and Warren Merriam. Seven years afterwards Mr. John Alcock wrote his name in large indelible letters in the history of the twentieth century, by piloting the first aeroplane to make a direct crossing of the North Atlantic ocean.

50. THE AUSTRALIAN AIR FORCE: THE NEW FLANDERS

It will be recalled that the Australian Government had sent Mr. Lindsay Campbell to England to learn to fly, with a view to placing him in charge of the organization of a Flying Service for the Commonwealth, and I have described how he lost his life in the process.

The Australian authorities had a wealth of native talent in this country from which to choose his successor. Messrs. E. Harrison, H. Busteed, H. G. Hawker, Sydney Pickles, and V. P. Taylor, were all Australians, and there was also Mr. J. J. Hammond, who was a New Zealander.

Eventually, Mr. Harrison, who had been assisting Mr. Ronald Kemp to operate the Bristol Company's newly-established school of flying at Halberstadt, in Germany, and Mr. H. Petre were chosen to be the first instructors at the Australian School of Military Aviation. They sailed during December.

Mr. Howard Flanders had brought out a new monoplane for the use of the R.F.C. Mr. F. P. Raynham was charged with the delivery of the machines to Farnborough, and with piloting them through their acceptance tests before the examining officers. This new type was a great improvement on the previous model and was fitted with a 70 h.p. Renault engine. In the official tests it climbed to 1,000 feet in 3½ mins., and to 2,000 feet in 8 mins., whilst its maximum speed was 67·2 m.p.h. As the machine stalled at 41 m.p.h., it had a speed range of 26·2 m.p.h., which was better than that of any competitor in the Military trials, and was only inferior to that of the B.E.2.

51. THE DEATH OF WILFRED PARKE: GREAT FLIGHT BY VERRIER

British aviation suffered a severe blow as a result of a catastrophe to the Handley-Page monoplane at Wembley, on December 15th.

The machine had taken off from Hendon aerodrome for Oxford at 11.50 a.m., with Mr. A. Hardwick, manager of Handley-Page, Ltd., in the passenger's seat, and with Lieut. Wilfred Parke, R.N., at the controls. The engine was not running well, and it is difficult to find any justification for Lieut. Parke's action in starting on a long cross-country flight with a passenger under such conditions.

After staggering off the ground the machine flew for about ten minutes until it was over Wembley. At this point it became obvious that the pilot could no longer maintain height with the power available, and apparently he determined to try to turn back to the aerodrome. The machine was only about forty feet above some trees at the time, and it is not surprising that Parke stalled in attempting the difficult feat of turning down-wind with insufficient reserve of flying speed. The monoplane dived vertically to the ground, and both occupants were killed instantaneously.

Lieut. Parke, R.N., who had taken his R.Ae.C. certificate (No. 73) on April 25th, 1911, was a pilot of great experience. He had flown Bristol, Sanders, Avro, Farman, Caudron, Short, and Cody biplanes, and Avro, Deperdussin, and Handley-Page monoplanes. He was the first British pilot to fly an all-enclosed cabin aeroplane, and the second to recover from a spinning nose-dive. It is for his cool resource in connection with the latter episode that he will always be remembered.

One of the finest flights yet attempted in this country was one from Hendon to Brooklands, which was carried out by M. Pierre Verrier on a British-built Maurice Farman biplane (70 h.p. Renault), in the middle of December. Verrier, who was accompanied by Lieut. Mapplebeck, took off into the teeth of a 45 m.p.h. gale, on a machine which had a maximum speed of 55 m.p.h. It was obvious from the start that they were making little progress, and, indeed, Mr. Clement Gresswell, then the assistant manager of the Aircraft Co., Ltd., who was "following" the flight in a car, had to keep stopping by the roadside to allow the biplane to overtake him!

Verrier never thought of turning back. For 2 hrs. 10 mins. he fought the gale, and eventually landed safely at Brooklands, having averaged 9 m.p.h. for the journey.

52. SABOTAGE AT HENDON: THE DEATH OF "PETRE THE PAINTER"

Some cowardly "person or persons unknown" evidently had a spite against the British Deperdussin Co., Ltd., or their pilots, for, on December 21st, it was discovered that the carburettors of two of the monoplanes had been filled with water. That might well have been the work of a practical joker, but on the following day a much more serious incident occurred.

Lieut. J. C. Porte, R.N., had just taken off in a considerable wind, with a distinguished Naval officer in the passenger's seat, when his engine stopped suddenly. Porte made a skilful forced landing six feet from the aerodrome fence, and got out to examine his motor. He found it completely smashed to pieces. A close inspection revealed the fact that someone had inserted a large nut, of a type not used at all on that particular engine, in the crank-case.

Mr. Edward Petre, known as "Petre the Painter" to distinguish him from his brother, Mr. H. A. Petre, whose nickname was "Petre the Monk," had long cherished an ambition to make a non-stop flight from Brooklands to Edinburgh before Christmas.

He was delayed owing to one cause and another, and it is probable that he persuaded himself to start on Christmas Eve, in the face of bad weather and the advice of his friends, against his own better judgment.

In any event, he took off at 9.10 a.m., in a Martin-Handasyde monoplane (65 h.p. 8-cylinder Antoinette engine), and headed north. The wind was broad on his left hand and became more and more violent as he proceeded on his long journey. He failed to allow enough for drift and, after battling with the gale for three hours and five minutes, he found himself above the coast at Marske-by-the-Sea, in Yorkshire.

Evidently he decided to land, fearing that the violence of the wind would drive him out over the North Sea, and his machine was seen to glide down from 500 to 400 feet. Then it rose again, and suddenly both wings collapsed, and the machine fell in scattered pieces.

"Petre the Painter," who was killed instantaneously, had covered more than 200 miles non-stop in a straight line, and thus set up a splendid new record for British pilots, although the flight could not count for the all-British record because the engine used was of French manufacture.

Mr. Petre had been intimately concerned in the flying tests of the original Handley-Page monoplane at Barking, but had not bothered to take out his R.Ae.C. certificate (No. 259) until July 24th, 1912.

53. 1912 REVIEWED: THE PRINCIPAL EVENTS

The most important happenings of 1912 were, of course, the establishment of the Royal Flying Corps and the Military trials. This sudden awakening on the part of the politicians to the growing importance of the aeroplane as a weapon, directed everyone's attention to the Military and Naval aspects of flying.

Men's minds were much concerned with the problems connected with the use of aircraft in conjunction with warships, and it is difficult to exaggerate the importance of the work of the Naval Wing, R.F.C., with float seaplanes, and of the dangerous experiments in deck flying carried out by Com. C. R. Samson, R.N., and Lieut. L'Estrange Malone, R.N.

From its very inception the spirit of the Royal Flying Corps was magnificent. The officers of the Military Wing impressed the civilian competitors in the Military trials by their disregard for weather which confined the competing aircraft to the hangars. They suffered heavy losses in men and material; losses which were the harder to bear because of the pathetically small personnel of the Corps, and the inadequacy of their stock of machines. Sqdrn.-Com. J. C. Burke of No. 2 Squadron, summed up the spirit of the Service when he stated at the inquest on one of the victims, "*We fly when it is our duty to fly.*" Moreover, the senior officers were all pilots themselves, and they made it clear that it was the duty of the Corps to fly whenever an aeroplane was available, and whenever the weather was at all possible: and very often when it was not.

54. ACCIDENTS IN 1912

The year had been a black one, indeed, as far as accidents were concerned.

The R.F.C. alone had lost six officers and one N.C.O. pilot in four crashes.

There had been eleven fatal accidents altogether, in which no less than fourteen pilots had paid the extreme penalty. It is probable, however, that the increase in the number of hours flown was almost proportionate to the increased death-roll, which was exactly double that for 1911.

The alarming feature of the accidents of 1912 lay in the fact that the pilots of the wrecked aircraft were all, with one exception, experienced men, and that in five cases deaths were brought about by failure of machines in the air. All the aeroplanes which broke up or failed to respond to their controls were monoplanes, and they comprised two Martin-Handasydes, an experimental Mersey, a Deperdussin, and a Bristol. These accidents accounted for seven of the deaths.

Of the other fatal smashes two were due to pilots stalling whilst gliding, two to side-slipping out of tight turns performed too close to the ground, one to the pilot taking off with a failing engine, and one machine was lost at sea.

55. THE PROGRESS OF THE SCHOOLS IN 1912

During 1911 the basis of a wide flung system of schools of flying had been laid in England. During 1912 that system was consolidated and expanded. Of the twelve civilian establishments which were working in 1911, five, namely: the Hanriot, Aeronautical Syndicate, McArdle and Drexel, Blackburn, and Spencer schools, had ceased to function during 1912, but nine fresh schools had arisen in their places and, in addition, the Naval school at Eastchurch now had a military rival at Upavon.

Thus, during 1912, there were sixteen civilian and two Government establishments engaged in training pilots *ab initio*, and between them they turned out no less than 211 new pilots. This was almost twice the number trained in this country during 1911, and, although it included fourteen foreign subjects, the net increase in the number of British pilots was actually 214, for eight Englishmen had qualified in France and six in the U.S.A., whilst three more had taught themselves to fly.

The record of the British schools for 1912 was as follows :—

School	*Aerodrome*	*No. of Pupils trained during 1912*
Bristol	Brooklands 63 Salisbury Plain 35	98
Grahame-White	Hendon	20
Naval School (R.F.C.) ..	Eastchurch	16
C.F.S. (R.F.C.)	Upavon	14
Deperdussin ..	Brooklands 5 Hendon 9	14
Sopwith	Brooklands	11
Bleriot	Hendon	8
Ewen	Hendon	7
Vickers	Brooklands	6
E.A.C.	Eastbourne	6
Avro	Brooklands	3
Melly	Freshfield (Lancs)	2
Hewlett and Blondeau ..	Brooklands	1
Ducrocq	Brooklands	1
Ogilvie	Eastchurch	1
Cody	Farnborough	1
Handley-Page	Fairlop	1
Lakes F. S. (seaplanes)	Windermere	1
		Total 211

The Bristol Company's effort was truly prodigious. Their gross output of pilots was almost two per week, and their Brooklands branch alone had trained more than three times as many pilots as any other firm in the country.

Few of the subsidized flying clubs of the present day could equal the output of the Brooklands branch of Bristols, in spite of the accumulated knowledge of twenty years, the dual controls, the telephones, the modern light training aircraft and the elaborate equipment with which they are provided. And if the Government was to equip a modern club with Bristol "boxkites" and set them to obtain the same results. . . .!

Great Britain now stood second amongst the nations of the world in the number of her pilots. Here is a list, which is only approximately accurate, of the aviators certificates issued by the various countries at the end of the year, wherein the immense superiority of the French, with nearly three times as many pilots as any other nation, is strikingly displayed :—

1. France	966	10. Holland		26
2. Great Britain	382[1]	11.	Argentine Republic	15
3. Germany	335		Spain	15
4. U.S.A.	193	13. Sweden		10
5. Italy	186	14. Denmark		8
6. Russia	162	15. Hungary		7
7. Austria	84	16. Norway		5
8. Belgium	58	17. Egypt		1
9. Switzerland	27			
		Total		2,480

This is not the sum total of the world's pilots, as there were a few others in countries which were not members of the *Fédération Aéronautique Internationale.*

56. THE PILOTS OF 1912

Now for a *résumé* of the work of the leading British pilots during the year.

Detailed performances of individual service pilots are not available and, as this is intended to be a history of aviation as a means of transport rather than as a fighting arm, I propose to confine my list of the ten best British pilots at the end of 1912 to civilians. I will merely record the impression that Lieuts. A. G. Fox, Mackworth, and Barrington-Kennett, were the best pilots in the squadrons of the Military Wing, R.F.C., whilst Com. C. R. Samson, R.N., and Lieut. Spencer Grey, R.N., were outstanding amongst the officers of the Naval Wing. It is probable that by the end of the year the R.F.C. could boast of several pilots who were quite capable of equalling any feat that the civilian experts could perform.

Whilst there had been no performances of such outstanding merit as Valentine's great flights of 1911, there had been a steady broadening of the general activity, and lengthy cross-country flights were becoming quite common.

Probably the best individual effort was Mr. E. Petre's non-stop flight in a gale for 200 miles from Brooklands to Marske-by-the-Sea, but Mr. Hucks' journey from Paris to Hendon in stages was almost equally good, and Mr. H. J. D. Astley's tour from Hendon to Bonn via Paris and back to Lille, was a great achievement.

The Channel had been crossed twelve times by British pilots during the year, Gustav Hamel having made the passage four times, and James Valentine three times. Other pilots who had ventured across were Messrs. H. J. D. Astley, W. H. Ewen, B. C. Hucks, Grahame-White, and Rhodes-Moorhouse.

[1] If the certificates issued by the R.Ae.C. to foreign subjects be deducted, and the certificates taken by British subjects in France and the U.S.A. be added, it will be found that the actual number of British subjects who had qualified as pilots at this date was 385, of whom twenty-one had been killed in flying accidents.

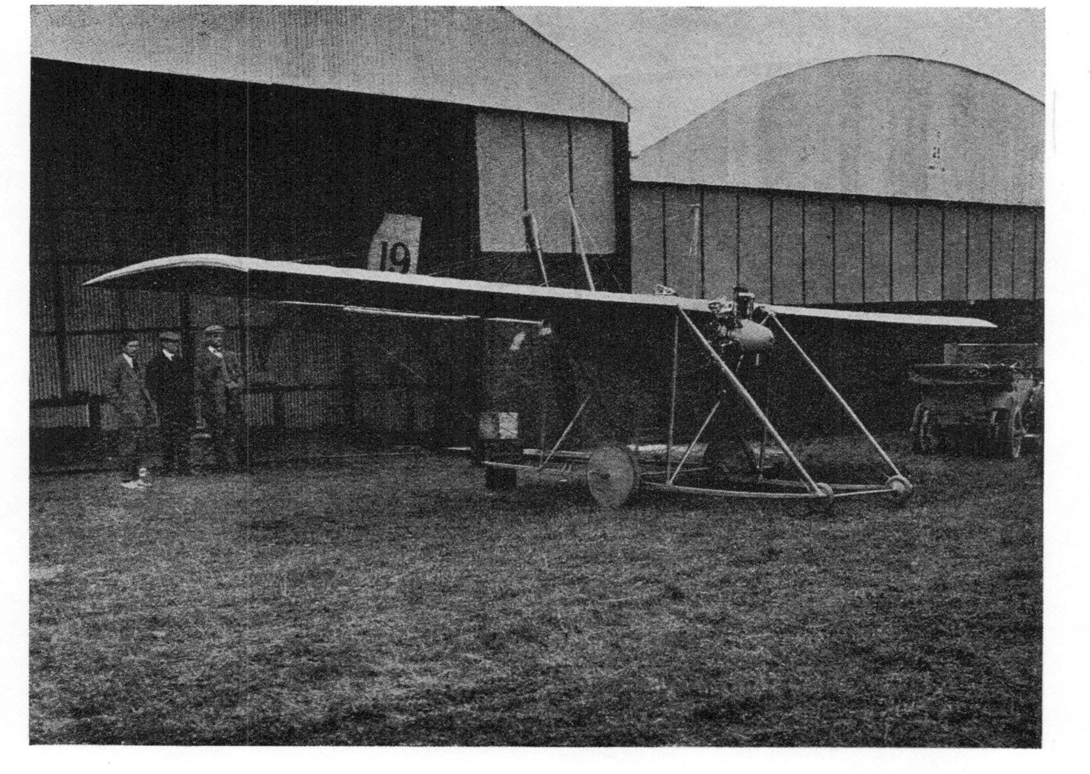

"Flight" photo

29.—The Military Trials: the Mersey Pusher Monoplane (Isaacson), which killed its designer, Mr. R. C. Fenwick.

Facing page 204

Mr. Corbett-Wilson had performed the astonishing feat of flying twice from the neighbourhood of London to his home in Ireland, and the dangerous crossing of the Irish Sea had also been accomplished by Mr. Vivian Hewitt.

It is very difficult to select the best ten from such a bunch of budding talent. I think, however, that Mr. Howard Pixton deserves the premier place. He had flown his company's machines from difficult aerodromes all over Europe. Pilots in Spain, Italy, Roumania, and Germany, had all been impressed by his masterly handling of the Bristol monoplanes, and he flew in the Military trials with great accuracy and dash.

Next I pick Mr. Geoffrey de Havilland, whose work on the various B.E. aeroplanes of his own design attracted little public notice, but was none the less invaluable to British aviation. He flew his machines with great intelligence and skill, and was the first British test pilot to carry out accurate observations of performance in the air by means of scientific instruments.

The pilots who were engaged in the *Daily Mail* tours flew magnificently under most difficult conditions, and each of them put in a great number of hours and gained a vast amount of useful experience. I think that the best performances of this little band were put up by Messrs. Gustav Hamel and B. C. Hucks, each of whom had many competition successes and long cross-country flights to his credit, in addition to those incidental to the tour.

A young pilot who must be put in the front rank was Mr. Gordon Bell, whose work in France for the R.E.P. firm was first-class in every respect, and with him must be included Mr. S. V. Sippe, whose exploits at Rheims received little attention in this country until the quality of his airmanship was displayed at the Military trials.

Of those who occupied places of honour in the list for 1911, Graham Gilmour was dead, Messrs. O. C. Morison, C. H. Gresswell, and H. Barber had retired from practical aviation and Messrs. T. O. M. Sopwith and C. Grahame-White were interesting themselves more in the manufacturing side, although both still flew occasionally, and the former had achieved many competition successes at Brooklands in addition to winning the first Aerial Derby.

Cody had done well to win the Military trials and the Michelin Trophy No. 2, but he still lacked experience of any other type of machine than his own, and I must reluctantly leave him out of this list. Valentine must still be included, although he had been less active of late, and the claims of Messrs. F. P. Raynham, H. G. Hawker, W. H. Ewen, Collyns Pizey, H. Busteed, Lewis Turner, and F. Warren Merriam, demand consideration.

Although Hawker beat Raynham in the contest for the Michelin Trophy No 1, he was inexperienced as yet and I should prefer to include the last-named, whose great experience and masterly flying of the Flanders monoplanes deserve recognition. I must also give a place to Mr. Warren Merriam as, although he had done nothing of a startling nature, he had probably flown more hours than any other civilian pilot in England during 1912, and had achieved a remarkable success, first as assistant, and finally as chief instructor at the Bristol school at Brooklands.

The list then is as follows :—

1. Howard Pixton (Avro and Bristol biplanes, and Bristol monoplanes).
2. Geoffrey de Havilland (de Havilland—B.E. biplanes).
3. Gustav Hamel (Bleriot monoplane and Howard-Wright biplane).
4. Gordon Bell (Farman and Avro biplanes, and R.E.P., Bleriot, Martin-Handasyde, Hanriot, and Deperdussin monoplanes).
5. B. C. Hucks (Blackburn and Bleriot monoplanes).
6. James Valentine (Deperdussin and Bristol monoplanes).
7. F. P. Raynham (Farman, Howard-Wright, Burgess-Wright, and Avro biplanes, and Flanders monoplanes).
8. S. V. Sippe (Avro biplane and Hanriot monoplane).
9. Corbett-Wilson (Bleriot monoplane).
10. F. Warren Merriam (Bristol biplanes and monoplanes).

57. BRITISH AIRCRAFT OF 1912

The outstanding feature on the manufacturing side was, of course, the development of Mr. Geoffrey de Havilland's B.E. tractor biplane at the Royal Aircraft Factory at Farnborough. I have already recorded the remarkable achievements of this machine, which was far ahead both in design and construction of any other aeroplane produced in England at that time.

Next in importance were Mr. A. V. Roe's products. The open-cockpit tractor biplane with the 50 h.p. Gnôme gave excellent service in the R.F.C., and the all-enclosed type which was flown in the Military trials was a notable step forward in design. It failed in the trials solely because it was grievously underpowered. A monoplane version of this machine had also been tried out. No one deserved to succeed more than did A. V. Roe, and it was a good sign when he was able to form a limited company with substantial capital, towards the end of the year, and thus equip his Manchester factory for quantity production to meet the requirements of the R.F.C.

The Bristol firm continued to expand. Their products were known all over Europe ; a Bristol school of flying was in operation in Germany, Bristol monoplanes were being built under licence in Italy, and the Governments of Spain, Roumania, and Bulgaria, were also buying Bristol aeroplanes. The Bristol schools at Salisbury Plain and Brooklands were training pupils from all over the world to use Bristol products. A further issue of capital was floated and promptly subscribed. The Company was the first British aviation firm to enter the ranks of " Big Business," and to acquire an international reputation.

The Short brothers were turning more and more towards the float seaplane type, and their latest tractor biplane had proved very successful in the hands of the pilots of the Naval Wing, R.F.C.

The Coventry Ordnance machine was full of clever ideas, but suffered an unusual multitude of " teething troubles." The new Flanders monoplanes were very promising; they flew strongly and well with their 70 h.p. Renault motors, and were beautifully made.

None of the other constructors had made any notable advance.

58. WORLD'S RECORDS AT THE END OF 1912

It is surprising to have to record that the *Fédération Aéronautique Internationale* still confined its official recognition to performances by aircraft round closed circuits, and to the altitude record. Thus, no official attempts had been made upon the absolute speed record over a straight measured distance, and the circuit records were valueless, as I have previously pointed out, because so much depended upon the cornering ability of the pilot. There can be no doubt, however, but that the two Deperdussin monoplanes which flew in the Gordon-Bennett contest were the fastest aeroplanes in existence at the end of the year. Their speed in still air cannot have been far short of 120 m.p.h.

I have omitted the record for distance flown in a straight line this year because, as this was also unrecognized officially, it is difficult to discover whether or not anyone had actually beaten M. Pierre Prier's non-stop journey of approximately 210 miles from Hendon to Paris. Many French pilots had covered long stages in their attempts on the *Coupe Pommery*, but verification of the actual distances is impossible. The most probable holder of the record was Sergt. Feierstein of the French Army, who flew from Casablanca to Mogador non-stop in 3 hours, with Lieut. Van den Vaero as passenger, in a Bleriot monoplane (Gnôme) on Boxing Day 1912. The distance covered was approximately 350 kilometres (217 miles). This flight was very little longer, however, than the tragic last journey Edward Petre had made two days previously from Brooklands to Marske, in Yorkshire.

It is good to note that an English pilot's name stood in the record book at the end of a year for the first time. This was that of Lieut. B. H. Barrington-Kennett, Adjutant of the R.F.C., who had covered 249 miles 840 yards non-stop in a closed circuit with a passenger, on a French machine. I have not included his performance in the table as there is only room for the more important records.

It will be noted that the duration and altitude records were still held by the same pilots as at the end of the previous year, and that the former had been extended by 2 hrs. 21 mins., and the latter raised by 4,457 feet.

Fourny had wrested the distance record (closed circuit) from Gobe, and added 171 miles to it during his flight for the duration record.

WORLD'S RECORDS AT THE END OF 1912.

Pilot	*Nationality*	*Aircraft*	*Nationality*	*Engine*	*Nationality*	*Time or Distance*	*Place*
			DURATION				
Fourny	French	Maurice Farman	French	Renault	French	13h. 22m.	Etampes
			DISTANCE IN A CLOSED CIRCUIT				
Fourny	French	Maurice Farman	French	Renault	French	1017 Km. (631·5 miles)	Etampes
			ALTITUDE				
Roland Garros	French	Morane-Saulnier	French	Gnôme	French	5,610 m. (18,400 ft.)	Tunis

59. ALL-BRITISH RECORDS AT THE END OF 1912

I have been forced to omit the record for distance flown in a closed circuit from the list, because the distances covered by Messrs. Raynham and Hawker in their long flights for the Michelin Trophy No. 1 had not been officially recognized. It is obvious that both pilots must have exceeded the 261·5 miles covered by Cody in the same competition in 1911 by a substantial margin, and it is a pity that their figures are not available.

There had still been no attempt to capture Sopwith's all-British record for distance flown in a straight line, which reappears for the third year in succession.

I have been able to add the record for speed over a measured distance in a straight line as a result of the Military trials, although this record was not recognized officially.

ALL-BRITISH RECORDS AT THE END OF 1912

Pilot	*Aircraft*	*Engine*	*Time, Distance or Speed*	*Place*
		DURATION		
H. G. Hawker	Sopwith-Wright	40/50h.p.A.B.C.	8 hrs. 23 min	Brooklands
		DISTANCE IN A STRAIGHT LINE		
T. O. M. Sopwith	Howard-Wright	60 h.p. E.N.V.	169 miles	Eastchurch to Thirimont (Belgium)
SPEED IN A STRAIGHT LINE :—MESNE OF TWO RUNS IN OPPOSITE DIRECTIONS (Unofficial)				
W. Parke	Avro	60 h.p. Green	61·8 m.p.h.	Salisbury Plain

INDEX A

AIRCRAFT

NOTE:—The nationality of foreign aircraft is indicated by the symbols in brackets.

INDEX B

AERO ENGINES

NOTE :—The nationality of foreign engines is indicated by the symbols in brackets.

[1] There are innumerable references to Gnôme engines throughout this book. Only the pages containing the most important passages are indexed.

INDEX C

PILOTS

NOTE :—The nationality of foreign pilots is indicated by the symbols in brackets.

HISTORY OF BRITISH AVIATION

1908—1914

"Flight" photo

1.—Mr. S. F. Cody: the great Anglo-American pioneer

HISTORY OF BRITISH AVIATION 1908—1914

By

R. DALLAS BRETT

Late Honorary Secretary of the Cinque Ports Flying Club, Lympne.

Volume II

AIR RESEARCH PUBLICATIONS

in association with

KRISTALL PRODUCTIONS

LIST OF DIAGRAMS

CHAPTER I

1913

1. ANOTHER DOUBLE FATALITY

The wave of fatal smashes which disfigured the history of British aviation for the closing months of 1912 showed no signs of abatement in the New Year.

Messrs. Vickers Ltd. had established a private aerodrome adjoining their works at Erith, on the banks of the Thames, where new designs were tried out before making their public appearance at Brooklands, and Mr. L. F. Macdonald was engaged in making test flights there on a new tractor biplane during January.

On the 13th of that month he took off with Mr. H. England, one of the firm's mechanics, in the passenger's seat, with the intention of making some tests.

The engine, a 70 h.p. Gnôme, was running badly on the ground, but Macdonald, following Lieut. Parke's bad example, ignored this and took off across the river. After staggering out of the aerodrome and over the river bank, the machine began to lose height, so the pilot made a feeble attempt to turn back, and flew about 100 yards upstream until the wheels dipped into the water and dragged the machine after them.

The aircraft, which hit the water with engine still on, sank in two minutes. Macdonald was evidently trapped in his seat and drowned, but the mechanic struggled clear and swam a few yards before he too disappeared.

This accident should never have occurred, any more than should that in which Lieut. Wilfred Parke, R.N., lost his life. It provided one more instance of a pilot taking an entirely unjustified risk by leaving the ground with a faulty engine.

Mr. L. F. Macdonald was the very first pilot to take his certificate (No. 28) as a pupil of the Bristol school of flying. His *brevet* was granted on November 15th, 1910, and he had seen a great deal of flying on Bristol biplanes and Vickers monoplanes, although he was only twenty-two years of age at the date of his death. His best achievements had been performed in Australia where he had toured with Mr. J. J. Hammond, the New Zealand pilot, on Bristol " boxkites " during 1911.

2. THE " MONOPLANE COMMITTEE'S " REPORT

A departmental committee had been appointed to investigate the fatal accidents to the Deperdussin and Bristol monoplanes flown by Capt. Hamilton and Lieut. Hotchkiss, and especially charged with the duty of discovering whether or not either accident was attributable to a defect inherent in the monoplane, as distinct from the biplane, type of aircraft.

Their report, which was presented to the Government on December 3rd, 1912, was not published until the beginning of February 1913. In effect it completely exonerated the monoplane, as such, but it made several sound suggestions as to desirable modifications of current monoplane design and construction.

It criticized adversely the haphazard mounting of the 100 h.p. Gnôme engine in the Deperdussin machine, and pressed for extensive alterations both in design and in the material used in the construction of the Gnôme motors.

It pointed out that flying wires should not be anchored to undercarriages, and thus subjected to continual strain on landing or taking off, that all flying and control wires should be duplicated, and that quick-release catches should only be used after most careful tests.

A most important recommendation was that a sufficient number of permanent officials should be appointed, whose duty it would be to carry out regular inspections of aircraft and engines, both in course of construction and in actual service, and to examine and report on every accident and repair.

Thus the committee, which included Brig.-Gen. D. Henderson, Maj. F. H. Sykes, Maj. R. Brooke-Popham, and Lieut. Spencer Grey, R.N., struck right at the roots of the growing menace.

In the early days the majority of aeroplanes were so slow that the strains imposed upon their various parts in the air were never very great, but now that air speeds were increasing, and now that pilots were becoming so proficient that they were beginning to perform more and more violent evolutions, the inadequacy of the safety factors of many of the more progressive designs was being laid bare. British aviation had entered upon the most dangerous phase of its career, when practical progress and the confidence and ability of pilots had far outstripped scientific knowledge of the subject.

The immediate result of the Committee's recommendations was that all the monoplanes belonging to the R.F.C. were dispatched to the Royal Aircraft Factory for extensive modification, and the total prohibition on the flying of monoplanes by pilots of the Military Wing was lifted as regards those machines which had been so dealt with.

3. THREE NEW G.W. MODELS

Mr. Grahame-White kept the public demand well in mind when he induced Mr. J. D. North to design his "Popular" biplane, which was produced during January.

The object of this little machine was to provide a cheap, handy aeroplane for school work or for the impecunious private owner. Its design owed a good deal to Henry Farman and René Caudron. It was a small pusher biplane, having the top wing of considerably greater span than the bottom one. The tail was carried on booms in the usual manner, a substantial four-wheeled undercarriage was fitted, and a 35 h.p. Anzani 3-cylinder radial engine was mounted at the back of the *nacelle* in which the pilot and passenger sat.

The machine, which sold at under £400 complete, was designed for a speed of 50 m.p.h. with fuel for four hours.

The Grahame-White firm had also produced a fantastic " Military biplane " the chief feature of which was that the propeller used the topmost of the three tail booms as a bearing, and the control wires passed through the centre of its boss ! No more need be said about this amazing machine. It owed its conception to Mr. Barber, who ought to have known better, and Mr. J. D. North worked out the details. Apparently it never occurred to either of them to speculate as to what would happen should the propeller break.

A far more practical model from the same stable was a two-seat tractor biplane on floats. This machine, which had pleasing lines, was fitted with a 60 h.p. Anzani engine, and was intended to cater for the private owner who wished to fly a seaplane purely for pleasure purposes. The floats, which were apparently designed to go backwards, that is with the thin end first, were each provided with two little airscoops which collected the air as the machine rushed forward and forced it down channels through the float so that it emerged underneath just abaft the step and broke up the water's adhesion to the under skin of the float.

4. THE AERO SHOW

(a) *The Aircraft*

As no exhibition had been staged in England during 1912, all the more interest was attracted by the Aero Show which opened in February 1913 at Olympia, since the exhibits represented two years' progress in design and construction.

The most important feature was the advent of the seaplane. No marine aircraft had been seen at the previous show in 1911, but the 1913 exhibition contained no less than five float seaplanes and one flying boat out of a total of twenty-five aircraft on view.

Three of the float seaplanes were straightforward monoplane designs produced by Borel, Nieuport, and Deperdussin respectively. The last-named, which was British built, was very carefully streamlined and the wing was rigidly braced to an auxiliary spar, which projected from the bottom of the fuselage, in order to avoid the necessity for a *cabane* and top wire bracing. This system started a new trend of thought which was eventually to develop into the well-known *sesquiplane* design, for in course of time, the auxiliary spar grew into a small wing. The Borel was of a type which had done well in the various French seaplane trials during 1912.

I have already described the Grahame-White seaplane, and a similar straightforward tractor biplane type was the standard Short twin-float machine which was similar to the model supplied to the Naval Wing R.F.C., on which Com. C. R. Samson, R.N., had put up so many fine flights.

A very interesting development was the entry into marine aviation of two famous boat-builders of Cowes, I.O.W., in Messrs. J. Samuel White & Company, and Messrs. Saunders. The former had constructed a large two-seat pusher biplane (160 h.p. Gnôme) to the design of Mr. T. Howard-Wright, who had invented a new wing section in which the top surfaces were cambered in such a way as to form a depression in the centre of the chord. The chief interest in this machine lay in the enormous floats which had three steps each, and a water rudder similar to that fitted to a racing eight.

Messrs. Saunders had collaborated with Mr. T. O. M. Sopwith and with Mr. Sigrist, who had already joined the Kingston works as manager, in producing a delightful little two-seater flying boat. This, the first British flying boat, consisted of two parts, the hull, which was a twenty-one foot cedar-built hydroplane of beautiful proportions, seating pilot and passenger side by side, and the air-frame, which was a simple pusher biplane superimposed upon the back deck of the hull. A 90 h.p. Austro-Daimler engine was mounted high up between the wings, and the tail was carried on outriggers well clear of the water. This revolutionary and brilliant design included a retractable wheel undercarriage for emergency landings on *terra firma*.

The land machines exhibited comprised seven monoplanes, five pusher biplanes, and six tractor biplanes.

In the first-named category there was little of especial interest as the Bleriot, Caudron, Handley-Page, and Martin and Handasyde machines were of established types, and the Vickers a mere development of the original R.E.P. Deperdussin exhibited a pretty single-seater monoplane from his Paris factory, which was a low-powered version of the Gordon-Bennett winner. An interesting development on the Military trials type Bristol was the provision of band brakes on the wheels which could be operated independently by bowden-wire mechanism. The pilot could thus apply one brake or the other by pressing pedals attached to the rudder bar and thus assist his machine in turning on the ground.

The pusher biplanes included the Cody, the latest products of the brothers Farman, the Grahame-White freak which I have already described, and one interesting new-comer from the Vickers factory. This was a two-seater fighter and was shown with a

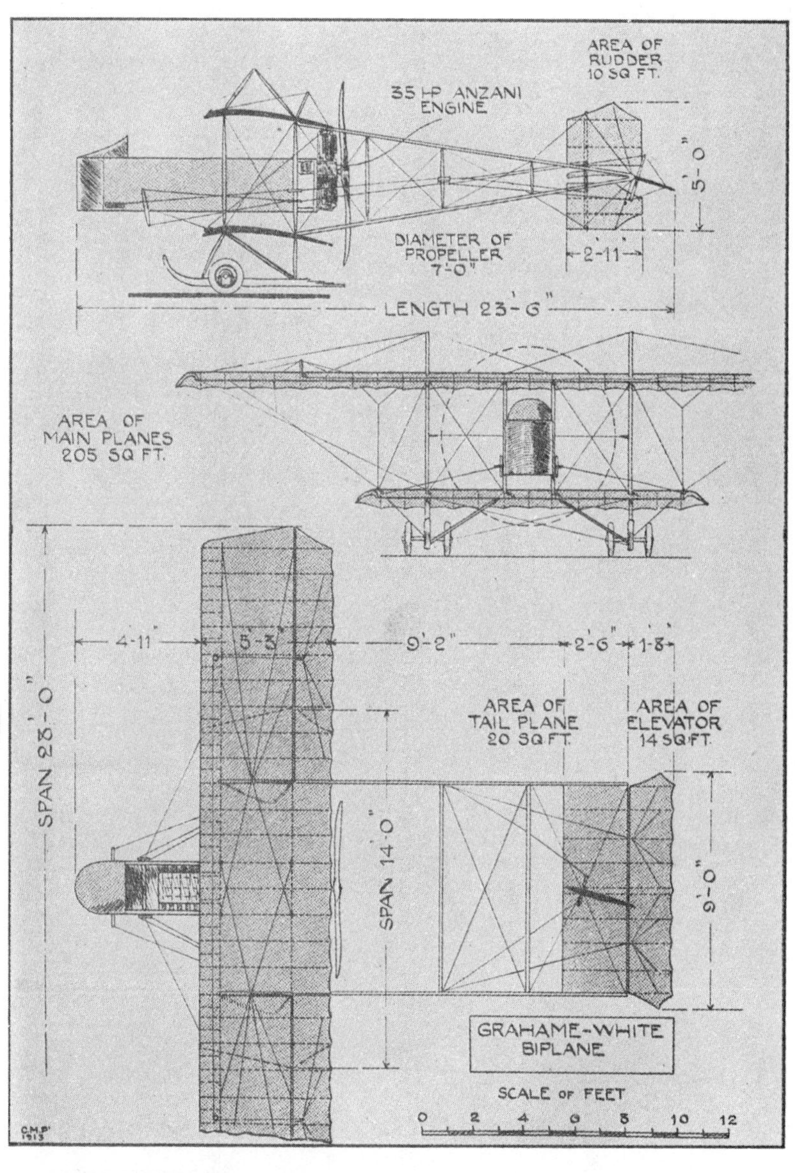

"*Flight*" *copyright*

1.—Designed to sell at under £400: the Grahame-White Popular Pusher Biplane (35 h.p. Anzani), designed by Mr. J. D. North.

Facing page 16

"*Flight*" *photo*

2.—THE SOPWITH THREE-SEATER TRACTOR BIPLANE (80 H.P. GNÔME)
WHICH CREATED A SENSATION AT THE AERO SHOW

machine gun protruding from a slot in the nose of the *nacelle*. One of the new 60-80 h.p. Wolseley engines drove the propeller direct. The wings, which were of narrow chord, were staggered, and the tail was carried very high and equipped with a steerable tail skid. This was a very promising machine.

It was in the tractor biplane class that some radical changes were to be seen.

The Avro open-cockpit type (50 h.p. Gnôme) was already well known and had been supplied in numbers to the R.F.C., as had the B.E.2, which formed part of the Government's official exhibit. Breguêt showed a cleaned-up version of his well-known type, which was also in use in the Service.

The remaining two machines were of great interest. M. Henri Coanda, Bristol's brilliant Roumanian designer, had applied the general principles of his successful monoplane to the tractor biplane type and evolved a remarkably neat machine to replace Mr. Gordon England's unsuccessful designs. It was designed to carry a useful load of 880 lbs. at 62 m.p.h. with a 70 h.p. Renault engine, and to climb to 1,000 feet in four minutes. The wings could be folded quickly and easily, and the engine was almost completely cowled in. Provision was made for substituting floats for the wheels.

The most promising machine in the show, however, was another product of Sopwith and Sigrist, who, not content with their clever flying boat, had produced a three-seater tractor biplane as well.

The pilot sat in the back seat and the two passengers were disposed side by side in the front cockpit above the centre of gravity. The machine was designed to carry a useful load of 450 lbs. at 70 m.p.h. with an 80 h.p. Gnôme. This was easily the most workmanlike and handsome aircraft in the exhibition, and fairly bristled with clever detail refinements.

(b). *The Engines*

It had been made very clear at the Military trials that the chief obstacle to the progress of British aviation was the lack of a reliable British Aero engine with a reasonable power-weight ratio.

The engines exhibited at Olympia held out little hope of any immediate improvement.

The Green Engine Company, Ltd. showed their 30-35 h.p., 50-60 h.p., and 100 h.p. water-cooled models, with the last of which Cody had won the Michelin Cup No. 2 for 1912. These were probably our most reliable motors, but they were very heavy.

The only other British firm represented was the Wolseley Company who displayed two water-cooled engines of 60-80 h.p. and 120 h.p., respectively, and a new model of 60-80 h.p., which resembled a Renault except for the fact that small water jackets covering the exhaust valve seatings only were provided, thus incurring all the disadvantages of both the air-cooled and the water-cooled types simultaneously.

France was represented by Gnôme, Renault, Anzani, Salmson, Clergêt, and Laviator engines, Germany by Benz, Mercedes, and N.A.G., and Austria by the well-known Austro-Daimler motor.

It was quite obvious that British constructors would have to go abroad for their power-plants for some time to come.

5. NO. 2 SQUADRON'S LONG TREK

The Government had prepared a new air station at Montrose in Scotland, and No. 2 Squadron of the Military Wing, R.F.C. were ordered to move there from Farnborough.

Most of the unit's equipment travelled by rail and road, but Sqdrn.-Com. J. C. Burke decided that it would be fitting to dispatch five aircraft by air.

Accordingly, on February 13th, 1913, Capts. C. A. H. Longcroft and J. H. W. Becke in B.E.2 tractor biplanes, and Capt. G. W. P. Dawes and Lieuts. F. F. Waldron, and P. W. L. Herbert in Maurice Farman pusher biplanes, left on their long journey of some 450 miles to the north. All the machines were fitted with 70 h.p. Renault engines.

Unfortunately, the squadron encountered fog immediately after taking off, with the result that Capt. J. H. W. Becke (B.E.2) and Lieut. F. F. Waldron (Maurice Farman) returned to Farnborough, whilst the other pilots landed at Reading.

Four days later the weather improved, and Capt. Becke flew his B.E.2 to Towcester, and Lieut. Waldron brought his M. Farman to Oxford, where he was joined by Capt. Longcroft's B.E.2. Capt. Dawes got his M. Farman up to Banbury, but Lieut. Herbert was forced down at Moreton in the Marsh, and did not reach Banbury till the following day, when Capt. Longcroft joined them in his B.E.2. All three machines then left Banbury for Towcester, but Capt. Dawes was forced down by engine trouble two miles short of the chosen field. Meanwhile Lieut. Waldron had left Oxford, but suffered a similar fate at Bicester.

Thus the morning of the 20th found the two B.E.2's and the M. Farmans flown by Lieut. Herbert and Capt. Dawes, at Towcester, but the last-named was still struggling to set his engine in order, as was Lieut. Waldron a few miles behind at Bicester. Without waiting for these stragglers, Capts. Becke and Longcroft and Lieut. Herbert flew on to Kelham, near Newark, and Lieut. Waldron managed to proceed to Towcester, where he rejoined Capt. Dawes.

Early on the 21st Lieut. Waldron caught up the leaders at Newark, refuelled, and pushed on immediately to York, followed by Capt. Longcroft's B.E.2, and Lieut. Herbert's Maurice Farman. Capt. Becke waited at Newark until Capt. Dawes arrived, but the latter damaged his undercarriage in landing, so Capt. Becke took off for York and left him to repair it. Unfortunately, the engine of Capt. Becke's B.E.2 gave serious trouble, and he was forced down near Doncaster.

On the following day the three leaders flew from York to Newcastle-on-Tyne, but all the pilots found difficulty in locating Gosforth Park, which had been selected as the landing place, and became scattered. Capt. Longcroft (B.E.2) and Lieut. Herbert (Maurice Farman) arrived eventually after several landings to inquire the way, but Lieut. Waldron remained at Benwell, about four miles away, with a damaged elevator. Capt. Dawes had repaired his undercarriage and left Newark for York, but eventually had to land twenty miles south of his destination after two forced landings for engine adjustments. Capt. Becke remained on the ground all this time and the following day, which was a Sunday, fitting a new engine in his B.E.2.

On Sunday and Monday, February 23rd and 24th, the leaders rested at Newcastle, but on the 24th, Capt. Dawes came right through and joined them, after one landing to inquire the way. There was much fog about on this day, and Capt. Becke had to land five times between Doncaster and Newcastle for the same purpose.

Thus Tuesday, February 25th, saw the whole Squadron assembled together for the first time since the departure from Farnborough, twelve days previously. All the machines left for Edinburgh and all arrived safely except Lieut. Waldron who was forced to bring his Maurice Farman down at Stamford Bridge, twenty-eight miles south of Berwick, owing to engine trouble. He got going again in the afternoon and reached Berwick that night.

On the following day Lieut. Waldron stole a march on his brother pilots by flying straight through from Berwick to Montrose. A short time later Capts. Becke and Longcroft (B.E.2's) and Capt. Dawes (Maurice Farman) arrived almost together, and finally Lieut. Herbert, on the remaining Maurice Farman, completed the journey during the afternoon.

This migration of approximately 450 miles in nine flying days was a remarkable feat on the part of pilots unused to long-distance cross-country work, especially when it is remembered that it was carried out in the middle of winter and that the visibility was bad throughout.

The only trouble experienced with the airframes was the damage occasioned by Capt. Dawes' heavy landing at Newark, and the broken elevator on Lieut. Waldron's Maurice Farman at Newcastle. In both cases repairs were speedily effected.

The Renault engines in Capt. Becke's B.E.2 and the Maurice Farmans flown by Capt. Dawes and Lieuts. Waldron and Herbert gave a great deal of trouble and anxiety, and the only machine which flew perfectly from start to finish was Capt. Longcroft's B.E.2.

6. ENGLISH WORLD'S RECORD BEATEN: BRITISH PILOTS IN FRANCE

On February 11th, 1913, M. Guillaux, the Caudron pilot who had flown so well in the first aerial Derby, covered forty-one laps of a ten-kilometre circuit at Etampes, in a Clement-Bayard monoplane (60 h.p. Gnôme), accompanied by a passenger, in 4 hrs. 10 mins. 45 secs. The official distance of 410 kilometres represents 254·610 miles, and this flight thus beat the world's record for distance flown in a closed circuit with one passenger, set up by Lieut. B. H. Barrington-Kennett at Salisbury Plain nearly a year previously by the narrow margin of five miles.

Mr. J. L. Hall, who had been flying a Bleriot monoplane at Hendon, had arrived at Issy where he flew the Clement-Bayard machines with great success.

The Irish pilot, Corbett-Wilson, had purchased one of the latest models of the Bleriot monoplane, and he went over to Pau to take delivery. Whilst there he made some splendid flights, notably one from Pau to Orthez and back, and a two-hours tour of the Gave Valley. Meanwhile Lieut. Boothby, R.N., had been learning to fly at one of the Farman schools, and he took his *brevet* in fine style at Buc on February 13th. That indefatigable enthusiast, Miss Trehawke Davies, had purchased yet another Bleriot, and Mr. James Valentine flew her in it from Issy to Rouen in a high wind and bad visibility. On the following day they continued to Dieppe, where the machine was dismantled and sent across to England by boat.

7. ANOTHER FATALITY: NARROW ESCAPE OF LIEUT. SPENCER GREY, R.N.

On March 5th, Mr. Geoffrey England, brother of Mr. E. C. Gordon England, was killed by the breaking up of another of M. Coanda's military-type two-seater Bristol monoplanes.

Mr. England had learned to fly at the Bristol school on Salisbury Plain, and had volunteered to carry out a flight of more than one hour's duration, by way of an acceptance test of the monoplane, prior to delivery to the Roumanian Government.

He took off in a 30 m.p.h. wind and flew round the aerodrome for thirty-two minutes at a height of 3,000 feet. The machine was then seen to be descending in a steep glide whilst the pilot switched his 80 h.p. Gnôme engine on and off, as was then the usual practice. At a height of 600 feet all the ribs for a distance of about six feet from the left-hand wing tip fell off the steel spars, and the machine dived into the ground, killing the pilot instantaneously.

It would appear that Mr Geoffrey England, who had been granted

"Flight" photo

3.—One of the best instructors: Mr. Lewis W. F. Turner standing by a Caudron Training Biplane (35 h.p. Anzani).

"Flight" photo

4.—Mr. H. G. Hawker flying the record-breaking Sopwith at Brooklands

his R.Ae.C. certificate (No. 301) on September 17th, 1912, noticed something wrong with the wing, and endeavoured to bring the machine down as gently as possible, but had too much height to lose.

The Admiralty, under the able direction of Mr. Winston Churchill, had made several wise purchases at the Aero Show, including the Short seaplane, one Avro and two Bristol tractor biplanes, the Vickers pusher biplane, the Sopwith flying boat, which was christened the "Bat-boat," and two of the Sopwith three-seater tractor biplanes.

Lieut. Spencer Grey, R.N., was ordered to take delivery of the last-named machines, and he flew the first one from Brooklands to Hendon on March 1st, accompanied by Lieut. L'Estrange Malone, R.N. Later he went up alone and proceeded to show off the machine's capabilities. Suddenly the spectators noticed with horror that the rudder was flapping idly in the slipstream. Fortunately Lieut. Grey kept his head, and by skilful use of his warp, succeeded in landing safely.

This machine had been clocked to attain 70 m.p.h. whilst being flown by Mr. H. G. Hawker, who had already been appointed test pilot to the Sopwith firm, in spite of his lack of experience.

Mr. Robert Barnwell, who had superseded Mr. Leslie Macdonald as chief pilot to Vickers, Ltd., was testing the new pusher biplane in a strong wind on March 1st, and this machine also gave excellent results.

8. INSTRUCTIONAL METHODS IN 1913

Mr. Lewis Turner, who was one of the most experienced flying instructors in England, having held the post of chief pilot to the Grahame-White and Ewen schools at Hendon successively, contributed an article to *Flight* of March 22nd, 1913, in which he described the training system then in vogue.

After emphasizing the necessity for careful preliminary ground instruction in use of controls, rigging, and maintenance of engines he continued as follows :—

"After a series of passenger flights he" (the pupil) "is allowed his first practical lesson, commonly termed 'rolling.' He is put on to a low-powered machine and is permitted to drive it across the aerodrome without leaving the ground. At first he may find a difficulty in keeping the machine on a straight course, but very soon he will pick up the 'feeling' of his rudder and be able to run along the ground in a straight line without difficulty. . . . Having got to that stage, and still keeping up the passenger flight treatment, he is allowed to go out on a higher-powered machine. At first he keeps his engine throttled down and continues to roll until he gets used to being on a different machine. Then he is told to speed up his engine and is permitted to make short hops, using his elevator control gently to lift the machine from the ground, and then immediately to return to it.

"In his early flying practice there is a most important point for the pupil to learn, and that is, never to switch off the motor should he find himself in a difficulty. On a motor-car, if there is some difficulty ahead, it is usually right to throttle down the engine and throw out the clutch. But with an aeroplane it is the reverse, for the greater the difficulty you get into, the greater is the engine power necessary to get you out of it.

"Gradually the length of his hops increase, until he is capable of making straight flights the full length of the aerodrome, keeping a few feet off the ground. He is kept at this for some little while, increasing the height of his flights as he gains confidence. The pupil should not be hurried over this stage because, above all, he is getting good practice at *vol planés* and landings, which are very important.

"He is now ready for a left-hand turn, and is sent out to make half-turns, using his rudder very slightly at first. He progresses and eventually succeeds in flying a complete circuit. On reaching this stage he can consider himself well on the way to getting his much-coveted 'ticket.'

"Having had plenty of practice at turning to the left, he will attempt to turn to the right. This, in the past, was considered the most difficult task for the pupil, but familiarity has brought with it contempt, and now the right-hand turn is considered to be quite as easy as turning to the left. When proficient with the right-hand turn it is quite a simple matter to fly a figure of eight.

"With all the experience that he has had, up to that point, he will not feel any anxiety about flying up to a height of 50 metres" (164 feet), "which is the altitude a pupil must obtain before he can be granted his certificate."

It will be noted that the fact that height is, in itself, a measure of safety, except in the case of structural failure, had not yet been fully appreciated, and that this system of instruction ensured that each pupil learned to perform his evolutions at dangerously low altitudes. It is, of course, the best modern practice to take pupils up to at least 1,000 feet before handing over control to them, so that the instructor may have sufficient room to recover should the pupil stall the machine accidentally.

The modern system necessarily involves dual controls, but these were available in 1913. Here is what Mr. Lewis Turner had to say about them:—"Another system of tuition is that of dual control. This method consists of the pupil taking numerous flights with an instructor on a machine that is fitted with two sets of controls, so that either may take charge of the machine in the air. Thus the instructor can correct any mistakes that the pupil may make. By this method of instruction a pupil can probably be put through his course of training in a little shorter time; but in my opinion, it is apt to make him rely too much upon the capabilities of his instructor, thus robbing him of that self-confidence which is so necessary."

The same issue of *Flight* contained a letter from a disgruntled pupil, calling for the adoption of the dual control system and alleging that at many schools pupils were deliberately kept on the ground in the "rolling" machines for months at a time. The writer suggested that this was due to the system of payment whereby each pupil was called upon to put down a lump sum in advance. He complained that the proprietors of some schools, having pocketed the fee, were unwilling to risk such of their machines (if any) as could actually fly, as they could earn further money by giving exhibition flights in the hands of the instructors with less risk of damage than if the pupils were allowed to take them into the air.

There was a great deal of truth in these complaints.

Some persons—there was a notable example at Hendon—actually advertised for pupils at their "schools," took fees from them in advance and used these fees for the purpose of teaching *themselves* to fly on their school machines, so that, as soon as they had taken their certificates, they would be "qualified" to instruct the said pupils. Meanwhile the pupils had the joy of watching their would-be instructor teaching himself to handle a machine on the ground at their expense, and of wondering what would happen when their turn came to receive instruction from him in the air!

As a matter of fact, there were only four schools in operation at that time which were adequately equipped with training aircraft and which could boast of an instructor who was really fit to instruct. The Bristol Company had five good men in Messrs. Jullerot, Merriam, Pixton, Busteed, and Gordon England, and was well equipped with Bristol monoplanes and biplanes. The Ewen school at Hendon had Mr. Lewis Turner, who taught on the excellent little Caudron biplane, the Grahame-White school had M. Louis Noel, who used Henry Farmans and Bleriot monoplanes, and Mr. Robert Barnwell did good work at Brooklands on the Vickers monoplanes. The conditions at all the other establishments were more or less deplorable and, in the more flagrant cases, the operation of these so-called schools of flying almost amounted to obtaining money by fraud.

9. FLIGHTS IN HIGH WINDS

On Easter Saturday a gale was blowing, but this did not deter Mr. Gordon Bell from leaving Eastchurch with a mechanic on one of the new Short pusher biplanes (50 h.p. Gnôme). He was forced down at Edmonton with engine trouble, but restarted after a delay of twenty minutes, and landed safely at Hendon 1 hr. 5

mins. after leaving Eastchurch, having averaged about 70 m.p.h., allowing for the stop. Unfortunately, however, the biplane was not taken into the hangar immediately, and a few minutes afterwards a terrific gust caught the machine as it stood on the aerodrome, lifted it off the ground, turned it over in the air, and smashed it down with such force that the airscrew was buried fourteen inches deep in the turf. Under such conditions Mr. Gordon Bell's cross-country flight was a plucky performance.

During March, news leaked out concerning two memorable flights by officers of the Central Flying School of the R.F.C. In accordance with the tradition of the Service, the names of these two pilots were kept secret, as also were the particulars of the aircraft used.

The authorities desired definite information regarding the possibilities of an aeroplane surviving a flight in a really violent gale of wind. Volunteers were called for, and, on the first occasion when the wind reached gale force, a machine, presumably a Maurice Farman biplane (70 h.p. Renault), having a maximum speed in still air of 57 m.p.h., was brought out and held down on the tarmac whilst one of the many volunteers took his place at the controls.

As soon as the aircraft was released it rose vertically upwards for 300 feet and the pilot then flew it up-wind over a measured distance of 400 yards and landed it successfully. It took him sixteen minutes to cover the 400 yards, an average rate of progress of 1,500 *y.p.h.* ! As the throttle was wide open during this amazing flight, it is clear that the wind velocity must have been approximately 55 m.p.h. throughout.

Naturally, no attempt was made to turn the machine out of wind during this initial experiment, but an even more remarkable feat was performed a few days later by another officer at the C.F.S.

This time it was decided to try to accomplish a cross-country flight in a gale, and a point was selected twenty-one miles away up-wind from Upavon. Probably the same Maurice Farman was used, but no details are available. The volunteer pilot reached his turning point in 1 hr. 15 mins., having averaged just under 17 m.p.h., and he turned successfully round the mark and was wafted back to the aerodrome at 105 m.p.h. in 11 mins. 56 secs.

On April 5th, another gale swept over Hendon, causing the anemometer to register a jagged line between the 40 and 55 m.p.h. marks. There was great astonishment when the little Deperdussin monoplane (35 h.p. Anzani) was brought onto the tarmac and held down by a number of mechanics. As soon as the engine was started, Mr. W. L. Brock, the American instructor at the Deperdussin school, climbed in, and in a few seconds he rose almost vertically off the tarmac, fought his way across the aerodrome and then turned, being swept far to leeward before he once more faced the wind. It took him fifteen minutes to cross the aerodrome a second time, but, to everyone's surprise, instead of landing, he turned once more and flew to Brooklands, where he made a safe descent thirty-eight minutes after taking off.

Not to be outdone, Mr. Gustav Hamel and Miss Trehawke Davies took off in the latter's new Bleriot (70 h.p. Gnôme) and in the course of half an hour's exciting flying reached a height of 4,000 feet. On the following afternoon the wind was even more violent, but Hamel made two flights alone in his own single-seater Bleriot (50 h.p. Gnôme) during which he received a tremendous buffeting from the gusts.

10. SOME R.F.C. STATISTICS: THE DUNNE MONOPLANE: HAMEL'S CROSS-CHANNEL FLIGHTS

During the ten months which had passed since the establishment of the R.F.C. on May 13th, 1912, its pilots had flown an aggregate of 1,550 hours, of which about half had been performed at the C.F.S.

By the middle of March 1913, there were 126 officers, of whom all but three were pilots, on the strength of the Corps, although only forty-five of these had passed the tests imposed at the Central Flying School.

A specimen of the monoplane version of the Dunne automatically stable aircraft had been built in France for experimental purposes, and Mr. Percival flew it in trials at Villacoublay. The climbing powers of this machine were exceptionally good, and great interest was taken in it by the French military authorities.

On April 2nd, Mr. Gustav Hamel carried out his tenth crossing of the Straits of Dover, when he flew his own Bleriot monoplane from Dover to Malines. He had intended to reach Cologne, but was brought down by engine trouble. Nine days later he left Dover once more, with Mr. Dupree in the passenger's seat, and struck the French coast to the east of Calais. Here he turned and flew up the shore to Dunkerque, where he swung left and returned across the water to Dover. During this flight Hamel maintained a height of 2,000 feet just below the snow clouds, except when he glided down in mid-Channel and "spoke" a German liner, whose passengers lined the rails and cheered him. Mr. Hamel was thus the first pilot to complete a dozen crossings of the Channel. Three days later he flew Miss Trehawke Davies in her Bleriot along the coast from Shoreham to Dover, covering the seventy-four miles in three minutes over the hour, in spite of pauses for stunt flying along the promenades of Brighton, Eastbourne, and Hastings.

11. THE FIRST SCHNEIDER TROPHY CONTEST

The announcement that M. Jacques Schneider had presented the beautiful trophy, which bears his name, for competition amongst pilots of hydro-aeroplanes caused little stir at the time.

No one could foresee then that the struggle for this *objet d'art* was to become an affair of nations, that the whole skill and resources of the air services of the world would become engaged, that the lives of the pick of the world's fighting pilots would be sacrificed to it, and that millions of pounds and tens of millions of francs, liras, and dollars, would be poured out in order to decide the question of which national aero club should secure permanent possession of this trophy.

Certain it is that M. Jacques Schneider never imagined for one moment the tremendous consequences of his gift.

It is equally certain that Great Britain owes a debt of gratitude to M. Schneider, for it is very largely due to the stimulus afforded by this amazing sporting contest, that British Military and Naval aircraft enjoy their present superiority to those of other nations.

The trophy itself, which is of comparatively small monetary value, can be inspected by the curious in its permanent home at the Royal Aero Club.

The organization of the initial contest was placed in the hands of the Aero Club de France, who arranged for it to be flown off over twenty-eight laps of a ten-kilometre course, a total distance of 174 miles, as a kind of side-show at the annual seaplane competition at Monaco.

The actual contest was preceded by eliminating trials involving observed descents on to the water and subsequent take-offs. The contest itself took place on April 15th.

France was represented by Prevost (Deperdussin, 160 h.p. Gnôme), Garros (Morane-Saulnier), and Espanet (Nieuport), whilst Weymann flew another Nieuport under American colours. Garros and Espanet fell out in the first lap and Weymann in the fourth lap, so that Prevost finished alone to win the trophy for France. He completed his twenty-eight laps in 2 hrs. 50 mins. 47 secs., at an average speed of approximately 61 m.p.h., but, unfortunately, he failed to fly across the finishing line properly and the officials made him take off again and repeat his last lap. This process occupied about an hour, so that the official time was recorded as 3 hrs. 48 mins. 22 secs., and the speed as 45·75 m.p.h.

12. THE DYOTT AND E.A.C. MONOPLANES: SCIENTIFIC AERIAL NAVIGATION

Mr. C. M. Dyott, who had acquired a great deal of practical experience during his "barnstorming" tour of the U.S.A., Mexico and Central America with Capt. Patrick Hamilton, embodied his ideas in an attractive single-seater monoplane. This elegant little craft was constructed at Clapham by Messrs. Hewlett and Blondeau. It had a span of twenty-nine feet and an overall length of twenty-three feet. Special features were the accessibility of the various parts, and the provision made for quick replacement in the event of damage. The only serious fault in this design lay in the fact that the flying wires were made fast to the undercarriage and thus subjected to undue stress on taking off and landing. The engine was a 50 h.p. Gnôme, which sufficed for a maximum speed of 75 m.p.h. and lateral control was obtained by warping the wings in the usual manner.

Another single seat monoplane of similar dimensions had been designed by Herr Gassler, an Austrian pupil of the Eastbourne Aviation Co., Ltd., who had built the machine for him at Eastbourne. This aircraft was, in several respects, an improvement on Mr. Dyott's design. In particular a *cabane*, or pyramid of struts, had been placed under the belly of the fuselage for the express purpose of providing a point of attachment for the flying wires, which would thus be insulated from undercarriage shocks. But the machine was chiefly notable as being the first monoplane to rely on the modern type of aileron for lateral control. Hitherto, monoplane wings had either been made sufficiently flexible to allow of their being warped upwards and downwards to simulate ailerons or else the whole wing tip had been made to revolve about the centre line of the wing. The obvious disadvantage of this was the risk of breakage of the wing in the air. The E.A.C. monoplane thus set a valuable example to other constructors. The power-unit was a 35 h.p. three-cylinder Anzani radial engine. The Eastbourne aviation school's equipment at this time consisted of a Bristol "boxkite" biplane and three Bleriot monoplanes, whilst three Henry Farman float seaplanes were under construction in the factory.

The first experiment in scientific aerial navigation was carried out from the Eastbourne aerodrome, when the proprietor, Mr. Fowler, took Mr. Rainey, one of the watch-keeping officers of the Royal Mail Steam Packet Company, for a flight out to sea. Mr. Rainey used a sextant and a chronometer, and determined his latitude by the double altitude method. He claimed to be able to fix the machine's position to a quarter of a mile, whilst out of sight of land.

Prior to this experiment no one had seriously contemplated navigating an aircraft by any other method than dead reckoning, and few pilots paid much attention to this. For instance, such an experienced man as Mr. G. M. Dyott fitted a special Kelvin compass to his new monoplane on which only the four cardinal points were marked, as he found great difficulty in keeping an accurate course except in still air, and therefore concluded that the instrument was useful only as a very rough guide. It must be borne in mind, however, that compasses for use on aeroplanes had not been developed to any great efficiency at that date and no doubt they were much addicted to oscillating.

13. HAMEL'S GREATEST FLIGHT

In the third week in April Mr. Gustav Hamel took off from Dover in a Bleriot monoplane (80 h.p. Gnôme) with Mr. Frank Dupree in the passenger's seat, intending to fly to Cologne. The machine carried forty gallons of petrol, giving a range of five and a half hours.

The French coast was crossed just to the south of Dunkerque, and Hamel struck off across the flat fields of Belgium and Holland. After about two hours in the air he encountered several storms of wind and rain which set him off his course, although he never considered abandoning the flight. Eventually he sighted the Rhine at a point about 60 miles to the north of Cologne, picked up his bearings and flew up the river until the cathedral city came in sight. He landed at the military aerodrome there after spending 4 hrs. 18 mins. in the air. The distance from Dover to Cologne in a straight line is approximately 245 miles, but Hamel had actually covered about 320 miles, owing to the deviations occasioned by the storms through which he had passed.

This magnificent flight, which involved Hamel's thirteenth crossing of the Channel, was the first non-stop flight between England and Germany, and quite the finest performance so far accomplished by a British pilot.

14. R.F.C. PILOT KILLED ON CODY BIPLANE: DE HAVILLAND INJURED: NEW HEIGHT RECORD

On April 28th, Lieut. L. C. Rogers-Harrison, R.F.C., who had been especially trained to handle the awkward Cody biplane, was killed at Farnborough. The particular machine which he was flying was the original "Cathedral" with which Cody had won the first prize at the Military trials, and which was composed largely of bits and pieces taken from his earliest experimental types.

Lieut. Rogers-Harrison flew around the aerodrome for twenty minutes and was then observed to commence a glide as if he was about to land. He glided normally from 1,200 feet to 500 feet, at which point the front elevator collapsed, followed by the wings. The aircraft disintegrated completely before the pieces hit the ground, and the pilot was killed instantaneously.

The set of the wings had been altered a few weeks prior to the accident from the *kathedral* angle, which gave the machine its nickname, to a more normal *dihedral* angle, but it is unlikely that this in any way contributed to the disaster. Indeed, it should have served to enhance the machine's safety in the air.

It is clear that the fabric covering the wings and elevator was old and threadbare, and that the whole crazy contrivance was quite unsuitable to withstand the strain of being thrust through the air at 70 m.p.h. by the powerful Austro-Daimler motor.

"Flight" photo

5.—Mr. Gordon Bell, who flew more different types than any other pilot of his time.

"*Flight*" *photo*

6.—Mr. Sydney Pickles flying a Caudron Biplane (35 h.p. Anzani) at Hendon.

The death of Lieut. Rogers-Harrison, who had been granted his aviator's certificate (No. 205) on April 16th, 1912, was directly traceable to the extraordinary decision of the judges, who had awarded the Cody biplane the first prize in the Military trials of the previous August and thus encouraged its use in the R.F.C.

The authorities were now faced with the fact that, since the judges' decision, every single one of the machines to which prizes had been awarded had collapsed in the air and killed their pilots.

Great secrecy was observed in regard to the details of an accident which occurred to Geoffrey de Havilland at Farnborough during April. It appears that he was testing his latest model of the B.E. tractor biplane, which had been modified with a view to obtaining a very high maximum speed. In fact, the machine concerned had been carefully timed to achieve a mesne velocity of 91·4 m.p.h. as an average of two runs in each direction over a measured course. This speed probably constituted a world's record for a biplane and was nearly 20 m.p.h. faster than that achieved by any other British-built aircraft, whether monoplane or biplane. As a result of the smash, Mr. de Havilland spent about a fortnight in hospital.

On May 2nd, Maj. E. L. Gerrard, of the Naval Wing, R.F.C., set up a new British passenger altitude record by taking two passengers to a height of 8,400 feet in a B.E. tractor biplane, which had been equipped with a fourteen-cylinder Gnôme rotary engine of 140 h.p.

15. A CROSS-COUNTRY FLIGHT BY NO. 3 SQUADRON, R.F.C.: DISCIPLINARY ACTION AGAINST BELGIAN PILOT

On May 9th, No. 3 Squadron of the Military Wing, R.F.C., flew from Salisbury Plain to Farnborough as a unit. Sqdrn.-Com. Brooke-Popham tested the air and then gave orders for the nine aircraft to take off at five-minute intervals.

Capt. Allen and Lieut. Wadham of "A" Flight led the way on B.E.2 tractor biplanes (70 h.p. Renaults), followed at the appropriate intervals by Lieuts. Cholmondeley, Carmichael, and Allen, and Maj. Higgins of "B" Flight on their Henry Farman pusher biplanes (70 h.p. Gnômes). The last named pilot was forced down by engine trouble shortly after taking off, but this was put right in twenty minutes, and he continued to Farnborough. "C" Flight, represented by Sergt. Frank Ridd, Lieut. Ashton, and Capt. Connor, brought up the rear on their Maurice Farman pusher biplanes (70 h.p. Renaults). Sergt. Ridd was the only pilot who failed to complete the course, as he had to make a forced landing near Andover with serious engine trouble.

M. Brindejonc des Moulinais, one of the greatest European pilots of the time, found himself at Bremen on the conclusion of an unsuccessful attempt to capture the Pommery Cup. He determined to try to fly his Morane-Saulnier monoplane to London, a distance of 450 miles, in order to take part in the Whitsun meeting at Hendon.

Leaving Bremen at 8.40 a.m. on May 9th, he flew to Wanne in Westphalia and thence via Liège, to Etterbeek near Brussels. Here he stayed two nights, waiting for an improvement in the weather, and on May 11th he continued to Calais, where he landed. After a short rest he crossed the Channel and passed over Canterbury and Gravesend, where he flew into fog. Keeping close above the river he passed right through London, and eventually found himself over Hyde Park, whence he flew up the Edgware Road to Hendon.

On hearing of this the R.Ae.C. cancelled the pilot's competitor's certificate, and thus prevented him from competing in this country. It would seem that this action was somewhat hasty and ill-considered in view of the fact that M. Brindejonc des Moulinais was a stranger in these parts and that the visibility was practically nil. Moreover, it is obvious that a *competitor's certificate* can properly be revoked only in consequence of an offence committed during a competition, and if the club felt compelled to inflict a penalty, their only logical course was to suspend the pilot's *aviator's certificate* for a stated period.

However, this unpleasant incident served as a warning that the Royal Aero Club was determined to enforce the regulations against low flying over towns. Possibly that was the club's intention, but if that was so, then it was a pity that a Belgian gentleman, who was one of the world's greatest pilots, should have been picked as the victim of the demonstration, when there were innumerable examples of similar dangerous flying to be seen at Hendon every week-end.

The Crown adopted a far more reasonable and logical point of view when M. Brindejonc des Moulinais appeared at Bow Street to answer the first two summons issued under the Aerial Navigation Acts, 1911 and 1913, which charged him with having, as a person having control of an aeroplane, failed to send notice to the Home Office stating the proposed landing place, the approximate time of arrival, and his name and nationality, prior to commencing a journey to the United Kingdom ; and further with navigating an aircraft, coming from a place outside the United Kingdom, over the County of London, without having first landed in one of the officially prescribed areas. The defendant pleaded guilty.

Mr. Muskett (for the Home Office), after mentioning that M. Brindejonc des Moulinais had flown over the prohibited areas at Dover, Purfleet, and Woolwich Arsenal, congratulated him in court on his marvellous achievement, and craved the magistrate to exercise the utmost indulgence. When the defendant pleaded ignorance of the regulations Mr. Dickinson gave him an address of welcome to this country from the Bench, describing him as " a brave and clever airman," and bound him over in 1,000 francs to come up for judgment if called upon within twelve months.

Thus did the majesty of the Law unbend to alleviate the harsh treatment meted out to a distinguished foreigner by the Royal Aero Club.

16. BRITISH PILOTS ABROAD: FATAL SMASH AT MONTROSE

On May 15th, Lord Carbery, who was destined to become one of the best amateur pilots in the world, began to learn to fly at the Morane-Saulnier school of flying at Villacoublay.

Meanwhile, Mr. George Newberry, the English president of the Argentine Aero Club, soared once more into the news when he raised the Argentine altitude record again by climbing to 4,075 metres (13,366 feet) in his Bleriot monoplane (Gnôme) on May 18th. Not content with this fine performance, he set off five days later and succeeded in breaking his own record by attaining a height of 4,400 metres (14,432 feet).

Mr. Corbett-Wilson had a *flair* for seeking out and overcoming natural obstacles. One would have thought that his two crossings of the Irish Sea would have satisfied his thirst for adventure, but he determined to tackle a flight over the Alps. On May 21st, he left Buc, in his new 2-seater Bleriot monoplane (Gnôme) accompanied by a mechanic, and flew non-stop to Dijon in three hours. After resting there for a while and refuelling his machine, he took off again and reached Lausanne after a further flight of 2 hrs. 25 mins., during which he crossed the Jura Alps at a height of 4,000 metres (13,120 feet). This performance deserves to rank with Hamel's great flight from Dover to Cologne as an example of brilliant airmanship, skilful navigation, and cool courage.

In accordance with the established tradition of the Squadron, it was decided that new machines produced at the Royal Aircraft Factory for No. 2 Squadron, R.F.C., should be delivered by air to Montrose.

Three B.E.2 tractor biplanes (70 h.p. Renaults) were ready for delivery towards the end of May, and Maj. Burke took Capts. Becke and Longcroft to fly them back. All three pilots brought their machines through successfully.

Unfortunately, the B.E.2 which had been ferried north by Maj. Burke broke up in the air on May 27th whilst being flown by Lieut. Desmond L. Arthur, who was killed. This aircraft was not a new one, having been built in June 1912 and fitted with new wings in August 1912, since which date it had been in regular service with the R.F.C.

Lieut. Arthur was descending in a gliding turn at a height of 2,500 feet, when the right-hand top wing collapsed. The pilot fell from the wrecked aircraft shortly afterwards, and his belt was subsequently found to be broken.

It was clearly established at the investigation carried out by the Accidents Investigation Committee of the R.Ae.C. that the death of this pilot, who had been granted his aviator's certificate (No. 233) on June 18th, 1912, was entirely due to criminally negligent repair work carried out on the machine, either at the Royal Aircraft Factory or in the Service.

The main rear spar had previously been broken at a point about eleven inches from the top right-hand wing tip. It had been repaired by making a taper splice seven and a half inches long, which was so badly made that, in places, the glue was one-eighth inch thick. This crude splice was bound with whipcord, which was not varnished or treated with cobbler's wax. The carpenter had then covered his botched job with new fabric, without even troubling to varnish the new section of spar, and the fabric used was of different material from the rest of the wing covering. It was this joint which had broken and started a general collapse of the whole wing structure.

No entry of this repair could be found in the records of either the Factory or the R.F.C., and the Committee made strong representations that all future repairs to service aircraft should be properly inspected, and that each such job should be marked both by the workmen concerned, and by the inspector, so that in future cases stern justice could be meted out to the culprits.

17. FIRST-HAND ACCOUNT OF PARIS-WHITSTABLE FLIGHT

Mr. Gordon Bell was commissioned to go over to Buc and to bring back a new Borel 2-seater monoplane (80 h.p. Gnôme) which was to be delivered to Eastchurch for the use of the pilots of the Naval Wing, R.F.C. He had never handled a Borel before, but he was always ready to fly anything that was given to him, and he asked Mr. C. C. Turner to cross over with him in the passenger's seat. Below I quote from Mr. Turner's own account of their adventurous journey on May 28th, which gives an admirable picture of the trials and tribulations of cross-country flying in 1913.

" We started at 4.30 a.m., and headed for Versailles. When over Versailles the great wooded slopes, the winding Seine, the blur of mist that hid Paris, of which city the only visible feature was the Eiffel Tower, and the sun rising in a mist made an unforgettable picture. Mont Valerian, our first landmark, looked like a black limpet among tangled weeds.

" After flying for half an hour we found we were only progressing at the rate of about 42 m.p.h. Gordon Bell had a roller map, and I had provided myself with some ordnance maps, which I cut into strips for the route, so that we could both observe the course. By turning my head I could see the compass also.

" As we approached Meru, Gordon Bell borrowed my note-book and wrote in quite his best hand the following question : ' This is

"Flight" photo

7.—The end of a great flight: Mr. Robert Slack's arrival at Hendon.

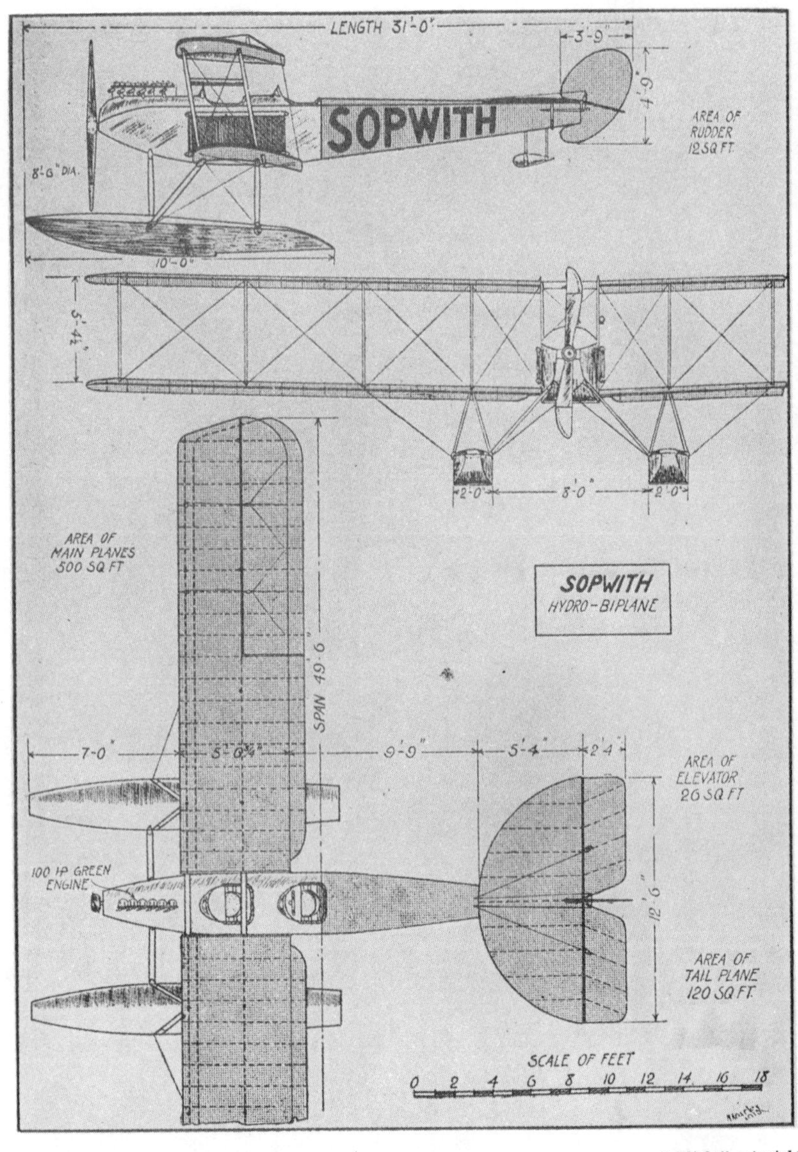

"Flight" copyright

2.—"DAILY MAIL" SEAPLANE TRIAL: THE SOPWITH TRACTOR BIPLANE (100 H.P. GREEN).

Facing page 33

Meru. How far have we come, and in how many minutes ?' I measured it up and replied, '60 kilos in 58 mins. !' An old biplane of the 40 m.p.h. order would scarcely have got away from Buc at all." (They had averaged only 38½ m.p.h. in a 70 m.p.h. machine.) "But the wind, though strong, was steady. As a rule when Gordon Bell wanted to speak to me he cut off for a few seconds, and while we planed down a few yards we discussed the situation.

"At 5.43 a.m. the windscreen was suddenly blurred with a stream of petrol which also blew sharply into my face and began to pour down my arms and hands. The vent on the tank cap was leaking, and, to stem the flow, I put out my hand and kept a finger on the hole, lifting it for a moment or two at frequent intervals to let the air in. This lasted for five minutes; and then a new trouble arose. The course ahead became obscured in a dark mist, and nearer at hand came a legion of small scurrying clouds below us. As we got over them more and larger ones succeeded, and soon we were in the thick of it.

"We flew lower, only to find the land fog-bound; and so we decided to stop. Gordon Bell brought the machine down into a large field, only seeing and clearing just in time a black iron fence dividing the field into two parts.

"Some cattle promptly trotted up and surrounded us. They were young bulls and their curiosity knew no bounds. They attempted to eat the planes and tried various other experiments. Gordon Bell and I had to keep a bold front; the slightest sign of yielding brought them on boldly with lowered horns. Some labourers came up and helped us.

"I would have given anything for a camera when we started from that field twenty minutes later. The moment the machine moved the bulls broke loose and galloped after us, heads down. We turned to the left at the bottom of the field, and they turned also and tried to head us off. Had the engine stopped then the Borel would have become so much cud; but she got up and away.

"No sooner were we up than something struck me on the head, apparently thrown back from the propeller. Gordon Bell drew my attention to the top of the tank. One of the taps" [filler-caps ?] "had disappeared. I replaced it with one from the tank inside the cockpit.

"After fifty minutes flying we were forced to descend again by thick fog. This time we were at Theuilly L'Abbaye, where we were held up for over an hour." [Here they were troubled by some more bulls.]

"We had no sooner got away than we began to feel doubt about the route. At times the country seemed recognizable from the map and the compass pointed about right, but after a time we knew we were astray. We forged steadily ahead for two hours, the country very slowly rolling back below us. Soon after 9 o'clock the horizon ahead had become a sharp white line, and we concluded we were approaching the sea. At 9.45 we were in no doubt whatever, and soon after we caught a glimpse of the water in a rift in the fog.

"I would like to say a word about Gordon Bell's fine piloting when looking for a resting place. He swooped about like a hawk after its prey until he found there was nothing better than a big clover field near the edge of the cliffs, over which the mist was streaming inland. There was no other place for miles, and on it he brought the machine cleverly to rest."

The travellers were at St. Valerie-en-Caux and here they were delayed for over four hours by French officials.

"Leaving St. Valerie at 2.30 p.m., the machine got off the thick clover and uneven ground in fine style, and as we soared aloft the sea down on our left was hidden by low-lying clouds, while the land below and to the east was brightly lit by the sun.

"We passed Dieppe at 2.45, and in the far distance could see the mouth of the Somme, where our first halt was to be. Le Crotoy adjoins another St. Valerie, a little village which gradually came into view. To the left of it I could distinguish some sheds, and pointed them out to Gordon Bell.

"While we crossed the estuary we were descending rapidly, and could see men on the sands waving to us and pointing out the landing place. Landing on smooth sand is delightful. There was plenty of space too, so that the long run was of no account, but it was judged so nicely that we came to a stop a few yards from our friends.

"We replenished the tanks, chatted with the Caudron pilots, and saw a new 80 h.p. Gnôme Caudron. Then, at 4.40, having received instructions as to where to look for the landing place at Calais, should it be advisable to descend there, we resumed our coast journey.

"Etaples was soon reached, and Boulogne came into clear view, but far below, for we were then steadily climbing. We left Grisnez about five miles to the east and, nearing Sangatte, attained a height of 1,800 metres" (5,900 feet). "Then as we turned north-westwards and approached the coast a faint line across the Channel slowly emerged from uncertainty and appeared as the English coast.

"From Boulogne to Sangatte the cap vent was leaking badly—indeed, both of them. I was drenched with petrol, and breathed it for twenty minutes. Perhaps it is good for one. For twenty minutes I kept my finger on the vent with brief intervals, and got very cold. Then it stopped.

"England being in view, and the motor going strong, Gordon Bell kept ahead, steering an almost due-westerly compass course, although we wanted to cross a few miles east of Dover. We left the French side at 5.20, and for a long time seemed to make no progress. Under the declining sun the sea in the far distance, somewhere about Hastings or Brighton, gleamed white. Below it was a light grey, and here and there a ship could be seen—a four-master in tow, two large steamships and specks of fishing boats. Very slowly we left the French coast behind, and Dover began to stand out, marked by the thin lines of its pier and breakwater. At 5.37 we appeared to be half-way across and the view was one of the most magnificent I have ever seen. We could see the whole of Kent; the coastline from Hastings, past Dover and Deal, Ramsgate, and the Nore, and the Thames estuary, past the mouth of the Medway, and probably as far west as Tilbury, was in view. Behind us lay France.

"We were obviously drifting considerably to the east" [north ?], "for as we neared England the South Foreland was well to the left, and we continued over the Downs, with Deal five miles or so to the west. A little farther on Gordon Bell dipped the head of the machine down and we descended rapidly, switching on and off. We crossed the coast at 6.2, having taken forty-five minutes to cover about thirty-two miles of sea. It was pleasant to be over land again, for, unquestionably, the Channel crossing has certain terrors.

"The end came soon after we got to England.

"Suddenly, when just south of Whitstable and on the point of turning to cross to Sheppey, the engine stopped dead. The next instant I found her head sharply down and the land hurrying up to us. At first I expected Gordon Bell would switch on, but as the engine continued silent it was evident that, for some reason, a landing not in our programme had become necessary.

"We were heading towards some tall trees, and I thought Gordon Bell would bring her up a bit and glide over their tops Then I saw that the field below was crowded with sheep.

"It began to look like trouble, and even now I cannot quite understand how we steered between the trees. But when I tell you that the rush of air for a few minutes was on the side of my head instead of in my face, you will understand that a stunt was in progress.

"We came down through those trees, swaying from right to left, and almost touching them, and then straightened out to land. The sheep had now cleared away save one ewe and her lamb, and over this family group the machine lifted, then landed gently as a feather, and ran forwards, stopping with forty yards to spare."

Thus ended a grand flight of approximately 291 miles. An inspection revealed that the magneto was permanently out of action.

It was Gordon Bell's first Channel crossing and it is clear that he flew magnificently throughout the 6 hrs. 46 mins. they were in the air. From the graphic description of the final forced landing it is obvious that the young pilot saved his machine by a skilful use of the sideslip. It is probable that he was the first British pilot to utilize this manœuvre deliberately as a means of approach to an awkward field, for at that time a sideslip was popularly regarded as being in the nature of a preliminary funeral rite.

18. SEAPLANES AT SHOREHAM: A ROYAL REVIEW: NEW NAVAL AIR STATIONS

Mr. James Radley, the Bleriot expert from Huntingdon, had collaborated with Mr. E. C. Gordon England in producing a remarkable seaplane. This machine was a large pusher biplane of forty-five feet span and some thirty feet in length. The centre section was occupied by no less than three 50 h.p. Gnôme engines arranged in a row, like three catherine wheels on a pin. Each of these engines was coupled by means of a roller chain to a counter-shaft overhead, on the back end of which was a ten-foot propeller, geared down to three-quarters of the engine speed.

The whole arrangement was supported on the water by two very large flat-bottomed floats which were fitted with small turtle decks extending some four feet back from the nose or bow. Behind each turtle deck was a well provided with three seats arranged in a clover-leaf pattern. The front seat of the right-hand float was intended for the pilot, and behind him sat two passengers, side by side. The other float had similar accommodation for three more passengers, who were thus able to wave and shout to the pilot and his companions on the other side, but could take no part in controlling the machine.

Gordon England succeeded in flying this strange aircraft off the river at Shoreham, but, unfortunately, the water was devoid of ripples, and very deceptive in consequence, so that he banked over to turn too low down, and the pilot's float hit the water, wrecking the machine.

The Avro company were more successful with their new seaplane, which was a large tractor biplane fitted with a 100 h.p. Gnôme engine. Mr. F. P. Raynham was entrusted with the trial flights, and he went down to Shoreham with Mr. John Alcock to test it at the end of May.

The machine left the water at the first attempt in ten seconds, loaded with one passenger, an anchor, and fuel for two hours. After that, Mr. Raynham carried out a number of successful flights with it up and down the coast.

A country club, very similar in its general arrangements to a modern flying club, had been organized on the Shoreham aerodrome, under the title of the Sussex County Aero Club. The moving spirits were the brothers Cecil and Eric Pashley, who had acquired an old Henry Farman pusher biplane (50 h.p. Gnôme) in which a lot of flying was done. This club soon became quite a popular social *rendezvous* for residents in Brighton, Hove, and Worthing.

"*Flight*" *photo*

8.—"Daily Mail" Seaplane Trial: Mr. H. G. Hawker, the gallant pilot of the Sopwith, photographed at Hendon.

Facing Page 36

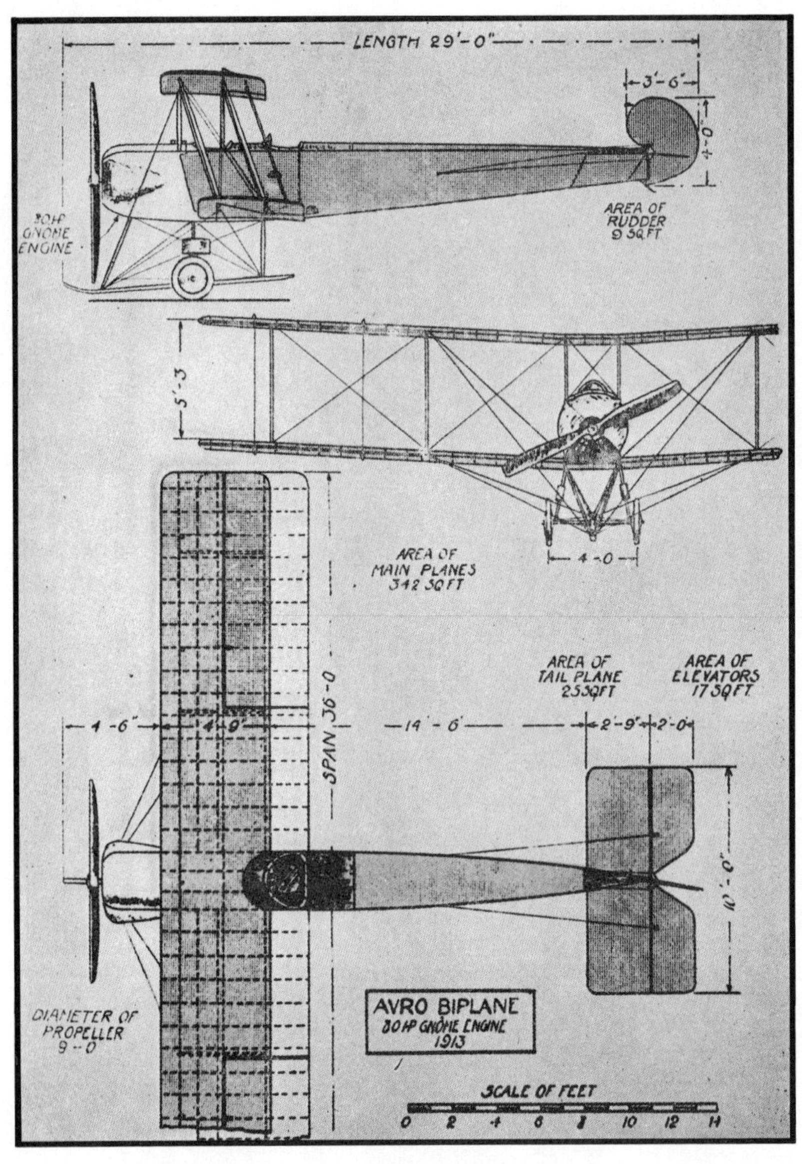

"Flight" copyright

3.—THE PRECURSOR OF THE FAMOUS TYPE 504: THE AVRO TRACTOR BIPLANE (80 H.P. GNÔME) WHICH FINISHED FOURTH IN THE AERIAL DERBY.

On June 3rd, a great review was held on Laffan's Plain in honour of the King's birthday, which was attended by His Majesty in person. The Royal Flying Corps was represented by six Maurice Farman biplanes, four B.E.2 tractor biplanes, two Henry Farman pusher biplanes, and one Bleriot monoplane. These machines first taxied past in line ahead at fifty yards intervals, and later took-off and flew past at 150 feet. As each machine came to the saluting base the pilot dived and pulled up again to the regulation height. This was the first occasion on which this now-established form of ceremonial salute from the air was carried out.

The Admiralty had established a naval air station at Yarmouth, and Lieut. C. L. Courtney, R.N., flew the first machine, a Maurice Farman pusher biplane (70 h.p. Renault), from Hendon to the new aerodrome. This station was destined to have an exciting history during the War, 1914–18. A section of the Naval Wing, R.F.C., was already quartered at Calshot Castle and plans were afoot for a new seaplane base at Cromarty.

19. GREAT FLYING BY HUCKS AND HAMEL

Mr. B. C. Hucks, profiting by his experience as one of the *Daily Mail's* exhibition pilots during the previous year, had placed himself and his Bleriot monoplane under the managership of Mr. J. C. Savage, who arranged for him to tour the Midland counties, giving demonstrations at garden parties, flower shows, political fêtes, and suchlike social occasions. The work was both arduous and remunerative, and Mr. Hucks performed many notable feats during his short cross-country flights from one engagement to another. Often these trips were made in the worst of weather conditions and often the fields or parks, which had been picked for his use as temporary aerodromes, were so small as to test the pilot's ability to the utmost. This "barnstorming" tour was the best possible training for a cross-country pilot, and it served to bring Mr. Hucks into the very front rank.

Mr. Gustav Hamel, who was already acknowledged to be the outstanding British pilot of 1913, had an engagement to give exhibition flights at Brooklands every Sunday. He kept these appointments with unfailing regularity, flying over from Hendon in any kind of weather so as not to disappoint his sophisticated audience at Brooklands. On one occasion, he set out in the teeth of a full westerly gale of such violence that the warp was insufficient to counteract the force of the gusts, and he was unable to keep the Bleriot level laterally. He landed to wait for the wind to drop, but was so afraid of his machine being blown away out of the field in which he had descended, that he decided that it would be safer in the air; so he took off again and reached Brooklands intact after taking 1 hr. 20 mins. to cover the twenty-one miles from Hendon.

20. HAWKER BREAKS THREE BRITISH RECORDS

Mr. H. G. Hawker was revelling in the performance of the new Sopwith three-seater tractor biplane (80 h.p. Gnôme), which he was privileged to demonstrate in his new official position as test pilot to the Sopwith firm.

He had won the cross-country race at Brooklands on Whit-Monday in driving rain and a strong wind, and he had taken the machine to Hendon and beaten the London experts in their altitude contest by climbing to 7,500 feet in fifteen minutes.

This latter performance had set him thinking about the new biplane's phenomenal climbing capacity, and he determined to make a formal attempt on the British altitude record, which was still held by Mr. Geoffrey de Havilland and his B.E.2, with 10,560 feet.

The first attack was made at Brooklands on May 31st, and the Sopwith roared up into a clear sky with Hawker alone on board. He climbed steadily for forty-five minutes until the carburettor froze up at a height of 11,450 feet, and he was compelled to shut off his engine and glide back to the aerodrome, where he received a great ovation.

This fine flight still left Mr. Geoffrey de Havilland in possession of the British record for altitude with one passenger, as it will be recalled that Maj. F. H. Sykes had accompanied him on his climb to 10,560 feet. Moreover, the British record for altitude with two passengers stood to the credit of Maj. E. L. Gerrard's B.E.2 (140 h.p. Gnôme) with 8,400 feet.

Hawker had a three-seater machine with a notable capacity for climbing, although it was of only about half the power of the special B.E., and he therefore decided to try to annex these two records as well.

Accordingly he took off from Brooklands on June 16th, with one passenger aboard, and set off for the higher layers once more. At 7,000 feet it became bitterly cold, but Hawker persevered and eventually forced the machine up past his own solo record level, until he had reached 12,900 feet, where the cold was so intense that he was unable to move his limbs and was forced, on that account, to switch off and go down.

After resting for half an hour and warming himself a little, Hawker took two passengers aboard, and went up to capture Maj. Gerrard's record. This time the rate of climb was much slower, but still the 80 h.p. Gnôme kept pulling grandly, and the biplane lifted well in spite of the heavy load. Eventually the ceiling was reached at 10,600 feet and Hawker landed once more, the proud possessor of four British records, i.e., altitude, solo and with one and two passengers, and duration.

It was then almost exactly nine months since he had learned to fly !

21. GORDON BELL WRECKS THE MARTIN-HANDASYDE

Mr. Gordon Bell had been deputed to fly the new Martin-Handasyde monoplane, which was of similar design to its predecessors although it had been fitted with one of the powerful 120 h.p. 6-cylinder Austro-Daimler engines, which gave it a maximum speed of over 75 m.p.h. He had done a good many hours on the machine and was already exhibiting signs of over-confidence, and an inclination to show off by making steep turns close to the ground.

On June 13th he left Eastchurch for Brooklands with Lieut. J. R. B. Kennedy, one of the pilots of the Naval Wing, R.F.C., in the passenger's seat. They arrived above Brooklands at 5.15 p.m. and Gordon Bell proceeded to " shoot-up " the aerodrome.

For fifteen minutes he roared in and out and round about the hangars, diving on the spectators and waving his hand to them as he almost scraped his wing tips on the grass in vertically-banked turns. Finally he flew between two of the sheds with only inches to spare, pulled up sharply to clear another hangar, went into a steep climbing turn, stalled, and dived into the ground on to his left wing tip and nose.

Lieut. J. R. B. Kennedy, who had been granted his aviator's certificate (No. 423) on February 18th, 1913, was crushed to death as the front seat telescoped. Mr. Gordon Bell was taken to hospital with very serious injuries, from which he subsequently recovered.

All the expert witnesses who were called at the inquest were unanimous in condemning the pilot for dangerous flying, and the jury added a rider to their verdict of death from misadventure to the effect that no pilot should be allowed to take such grave risks whilst carrying a passenger.

This rider was communicated to the R.Ae.C., but the Accidents Investigation Committee neglected to take any disciplinary action, although they agreed that the smash was caused solely by the handling of the aircraft, and that the pilot had shown " a grave error of judgment " in flying as he did over a place reserved for spectators, where low flying was prohibited by the club. They pointed out that the practice of steep turns might " be highly valuable, provided this be done with due regard for the life and property of others."

Compare this official " white-washing " of a prominent British pilot, with the drastic treatment meted out to M. Brindejonc des Moulinais. In the one case the life of a Service pilot had been recklessly thrown away by criminal negligence to satisfy a pilot's vanity, whilst in the other case the pilot trespassed over forbidden territory unwittingly in an endeavour to reach his destination through bad visibility.

It is only fair to point out, however, that Mr. Gordon Bell was brought up before the General Committee of the Club four months later and cautioned as to his future flying.

22. SOME FAMOUS PUPILS: CORBETT-WILSON FLIES HOME

A number of the pupils under instruction at the various schools at this time were destined to make their mark in British aviation. On June 2nd, Mr. R. H. Carr, who had seen much flying as a assenger whilst acting as chief mechanic to Mr. Grahame-White, qualified at his employer's school at Hendon. On the following day Mr. F. W. Gooden, who was later to take Mr. de Havilland's place as chief test pilot to the Royal Aircraft Factory at Farnborough, passed his tests on one of the Caudron biplanes at the Ewen school. Ten days later Mr. Wm. Birchenough, who was to become a great pilot of de Havilland machines, took his certificate on the Grahame-White biplane. It was shortly after this that Mr. L. A. Strange, now well-known as a pilot of Spartans, and Mr. Hereward de Havilland, who now looks after de Havilland interests in Australia, began to learn to fly on Caudrons at the Ewen school.

At Brooklands Mr. Waterfall and Maj. Sefton Brancker, who had now returned from India, were receiving instruction on the Vickers monoplanes and biplanes from Messrs. Barnwell and Knight.

Mr. Corbett-Wilson left Rheims in his Bleriot in which he had crossed the Jura Alps, accompanied by his faithful French mechanic, and tried to fly to Hendon in the teeth of a westerly gale. After experiencing some exceptionally violent bumps, he decided to land at Peronne, 120 kilometres (75 miles) from Rheims. The next day he continued to Hardelot and, leaving there at 4.50 a.m. on the following morning, he crossed the Channel and arrived safely at Hendon, having covered 120 miles in eighty minutes at an average speed of 90 m.p.h.

23. TWO NEW BRITISH ENGINES

A very important development was the entry into the aviation world of the great armament firm of Armstrong-Whitworth and Co., Ltd.

During June they took up the manufacture of the 100 h.p. A.B.C. aero engine. This was an 8-cylinder vee-type motor, each cylinder of which was surrounded by its own separate water jacket for cooling. The valves were placed in the cylinder heads and operated by push rods from the central camshaft between the banks of cylinders. The engine developed 100 h.p. at 1,300 r.p.m. for a weight of 3¾ lbs. per b.h.p.

The new edition of the Isaacson motor was an extremely neat 7-cylinder radial engine, which developed a maximum of 67·9 b.h.p. at 1,080 r.p.m. The weight complete was only 196 lbs. so that the power/weight ratio was better than 3 lbs. per b.h.p. Moreover, it was economical to run, as the petrol consumption worked out at only 3·8 gals. per hour at cruising speed. This promising engine was made at Leeds by Messrs. Manning, Wardle and Co., who had arranged matters so that it could be fitted in place of the ubiquitous Gnôme without any structural alteration to the airframe.

24. THREE CROSS-CHANNEL FLIGHTS

Mr. Sydney Pickles had thoroughly mastered the Caudron biplanes in the course of a number of cross-country flights, including one from Hendon to Shoreham and back, which qualified him for his superior aviator's certificate. He had also been practising tight spiral descents from considerable altitudes, and was already regarded as the best exponent of the Caudron type in England.

It fell to his lot to be sent to Crotoy to take over a new Caudron seaplane for delivery to the Naval Wing, R.F.C., at the Isle of Grain, and he had asked a friend to accompany him. Just as the boat train was leaving the friend turned up with another man and stated that he was unable to go, so Pickles jokingly suggested that the stranger, who turned out to be Mr. W. R. M. Oddey, should take his place. Although this sportsman had never been in an aeroplane, he readily consented. I quote below from his own account of his strange *baptême de l'air*, which took place on June 23rd.

" At 5 p.m. I donned overcoats, and such wraps as I could secure, and very gingerly accommodated myself in the seat of the Caudron 'bus.' Then Pickles got aboard and proceeded to start the engine from a handle, for all the world like a motor-car. Waving 'good-bye' to our hosts, we roared across the sands, and started the flight at exactly five minutes past the hour.

" Rising gently as we flew along the coast, we gradually climbed higher and higher until the ground lay 3,000 feet below. It was glorious. At this height the country was one vast picture map. Still following the coastline we forged steadily through the air, and fifty-five minutes from the time of starting had reached Boulogne. My word, it was cold up there. I had arranged with Pickles to write a log of the flight, but I shivered so much that I could scarcely hold the pencil. Noticing this, Pickles switched off for a glide to warmer levels. But it was only for a little while, for very soon we were fighting our way full speed through the wind again, and the shivering fits came on worse than ever. It was horrible. . . .

" And so we flew on against the wind to Cap Gris Nez, the name of which Pickles yelled at me through the hurricane draught as a reminder that, shivers or no, I must keep my log. Thence we headed out to sea, and I left behind with the land a heartfelt wish that we had alighted, if only for a moment or two, to ease the strain on my cramped, cold, shivering body and limbs.

" The idea of the non-stop flight was strong in the mind of the pilot, and he kept going. Clouds loomed thick ahead, and there was no sight of the coast. A steamer came into view on the water below and remained in sight for a minute or two ere it was blotted out by the mist. Presently Pickles switched off and glided down from 4,000 feet, where we had been flying, to 2,000 feet, where he switched on again.

" There was still no sign of land. . . . It seemed years since we started, and the memory of the French coastline had almost faded out of the sense of reality, so long did it seem since we had left it behind.

" Occasionally I noticed that the machine would rock quite a lot, and then fly steadily again for a while, until it had another spasm. Ordinarily I should have been much interested in the performance, and possibly a little alarmed. But, under the present circumstances, I think I was willing to accept anything that fate might ordain, were it only a change.

" At seven o'clock in the evening, signs of land ahead were still absent, but, looking backwards, I could dimly discern the outline of France. Three minutes later, however, a tap on the back from Pickles caused me to strain my eyes against the blast. There, in the distance, I could just make out a narrow, dark excrescence on the horizon—the first glimpse of the shores of home.

" Two steamers and a lightship that presently came into view gave an air of civilization to the otherwise deserted space, and cheered my drooping spirits immensely. I rubbed my hands together with renewed vigour, so that I might hold the pencil with better effect, but it was a sorry business.

" Keeping Dover well to the left, we made for the mouth of the Thames, and by 8 o'clock we came up with the coastline and followed it round to Margate. About this time, too, Pickles was beginning to get particularly interested in his petrol gauge, and as I obstructed the view in my normal position, I found myself once or twice summarily pushed out of the light.

" At Margate Pickles switched off and alighted on the sea alongside the pier, where the machine rocked about like a row-boat on the swell. . . .

". . . Having filled up with petrol and oil, we once more ascended into the air, after considerable preliminary bumping over the rough surface of the water.

" Dusk was now falling, for it was 8.45 when we passed Herne Bay pier. Presently came Sheerness, with the lights of the town and the steamers, and the flashing buoys, making a scintillating picture. Suddenly three searchlights shot their beams across the water, and passing over a little bay, Pickles switched off and made a smooth landing on the Medway precisely at 9 o'clock."

The Caudron was not a fast machine, but there must have been a considerable head-wind to cause Pickles to spend 2 hrs. 55 mins. in the air on the section from Crotoy to Margate, a distance of about 140 miles. This was Sydney Pickles' first cross-Channel flight and the third occasion on which he had flown a seaplane.

Intense interest had been aroused at Hendon by the arrival of M. Brindejonc des Moulinais in one of the latest Morane-Saulnier monoplanes (60 h.p. Le Rhone). These machines were undoubtedly the best aeroplanes in the world at that time and stupendous feats were being performed on them daily in France.

The Grahame-White Co. had ordered two of them, one land machine and a float seaplane, and Mr. Robert Slack went across to Villacoublay to fetch back the former.

He made a trial flight on June 24th and left for England just after 5 a.m. on the following morning. Almost immediately he flew into heavy rain and low cloud and was forced to fly blind, trusting to his compass. He caught only an occasional glimpse of the ground and very soon lost all idea of his whereabouts.

On the top of the forward fuel tank of the Morane-Saulnier was a glass cup in which the petrol could be seen when being pumped from the reserve tank to the main one. This cup had evidently been cracked prior to taking off, and a piece of glass had been shaken out during the flight. After flying for about three hours, Slack decided that it was necessary to pump up some fuel, but as soon as he started to do so, the petrol came out through the gap in the cup and was blown back in his face, very little passing on into the service tank.

Slack did not know where he was, and he could see neither land nor water below, but in any case the situation was desperate, and he set himself to pump for his life. The more he pumped the more petrol was sluiced over him until he sat drenched in the icy spirit, almost blinded and nearly suffocated by the fumes.

At last the engine stopped, and, as Slack put his nose down, the clouds parted and he saw the town of Folkestone straight in front of him and about a mile away. He was just able to reach a small field, where he made an extremely able landing on the summit of a steep ridge.

So far he had put up a wonderful performance under the worst possible conditions and had covered 170 miles in 3 hrs. 40 mins. of blind flying at an average speed of 46 m.p.h.

He blocked up the hole in the glass cup with insulating tape, that panacea of the early pilots, refuelled his machine and took off after a stoppage of 1 hr. 35 mins.

The ceiling was 1,000 feet over Kent, but Slack climbed up through the cloud layer and set a course for Kempton Park. He held this for two hours and then came down, thinking that he must have overshot his turning point. On landing he found he was at Headley, twelve miles short of Kempton, and that his average speed had been reduced to 33 m.p.h. As the Morane-Saulnier cruised at 75 m.p.h., the wind must have been at least 40 m.p.h.—gale force.

Slack bought more petrol at Headley, and then set off on the last stretch to Hendon, where he landed safely at 1.41 p.m., having spent 6 hrs. 36 mins. in the air in covering a total distance of about 260 miles.

This magnificent struggle against adversity, established Mr. Robert Slack's claim to be counted amongst the best British pilots.

Mr. Grahame-White himself went to Paris to fetch the Morane seaplane. He left the Ile de Jatte on the Seine the day after Robert Slack's crossing, and flew down the river to le Havre, where he stopped for breakfast. Thence he followed the coast up to Boulogne and crossed to Dover, where he lunched with Mr. Algernon Guinness in his yacht. In the afternoon he took off and flew round to the mouth of the Thames, alighted on the water, taxied past the prohibited areas, took to the air again at Greenwich, and flew on to Putney, where the final landing was made.

25. FIRST FATAL SMASH AT SHOREHAM: HAWKER WINS MORTIMER SINGER SEAPLANE PRIZE

On June 29th Mr. Richard Norton Wight, a pupil of the Avro school at Shoreham, was killed whilst flying an old Avro tractor biplane (60 h.p. E.N.V.)

This was another case of a pilot taking off with an engine which was not pulling properly. Mr. Geere, who was acting as instructor to the Avro school, had warned Mr. Wight not to attempt to fly circuits as the engine was running 100 r.p.m. below normal speed owing to an unsuitable airscrew.

Mr. Wight chose to ignore this advice and proceeded to clamber into the air and commence a sharp left-hand turn, with the tail drooping. He got round this first turn, but in attempting another one in order to get back to the aerodrome he stalled the machine and dived into the ground. The wreckage caught fire and the pilot was trapped by the foot and burned to death, in spite of heroic efforts on the part of Mr. Geere and others to release him.

Mr. R. N. Wight had been granted his aviator's certificate (No. 462) two months previously on April 22nd, 1913.

On July 8th, Mr. H. G. Hawker won the prize of £500 presented by Mr. Mortimer Singer for the first flight by an all-British amphibious aircraft to comply with the difficult conditions he had laid down.

These rules called for six consecutive out-and-home flights between two points five miles apart, one of which was on water and the other on the land. At each point a descent had to be made before resuming the journey. Thus the aircraft was subjected to six landings and take-offs on the water and six on the land, and a period of five hours was allowed for completion of the tests. A further stipulation was that a height of at least 750 feet had to be attained during each of the twelve separate flights, and on one

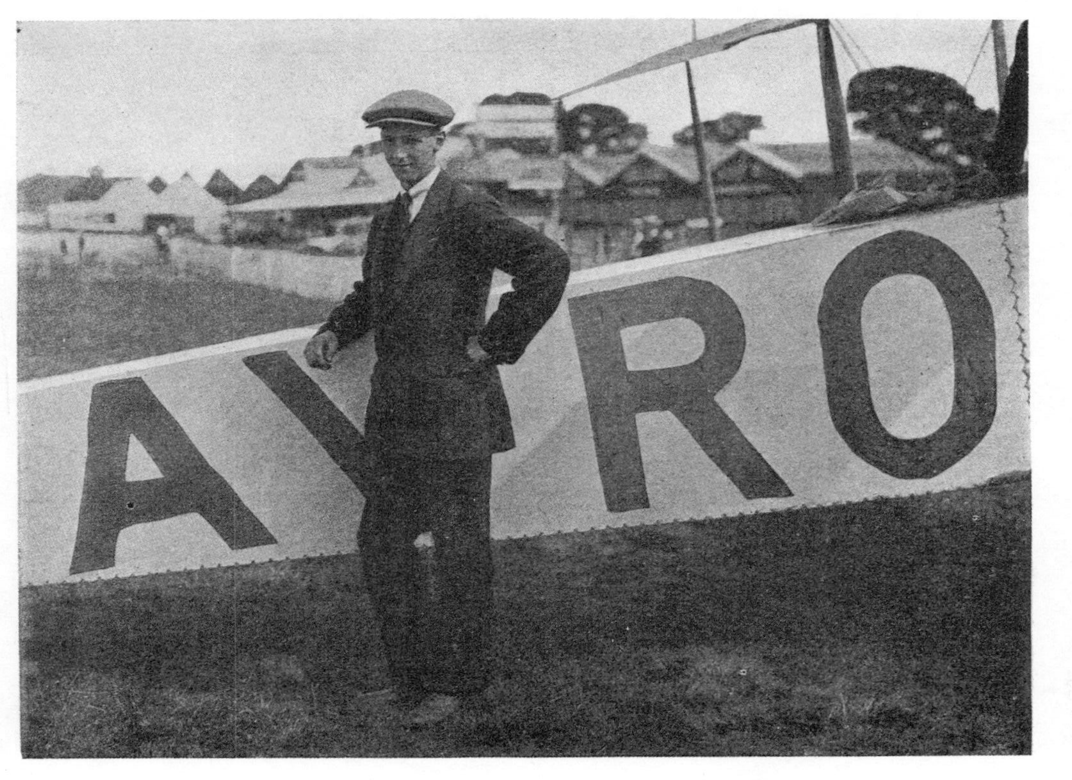

"Flight" photo

9.—The Aerial Derby: the pilot of the Avro, Mr. F. P.

"*Flight*" *photo*

10.—Survivor of a terrible smash: Mr. Sydney Pickles, the Caudron expert.

Facing page 45

single occasion during the tests the machine was to be taken up to 1,500 feet.

This was a competition which called not only for clever design and good workmanship if the machine was to withstand the various strains imposed by such a severe test, but also for piloting of quite an exceptional order. The combination was forthcoming in the Sopwith "Bat-boat," which was fitted with a 100 h.p. Green engine in order to bring it into the all-British category, and Mr. Harry Hawker.

The machine was flown backwards and forwards between a field close to the present site of Hamble aerodrome and a buoy in the Solent and, thanks to a series of beautiful landings by Hawker, everything went without a hitch, and the test was completed in 3 hrs. 25 mins.

26. ANOTHER OFFICER KILLED: WORLD'S RECORD FOR HAWKER

The first fatal accident to happen to a pupil whilst flying through the tests for his aviator's certificate occurred at Larkhill, Salisbury Plain, on July 17th.

The pupil was Maj. Alexander Wm. Hewetson, and he had been under instruction at the Bristol school of flying for about two months. He was sent for his tests on a sociable (side by side seater) monoplane (50 h.p. Gnôme), and he overbanked the machine whilst performing the figure-of-eight test and sideslipped into the ground from 100 feet.

It was a sheer error of judgment, arising from inexperience. His instructor, M. Henri Jullerot, stated at the inquest that he considered it inadvisable for men of Maj. Hewetson's age, he was forty-four, to take up flying.

Mr. H. G. Hawker was never one to rest on his laurels and, not content with having captured the British records for altitude in the solo, and one and two passenger categories, he determined to set up a new record for pilot and three passengers.

The attempt was made at Brooklands on July 27th, in the same Sopwith tractor biplane (80 h.p. Gnôme) with which the earlier records had been secured. The results exceeded all expectations, for the machine soared steadily up to 8,400 feet (2,560 metres), thus easily breaking the world's record of 1,680 metres (5,486 feet) then held by Mons. E. Marty (Caudron).

This was the fourth time that a world's record had been captured by a British pilot, and Mr. H. G. Hawker now held five British records as well, although it was still less than a year since he first learned to fly.

27. THE GREAT WAR OFFICE SCANDAL: POSITION OF THE R.F.C.

It is now necessary to give an account of one of the most amazing scandals which have ever disgraced the political life of this country. Generally speaking, such mud is better left undisturbed once it has settled on the bottom, but there are reasons why it is essential that the facts of the matter be included in any history of British aviation.

It is true that this history is intended to set out the story of Britain's part in the development of aviation as a means of transport only, and that I am not concerned with purely military affairs, except so far as they affected aviation as a whole. But here we come up against the fact that in 1913 military aviation, as such, was scarcely to be distinguished from civil aviation. The whole of the R.F.C. at that time was nothing but one large flying training school, rather better organized and disciplined than a civilian school of flying, but none the less, a school. A few experiments of a warlike nature were carried out by the pupils, such as signalling from the air, observing the movements of troops on the ground, and firing off machine guns and rifles from the cockpits of the machines, but the primary aim of the officers of the Corps was to obtain flying practice, and yet more flying practice, and to try out as many different types of aeroplane as could be obtained.

It is obvious, therefore, that the supply of machines to the R.F.C. was a great factor in the lives and hopes of the aircraft constructors in this country, and that the results of the Service tests of those machines were of great value to aeronautical science as a whole. In fact, the R.F.C. represented the manufacturers' laboratory in which full-scale tests to destruction could be made of their products. For that reason it had become a vitally important factor in the development of the aeroplane as a reliable conveyance, and any neglect of its requirements tending to hinder its work was of serious concern to British aviation as a whole.

In order to understand the development of this scandal it is necessary to appreciate the state of men's minds at the time.

Europe was dwelling in fear. The black shadows of Vickers, Armstrongs, Maxim-Nordenfelts, Krupps, Creusots, and the sinister shade of the Greek, Zaharoff, darkened men's lives.

" Incident " after " incident " occurred, each of which threatened to strike the spark which should set Europe aflame. Armies of spies peered and pried into the private affairs of every state. There were swift assassinations, secret trials, hideous oppressions, and sporadic outbursts of open warfare amongst the smaller nations. Trial runs these last, in which the armament experts could test their latest devices for torturing the common soldier.

Into this seething cauldron of hatred and mistrust had been flung a new weapon of incalculable possibilities, promising hitherto unimagined facilities for promoting death and destruction—especially in England.

Four years had passed since that portentous Sunday, July 25th, 1909, on which Louis Bleriot had shattered for ever Nature's barrier against the invasion of England. If Bleriot had flown across the Straits of Dover waving a red flag, the danger signal could not have been more obvious, but it takes a long time for simple facts to penetrate the dim recesses of the military mind. For three vital years the Government had sat back and gaped in wonderment at the glorious spectacle of France conquering a new element single-handed; whilst the English people became increasingly alarmed.

When, at long last, the politicians acted there was a general sense of relief. The initial scheme for the establishment of the R.F.C. was sound and generally approved. But the people expected that the Government's promise to establish seven squadrons of twelve aeroplanes, each with six machines in reserve, and manned by eighty-four officer pilots, would be carried out promptly and effectively.

It was, therefore, a shock to the public when it became known on the introduction of the Army Estimates for 1913, that only £501,000 was to be expended on the maintenance and development of the C.F.S., the Military Wing, R.F.C., and the Royal Aircraft Factory. Obviously there was something wrong, for the amount was clearly inadequate to carry out the Government's promises.

Once more the people became alarmed and a great campaign was started in the Press, led by the *Daily Mail*, and public meetings were held in all parts of the country at which resolutions were passed urging the Government to take vigorous action.

The newspapers pressed home the attack by publishing exaggerated reports of the wonderful efficiency of the French and German Air Services, and finally a rumour was started, probably deliberately, to the effect that a foreign aircraft had been observed cruising unchallenged over Sheerness Dockyard in the dead of night.

The powerful Navy League took the matter up, and organized a meeting at the Mansion House, under the chairmanship of the Lord Mayor, which was attended by many Members of Parliament.

The whole populace was whipped into a perfect frenzy of anxiety.

Such was the state of affairs when back-bench Members of Parliament began to make searching inquiries into the condition of the R.F.C. The results were not encouraging. The investigators found that the pilots of the Corps were second to none and their spirit magnificent, but they could only discover three of the seven squadrons which had been promised, and it was clear from the start that not one of them was adequately equipped.

The Members, led by Mr. William Joynson-Hicks, a London solicitor of good standing in his profession, began to ask a great many awkward questions in the House of Commons. Col. J. E. B. Seely, Secretary of State for War, and thus wholly responsible for the Military section of the R.F.C., gave a series of evasive replies. When pressed he would stave off the attack by declaring that it was "not in the public interest" to make further disclosures.

The movement gathered force steadily, week by week, throughout the early summer, and it is probable that no politician has ever been subjected to such a concentrated fire of questions on a subject of such vital importance.

In considering this amazing affair it should be borne in mind that Col. Seely was not in the position of the ordinary politician who suddenly finds himself in charge of a Department of State of whose business technicalities he is in complete ignorance. Col. Seely knew more about aviation than most people. He was an enthusiast for the air. He was personally acquainted with many pilots and had made numerous flights as a passenger.

When he introduced the estimates on March 19th, 1913, he stated categorically :" We have in our possession 101 aeroplanes capable of flying." Mr. Joynson-Hicks flatly denied that this was true, and five days later Col. Seely spoke as follows :—" I say on my full responsibility as a Minister that we have got 101 aeroplanes ; I understand the honourable gentleman to say that this is not true—that is a very unusual statement to make ; we certainly have got 101 aeroplanes." On June 4th, Col. Seely stated that he then had " 126 aeroplanes, of which thirty-one were in various stages of repair."

Mr. Joynson-Hicks and his little band of followers disbelieved these unequivocal announcements and refused to be thrown off the scent by a series of graphic stories with which Col. Seely regaled the House concerning the more spectacular performances of the pilots of the R.F.C. They decided to issue a definite challenge and, on July 12th, Mr. Joynson-Hicks asked permission for a Committee of the House to tour the Government aerodromes and count the machines for themselves.

Col. Seely had his back to the wall.

It was impossible to refuse altogether and the best course he could take was to try to minimize the importance of the Committee as far as he was able. " Public interests" were invoked once more and, on the grounds of official secrecy, he refused to allow more than two members of the House to set eyes on the innocuous collection of B.E.'s, Farmans, and Bleriots which comprised our aerial fleet. By this means the odds in the final battle, when the Committee presented their report to the House, would be reduced to two back-bench Members versus one Minister of the Crown.

Mr. Joynson-Hicks and Mr. Sandys, his chosen partner in the enterprise, requested the Minister for War to instruct a Military expert to accompany them on their tour of investigation, but this facility was withheld. Mr. Joynson-Hicks then asked that Mr. du Cros, M.P. for Hastings, and a civilian authority on aircraft, should be permitted to join the party, but this request was also rejected.

The basis of the investigation was to check the accuracy of Col. Seely's statement, made when he accepted the challenge, that : " We have now got 120 machines—I take only those in first-class order."

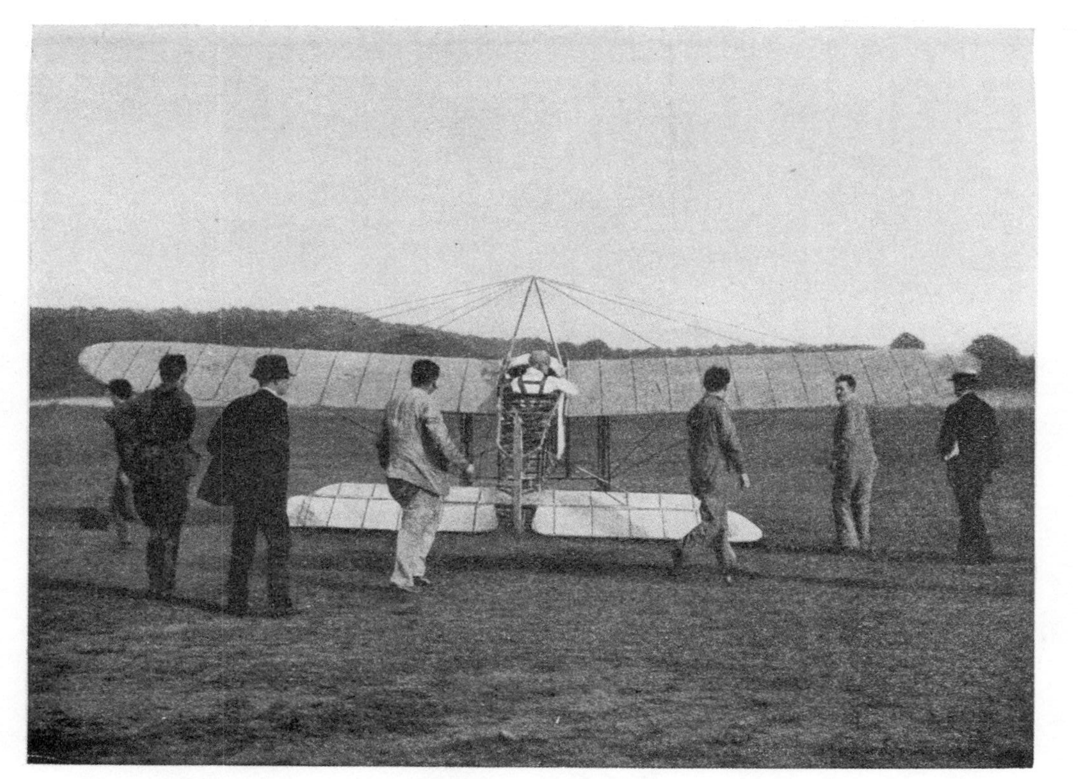

"Flight" photo

11.—A tense moment. Mons. E. Pégoud ready to take off from Brooklands to loop for the first time in England.

"*Flight*" *photo*

12.—London–Brighton Race: Mr. Robert H. Barnwell, the pilot of the Martinsyde.

Facing page 49

As a preliminary safeguard Mr. Joynson-Hicks wrote to the War Office for an official list of the 120 machines. Here is the list which was supplied by Col. Seely's own department :—

At the Central Flying School	
Biplanes—	
Ready to fly	20
Under repair	5
Awaiting authority to strike off	2
Monoplanes	2
At Larkhill.	
Biplanes—	
Ready to fly	9
Under repair	2
Damaged	2
At Farnborough	
Biplanes	
Ready to fly	10
Under repair	11
Monoplanes	11
Damaged	4
Montrose.	
Biplanes—	
Ready to fly	4
Under repair	4
Wrecked	1
Royal Aircraft Factory	
Biplanes	
Experimental, ready to fly	3
Under test, ready to fly	7
Monoplanes—	12
Under repair	2
Under reconstruction	9
Total	120

There were the 120 aeroplanes right enough—and the investigation proved that the above list was substantially accurate. But let us analyse this schedule of these 120 aeroplanes, bearing in mind the fact that Col. Seely, in counting them up, had taken "only those in 'first-class order.'"

There were fifty biplanes ready to fly, three experimental biplanes which had not yet passed their manufacturer's test, twenty-two biplanes under repair, and five biplanes damaged or wrecked.

The remaining forty machines were monoplanes, of which only two were in service, as I will explain shortly.

The number of machines then in first-class order and in active use by the Service pilots was therefore approximately fifty-two—or less than half the number stated by the Minister for War. By stretching the imagination a little it might be said that the twenty-two biplanes listed as "under repair" were actually in service, as, no doubt, many of them were merely undergoing routine overhaul, but, even if we count these as being "in first-class order," the total of machines in service could not exceed seventy-four, or forty-six short of Col. Seely's figure.

The investigators saw only twenty-four of the forty monoplanes included in the list, and were informed that two Bleriots were the only machines of this type that were actually being flown in the Service. The position with regard to the remainder was as follows: The ban on monoplanes had been officially lifted consequent upon the "Monoplane Committee's" report, but only in regard to those machines which had been modified at the Royal Aircraft Factory in accordance with the Committee's recommendations.

Now the Royal Aircraft Factory was an institution run by Civil Servants, and was consequently obsessed with a sense of its own importance. The business of modifying a number of monoplanes, which would subsequently compete against their own biplanes of the B.E. type, failed to appeal to these people. So the Bristols, Deperdussins, Bleriots, and Nieuports were snatched away from the pilots and left to moulder into decay in odd corners of the sheds at Farnborough.

Obviously the monoplanes, always excepting the two Bleriots which had somehow escaped the clutches of the Factory, had to be left out of the calculations.

The position at the time of the investigation was actually as follows: According to Col. Seely there were 191 officers and men in the R.F.C. who were certified flyers, of whom eighty-two were fully qualified Military pilots who had passed through the C.F.S. tests. There were at the most, seventy-four aeroplanes in commission on which they could fly, a ratio of five pilots to every two machines.

This is how it worked out in practice.

At the Central Flying School Mr. Joynson-Hicks found eighteen machines ready to fly, on which twenty-five pupils were under instruction. This was the best equipped station in the Service.

He did not trouble to go to Montrose, but reported that he had been informed that the eleven officer pilots of No. 2 Squadron had three serviceable machines between them, and one of these was a training machine, useless for purposes of war.

No. 3 Squadron at Larkhill had ten machines in all, two of which were under repair. The proper equipment of each Squadron had been fixed at eighteen machines, so that No. 3 was eight aeroplanes deficient, and of the ten machines on hand, two were unsuitable for active service. The two Bleriots were understood to be in transit between Farnborough and Larkhill.

On visiting Farnborough the investigators found such a muddle that they were unable to distinguish between the equipment of No. 4 Squadron, then in embryo form, and that of the Royal Aircraft Factory. They were shown twelve aeroplanes in flying order, which apparently belonged to the Squadron, and seven more machines in charge of the Factory's civilian staff, which were destined for the C.F.S. They also saw three experimental biplanes which were being flown by civilian pilots.

Counting the two Bleriots, and allowing four machines to No. 2 Squadron at Montrose, the investigators found forty-four aeroplanes actually capable of flight and at the disposal of the officers of the R.F.C. No single one of the three Squadrons of the Royal Flying Corps had more than one half of its war-time equipment, and, as a large proportion of the forty-four aeroplanes were school machines, it is doubtful if at that time a single squadron could have been set up on a war basis.

Col. Seely's answer to this alarming exposure began as follows: "With regard to the number of aeroplanes, I said in the course of the debate that it seemed to me that the whole controversy was uninteresting, and I think so still. . . ." He went on to gloss over the matter by talking about the undoubted excellence of the pilots.

The late Mr. Bonar Law closed a heated debate with the following stern rebuke: "My honourable friend" (Mr. Joynson-Hicks) "made a challenge that there were not 120 aeroplanes, but only eighty, which could efficiently fly. What was the result? There were not eighty, but fifty-one on the most liberal computation. Further, the right honourable gentleman" (Colonel Seely) "said they had 120 machines in first-class working order. From their own official statement this number included some that were described as damaged and awaiting instructions as to disposal, and others regarded as wrecked and awaiting authority to 'knock-off.' All this proves that the right honourable gentleman was rash in the extreme in the statement he made to the House, and if we cannot accept a deliberate statement made in a case of that kind, how can we be expected to accept his assurances on other matters in regard to which it was impossible to have such a test?"

So the cat was out of the bag at last, and everyone knew how the flying officers had been let down by the politicians and Civil Servants at the War Office. Everyone knew now that the Royal Flying Corps was unfit for active service after eighteen months of preparation, that as a fighting force it was completely worthless, and that this position had arisen in spite of the most intense loyalty, stern devotion to duty, and disregard of danger on the part of officers and men. Never had a Government department suffered such bitter disgrace.

There was one bright spot in this unpleasant prospect. Mr. Winston Churchill, guided by that great personality, Com. C. R. Samson, R.N., had resisted all the wiles of the Royal Aircraft Factory and steadily pursued an open policy of free experiment. He had first shown his independence by refusing to co-operate with Col. Seely in imposing the ban on monoplanes, and since that time the Admiralty had purchased aeroplanes of many different types, both at home and abroad, and had encouraged the pilots of the Naval Wing, R.F.C., to use them impartially and to criticize them freely. There were fifty-seven Naval pilots at the end of May, and they were well equipped with Deperdussin, Bristol, Bleriot, Borel, and Nieuport monoplanes, and Short, Vickers, Bristol, Caudron, Farman, Sopwith, and B.E. biplanes. It was obvious that the Naval Wing would not form part of the R.F.C. much longer.

28. THE DEATH OF S. F. CODY: THE BURTON MEETING

British aviation lost one of its most popular characters on the morning of August 7th, when Col. S. F. Cody's new biplane collapsed in the air above Laffan's Plain, which had been the scene of the pilot's earliest experiments.

The machine had been constructed, largely with Col. Cody's own hands, for the express purpose of competing for the prize of £5,000 which had been offered by the *Daily Mail* newspaper to the winner of a seaplane race round Britain. It differed scarcely at all from the famous "Cathedral." Bamboo was still utilized for the principal longitudinal members, but the split elevator in front, which formerly did duty as a substitute for ailerons in maintaining lateral control, had given place to warp. The tail had been brought nearer to the main wings and one large rudder now took the place of the twin rudders previously fitted.

The new biplane was being tested with a land undercarriage when the accident took place. For eight minutes it had flown satisfactorily, and Cody was gliding in to land, at a height of 200 feet when, without any warning, the front spar of the lower wing on the left-hand side broke, and the whole aircraft collapsed.

Neither the pilot, nor Mr. W. H. B. Evans, who was riding as passenger, was strapped in, and both were thrown clean out into space when the machine turned over in the air. The wreckage landed on some trees and the centre section was found undamaged, so that it is possible that, had the ordinary precaution of using safety-belts been adopted, neither would have been killed.

Col. Cody had taught himself to fly early in 1909 on the primitive British Army Aeroplane, which he had designed and helped to construct, and his aviator's certificate (No. 9) was granted to him on June 7th, 1910.

For many months he was far in advance of any other British experimenter, although his aeroplanes were never safe to fly.

"Flight" photo

13.—Mr. R. H. Carr, winner of the Michelin Cup No. 1 with his Grahame-White Charabancs (100 h.p. Green).

Facing page 52

"Flight" photo

14.—England's greatest stunt pilot: Mr. B. C. Hucks adjusting

He knew nothing of aerodynamics, and cared less. Never has there been a more remarkable instance of a man attaining considerable success by pure trial and error, whilst remaining in profound ignorance of what he was doing.

It was this persistent disregard for theoretical knowledge which caused Cody to lose the place which he had won for himself at the outset. He continued to produce aeroplanes by guess-work long after other constructors had mastered the elements of aerodynamics, and to use materials which had long since been condemned as dangerous and impractical.

I have already said enough to show that what the uninitiated regarded as his culminating triumph at the Military trials in 1912, was in reality a fluke, occasioned first by the possession of a magnificent engine, and, secondly, by the ignorance of the judges.

But however incompetent Cody may have been as an aeroplane designer, he was immensely popular as an individual—and rightly so—for no man was ever more candid, more straightforward, or more likeable.

Cody's principal achievements—and the earliest of them were genuine triumphs—included the winning of the British Empire Michelin Cup No. 1, for distance covered in a closed circuit in the years 1910 and 1911, and the Michelin Cup No. 2 for speed over a cross-country course in 1911 and 1912. He held the all-British records for distance and duration in a closed circuit at the end of 1910 and 1911, and was amongst the ten best British pilots throughout the years 1909, 1910, and 1911.

His death, following so closely upon that of Lieut. Rogers-Harrison, was not without one beneficial result in that the authorities abandoned all attempts to make use of his designs for army purposes, so that no more valuable lives were sacrificed in flying a type which had been proved to be highly dangerous.

A four-day flying meeting was held at Burton-on-Trent during the August Bank Holiday week-end, at which some good flying took place, although the entries were confined to Messrs. F. P. Raynham (Avro tractor biplane, 50 h.p. Gnôme), Sydney Pickles (Bleriot monoplane, 60 h.p. Anzani), and E. R. Whitehouse (Handley-Page monoplane, 50 h.p. Gnôme).

Raynham won the cross-country race to Repton, and the quick take-off competition, whilst Whitehouse brought the Handley-Page in first, in a race round six laps of a closed circuit. Pickles won the prize in the altitude contest, by climbing to 6,100 feet.

29. THE "DAILY MAIL" SEAPLANE TRIAL

The regulations governing the competition for the £5,000 prize offered by the *Daily Mail* newspaper were of a most stringent nature. The course was divided into nine stages as follows:—

Southampton–Ramsgate, 144 miles; Ramsgate–Yarmouth, 96 miles; Yarmouth–Scarborough, 150 miles; Scarborough–Aberdeen, 218 miles; Aberdeen–Cromarty, 134 miles; Cromarty–Oban, via the Caledonian Canal, 94 miles; Oban–Dublin, 222 miles; Dublin-Falmouth, 280 miles; and thence back to Southampton, 202 miles.

The total distance of 1,540 miles had to be covered by each competitor within seventy-two hours of starting. Attempts could be made at any time between August 16th and 30th.

The contest was restricted to all-British aircraft, and four machines had been entered. They were the Cody, a Short biplane (100 h.p. Green), the Radley-England pusher biplane, which had been re-designed after its smash at Shoreham and fitted with a Sunbeam engine of 150 h.p., in place of the three Gnômes, and one of the three-seater Sopwith tractor biplanes, in which a 100 h.p. Green engine had been installed as a substitute for the 80 h.p. Gnôme.

The Cody had been eliminated in the tragedy at Laffan's Plain, the Sunbeam engine in the Radley-England refused to work, and the Green motor in Mr. F. K. McClean's Short also proved refractory.

The Sopwith therefore started alone on its long journey at 11.47 a.m. on the morning of Saturday, August 16th, with Mr. H. G. Hawker at the controls, and Mr. H. Kauper of the Sopwith Company in the passenger's seat.

Hawker flew steadily eastwards at a height of 1,000 feet past Brighton, Eastbourne, and Dover, with a light southerly wind on his right hand, and glorious hot sunshine. He checked in at Ramsgate at 2.11 p.m., having averaged exactly 60 m.p.h. for 144 miles.

At 3.2 p.m. he took off for Yarmouth. There was mist over the Thames Estuary, but Hawker flew a good compass course, and reached the next control at 4.38 p.m., having maintained his average speed of exactly a mile a minute.

Unfortunately the moment Hawker got ashore he collapsed. The sun and the fumes from the engine had been too much for him and it was obvious that he could not continue.

At this stage there took place a pleasant interchange of courtesies, which demonstrated the sporting spirit of the competitors. The Short seaplane was still at the Isle of Grain, where Mr. McClean was wrestling with its Green engine. Mr. Sopwith offered to lend him a radiator, similar to that fitted to Hawker's machine, which he had found to be efficacious in overcoming the cooling troubles to which the Green motors were subject. In return Mr. McClean offered to let his own pilot, Mr. Sydney Pickles, take over the Sopwith biplane from Hawker.

Unfortunately neither of these sporting offers was to prove helpful, for the trouble in the Short's engine was traced to a cracked cylinder which necessitated its withdrawal, and Pickles was unable to continue on account of a violent gale which made the sea far too rough to permit the Sopwith to take off from Yarmouth.

Hawker's machine was therefore dismantled and sent back to Cowes, where longer exhaust pipes were fitted in order to carry the gases clear of the pilot's cockpit. This modification was to prove costly, for the new pipes were placed too close to a rubber water connection, which perished from the heat and allowed the cooling fluid to escape.

The final attempt on the prize began at 5.30 a.m. on August 25th, when Hawker and Kauper took off once more from Southampton Water in still, misty weather, which called for careful attention to the navigation.

Ramsgate was reached in two hours thirty-nine minutes at an average speed of 55 m.p.h. and, after a stop of one hour, the Sopwith left for Yarmouth, where a descent was made one hour twenty-eight minutes out from Ramsgate, the ninety-six miles having been covered at 65 m.p.h. ; so that the average for the first two stages was 58 m.p.h., or 2 m.p.h. slower than on the previous attempt.

The machine remained for one hour eight minutes in the Yarmouth control taking in petrol and oil whilst the crew rested. There were unpleasant bumps and thick mist off the Norfolk coast, but Hawker brought her safely through to Scarborough, a distance of 150 miles, although the speed had dropped to 50 m.p.h., and it took him two hours fifty-eight minutes.

Here the pilot was faced with the first of the long stages, and he arranged to call at Berwick for petrol, as he was doubtful if he could fly the 218 miles to Aberdeen non-stop at such a slow speed. It was one hour forty minutes before he took off again, and it was on this section that he and Kauper, who was already exhibiting signs of the strain imposed by the long flight, were to begin their losing struggle against bad luck.

The water connection had begun to feel the effects of the heat from the exhaust pipe, and a hot engine forced them down at Seaham Harbour, where sixty-five precious minutes were lost in filling the radiator with sea water and strapping up the joint. They left again at 6.40 p.m., but their makeshift repair could not stand the intense heat, and the engine lost so much water that a descent became imperative at Beadnell, twenty miles south of Berwick, after an hour's flying.

It was now 7.40 p.m. and getting dark, so Hawker decided to stay the night at Beadnell. He had covered 495 miles, and had been working hard for fifteen hours that day.

At 8.5 a.m. on the following morning the Sopwith took off and flew northwards for one hour fifty minutes to Montrose, where a stop of half an hour was made for refuelling. The Aberdeen control was reached at 10.58 a.m., and by 11.52 a.m. the machine was in the air once more, bound for the northernmost turning point at Cromarty. Hawker covered the 134 miles non-stop, in two hours three minutes, at an average speed of just under 60 m.p.h.

The course now led south-westwards along the Caledonian Canal to Oban, and was bounded by steep hills for the whole length of ninety-four miles. Although this was the shortest stage, it was also the most difficult, and the Sopwith was subjected to the most violent buffeting in the down-draughts from the mountains. Hawker had left Cromarty at 3.5 p.m., but the conditions were so bad that it took him two hours fifty-five minutes to reach Oban, and his average speed had dropped to 32 m.p.h.

It was 6 p.m. when he battled his way into Oban, and it was out of the question to attempt to start on the exposed stretch of 222 miles to Dublin that night. He had flown 341 miles that day and was already on his way home.

Accordingly both men had a good night's rest, and at 5.42 a.m., the Sopwith took off ; but sluggishly. Hawker was worried and decided to land and beach the machine. On inspection it was found that one of the floats was leaking, and an hour was spent in getting the water out of it. Hawker had arranged to refuel in Larne Harbour, and as soon as he got into the air again, at 6.42 a.m., he settled down to fly a direct compass course along the Firth. He had only flown for thirty minutes, however, when the water connection gave trouble once more, and he had to come down at Kiells and spend an hour and a quarter tinkering with it. Eventually he got away and alighted in Larne Harbour at 9.30 a.m.

Having refuelled, Hawker took off at 11 a.m. for Dublin. Everything went well until they were within sight of the control, when a sudden loss of r.p.m. caused Hawker to suspect that some of the valve springs had given out. He therefore decided to descend and investigate.

It was whilst the machine was losing height by means of gliding turns that luck dealt out a final blow. Hawker's shoe had picked up some grease during the repairs at Kiells, and his foot slipped off the rudder bar at a critical moment, so that he was unable to flatten out in time and the biplane struck the sea with a wing tip, and was broken up by the impact.

Hawker was picked up unhurt, but plucky little Kauper was taken to hospital with a cut head and a broken arm.

Thus ended a grand performance on the part of man and machine. Except for the leaking floats the Sopwith had behaved irreproachably, and the Green engine had emerged creditably from an exacting trial, for the water trouble was not due in any way to the engine itself, but was the result of a hasty and ill-considered modification not authorized by the makers.

For the crew no praise can be too high. Hawker's navigation had effectively overcome conditions of bad visibility over open water, and his flying of the seaplane on the rough stretch across the north of Scotland was skilful and courageous. Kauper had worked very hard, in spite of not feeling well, and had it not been for his capable handling of the damaged cooling system and floats, the machine could not have reached Ireland.

The Sopwith had covered 1,043 miles in approximately twenty hours flying time, at an average speed of about 52 m.p.h. Recognizing that this was the greatest feat of air pilotage yet achieved by any British pilot, the *Daily Mail* generously awarded Mr. H. G. Hawker a special personal prize of £1,000, whilst retaining their £5,000 award for competition in the following year, and the R.Ae.C. very properly bestowed its Silver Medal upon the pilot and its bronze medal upon Mr. Kauper.

30. TWO NEW AIRCRAFT: SOME DISTINGUISHED PUPILS

Messrs. John Alcock and Jack Humphries were putting the new Parsons biplane through its tests at Brooklands. This machine had already flown more or less successfully with a heavy 40 h.p. motor-car engine, and, now that a 70 h.p. Gnôme had been installed, it was found to have a surprisingly good climb.

Mr. Robert Blackburn had been experimenting quietly at Leeds throughout the summer and had at last produced a really fine-looking monoplane. This machine was designed to the order of Dr. M. G. Christie, who had learned to fly on a Deperdussin at Hendon, and it was intended for touring purposes. On its first test flights, Mr. H. Blackburn took it up to 7,000 feet in ten minutes, and it was claimed that the speed range was from 40 to 70 m.p.h. This represented a very great advance upon anything previously produced by the Blackburn family.

Lord Carbery purchased a Morane-Saulnier monoplane (Le Rhone) for his private use and, as soon as he had passed the tests for his certificate at Villacoublay, he set off to fly it to England. He arrived safely above Hendon after an uneventful journey, during which he had made stops on both sides of the Channel. Evidently he had not yet learned to make three-point landings, for he nosed over on touching down at Hendon. The new monoplane was wrecked, but fortunately the owner emerged unhurt.

The Bristol school had two important pupils at this time, for Lord Wellesley was learning to fly at Salisbury Plain, and Lord Edward Grosvenor, who was destined to do so much to foster sporting flying in England after the War, was receiving instruction from Mr. Warren Merriam at the Brooklands branch.

Incidentally, the Bristol headquarters staff had been strengthened by the engagement of the Hanriot expert, Mr. S. V. Sippe, who had taken Mr. Gordon England's place, whilst Mr. Bendall, who had proved such an able assistant to Mr. Merriam at Brooklands had been forced to give up flying on account of his health. His place was taken by Mr. Skene, a recent pupil of the School. Early in September the Bristol Company lost the services of Mr.

Collyns Pizey, who had undertaken the task of organizing the Greek Naval Air Service, which involved his acceptance of the rank of *Capitaine de Freigate* in the *Marine Royale Hellenique*.

31. A BRITISH RECORD BROKEN BY CAPT. LONGCROFT: FIRST OVERSEA FLIGHT BY R.F.C.

Capt. C. A. H. Longcroft performed a magnificent feat on August 19th, when he flew Col. F. H. Sykes, Commandant of the Military Wing, R.F.C., to Montrose from Farnborough on a visit of inspection to No. 2 Squadron.

He used a new B.E.2 tractor biplane (70 h.p. Renault), which had been built for the Squadron at the Royal Aircraft Factory, and he flew the whole distance of approximately 450 miles with only one stop in a net flying time of 7 hrs. 40 mins.

The machine took off from Farnborough at 9.40 a.m., and flew steadily northwards all the morning at an average speed of 52 m.p.h. By three o'clock in the afternoon the fuel supply was getting low, so Capt. Longcroft brought the machine down at Alnmouth in Northumberland at 3.10 p.m., after covering 287 miles non-stop.

The *Fédération Aéronautique Internationale* had at last consented to recognize point-to-point cross-country flights as records, and Capt. Longcroft's performance was thought at first to have broken the existing world's record for distance flown in a straight line with one passenger, and his name was actually inscribed in the record book. As a matter of fact, the French pilot, Deroye, had flown non-stop from Milan to Bani, a distance of 784 kilometres (487 miles) on an S.I.A. monoplane with a passenger on July 17th and, when these figures had been confirmed, Capt. Longcroft's name was erased from the book and that of Deroye substituted, the record being officially credited to Italy.

No. 2 Squadron of the Military Wing, R.F.C., had been ordered to assist in the Irish manœuvres, and the problem arose of how to get there. The aerial crossing to Ireland had only been accomplished five times up-to-date, by Robert Loraine, Corbett-Wilson (twice), Vivian Hewitt, and H. G. Hawker. It was a hazardous passage and no doubt the War Office would gladly have arranged for transport by train and boat; but No. 2 Squadron had a tradition to uphold, and it was decided that the journey should be made by air as a unit.

Capt. Dawes started first on his Maurice Farman pusher biplane (70 h.p. Renault), and flew to Stranraer in bad visibility on August 26th, and he was followed on the next day by Captains Longcroft, Tucker, and MacLean, and Lieut. Dawes, on B.E.2 tractor biplanes (70 h.p. Renaults). Capt. Tucker failed to arrive, as he collided with a wall in executing a forced landing in Fifeshire, and Lieut.

Dawes had to spend the night at Inverkeithing whilst he repaired a broken petrol pipe. A few days later the party at Stranraer were reinforced by two more B.E.2's flown by Capt. Becke and Lieut. F. F. Waldron.

On September 2nd, Capt. Dawes (M. Farman), and Capts. Longcroft and Becke, and Lieuts. Waldron and Dawes, all on B.E.2's, started off across the sea to Ireland. Capt. Longcroft had to return to make an adjustment to his machine, but the other four pilots arrived safely at Rathbone near Limerick.

This was the first occasion upon which a unit of the R.F.C. had flown overseas.

32. HAMEL *v.* HUCKS: AVRO SUCCESS IN GERMANY

B. C. Hucks' enterprising manager, J. C. Savage, had issued a challenge to Gustav Hamel to race his man round a circuit near Birmingham for £500 a side; both pilots to use Bleriot monoplanes (80 Gnômes).

The challenge was accepted and a course was chosen, starting and finishing at Edgbaston and with turning points at Redditch, Coventry, Nuneaton, Tamworth, and Walsall. It was agreed that a stop of thirty minutes should be made at each control, except Tamworth, where a tea interval of forty minutes was arranged, almost as if it was a cricket match.

This contest between two pilots who had every right to claim that they were as good as any others in this country, and better than most, aroused intense excitement in the Midlands, where Hucks was a great favourite. Unfortunately, Hamel was unable to obtain a Bleriot similar to his opponent's, so he borrowed a Morane-Saulnier monoplane (80 Le Rhone), on which he flew from Hendon to Birmingham, a little over 100 miles, in ninety minutes, including a short stop at Nuneaton. This was a much more formidable machine than Huck's Bleriot, so the bet was withdrawn, and it was agreed that Hamel should carry his mechanic by way of handicap whilst Hucks flew alone.

The match took place on August 30th in bad visibility and proved a most exciting affair, for what Hamel gained in superior speed, Hucks made up by better course-keeping, in which he was assisted by his local knowledge.

Thirty thousand people cheered wildly as the Bleriot and the Morane took off from the Tally Ho Grounds at 2.30 p.m. At the first control Hamel led by twenty-four seconds, but by the time Coventry was reached Hucks had cut this down and established a useful lead of two minutes. At Nuneaton Hucks had lost half his lead and before Tamworth Hamel had overtaken him and landed there, fifty-five seconds ahead. Hucks made a great effort on the next stage to Walsall, and reduced the deficiency to a mere nine seconds, but on the home stretch, Hamel drew away once more and finished 20⅗ secs. ahead after one of the most thrilling races ever flown.

The German pilot, Lieut. Langfeld, made a fine flight with a passenger over the open sea, from Wilhelmshafen to Heligoland, on September 6th. He had to face a strong northerly wind, and took about three hours for the journey, as he was forced to alight several times *en route* upon the rough water. He was using one of the new Avro twin-float seaplanes similar to that which was tested by Mr. F. P. Raynham at Shoreham.

33. LEARNING TO FLY BEFORE BREAKFAST

Mr. Pemberton Billing will be remembered as the enterprising individual who developed and equipped an aerodrome at Fambridge, Essex, in the latter part of 1908, before anyone had flown successfully from English soil, and who had himself built three experimental aeroplanes during that year, one of which is supposed to have covered twenty yards in flight before it was smashed to pieces. Nothing had been heard of him in aviation circles for some years, although he was still keenly interested in flying, until he met Mr. Handley-Page and started an argument about the shortest length of time in which it was possible for a man to learn to fly.

The result of this conversation was a wager of £500 to the effect that Mr. Pemberton Billing would obtain his Royal Aero Club's aviator's certificate within twenty-four hours of first sitting in an aeroplane.

The bet was taken up and Mr. Billing was forced to purchase a very old Henry Farman biplane on which to make his attempt, as none of the school proprietors would accept his risk. He had the ancient machine sent down to Brooklands, and arranged with Mr. Robert Barnwell of the Vickers school to act as instructor. Finally, he arrived on the aerodrome at 5.45 a.m. on September 17th, ready for his attempt. The machine was brought out, and the 50 h.p. Gnôme engine was started up, whilst Mr. Pemberton Billing seated himself at the controls with Mr. Barnwell behind him. There was a drizzling rain and the wind was gusty and uncertain.

Here is his own account of one of the most amazing feats in the whole annals of aviation :—

" After four minutes taxying Mr. Barnwell gave the sign to shove her up in the air. I did so, and we attained a height of 200 feet flying steadily. Mr. Barnwell accompanied me for about twenty to twenty-five minutes in the passenger seat, during which time I succeeded in doing some dozen circuits of the aerodrome. Several figure eights, two or three *vol planés*, landings, and some landing under power were carried out, and as it was raining, and the machine was sodden and sluggish in consequence of carrying two thirteen

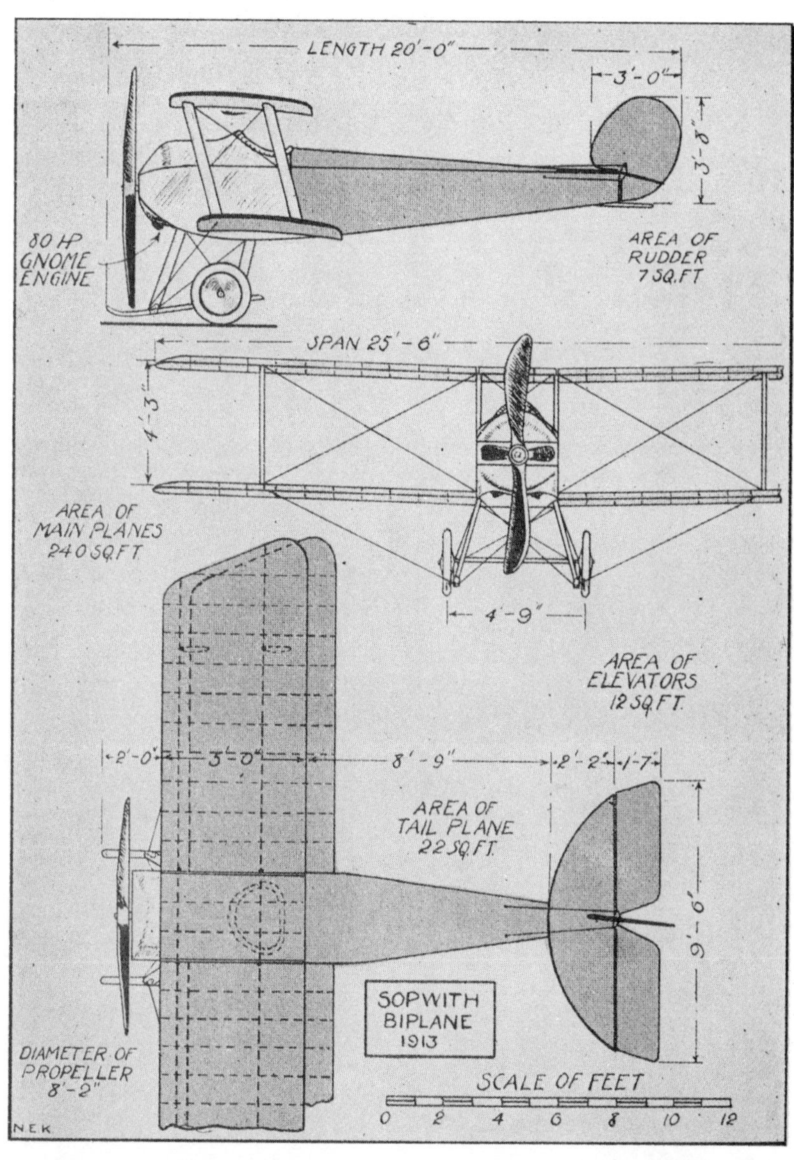

"Flight" copyright

4.—The first of the Scout Class: the revolutionary Sopwith Tabloid (80 h.p. Gnôme) which set up new standards in design.

Facing page 60

"*Flight*" *photo*

15.—THE FIRST WINNER OF THE BRITANNIA TROPHY: CAPT. C. A. H. LONGCROFT, OF No. 2 SQUADRON, R.F.C., ON AN OLD HENRY FARMAN

stone men, this made the landing rather speedy and much more difficult in consequence. At the end of twenty-five minutes Mr. Barnwell left me, and told me to get up and get on with it.

"I immediately started away without any taxying, rose straight in the air at an exceedingly dangerous angle, amid the yells and shrieks of the spectators.

"I did a half-circle and landed successfully, got up again immediately and did a circle and landed successfully, and then rose again and did five circuits. It was my intention to do twelve, but the petrol running out brought me down, the idea of coming trouble dawning upon me by the missing of the engine and the frantic waving of petrol cans by agitated spectators below.

"The rain had then set in so heavily that I was obliged to put the machine away for half an hour, at the termination of which time the machine was brought out again, and Mr. Barnwell went once again as passenger for three or four minutes to test my right-hand turns before allowing me to essay the figure eight alone.

"Immediately on descending, Mr. Barnwell jumped out of the machine, and I took her up at once, doing three successful eights. During the right-hand turns of these I managed to execute the most alarming banks, and, from inexperience, startled by the angle, at first hung on to the struts.

"When I had descended from this stunt, on Mr. Barnwell's orders, I proceeded to practice *vol planing* from an altitude of about one hundred feet, with the engine cut off, which experience I found about the most arduous of all.

"While I was performing my gyrations in the air, Mr. Barnwell thought it about time to send for Mr. Rance, the R.Ae.C. official observer. There was some delay in finding him, as the weather, which was puffy and wet, never led him to believe anyone would want his services on such a morning. Eventually he was found and kindly consented to observe, notwithstanding the short notice given. Incidentally this entailed a loss of an hour or more in the time in which it would have been possible for me to have taken my ticket, because it stands to reason that if I was capable of doing the test at a quarter-past nine I was quite as capable of doing it at a quarter to eight, so I was practically waiting during that time to go through the regulation tests. Although Mr. Rance expressed himself as exceedingly dubious about the advisability of attempting, he consented to act in his official capacity.

"I then rose in a very steep climb to a height of about 250 feet, so as to make sure of the altitude test once and for all. Then I came round with a left-hand bend, and proceeded on my first five figure-eights.

"The five, so I was told afterwards, were good sound flying of an experienced airman, although the fifth right-hand turn proved an alarming one. I was flying over the paddock, where my wife was watching very anxiously, and to give her confidence I waved my hand to her, taking my attention off the elevating plane for the moment." [On these machines the elevator protruded in front of the pilot, on outriggers, and formed the natural guide for observing the attitude of the aeroplane in relation to the ground]. "The machine, as machines will on right-hand turns, shot up, throwing me back on my seat. The position was rendered more hopeless, undoubtedly, by my grabbing hold of the 'joy stick' to recover myself, which caused her to stand on her tail.

"She stopped dead in the air, about 200 feet up, and then fell about 100 feet *tail first*.

"From the looseness of the control, caused by the machine being stationary, I jumped to the conclusion that the wires were broken, and tried to save the position by throwing all my weight forward, with the result that when about fifty feet from the ground the machine righted itself and dived head first.

"This, of course, was not attributable so much to my throwing my weight forwards as to the fact that with me also came the joy stick, bringing the elevator down and causing the machine to dive, which immediately tightened up the controls.

"I instantly realized that I had the control of the machine again, and, thinking I would be disqualified for this stunt, saved her from landing about twenty feet from the ground, climbed up again to 160 feet, and did an extra figure-eight to make sure.

"Then followed a *vol plané* landing, and after listening with some impatience to Mr. Barnwell's illuminating and very forcible remarks on right-hand turns, I started off for the last half of the test, which was accomplished most successfully, finishing off with a *vol plané* from 100 feet with the engine cut off, and brought the machine to rest without switching on again, with the elevating plane over the heads of the observers, thus succeeding in obtaining my pilot's certificate before breakfast on the morning when I had for the first time in my life sat in a flying machine that flew."

Actually the whole process had taken a few minutes over four hours, and it proved, not only that Mr. Pemberton Billing was blessed with unusually quick reflexes and exceptionally steady nerves, but also that the possession of an aviator's certificate did not necessarily indicate that one was a capable pilot ; any more than it does now.

This extraordinary feat, which so nearly cost the pupil his life, probably still stands as a world's record for quick tuition, but it is to be hoped that no one will be so foolish as to attempt to beat it, as even with modern equipment the risk would be entirely unjustifiable.

34. THE SECOND AERIAL DERBY AND THE DÉBUT OF THE AVRO 504

The second Aerial Derby was flown off on September 20th, round a circuit starting and finishing at Hendon, with turning points at

Kempton Park, Epsom racecourse, West Thurrock, Epping, and Hertford, a total distance of ninety-four and a half miles.

There was a formidable entry list of fifteen machines, of which eleven started. The starters comprised three British aeroplanes with foreign engines, flown by British pilots, and eight French machines, of which four were in charge of Englishmen, three had French pilots, and the remaining one was handled by the American, W. L. Brock. None of the competing machines was fitted with a British engine.

Gustav Hamel had a Morane-Saulnier (80 h.p. Gnôme) which had been specially prepared for the race. The passenger's seat had been removed and the wings had been heavily clipped down from the normal span of thirty feet six inches to a mere twenty feet. The machine looked dangerous, but it looked fast, and it was obvious that if Hamel could control it he would win.

The most interesting of the English entries was the new Avro tractor biplane (80 h.p. Gnôme) flown by Mr. F. P. Raynham. This was none other than the precursor of the world-famous 504 type. Its appearance brought Mr. A. V. Roe into the front rank of the world's aircraft constructors. This wonderful machine has developed, solely by means of detail refinements, into the Avro Tutor of to-day. In essentials the general lay-out is the same. If the identical biplane which Raynham flew in the Aerial Derby on September 20th, 1913, could land at Heston or Hanworth to-morrow its appearance would excite little comment; for it would not be conspicuously old-fashioned. Avros of the 504 type have flown millions of miles in the hands of "joy-ride" concerns and more people have had their first flights in them than in any other type. Their freedom from vices in the air, the ease with which they can be flown in and out of small fields which would be dangerous for ordinary light aeroplanes, and their ability to perform many kinds of aerobatics have made them immensely popular with pilots all over the world. With the possible exception of the de Havilland Moth, the Avro 504 in its various stages of development can claim to have proved the most successful aeroplane, judged by the number sold, that has ever been produced.

The other two English entries consisted of a standard three-seater Sopwith tractor biplane (80 h.p. Gnôme) and a Martin-Handasyde monoplane (120 h.p. Austro-Daimler) flown by Mr. R. H. Barnwell.

The competitors were started at one minute intervals in the following order: 1, Mons. E. Baumann (Caudron biplane, 60 h.p. Anzani); 2, Mons. P. Verrier (Henry Farman pusher biplane, 80 h.p. Gnôme); 3, Mr. W. L. Brock (Bleriot monoplane, 80 h.p. Gnôme); 4, Mr. B. C. Hucks (Bleriot monoplane, 80 h.p. Gnôme); 5, Mr. F. P. Raynham (Avro tractor biplane, 80 h.p. Gnôme); 6, Mr. H. G. Hawker (Sopwith tractor biplane, 80 h.p. Gnôme); 7, Mons. P. Marty (Morane-Saulnier monoplane, 50 h.p. Le Rhone);

8, Lieut. J. C. Porte, R.N. (Deperdussin monoplane, 110 h.p. Anzani); 9, Mr. R. Slack (Morane-Saulnier monoplane, 80 h.p. Le Rhone); 10, Mr. R. H. Barnwell (Martinsyde monoplane, 120 h.p. Austro-Daimler), and 11, Mr. Gustav Hamel (Morane-Saulnier monoplane, 80 h.p. Gnôme).

Baumann (Caudron) abandoned the race before the first turn, and Porte lost himself between Epsom and West Thurrock and landed, his machine being wrecked whilst he was attempting to take off again. The others fought out a tremendous race.

At Kempton Park, Brock was leading, with Raynham, who had already passed Hucks and Verrier, in second place.

At the Epsom turn Raynham (Avro) had overtaken Brock's Bleriot and led him round the mark with thirty seconds to spare Hawker (Sopwith), who had given Raynham a minute's start, passed this control just that amount behind him and level with Hucks, on whom he had gained two minutes. Hamel was still with the rearguard, but he was going fast.

On the long run of twenty-six and a quarter miles across the south of London to the third mark at West Thurrock, Raynham held his lead and gained thirty seconds from Hawker. But the two fastest men had started last, and Raynham went into the West Thurrock turn with Hamel (Morane-Saulnier) tearing through the air only thirty seconds behind him. Barnwell (Martinsyde) had also overtaken Slack, Marty, Hucks, Brock, and Verrier, and was only one minute behind Hawker, who lay third.

Between West Thurrock and Epping, Hamel was the victim of a disturbing incident, which nearly cost him the race. The drain tap at the bottom of his petrol tank unscrewed itself and fell on to the floor of the fuselage. Petrol poured out over the pilot's legs as he tried frantically to reach the tap. It was just out of reach, so Hamel leaned forward and stuck his finger in the hole. He found that he could stop the leak in this way, but he was forced to crouch in a very uncomfortable position in which it was difficult to fly the machine. Many pilots would have landed at once and abandoned; but not Hamel. He had lost a lot of time and gone off his course whilst trying to pick up the petrol tap, but now he settled down to regain the lead, keeping his finger firmly in the hole.

At Epping, Barnwell was one minute in front of Raynham and Hawker, who were flying level in second place, whilst Hamel came rushing along behind them.

Hamel swept past the Avro and the Sopwith, and overtook Barnwell whilst rounding the Hertford turn, and it was only a question of whether he could hold his cramped position over the last stretch of sixteen miles to Hendon, and whether he had still got sufficient petrol to carry him home. Fortunately all went well, and he dived across the line, a popular winner, having covered ninety-four and a half miles in 1 hr. 15 mins. 49 secs., at

"Flight" photo

16.—The Sopwith Tabloid Scout (80 h.p. Gnôme): the best aeroplane of the year.

Facing page 64

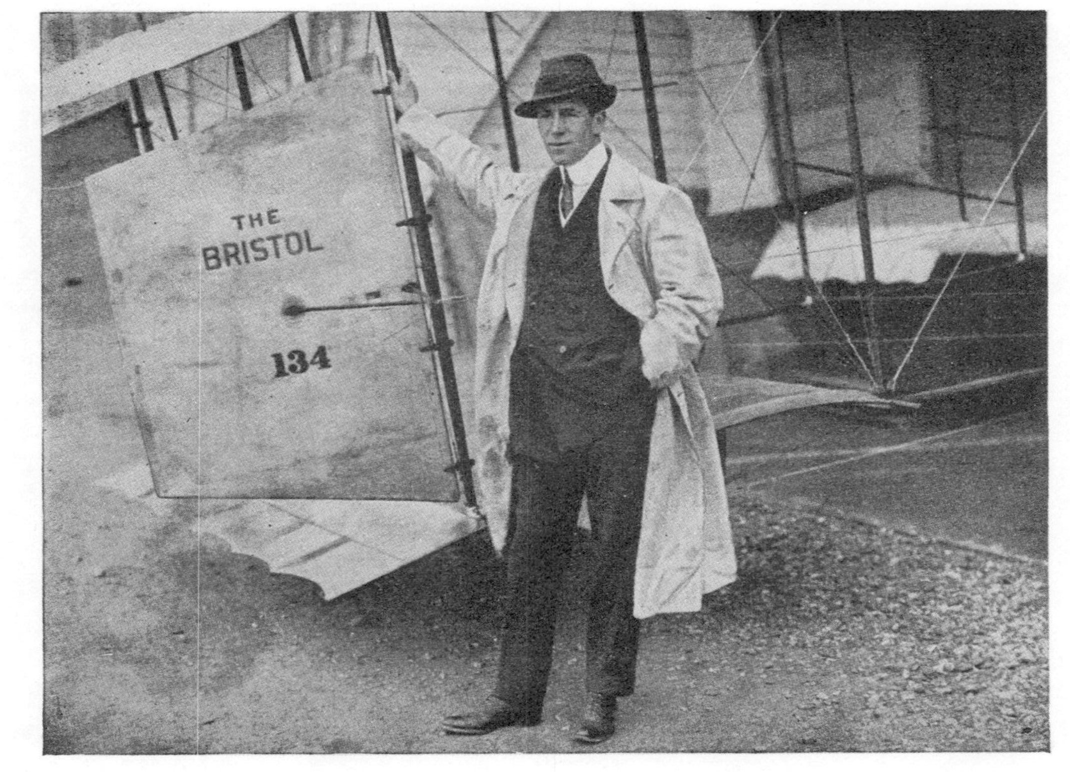

"Flight" photo

17.—England's greatest instructor: Mr. F. Warren Merriam of the Bristol School of Flying, Brooklands.

an average speed of 76 m.p.h. The three British aeroplanes captured the next three places as follows :—

Pilot	*Aircraft*	*Engine*	*hr. min. sec.*	*m.p.h*
1. G. Hamel ...	Morane-Saulnier monoplane	80 Gnôme	1 15 49	76
2. R. H. Barnwell	Martinsyde monoplane	120 Austro-Daimler	1 18 44	72.5
3. H. G. Hawker	Sopwith biplane	80 Gnôme	1 25 24	67
4. F. P. Raynham	Avro biplane	80 Gnôme	1 26 1	66.5

It had been a great race and the struggle between Hawker and Raynham on their tractor biplanes was especially interesting, as the difference between their times over a distance of nearly 100 miles amounted to a mere thirty-seven seconds. The performance of these two machines was a surprise to many, who never anticipated that biplanes could be made fast enough to beat the Bleriots and Moranes. Their success augured well for the future of the British industry. Gustav Hamel won a Gold Cup and a cheque for £200 presented by the *Daily Mail* newspaper.

35. A PILOT'S ACCOUNT OF A BAD CRASH

After the race was over a number of machines made exhibition flights, but the evening was marred by a serious accident to a Champel pusher biplane (110 h.p. Anzani) which was being demonstrated by Mr. Sydney Pickles. The pilot suffered a broken leg and other injuries, whilst his passenger, Mrs. de Beauvoir Stocks, who was then the sole active British woman pilot, since Mrs. Hewlett had given up flying, was picked up unconscious with concussion and serious injuries to her back. Mr. Pickles subsequently wrote down a detailed account of his sensations during the accident, which is of such interest that I quote it *verbatim* below.

" Mrs. Stocks and I climbed on board the machine, and started away from No. 1 pylon, and making in the direction of pylon No. 4. We lifted very quickly, and on reaching the other side of the aerodrome we were up quite a good height. I then flew round pylons Nos. 4, 5, and 6, keeping to the usual course followed in the speed races, and at a height of about 250 feet. Somewhere near No. 6 pylon I turned and spoke to Mrs. Stocks, saying how glorious the lights of Hendon looked in the distance. As it was beginning to get dark I decided to curtail the flight and land, so I continued along down the middle of the racing course until I was nearly opposite No. 1 pylon. Here I intended to throttle down the motor, and glide down, and also to turn the machine towards a point near No. 4 pylon. This meant a fairly sharp left-hand turn during the glide. Then I intended to cross the aerodrome to somewhere near No. 4 pylon, turn back again, and land.

"Well, I throttled the motor down, and then ruddered over to the left to make the turn. After completing the turn I pressed on the right side of the rudder bar to bring the rudder straight again, and to my unpleasant surprise the bar refused to move. By this time the machine had made a complete circle, and naturally taken a terrific bank owing to the small diameter of the circle. I now instantly resorted to my lateral control in order to reduce the bank, which felt as if it were vertical. This appeared to have a little effect, but the machine still kept spinning and side-slipping. Then, curiously enough, I seemed to realize fully the fate of Paul Beck, in America, and how one person remarked to me that had he switched his motor on he might have saved himself. I thought I was in a similar position to his, so I would try what he apparently did not. I then reached for the throttle lever and opened the throttle wide, at the same time bringing the elevator lever back towards me, as the machine had by now got its nose down. The object of this manœuvre was, of course, to try and get the nose up. After doing nearly a complete circle with the throttle open I could see no improvement in my position, and, realizing that it was increasing my speed towards the ground, I closed the throttle. By this time my machine was in a hopeless position, and I reached forward and turned the switch off, thinking, 'Well, we won't have a fire anyway.' I now fully realized that a smash was inevitable, and then the green megaphone-stand flashed past me, and I realized, much to my astonishment, that I was falling behind this stand, and how near the ground I was, and I pulled the elevator lever right back against my chest as a last effort to flatten out the machine, and also in order to hold my passenger in her seat, and prevent her being thrown out on her head. (I was surprised at falling behind the stand as, when I first lost control, I was 300 feet up, or more, over the flying ground, about half-way between No. 1 pylon and the enclosure. How I got there I cannot explain, except that possibly the rotation of the machine caused a drift, which was perhaps increased when I opened the throttle in my attempt to save the accident.) Then we struck! I distinctly heard the crash, and was momentarily dazed with the shock. When all seemed quiet I opened my eyes, and felt rather surprised at realizing that I was still alive. During the whole of the struggle I had had, my anxiety was with my lady passenger, Mrs. Stocks, and I felt sure that we should both 'go out.' The whistling of the wires gave me an idea of the speed at which we were about to strike. As Mrs. Stocks was herself an experienced flyer, the ordeal she must have gone through, sitting there helpless, while the machine was dashing to the ground, must have been terrifying, yet she did not make a sound.

"Then I could hear people's footsteps coming round the machine, and the petrol trickling away from the petrol tank, and I also heard the shouts of 'Put out matches, pipes, cigarettes, etc.'

quite distinctly, although I had my eyes closed. I only have a very dim recollection of being lifted out of the machine, but directly they laid me out on the stretcher I felt pain, real pain, in my back. The ambulance men quickly arrived on the scene, and I distinctly heard them pronounce 'Compound fracture right leg.' This I did not feel at all, but in addition to the pain in my back I felt a burning sensation in my body, which turned out afterwards to be caused by a wound three and a half inches deep. I thought I would make an effort to see, and found it very difficult. I said, 'How is she?' and somebody asked 'Who?' This exasperated me, as I felt irritable. I said, 'My passenger.' They replied, 'She's all right, we gave her something, and she was able to be carried away.' As I lay on my back I felt curious as to the damage done to the machine, so I turned my head to the left and opened my eyes in order to have a look at the machine. I also recollect hearing quite distinctly a person's voice sympathizing with me when I complained of pain. One of the sentences was, 'Never mind, you'll be all right. I'm your friend, Pickles.' I then said, 'The control wouldn't work,' and a voice answered 'Yes, I know.' I was feeling frightfully exhausted from shock, and thought that should anything happen to me this would be an explanation, however meagre. As I still lay on my back beside the machine I was looking at the irregular row of heads, when everything slowly darkened and went black. I knew I had my eyes open, so I complained about not being able to see. They got me some liquid, which they wanted to put in my mouth, and I asked what it was, because I am a strict teetotaller. (Of course, in a case of emergency such as this I would not have refused it, but I just wanted to know first.) Then the ambulance men lifted me and proceeded to carry me away on the stretcher. Each pace they took gave me terrific pains in my back, which caused me to complain and ask them to take it easily. After a short while we arrived outside the Grahame-White offices, and here they rested a minute. I looked at the many people around me for a familiar face, and soon discovered one. I have since found out that it was Mr. Harry Delacombe. As I was looking up at him he had his head turned away a little, so I proceeded to speak to him, saying, 'Will you do something for me?' and he naturally replied, 'Yes.' I then added, 'I want you to telegraph my mother. The address is Lancaster Court Hotel, Lancaster Gate. Tell her I'm fairly all right—you know.' I was next taken inside the aerodrome hospital to await the return of the motor which had taken Mrs. Stocks to the hospital. I was then taken to the hospital nearby, where they proceeded to cut the clothes off my legs, and get me ready for the surgeon, who was coming down from London to perform an immediate operation. I clearly remember my mother coming into the ward to see me before the surgeon arrived. They put me under an anaesthetic for the operation, and I awoke the next day fully realizing that I was to be a patient for a long time. As a matter of fact, as I write these lines I am still lying on my back since the accident seven weeks and three days ago, and I am certain the accident was entirely due to my heel becoming fixed between the rudder bar and the flooring of the *fuselage*, with the result that the machine kept turning, and which turning was in all probability aggravated by my opening the throttle.

"By doing the latter very considerable forward impetus was imparted to the machine, and it is possible, as I have already said, that had I left the throttle alone, the smash would have happened in the aerodrome instead of in the enclosure."

Both pilot and passenger recovered from their injuries, but Mrs. Stocks never flew again.

36. TWO WORLD'S RECORDS BROKEN BY THE GRAHAME-WHITE "CHAR-A-BANCS": HAWKER'S WORLD'S RECORD BROKEN

Mr. Claude Grahame-White had been impressed by the increasing popularity of passenger flights at Hendon and decided to produce a machine which could cope adequately with the demand. Mr. J. D. North accordingly designed a large pusher biplane for him which had a span of sixty-two feet. The top wing was larger than the bottom one, and the customary front elevator was dispensed with, control being provided by a "boxkite" tail carried to the rear on the usual framework of booms. Lateral balance was maintained by means of ailerons on both top and bottom wings. A large *nacelle* rested on the centre of the bottom wing and protruded well forward. The pilot sat in the extreme front, and thus obtained a very good view, whilst there were seats for four passengers in pairs behind him. The 120 h.p. water-cooled 6-cylinder Austro-Daimler engine was mounted at the back of the *nacelle* and drove a propeller of nine feet three inches diameter between the tail booms.

This machine proved an instantaneous success. After a series of test flights M. Louis Noel, chief pilot of the Grahame-White Company, decided to make an attack on the world's record for duration with a pilot and seven passengers, which then stood at 6 mins. 49 secs. Having stowed away his living freight, which, including himself, totalled just over eighty-one stone (1,134 lbs.), he took off from Hendon on September 22nd, and succeeded in staying in the air for 17 mins. 25⅗ secs. This feat proved once again the amazing efficiency of the Austro-Daimler motor, which was far in advance of any other aero engine in existence at that time.

Louis Noel was not content with one world's record, and he firmly believed that the biplane would lift an even greater load. On October 2nd he piled no less than nine passengers on to the machine and succeeded in taking off from Hendon and flying round the aerodrome for 19 mins. 47 secs., with a total live load of

"*Flight*" *photo*

18.—Miss Trehawke-Davies in the passenger's seat of one of her Bleriot monoplanes.

"Flight" photo

19.—The first British Aeroplane to reach Khartoum: The big Short

more than ninety-eight stone (1,372 lbs.) This fine performance set up another world's record in a new category.

As if to prove that his latest machine was no freak, Mr. Grahame-White personally flew it across-country from Hendon to Brooklands and back again with Mr. and Mrs. Gates, Messrs. Chapman and Carr, and the designer himself, Mr. J. D. North, as passengers. On the return journey the party covered nineteen miles in fifteen minutes, at an average speed of 76 m.p.h.

Messrs. J. D. North, Grahame-White, and Louis Noel had reason to congratulate themselves on having made a very great step forward towards establishing aviation as a practical means of transport.

The world's altitude record for pilot and three passengers, which Hawker had set up by climbing to 8,400 feet, was not destined to remain intact for long as the German pilot, Sablatnig, succeeded in taking three passengers to a height of 2,830 metres (9,282 feet) at Johannisthal, on September 28th in an Albatros biplane.

37. THE DISCOVERY OF AEROBATICS BY MONS. E. PÉGOUD

It is curious that no serious attempt was made for more than three years after the beginning of practical aviation in Europe to accomplish any free evolutions in the air other than such as were strictly necessary for the purpose of changing direction or of going up or down.

Pilots were very nervous of attaining any unusual attitude in the air, and it was generally considered that if an aeroplane was turned vertically on its side, or inverted, it would inevitably become uncontrollable and crash.

Until the summer of 1913 the majority of pilots performed very flat turns and brought their machines down cautiously at a shallow angle with their engines running. The more accomplished descended by means of glides, known as *vols plané*, and some of the experts introduced gliding turns (spiral *vols plané*) or even gentle dives, which were regarded with awe and alluded to as *vols piqué*. Gustav Hamel, B. C. Hucks, H. G. Hawker, Warren Merriam, F. P. Raynham, and Sydney Pickles were the best English exponents of these simple manœuvres.

The first exhibition in the nature of genuine stunt flying to be seen in England took place at Hendon at Easter 1913, when M. Manuel Chevillard brought over a Henry Farman pusher biplane, on which he had taught himself to do a mild form of stalled turn. This feat consisted of a dive followed by a climbing turn at an angle of some 60° from which the machine was allowed to sink sideways into a dive once more. Huge crowds were attracted to the weekly meetings at Hendon to witness this performance, which was known as the *chute de côté*. This pilot also performed tight turns with almost vertical banks.

It was with some astonishment, therefore, and no little incredulity, that the aviation world received the news of the experiments carried out at Juvisy by Mons. E. Pégoud on September 1st.

For a fortnight thereafter reports came in thick and fast concerning his amazing feats, whilst his popularity in Paris surpassed any example of hero-worship thitherto seen, even in France. Crowds surrounded the Bleriot aerodrome at Buc all day long in the hope that he would fly, whilst on one occasion his presence was discovered in the audience at a theatre and the performance was held up for fifteen minutes whilst the people cheered themselves hoarse.

At first the British pilots remained incredulous and the general tendency was to condemn Pégoud as a mountebank and to regard his flying as a trick in the nature of a circus turn. The authorities at Brooklands, however, managed to persuade him to come over and give a demonstration.

On September 25th, 26th, and 27th, Pégoud flew his Bleriot monoplane above the Weybridge track in a manner which dumbfounded the sceptics and silenced every accusation of chicanery.

To say that the British pilots were staggered would be inadequate to express the complete stupefaction which was felt by all who witnessed his beautiful exhibition of perfect control.

Even to-day there are few people who realize the magnitude of the feats which Pégoud performed. He is universally credited with the invention of the loop, which everyone now knows to be a perfectly simple evolution, but it is not understood that his repertoire also included the tail slide, the half-roll and the bunt.

In fact the bunt was the first feat which Pégoud performed during that epoch-making flight on September 1st. He dived the Bleriot, until he had passed the vertically head downward position, and attained an inverted glide, which he held for more than thirty seconds. He then pulled back on the stick and dived out, having traced a large vertical S in the sky.

In spite of repeated attempts he was unable to accomplish a half-roll on to his back from the normal flying position, although he was able to regain that position from the top of a loop by a half roll at any time. Within a month of his first experiment Pégoud was making flights up to 1 min. 30 secs. in length on his back, with his engine on, and executing turns whilst inverted.

All his flying was exquisitely smooth, in fact he even imparted grace to that most violent and horrible of all manœuvres, the tail slide, in which the machine is stalled with the nose pointing vertically upwards and allowed to slide back until the elevator brings it up with a jerk and the machine is thrown forward into a dive.

These stunts, especially the tail slide and the bunt, put an enormous strain upon the machine, and no praise can be too high for the man who willingly and knowingly risked death in carrying out these tests. The flights were made under the personal supervision of M. Louis Bleriot, the designer and constructor of the machine, which was perfectly standard except for the fitting of a *cabane* about twelve inches higher than that normally used and the substitution of a tail unit taken from the two-seater model.

It was no circus trick, but a scientific experiment of the utmost importance, the details of which were worked out beforehand with great care by all concerned.

Pégoud knew the chance he was taking. Too many pilots had been killed by the breaking of machines in the air for the thought of that probability to escape his notice. But Pégoud had risked his life before in the cause of science.

On August 20th he had conducted an even more perilous experiment at Buc. Mons. Bonnet had invented a parachute which he desired to test under actual service conditions. It was a very primitive device, and it was designed to open whilst the pilot was still seated in the machine, so that the danger of the envelope fouling the tail of the aeroplane was all too patent ; but Pégoud readily agreed to try it.

He took off in an old Bleriot monoplane with a 5-cylinder Anzani engine, which was in itself thoroughly decrepit and unairworthy, climbed to a height of 700 feet, released the box containing the parachute, stopped the motor, pushed the stick forward ; and awaited events. Fortunately the parachute opened, swung up clear of the machine, plucked Pégoud out of his seat and, in due course, deposited him gently in the branches of a tree. Meanwhile the ancient monoplane, relieved of its load, stalled, turned on to its back, righted itself and glided to earth, where it landed quite gently in a convenient field.

Aviation owes a deep debt of gratitude to Pégoud, whose cool courage and exceptional skill gave men an entirely new conception of the art of flying, and whose example instilled added confidence into pilots all over the world. Thitherto aviators had travelled through the air humbly, dreading what new terrors the unknown might bring. Thenceforth they flew boldly, their fears dispelled, confident that what Pégoud had done, they also might do.

Pégoud had altered the whole attitude of men's minds towards the air.

38. THE WIGHT SEAPLANE : THE DEATH OF CAPT. DICKSON

Mr. Gordon England was busy throughout September testing the Wight seaplane, built at Cowes by Messrs. J. Samuel White & Co., Ltd. The machine had been designed by Mr. Howard-Wright, and was a large pusher biplane fitted with a Gnôme double-row rotary motor of 160 h.p.

The tests were eminently satisfactory, as it was found that the top speed was 63 m.p.h., in spite of the fact that the propeller was too heavy for the engine, whilst the stalling speed was as low as 27 m.p.h. The machine left the water in sixty yards, and climbed to 3,000 feet in ten minutes and, moreover, the long narrow floats proved capable of standing up to quite choppy seas. This was an excellent performance for a new design.

On September 28th Capt. Bertram Dickson, one of the greatest of the British pioneer pilots, died at Lochrosque Castle, Ross-shire, N.B. It will be recalled that he had, through no fault of his own, been the victim of the first aerial collision, which occurred at Milan on October 2nd, 1910. For almost exactly three years Capt. Dickson had slowly struggled towards a complete recovery from the terrible injuries which he received. He had never lost hope that one day he might be able to take his seat at the controls again ; but it was not to be.

39. THE GORDON-BENNETT CONTEST : ANOTHER MATCH RACE

No English entry was received for the Gordon-Bennett contest which was flown off at Rheims on September 29th, over twenty laps of a ten-kilometre circuit. There were four starters, all monoplanes, consisting of three Deperdussins and a Ponnier, the latter being a development of the Hanriot racer. One of the Deperdussins had a Le Rhone rotary engine of 160 h.p., but each of the other three was fitted with the 160 h.p. Gnôme.

Prevost's Deperdussin had clipped wings, and was beautifully streamlined, so that it was considerably faster than its team mates. In fact, its speed astonished the spectators, for Prevost covered his twenty laps in fifty-nine minutes $45\frac{3}{5}$ secs. at an average speed of $124\frac{1}{2}$ m.p.h., having smashed eight world's speed records *en route*. Emile Vedrines did well to secure second place in the Ponnier, 1 min. 5^{4} secs. behind the winner.

It was only three years since Grahame-White had won the cup in America by taking 1 min. 15 secs. *longer* than Prevost's time to cover only *half* the distance !

Mr. Harold Blackburn had been doing a lot of flying in Yorkshire on Dr. Christie's new Blackburn monoplane, which had fulfilled the promise of its early trials. A challenge was thrown out for a cross-country race and the *Yorkshire Evening News* offered a cup to the winner.

The Avro firm picked up the gauntlet and Mr. F. P. Raynham flew the new tractor biplane, which had finished fourth in the Aerial Derby, from Brooklands to Leeds, with one stop at Rugby, to take part in the contest.

A circuit of just under 100 miles had been chosen, with Leeds as the starting and finishing point. The controls were at York, Doncaster, Sheffield, and Barnsley.

A crowd of 60,000 people saw the two machines take off side by side at 2.14 p.m. on October 2nd. Dr. Christie flew as passenger in his own machine, and Mr. H. V. Roe accompanied Raynham.

Visibility was very bad and this gave Mr. Blackburn a great

advantage, as he had flown over almost every inch of Yorkshire, whilst Mr. Raynham was in strange country.

The Avro proved to be the faster machine, and led by $48\frac{4}{5}$ secs. at York, but Blackburn flew straighter on the leg to Doncaster, where he arrived three seconds ahead. On the stretch between Doncaster and Sheffield the racers encountered some really thick weather and Raynham became thoroughly lost, and landed twice to ask the way, thereby losing a further 3 mins. 57 secs. At Barnsley the Avro flew right past the control and eventually landed at Dewsbury, where Raynham abandoned the race and flew back to Leeds direct.

Blackburn stuck to his task and completed the course in a net flying time of 1 hr. 58 mins. 34 secs., at an average speed of approximately 50 m.p.h.

40. A FATAL SMASH AT THE C.F.S.: TWO FAMOUS PUPILS

Many pilots still had strong objections to strapping themselves into their seats, although quick-release belts were available. Presumably it was the fear of fire which gave rise to this reluctance to take such a commonsense precaution. It is extraordinary that the authorities had not yet made the wearing of belts compulsory for pilots of the R.F.C. Yet another officer lost his life on October 3rd through neglecting to secure himself in his seat.

Maj. G. C. Merrick, who had taken his aviator's certificate (No. 484) on May 17th, 1913, took off in perfect weather from the C.F.S. aerodrome at Upavon in a Short biplane (70 h.p. Gnôme) for a practice flight.

He was seen to be gliding steeply at a height of 300 feet, apparently with the object of coming in to land. The angle of descent became steeper until the machine was diving. It is probable that the pilot then slipped forward out of his seat on to the control column, thus pushing it forward, for the aircraft plunged violently downward and performed a bunt on to its back. Maj. Merrick fell out as it passed over the vertical, and was instantly killed.

On October 2nd Mr. F. B. Halford, one of the most brilliant internal combustion engineers in the world, and designer of the Cirrus, Hermes, and Gipsy engines for light aeroplanes, qualified for his R.Ae.C. aviator's certificate (No. 639) at the Bristol school at Brooklands. He was so good that within two months he was acting as assistant instructor at the school under Mr. Warren Merriam, in the place of Mr. Skene, who had left.

A week later Mr. Christopher Draper, who was to have a most spectacular career during the War 1914–18 in the Royal Naval Air Service, and who was to become one of the greatest pilots of Sopwith Camels in the World, also passed his tests as a pupil of the Grahame-White school at Hendon.

41. A BRITISH PILOT KILLED IN S. AFRICA: THE CURTISS FLYING BOAT

Mr. Compton Paterson had established a school of flying at Kimberley in South Africa, whither Mr. E. W. Cheeseman had gone to join him as instructor. Mr. Cheeseman was a pupil of the Grahame-White school at Hendon, and during the summer he had been acting as assistant instructor to M. Louis Noel.

The school was equipped with two Paterson pusher biplanes, and they operated from an aerodrome at an altitude of 4,000 feet, which naturally caused certain difficulties for slow, underpowered machines.

On October 13th Mr. Cheeseman was instructing Lieut. Dunlop on one of these biplanes, when, according to the reports received here, the machine " was caught in an airpocket " and fell 100 feet to the ground. It is probable that the accident was actually due to a stall, which would, of course, take place at a higher air speed than usual, owing to the rarefied atmosphere in which the aerodrome was situated.

Lieut. Dunlop escaped with a shaking but Mr. Cheeseman sustained such severe injuries that he died in hospital two days later.

Mr. Magnus Volk, the proprietor of the little electric railway which runs, or used to run, along the shore beneath the Madeira Drive at Brighton, had put up a hangar for seaplanes and had been organizing exhibition flights there during the summer. When the great American pioneer designer, Mr. Glenn Curtiss, brought the latest model of his flying boat to England he housed it in Mr. Volk's hangar, and it was flown from Brighton beach by Mr. J. D. Cooper, an Englishman who had learned to fly at the Curtiss flying school in the U.S.A.

Capt. E. C. Bass acquired the British rights for the Curtiss products, and with him was associated Lieut. J. C. Porte, R.N., who had severed his connection with the Deperdussin Company when their school at Hendon had been forced to close down in August.

42. ANOTHER ARMAMENT FIRM STEPS IN: THE FOUNDING OF SUPERMARINES

At the end of October two very important events took place on the manufacturing side. The extraordinary success of the Austro-Daimler aero engine, which was designed by Herr Porsche, resulted in negotiations being opened with its manufacturers by the great armament firm of Beardmore and Co. Ltd. They secured the exclusive rights to build Austro-Daimler engines for aviation purposes in this country and were instantly rewarded by an order from the Government for a batch of two dozen.

Mr. Pemberton Billing, fresh from his amazing feat at Brooklands, decided, with his customary impetuosity and efficiency, to enter the ranks of the aircraft constructors and planned to produce several flying boats immediately.

He secured premises at Southampton and adopted the word "Supermarine" as his telegraphic address.

From this small beginning sprang the largest, most famous and most successful seaplane factory in the world :—that of the Supermarine Aviation Co., Ltd., winners of the Schneider Trophy, and several times holders of the world's record for absolute speed.

43. NIGHT RACING AT HENDON : LONDON–BRIGHTON HANDICAP

Successful flying meetings had been held at Hendon every Saturday and Sunday throughout the year, in spite of everything that the weather could do. Nearly every Saturday the programme included a race round the pylons erected on the aerodrome and several of the pilots had become exceedingly expert at cornering round these marks. Once or twice exhibitions of night flying had been given, concluding with a firework display.

The management decided to give their patrons a real thrill, and on November 6th they staged the first aeroplane race to be flown at night.

There were three starters and the course was over four laps of the aerodrome. The competitors were very evenly matched and M. Louis Noel (scratch) gave Mr. Marcus D. Manton 26 seconds, and Mr. R. H. Carr 56 seconds.

The contest produced a magnificent struggle, the three biplanes racing close together in the darkness and finishing "in a heap" with $1\frac{1}{5}$th sec. between them. Louis Noel came through from scratch on his M. Farman (70 h.p. Renault) to beat Carr's G.W. pusher biplane (50 Gnôme) by one second, with Manton's G.W (50 Gnôme) only one-fifth of a second behind.

Considering the small size of the circuit and the sharpness of the turns it is remarkable that no accident occurred, which was in itself a cogent testimonial to the skill of the three pilots.

Two days later, on November 8th, an important race was held from Hendon to Brighton and back, on a handicap basis, for a trophy presented by the Sussex Motor Yacht Club and a cash prize of £100. Mr. Barclay Walker had offered a second trophy and £50 in cash to the pilot who made the fastest time.

The course was from Hendon to Harrow Church and thence to the Palace Pier, Brighton, where the competitors were timed to finish the outward journey. The machines were to fly on to Shoreham to refuel and return over the same route, their times of commencing the homeward journey being taken as they re-entered the course at the Palace Pier.

Nine machines started, including Mr. G. M. Dyott's fascinating little monoplane, on which he had been doing many hours flying in the United States.

There was a very strong westerly wind blowing when the machines took off in the following order:—

Pilot	Machine and Engine	Handicap h.	m.	s.
1. P. Verrier (French)...	M. Farman pusher biplane (70 Renault)	1	4	14
2. G. Lee Temple ...	Bleriot monoplane (50 Gnôme)		53	44
3. G. M. Dyott... ...	Dyott monoplane (50 Gnôme)		32	47
4. W. L. Brock (U.S.A.)	Bleriot monoplane (80 Gnôme)		22	26
5. F. Marty (French)	Morane-Saulnier monoplane (50 Le Rhone)		20	30
6. R. Slack	Morane-Saulnier monoplane (80 Le Rhone)		16	23
7. F. P. Raynham ...	Avro tractor biplane (80 Gnôme)		15	10
8. R. H. Barnwell ...	Martinsyde monoplane (120 Austro-Daimler)		5	26
9. G. Hamel	Morane-Saulnier monoplane (80 Gnôme)	Scratch		

Temple soon retired, as his compass came adrift and fell into his lap, whilst Marty came down at Ealing with engine trouble, and Raynham brought off a brilliant forced landing into a very small field near Horley when the wire controlling the air valve of his carburettor broke. Dyott failed to allow enough for drift and found himself over Eastbourne. He landed on Beachy Head where a gust of wind overturned his machine on the ground, fortunately without injuring the pilot.

The remaining five reached Brighton and started on the return journey. The start of the race had been delayed, and Barnwell had been warned by his firm not to risk arriving at Hendon in the dark, so, as the light was failing when he left Shoreham, he abandoned the race and flew straight home to Brooklands.

Verrier brought the Maurice Farman in first, and was followed four minutes fifty-five seconds later by Hamel, with Brock just behind.

As expected Hamel clocked the fastest time of the day by a clear margin of twenty-three minutes, the actual net times for the round trip being as follows:—

	h.	m.	s.
1. G. Hamel (Morane-Saulnier)	1	40	14
2. W. L. Brock (Bleriot)	2	3	20
3. R. Slack (Bleriot)	2	5	51
4. P. Verrier (M. Farman)	2	39	43

44. THE MICHELIN CUPS

The rules governing the award of the British Empire Michelin Cup No. 1 had been considerably modified for the 1913 competition. The old idea of flying round and round a small circuit marked out on an aerodrome had been abandoned, and this year each competitor had to fly backwards and forwards between Brooklands and Hendon, making a compulsory stop of five minutes at the conclusion of each third journey. The minimum distance of 300 miles was to be covered between 7 a.m. and one hour after sunset, and the

"Flight" photo

20.—Mr. F. P. Raynham flying the record-breaking Avro (80 h.p. Gnôme) at Hendon.

"*Flight*" *photo*

21.—" Lizzie," a Grahame-White aerobatic Biplane built round the fuselage of a Morane Saulnier Monoplane.

engine had to be stopped during each halt. It was not permitted to refuel or repair a competing machine once it had started, and any intermediate landing between the controls entailed disqualification.

The competition was confined to all-British aircraft, and the competitors were faced with the customary difficulty of finding a British aero engine which was sufficiently reliable to accomplish the minimum distance without breaking down.

As usual, the intending competitors waited until the last minute before making their arrangements, with the result that no one had qualified when the closing date, October 31st, arrived; but the Michelin Company generously agreed to extend the period for fourteen days.

The first attempt was made on October 31st by Mr. H. G. Hawker in one of the Sopwith three-seater tractor biplanes, which had been fitted with a Green engine of 100 h.p. in order to bring it into the all-British category. He started from Brooklands and made ten return trips, but was taken ill during his eleventh passage and landed at Hendon, where he abandoned the struggle after covering about 220 miles.

Hawker's greatest handicap was his ill-health, against which he struggled manfully for many years. It seemed extraordinary that such a sick man could fly so brilliantly and those who accused him of shirking during the War 1914–18, when he was employed in testing the output of the Sopwith factory at Brooklands, little realized how ill he was.

The record breaking G.W. "Charabancs" had also been prepared for an attempt on the Cup. A larger petrol tank was fitted and one of the 100 h.p. Green engines was substituted for the Austro-Daimler. This entry was entrusted to Mr. R. H. Carr, who left Hendon at 8 a.m. on November 6th.

Throughout the morning and the early afternoon the great biplane flew backwards and forwards until it had completed fifteen journeys. During the day the visibility had been deteriorating, and after leaving Brooklands at 4.47 p.m., for the last part of his sixteenth lap, Carr ran into very thick fog and was forced to land in a field. He had covered a distance of 315 miles, but the last stage had to be discounted for the purpose of the competition as he had failed to complete it.

Hawker made a second attempt on the closing date, November 14th, but the weather conditions were terrible, and he was soon forced to give up.

The stewards of the R.Ae.C. decided that Carr had just succeeded in covering the minimum distance of 300 miles required by the rules, and he was duly awarded the cup and its accompanying prize of £500.

Having disposed of the Michelin Cup No. 1, both these enterprising pilots turned their attention to the British Empire Michelin Cup No. 2, which carried with it a prize of £800. The closing date was November 30th, so that they had a fortnight in which to make their attacks.

This was a more difficult competition altogether, as the rules called for a cross-country circuit of 297 miles, to be flown without alighting. The entries were confined to British pilots flying all-British aircraft, and the prize was to go to the pilot making the fastest time round the course.

The difficulty was to get round at all with a British engine, even at a slow speed.

The chosen circuit had turning points at Hendon, Salisbury, Shoreham, Eastchurch, and Brooklands, and competitors could start and finish at any one of those points, and fly in either direction.

Both pilots set out on November 18th in spite of a gale of wind.

Mr. R. H. Carr (G.W. "Charabancs" 100 h.p. Green) started in an anti-clockwise direction from Hendon at 8.20 a.m., struggled past the Salisbury turn, where he encountered the full force of the gale, and fought his way as far as Shoreham. He reached the half-way point at 1.30 p.m., after five hours ten minutes of severe buffeting and bumping, and was faced with the fact that he could not hope to complete the course on his rapidly diminishing supply of petrol. He therefore landed after covering 140 miles at an average speed of 27 m.p.h. It had been a game struggle against almost impossible conditions.

Meanwhile Mr. H. G. Hawker had left Brooklands at 9.45 a.m. in an attempt to get round in the reverse direction. With his faster and more stable machine he stood a better chance of beating the weather and, although he failed, he accomplished one of the greatest feats of his career.

After a swift passage down-wind to Eastchurch, he battled his way to Shoreham, where he turned and flew with the wind abeam to Salisbury, whence he was wafted rapidly to Hendon. In order to win the prize he had only to succeed in forcing his way against the gale over the short stretch back to Brooklands, but his machine let him down, and he was compelled to land at Hendon and abandon the contest owing to a broken pressure pipe.

In spite of the appalling conditions he had covered 265 miles in five hours at an average speed of 53 m.p.h., and it was the worst possible luck that he should lose a handsome reward by such a small margin through no fault of his own.

On November 27th Mr. Hawker made a second attempt, but flew into a fog bank between Croydon and Eastchurch and was compelled to turn back. No further attempts were made in this competition, so the Cup was withdrawn for the year.

45. THE FIRST BRITISH AEROBATIC PILOTS

Pégoud's demonstration of *haute école* airmanship had fired the enthusiasm of pilots all over the world, and there was a rush to imitate his feats as soon as the initial astonishment had subsided.

Mr. B. C. Hucks was the first Englishman to look into the matter seriously, and he adopted the sensible course of going over to France and obtaining first-hand information on the subject from M. Louis Bleriot himself.

Under the latter's direction his monoplane was modified with a view to affording extra strength and increasing the power of the controls. Meanwhile, Mr. Hucks went into training by having himself strapped in a chair, and suspended upside down for periods of from five to fifteen minutes at a time.

The modifications were completed on November 15th and, in spite of a high wind and rain, Mr. Hucks took off from Buc, climbed to a safe height and commenced his experiments.

Like Pégoud he first essayed the bunt, or vertical S, which he accomplished successfully, the machine gliding inverted for nine seconds during the manœuvre. He then flew on his back for thirty seconds and did two loops.

On the following day he flew inverted twice for periods of thirty-five and forty seconds, and made five loops. On the next day he performed ten successive loops and mastered the half roll off his back. He then returned to England, and was met by a party of enthusiastic friends, who chaired him head downwards at Charing Cross Station.

The first attempt by an English pilot to perform the bunt in England was made at Hendon on November 24th by Mr. G. Lee Temple, who was the owner of a Bleriot monoplane which he had flown across from France in the early autumn. He had carried out the modifications necessary for inverted flying in his own shed.

The attempt was not particularly successful and was very nearly disastrous. He went into a steep dive from a turn and the tail continued to swing over after the machine had passed beyond the vertical. This promoted an inverted sideslip from which the pilot did not know how to recover. Luckily the nose swung downwards of its own accord and the machine resumed a normal vertical dive, from which Temple was able to pull out with a few feet to spare. It was a very narrow escape, and sufficed to discourage Mr. Temple from making any further experiments in inverted flying.

On November 27th, Mr. B. C. Hucks gave a demonstration of the new art at Hendon, when he made six perfect loops, but he did not attempt any inverted flying, bunts, or half-rolls.

In the meantime Mr. Gustav Hamel had been strengthening his Morane-Saulnier monoplane, and on November 29th he climbed to 5,000 feet above Hendon and tried to loop it. On his first attempt he stalled half-way up, and had the horrible experience of sliding down tail first for a full thousand feet before he could recover control. He tried again immediately and this time he got on to his back, but stalled on the top and the machine fell out sideways.

Thereafter he contented himself with tight turns and dives, and it was not until Boxing Day that he gained the distinction of being the second British pilot to loop the loop.

For nearly six weeks Mr. B. C. Hucks was the sole exponent of aerobatic flying in England, and he continued to give magnificent exhibitions of looping, bunting, and half-rolls. He invented the delayed loop in which he flew inverted for some seconds after reaching the top, and then pulled back on the stick and dived out. His loops became lower and lower until he was flattening out a mere 300 feet above the ground. Within a fortnight he was flying steadily on his back with engine on. He was not even deterred by the discovery that the tubular tail struts had buckled during one of his aerobatic flights to such an extent that the whole tail unit was twisted in relation to the fuselage, an indication of the great risk involved in performing stunts on a machine with an inadequate factor of safety.

Commenting upon the spread of aerobatics abroad, a contributor to *Flight* wrote as follows :—" Mr. Beachey, the American aviator, I see, has added the letter z to his repertoire of fancy flying . . . so I suppose it will not be very long now before some of our most skilled pilots will sail on high and go through the whole alphabet, forwards and backwards. I will even go so far as to imagine the time as not far off, when, on seeing an airman climb skywards, we shall watch to see whether he is going to tell us in aerial evolutions to 'Give him Bovril.' "

Less than ten years later this extravagant prophecy was literally fulfilled and Mr. J. C. Savage, who was acting as manager to Mr. B. C. Hucks in 1913, rode the skies in an S.E.5A, and wrote the words *Daily Mail* in letters of smoke two miles high.

46. CAPT. C. A. H. LONGCROFT WINS THE BRITANNIA TROPHY : THE CEDRIC LEE "FLYING SAUCER"

Capt. C. A. H. Longcroft, the star pilot of No. 2 Squadron, R.F.C., and holder of the British record for distance flown in a straight line with one passenger, surpassed his previous performance on November 22nd when he carried out a truly amazing journey.

A B.E.2 tractor biplane (70 h.p. Renault), built by the Bristol Company under licence from the Royal Aircraft Factory, had been fitted with a large petrol tank of fifty-four gallons capacity and Capt. Longcroft took off from Montrose with his commanding officer, Col. F. H. Sykes, in the passenger's seat, at 8.55 a.m. All day they flew southwards and eventually reached Farnborough, whence they continued without stopping to Portsmouth, where they turned round and headed back to Farnborough again, landing there at 4.10 p.m. They had spent seven and a quarter hours in the air and covered approximately 600 miles non-stop at an average speed of over 80 m.p.h.

Les vainqueurs de la Coupe d'Avion Maritime 'Jacques Schneider' 1er Howard Pixton _ 2e Burri (20 Avril 191

Photo: Mons. E. Marchessaux

22.—THE SCHNEIDER TROPHY: PIXTON (SOPWITH—100 H.P. GNÔME) ABOUT TO OVERTAKE BURRI (FRANCO-BRITISH FLYING BOAT).

Facing page 80

"Flight" photo

23.—The Schneider Trophy: Mr. Howard Pixton talking to

This great flight was the longest non-stop cross-country journey ever made with a passenger, but it does not seem that it was ever put forward officially to rank as a world's record, no doubt because the actual distance in a straight line between Montrose and Farnborough is only about 445 miles, which was forty-two miles short of the distance covered by Deroye in Italy.

Mr. H. Barber had presented the Britannia Trophy for the most meritorious performance accomplished by a British pilot during the year 1913, and when the various feats came to be reviewed by the Committee of the R.Ae.C., it was unanimously decided to award this, the highest prize in British aviation, to Capt. C. A. H. Longcroft in recognition of this wonderful flight.

Mr. E. C. Gordon England, ever ready to take on the wildest propositions, had agreed to carry out the flying trials of an extraordinary aeroplane which had been designed and built by Mr. Cedric Lee at Shoreham. This strange machine consisted of an annular wing across the diameter of which was set a normal fuselage, with a 50 h.p. Gnôme engine driving a tractor airscrew at one end and a biplane tail with twin rudders at the other. The pilot sat in the centre of this flying disc entirely surrounded by the annular wing.

The first flight was attempted on November 23rd and, much to everyone's surprise, Mr. England succeeded in getting it well off the ground and found that it travelled very fast indeed. He was in difficulties almost at once, for the machine was tail heavy and, as soon as he throttled back his engine in order to bring it down, the tail dropped and the machine stalled and fell upside down 150 feet on to the telegraph lines bordering the railway. Mr. Gordon England had yet another miraculous escape, as he suffered no injury other than shock.

47. AVRO PERFORMANCE FIGURES: THE SOPWITH "TABLOID"

On November 24th, the new Avro tractor biplane (80 h.p. Gnôme), the first model of the world-famous 504 type which had finished fourth in the Aerial Derby, was flown from Brooklands to Farnborough by Mr. F. P. Raynham and passed through the Government's tests. The figures are of great interest.

With one passenger and fuel for three hours the machine climbed to 1,000 feet in 1 min. 45 secs., and clocked a high speed of 80·9 m.p.h. over the measured distance. The stalling speed was 43 m.p.h., which gave a speed range of 37 m.p.h. It will thus be seen that the performance was much the same as that of the original de Havilland Moth (Cirrus I), which was produced twelve years later.

The Avro biplane had made a profound impression, but Mr. A. V. Roe was not allowed to occupy the limelight for very long, as his new machine was completely eclipsed by the latest product of Messrs. Sopwith and Sigrist, destined to achieve world-wide fame as the Sopwith Tabloid.

The Sopwith Tabloid was a revolutionary design. It set up a new standard of aeroplane construction altogether. It upset all the established theories of the time. It did a great number of things that nearly everybody thought were impossible of achievement for a biplane, and, generally speaking, it came as a distinct shock to everyone in aviation, not only in this country, but all over the world.

It is necessary to describe this wonderful aeroplane in considerable detail. It was a very small tractor biplane having wings of equal chord and span. The overall width was twenty-five feet six inches and the overall length was twenty feet. It was the first single bay biplane in the world, that is to say, it was the first biplane to be fitted with only one pair of interplane struts on either side. The chord of each wing was three feet throughout and no ailerons were fitted, lateral control being by warp. The top wing was staggered about one foot in advance of the bottom wing and the gap was four feet three inches. The fuselage was a simple square section job tapering from a point just abaft the trailing edge of the bottom wing to a vertical knife edge at the rudder, and fitted with a turtle back along the top. The 80 h.p. Gnôme engine was almost completely cowled in, but a horizontal gap about six inches wide was left in the middle of the cowling for cooling purposes. The undercarriage had a track of four feet nine inches and two large wheels, with a pair of light skids projecting forward to protect the airscrew. A very small cockpit, situated under the top wing and immediately above the centre of the bottom wing, contained seats for the pilot, on the left, and the passenger side by side. The machine weighed 670 lbs. empty and 1,060 lbs with pilot and fuel for three and a half hours.

The aircraft had been constructed in considerable secrecy and, as soon as it had been assembled and flown through some preliminary tests at Brooklands, Mr. H. G. Hawker took it over to Farnborough on November 29th and put it through the official trials there.

The results were astounding. With a load of pilot, passenger, and fuel for two and a half hours, the Tabloid climbed to 1,200 feet in one minute and attained a maximum speed of 92 m.p.h. Most remarkable of all was the fact that the stalling speed was only 36·9 m.p.h., which gave the extraordinary speed range of 55·1 m.p.h., a figure which had never previously been approached by a biplane.

As soon as the tests were over, Hawker flew the machine to Hendon, where the usual Saturday meeting was in progress and where over 50,000 people were gathered to see Hucks perform aerobatics. He roared over the enclosure low down and proceeded to put in two laps of the racing course at a speed which amazed the Hendon pilots.

The impression created was immense. Here was a biplane

which could fly rings round any monoplane in England. Thitherto the biplane had been despised as a slow, cumbrous and inefficient type, and it was universally accepted that the monoplane was the only design to adopt where speed and manœuvrability were required. The B.E.2, the Sopwith three-seater, and the Avro had served to modify this opinion to a certain extent, but the Tabloid represented such a giant stride forward in biplane development that it necessitated an entirely new conception of the respective possibilities of the two types. It took some time for people to adjust their ideas to the new state of things.

As soon as the lesson had been grasped the British manufacturers turned with one accord to follow Sopwith's lead and the monoplane type was almost completely neglected, until the Bristol Company revived it just before the end of the War 1914–18.

Mr. H. G. Hawker took the first Tabloid home with him to Australia, and Mr. Howard Pixton, who had left the Bristol Company in the early autumn, was engaged to take over Mr. Hawker's duties as test pilot for the Sopwith Company at Brooklands. Herr Voigt was appointed to take Mr. Pixton's place at the Bristol school on Salisbury Plain.

48. A NAVAL PILOT KILLED: A HANDLEY-PAGE BIPLANE

On December 2nd, Capt. G. V. Wildman-Lushington, R.M.A., met with a fatal accident at Eastchurch. He was returning from a flight to Sheerness with Capt. Fawcett, R.M., as passenger on his Short biplane, when apparently he overbanked on coming in to land, and the machine sideslipped into the ground. The pilot was crushed beneath the petrol tank and received fatal injuries, but the passenger was thrown clear and escaped with a broken collar-bone.

On the previous day, Capt. Lushington had been giving dual instruction for three-quarters of an hour to Mr. Winston Churchill, First Lord of the Admiralty, on the same machine. He was one of the four officers originally selected by the Admiralty to receive flying training at Eastchurch on the two Short biplanes, which had been placed at the disposal of the Naval authorities by Mr. Frank McClean.

Mr. Handley-Page had produced a tractor biplane designed for exhibition purposes which was in reality a two-decker version of his well-known monoplane. The characteristic curved and swept-back wings were retained and large ailerons were provided at the extremities of the top wing for lateral control. The span was forty feet, and the overall length twenty-seven feet. No less than three pairs of interplane struts were fitted on each side, and the whole machine had a clumsy and awkward appearance. The fuselage was set midway between the upper and lower wings, and a 10-cylinder Anzani radial engine of 100 h.p. drove the airscrew direct.

Mr. E. R. Whitehouse, who was now acting as test pilot for Mr. Handley-Page, put the machine through the official tests at Farnborough on December 11th, when it climbed to 3,000 feet at a rate of just under 300 feet per minute, carrying two passengers besides the pilot, and a full load of petrol and oil. The maximum speed with this load was 70 m.p.h. and the stalling speed 35 m.p.h., giving a speed range of 35 m.p.h.

49. A NEW BRITISH ALTITUDE RECORD: THE PARIS SALON

On December 13th, Capt. J. M. Salmond, of the R.F.C., took off alone from Upavon in a B.E.2 tractor biplane (70 h.p. Renault) with the object of attacking the British altitude record of 12,900 feet, established by Mr. H. G. Hawker. In spite of the most intense cold he stuck to his task and eventually reached a height of 13,140 feet. This record could not count in the all-British category, as the engine used was of French design and manufacture. Mr. Hawker's climb to 12,900 feet on the Sopwith three-seater still stood as a British record for pilot and one passenger.

As usual the Bristol Company was the sole English representative at the Paris Salon, which opened just before Christmas, but this year the monoplane was not exhibited. In its place the company showed the latest model of M. Coanda's tractor biplane (80 h.p. Gnôme), in which were incorporated several interesting modifications which had been suggested by actual experience in warfare.

It will be recalled that the Roumanian Air Force was equipped almost entirely with Bristol aircraft, and that the pilots of that Service had been trained in the Bristol school at Salisbury Plain. Naturally the Company had received much useful information as to how their machines had behaved under active service conditions during the Balkan wars, and the results were embodied in the biplane shown in Paris.

The wheel brakes which had been fitted on the model displayed at Olympia had proved unsatisfactory and had been removed. Probably the item which attracted most attention was the bomb-rack, which was situated under the fuselage and which held twelve bombs. The observer could release these, either singly or simultaneously, by pulling a lever.

Another innovation was an instrument for calculating ground speed, which consisted of a rectangular box projecting down through the bottom of the fuselage. The observer looked through a sight in the top of the box and watched an object on the ground pass between two wires running across the lower aperture. The time taken to complete the transit was checked on a stopwatch, compared with the altimeter and the ground speed read off from a

"*Flight*" *photo*

24.—The first parachute drop from an aeroplane in England: Mr. Guy Newall on the G.W. Charabancs (120 h.p. Austro-Daimler).

"Flight" photo

25.—AERIAL DERBY DAY: A BUSY SCENE AT HENDON.

Facing page 85

table supplied with the box. Needless to say, the result was usually a long way from the truth.

Another ingenious, but unnecessary, aid to navigation were the two sights mounted on the fuselage. The pilot was supposed to keep them in line with some landmark, and if they refused to stay in line then he could move the back one to one side or the other to compensate for drift.

Yet another fascinating toy was a full equipment of coloured signal lights. The observer pressed a button and a lamp lit up in front of the pilot, signifying " Turn to the right," " Descend," or " Climb," as the case might require.

It is difficult to suppose that the Bristol Company intended these toys to be taken seriously, always excepting the bomb-rack, but they served to attract attention to the biplane, which was well made and compared favourably with some of the French exhibits.

There was nothing very striking in the Salon. Only forty aeroplanes were on view altogether. Amongst them was a Dunne biplane, which had been constructed by the Nieuport firm. Commandant Felix had made a number of most successful flights on this original British design, including a passage of the Straits of Dover, and the French military authorities were keenly alive to its possibilities.

Bleriot had produced a pusher-biplane on Farman lines in addition to a new *monocoque* monoplane. Bathiat-Sanchez, Clement-Bayard, Borel, Nieuport, and R.E.P., all showed neat monoplane types, whilst Morane-Saulnier struck a new note with their " parasol " model in which the wing was set up clear above the fuselage in order to improve the pilot's view. Ponnier (Hanriot) and Deperdussin showed their 160 h.p. Gordon-Bennett racers, the two fastest aeroplanes in the world, and the former displayed a very beautiful little single-seat touring version of the racer fitted with a 60 h.p. Le Rhone rotary engine.

Generally speaking there was an increasing tendency to use steel in place of wood and to pay more attention to the reduction of drag, especially by means of the simplification of undercarriages.

It was a pity that the Sopwith and Avro Companies were not represented, as the Tabloid and the 504 would have created a sensation in the Salon.

50. 1913 REVIEWED : BRITISH AERO ENGINES AND AEROPLANES

The year had shown a very great advance in all departments of British aviation, except that the position with regard to aero engines was even worse than it had been before. The E.N.V. ; A.B.C. ; N.E.C., and Wolseley engines had practically disappeared, leaving the 100 h.p. Green as the sole survivor of the original British aero engine industry. It is true that one single example of the Isaacson radial was flying in the Flanders biplane, and that

Mr. John Alcock was testing a Sunbeam aviation motor for Mr. Louis Coatalen in a Maurice Farman; but for all practical purposes the industry was dead. The Green engines were only used by people who were compelled to fit a British engine in order to qualify for some competition; no one chose them voluntarily on their merits. It was a black outlook.

Very different was the position with regard to aeroplanes. At the end of 1912, we had only one type, the B.E.2, which compared favourably with the best French aircraft. During 1913 Mr. de Havilland had improved this machine and it still ranked amongst the world's best aeroplanes. Mr. A. V. Roe had secured a major triumph with his type 504, which was a definite advance on the B.E. design, whilst Messrs. Sopwith and Sigrist had made the most notable contribution to the world's progress in aviation.

If anyone had dared to suggest in 1912 that within twelve months England would lead the world in aircraft design and construction, they would have been ridiculed, such was the overwhelming superiority of the French. But Sopwith and Sigrist almost brought it to pass by designing, first the Bat-boat amphibian, winner of the Mortimer Singer prize, next the three-seater tractor biplane, breaker of one world's and four British records, and finally the Tabloid, the fastest biplane in the world. Even the French, who still held every one of the world's records of first-class importance, had no machine with an *all-round* performance equal to that of the Sopwith Tabloid.

In addition to this, Messrs. Grahame-White and J. D. North had evolved a remarkably efficient weight-carrier in the G.W. "Charabancs," which had brought two world's records to Britain, the Bristol Company were obtaining a very fine performance from the latest model of Mons. Coanda's tractor biplane, and Messrs. Robert and Harold Blackburn were at last well started on the right track with the excellent monoplane designed for Dr. Christie.

In the seaplane category it was obvious that the Wight machine built by Messrs. J. Samuel White and Company was showing great promise, whilst Messrs. Short Bros. continued to conduct their full-scale experiments at the Isle of Grain with satisfactory results, and the large Avro seaplane had proved to be capable of performing creditably on rough water.

Altogether the position at the end of 1913 was extremely satisfying, and it was a good sign that our most advanced designers were no longer content to imitate French types, but were striking out an original line of their own, which bade fair to surpass even the best that the French could produce.

51. THE PILOTS OF 1913

In contrast to 1912 there had been many spectacular feats performed by British pilots during the year, and it is difficult to choose the best ten from the increasing number of really sound pilots then operating in England.

Probably the best individual flight of 1913 was Capt. C. A. H. Longcroft's non-stop journey from Montrose to Farnborough, via Portsmouth, on a B.E.2, for which he was awarded the Britannia Trophy. Capt. Longcroft was the outstanding pilot of the R.F.C. at that time, but I do not propose to admit his name to the list, which will be confined once more to civilian pilots.

The next best performance was undoubtedly Hawker's unsuccessful attempt on the *Daily Mail* seaplane prize and, if that were not sufficient, his flight for the Michelin Cup No. 2, his race with Raynham in the Aerial Derby, his success in the Mortimer-Singer competition and his record-breaking ascents for the various altitude records would ensure that his name would be somewhere near the top of the list.

Mr. Gustav Hamel had crossed the Channel more times than any other pilot in the world and his flight from Dover to Cologne non-stop was a great achievement. In addition he had flown magnificently to win the Aerial Derby and he was the second British pilot to loop the loop.

Mr. B. C. Hucks had established himself as the greatest exhibition pilot in England and he was the first and only English pilot to display a full repertoire of aerobatics in 1913. His stunt flying was smooth and polished, and was generally considered to be better than that of any other pilot in the world, not excepting the great Mons. E. Pégoud himself. So far as the actual ability to control an aeroplane is inferred by the term "pilot," Mr. B. C. Hucks was undoubtedly the best British pilot of the year.

Mr. Robert Slack died on December 21st as the result of a motor-car accident, otherwise his name would have been high in the list in recognition of his grand flight from Paris to Hendon, made under conditions which would have caused most modern pilots to seek safety on the ground.

One of the greatest feats of the year was Mr. Corbett-Wilson's wonderful flight from France into Switzerland over the Jura Alps.

Other notable cross-country journeys had been made by Mr. Gordon Bell from Paris to Whitstable, by Mr. Sydney Pickles from Crotoy to the Isle of Grain (twice), by Mr. G. Lee Temple and Lord Carbery from Paris to Hendon, by Mr. James Valentine from Paris to Dieppe, and by Mr. Grahame-White from Paris to Putney, via Le Havre.

Mr. F. P. Raynham had steadily improved in his flying and had put up a splendid performance in the Aerial Derby. He had carried out a number of cross-country journeys between Brooklands and Manchester, and had flown many types of machines on test, including the Avro seaplane.

Mr. Warren Merriam continued to uphold his peerless reputation as an instructor, and had performed the remarkable feat of training no less than seventy pupils during the year without a serious accident; a truly wonderful record. Mr. R. H. Barnwell had also established an enviable reputation as an instructor, and had proved himself to be a test and racing pilot of great ability.

Of the other men who appeared in the list for 1912, not very much had been heard of Mr. Geoffrey de Havilland, who had been quietly continuing his work of testing his machines as they were produced by the Royal Aircraft Factory, or of Mr. S. V. Sippe, who was engaged on testing the output of the Bristol works. Both pilots had been doing fine work unobtrusively. Mr. Howard Pixton had also been carrying on quietly as a test pilot, first for the Bristol Company, and afterwards for Messrs. Sopwith and Sigrist, and had had little opportunity of showing what he could do in public.

My list of the best British pilots at the end of 1913 is as follows:—

1. H. G. Hawker (Farman, Sopwith-Wright, Sopwith three-seater, Sopwith Bat-boat, and Sopwith Tabloid biplanes).
2. B. C. Hucks (Blackburn and Bleriot monoplanes).
3. G. Hamel (Bleriot and Morane-Saulnier monoplanes and Howard-Wright biplane).
4. F. P. Raynham (Farman, Howard-Wright, Burgess-Wright, Avro, and Flanders biplanes, and Flanders monoplanes).
5. Corbett-Wilson (Bleriot monoplanes).
6. Sydney Pickles (Caudron and Champel biplanes and Bleriot monoplanes).
7. R. H. Barnwell (Vickers and Farman biplanes and Vickers and Martinsyde monoplanes).
8. F. Warren Merriam (Bristol biplanes and monoplanes).
9. Howard Pixton (Avro, Bristol, and Sopwith three-seater biplanes, and Bristol monoplanes).
10. S. V. Sippe (Avro and Bristol biplanes and Hanriot and Bristol monoplanes).

52. FURTHER PROGRESS OF THE FLYING SCHOOLS

At the close of 1912 there had been sixteen civilian and two military schools of flying in operation. During 1913 the Sopwith, Hewlett and Blondeau, Ogilvie, Cody and Handley-Page organizations had ceased to train pupils, but their loss was more than counter-balanced by the establishment of the Temple, Blackburn, Hall, and Beattie schools at Hendon, the Percival school at Brooklands and the Shoreham flying school.

Pilots were now being trained *ab initio*, not only by the C.F.S. at Upavon, but also within the ranks of the squadrons of the Military Wing, R.F.C.

During the previous year sixteen civilian schools had trained 181 new pilots, but, owing to the increasing efficiency of the larger establishments, the seventeen civilian operators passed 243 pupils through their tests in 1913.

Including the pilots trained at the Naval and Military schools no less than 336 new pilots were manufactured during the year. This total included seventeen foreign subjects, but as twenty-four Englishmen qualified in France and three in the U.S.A., and one taught himself to fly at Brooklands, the net increase of British pilots in 1913 was 347, thus bringing the grand total of British subjects who had qualified as pilots since the beginning of aviation to 732, of whom thirty-two had been killed in flying accidents.

The record of the British schools for 1913 was as follows :—

School	*Aerodrome*	*No. of pupils trained during* 1913
Bristol	Brooklands 70 Salisbury Plain 47	117
C.F.S. (R.F.C.)	Upavon	56
Vickers	Brooklands	35
Naval School (R.F.C.)	Eastchurch	29
Ewen	Hendon	25
Grahame-White	Hendon	19
Deperdussin	Hendon	12
E.A.C.	Eastbourne	12
Bleriot	Hendon	8
R.F.C. (Military Wing)	Netheravon 4 Montrose 4	8
Temple	Hendon	3
Blackburn	Hendon	2
Ducrocq	Brooklands	2
Avro	Shoreham	2
Shoreham F.S.	Shoreham	1
Hall	Hendon	1
Beattie	Hendon	1
Melly	Freshfield (Lancs)	1
Percival	Brooklands	1
Lakes F.S. (seaplanes)	Windermere	1
		Total 336

The Bristol school had now reached its peak. Mr. Warren Merriam had achieved the apparently impossible by forcing the output of the Brooklands branch up to seventy, and an improvement in the Salisbury Plain section had resulted in a gross output from the two schools of almost one pilot every three days, or well over two pilots weekly. This was surely one of the most astonishing feats in the whole history of aviation. Mr. Warren Merriam, Mons. H. Jullerot, and their able assistants deserve the very highest praise. Between them they had trained only nine short of the total number of pupils who qualified at all the sixteen other civilian schools of flying put together. It was phenomenal.

Another interesting development was the swift advance of the Vickers school under the management of Mr. Robert Barnwell. In 1912 they had trained only six pupils, but the output had grown to thirty-five in 1913, an average of one new pilot every eleven days. At Hendon the Ewen organization, profiting by the installation of Caudron training biplanes, had surpassed the Grahame-White school, which had thitherto held the lead.

53. ACCIDENTS IN 1913

There had been twelve accidents involving loss of life during the year as against eleven in 1912. This was a very great improvement considering the fact that a much larger number of hours had been flown during 1913. Only four machines had broken in the air and killed their pilots, as against five in the preceding year. Of these, two were Cody biplanes, one was a Bristol monoplane, and one was a B.E.2. In the last-mentioned case it was clearly established that the failure was the result of a bad repair and not due to faulty design or construction.

An analysis of the eight remaining accidents shows that two were due to taking off with failing engines, two to pilots overbanking and side-slipping into the ground, one to a pilot stalling on a gliding turn, one was caused by a pilot slipping out of his seat and jamming the controls on a steep glide, another by sheer reckless stunting, and the last was due to the victim being struck by an airscrew on the ground.

In one case the pilot was a pupil who had not then qualified for his certificate.

This is not a bad record for a year's hard flying, including, as it does, not merely civilian accidents, but the results of Service smashes as well.

54. WORLD'S RECORDS AT THE END OF 1913

The authorities had not yet realized the necessity for timing aeroplanes over two runs in opposite directions on a straight course, if any accurate figures as to maximum speeds were to be obtained. Actually the fastest record on the book at the end of the year was that for one lap of a ten-kilometre circuit, which had been covered by Mons. M. Prevost on a Deperdussin monoplane (160 h.p. Gnôme), during the Gordon-Bennett contest, in 2 mins. 56⅗ secs., at a speed of 127 m.p.h. The futility of timing machines round corners can be gauged from the fact that a heated dispute arose as to whether or not the Deperdussin was actually faster than the Ponnier monoplane (160 h.p. Gnôme), which finished second in the same race. Many people thought that Prevost had won by reason of his wonderful cornering, and that the Ponnier was actually the faster machine. In any case, it is certain that one or other of these two aeroplanes was the fastest aircraft in the world at that time.

Although the F.A.I. now accepted records for distance flown in a straight line in various categories, no claim had been put forward for homologation in respect of this most important record as regards the class for pilot alone.

Deroye's Italian record of 487 miles with one passenger stood alone on the books under this heading, although much longer non-stop flights had been made during the various attempts on the Pommery Cup. There had been two flights from Paris to Vittoria in Spain, a distance of about 900 kilometres, and the 568 miles between Paris and Berlin had been covered non-stop no less than three times, by Letort (twice) and A. Seguin. I have included the former in my list as the unofficial holder of the record.

It will be seen that France still held every important record and that no one had beaten Fourny's wonderful duration flight of thirteen hours twenty-two minutes, although Seguin had come within seventeen minutes of doing so during his journey from Paris to Bordeaux and back non-stop, which raised the closed circuit distance record by the narrow margin of three and a half miles.

The altitude record had been raised by 1,614 feet and Legagneux used oxygen on his record-breaking climb. This was the first occasion on which this was deemed to be a necessary precaution.

No English pilot held a world's record at the end of the year, but the weight-lifting feats of Louis Noel in the English-built Grahame-White "Char-a-bancs" remained unbeaten, and these two records were officially credited to Great Britain.

WORLD'S RECORDS AT THE END OF 1913

Pilot	*Nationality*	*Aircraft*	*Nationality*	*Engine*	*Nationality*	*Time or Distance*	*Place*
			DURATION				
Fourny	French	Maurice Farman	French	Renault	French	13 hrs. 22 mins.	Etampes
			DISTANCE IN A CLOSED CIRCUIT				
A. Seguin	French	Henry Farman	French	Gnôme	French	1,021·2 Km. (634 miles)	Paris to Bordeaux and back
			DISTANCE IN A STRAIGHT LINE (Unofficial)				
Letort	French	Morane-Saulnier	French	Le Rhone	French	915 Km. (568 miles)	Villacoublay to Johannisthal
			ALTITUDE				
G. Legagneux	French	Nieuport	French	Le Rhone	French	6,120 metres (20,014 ft.)	St. Raphael

55. ALL-BRITISH RECORDS AT THE END OF 1913

No advance whatever had been made during 1913 from the position established at the end of 1912 so far as the all-British records were concerned, so the reader can refer back to the table set out on page 188 *supra*, which gives all the information available. The Sopwith three-seater, as fitted with a Green engine, was obviously capable of beating the unofficial speed record of 61·8 m.p.h. set up by Wilfred Parke on the Avro cabin biplane, but no attempt had been made to do so.

A clear distinction must be drawn between these all-British records and British records.

British aeroplanes fitted with foreign engines had put up some very creditable performances, the B.E.2 having set up an altitude record of 13,140 feet, and a record for distance flown in a straight line of some 445 miles, whilst the Sopwith Tabloid had achieved a mesne speed of 92 m.p.h. for two runs over a straight course in opposite directions.

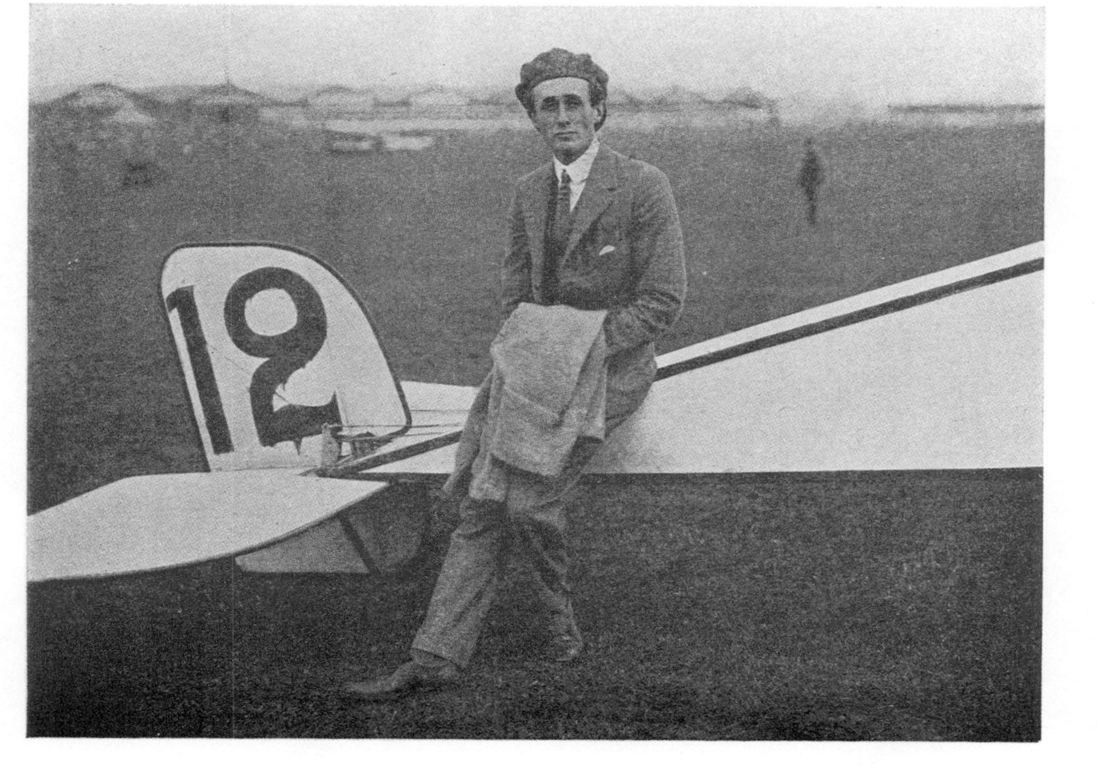

"Flight" photo

26.—The Aerial Derby: Lord Carbery (Morane-Saulnier Monoplane).

Facing page 92

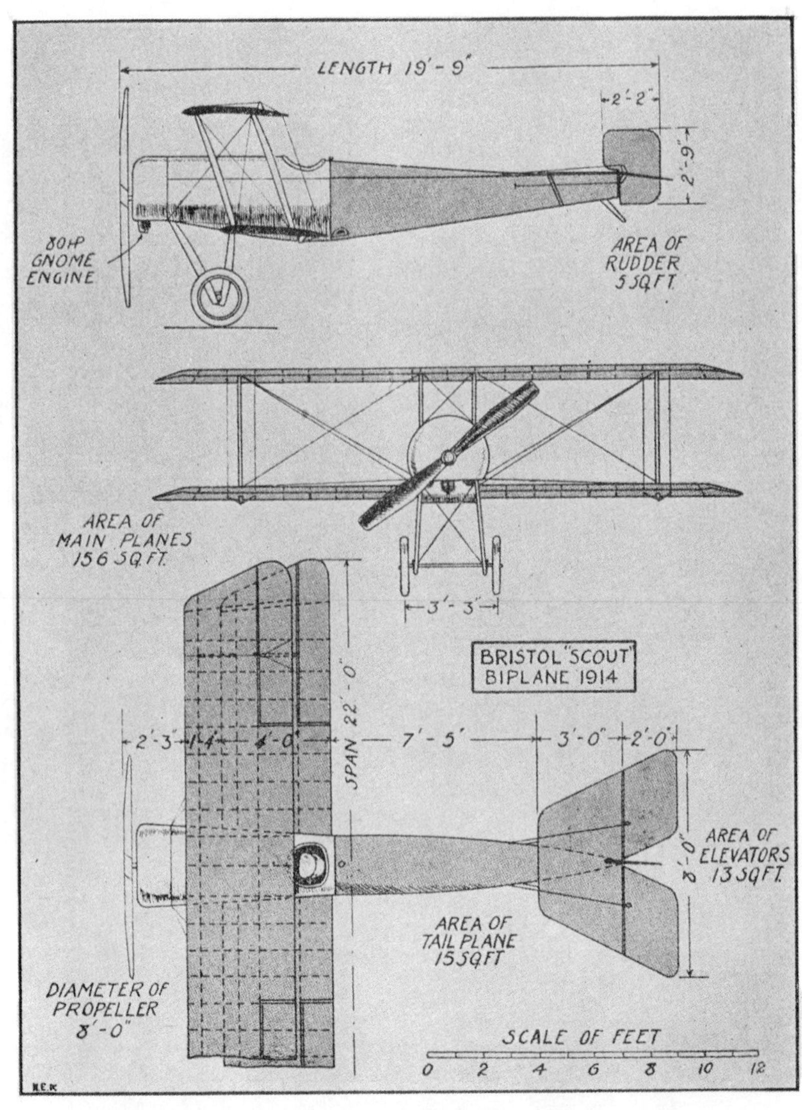

5.—A worthy rival of the Tabloid, the fast Bristol Scout (80 h.p. Gnôme).

Facing page 93

CHAPTER II

JANUARY 1ST–AUGUST 4TH, 1914

1. MISS TREHAWKE DAVIES: THE R.F.C. INSPECTION DEPARTMENT

AT the beginning of 1914 there were no English women pilots flying. Only three had qualified during the first five years of practical aviation. One of these, Mrs. Maurice Hewlett, gave up flying soon after taking her certificate, another had married and become an American citizen, whilst the remaining one, Mrs. de Beauvoir Stocks, who had become a capable pilot of Bleriot monoplanes, so far as flying round an aerodrome was concerned, had been badly hurt in the accident to Sydney Pickles.

Mention must be made, however, of Miss Trehawke Davies. This remarkable enthusiast, although not a pilot herself, had done far more serious flying than the great majority of English pilots. She had purchased two Bleriot monoplanes of her own and had travelled in them for great distances across the Channel into France and Germany. She had flown without hesitation in really bad weather, and her serious smash with Mr. H. J. D. Astley, at Lille, had not impaired her nerve. She had a gift for picking the soundest pilots to fly her about, and her machines were generally handled by Gustav Hamel, B. C. Hucks, or James Valentine. Later on she also flew with Mr. R. O. Crawshay, an English pupil of the Bleriot school at Buc, who was the third English pilot to loop the loop, which he did at Buc on January 7th.

She was naturally interested and excited by the discovery of aerobatic flying, and decided that she must be the first woman in the world to experience a loop. Hamel having at last succeeded in pulling his Morane-Saulnier over the top on Boxing Day, Miss Davies became so determined to achieve her object that, although she was ill in bed, she insisted on getting up and going down to Hendon on January 2nd, against her doctor's orders.

Hamel and Miss Davies took off at 4 p.m., in the gathering dusk, and performed a loop at 1,000 feet. After this Hamel succeeded in doing a half-roll onto his back, from which position he dived out to regain normal flight.

Having satisfied her ambition of being the first woman in the world to loop-the-loop and the first passenger of either sex to loop with an English pilot, Miss Trehawke Davies returned home to bed and underwent a minor operation.

It was a pity that a woman of such unusual pluck and determination did not actually learn to fly herself. No doubt she would have become a brilliant pilot.

It will be recalled that the terrible accidents to the Deperdussin and Bristol monoplanes in 1912, followed by the collapse of a B.E.2 at Montrose, and the complete disintegration of two Cody biplanes at Farnborough during 1913, had indicated unmistakably the necessity for more adequate and careful maintenance of the machines of the R.F.C. The strongest recommendations had been made, first by the "Monoplane Committee" on December 3rd, 1912, and later by the Accidents Committee of the R.Ae.C., to the effect that an independent inspection department should be established forthwith and charged with the duty of examining every repair carried out by the mechanics of the Squadrons of the Military Wing, R.F.C., or at the Royal Aircraft Factory.

These recommendations were ignored by Col. Seely and his advisers for more than a year, but Army Orders of January 2nd, 1914, announced the formation of the Inspection Department of the Military Wing, R.F.C. Maj. J. D. B. Fulton, C.B., was appointed chief inspector, Mr. Geoffrey de Havilland became inspector of aeroplanes, and Capt. R. K. Bagnall-Wild was to act as inspector of engines.

This long overdue decision laid the foundations of the Aeronautical Inspection Directorate, which has performed such valuable services to British aviation in the past, and which still does so much to ensure that British aeroplanes remain the strongest and safest in the world.

2. MR. F. K. McCLEAN'S EGYPTIAN TOUR: MR. GORDON BELL FLYING AGAIN

Mr. F. K. McClean had been conducting experiments with seaplanes for a considerable time and he conceived the idea of having a large powerful machine built on which he could tour through Egypt, using the river Nile as his aerodrome.

The Short brothers constructed a three-seater pusher biplane for the purpose. It was, generally speaking, of the traditional Farman type, the upper wing being longer than the bottom one, and fitted with very large ailerons. There was a diminutive front elevator attached to the nose of the *nacelle*, and the monoplane tail was equipped with twin rudders and twin tail floats. The main floats were of the normal Short punt-shape, and the engine was one of the 160 h.p. Gnômes.

During a test flight at Eastchurch on November 19th, 1913, Mr. McClean had flown with four passengers, Com. Samson, R.N., Lieut. I. T. Courtney, R.N., Mr. Alec Ogilvie, and Mr. Horace Short, at an estimated speed of 72 m.p.h.

The machine was shipped out to Alexandria and re-erected there, and Mr. McClean, Mr. Ogilvie, and their mechanic began their long journey on January 3rd, 1914, by flying to Cairo, a distance of 160 miles, in 2 hrs. 55 mins., at an average speed of 55 m.p.h. On January 6th they proceeded to Minieh against a strong headwind.

Thereafter the flight was dogged by trouble. The 160 h.p. Gnôme let the machine down on thirteen separate occasions, notably at Assiut, where a ball race broke and distributed itself amongst the machinery in the crank case; and three times the floats were damaged in bad "landings."

On January 16th, the expedition arrived at Luxor and left on the same day for Assuan. On March 23rd, about eleven weeks after leaving Alexandria, the machine reached the main objective at Khartoum, having covered about 1,400 miles in all. It was then dismantled and shipped back to England.

The Short was the second aeroplane to penetrate to Khartoum, the first being a Morane-Saulnier monoplane flown by Marc Pourpe, who landed there on January 12th.

Mr. Gordon Bell had now recovered from his terrible smash at Brooklands, and he was employed by the Short brothers in testing their new machines at Eastchurch. He made a number of fine flights on the latest Short tractor biplane (100 h.p. Gnôme) at the beginning of January, during which he was accompanied by Mr. C. R. Fairey. On January 8th, he flew alone in this machine from Eastchurch to the Isle of Grain in a terrific storm of wind, rain, and hail, which sufficed to keep everyone else, even the Naval pilots, indoors.

The Short brothers were already building their large new factory at Rochester, and they were in process of developing the first satisfactory method of folding the wings of their seaplanes back alongside the fuselage. The Hon. Maurice Egerton had purchased a Short pusher biplane on which he did a good deal of flying at Eastchurch, where Professor Huntingdon was obtaining satisfactory results from the machine of his own design.

3. AN INVERTED DINNER: FINE FLIGHT BY NAVAL PILOT

On January 16th, the Hendon pilots gave a dinner to Messrs. B. C. Hucks and Gustav Hamel, designed to commemorate their achievements as the first two Englishmen to fly upside-down under control. It is unlikely that any of those present will ever forget it.

The rite was performed at the Royal Automobile Club under the chairmanship of Mr. Claude Grahame-White. Proceedings began with the announcement, by megaphone, that coffee was served, whereupon the company drank the loyal toast in liqueurs.

The waiters, dressed in mechanic's overalls, then served the savoury, followed by the sweets, until the tortured palates of the guests had grappled with various joints and *entrées* and arrived, via lobster and soup, at the *hors d'oeuvres*.

Amongst those who lent themselves to this gastronomic perversion were the following well-known British pilots :—Messrs. E. Bass, W. Birchenough, R. H. Carr, R. T. Gates, F. W. Gooden, C. Gresswell, Robert Loraine, M. D. Manton, J. C. Porte, L. A. Strange, and R. Whitehouse, and Sir Bryan Leighton. France was represented by MM. Marcel Dessouter, P. Marty, Louis Noel, and P. Verrier ; America by Messrs. G. W. Beatty and W. L. Brock, and Switzerland by Mons. E. Baumann. Other notabilities present were Messrs. Stanley Spooner and C. G. Grey, editors of *Flight* and *The Aeroplane* respectively ; Messrs. G. Holt Thomas, J. D. North, Handley Page, and Norbert Chereau representing the manufacturers, and Messrs. Harold Perrin, secretary of the R.Ae.C., and A. G. Reynolds, the famous timekeeper.

A serious accident occurred to H.M. Submarine A7 off Plymouth in the third week of January, and the Naval authorities thought that an aeroplane should be used to assist in the endeavours to locate the wreck. Acting under orders, Com. Seddon left the Isle of Grain with a mechanic on a Maurice Farman float seaplane (70 Renault) at 9.15 a.m. on January 21st, and flew round the coast towards Plymouth.

He passed Beachy Head at 11.40 a.m. and landed at the Calshot seaplane station at 12.40 p.m. He took off once more at 2.20 p.m. and alighted in Plymouth sound at 4.40 p.m., after spending five hours twenty-five minutes in the air. The submarine had been found before he arrived and, although he flew over the spot, he was unable to see it.

4. TWO FATAL ACCIDENTS

A terrible accident occurred at Hendon on Sunday, January 25th, before a large crowd of people. Mr. G. Lee Temple had been in bed for a fortnight suffering from a bad attack of influenza, but he came down to the aerodrome and insisted on getting out his Bleriot monoplane (50 Gnôme) and making an exhibition flight in a very cold and gusty wind. For ten minutes he flew round the enclosures at 500 feet, and then came down to 150 feet. At this height he flew level for about 200 yards, and then his engine suddenly stopped. The machine went into a steep dive, passed beyond the vertical, executed a complete bunt, and landed upside-down in the middle of the aerodrome.

From the medical evidence it was established beyond reasonable doubt that the pilot had lost consciousness in the air. The doctor stated that he incurred the gravest risk by flying at all in his then state of health, and no doubt he fainted from the cold and fell forward on to the control column.

Mr. Lee Temple had taught himself to fly on a Caudron biplane at Hendon, and had taken his Aviator's certificate (No. 424) on February 18th, 1913.

"Flight" photo

27.—London–Manchester Race: Mr. Jack Alcock and his Maurice Farman (100 h.p. Sunbeam), the first all-British Aeroplane to finish a long distance race

"Flight" photo

28.—London–Paris Race: the scratch machine, Lord Carbery's Bristol Scout (Le Rhone).

Mr. Warren Merriam, the most brilliant of the English instructors, was transferred for a short time from Brooklands to the Bristol Company's school on Salisbury Plain. On January 26th, he took off in a Bristol "sociable" monoplane (50 Gnôme) with one of the more advanced pupils, Mr. G. L. Gipps, who had taken his Aviator's certificate (No. 513) as long ago as June 13th, 1913, for the purpose of giving him dual instruction. This machine was not equipped with an air speed indicator, revolution counter, or bank indicator, and neither pilot nor passenger was strapped in or wearing a crash helmet.

After completing a circuit at a height of about eighty feet the monoplane performed a violent flat turn, stalled, and dived into the ground. Mr. G. L. Gipps was killed and Mr. Merriam was severely hurt, but eventually recovered. There is little doubt but that the pupil resisted his instructor's initial application of rudder and then suddenly relaxed his leg, with the result that Mr. Merriam jerked on full rudder, and the machine stalled before he could counteract its effect.

Apart from a slight misadventure in the sewage farm at Brooklands, this was the first accident in which Mr. Merriam had been implicated. Mr. S. V. Sippe took charge of the Bristol school at Brooklands pending his recovery, whilst Mr. F. B. Halford continued to act as assistant instructor.

5. TWO BRITISH PILOTS ATTACK ALTITUDE RECORDS

On February 4th Mr. F. P. Raynham took off from Brooklands alone in one of the new Avro tractor biplanes (80 Gnôme) with a barograph on board, intending to test the machine's climbing capacity. The engine was in great form, and he went up and up into the cold winter sky until he had passed Capt. J. M. Salmond's record height, and reached an altitude of more than 15,000 feet. Switching off his engine he went into a glide and pointed the machine's nose in the direction of Hendon, some twenty miles away. For twenty-five minutes he slid down the air and arrived over Hendon with 5,000 feet still in hand, so he continued his silent descent in a spiral and landed safely, without using his engine again, after having made one of the greatest flights yet achieved in England. Unfortunately this feat, though well authenticated, was not officially observed, and no claim could be made for the British record.

Six days later, on February 10th, Mr. Raynham made a formal attack on the record. This time he carried Mr. MacGeagh Hurst as passenger. The attempt was highly successful for, not only did he beat Mr. Hawker's British record of 12,900 feet for pilot and one passenger, but, in spite of the extra load, he exceeded Capt. Salmond's achievement once more by taking the Avro up to 14,420 feet.

Mr. George Newberry, President of the Argentine Aero Club, had purchased a Morane-Saulnier monoplane, and he decided to see if he could break the Argentine height record of 14,432 feet, which he had set up himself on his Bleriot monoplane in May 1913. The attempt was made at Buenos Aires on February 11th, and he not only broke the Argentine record, but actually surpassed the world's record, held by M. Legagneux, by climbing to no less than 6,220 metres (20,400 feet). It was a rule of the *F.A.I.* that, in order to count as a fresh record a climb must exceed the previous best by at least 150 metres. Mr. Newberry had only beaten M. Legagneux's record by 100 metres, so that he had failed by a mere 164 feet to capture one of the three most important world's records, which was very hard luck indeed.

This was the last great feat of a great career as a pilot, for Mr. George Newberry was killed on March 1st whilst starting on an attempt to fly across the Andes. His passenger, Lieut. Rastra, was seriously injured.

Mr. George Newberry's speciality was high flying, and he had broken the altitude record for his adopted country on four separate occasions. He was also a cross-country pilot of outstanding ability, and his death was an irreparable loss to aviation in the Argentine.

6. GARROS V. HAMEL: A SERIOUS ACCIDENT AT WITTERING

Mr. Gustav Hamel had issued a challenge to M. Roland Garros to fly a series of match races against him at Juvisy. The contest took place on February 22nd, and attracted a large crowd. Each race was flown over twelve laps of a small circuit of two kilometres circumference, designed to test the cornering ability of the pilots to the utmost, and each pilot flew an identical Morane-Saulnier monoplane (80 Gnôme).

The machines were sent off at an interval of one minute, Garros starting first. The Frenchman completed his first ten laps in 12 mins. 6 secs., and Hamel, finding that he could not hold his eminent rival, gave up in the ninth round. The pilots then exchanged machines and Hamel started first. This time he completed the course in 11 mins. 11⅕ secs., but Garros was just getting his hand in, and he finished in 11 mins. 4⅗ secs., at an average speed of 67 m.p.h., which was very good for such a small circuit. Garros, having won two out of three contests, was adjudged the winner, and both pilots proceeded to give displays of aerobatics.

On February 23rd, Mr. Ronald Kemp, who was now engaged as a test pilot at the Royal Aircraft Factory, was flying an experimental biplane known as the F.E.2 (70 h.p. Renault), which had been built at the Factory in August 1913, with Mr. E. T. Haynes, one of the civilian experts at Farnborough, as passenger.

When above Wittering, about seven miles from Chichester, the machine went into a steep spiral glide at a height of about 500 feet, which continued until it struck the ground. The biplane was wrecked, and Mr. Haynes was so badly hurt that he died almost immediately, whilst Mr. Kemp suffered a broken leg and other injuries. In spite of his wounds the pilot calmly directed the helpers in their task of extricating his passenger's body from the wreckage.

Mr. Kemp was unable afterwards to recall anything that happened on the day of the accident, but it was thought that the disaster was caused by the pilot's foot slipping off the rudder bar.

7. DEVELOPMENTS AT BROOKLANDS: SOME MORE ENGLISH STUNT PILOTS

There was intense activity at Brooklands throughout February and the early part of March. Three British engines were undergoing the most strenuous tests. One was the 100 h.p. Sunbeam which had been installed in a Maurice Farman pusher biplane in which Mr. Jack Alcock spent several hours in the air every week. He was usually the first up in the morning and often the last down at night. He flew in weather which kept all the other pilots indoors, and he ranged far and wide over southern England. He took many passengers for high flights above the clouds, including Mr. Louis Coatalen, the designer of the engine. The new motor proved very reliable under this continued strain, and the intense flying practice served to develop Mr. Alcock into one of the soundest pilots in the country. Probably he was putting in more hours in the air during this period than any other pilot.

The Isaacson radial engine in the Flanders biplane was also giving a very satisfactory account of itself and Mr. Dukinfield Jones, who was engaged to fly the machine for Mr. Howard Flanders, spent almost as much time in the air as did Mr. Alcock.

Mr. Howard Pixton was putting a series of Sopwiths through their tests, one of which was a new model fitted with the first A.B.C. engine constructed by Messrs. Armstrong Whitworth & Co., Ltd. Mr. F. P. Raynham was very busy with the increasing output of the Avro firm, who had sold several 50 h.p. training machines to private owners and one to Mr. J. L. Hall, who had started a new school at Hendon. The Bleriot Company had leased a row of sheds at Brooklands, and were busy converting them into an up-to-date repair and service station, and Vickers had produced a new monoplane and were still carrying out tests with their gun-carrying pusher biplane. The Martinsyde firm also had a new monoplane on test in the hands of Messrs. Robert Barnwell and Vincent Waterfall.

All things considered, Brooklands had become the very hub of the industry in this country by the spring of 1914.

The fourth and fifth British pilots to loop were Lord Edward Grosvenor and Mr. Robert Skene, who had both gone over to the Bleriot school at Buc to receive instruction in aerobatics. Lord Edward Grosvenor performed the feat on February 26th and Mr. Skene initiated himself on the following day.

It was not until nearly a month later that the next English pilot joined the select band. Mr. J. E. B. Thorneley had passed the tests for his aviator's certificate in November 1913, as a pupil of the Eastbourne aviation Co., but he was only just over seventeen years of age at that time and the R.Ae.C. was compelled to withhold the certificate until July 1914, when he would reach the minimum age limit then in force. On March 23rd this young man performed the astonishing feat of looping an old Henry Farman pusher biplane (70 h.p. Gnôme), which was used as a school machine. He had to dive it almost vertically for 1,500 feet before he could gain enough speed to pull it over the top. This was an extremely courageous, if foolhardy, performance.

Three days later a perfect epidemic of aerobatics broke out at Hendon. Mr. F. W. Gooden made two perfect loops in an old Caudron biplane (45 h.p. Anzani), which had been built early in 1912, and Mr. R. H. Carr looped the new Grahame-White tractor biplane, which had been constructed around the fuselage of a Morane-Saulnier monoplane, and was familiarly known as "Lizzie." On the same afternoon both M. Louis Noel and Mr. L. A. Strange succeeded in inverting "Lizzie," whilst Mr. J. L. Hall looped his Avro tractor biplane (50 h.p. Gnôme).

During all this time Mr. B. C. Hucks maintained his unchallenged supremacy as an aerobatic pilot and he continued to tour the country giving peerless exhibitions of his perfect control over the single-seat Bleriot. As early as March 5th he had completed his two hundredth loop, and two days later he flew on his back for more than a mile at Nuneaton.

8. NAVAL PILOT BREAKS THE BRITISH HEIGHT RECORD: FOUR OFFICERS KILLED ON SALISBURY PLAIN

On March 11th, Eng.-Lieut. E. F. Briggs, R.N., who was one of the most determined of the small band of Naval pilots at Eastchurch, set out in a Bleriot monoplane, fitted with an 80 h.p. Le Rhone rotary engine, on an attempt to beat the British altitude record for pilot alone. This record stood officially to the credit of Capt. J. M. Salmond of the Military Wing, R.F.C., who had reached 13,140 feet on a B.E.2 (70 h.p. Renault), although Mr. F. P. Raynham had exceeded this height by 1,280 feet with a passenger in the Avro tractor biplane.

Eng.-Lieut. Briggs chose a very cold day for his attempt, but the dreadful conditions did not deter him. As he approached the record height his cheeks became frost-bitten, but he kept on in

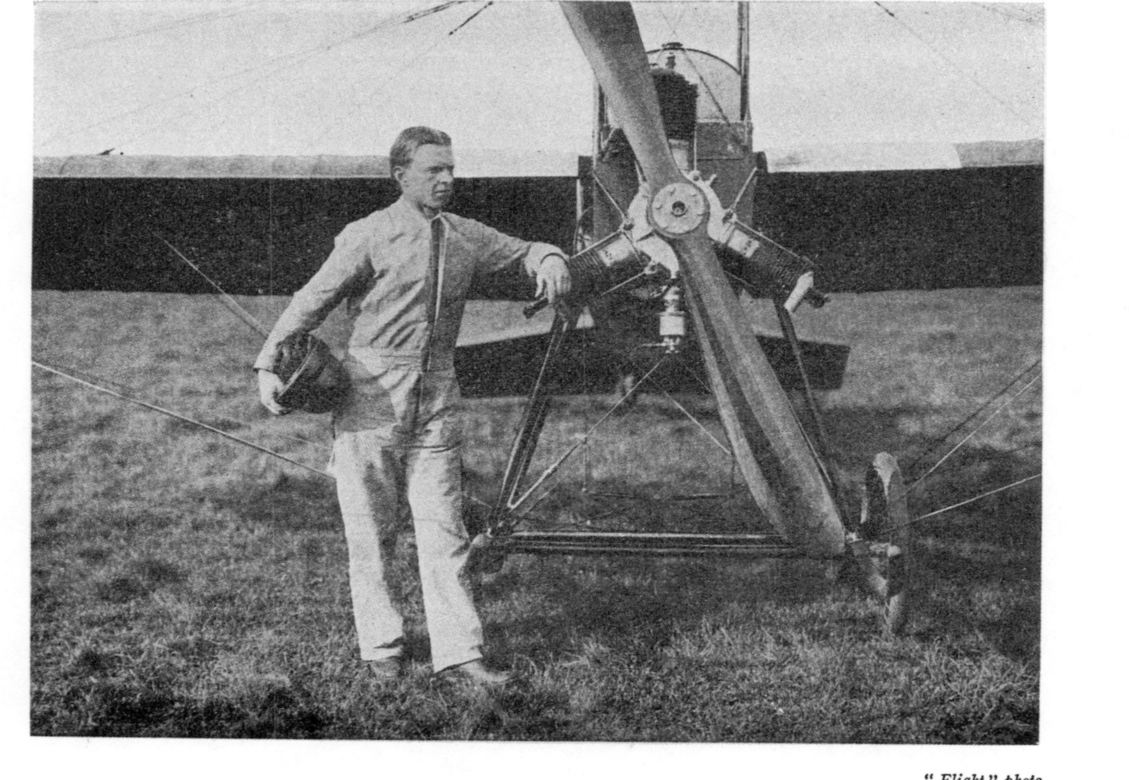

"*Flight*" *photo*

29.—London–Paris Race: the winner, Mr. W. L. Brock, the American racing pilot.

Facing page 100

"*Flight*" *photo*

30.—An English stunt pilot: Mr. Marcus D. Manton,
the dashing partner of Mr. B. C. Hucks

spite of the pain until his barographs recorded 14,920 feet. When he landed after beating the record he was unrecognizable, as his face was swollen and blackened by the frost. He was taken to hospital and, fortunately, he soon recovered.

Early in March three terrible calamities occurred at Salisbury Plain and resulted in the death of four officer pilots of the Military Wing, R.F.C.

The first happened on March 10th when Capt. C. P. Downer took off alone in a B.E.2 tractor biplane (70 h.p. Renault) with the intention of practising gliding turns. From a height of 2,000 feet the machine descended in an almost vertical rotating dive until it was some 500 feet above the ground, when the right-hand pair of wings collapsed and the wreckage dived into the ground. Capt. Downer, who had been granted his R.Ae.C. certificate (No. 608) on August 29th, 1913, was killed instantaneously.

An examination of the wreckage revealed the facts that both the elevator planes were bent downwards to the extent of several inches and that the control column was bent backwards. The Accidents Committee of the R.Ae.C. expressed the opinion that the accident was due solely to the pilot, who was inexperienced, attempting to flatten out suddenly from a fast dive and thus tearing the wings off. It would seem probable, however, that the machine, which had been built in September 1913, by Vickers Ltd., was partially to blame.

As I see it the accident happened in this way. Capt. Downer pushed the stick forward to begin his glide and the elevators promptly jammed in the downward position. This would account for the excessive steepness of the dive and for the bent control column. One can imagine the frightened pilot tugging with both hands, and exerting all his strength to pull the stick back, until suddenly the elevators freed themselves and came up with a jerk. The violent reversal of the elevator control would have thrown a terrific strain upon the wing structure, and thus brought about the collapse of the whole machine.

The second disaster, which occurred on the following day, was definitely due to the breaking of the rudder post of an old B.E. (80 h.p. Gnôme), which had been built at the Royal Aircraft Factory in June 1912.

Capt. C. R. W. Allen of No. 3 Squadron, R.F.C., was flying the machine, with Lieut. J. E. G. Burroughs as passenger. They took off from Netheravon in a perfect calm and began to circle the aerodrome. After flying for five minutes, and having nearly completed a circuit, the whole rudder fell off the machine at a height of 350 feet. The biplane flicked into a spin and both occupants were killed instantaneously as it hit the ground.

The pilot was a most experienced officer who had taken his certificate (No. 159) as long ago as November 14th, 1911, and his passenger was also a pilot, having qualified in France and been awarded his *brevet* (No. 1213) on January 31st, 1913, by the Aero Club de France.

An investigation showed that the steel tube which formed the rudder post was fractured at the base of the rudder, just below where it passed through the frame of the rudder itself and was welded to it.

The rudder post was examined miscroscopically at the National Physical Laboratory and the general conclusion was that the factor of safety of such a tube was three, and that it was of such design and construction that it should have been capable of withstanding all normal strains in flight. It was thought possible that the material had been weakened by overheating during the welding process and that the flaw thus caused was masked by the fracture itself. This particular machine had been subjected to severe stresses during its life and the Accidents Committee of the R.Ae.C. found that it had "probably been damaged prior to this particular flight."

Whatever may have been the exact cause of this double tragedy, it was abundantly clear that there was still room for improvement in the maintenance of the machines of the R.F.C., and that the sooner the long-awaited inspection department came into action the better it would be for the pilots.

The third fatality occurred eight days later, on March 19th, and on this occasion there was no question of any failure on the part of the machine. Lieut. H. F. Treeby, who had learned to fly on a Bristol biplane and taken his certificate (No. 687) on November 16th, 1913, took off from Upavon in a Maurice Farman pusher biplane (70 h.p. Renault), and flew round the aerodrome for twenty minutes. He then turned into wind and approached the landing ground at 350 feet as if about to alight. He throttled back his engine and apparently he failed to depress the nose sufficiently, for the biplane stalled and dived into the ground. Lieut. Treeby was crushed to death beneath the engine.

9. THE AERO SHOW

On March 16th the fifth exhibition of aeroplanes and aero engines was opened at Olympia by His Majesty the King.

I propose to describe this exhibition in some detail, because it afforded the last comprehensive view of the British aircraft industry which was vouchsafed to the public before the War came to deflect the course of progress, and to set back the development of aviation as a means of transport for a number of years.

(*a*) THE AIRCRAFT.

(i) *The Flying Boats*

The chief feature was the increase in the number and a vast improvement in the design of marine aircraft. Out of twenty-five complete machines on view no less than nine were intended to operate from water, and this in spite of the fact that four of the most successful constructors of seaplanes in Messrs. Short Brothers, and the Caudron, Deperdussin, and Borel firms were not represented at Olympia. The Short brothers were in the throes of organizing their new works at Rochester, and were working hard on orders for seaplanes from the Admiralty, but it was a great pity that they were unable to display their latest types.

There were three flying boats in the exhibition. The Sopwith Company showed the latest version of the Bat-boat, which had been redesigned since its victory in the Mortimer Singer Competition, and which was now built entirely in the Sopwith works at Kingston. The auxiliary wheeled undercarriage had been abandoned and the engine now fitted was one of the new 200 h.p. Salmson water-cooled radials, which was started from the cockpit by means of two compressed-air self-starters. A wireless transmitting set driven by a small motor-cycle engine was installed in front of the passenger's seat. The whole machine had been strengthened considerably and the workmanship was of the very highest quality. A novel feature was that the bottom wings were set at a considerable dihedral angle, whereas the top wing was flat ; an arrangement which was later repeated in the world-famous Sopwith Camel.

Next in importance was the first Supermarine designed and constructed by Mr. Pemberton Billing at Woolston and known as the P.B.1. There were many clever ideas embodied in this design and the cigar-shaped hull, which weighed only 200 lbs., was beautifully made. The lower wing passed through the upper part of the hull and the upper wing was supported on six pairs of struts. A 50 h.p. Gnôme engine was set in a small *nacelle*, mounted high up in the centre section and it drove a three-bladed airscrew direct. The whole of this power-egg was tilted backwards so that the thrust of the airscrew was directed downwards on to the tail. This was the weak point in an otherwise promising design.

The other flying boat was built by Messrs. Perry, Beadle & Co., and it was fitted with two airscrews mounted in front of the wings on either side, which were driven through long chains and sprockets by a 60 h.p. E.N.V. engine housed inside the bow of the boat. This was not a very practical arrangement. The hull, which was built by Messrs. Saunders at Cowes, consisted of two skins of mahogany sewn together with copper wire, and the tail plane and fin formed part of, and merged into, the hull itself. The lower of the two wings was set so low that the trailing edge was submerged when the boat was at rest on the water. This wing was covered with mahogany in the same way as the hull and thus rendered watertight ; but it was obvious that the whole idea was impractical.

(ii) *The Float Seaplanes*

There were two French monoplane float seaplanes, both of well-known standard types, shown by Bleriot and Nieuport respectively.

One of the remaining four float seaplanes was an ordinary Avro tractor biplane of the successful 504 type, which had been fitted with floats instead of wheels. Although designed primarily as a land machine the Avro formed the most imposing and workmanlike seaplane in the show.

The other three exhibits in this category were pusher biplanes. The Henry Farman was of normal type and the floats were sprung independently of one another. This machine was also equipped with a wireless transmitter.

The big Wight twin-float biplane had undergone several important modifications since it appeared in embryo form at the 1913 show. Mr. Gordon England had flown it for a great many hours during the year, and it was now a thoroughly practical machine. The particular model exhibited was fitted with a 200 h.p. Salmson water-cooled radial engine, and Mr. Howard-Wright's double-cambered wing section, which had caused much sceptical merriment when it was first introduced, had been retained, as it had amply justified its inventor's claims.

The remaining seaplane was the product of a new concern, Messrs. Hamble River, Luke & Co. It was an extremely workman-like pusher biplane which had been designed by Mr. F. Murphy, who had been trained in the drawing office of the Bristol Company. The two-seater *nacelle* was of the shape of a projectile, at the back, or flat, end of which was housed an N.A.G. engine of 150 h.p., which, though of German design, was built in England. The undercarriage was extremely neat and the twin floats were shaped like cigars, with deep steps cut into the under-surface for the last third of their length. Sopwith practice was followed in giving the bottom wing a large dihedral, whilst retaining a flat top plane, the idea being to raise the lower wing-tips clear of the sea. This promising design was shown in an incomplete condition, and it was obvious that much remained to be done before the machine became a practical proposition.

Although England was not represented by a monoplane, which was the type most favoured for marine work on the Continent, there was sufficient evidence at Olympia that the British manufacturers were ready to compete on level terms with the rest of the world in seaplane design and construction. The latest Sopwith Bat-boat was actually far in advance of any Continental design, the Avro and the Wight were both sound machines, and the Supermarine and Hamble River showed promise. It must be remembered that our premier firm of seaplane constructors were not represented at all, and that the Sopwith twin-float tractor biplane, which had so nearly won the *Daily Mail* prize, was also missing from Olympia.

Both the latest Short tractor biplane and the Sopwith were probably capable of a better all-round performance than any foreign seaplane.

(iii) *The Monoplanes*

The sixteen land aeroplanes which were exhibited, were divided into five pusher and five tractor biplanes and six monoplanes.

Five of the monoplanes were French, and included three Bleriots, one of which was the well-known two-seater, another a "parasol" type with the wing raised above the pilot's head, and the third a fast sports two-seater with *monocoque* fuselage. The other two foreign machines were a Nieuport, which was a close copy of the successful Morane-Saulnier, and an all-steel Clement-Bayard, which was armoured against rifle fire. The Blackburn Company exhibited the sole English monoplane, which was a replica of that sold to Dr. Christie in the previous year, on which a great deal of flying had been done. This machine was very strong and had good, clean lines, but the undercarriage was unnecessarily complicated and there was a great deal of external wire bracing. The workmanship could not compare with that of the highly-finished French monoplanes.

(iv) *The Pusher Biplanes*

The pusher biplane class produced some surprises. The Vickers Company showed their military type, fitted with a machine gun, which had been thoroughly tested by Mr. Barnwell at Brooklands, as a result of which certain modifications had been carried out since its first appearance at the Aero Show of 1913. The wings were no longer staggered, the undercarriage had been simplified, the Wolseley engine had been discarded in favour of the new 100 h.p. *monosoupape* Gnôme, and steel had been substituted for wood to a great extent. So altered, this biplane was a very fine aeroplane indeed, and compared favourably with the Farmans, the acknowledged leaders of the class.

The latest Maurice Farman was none other than the famous "Shorthorn," on which most of the pilots of the Royal Flying Corps received their initial flying training during the first two and a half years of the War 1914–18. I shall always think kindly of this cumbrous old aeroplane, for I had my first flight in one at Shoreham in 1916. It was very similar to the original "Longhorn" Maurice Farman, except that the enormous framework which carried the front elevator had been removed and the boxkite *empennage* had been reduced to a simple tail plane and elevator, with a pair of small rudders superimposed. A good specimen would achieve a mile a minute in still air with an ordinary 70 h.p. Renault, and the stalling speed was some 32 m.p.h. The view from the *nacelle*, which projected forward into space, was well nigh perfect.

Grahame-White displayed the record-breaking "Charabancs,"

in addition to a neat two-seater pusher biplane fitted with a 100 h.p. *monosoupape* Gnôme, which drove a huge propeller through a chain and sprocket, giving a gear ratio of 14:23. In contrast to most machines of this type the undercarriage was quite simple and no skids were employed. The tail plane, elevators, and stabilizing fin were carried on the top of the topmost tail boom, where they were practically outside the slipstream, and the whole *empennage* was dangerously close up to the main supporting surfaces. This machine was designed by Mr. J. D. North.

The surprise of the show was provided by Mr. A. V. Roe, the originator of the tractor type of aeroplane, who produced a pusher biplane which bore a remarkable resemblance to the Grahame-White machine described above. The position of the elevators may be criticized for the same reason, although Mr. Roe had not made the mistake of setting his tail too near to the wings. The undercarriage fitted to this machine was of the famous "hockey-stick," central skid pattern, as used on the model 504, and the engine was an 80 h.p. Gnôme.

(*v*) *The Tractor Biplanes*

Only one of the five tractor biplanes was of an established type. This was the two-seater Bristol, which was similar to that exhibited at the Paris Salon a few months previously, except that the bomb-rack had been removed.

The Vickers Company showed a new two-seater tractor biplane, designed for high speed reconnaissance and fitted with a 100 h.p. *monosoupape* Gnôme. This was an ugly looking machine, with a lifting tail plane, and its appearance did not inspire confidence. It was apparently untested.

The Eastbourne Aviation Co. exhibited another two-seater tractor biplane, fitted with an 80 h.p. Gnôme engine, which had an exceptionally clean fuselage and engine cowling. The undercarriage was also neat and well designed, and the tail unit followed modern practice. This otherwise excellent aeroplane was spoiled by the crude design of the wings, which were of very narrow chord and excessive camber. The speed range of the machine was given by the makers as 50–75 m.p.h., which was not very good.

The sensation of the show was the appearance of two fast single-seat tractor biplanes, similar to the Sopwith Tabloid, and of a type which was to be known as the Scout class.

One was a product of Mr. A. V. Roe, and was known as the Avro Scout. The fuselage, undercarriage, and tail unit followed the well-known 504 type on a reduced scale, but the wings were entirely unconventional. The planes themselves were flat on the under-surface, and cambered on the top, and were set in a wide horizontal V and at a slight dihedral angle. A single pair of interplane struts braced the main planes on either side of the centre section and these struts, which were set close together, were encased in fabric, so that each pair gave the appearance of a single very broad strut. A section of the trailing edge of each bottom wing near the root was pivoted in such a manner that it could be turned by the pilot until it stood vertically against the flight path and thus acted as an air brake. The engine was an 80 h.p. Gnôme, and lateral control was by ailerons on both upper and lower wings.

The *clou* of the show was the other single-seat Scout, which appeared on the Bristol stand. This delightful little aeroplane was closer to the Sopwith Tabloid design than the Avro Scout. Its span was only twenty-two feet, and its length nineteen feet nine inches. Its maximum speed with an 80 h.p. Gnôme was 94 m.p.h. and it weighed only 616 lbs. empty, and carried a useful load of 340 lbs. A curious wing section, designed by M. Coanda, was used, in which a sharp depression occurred in the camber of the underside. Lateral control was by double acting ailerons on both top and bottom wings. The machine stalled at 44 m.p.h., so that it could not be said to be so efficient as the Sopwith Tabloid, which carried two people at 92 m.p.h., and stalled at only 37 m.p.h. All the same, the Bristol Scout was a very fine aeroplane indeed, and a worthy rival of the famous Tabloid. It was a great pity that the latter was not exhibited at Olympia so that the two designs could be closely compared.

It was obvious that the example of Messrs. Sopwith and Sigrist had spurred the imagination of the other English designers, and it was extraordinarily satisfactory to see that, in the Tabloid and the Bristol Scouts, we had two machines, of a new type altogether, which could beat the all-round performance of any foreign aeroplane in the world. With the production of these two little aeroplanes Great Britain stood on the threshold of wresting the supremacy in aircraft design and construction from the French.

In the large pusher biplane class we had the Vickers, which was a worthy competitor of the Farmans and better made, and the record-breaking G.W. "Charabancs," whilst in the two-seater tractor biplane category we had the Avro 504, the Sopwith, the B.E., and the Bristol, any one of which could beat their French counterparts, although it is probable that there were several German machines of this type with better performance figures. As evidence of our definite superiority in this type of aircraft, I may quote the figures resulting from some tests of the latest Bristol two-seater tractor biplane, which were carried out near Paris before French Government officials by Mr. S. V. Sippe. The machine under test was a standard model fitted with a Le Rhone rotary engine of 80 h.p., and Mr. Sippe took it up to 3,280 feet in 7 mins. 35 secs., with a useful load on board of 715 lbs. With only 385 lbs. load the biplane reached the same height in 5 mins. 10 secs. In the speed tests a fast speed of 74·5 m.p.h.

was recorded and the stalling speed was only 35 m.p.h. These figures had not previously been approached in France, and the officials were so impressed that arrangements were made for a batch of Bristols to be built in the Breguêt works under government auspices. It must be remembered that both the Avro and the Sopwith actually had better performances than the Bristol.

When it came to monoplanes, the French still reigned supreme. But their Morane-Saulniers, Nieuports, Deperdussins, Bleriots, and Ponniers had to face the challenge of our new Scout biplanes and, except in the case of special racing craft, there was little doubt but that any one of the latter could outfly the French machines.

(*b*) THE ENGINES

If the position with regard to the aircraft was extraordinarily satisfactory, the same could not be said of the situation in the British aero engine industry. It will be noted that only two out of sixteen British aeroplanes exhibited were fitted with engines of English design. One was the G.W. "Charabancs," which was shown with a 100 h.p. Green, although its world's records had been captured by means of an Austro-Daimler motor, and the other was the Perry Beadle flying boat, whose makers admitted that the E.N.V. engine was not sufficiently powerful, and would have to be discarded. Six firms displayed engines designed and built in England. The Green Engine Co., Ltd. showed their well-known 65 and 120 h.p. models, which were the only tried and proven British aero engines in existence at that time.

The Sunbeam Company exhibited two large engines. One was an 8-cylinder Vee water-cooled model of 150 h.p., which was a development of that which had survived many strenuous hours flying in Mr. Jack Alcock's Maurice Farman. The other was a 12-cylinder model designed primarily for use in airships.

The Isaacson Company had developed a whole series of rotary and radial engines of various sizes and their 60 h.p. model had performed excellently in the Flanders biplane at Brooklands. They showed a very large double-banked rotary having eighteen cylinders, and rated at 200 h.p.

The Wolseley firm also produced a great number of different models, of which they displayed the 60–80 h.p. engine with the water-cooled exhaust valves, which had been seen at the previous year's show, and a large engine of 120 h.p. which was wholly water-cooled. Many of these Wolseley engines had been tried; and found wanting.

The most interesting exhibit, if we omit the Statax "wobble gear" freak design, was the new Argyll sleeve-valve motor which had been designed by M. Henri Perrot in collaboration with Mr. B. P. Burt. This was a very large 6-cylinder in line water-cooled engine of 120 h.p., which employed the sleeve-valve principle

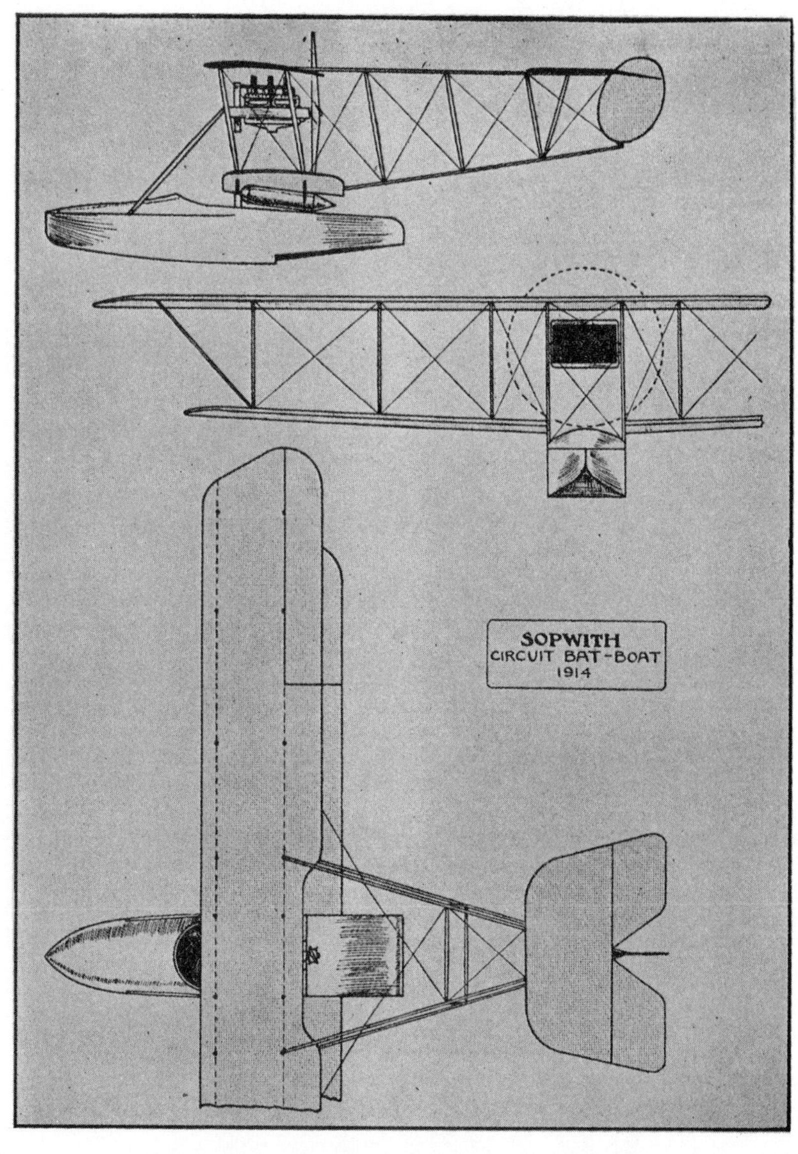

" *Flight* " *copyright*

6.—An enlarged version of the first British Flying Boat: the Sopwith Bat-Boat (200 h.p. Sunbeam) designed for the Circuit of Britain.

1914

"Flight" photo

31.—England's greatest pre-War pilot: Mr. B. C. Hucks.

Facing page 109

which had proved so successful in motor-car practice. The weight was 600 lbs., giving a weight/power ratio of 5 lbs. for one b.h.p.—which was extremely bad. It was clear that this engine was far too heavy to be of any practical use, but it was beautifully made, and of great academic interest to the student of engineering.

In addition to the above there were two foreign engines exhibited which were built under licence by British firms. The Beardmore Company showed the well-known Austro-Daimler 6-cylinder in line water-cooled motors of 120 and 90 h.p., which were the best aeroplane engines of their size in the world at that time. The Austin Motor Company displayed a water-cooled Vee 8-cylinder Curtiss engine of 100 h.p., which they had built for the Curtiss Company of America, and which it was proposed to instal in a Curtiss flying boat, which had been entered for the *Daily Mail* Circuit of Britain contest.

The A.B.C. engine built by Armstrong-Whitworth, Ltd., and the E.N.V. were not represented officially at Olympia.

To sum up the position of the British aero engine industry early in 1914, we may say that we had one moderately reliable but heavy engine in the Green, and two engines which showed considerable promise in the Sunbeam and the Isaacson. The rest were, for practical purposes, unworthy of serious consideration.

It was a humiliating situation.

France was represented at the show by the Gnôme, Renault, Salmson and Clement-Bayard engines, the most notable absentee being Le Rhone.

The Germans had made great headway in the development of the 6-cylinder in line water-cooled type, and displayed a series of magnificent models by Benz and Mercedes, which were typical of their native genius for sound solid engineering work. The last-named firm had just produced the first 6-cylinder in line inverted engine, designed to improve the view from the pilot's cockpit. This revolutionary model had already flown in a Rumpler Taube monoplane.

10. TWO BRITISH WORLD'S RECORDS BEATEN: AVIATION IN NEW ZEALAND

On March 17th, the French pilot Garaix beat one of the weight-lifting records set up by M. Louis Noel on the G.W. "Charabancs" by staying in the air with seven passengers on his Schmitt biplane (160 h.p. Gnôme) for forty-three minutes during an attempt on an altitude record, in which he attained a height of 1,650 metres (5,400 feet); a remarkable performance.

Garaix continued his experiments, and after capturing the world's height record for pilot and eight passengers, he took off on March 31st with nine passengers aboard, and succeeded in reaching an altitude of 1,580 metres (4,820 feet). This flight occupied fifty-nine minutes, so that he beat Louis Noel's other duration record by nearly forty minutes. As Garaix had declared that he was out to beat the height records only, the duration of his flights was not officially timed, and Great Britain was still credited with the "Charabancs" two duration records, although Garaix had beaten them both by a large margin.

Mr. J. J. Hammond, the well-known Bristol pilot who had acted as instructor at the Eastbourne school of flying, had returned to his birthplace in New Zealand, and was flying the Bleriot monoplane on which Mr. Gustav Hamel had flown to Cologne, and which had been presented to the New Zealand Government by the Imperial Air Fleet Committee. He was joined by Mr. J. W. H. Scotland, who had learned to fly during the summer of 1913, at Mr. Hall's school at Hendon. Mr. Scotland brought a Caudron biplane (45 h.p. Anzani) with him, and founded the New Zealand Aviation Co., Ltd., for the purpose of giving exhibition flights in the islands. Apart from Mr. A. W. Schaef, who was experimenting with a home-made monoplane, these were the only two pilots flying in New Zealand at that time. Unfortunately, Mr. Scotland crashed his Caudron on his second flight, through trying to fly it out of an unsuitable field, and although the pilot emerged unhurt, the lack of spare parts put this enterprise out of action for a considerable time.

11. A SERGEANT PILOT KILLED: LOOPING AT BROOKLANDS

On April 8th, 1914, another pilot lost his life as a direct result of the senseless prejudice against the use of safety belts.

Sergt. E. N. Deane of the R.F.C. had been receiving instruction from Mr. Warren Merriam at the Brooklands school of the Bristol Company for about six weeks, and had made good progress. On the day in question he had been sent up in a Bristol "Boxkite" pusher biplane to fly for his certificate. He passed the figure-eight and landing tests in a satisfactory manner, and he then took off for the height test, which involved a climb to about 400 feet. Deane went up to 1,000 feet and then began a steep spiral glide. At about 400 feet he fell out and was killed.

On the Bristol "Boxkite" the pilot sat on the leading edge of the bottom wing, and was quite exposed. This particular machine was not fitted with a belt of any kind. Could stupidity be carried further than that?

Once more the accidents committee of the R.Ae.C. published a strong recommendation for the general adoption of safety-belts, but many pilots continued to ignore this obvious precaution.

Sergt. Deane was the second British pilot to meet his death whilst actually engaged in flying through the tests for his certificate.

The first of the Brooklands pilots to attempt aerobatics was Mr. Robert Barnwell, who borrowed a Sopwith Tabloid (80 h.p.

Gnôme) from Mr. Sopwith and climbed up to 4,000 feet on April 12th. His first attempt was unsuccessful, as the machine fell sideways off the top of the loop, completed a half-roll, and thus regained normal flight. Mr. Barnwell was somewhat confused as to what had happened to him and landed to inquire. Finding that Mr. Sopwith and the other spectators were unable to enlighten him, he took off again to continue his experiments, and this time he made three perfect loops at 3,000 feet.

12. GREAT BRITAIN'S VICTORY IN THE SECOND SCHNEIDER TROPHY CONTEST

On April 20th the second contest for the Schneider Trophy was flown over twenty-eight laps of a quadrilateral course, marked out on the sea between Monaco and Cap Martin. This course, which measured ten kilometres to the lap, was a very difficult one, for the turn off Cap Martin was a hairpin of some 165°, and the two corners opposite the harbour at Monaco were only 260 yards apart. The longest straight section was about two and three-quarter miles.

The Schneider Trophy was already beginning to excite world-wide interest and entries had been received from France, Great Britain, Germany, Switzerland, and the U.S.A.

The British representatives were Lord Carbery, who had entered a Morane-Saulnier monoplane, and a special Sopwith Tabloid which had been converted into a single-seater and fitted with floats and one of the latest 9-cylinder *monosoupape* Gnôme rotary engines of 100 h.p. The Tabloid, which represented the last word in British aeroplane design and construction, was tuned by Mr. Victor Mahl and flown by Mr. Howard Pixton. Mr. T. O. M. Sopwith travelled to Monaco, and supervised the arrangements in person.

The principal opposition was expected to come from France, represented by two Nieuport monoplanes flown by MM. Espanet and Levasseur, and a Morane-Saulnier in charge of M. Roland Garros.

The German pilot, Herr Stoeffler, crashed his machine on the day before the race, as did Lord Carbery. The latter immediately made arrangements to borrow a Deperdussin monoplane (160 h.p. Gnôme) from M. Janoir.

The American entries were Mr. C. T. Weymann (Nieuport) and Mr. Thaw (Deperdussin), and Switzerland was represented by M. Burri on a Franco-British flying boat, which was a development of the well-known Donnet-Levêque type.

The rules called for each competitor to make a preliminary lap of the course, during which he had to alight twice at specified points before taking off for the last time and crossing the starting line in flight. Each entrant was at liberty to start at any time between 8 a.m. and sunset, the machines being timed over the course individually, and the one taking the shortest time being the winner.

There was an easterly wind of some 30 m.p.h. blowing when the starting bombs were discharged at 8 a.m., but the water was fairly calm. The French team wasted no time and sent the two Nieuport monoplanes out as soon as the signal was given, Roland Garros holding the fast Morane-Saulnier in reserve for an attempt later in the day, should the Nieuports be beaten. Pixton and Burri soon joined them in the air, and it became possible to calculate the probable result.

In spite of the fact that he had never flown a Deperdussin before, Lord Carbery started soon after Burri, but he had trouble with the high-tension wires on the 160 h.p. Gnôme and was forced to abandon his sporting effort after covering one lap.

Pixton went away at an astonishing speed and at fifty kilometres the times were as follows :—1, Pixton (Sopwith), 20 mins. 57 secs; 88·9 m.p.h.) ; 2, Espanet (Nieuport) 28 mins. 13 secs. (65·8 m.p.h.); 3, Burri (Franco-British) 29 mins. 17 secs. (63·5 m.p.h.); 4, Levasseur (Nieuport), 30 mins. 5 secs. (62 m.p.h.) Thus the British machine had already established a clear lead of 7 mins. 16 secs., and was lapping 23 m.p.h. faster than the leader of the French team.

The Tabloid continued to travel steadily and Pixton's cornering was above reproach as he drew further and further away from his pursuers, until at 150 kilometres the position was as follows :—1, Pixton, 1 hr. 2 mins. 31 secs. (89·4 m.p.h.) ; 2, Espanet, 1 hr. 16 mins. 47 secs. (68·9 m.p.h.) ; 3, Levasseur, 1 hr. 22 mins. 56 secs. (67 m.p.h.) ; 4, Burri, 1 hr. 27 mins. 36⅖ secs. (64 m.p.h.) It will be seen that Pixton was flying with splendid regularity, as there was but a fraction of a m.p.h. difference in his speed over the first fifty kilometres and over the first 150 kilometres, and he now led by a clear margin of 14 mins. 16 secs. The two Frenchmen had opened right out in a hopeless effort to catch the little Tabloid, and Espanet had increased his speed by 3 m.p.h., and Levasseur, who had caught and passed the Swiss entry, by 5 m.p.h.

It was clear that, if the Sopwith could keep in the air, a British victory was a certainty.

At 160 kilometres the engine of Espanet's Nieuport cracked up, and he retired, and his team mate, Levasseur, was also forced down at the end of his seventeenth lap. Pixton continued to tear round the course and the position at 200 kilometres, was: 1, Pixton, 1 hr. 24 mins., 4 secs. (88·5 m.p.h.) ; 2, Burri, 1 hr. 57 mins. 39 secs. (60 m.p.h.) Great Britain now led by 33 mins. 35 secs., and the Swiss flying boat was slowing down.

On his twenty-third lap, Burri ran short of fuel, and had to alight to replenish. Whilst this was being done, Pixton crossed the finishing line, having covered 280 kilometres in 2 hrs. 13⅖ secs.,

"Flight" photo

32.—BRITAIN'S BEST: A SOPWITH TABLOID SCOUT TAKING OFF FROM BROOKLANDS

"Flight" photo

33.—Already obsolescent: Four B.E. Tractor Biplanes and a Maurice Farman Longhorn Pusher Biplane (70 h.p. Renaults) of the R.F.C.

at an average speed of 85·5 m.p.h. Burri took off again and completed the course after refuelling, his time being 3 hrs. 24 mins. 12 secs., and his average speed 51 m.p.h.

After crossing the finishing line Pixton opened up his 100 h.p. Gnôme to its fullest extent and drove the Tabloid "all-out" for two extra laps, so that his time could be recorded over 300 kilometres. The little Sopwith responded magnificently, and clocked 2 hrs. 9 mins. 10 secs. for the whole distance, which gives a speed of no less than 92 m.p.h.; a world's record for seaplanes.

It was not yet half-past ten in the morning, and there was nothing in the rules to prevent Roland Garros, or the Americans, Weymann and Thaw, from taking off in an attempt to better Pixton's time. No such attempt was made. The foreign competitors simply stood about, stupified by the Tabloid's wonderful performance. Levasseur, it is true, restarted during the afternoon with the idea of obtaining third place, but he abandoned with engine trouble after covering nine more laps.

It is difficult to convey the atmosphere of astonishment created by Pixton's flight. Thitherto the English pilots had been regarded with mild amusement whenever they had dared to compete with the French experts, and the English aircraft were frankly ridiculed in France. The French had been taken by surprise, but it was not as if some English machine had snatched a lucky victory through the misfortunes of the other competitors. On the contrary, it was abundantly clear that the combination of Howard Pixton and the Sopwith Tabloid was immeasurably superior to any other combination of pilot and seaplane on the continent of Europe. For the first time a British aeroplane handled by a British pilot had completely outflown the pick of the world's best. It was a staggering blow at the French national pride and a portent of the dawning ascendancy of the British aircraft industry. It was the most important event which had ever happened in the history of British aviation.

An editorial on the subject in *Le Temps* newspaper may be translated as follows: "We know that our French representatives, Levasseur and Espanet, have, by bad luck, not been able to finish the course. These two excellent aviators, who piloted Nieuport monoplanes, were stopped by engine trouble, but in any case, their machines were not as fast as the Sopwith. As to Garros, who is not afraid of 280 kilometres, he doubtless preferred not to start, rather than put up a performance which, in his opinion, could not possibly beat that of the Englishman, Howard Pixton, who had covered, complying with all the regulations of the race, the 280 kilometres for the Schneider Cup, in 2 hrs. 13 secs. . . .

"This absolutely remarkable performance had, up to the present, never been accomplished on any hydro-aeroplane; that is why this English victory is particularly meritorious, all the more so because it was gained on a biplane specially constructed by the

Sopwith Company. We have had our part of the success because the machine was fitted with a 9-cylinder Gnôme *monosoupape* engine of 100 h.p., the name of which may be associated with the British victory, but that is no more than half a consolation."

That graceful acknowledgment of defeat was a fair testimony to the magnitude of the Sopwith Company's achievement.

13. A STRANGE ESCORT: TAKING MOTION PICTURES FROM A BLERIOT

On April 21st, H.M. the King left Dover in the royal yacht, *Victoria and Albert*, on a visit to Paris. The yacht was escorted out of Dover Harbour by a strangely mixed squadron of the Naval Wing, R.F.C., led by the commanding officer, Com. C. R. Samson, in a B.E.2 tractor biplane (70 h.p. Renault). The other machines consisted of the Bleriot monoplane (80 h.p. Le Rhone) which held the British altitude record, with Eng.-Lieut. Briggs at the helm, a Caudron biplane flown by Lieut. Osmond, a Sopwith three-seater tractor biplane flown by Sub.-Lieut. Littleton, an Avro tractor biplane in the hands of Sub.-Lieut. Pierse, a Short tractor biplane flown by Sub.-Lieut. Rainey, and an old Short pusher biplane (50 h.p. Gnôme) in charge of Pte. Edmonds of the R.M.L.I. This motley fleet flew from Eastchurch, and it was augmented over Dover by a seaplane from the Isle of Grain, flown by Com. Seddon. It was a remarkable demonstration of the versatility of the Naval pilots.

This was the first occasion upon which a film company chartered an aeroplane for the purpose of obtaining news pictures of topical interest. Mr. B. C. Hucks was the pilot, and here is his own account of this interesting flight.

"On Sunday a landing ground at Calais was chosen, and a starting ground at Folkestone. The latter was a field at Capel, right on the top of the cliffs and about three miles from Folkestone. My machine arrived at Folkestone on Monday midday, and was conveyed by motor to the ground, and was erected and ready for flight by 5 p.m. I made a trial trip over the sea front at Folkestone about 6 o'clock the same evening, and found everything in order.

"On Tuesday morning, after a trial flight with the operator to get him used to his peculiar position—he faced towards the tail—I started off across the Channel at exactly 11 a.m., in brilliant sunshine and very little wind, exactly half an hour after the departure of the royal yacht from Dover.

"It took me some time to pick up the royal yacht as there was a considerable mist on the surface of the sea, but after about fifteen minutes flying, I noticed a haze of smoke and, as this was the only sign of activity in the neighbourhood, I made for it, and discovered my quarry.

"The French cruisers had already joined the escort, and to give my operator every possible facility I dived down to about

400 feet, and enabled him to get a fine picture of the mid-Channel scene. I circled the fleet completely on three occasions, being then right out of sight of land.

"As we were nearing Calais I hovered about and flew over Calais harbour at the precise moment of the entry of Their Majesties' yacht, when my photographer obtained what turned out to be a most magnificent and novel film.

"I then made direct for the Calais aerodrome, flying over the town at 800 feet. I landed at twelve noon, when I was presented with a bouquêt from the Mayor of Calais and also learned that I was the first English airman to land at Calais.

"The operator then extracted the exposed film which I fixed in the passenger seat of my machine, together with the bouquêt, and at 1.45 I started off for Hendon.

"I struck the English coast at the exact point of my departure, followed the railway line to Ashford, and on reaching the outskirts of London, I took last year's Aerial Derby course to Hendon, where I arrived at 2.35. I had covered the 125 miles in 110 mins. The journey over land was a very bumpy one, there being a terrible lot of *remous* owing to the extreme heat of the sun.

"On landing, the film was handed to a representative of the Warwick Bioscope Chronicle Film and rushed off to Charing Cross Road, where it was developed, a print made, and a complete record of the King's journey from London to Calais was shown at the *matinée* performance at the Coliseum at 5.20. Actually the film was delivered to the Coliseum at 4.45."

14. DESOUTTER'S LEG: A PARACHUTE DROP AT HENDON

The plucky young French pilot, Marcel Desoutter, had been badly hurt in a smash at Hendon during 1913, in which his Bleriot monoplane was wrecked. His injuries necessitated the amputation of one of his legs and the doctors prescribed the customary wooden limb as a substitute. Desoutter found this large baulk of timber altogether too heavy and clumsy for his liking and decided to redesign his own anatomy more in accord with the principles of modern aeronautical science.

The result was the first model of the world-famous Desoutter automatic leg. The whole construction, which consisted of a framework composed of a light aluminium alloy covered with leather, weighed only two pounds.

So many legless people wrote and asked him to build similar legs for them that he patented the invention, which, unfortunately, enjoyed a boom during the years 1914–18.

This leg was so satisfactory that the inventor was able to take up flying again, using the ordinary controls, and on May 3rd he flew one of Lord Edward Grosvenor's Bleriot monoplanes from Brooklands to Hendon.

Another pilot who was flying once more after being maimed in an accident was the Australian, Sydney Pickles, who was operating a Bleriot (Anzani) from Eastchurch as a private owner.

The first descent by parachute from an aeroplane to be carried out in England was made by Mr. W. Newell at Hendon on May 9th. A small rope seat was slung between the left hand undercarriage struts of the G.W. "Charabancs" and Mr. Newell took his place on this with his feet braced against the skid below. Mr. F. W. Gooden, who had himself made a number of jumps from balloons, sat on the leading edge of the lower wing just behind the parachutist. The machine was flown by Mr. R. H. Carr, with Mr. J. Lillywhite as passenger.

The parachute was twenty-six feet in diameter, and weighed forty pounds. Mr. Newell held it on his lap until the machine had climbed to 2,000 feet, when Mr. Gooden prised him off his perch with his foot. The parachute opened promptly, and Mr. Newell made a good landing in the centre of the aerodrome after a descent lasting 2 mins. 22 secs.

15. A FATAL COLLISION : NO. 2. SQUADRON'S TRAGIC JOURNEY

The first collision in the air between two aeroplanes of the R.F.C. occurred at Farnborough on May 12th, and resulted in the death of an officer and an air mechanic, and serious injuries to another officer.

Both the machines involved belonged to No. 5 Squadron R.F.C., and each was a standard Sopwith three-seater tractor biplane (80 h.p. Gnôme). Lieut. C. W. Wilson took off alone in one of the Sopwiths at about 4 p.m., with the object of flying to Brooklands. Nearly an hour later, Capt. E. V. Anderson, who had not previously flown a Sopwith, although he was accustomed to flying tractor biplanes, went up in the other machine accompanied by Air Mechanic Carter, with a view to getting used to the new type.

Just after Capt. Anderson had taken off, and whilst he was still climbing, witnesses saw Lieut. Wilson's Sopwith returning from Brooklands, and gliding down from a height of about 2,000 feet. The two machines collided and fell out of control quite near to one another. Capt. Anderson and Air Mechanic Carter were killed instantaneously, but Lieut. Wilson had a miraculous escape, and was able to extricate himself unaided from the wreckage of his machine. He suffered extensive bruises and a broken jaw.

It is impossible to apportion the blame for this accident between the two pilots, although, of course, Lieut. Wilson was technically responsible, as being the pilot in charge of the higher of the two machines. It would seem probable that neither pilot saw the other at all until the moment of impact.

No. 2 Squadron was ordered to leave its station at Montrose

in order to take part in a general mobilization of the Military Wing, R.F.C., on Salisbury Plain.

This premier Squadron of the R.F.C. was now completely equipped with B.E. tractor biplanes (70 h.p. Renaults), and ten of these machines left for the South on May 11th, led by the commanding officer, Maj. C. J. Burke. The other pilots were Capts. G. W. P Dawes, F. F. Waldron, and Todd, and Lieuts. Martyn, Corballis, Empson, Rodwell, Dawes, and Harvey-Kelly. The machines were followed by thirty-four transport vehicles with tools, spares, and the rest of the personnel of the Squadron, and it was arranged that the whole force should move down as a unit, i.e., that the aeroplanes should halt at short intervals, in order to allow the transport to catch up with them every night.

Maj. Burke had engine trouble at the start, but the other nine machines reached Edinburgh on the first day, and the commanding officer caught up with his squadron at Berwick the next evening. On the third day all ten aircraft reached Blyth, and on the fourth night the Squadron camped at West Hartlepool.

On May 15th the machines took off for York, and tragedy overtook them. They had flown only a short distance when they encountered a bank of thick fog. The effect was disastrous. Capt. F. F. Waldron and Lieut. Harvey-Kelly wrecked their B.E.'s in trying to get down, fortunately without injuring themselves or their mechanics. Another pilot damaged his undercarriage in a forced landing, and Lieut. J. Empson and Air Mechanic George Cudmore were killed instantaneously, when their biplane hit a hedge at high speed and crashed on to its back.

As soon as the fog cleared Maj. Burke concentrated the six surviving B.E.'s at Knavesmire near York, where a week was spent in repairing the undercarriage of the slightly damaged machine. Meanwhile Capt. F. F. Waldron, and Lieut. Harvey-Kelly were sent back to Montrose to fetch two spare B.E.2's to replace those which they had wrecked. These two officers rejoined the unit on May 19th, with their fresh mounts.

On May 22nd nine machines reached Lincoln, where they were delayed for one day by continuous heavy rain. Thence the Squadron proceeded to Northampton, and eventually arrived at Netheravon, by way of Oxford, on May 30th.

The journey of nearly 500 miles had lasted twenty days and had cost the lives of one officer and one airman, and the total loss of three aeroplanes. The scheme was originally conceived as a test of the Squadron's mechanical transport rather than of its pilots and machines, and, no doubt, a great deal of useful knowledge was acquired as to the mobility of a complete Squadron in the field.

The chief lesson to be learned, however, was the imperative necessity for an adequate meteorological service. It is almost incredible that this whole Squadron of ten machines was allowed to take off on that fateful morning in complete ignorance of the weather conditions along their route, and to plunge into a fog-bank within five miles of the field in which they had spent the night.

16. AN ENTERPRISING NEWCOMER: A GOOD "FIRST SOLO" STORY

Mr. T. Elder Hearn, well-known on the "boards" as "The Lazy Juggler," went to Buc to learn to fly, as he proposed to use an aeroplane for travelling from music hall to music hall on a tour of the provinces. He ordered a standard two-seater Bleriot monoplane, and began his tuition whilst the machine was being built. He took his *brevet* after only four hours instruction and, finding that his new machine was not ready for him, he decided to improve his technique with a little aerobatic practice. M. Bleriot lent him one of his specially strengthened looping monoplanes, and Mr. Hearn promptly took off and made four loops!

A day or two later this spirited pupil took delivery of his own new machine and set off for England without more ado, although there was a gale blowing. After bumping and boring his way into the wind for two hours forty minutes, and passing through several rainstorms, he landed at Amiens to wait for better weather. It was still blowing hard on the following day, but at 3 p.m. he took off again and flew to Folkestone, via Boulogne. It was so rough that he took more than an hour to cross the Channel. After resting for thirty minutes at Folkestone he left for Hendon, but the headwind slowed him so much that he ran out of oil and had to land at Gillingham, where he bought a stock of castor oil from a chemist and refuelled.

It was too dark to continue that day, but on the following morning he took off at 6.30 a.m. This time there was a ground mist to make things difficult, and he lost himself and eventually landed on Hounslow Heath, where he buckled a wheel.

Three days later the machine was repaired, and Mr. Hearn took off from Hounslow and flew to Wolverhampton. Here he refuelled and left again the same afternoon for Liverpool, where he arrived safely after putting up a most gallant performance.

Prior to tackling this long and difficult cross-country journey of about 500 miles Mr. Hearn had flown less than ten hours alone!

A very good story, for the truth of which I cannot vouch, was going the rounds at this time. It concerned an absent-minded pupil at Brooklands, who was dispatched on his first solo flight on one of those strange old "Boxkite" biplanes, all the control wires of which were fully exposed. It was one of those aeroplanes which were so festooned with wires and cables that the accepted method of checking their rigging was to insert a small bird into the space between the wings and await developments. If the bird succeeded in flying out, it was a sign that a wire was missing somewhere!

It appears that this pupil started off in fear and trepidation towards the River Wey, which flows across the eastern end of the aerodrome. He succeeded in yanking the biplane off the ground about three inches from the edge of the river bank, and was then faced with the test hill, which he had no chance of surmounting.

He decided to turn to the left, and proceeded to rudder sharply in that direction. Unfortunately he forgot to apply any bank, and the old machine began to skid outwards. Just before she stalled the pilot remembered that there was something else he ought to do and, looking about him, he caught sight of the sagging aileron cables.

Letting go of his control lever, he leaned over the side, caught hold of one of the cables and proceeded to haul it in, hand over hand, as though it was the main sheet of a sailing boat !

The machine responded promptly to this unusual treatment, and banked round in splendid style. After he had missed the hill the pupil let go the slack on the cable, and the old biplane straightened itself up.

Presently he found himself approaching the dreaded sewage farm at the other side of the aerodrome, so he repeated the manœuvre as before. As soon as he was facing the landing area again he let go of everything, switched off the engine, and the "Boxkite" sat down quite gracefully of its own accord !

17. GREAT FLIGHT BY NAVAL PILOT: MR. ROWLAND DING AND THE HANDLEY-PAGE

The Admiralty had acquired a specimen of the magnificent D.F.W. two-seater tractor biplane (100 h.p. Mercedes 6-cylinder in line water-cooled engine), which had been designed by Mr. Cecil Kny, and was built at Leipzig. This machine, which was constructed entirely of steel, except for the airscrew and the fabric covering, had a remarkable performance, as its top speed was 78·4 m.p.h., and it climbed to 3,500 feet in four minutes with pilot, passenger, and fuel for five and a half hours.

Lieut. C. H. Collet was given charge of the new machine and, after a few preliminary flights in order to accustom himself to the controls, he took it to the air station at Gosport and prepared to make a long-distance journey. Unfortunately, he chose a day on which a strong north-easterly wind was blowing, so that, as he was bound to fly north, he stood no chance of beating the record for a point-to-point flight.

The biplane took off at 7.30 a.m., on May 13th, with a useful load of 1,400 lbs, including 125 gallons of petrol, and Lieut. Collet fought his way against the wind for seven and a half hours, landing eventually at a point between Hull and Grimsby, at three o'clock in the afternoon.

The American pilot, Mr. G. W. Beatty, had established a new school of flying at Hendon, where Mons. E. Baumann, the Swiss

Caudron pilot, instructed on Wright biplanes (50 h.p. Gyros) equipped with dual controls. One of their first pupils was Mr. Rowland Ding, who showed great natural aptitude for flying, and passed his tests for his aviator's certificate on April 28th.

Mr. Handley-Page was quick to recognize this newcomer's outstanding ability and he actually nominated him as his pilot for the Aerial Derby, which was due to be flown off on May 23rd.

During some preliminary trials Mr. Ding showed that he could handle the Handley-Page biplane as easily as he could the Wright, and on May 21st he set off on his first cross-country flight.

He took off from Hendon at 7.40 a.m. with Princess Ludwig of Lowenstein-Wertheim in the passenger's seat, and flew to Eastbourne in sixty-five minutes. There was fog over the Channel, so Mr. Ding waited all the morning for conditions to improve, and it was not until 3.30 p.m. that he left Eastbourne, flew along the coast to Dover, crossed the Channel in fifteen minutes, and landed at Calais at 4.20 p.m., having made a very fast passage.

Mr. Ding stayed the night at Calais and his passenger proceeded to Paris by train. At 8 a.m. on the following morning the young pilot set off alone to fly back to England. He had a nasty moment when his 100 h.p. Anzani engine almost stopped in mid-Channel, but it picked up again whilst he was preparing to land on the water, and he continued to Staplehurst in Kent, where he refuelled. Eventually he arrived safely at Hendon.

Four days later Mr. Rowland Ding made another fine cross-country flight, from Hendon to Bath, via Southampton and Salisbury Plain. All these long and difficult journeys were carried out within four weeks of passing his tests as a pilot.

18. THE LOSS OF GUSTAV HAMEL

On Saturday, May 23rd, British aviation suffered an irreparable loss through the death of Gustav Hamel.

It was Aerial Derby day, and Mr. Hamel had travelled to Paris on the previous evening in order to fetch the new racing Morane-Saulnier monoplane (80 h.p. *monosoupape* Gnôme), which he was to fly in the race on the following afternoon.

He found the machine ready for him, although he was warned that the engine had been giving a certain amount of trouble, and he took off from Villacoublay at 4.40 a.m., so as to arrive in plenty of time to make any adjustments which might be necessary before the race.

At 5.22 a.m. he landed at the Caudron aerodrome at Crotoy, where he had breakfast. At 8.30 he left for the Bleriot landing ground at Hardelot, and he arrived there safely half an hour later. He refuelled the machine and took off for Hendon at 12.15 p.m.

That was the last that was seen or heard of this very gallant pilot. No doubt his engine failed in mid-Channel, when he was out of sight of land or shipping, and he was drowned.

The Admiralty sent out a flotilla of destroyers which scoured the Straits of Dover for two days and nights, but failed to find any trace of the machine.

Gustav Hamel was the son of a well-known English surgeon. He learned to fly in France on a Morane-Saulnier monoplane, and was granted his French *brevet* on February 3rd, 1911. He then returned to England and took his R.Ae.C. aviator's certificate on a Bleriot monoplane, eleven days later.

He had made many flights across the Channel, his most notable achievement being the first non-stop journey by air from England to Germany, in April 1913.

He was not only a cross-country pilot of great experience but also a most successful racing pilot. He was placed second in the first Aerial Derby in 1912, and he won the race in the following year. He made fastest time of the day under very difficult conditions in the London–Brighton–London race on November 8th, 1913, when only four competitors finished out of nine starters.

Hamel was the second British pilot to attempt aerobatics, and although he never acquired the exquisite skill in this branch of flying which was attained by Mr. B. C. Hucks, he was, nevertheless, a daring and competent stunt pilot, and three times he had the honour of flying for H.M. the King.

Dr. Hamel received the following letter of sympathy dated from Buckingham Palace, May 27th, 1914 :

" DEAR SIR,

" The King and Queen, fearing that the worst must now be realized as to the fate of your son, desire me to assure you how deeply they feel for you in your sudden and grievous sorrow. Their Majesties knew your son personally. They had seen him fly on two occasions at Windsor this year, and were struck by the skill, courage, and mastery with which he controlled the aeroplane, no less than by his modest and unassuming bearing. In offering you their heartfelt sympathy Their Majesties recognize that in this young, useful life the country loses its most accomplished and experienced aviator. Believe me, dear Sir, yours very truly,

Stamfordham."

When it was reluctantly decided to suspend the search for his body, the Admiralty issued a *communiqué* which contained the following remarks : " His qualities of daring, skill, resource, and modesty merited the respect of those who pursue the profession of arms ; and his loss, if this must be accepted, is received with deep regret by the officers and men of the Naval Wing of the Royal Flying Corps."

Such an epitaph is seldom accorded by a Military Department of State to a mere civilian, and it emphasizes the great respect and admiration with which Gustav Hamel was regarded by the whole nation.

One of Great Britain's national heroes had fallen.

19. PREPARATIONS FOR FLYING THE ATLANTIC

Had it not been for this calamity it is probable that Gustav Hamel would have made the first attempt to fly across the Atlantic Ocean from Newfoundland to Ireland. Mr. Mackay Edgar had put up the capital to finance the attempt, and Messrs. Martin and Handasyde had almost completed the construction of a large monoplane of sixty-five feet span, which had been specially designed for the purpose. This machine was fitted with a Sunbeam engine of 215 h.p. and equipped with a telescopic mast, which could be raised for signalling purposes in the event of a forced descent on the water.

Another British aspirant for the *Daily Mail* prize of £10,000, which had been offered during the previous year to the pilot of the first aeroplane to make the crossing, was Lieut. J. C. Porte, R.N. He had been chosen by Mr. Glenn Curtiss as one of two pilots for his long-range flying boat, then under construction at Hammondsport, N.Y. This machine, which was fitted with two Curtiss O.X. engines of 100 h.p. each, had a span of seventy-two feet, and was designed to carry 300 gallons of petrol, 25 gallons of oil, and a crew of two.

20. THE THIRD AERIAL DERBY

Everyone had been looking forward eagerly to the Aerial Derby, as it was anticipated that the Sopwith, Bristol, and Avro Scouts would race against each other for the first time, and that the public would have an opportunity of discovering which of these new machines was really the fastest.

A Sopwith Tabloid and a Bristol Scout had already met in a handicap race at Brooklands, when the Sopwith beat its rival by a small margin, but the Avro was an unknown quantity.

Apparently Mr. A. V. Roe was not entirely satisfied with it, for he abandoned the swept-back wings, which were its most unusual feature, and substituted a more normal *cellule* derived from his type 504. In order to increase the speed still further, the "hockey-stick" undercarriage was removed, and a very light rigid framework carrying two unsprung wheels, was substituted for it.

Mr. F. P. Raynham tried out the modified machine at Brooklands on the eve of the race, but the new undercarriage proved unequal to its task and collapsed, causing such extensive damage that it was impossible for the Scout to compete on the following day.

Conditions were so bad on the day of Hamel's death that the race had been postponed, for a fortnight, until June 6th. As it happened, the authorities were faced with equally bad conditions on the second occasion, and they would have been quite justified in authorizing a further postponement. Unfortunately, the presence of a large crowd at Hendon, coupled with a natural anxiety to avoid giving any more trouble to the officials and competitors, led them to allow the race to be started.

The visibility was so bad as to render it thoroughly dangerous for the pilots, and the Bristol Scout, which was to have been flown by Mr. S. V. Sippe, was not allowed to leave Brooklands. The Martinsyde machines also stayed in their hangar, as their entrants felt certain that the race would be postponed once more.

Twenty-one machines had been entered, but under these conditions only eleven of them started. The course was the same as that used in 1913, and measured ninety-four and a half miles round.

The competitors were sent off at intervals of one minute in the following order :—

1.	Filip Bjorkland (Sweden)	Bleriot monoplane	50 h.p. Gnôme
2.	Wm. Birchenough ...	Maurice Farman pusher biplane	70 h.p. Renault
3.	R. H. Carr	Henry Farman pusher biplane	80 h.p. Gnôme
4.	P. Verrier (French) ...	Henry Farman pusher biplane	80 h.p. Gnôme
5.	L. A. Strange	Bleriot monoplane	80 h.p. Gnôme
6.	J. Alcock	Maurice Farman pusher biplane	100 h.p. Sunbeam
7.	W. L. Brock (U.S.A.)	Morane-Saulnier monoplane	80 h.p. Le Rhone
8.	L. Noel (French) ...	Morane-Saulnier monoplane	80 h.p. Le Rhone
9.	Lord Carbery	Morane-Saulnier monoplane	80 h.p. Le Rhone
10.	H. Pixton	Sopwith Tabloid tractor biplane	80 h.p. Gnôme
11.	R. H. Barnwell ...	Sopwith Tabloid tractor biplane	100 h.p. Gnôme

The Bleriot flown by F. Bjorkland was the identical machine on which Mr. Rhodes-Moorhouse had secured third place in the first Aerial Derby in 1912, and Mr. Barnwell's Sopwith was the Schneider Trophy winner, which had been stripped of its floats, and fitted with a light racing undercarriage. The latter was easily the fastest aeroplane in the race, and was capable of well over 100 m.p.h.

Under good conditions there is no doubt but that Barnwell would have finished first, with Pixton second and one of the three Moranes third. But the thick mist turned the race into a grim farce.

The American pilot, Brock, who started seventh, led the competitors round the Kempton Park turn. He was followed by Carr (H. Farman), Pixton (Sopwith Tabloid), who had also overtaken six machines already, Verrier (H. Farman), and Barnwell (Sopwith Tabloid). Birchenough (M. Farman) gave up, and landed in Richmond Park.

On the second leg of the course the visibility, which was already poor, began to deteriorate still further, and at the Epsom turn the Swedish pilot landed his Bleriot on the racecourse, and Jack Alcock turned his Maurice Farman out of the race and went home to Brooklands. Brock, whose Morane-Saulnier was going magnificently, still led at this point, but the two Tabloids had already passed everyone else and were roaring along together close on his tail, Barnwell leading. Carr (H. Farman) and Noel and Carbery (Moranes), came by in a bunch, two minutes behind the leaders.

At West Thurrock the competitors ran into really thick fog and the observers had the greatest difficulty in distinguishing the machines as they flashed past. Some were heard but not seen, and only Brock (Morane-Saulnier) and Carr and Verrier (H. Farmans) were officially reported as having turned round the mark. Louis Strange and Lord Carbery went out on this leg of the course, the former landing his Bleriot at W. Wickham in Kent, with its petrol pressure pump out of action, and the latter putting his Morane down at Purfleet. The two Sopwith Tabloids were also brought out of the race on this section, as Pixton decided to fly back to Brooklands, but was forced to land near Croydon, whilst Barnwell, who had actually passed the West Thurrock turn unseen in the fog, gave up shortly afterwards, and arrived safely at Brooklands at 6.20 p.m.

These important withdrawals put quite a different complexion on the race, and the four survivors struggled across the river into better visibility, although the conditions were still quite unfit for racing.

At Epping, Brock (Morane) was still leading, with Noel (Morane) close behind and Carr and Verrier (H. Farmans), following.

Noel missed the last turn at Hertford, but Brock still kept the course, trailed by Carr and Verrier.

The first machine to finish was the Morane-Saulnier, flown by Louis Noel, who crossed the line 1 hr. 15 mins. 9 secs. after taking off, only to be disqualified for missing the turns at W. Thurrock and Hertford.

The other three machines finished, and the results were as follows :—

Pilot	*Aircraft*	*Engine*	*h.*	*m.*	*s.*	*m.p.h*
1. W. L. Brock (U.S.A.)	Morane-Saulnier	80 Le Rhone	1	18	54	71·9
2. R. H. Carr ...	Henry Farman	80 Gnôme	1	46	27	53·2
3. P. Verrier (French)	Henry Farman	80 Gnôme	1	49	50	51·6

Each of the three pilots who finished had every cause to congratulate himself on having accomplished a magnificent feat, and their rivals, who deemed it prudent to retire, suffered no disgrace through the exercise of such discretion.

For the American victor no praise can be too high. Carr and Verrier were flying very safe, slow machines, from which the view was exceptionally good, and which could be landed with great ease should the necessity arise. Brock, on the other hand, was flying a fast monoplane, from which the view was notoriously bad and which was exceedingly difficult to land, even under the most favourable conditions. His determination and dauntless courage in such circumstances marked him as one of the greatest racing pilots in the world.

Brock not only won the *Daily Mail* Gold Cup and 200 sovereigns, but he also won the "Shell Trophy," and a further prize of 100 sovereigns, awarded in connection with a sealed handicap.

Lord Carbery had an adventurous day, for, having landed at Purfleet and discovered where he was, he set out to fly back to Hendon, and was very soon lost again. After flying about for some time he saw a large open space, and proceeded to descend once more to ascertain his position.

A forced landing on a Morane-Saulnier was always a ticklish business, for they had a trick of swinging wildly as soon as they touched down and whipping over on to their backs. With infinite skill Lord Carbery eased his machine down onto the rough ground and, as soon as she had rolled to a standstill, he found himself surrounded by a huge crowd. He was on Hampstead Heath! A number of policemen arrived and took charge of the crowd, a courageous bystander was prevailed upon to swing the airscrew, and Lord Carbery took off and completed his journey to Hendon, where he performed three loops and some tail slides at 1,000 feet; no doubt as an expression of his relief at having come through such a race alive.

21. THE FIRST FATAL ACCIDENT TO A SEAPLANE: HAWKER'S RETURN

On June 4th, the first accident to a British seaplane involving the death of its pilot, took place at the Calshot Air Station of the Naval Wing, R.F.C. The machine was a Short twin-float biplane No. 128, and Lieut. T. S. Cresswell had made a series of flights with passengers immediately before he took off for the last time, accompanied by Com. A. Rice, R.N.

Mr. Gordon Bell and Lieut. Spencer Grey, R.N., were in a motor boat on Southampton Water, and the former gave evidence at the inquest to the effect that the machine took off right over their boat, and that the pilot waved to them as he passed. The seaplane was then at a height of between 200 and 250 feet, and it flew on steadily for about three-quarters of a mile. Mr. Gordon Bell looked away, and when he next saw the machine it was diving vertically at a height of 100 feet, and the outer portion of the left-hand pair of wings was beginning to fold up. The whole wing structure broke into pieces before it hit the water, and a black object, believed to be the body of Com. Rice, fell out just before she struck.

Another witness saw the biplane turn and then rise slightly, immediately before the dive commenced.

Lieut. Cresswell's body was found in the pilot's seat, but his passenger had disappeared. The elevator controls were examined and found intact.

The probable explanation of this mysterious affair is that the pilot stalled on a turn, and, when the machine began its dive, he became so perturbed at the steep attitude, and at the fact that he had little height to spare, that he jerked the control column violently backwards, thus applying full elevator. Such a sudden wrench might well have caused the wing structure to fail under the excessive stress imposed. After that, of course, the machine became quite uncontrollable.

Mr. H. G. Hawker, who had taken the original Sopwith Tabloid to Australia, where his flying had made a great impression, returned to England on June 6th. On the following day he resumed his duties as chief test pilot to the Sopwith Company, and treated the Brooklands *habitués* to a thrilling exhibition on the 100 h.p. Schneider Trophy winner. Mr. Victor Mahl, who had been the engineer responsible for tuning this machine at Monaco, had since learned to fly and was already proficient on the standard three-seater Sopwiths, although he had not yet tackled the formidable Tabloids. The firm was in a very strong position with H. G Hawker, Howard Pixton, and Victor Mahl, as their regular pilots, and with Robert Barnwell of Vickers, Ltd. always ready to fly for them if called upon to do so.

22. A RESHUFFLE OF PILOTS

Mr. Geoffrey de Havilland, designer and chief test pilot of the B.E., R.E., F.E., and S.E. tractor biplanes produced by the Royal Aircraft Factory at Farnborough, joined the Aircraft Co., Ltd. in June. Mr. Holt Thomas, managing director of the company, showed great foresight in engaging the services of one of the most experienced designers in the world. Mr. de Havilland had not only flown every one of his own types, most of which were variations on the original B.E. theme, but had also had numerous opportunities of examining and flying the products of private manufacturers, which were sent to Farnborough to pass through the Government acceptance tests. In this way he had acquired an immense knowledge of aircraft design and construction.

Messrs. Norman Spratt and E. T. Busk joined Mr. Ronald Kemp as test pilots at the Royal Aircraft Factory, and Mr. R. Skene had taken over the post of chief pilot to Messrs. Martin and Handasyde from Mr. Vincent Waterfall, who had accepted a commission in the R.F.C. Mr. Dukinfield Jones had left Mr.

Howard Flanders and was engaged by Mr. Cecil Kny to put the D.F.W. all steel tractor biplanes through their tests. These machines were now being built in England under licence. Mr. J. Clappen, a pupil of the Bleriot school at Hendon, was appointed assistant instructor at Mr. J. L. Hall's school there.

Mr. F. W. Gooden was now giving exhibitions of aerobatics on Mr. Hamel's Morane-Saulnier, and Mr. Marcus Manton, who had been acting as an assistant instructor at the Grahame-White school at Hendon, had allied himself with Mr. B. C. Hucks, and was touring the Midland Counties under the management of Mr. J. C. Savage. Mr. Manton had developed into a most polished stunt pilot, and there were few tricks in his famous partner's repertoire which he could not imitate. Both men used specially-strengthened Bleriot monoplanes for their exhibitions.

Mr. S. V. Sippe had replaced Mr. Busteed as chief test pilot for the Bristol machines. On June 8th, Lord Carbery asked his permission to fly a Bristol Scout, and became so enamoured of its beautiful flying qualities and its high speed that he instantly decided to buy one. His machine was duly delivered two days later.

23. THE FOUNDING OF THE R.N.A.S.

There had been another political scandal arising out of the debate on the Army Estimates for 1914. Once again Mr. Joynson Hicks had set himself to champion the cause of the pilots of the Military Wing, R.F.C., and had challenged the accuracy of Col. Seely's figures as to the number of machines available for their use.

It is unnecessary to go into the details of this affair, which followed closely upon the lines of the dispute in 1913, and served to demonstrate once more that there was something radically wrong with the administration of the Military Wing.

Matters were not improved by the discovery that the Government had departed from the principle clearly laid down when the Royal Aircraft Factory had been established, that it should not be permitted to compete with the private manufacturers, but would be confined to experimental and repair work. The disclosure that the staff at Farnborough had been doubled, and that nearly 1,000 men were employed upon the construction of a large batch of aeroplanes, caused a very natural feeling of alarm and a great deal of dissatisfaction in the industry.

Early in April Col. Seely had resigned his post as Secretary of State for War, and was succeeded by the Prime Minister, Mr. Asquith.

Flight, in a valedictory editorial, in which it was pointed out that Ministers often had to take the blame for the sins of others, summed up the position in the following terms: "In the matter of aviation, however, we believe that Col. Seely really took a keen personal interest, and even if at times he found it expedient to enunciate statements which did not always coincide with the facts, we, nevertheless, credit him at heart with the sincere desire to set our aerial defences on a satisfactory basis."

The Military Wing of the R.F.C. had developed rapidly throughout the summer, either as a result of Col. Seely's efforts in the past, or of those of his distinguished successor, or through the organizing ability of Sir David Henderson, who was then in charge of the aviation department of the War Office.

At the concentration camp at Netheravon in June there were present upwards of 700 officers and men of the Headquarters Flight, Aircraft Park and Nos. 2, 3, 4, 5, and 6 Squadrons of the Military Wing, R.F.C.

The first four of these Squadrons were fairly completely equipped with B E., Maurice and Henry Farman, and Avro biplanes, and there was also a limited number of Sopwith tractor biplanes and Bleriot monoplanes ; but No. 6 Squadron was neither fully equipped nor up to strength.

The airship equipment and the balloons had been passed over to the Naval Wing at the end of March and No. 1 (Airship) Squadron of the Military Wing was in process of conversion into an aeroplane Squadron, whilst No. 7 Squadron was in course of formation at Farnborough.

The position was, indeed, much more satisfactory.

Whilst Col. F. H. Sykes and the officers of the Military Wing had been welding their Corps together, despite the political upheavals, the Naval Wing of the R.F.C., unhampered by the festoons of red tape in which their Military colleagues were hopelessly entangled, continued to forge ahead with astonishing rapidity.

Mr. Winston Churchill had given the officers a free hand to experiment more or less as they thought best, with the result that real progress had been made, and the pilots had collected a mass of information about all sorts of different types of aeroplanes.

The policies of those directing the two branches of the Corps were definitely antagonistic. The War Office lent a ready ear to the theorists and the scientific experts, especially those at the Royal Aircraft Factory, and was all in favour of standardization. The Admiralty adopted the sounder principle of listening to what the pilots said, and giving the pilots what they wanted, whilst at the same time experimenting freely with any aeroplane which appeared to have possibilities, whatever its source of origin, and whether the civil servants at Farnborough approved of it in theory or not.

The R.F.C. was split in twain at the end of June 1914, when the Admiralty announced the formation of the Royal Naval Air Service, consisting of the Air Department (Admiralty), the Central Air Office, the Royal Naval Flying School, and the Royal Naval Air Stations.

All seaplanes, aeroplanes, and airships which might from time to

"Flight" photo

34.—Supplying the thrills: A Morane-Saulnier (bottom) and a Bleriot racing round the pylons at Hendon

"Flight" photo

35.—A CONTRAST TO THE LAST PICTURE: A B.E. (70 H.P. RENAULT) FLYING PEACEFULLY ABOVE THE ROLLING GRASSLANDS OF SALISBURY PLAIN.

time be employed for Naval purposes were to belong to the R.N.A.S.

Thenceforth the Central Flying School was to be administered by the War Office alone, and all officers of the R.N.A.S. were to be Naval officers, and to serve a term every year in a ship of war at sea; although the Admiralty prudently pointed out that flying officers would never be permitted actually to take charge of the ship.

Capt. Murray F. Sueter, C.B., became the first Director of the Air Department of the Admiralty, and the names and ranks, in order of seniority, of the original flying officers of the R.N.A.S. were as follows :—

Wing Commanders.—O. Schwann, E. A. D. Masterman, F. R. Scarlett, E. M. Maitland, N. F. Usborne, and C. R. Samson.

Squadron Commanders.—F. M. L. Boothby, E. L. Gerrard, R. Gregory, A. M. Longmore, R. Gordon, C. M. Waterlow, H. L. Woodcock, J. W. Seddon, R. H. Clark-Hall, G. W. S. Aldwell, C. R. J. Randall, Spenser D. A. Grey, C. J. L'Estrange-Malone, P. A. Shepherd, R. B. Davies, E. F. Briggs, I. T. Courtney, C. E. Risk, and C. L. Courtney.

Flight Commanders.—C. E. Rathbone, R. Pigot, D. A. Oliver, W. R. Crocker, T. G. Hetherington, J. N. Fletcher, Hon. J. D. Boyle, J. D. Mackworth, W. P. de C. Ireland, J. L. Travers, J. T. Babington, and F. E. T. Hewlett.

In addition there were forty-seven Flight Lieutenants, four Acting Flight Lieutenants, and seven Probationary Flight Sub-Lieutenants.

The creation of such a formidable flying force as a separate unit, yielding no form of allegiance to the civil servants at Farnborough, was a source of much gratification to the private manufacturers, who had begun to fear, not without justification, that their budding business was to be stolen from them *in toto* by the Royal Aircraft Factory.

24. LONDON–MANCHESTER RACE

On June 20th an important cross-country handicap race was flown from Hendon to Manchester and back. The competitors had to land in a control at Birmingham on both outward and homeward journeys. There were eight starters as follows :—

Pilot	*Aircraft*	*Engine*	*Handicap* h.	m.	s.
1. W. Birchenough	Maurice Farman pusher biplane	70 h.p. Renault	2	50	32
2. J. Alcock ...	Maurice Farman pusher biplane	100 h.p. Sunbeam	2	14	38
3. L. A. Strange	Bleriot monoplane	80 h.p. Gnôme	1	51	44
4. L. Noel (Fr.)	Morane-Saulnier monoplane	80 h.p. Gnôme	1	17	10
5. W. L. Brock (U.S.A.) ...	Morane-Saulnier monoplane	80 h.p. Gnôme	1	13	52
6. R. H. Carr ...	Morane-Saulnier monoplane	80 h.p. Gnôme	1	10	50
7. Lord Carbery	Bristol Scout	80 h.p. Le Rhone		24	42
8. H. G. Hawker	Sopwith Tabloid	100 h.p. Gnôme	Scratch		

Here was another opportunity to judge between the Bristol and Sopwith Scouts, the two most formidable aeroplanes in England at that time. In preliminary trials over a straight quarter of a mile Lord Carbery had clocked a mesne speed of over 100 m.p.h. for a series of three runs in opposite directions, and Hawker was expected to be several miles per hour faster in the Schneider Tabloid.

Unfortunately the weather and bad luck again conspired together to prevent the match being fought to a finish. Visibility was but half a mile at Hendon when the first competitor was sent off at 9.30 a.m. on his long journey of 325 miles.

Two of the pilots were soon in trouble, for Birchenough had to bring his M. Farman back after covering fifty miles, owing to a bad leak in the petrol tank, and Jack Alcock found a hole in the float of his carburettor just before he was due to start, and lost 49 mins. 46 secs. in repairing it.

Hawker roared away to time, and it was confidently anticipated that he would just be able to make up the 24 mins. 42 secs. which he had to allow to Carbery's Bristol. Once again his frail physique proved unequal to the strain of long-distance racing, and by the time he reached Coventry he was feeling ill. The visibility was very bad around the Birmingham control, and Hawker decided to give up. He therefore returned to Hendon and landed in a dazed condition, being quite unable to remember how he had found his way back.

Louis Strange brought his Bleriot into Birmingham in first place, 31 mins. 23 secs. ahead of Carr's Morane, which had overtaken Brock's similar machine, which had started 3 mins. 2 secs. before it. Alcock's M. Farman lay fourth in spite of the long delay at the start, but the Bristol Scout came tearing in less than one minute behind. Unfortunately, Lord Carbery, who was not yet accustomed to his new mount, misjudged his landing, broke up his undercarriage, and was compelled to retire from the race. Louis Noel damaged his Morane when he landed on Birmingham racecourse instead of the Castle Bromwich Playing Fields, where the control was situated, and he also was forced to withdraw.

Already half the starters were out of the race, but the four survivors carried on, and Louis Strange still led at Manchester, although Brock, who had repassed Carr's Morane, had cut his lead down to 12 mins. 18 secs. Carr lay third, 26½ mins. behind Brock, and Alcock kept plugging away in the Maurice Farman three-quarters of an hour behind the leader.

A number of civic dignitaries had gathered to welcome the competitors at Manchester, and as soon as Strange landed they dashed on to the field to greet him. The Lord Mayor, anxious to be the first to shake the pilot's hand, clambered on to the Bleriot, using the flying wires as a ladder. His weight proved too much for one of the fittings, and when Strange came to take off for the return journey it snapped, the wire flew into the airscrew, and the airscrew flew into pieces. Thus one more competitor retired.

It was now evident that Brock had the race well in hand, provided that he did not lose himself in the mist, or have trouble with his engine. He checked in at Birmingham, 1 hr. 10 mins. 58 secs. ahead of Carr, who had gone off his course near Manchester. Alcock's Maurice Farman brought up the rear, 23 mins. 54 secs. behind Carr's Morane.

Brock continued to maintain his long lead and the finishing order was as follows :—

Pilot.	*Aircraft.*	*Engine.*	*h.*	*m.*	*s.*	*m.p.h.*
1. W. L. Brock (U.S.A.)	Morane-Saulnier	[illegible] h.p. Gnôme	4	42	26	69
2. R. H. Carr ...	Morane-Saulnier	80 h.p. Gnôme	5	56	12	54
3. J. Alcock	M. Farman	100 h.p. Sunbeam	7	56	17	45

The American pilot thus confirmed the impression he had created by winning the Aerial Derby. There was no doubt but that he was one of the greatest racing pilots in Europe. He had flown a marvellously straight course, and only lost himself once, on the first stage, when he had to land about fourteen miles short of Birmingham to inquire the way. It was this stop which had enabled Carr to overtake him. Brock thus won the *Daily Mail* Gold Trophy, and two cash prizes of £400 and £250, presented by the Anglo-American Oil Company.

Carr was flying a fast monoplane in a big race for the first time, and he evidently found that the view out of his Morane was inferior to that afforded by the old "boxkites" to which he was accustomed. He lost himself repeatedly and flew a great deal further than he need have done. But in such conditions a certain amount of deviation from the straight and narrow racing track could be excused. It was creditable to finish at all.

If the 49 mins. 46 secs., which Alcock lost at the start be subtracted from his flying time it will be seen that he took 2 hrs. 24 mins. 5 secs. longer to complete the course than did the winner, and that his actual average speed was 50 m.p.h. It would have been higher than this if Alcock had not flown into the thick of a storm, which swept across the last stage after Brock and Carr had finished.

The Sunbeam engine in the Maurice Farman was the first British aero engine to finish the course in a big cross-country race in the whole history of aviation.

25. THE FIRST INVERTED SPIN : LOOPING IN FORMATION

Mr. H. G. Hawker had a very narrow escape from death at Brooklands at the end of June. He had been putting in a great deal of practice in stunt flying on the Schneider Trophy Tabloid, and had been engaged to give aerobatic exhibitions every Sunday throughout the summer.

On this occasion he attempted to loop without engine in an endeavour to see how slowly he could go over the top. Unfortunately, he failed to attain sufficient speed in the initial dive, and he stalled upside down on the summit of the loop at a height of just over 1,000 feet.

The Tabloid immediately went into an inverted spin, from which Hawker managed to recover but a few feet above the ground. The spectators thought he was dead, as the biplane was still in a steep dive when it disappeared from their view behind some tall trees. The machine hit one of the trees and hung in the branches for a moment or two before dropping gently to the ground. Hawker stepped out unhurt after one of the narrowest escapes in his hectic career ; and he was in the air again on the following day.

This is the first recorded instance of a British pilot recovering from an inverted spinning nose dive.

The spectacle of two aeroplanes performing aerobatics at the same time had been afforded by Mr. B. C. Hucks and Mr. Gustav Hamel at Hendon during the early spring. But in that case the pilots were flying independently, and at a considerable distance apart.

The first attempt at organized aerobatics in close formation was made by Messrs. B. C. Hucks and Marcus Manton during a combined demonstration at Glasgow. Each pilot had a single-seater Bleriot monoplane (50 h.p. Gnôme), and they looped simultaneously in line abreast. The manœuvre was perfectly timed, so that it looked as if the two machines, which were very close to each other, were linked by an invisible bar.

26. THE LAST GREAT RACE : LONDON–PARIS–LONDON

The last of the big long-distance cross-country races in which British pilots competed, prior to the outbreak of war, was the longest, most difficult and most dangerous contest held in 1914.

The course was from Hendon to Buc and back, but, in order to avoid the risks of crossing the city of London, and of making long sea passages, turning points were established at Harrow, Epsom, Folkestone, and Boulogne. Buc lies a few miles to the S.W. of Paris, a little south of Versailles, and the actual distance to be flown worked out at 508½ miles, which included nearly sixty miles of water.

It was an extremely formidable undertaking, but the romance associated with the first race between the British and French capital cities appealed to the pilots, and fourteen entries were received, representing Great Britain, France, Germany, the U.S.A., and Switzerland.

Unfortunately there was an epidemic of engine trouble amongst the racing machines immediately before the race and only half of the field left Hendon on July 11th.

Once again the weather was thick, and at 6.30 a.m., the hour fixed for the start, the visibility at ground level was hazy, and the clouds were down at 100 feet above the aerodrome. The authorities decided to postpone the start for an hour, and at the end of that time, although there was little improvement at Hendon, a report came in from Dover indicating good conditions in the Channel. Accordingly, the competitors were dispatched on their hazardous journey at five minute intervals in the following order :—

Pilot	*Aircraft*	*Engine*	*handicap* *h.*	*m.*
1. T. Elder Hearn ...	Bleriot monoplane	80 h.p. Gnôme	3	18
2. E. Renaux (French)	Maurice Farman pusher biplane	120 h.p. Renault	2	21
3. L. Noel (French) ...	Morane-Saulnier monoplane	80 h.p. Gnôme	1	43
4. W. L. Brock (U.S.A.)	Morane-Saulnier monoplane	80 h.p. Gnôme	1	36
5. R. H. Carr	Morane-Saulnier monoplane	80 h.p. Gnôme	1	30
6. R. Garros (French)	Morane-Saulnier monoplane	80 h.p. Gnôme		32
7. Lord Carbery ...	Bristol Scout biplane	80 h.p. Le Rhone	scratch	

The limit man, Hearn the juggler, had not cleared the aerodrome fence before his engine stopped. He managed to land safely, and soon had it running once more, but, after making a couple of circuits, he decided that it was not pulling well enough to continue, so he came down again and retired.

Meanwhile Renaux had taken off in the powerful Maurice Farman "Shorthorn," and disappeared in the mist. A few minutes later he returned and landed, saying that the conditions were impossible and that he could see nothing of the ground.

The three Morane-Saulniers flown by Noel, Brock, and Carr, all of which had been built under licence at Hendon by the Grahame-White Company, left promptly to schedule.

Two last-minute withdrawals caused a wait of fifteen minutes before the great French pilot, Roland Garros, roared away into the fog on his very fast Morane racer.

Lord Carbery had fitted his little Bristol Scout with special long-range tanks, and he stalled off in a terrifying manner with his heavy load of petrol and oil. Shortly after his departure Renaux decided to risk another start, and plunged into the mist again, whilst the crowd at Hendon settled down to wait, with some anxiety, for news of the racers.

Carr was the first to lose his way, and he landed at Kenton, about five miles from the start, and remained for an hour on the ground waiting for the visibility to improve. He then took off again and eventually descended at Dymchurch near Hythe, on the Kent coast, where he gave up.

Noel led at the Epsom turn, followed by Brock and Garros, the latter circling the Downs for some time before he picked up his bearings, and struck off on the course for Folkestone. Carbery passed at speed a few minutes later, and Renaux appeared shortly afterwards and landed to discover his whereabouts. He soon started off again on his wanderings, and was next reported from Gravesend, many miles off his course.

It was quite plain that the three surviving Moranes and the Bristol Scout were the only serious contestants, and the conditions pointed to the probability of another win for the American pilot, Brock, whose ability to navigate himself about in thick fogs had already been demonstrated in the Aerial Derby and the London–Manchester race.

The issue was simplified by the retirement of Louis Noel, who had a very narrow escape when the petrol pipe of his Morane-Saulnier broke, a few minutes after he had begun the passage of the Channel. He was just able to glide back over *terra firma* and land at Camber near Rye. It is probable that he would have been disqualified in any event for missing the Folkestone control.

It was now a straight fight between the French Morane pilot, the American in the surviving English-built Morane, and Lord Carbery's Bristol Scout.

Brock flew a dead-straight course as usual, and passed Boulogne fifteen minutes ahead of Garros, and thirty-nine minutes ahead of Carbery, on actual flying time. He had only a limited fuel capacity, and he was compelled to make an excursion to Hardelot in order to replenish his tanks.

He increased his lead, however, and arrived at the Paris aerodrome forty-six minutes ahead of Carbery, who had caught and passed the Frenchman between Boulogne and Buc. Garros arrived six minutes after the Bristol had landed, and immediately began to dismantle his engine. There was a two hours compulsory stop at at Buc and, although the French mechanics worked feverishly on the Morane, it was found necessary to fit a new magneto and airscrew, and Garros was twenty-five minutes late in starting on the return journey.

Meanwhile Brock had left strictly to schedule, as had Carbery, and there was a possibility that if the latter could keep the Bristol on a straight course he might make up the forty-six minutes he had lost on the outward journey, as his machine was at least 20 m.p.h. faster than Brock's.

Unfortunately it was not to be, for Brock, never deviating from the direct track, landed at Hardelot at 3 p.m., where he refuelled in twelve minutes, passed Folkestone at 3.45 p.m., Epsom at 4.28 p.m., swept round the Harrow turn, and landed at Hendon at 4.48 p.m., having averaged 71 m.p.h. for the whole distance !

Meanwhile Carbery had also landed at Hardelot, but he did not leave there until after Brock had arrived at Hendon. He took off at 4.55 p.m. and set out across the Channel in the wake of

Garros, who had caught him up, and was then about ten minutes ahead. In mid-Channel the Le Rhone engine suddenly stopped, and Lord Carbery was faced with a descent onto the water. Fortunately, the sea was calm and he managed to alight close to a tramp steamer. He eased the little biplane down so skilfully that he did not even get wet, and the steamer picked up both pilot and machine. A little later Lord Carbery was transferred to H.M.S. *St. Vincent*, whose officers put him ashore on Folkestone Pier, none the worse for his narrow escape.

Garros, who had brought his Morane across safely, passed Folkestone at 5.12 p.m., and Epsom at 5.55 p.m., and landed at Hendon at 6.20 p.m. Here he was informed that he had missed the Harrow turn, and he accordingly took off again immediately, and flew round it, his official time being 8 hrs. 28 mins. 47 secs.

The indefatigable Renaux was still wandering about in the M. Farman. He had arrived at Buc from Gravesend, at 2.49 p.m., three and a half hours behind Brock, but he had no thought of giving up, and left Paris on the return journey at 4.49 p.m. He was overtaken by darkness at Boulogne, where he landed at 7.45 p.m. ; but still he refused to be beaten. On Sunday morning he set out again and eventually he reached Hendon, at 12.25 p.m., 26 hrs. 55 mins. after the start. For this display of determination he was awarded the third prize of £50.

Brock had obtained first place on handicap, in addition to making fastest time, and he won £300 presented by the R.Ae.C., as well as the trophy and £500 presented by the International Correspondence Schools, who had organized the race. Garros won the second prize of £150.

The official results were as follow :—

Pilot	*Aircraft*	*Engine*	*Flying Time* *h.*	*m.*	*s.*	*m.p.h*
1. W. L. Brock (U.S.A.)	Morane-Saulnier	80 Gnôme	7	3	6	71·5
2. Roland Garros (Fr.)	Morane-Saulnier	80 Gnôme	8	28	47	58.8
3. E. Renaux (Fr.) ...	Maurice Farman	120 Renault	26	55	0	—

Mr. Brock had won £1,750 in three races within five weeks, and in each case he had outflown faster machines solely by reason of his masterly navigation and the intrepid determination with which he forced his way through the most adverse conditions. None could grudge him these rich rewards.

27. TAIL-SLIDING A BLERIOT

The pilots who conducted the early experiments in aerobatics often suffered alarming experiences. There was no one to teach them how to recover from any awkward position into which they might get themselves, and their knowledge of the best methods of saving their machines in such circumstances was necessarily acquired solely by trial and error. Incidents such as Hawker's inverted spin on the Tabloid served to emphasize the necessity for experimenting at a considerable height in order to allow of plenty of room for the recovery, but, on the other hand, the exhibition pilots recognized their obligation to their public to do their tricks at a low altitude so that everyone should have a good view.

A striking instance of the very real perils to which the early stunt pilots were subjected is afforded by the following account of an incident which occurred to Mr. Marcus Manton. I quote from the pilot's own story of what happened :—

" The experience I am going to describe took place at Newbold Revel Hall, near Rugby, on Saturday, July 18th. The atmosphere was full of *remous* even at 1,500 feet.

" I had already given a demonstration of vertical banking and steeplechasing, and I then went out to loop the loop.

" I climbed to nearly 2,000 feet to try to get out of the *remous*. After completing one loop successfully, I immediately started another vertical dive for another loop.

" This preliminary dive, by the way, is very necessary on a looping Bleriot, as it is a comparatively slow machine, and has only a 50 h.p. Gnôme.

" Gently pulling the control lever towards me, the nose began to rear up, and I climbed until the machine was standing on its tail.

" Then, to my consternation, the motor started to splutter, and the next instant had ceased to work.

" For a fraction of a second the monoplane remained poised in the air, absolutely stationary.

" Then it commenced to fall backwards, tail first. The noise it started to make is almost indescribable. The wires vibrated and screamed and whistled. Each wing seemed to flap and rattle like a flag in a stiff breeze--this, of course, being due to the wind getting hold of the thin and flexible trailing edge—the metal engine cowl joined in the chorus of noise in a lower key, and for a few seconds it certainly seemed as though the machine was going to break up.

" Having plenty of altitude, I did not make any desperate efforts to get the machine back to its proper position. I just let her do what she liked.

" Down, down, we came, the speed increasing with every second until the rattling and roaring were simply deafening.

" All this time I kept my control lever pulled back in the normal position for looping. This would mean that the elevator was up, and in the ordinary way should have had the effect of bringing up the tail and levelling out the machine.

" But the tail-slide continued, so I thought I would make a little experiment. I pushed the lever forward until it was in a neutral position. I was able to do this quite easily, although, theoretically, it would seem that the rush of air on to the elevator would cause such a pressure that it would need great strength to alter the elevator's position.

"To my great surprise the fall was immediately checked, then with a hefty kick the machine made a forward plunge, slightly sideways, and then nose-dived, after which I got level once again.

"I must say that tail-sliding on a Bleriot is most unpleasant. . . .

"These experiences have, however, given me even greater confidence in the Bleriot, for although the machine underwent a very severe straining, there were no signs of weakness when I came to examine it after landing."

When it is remembered that the Bleriot monoplane had no covering over the after part of the fuselage, and that there was nothing to obstruct the air from rushing upwards with great force beneath the pilot's seat into the cockpit during a tail-slide, it seems astonishing that these machines withstood the colossal strain Mr. Manton probably owed his life to the fact that he remained cool and avoided any violent movement of the controls; although it should be borne in mind that many of the early stunt pilots performed this unpleasant manœuvre deliberately as part of their shows.

28. A FATAL ACCIDENT AT GOSPORT: MR. COLLYNS PIZEY IN GREECE

On July 20th, two days after this thrilling incident at Rugby, Lieut. L. C. Hordern of No. 5 Squadron, R.F.C., was killed in an accident to a Henry Farman pusher biplane at Gosport.

The machine had been circling round the neighbourhood of the aerodrome for a few minutes when the engine stopped at a height of 800 feet. Apparently the pilot omitted to depress the nose sufficiently to maintain flying speed, and the great biplane stalled and went into a left-handed spin.

The machine completed three and a quarter turns of the spin before it hit the ground and was wrecked. Sergt. Campbell, who was sitting behind the pilot, was very lucky to escape with a broken leg.

It will be recalled that the Australian pilot, *Capitaine de Freigate* Collyns P. Pizey, had become chief instructor to the *Marine Royale Hellenique* at the Eleusis air station. Mr. Pizey found the base singularly ill-equipped, as there were no sheds or workshops, and the only machine available, a Sopwith pusher biplane (Anzani), which had been specially designed to the order of the Greek Government, had therefore to be kept out at moorings, exposed to the weather.

This machine was a fine large biplane with wings of equal span and a neat tail unit somewhat akin to that of the Vickers "Gun-bus." A roomy *nacelle* provided comfortable seats for pilot and pupil in tandem, and dual controls were fitted. The two Astra floats were arranged in such a way that the engine and propeller were well clear of the water.

Mr. Pizey had taken the precaution of securing the services of four British mechanics, Messrs. Lapray, Gaskell, Simms, and Radley, who were enlisted as warrant officers, and by whose efforts the Sopwith was kept in good condition in spite of the meagre facilities afforded.

Amongst Mr. Pizey's pupils was Rear-Admiral Mark E. F. Kerr, commanding a section of the Mediterranean Fleet of the Royal Navy in Greek waters, who took his R.Ae.C. certificate at Eleusis on July 14th.

29. A NARROW ESCAPE FOR ROWLAND DING

Mr. Rowland Ding had been touring the provinces throughout the summer, and had already covered more than 10,000 miles by air in the Handley-Page biplane, and had carried 200 passengers.

Following the example of Messrs. Hucks and Manton, he always flew to his engagements, and it was during one such journey that he had the very narrow escape from destruction, which is described in his own words below :—

" The most terrifying experience I have had since I have been flying, and really the most marvellous that any aviator could well have, occurred to me when flying from Bath to Harrogate.

" Setting out from Bath very early one morning, about five o'clock, and intending to fly straight through to Harrogate without a stop, I found the conditions practically perfect, with the sky beautifully clear, and not a cloud to be seen.

" Before very many miles had been covered, however, in the distance I saw a little fleecy cloud just making its appearance. It looked quite thin and very innocent indeed, and I thought the best way would be to get over the top of the cloud and continue on my way by the aid of the compass.

" Having risen over the top of what appeared to be the little cloud, I found that it got larger and larger, the ground being quite hidden from sight ; there was simply a beautiful level sea of fleecy white clouds underneath me. I felt quite happy, because the compass appeared to be doing its work, the machine was going well, and the engine running beautifully.

" Then the sea of white cloud began to rise gradually, when I naturally pulled up the nose of the aeroplane a little and climbed up what looked like the side of a big snowy mountain. After keeping on for some time, getting higher and higher, one of the plugs of the engine, probably owing to becoming fouled with oil, mis-fired.

" Thus having one cylinder cut off, the machine could not climb quite so rapidly, and as the surface of the cloud itself seemed suddenly to take a very steep ascent, this meant that I had either to come down below it or else continue on straight through the cloud. The extent of the latter being an unknown quantity, I thought the best thing would be to dive down until I was underneath it.

" Switching the engine off, I started diving down from a height of between 3,000 and 4,000 feet, the cloud getting thicker and thicker until I could not see even the aeroplane itself. In fact, I could only just distinguish the instruments in front of me, about two feet from my face.

" Of course I was watching the height recorder very intently, and very anxiously, because it was a great surprise to find that the cloud was so deep. I thought I should soon be underneath it and have a clear view of the ground from about 2,000 or 3,000 feet.

" I went on diving for a long time, until, to my horror, the height recorder registered nothing, which meant that I must be very near the ground.

" As I was unable to see anything at all, I thought the best thing to do would be to make the machine fly as slowly as ever it could. I knew sooner or later I should have to hit something, and so the best thing was to hit it very slowly instead of very fast.

" Fortunately the engine I have—the Anzani—throttles down beautifully, and I managed to slow it down till the aeroplane was only travelling at about 35 m.p.h., and with teeth set I continued at this pace until, suddenly, we hit the ground.

" Under such conditions a perfect landing could hardly be expected, and it is something to record that there was very little damage done to the aeroplane itself—in fact it was flying again in two days' time.

" When the fog cleared, giving me an opportunity to take my bearings, I found that I had landed in a barley field, about a mile and a half outside Stroud in Gloucestershire, and the most wonderful part was, that it was the only field for many miles around on which a landing was possible. All round were thick forests and very high hills.

" I had motored to Stroud a good many times previously, and scoured the whole district round to look for a suitable ground on which to give exhibition flying, but there was never a one to be found, and ultimately I had to give it up as a hopeless job. However, from the above it will be seen that my Handley-Page biplane was more successful and found a ground of its own accord."

There is no doubt but that Mr. Ding was in the most acute peril during the period when he was holding his machine at its stalling speed and at the same time flying blind. It says a good deal for his touch that he managed to " pancake " on to the ground without actually stalling and plunging down in a spin.

30. WAR

On August 4th, Great Britain plunged into the greatest war in the history of mankind, which was destined to retard the normal progress of aviation, as a means of transport, for a considerably longer period than the four and a quarter years occupied by the actual hostilities.

The immediate result of the declaration of war was the complete cessation of all cross-country flying by civilian pilots in accordance with the following order issued from the Home Office :

"In pursuance of the powers conferred on me by the Aerial Navigation Acts, 1911 and 1913, I hereby make, for the purposes of the safety and defence of the Realm, the following Order :

"I prohibit the navigation of aircraft of every class and description over the whole area of the United Kingdom, and over the whole of the coastline thereof and territorial waters adjacent thereto.

"This order shall not apply to Naval or Military aircraft or to aircraft flying under Naval or Military orders, nor shall it apply to any aircraft flying within three miles of a recognized aerodrome.

R. McKenna.

One of His Majesty's Principal Secretaries of State."

The saving clause at the end was inserted to ensure that there should be no interference with the work of the civilian schools of flying, which had instantly assumed the greatest importance in view of the sudden demand for pilots to complete the gaps left in the ranks of the R.F.C. by the dilatory methods of the War Office.

Most of the foreign pilots who had long been associated with British aviation had already left the country. Most notable of these was M. Henri Jullerot, *doyen* of flying instructors in Great Britain, who had been in supreme charge of the Bristol Company's schools of flying for nearly four years, and who had supervised personally the training of the majority of the original officers of the Military Wing, R.F.C. With him went M. Jules Teulade, chief instructor to the Bleriot school at Brooklands, M. Pierre Verrier, chief pilot to the Aircraft Manufacturing Company, Ltd., M. Louis Noel, test pilot and instructor at the Grahame-White establishment at Hendon, and M. Henri Salmet, whose brilliant flying of a Bleriot monoplane under the management of the *Daily Mail* newspaper has already been recorded.

A veil of secrecy shut down over all aeronautical activities immediately after the declaration of war. The following notice, which was posted up in the vicinity of every Naval air station, served to discourage any undue interest in aviation :

"All persons are hereby warned that all Army sentries at the waterplane station or on the foreshore have orders to challenge once, and if not instantly obeyed, to fire.

"On the order to halt they must immediately do so.

"They will approach the air station at night at their peril——"

Civil aviation was at an end.

The various schools of flying redoubled their activity until such time as the Admiralty and the War Office had made the necessary arrangements for the training of pilots within their respective Services, but the flying at the schools was strictly regulated by the authorities, and strictly confined to tuition.

31. THE BRITISH FLYING SCHOOLS IN 1914

In the seven months and four days which had passed from the beginning of 1914 until the outbreak of war the British schools of flying had trained 143 pilots, of whom twenty-six received their instruction at the C.F.S., or in the Squadrons of the Military Wing, R.F.C., and the remaining 117 at civilian schools.

The Deperdussin, Temple, and Blackburn schools at Hendon had disappeared, as had the Ducrocq and Percival schools at Brooklands, and Mr. Melly's establishment near Liverpool. The Ewen school at Hendon had suffered disintegration during the year, but was reconstructed under the name of the British Caudron school of flying. At Brooklands the Sopwith firm had recommenced instruction after twelve months' inactivity.

The net result was that, where there had been seventeen civilian schools of flying at work during the previous year, there were but thirteen operating during the first part of 1914. Their records were as follow :—

School.	*Aerodrome.*	*No. of pupils trained between Jan. 1st and Aug. 4th, 1914, both inclusive*
Vickers	Brooklands	36
Bristol ..	Brooklands 27 Salisbury Plain 8	35
C.F.S. (R.F.C.) ..	Upavon	23
Grahame-White ..	Hendon	20
Ewen	Hendon	5
Bleriot	Hendon 3 Brooklands 2	5
Shoreham F.S. ..	Shoreham	5
R.F.C. (Military Wing)	Netheravon	3
Sopwith	Brooklands	2
British Caudron ..	Hendon	2
Beattie	Hendon	2
E.A.C.	Eastbourne	2
Hall	Hendon	1
Avro	Brooklands	1
Lakes, F.S. (seaplanes)	Windermere	1
		Total 143

This total includes seven foreign subjects, but during the period ten English pupils learned to fly in France, two in the U.S.A. and one in Greece, so that actually 149 British subjects became qualified pilots in 1914, prior to the outbreak of war.

It will be seen that there had been a pronounced slackening of activity after the tremendous urge to learn to fly which had kept the schools so busy in 1913. Only the Grahame-White and Vickers establishments had increased their output noticeably. Both the Bristol schools had fallen back and, for the first time, they do not figure at the top of the list. Mr. Barnwell and his assistants, Messrs. Knight and Elsdon, had driven their firm to the head of the table by increasing their output to one pupil every six days, which was a very fine performance, and the Grahame-White school was turning out a new pilot every ten days.

At the outbreak of war 809 British subjects had qualified for aviator's certificates in England, 60 in France, 11 in the U.S.A., and 1 in Greece, a grand total of 881.

Of these 43 or 4·8 per cent. had met their deaths in flying accidents.

32. ACCIDENTS IN 1914

There had been twelve fatal accidents to British pilots in the first seven months of the year, involving the deaths of thirteen pilots, and three unqualified passengers. Two of the pilots did not hold aviator's certificates, one of them being killed whilst actually flying in his qualifying tests.

These accidents were due to a strange variety of causes. In three cases the pilots stalled their machines, and in one of them the aircraft, a Short seaplane, broke up in the air during the resultant dive. Two of the three B.E.2's which were wrecked broke up in flight, and the other one hit a hedge in a dense fog. One accident was attributed to a misunderstanding between an instructor and his pupil as to the operation of the dual controls, and another was apparently caused by the pilot losing consciousness in the air. In the remaining four cases, one pilot simply fell out of his machine during a steep gliding turn, another was lost at sea, two aeroplanes were wrecked in a collision in the air, and the cause of the smash in the Argentine was never explained satisfactorily.

This was a black record, for more people had been killed in seven months than in the whole of the previous year, although there had been no commensurable increase in the number of hours flown. In fact, the marked decline in tuition probably indicated that actually rather less flying had been done throughout the country than during the hectic days of 1913. Moreover, the time had passed when it was reasonable to expect that three Service aircraft should break in the air within such a short period. These smashes pointed unmistakably to faulty maintenance in the R.F.C.

33. THE PILOTS OF 1914

Of the 881 British subjects who had qualified for aviators' certificates at the outbreak of war, 305 were serving as officers and 47 as N.C.O.'s or men in the Army or the R.F.C. (Military Wing), and 101 were officers, and 39 petty officers or ratings serving in the Royal Naval Air Services. Thus it will be seen that the fighting services claimed the allegiance of no less than 492, or more than half the sum total of the British pilots, and that only 389 civilians had qualified in all. Twenty of these civil pilots had been killed in accidents, several more had been seriously injured, and a great number had given up flying for various reasons.

Of the great men of the early years few were still flying.

The Farman brothers, Henry, Maurice, and Dick, still used aëroplanes for pleasure and business purposes in France, Grahame-White often flew in the short races at Hendon, and appeared to have lost none of his old skill, and Alec Ogilvie continued to fly his old-fashioned Wright at Eastchurch in open defiance of all progressive thought. Maurice Egerton had graduated to a Short, and Frank McClean, founder of British Naval aviation, amused himself with his seaplanes in the Thames Estuary.

Of the others, Latham, Cody, Rolls, Grace, Dickson, Astley, D. L. Allen, Macdonald, Gilmour, Fisher, Fenwick, Hamilton, Hotchkiss, Parke, Petre the Painter, Wildman-Lushington, Slack, and Hamel, were dead.

Moore-Brabazon, Cockburn, Mortimer-Singer, Loraine, McArdle, Gibbs, Radley, Colmore, Rawlinson, Valentine, Morison, Greswell, Barber, Paterson, Fleming, Hewitt, Corbett-Wilson, Ewen and Turner had blazed into prominence and faded away.

Roe, Sopwith, and Blackburn had abandoned the actual flying part of the business to younger men, and had settled down to design and construct aircraft for others to fly.

Probably there were not more than 100 qualified British pilots actively engaged in civil aviation in this country in August 1914, of whom fifty, at the most, were really sound aviators.

These fell readily into four classes. First there were the exhibition pilots, such as Hucks, Manton, Gooden, Hall, and Rowland Ding. A second class comprised the instructors, like Warren Merriam, Knight, Elsdon. Pizey, Howarth, Lillywhite, Fowler, and Clappen. A third group consisted of those who flew purely for sport, amongst whom must be mentioned Lord Carbery, Lord Edward Grosvenor, Dr. Christie, and Mr. Creagh. The last, and most important, section was that which included the experts who were retained by the constructors, and who were called upon to test new types, fly the firm's racing aircraft, put in a little instruction, and generally do anything which might be necessary in the firm's interests. The most famous names appear in this category, men such as Hawker, Raynham, Barnwell, Pixton, Sippe, de Havilland, Gordon Bell, Gordon England, Dukinfield Jones, Kemp, Skene, Alcock, Carr, and Pickles.

I propose to select twenty of the best British civilian pilots flying at the outbreak of war, and to endeavour to place them in order of precedence, taking into consideration all their achievements and their previous experience.

I do not think it can be questioned but that Mr. B. C. Hucks was the best all-round pilot in England at that time. It is true that he had never accomplished any spectacular long-distance flights, broken any records, or made any claim to fame, otherwise than as an aerobat.

But in his own line he was unequalled, his handling of a Bleriot was a joy to behold, and his stunt flying was fluid and effortless. In addition he had become a cross-country pilot of the greatest ability. He made all his journeys between the scenes of his exhibitions by air, regardless of the weather.

It is very difficult to choose the order of the next four pilots on the list, although the names select themselves. Pixton's magnificent performance in the Schneider Trophy contest must be considered, and pitted against the great all-round ability of Hawker, Barnwell, and Raynham. The last-named, although a pilot of greater experience than the other two, had not yet had experience of aerobatics, and nor had Pixton. To that extent their education was incomplete, and for that reason I shall place Hawker, who was already a polished stunt pilot, and Barnwell before them.

Young Marcus Manton had made astonishing progress under the tuition of Mr. Hucks, and he must be placed high in the list, and other newcomers worth mentioning are Lord Carbery and Messrs. Jack Alcock, R. H. Carr, and Rowland Ding.

My selection of the twenty best pilots, with the machines with which they were associated, is as follows :

1. B. C. Hucks (Blackburn and Bleriot monoplanes).
2. H. G. Hawker (S) (Farman, Sopwith-Wright, Sopwith three-seater, Sopwith Bat-boat, and Sopwith Tabloid biplanes).
3. R. H. Barnwell (Vickers, Farman, and Sopwith Tabloid biplanes, and Vickers and Martinsyde monoplanes).
4. H. Pixton (S) (Avro, Bristol, Sopwith three-seater, and Sopwith Tabloid biplanes, and Bristol monoplanes).
5. F. P. Raynham (S) (Farman, Howard-Wright, Burgess-Wright, Avro and Flanders biplanes, and Flanders monoplanes).
6. S. V. Sippe (S) (Avro and Bristol biplanes, and Hanriot and Bristol monoplanes).
7. M. Manton (Grahame-White and Farman biplanes, and Bleriot monoplanes).
8. S. Pickles (S) (Caudron and Champel biplanes, and Bleriot and Blackburn monoplanes).
9. W. Merriam (Bristol biplanes and monoplanes).
10. J. Alcock (Farman biplanes).

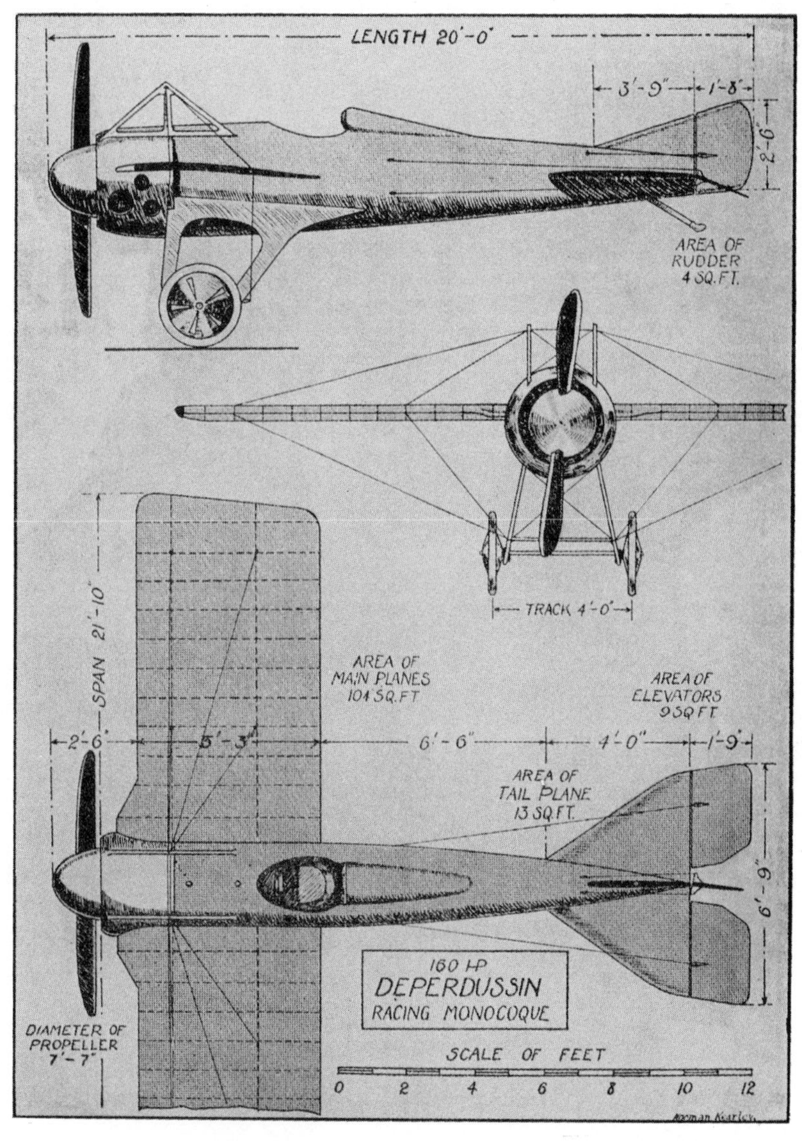

"*Flight*" *copyright*

7.—Probably the fastest aeroplane in existence at the outbreak of war: the Deperdussin Monoplane (160 h.p. Gnôme).

11. C. Pizey (S) (Bristol and Sopwith pusher biplanes).

12. G. de Havilland (B.E., R.E., S.E., and F.E. biplanes).

13. G. Bell (S) (Farman, Avro and Short biplanes, and R.E.P., Bleriot, Martinsyde, Hanriot, and Deperdussin monoplanes).

14. R. Kemp (Bristol, B.E., S.E., F.E., and R.E. biplanes, and Bristol monoplanes).

15. Lord Carbery (S) (Morane-Saulnier and Deperdussin monoplanes, and Bristol Scout biplanes).

16. R. H. Carr (Grahame-White and Farman biplanes, and Morane-Saulnier monoplanes).

17. G. England (S) (Weiss, Bristol, Cedric Lee and Bleriot monoplanes, and Bristol, Farman, Wight, Short, Radley-England, and Avro biplanes.)

18. F. W. Gooden (Deperdussin and Morane-Saulnier monoplanes and Caudron biplanes).

19. R. Ding (Wright and Handley-Page biplanes).

20. D. Jones (Bleriot, Flanders and Martinsyde monoplanes, and Flanders and D.F.W. biplanes).

The first twelve of the above were fit to fly on level terms with any of the French or German experts, and those marked (S) had had experience with seaplanes.

34. BRITISH AIRCRAFT AND ENGINES AT THE OUTBREAK OF WAR

I have given a comprehensive view of the British aircraft industry in Section 9 of this chapter, when I described the Aero Show of 1914. There is very little to add to that description, except to record that some interesting seaplanes had been constructed for the *Daily Mail* round Britain contest, which had been postponed from the previous year, and which was destined never to take place. Most of these machines had left the factories and were under test at the outbreak of war.

The most interesting was the Sopwith two-seater twin-float seaplane (100 h.p. English-built Gnôme), which was to have been flown by Mr. Victor Mahl. This was an enlarged version of the Tabloid with aileron control, and was designed for a top speed of 80 m.p.h. The span was thirty-six feet, and the overall length was thirty feet. It was an extremely handsome and workmanlike design.

Hawker had been dropped from the Sopwith team on account of his ill-health, and the firm's other entry was entrusted to the winner of the Schneider Trophy, Mr. Howard Pixton. This was the latest version of the Sopwith Bat-boat, which had been strengthened and modified in detail, and was now fitted with a Sunbeam engine of 200 h.p., which was expected to give a maximum speed of 75 m.p.h.

The D.F.W. entry was a standard all-steel tractor biplane, built by the Beardmore Company, who also built its 120 h.p.

Austro-Daimler engine. It was similar to that which had been flown with such success by Lieut. C. H. Collet, R.M., and was provided with twin floats. The maximum speed was intended to be 85 m.p.h.

Mr. J. D. North had designed the Grahame-White entry, which was to have been handled in the race by the great pioneer himself. This machine was a small tractor biplane, with a span of only twenty-seven feet ten inches, and an overall length of twenty-seven feet three inches. Superficially it bore a faint resemblance to Mr. A. V. Roe's unsuccessful Scout. It was equipped with very short twin floats, set close together, and an English-built 100 h.p. Gnôme. The speed was alleged to be in the neighbourhood of 85 m.p.h.

The E.A.C. entry was in the nature of a freak, and need not be described here, and Mr. A. V. Roe's machine, which was to have been flown by Mr. F. P. Raynham, was a twin-float tractor biplane, which did not compare at all favourably with the 504 type. It was indeed a clumsy-looking craft and its enormous size, the top wing had a span of sixty-three feet, rendered it unwieldy.

Mr. Sydney Pickles had joined the Blackburn firm as test pilot, and he was in charge of the firm's entry. This was a notable departure for the Yorkshire Company, in that it was a handsome tractor biplane fitted with a Salmson radial engine of 130 h.p. Previously the Blackburns had confined their attention to monoplanes. Although the machine was large, the span being fifty feet, yet it was well proportioned and, indeed, showed great promise. It was expected to develop a top speed of 75 m.p.h. with a useful load of 700 lbs.

The entry list was completed by two Curtiss flying boats, which had been constructed by Messrs. White and Thompson, except for the hulls, which were built by Messrs. Saunders of Cowes.

It was a great pity that these new seaplane types could not be tried out against each other under the strenuous conditions of the *Daily Mail* circuit.

The principal types of British aircraft in existence at the outbreak of war, together with the engines fitted to them and their approximate maximum speeds, are tabulated below.

Machine	*Engine*	*Approx. max speed, m.p.h.*
CLASS I. THE SINGLE-SEATER SCOUTS		
Sopwith Tabloid	100 Gnôme	105
Bristol Scout	80 Le Rhone	100
Sopwith Tabloid	80 Gnôme	95
Martinsyde (*Building*) ..	80 Gnôme	80
Pemberton-Billing P.B. IX (*Building*)	50 Gnôme	75

Machine	*Engine*	*Approx. max. speed, m.p.h.*
CLASS II. TWO-SEATER TRACTOR BIPLANES		
Sopwith Tabloid	80 Gnôme	90
Avro 504..	80 Gnôme	80
Sopwith	80 Gnôme	80
Bristol	80 Le Rhone	75
B.E.	70 Renault	70
CLASS III. PUSHER BIPLANES		
Vickers Gun-bus	100 Gnôme	65
M. Farman Shorthorn ..	70 Renault	55
Bristol Boxkite	50 Gnôme	50

In Class I Great Britain led the world. None of the French monoplanes of standard type could beat the performance of the Sopwith and Bristol Scouts, and Germany had given no serious attention to fast single-seaters as yet, although the D.F.W. firm had one building. The French house of Ponnier, lineal descendant of the Hanriot Company, had attempted to imitate the Tabloid, but their machine could not exceed 65 m.p.h. with a 50 h.p. Gnôme.

In Class II the Germans had established a firm lead, owing to the excellence of their 6-cylinder in line water-cooled engines, but the French had no two-seater tractor biplanes of equal performance to ours, and they relied upon their two-seater monoplanes, which were, generally speaking, neither so fast nor so reliable as our biplanes, and afforded little space for the occupants.

In Class III the Vickers Gun-bus could compete on level terms with the French Farmans, whilst the Germans had no pusher biplanes worthy of consideration at all.

There was no aeroplane of any type in America, with the sole exception of the Curtiss flying boat, which could be compared with the European designs.

Thus it will be seen that the British manufacturers had made a very real contribution to the science of aviation and that Great Britain had no cause to be ashamed of her position at the outbreak of war.

We had to bow to France and Germany when it came to breaking records with special aircraft especially designed for the purpose, but our standard aeroplanes were, generally speaking, as good as those of any other nation.

It will be noted, however, that in every case it was necessary for our manufacturers to use a foreign engine in order to obtain these excellent results. The Isaacson engines had dropped out of the running and the 100 h.p. Sunbeam in Mr. Jack Alcock's M. Farman was the sole individual aero engine of English design and construction in regular use at the outbreak of war. For all practical purposes Great Britain had no aero engine industry at all at this vital moment in her history.

35. WORLD'S AND BRITISH RECORDS AT THE OUTBREAK OF WAR

No attempts had yet been made to establish a record for absolute speed over a straight course.

The Gordon-Bennett racers of 1914 had not been tested when war broke out, and it is safe to assume that the Deperdussin and Ponnier monoplanes which flew in the previous year's contest were still unsurpassed for sheer speed, although it was still a debatable point as to which of them was actually the faster. The speed of both these remarkable monoplanes over a straight course must certainly have been in excess of 135 m.p.h., and it is a great pity that the question was never definitely settled. I have inserted the Deperdussin's record in the table, but it must be borne in mind that it was made on a circular course, and an allowance must be given for the pilot's cornering ability.

No attack had been made prior to August 4th, 1914, upon the record for distance flown in a straight line, and I can find no report of any unofficial flight which surpassed the three non-stop flights from Paris to Berlin made by Letort (twice), and Seguin in 1913. I have, therefore, again credited the former with the record unofficially.

A glance at the record table set out below shows that, whereas the French still held three of the five principal records, these had not been improved upon since the end of the previous year and, moreover, the Germans had come rapidly to the front, and had wrested two records away by such substantial margins as to leave no doubt as to their supremacy. It was the first time since 1910 that any record of first-class importance had been held by any country but France.

For the first time in history a man had stayed in the air for a whole day and a whole night without cessation. Herr Böhm's wonderful flight had added no less than ten hours fifty minutes to the world's duration record, and if the distance he had flown had been calculated, it is obvious that he would have been credited with beating M. Seguin's distance record as well.

No less extraordinary was the feat performed by Herr Oelrich in climbing to 25,780 feet. When M. Legagneux had topped 20,000 feet in December 1913, it was generally felt that the limit had been reached, but the German pilot had soared up nearly 6,000 feet higher, until he was almost five miles above the earth. It was a splendid achievement.

It was abundantly clear that the rush of French progress had been checked. For five years France had reigned supreme and unchallenged in the air, but now there was a visible slackening of effort, which coincided with a fresh burst of energy on the part of the German and British manufacturers and pilots. The former were reaping the fruits of the years of research which they had devoted to the perfection of the water-cooled aero engine, and the latter were threatening French supremacy with their new Scout biplanes, using engines of French manufacture.

No English pilot held a world's record of any sort at the outbreak of war, although Louis Noel's weight-carrying performances on the G.W. "Charabancs" still stood on the record book to the credit of Great Britain, in spite of the fact that they had been surpassed by Garaix, as previously described.

The following are the particulars of the five most important records standing at August 4th, 1914:—

WORLD'S RECORDS AT AUGUST 4th, 1914

Pilot	*Nationality*	*Aircraft*	*Nationality*	*Engine*	*Nationality*	*Time, distance or Speed*	*Place*
			DURATION				
Hr. Böhm	Ger.	Albatros biplane	Ger.	75 Mercedes	Ger.	24 hrs. 12 min.	Johannisthal
			DISTANCE IN A CLOSED CIRCUIT				
Mons. A. Seguin	French	H. Farman biplane	French	Gnôme	French	1021·2 Km. (634 miles)	Paris to Bordeaux and back
			DISTANCE IN A STRAIGHT LINE (Unofficial)				
M. Letort	French	Morane-Saulnier monoplane	French	Le Rhone	French	915 Km. (568 miles)	Villacoublay to Johannisthal
			ALTITUDE				
Hr. Oelrich	Ger.	D.F.W. biplane	Ger.	100 Mercedes	Ger.	7,860 m. (25,780 ft.)	Lindenthal
			SPEED (Round a Closed Circuit of 10 Km. (6·21 miles) in circumference)				
Mons. M. Prevost	French	Deperdussin monoplane	French	160 Gnôme	French	203·85 k.p.h. (127 m.p.h.)	Rheims

The idea of flying for hours at a time around an aerodrome failed to appeal to the British pilots, with the result that no attack had been made upon the British record for distance flown in a closed circuit since Cody had raised the figure to 261·5 miles in the year 1911. It will be recalled that Hawker must have beaten this record during his non-stop flight of 8 hrs. 23 mins., which won him the Michelin Cup in 1912, had the distance which he covered been officially measured. But that was not done; so Cody's record remained on the book, and no attempt had been made during 1913 or 1914 to better Hawker's time.

The British record for distance flown in a straight line was very satisfactory and was, in fact, only 123 miles short of the unofficial world's record, but the British altitude figure was scarcely a cause for congratulation. Not only was the height attained more than 10,000 feet below the world's record, but it had been achieved in a foreign aeroplane fitted with a foreign engine. The speed records quoted were very good, when it is realized that each was set up by a British aeroplane of a standard type, which bore no relation whatever to the freak racer which had set up the world's record mentioned above. Either the Bristol Scout or the Sopwith Tabloid could land at well under 50 m.p.h., but Prevost's Deperdussin and Emile Vedrine's Ponnier could only fly from specially prepared aerodromes, since their stalling speeds were in the nature of 75 m.p.h., or more, and their pilots took their lives in their hands every time they left the ground.

The fastest British aeroplane in existence in 1914 was the Sopwith Tabloid which won the Schneider Trophy. This machine, as subsequently fitted with a wheel undercarriage, could exceed 105 m.p.h.

The British records standing at the outbreak of war were as follow :—

BRITISH RECORDS STANDING AS AT AUGUST 4th, 1914

Pilot	*Nationality*	*Aircraft*	*Nationality*	*Engine*	*Nationality*	*Time, distance or speed*	*Place*
				DURATION			
Mr. H. G. Hawker	Br.	Sopwith-Wright biplane	Br.	40/50 A.B.C.	Br.	8hrs. 23 mins.	Brooklands
				DISTANCE IN A CLOSED CIRCUIT			
Mr. S. F. Cody	Br.	Cody biplane	Br.	60 Green	Br.	261·5 miles	Laffan's Plain
				DISTANCE IN A STRAIGHT LINE			
Capt. C. A. H. Longcroft, R.F.C.	Br.	B.E.2 biplane	Br.	70 Renault	French	445 miles	Montrose to Farnborough
				ALTITUDE			
Eng.-Lieut. E. F. Briggs R.N.	Br.	Bleriot monoplane	French	80 Le Rhone	French	14,920 feet	Eastchurch
				SPEED			
(i)—Mesne of 3 runs in opposite directions over a straight course of 440 yards (Unofficial)							
Lord Carbery	Br.	Bristol Scout	Br.	80 Le Rhone	French	100·6 m.p.h.	Hendon
(ii) 150 Km. (93·15 miles) round a closed circuit of 10 Km. (6·21 miles) in circumference							
Mr. H. Pixton	Br.	Sopwith Tabloid seaplane	Br.	100 Gnôme	French	89·4 m.p.h.	Monaco

As regards the *all-British* category there had been no change from the position obtaining at the end of 1912, for the simple reason that only one all-British aeroplane, namely the British-built Maurice Farman biplane fitted with a Sunbeam engine, was flying in regular service during 1914, and Mr. Alcock had made no attempt to break records with this machine.

36. CONCLUSION

I have now traced the development of British aviation from the time when it first began to be a practical proposition until its growth was abruptly cut off by the War in 1914.

I have shown how swift and certain that development was and demonstrated the quite remarkable degree of proficiency to which the art of flying had attained in the short space of five and a half years.

I have said enough to indicate that the British aeroplane constructors had drawn level with their French rivals and were about to enter upon a struggle with Germany for supremacy in the aeroplane markets of the world, a struggle in which they were heavily handicapped by the complete absence of any efficient British aero-engine.

I have also shown that the best British pilots had reached a stage at which they could compete on level terms with the pick of the pilots of any other nation.

It remains to review briefly the factors which had helped to bring about this satisfactory state of affairs, and the obstacles which had had to be overcome in the process.

The chief hindrance was, of course, the inertia of the Great British Public, whose members were only too glad to welcome flying as a new diversion and even, in some cases, to pay to see it, but to whom the idea of actually risking their necks by taking up aviation as a sport failed to appeal. This attitude of sceptical admiration from a respectful distance was accurately reflected by the public's chosen representatives in Parliament. The government of the day, faithful to their leader's motto of "Wait and see," duly waited, and eventually saw that, unless urgent steps were taken forthwith, British aviation would die out before their eyes for lack of funds, and we should be at the mercy of France and Germany. Long before this elementary fact had been grasped by the politicians, the public themselves were clamouring for an air force to protect them from they knew not what. The Government could have taken as many millions as it liked from the frightened taxpayers, but where previously it had waited with caution, now it acted with caution. Everything was in skeleton form, and cadre squadrons for the R.F.C. and niggardly orders for aircraft gave rise to a disquieting atmosphere of impermanence, which did little or nothing to encourage our manufacturers to continue their experiments.

Over all loomed the threat of the Royal Aircraft Factory at Farnborough. The industry had exacted a solemn promise from the Government that this institution should be strictly confined to its professed function of conducting experimental and repair work only, yet, within a year of its inauguration the Civil Servants in charge had prevailed upon the Government to break that undertaking and the Factory was working at full pressure turning out machines of its own design in direct, subsidized competition with the struggling inventors, upon whose shoulders the whole future of British aviation rested.

It was not until late in 1913 that the Government realized the futility of organizing an Air Arm which was entirely dependant upon foreign engines for its motive power, and it was not until early in 1914 that any steps were taken to encourage the production of British engines. A competition, for an inadequate prize, was actually in progress at Farnborough at the outbreak of war, but, such was the inefficiency of the Royal Aircraft Factory, that months of invaluable time had been wasted through the inadequacy and frequent breakdowns of the plant which had been devised by the "experts" there for testing the engines submitted. The war broke upon us before any useful data had been obtained, and for the first two and a half years of hostilities, our Air Arm went into action with French engines, or inferior British copies thereof.

Such was the muddled-incompetence in official circles, with which the British aircraft industry had to contend.

It was only through the indomitable individual pluck and determination of men like A. V. Roe, T. O. M. Sopwith, Robert Blackburn, the Short brothers, Messrs. Martin and Handasyde, Howard Flanders, Howard Wright, and the directors of the Bristol Company, that any results were achieved at all.

The story of the development of "Roe the Hopper" into Sir Alliot Verdon Roe, Managing Director of one of the most powerful combinations in British industry, is an epic tale of courageous struggle against adversity and ridicule. The story of the life of "Tom" Sopwith, can only be compared with the biography of "Tony" Fokker in its combination of physical daring and business brilliance.

But if there was any single individual or firm which did more than any other to push forward the development of British aviation, it was Sir George White and the British and Colonial Aeroplane Co. Ltd. In the black days of 1910 and 1911, when it really seemed as if the English people would never make a success of the new art, and when British aviation was regarded with contempt and ridicule in France, the Bristol Company alone upheld British prestige abroad. Their reliable old "boxkites" and sprightly monoplanes were flown all over Europe, and in India, the far East, and the Antipodes, and gained a reputation for sound workmanship which did much to undermine the overpowering influence of the French.

The existence of a group of flourishing schools of flying is almost as important a factor in the aviation of a nation as is the possession of a sound aircraft industry. The schools or clubs represent the very heart of aviation, pumping out a stream of new pilots into every vein and artery of the whole organization, some for the use of the manufacturers as test pilots, some to the Services as fighting men, and some, the amateurs, as prospective customers of the industry.

Great Britain was very fortunate in her schools of flying, and in the early development of a number of first-class instructors. During the four and a half years immediately preceding the outbreak of war there were twenty-eight civilian schools working at one time or another, and between them they trained 664 new pilots. The complete record of these schools is as follows :—

School	*Aerodrome*	*No. of pupils trained up to and including Aug. 4th, 1914*
Bristol	Brooklands 182 Salisbury Plain 127	309
Vickers	Brooklands	77
Grahame-White	Pau (Fr.) 1 Brooklands 1 Hendon 70	72
Ewen	Hendon	37
Bleriot	Hendon 32 Brooklands 2	34
Deperdussin ..	Brooklands 6 Hendon 21	27
E.A.C.	Eastbourne	20
Avro	Brooklands 12 Shoreham 2	14
Hewlett and Blondeau	Brooklands	13
Sopwith	Brooklands	13
Hanriot	Brooklands	7
Shoreham F.S. ..	Shoreham	6
Melly	Freshfield (Lancs.)	4
McArdle and Drexel ..	Beaulieu (Hants.)	4
Aeronautical Syndicate	Hendon	3
Temple	Hendon	3
Beattie	Hendon	3
Ducrocq	Brooklands	3
Lakes F.S. (seaplanes)	Windermere	3
British Caudron ..	Hendon	2
Hall	Hendon	2

School	*Aerodrome*	*No. of pupils trained up to and including Aug. 4th, 1914*
Blackburn	Hendon	2
Spencer	Brooklands	1
Percival	Brooklands	1
Blackburn	Filey (Yorks.)	1
Ogilvie	Eastchurch	1
Cody	Farnborough	1
Handley-Page	Fairlop	1
		Total 664

Once again the superiority of the Bristol Company's organization is apparent. The Company had not only taught almost half of the total number of pilots trained at the British schools, but they had also established a very great reputation for sound instruction. A Bristol pupil felt that he was superior to a pupil trained elsewhere; and he was justified in feeling so. Bristol pupils found it easier to obtain employment in the industry than did those of the other schools, for it was universally recognized that Bristol tuition was the best obtainable anywhere in the world.

It is interesting to note the fact that all except eight of the pupils trained at the civilian schools learned to fly in the south of England. No. 2 Squadron, R.F.C., trained four men to fly at Montrose, so that only a round dozen pilots were trained in the north. The record of the various aerodromes in regard to tuition works out as follows :—

Aerodrome	*No. of pupils trained at Civilian schools there up to and including August 4th, 1914*
Brooklands	 318
Hendon	 175
Salisbury Plain	 127
Eastbourne	 20
Shoreham	 8
Beaulieu (Hants.)	 4
Freshfield (Lancs.)	 4
Windermere (seaplanes)	 3
Filey (Yorks.)	 1
Fairlop	 1

Aerodrome	*No. of pupils trained at Civilian schools there up to and including August 4th*, 1914
Farnborough	 1
Eastchurch	 1
Pau (France)	 1
	Total .. 664

A glance at these figures is sufficient to dispose of the popular misconception that Hendon was the hub of all aerial activity in England prior to 1914.

Not only was Brooklands established first, but throughout the whole period it was the centre of three-quarters of the real work and effort behind British aviation.

At Hendon flying was ably exploited as an entertainment for the public. Pylon-racing, passenger flights, displays of aerobatics, night-flying by illuminated aeroplanes, fireworks, and cleverly organized bombing displays and comic events took place to a musical accompaniment in thoroughly congenial surroundings, within easy reach of London. The public flocked in excited crowds to witness the latest novelty, and it was not unusual for more than 20,000 people to pay for admission to the week-end meetings.

Some of the regular entertainers became quite expert at cornering round the mark towers, and, no doubt, it was all very exciting for those unused to seeing aeroplanes in flight. But as a method of furthering aviation as a practical means of transport such entertainments are well-nigh valueless.

None of the many firms operating at Hendon made any serious contribution to the science of aeronautics, with the sole exception of the Grahame-White Company, whose "Charabancs" captured two world's records.

Brooklands, on the other hand, saw the birth of many a sound design. T. O. M. Sopwith, A. V. Roe, Howard Wright, Martin and Handasyde, Howard Flanders, and the Vickers Company, all used Brooklands as the principal base for their experiments.

At Brooklands the public was a minor consideration. Sporadic efforts were made to entertain the few who were attracted to the Byfleet side of the track, but it was clearly understood that nothing was to be permitted to interfere with the free use of the aerodrome by those who were conducting practical experiments.

Brooklands devoted itself strictly and conscientiously to the business of inventing and perfecting new types of aeroplanes, and of training pilots to fly them.

Although Hendon appears in second place on our list with a total of 175 pupils trained there, yet it must be remembered that we are dealing solely with commercial schools of flying, and have taken no count of the Military schools.

No less than 153 pilots had been trained by the R.F.C., *ab initio*, of whom ninety-three had learned at the C.F.S., and eleven at Netheravon. If these be added to those who had qualified at the Bristol school there, we find that 231 pupils had been trained on Salisbury Plain. It is clear that the group of aerodromes at Larkhill, Upavon, and Netheravon formed collectively the second most important flying station in Great Britain. Quite apart from the tremendous amount of tuition accomplished there, Salisbury Plain saw the testing of the Bristol Company's latest types, as well as a great deal of practical flying on the part of the R.F.C.

After a lull, following the activity of the earliest days, the Royal Aero Club's ground at Eastchurch attained considerable importance as the centre of Naval aviation. Forty-nine Naval officers and men had learned to fly there, and by the middle of 1914, it had become an exceedingly busy aerodrome.

Taking everything into consideration it is apparent that Brooklands, Salisbury Plain, Hendon, and Eastchurch, were the four aerodromes which exerted the greatest influence for good upon British aviation.

Amongst other factors which contributed to the growth of the movement in England was the wise and steady guidance of the Royal Aero Club and the encouragement and constructive criticism afforded by the technical press.

From the very beginning the R.Ae.C. adopted and wielded the most extensive powers over everything appertaining to aeronautics. Closely allied to the international governing body, the club kept a rigid hold upon its members, both at home and abroad, and saw to it that any person who attempted to escape its jurisdiction should be outlawed wherever he went.

Generally speaking, these wide powers were used prudently and with intelligence. The members of the General Committee were chosen, it is true, more on account of their influence in politics or eminence in private life than on account of their knowledge of aeronautical affairs, but the club had an executive officer of rare ability in the secretary, Mr. Harold E. Perrin, and the sub-committees, which were formed to carry out the principal duties of the club, included a sprinkling of pilots in their ranks.

The club made some serious errors of judgment, notably in the cases of Mr. Graham-Gilmour, M. Brindejonc des Moulinais, and Mr. Gordon Bell, but the manner in which they backed up Mr. Grahame-White in the disgraceful affair of the Statue of Liberty prize, and the efficiency with which they handled the various big competitions entrusted to their care, were wholly admirable.

The most important work of the club lay in the self-appointed task so ably performed by the Accidents Investigation Committee. It is an illustration of the autocratic powers enjoyed by the club during this period, that this sub-committee was allowed by the Government to investigate accidents involving aeroplanes belonging to the R.F.C., and to cross-examine serving officers and men of the Corps with regard to details as to maintenance, and so forth.

It would be a fair parallel if a sub-committee of the Royal Automobile Club were empowered to descend upon a depot of the Royal Tank Corps, and to cross-question the officers and men as to the cause of any accident which had occurred to one of their secret tanks.

The R.Ae.C. performed their onerous duty exceedingly well, and their published reports on the various accidents were of great value to British aviation. That the reports were published was in itself a good thing. Nowadays this vital work is performed by a special department of the Air Ministry, which, for some inscrutable reason, known only to the civil servants concerned, withholds all the information thus obtained from the persons entitled to have it.

When an accident occurred to a de Havilland Moth X (Cirrus II) of the Cinque Ports Flying Club a few years ago, it became a matter of great importance that the club's executive should discover the primary cause. This was explained to the Inspector of Accidents, and he was implored to communicate the result of his investigation to the club. It would be assumed by any intelligent person that the club's officials, as operators of the aircraft, were the persons primarily entitled to the benefit of the inquiry, but they were informed that these investigations were secret, confidential, hush-hush, and the rest of it, and could not, in any circumstances, be disclosed to them.

So the inquiries conducted by the R.Ae.C. were of some practical benefit to aviators, even if they were not conducted in such a highly scientific manner as are those of Maj. Cooper and his satellites, which are, no doubt, models of scientific reasoning and deduction, and lasting ornaments to the secret recesses of the Air Ministry's filing system ; but of no practical use to practical aviators whatever.

British aviation owes a deep debt of gratitude to the members of the Accidents Investigation Committee of the Royal Aero Club, who gave up so much of their time, and took such an infinity of trouble to see that no gleam of knowledge which could be extracted from each tragic accident should be lost to humanity.

If aviation was fortunate in its self-appointed governing body it was no less fortunate in its press.

The technical press of Great Britain has always been a model to the world, but no sport or movement in this country has ever been so well served in this respect as has flying.

Flight, official organ of the Royal Aero Club, under the control of Mr. Stanley Spooner, opened its columns wide for the free discussion of any subject remotely connected with aviation. The most improbable theories were thrashed out in its pages, and the journal held out a helping hand, and offered encouragement and advice freely to everyone who appeared to have the good of aviation at heart, however curious his ideas. Through all this wild discussion of probabilities and impossibilities, *Flight* preserved an admirable restraint, and pursued a policy of steady encouragement of progress. Especially valuable were the excellent scale drawings of new types of aircraft, which were a feature of the newspaper from its earliest days, and the well-informed reports of the latest developments and achievements in France.

Mr. C. G. Grey, the witty editor of *The Aeroplane*, offered his readers that devastating, albeit constructive, criticism of aeronautical affairs which has made his newspaper famous throughout the world. *The Aeroplane* proved an admirable foil to the more sober pages of *Flight* and, unlike Mr. Spooner, its editor never suffered fools gladly, but preferred to expose them to the crushing forces of ridicule, which he knows so well how to invoke. The result was the same in either case, for views were ventilated freely, ideas interchanged, and thought and discussion promoted, to the lasting good of British aviation.

No account of these times would be complete without a word concerning the late Lord Northcliffe and the *Daily Mail*. During the four and a half years ending on August 4th, 1914, the proprietors of this newspaper had actually given the enormous sum of £24,050 in prizes for great feats in aviation, and the further sum of £15,000 was waiting to be won when the War put a stop to all competition flying.

It is not only the sheer amount of these prizes which compels respect, for the greatest credit must be given to Lord Northcliffe for the intelligence which he displayed in selecting the feats which were to be performed to win them.

The first man to fly the Channel, the first to fly from London to Manchester, the great races round Britain, the first man to fly across the Atlantic Ocean, these were stupendous achievements calculated to excite the utmost enthusiasm, and to attract the maximum of attention. They were clever ideas, and we must recognize the genius of the man who thought of them and his sound judgment in leaving the organization of the contests in the able hands of the R.Ae.C.

Those were the principal forces which had developed the little band of isolated experimenters of the years preceding 1909 into the vital movement which represented British aviation on August 4th, 1914, with its flourishing industry, its busy schools of flying, its small but efficient Royal Flying Corps and Royal Naval Air Service, its races, pageants, exhibitions and displays, and which had laid the foundations of the greatest air power the world has ever seen.

APPENDIX A

PART I

WORLD'S RECORDS HELD BY BRITISH PILOTS UP TO AUGUST 4TH, 1914

Date	*Pilot*	*Aircraft*	*Nat.*	*Engine*	*Nat.*	*Place*	*Time or distance*	*Length of time for which record stood unbroken.*
				DURATION WITH ONE PASSENGER				
1910 June 6th	Capt. Bertram Dickson	Henry Farman biplane	Fr.	Gnôme	Fr.	Anjou	2 hrs.	33 days
1911 Aug. 16th	Lieut. E. L. Gerrard, R.M.L.I.	Short biplane	Br.	Gnôme	Fr.	East-church	4 hrs. 13 mins.	114 days
		DISTANCE FLOWN IN A CLOSED CIRCUIT WITH ONE PASSENGER						
1912 Feb. 14th	Lieut. B. H. Barrington-Kennett, R.F.C.	Nieuport monoplane	Fr.	Gnôme	Fr.	Salisbury Plain	249 mls. 840 yds.	362 days
		ALTITUDE, PILOT AND THREE PASSENGERS						
1913 July 27th	Mr. H. G. Hawker	Sopwith tractor biplane	Br.	80 Gnôme	Fr.	Brooklands	2,560 m. (8,400 ft.)	63 days

Note.—It should be borne in mind that Mr. Henry Farman repeatedly broke the principal distance and duration records throughout the years 1909 and 1910. I have not included his performances, as, although English by birth, he was for all practical purposes a Frenchman, and his records were officially credited to France. For the same reason Mr. Hubert Latham's many records for altitude and speed have been omitted.

APPENDIX A

PART II

WORLD'S RECORDS GAINED BY BRITISH AEROPLANE (WITH FOREIGN PILOT) UP TO AUGUST 4TH, 1914

Date	*Pilot*	*Aircraft*	*Nat.*	*Engine*	*Nat.*	*Place*	*Time*	*Length of time for which record stood unbroken*
				DURATION, PILOT AND SEVEN PASSENGERS				
1913 Sep. 22nd	L. Noel (Fr.)	Grahame-White pusher biplane	Br.	120 Austro Daimler	Aus.	Hendon	17 mins. $25\frac{2}{5}$ secs.	176 days
				DURATION, PILOT AND NINE PASSENGERS				
1913 Oct. 2nd.	L. Noel (Fr.)	Grahame-White pusher biplane	Br.	120 Austro Daimler	Aus.	Hendon	19 mins. 47 secs.	180 days

APPENDIX B

RESULTS OF PRINCIPAL RACES AND COMPETITIONS

Year	*Winner*	*Speed m.p.h.*	*Pilot*	*Aircraft*	*Nat.*	*Engine*	*Nat.*	*Place*	*Contest described on page*
				THE GORDON BENNETT CONTESTS					
1909	U.S.A.	46	G. Curtiss	Curtiss	U.S.A.	Curtiss	U.S.A.	Rheims	—
1910	Gt. Britain	60	C. Grahame-White	Bleriot	Fr.	Gnôme	Fr.	New York	I., 62
1911	U.S.A.	78	C. T. Weymann	Nieuport	Fr.	Gnôme	Fr.	Eastchurch	I., 102
1912	France	105	J. Vedrines	Deperdussin	Fr.	Gnôme	Fr.	Chicago	I., 192
1913	France	124·5	M. Prevost	Deperdussin	Fr.	Gnôme	Fr.	Rheims	II., 72
				THE SCHNEIDER TROPHY					
1913	France	45·75*	M. Prevost	Deperdussin	Fr.	Gnôme	Fr.	Monaco	II., 25
1914	Gt. Britain	85·5	H. Pixton	Sopwith	G.B.	Gnôme	Fr.	Monaco	II., 111
				THE AERIAL DERBY					
1912	Gt. Britain	58·5	T. O. M. Sopwith	Bleriot	Fr.	Gnôme	Fr.	Circuit of London	I., 158
1913	Gt. Britain	76	G. Hamel	Morane-Saulnier	Fr.	Gnôme	Fr.	Circuit of London	II., 62
1914	U.S.A.	71·9	W. L. Brock	Morane-Saulnier	Fr.	Le Rhone	Fr.	Circuit of London	II., 122

*The pilot failed to cross the finishing line correctly, and was compelled to take off again after he had alighted and repeat his last lap. His actual speed was approximately 61 m.p.h.

RESULTS OF PRINCIPAL RACES AND COMPETITIONS

Year	Winner	Distance covered	Duration	Aircraft	Engine	Place	Contest described on page
			THE BRITISH EMPIRE MICHELIN CUP, No 1.				
1910	S. F. Cody	185·46 m.	4 hrs. 47 mins.	Cody	60 Green	Laffan's Plain	I., 69
1911	S. F. Cody	261·5 m.	5 hrs. 15 mins.	Cody	60 Green	Laffan's Plain	I., 120
1912	H. G. Hawker	——	8 hrs. 23 mins.	Sopwith-Wright	40/50 A.B.C.	Brooklands	I., 196
1913	R. H. Carr	315 m.	——	Grahame-White "Charabancs"	100 Green	Hendon to Brooklands and back, landing at every third turn.	II., 76
			THE BRITISH EMPIRE MICHELIN CUP, No. 2				
1911	S. F. Cody	125 m.	3 hrs. 6 mins. 30 secs.	Cody	60 Green	Cross-country circuit from Laffan's Plain	I., 119
1912	S. F. Cody	186 m.	3 hrs. 26 mins.	Cody	100 Green	Cross-country circuit from Laffan's Plain	I., 196
1913	H. G. Hawker*	265 m.	5 hrs.	Sopwith	100 Green	Cross-country circuit from Brooklands	II., 77

* Mr. Hawker was not awarded the prize as he failed, by twenty miles, to complete the course. I have inserted his name, however, as having made the best attempt. The prize was withdrawn.

Other Important Awards

Date	*Nature of Contest*	*Winner*	*Nat.*	*Aircraft*	*Nat.*	*Engine*	*Nat.*	*Prize*	*Awarded by*	*Contest described on page*
1908										
Jan. 13th	First circular flight of one kilometre in Europe	H. Farman	Br.	Voisin	Fr.	Vivinus	Fr.	50,000 fr.	Mons. D. Archdeacon	I., 21
1909										
July 25th	First flight from France to England	L. Bleriot	Fr.	Bleriot	Fr.	Anzani	Fr.	£1,000	*Daily Mail*	I., 30
Oct. 30th	First circular flight of one mile on all-British aeroplane	J. T. C. Moore-Brabazon	Br.	Short	Br.	Green	Br.	£1,000	*Daily Mail*	I., 35
1910										
April 26th and 27th	First flight from London to Manchester	L. Paulhan	Fr.	H. Farman	Fr.	Gnôme	Fr.	£10,000	*Daily Mail*	I., 43
Sept. 7th	Thirty-three miles cross-country race round Boston, U.S.A.	C. Grahame-White	Br.	H. Farman	Fr.	Gnôme	Fr.	£2,000	*Boston Globe*	I., 58
Oct.	Thirty-three miles race from Belmont Park, round the Statue of Liberty, in New York Harbour, and back	C. Grahame-White	Br.	Bleriot	Fr.	Gnôme	Fr.	£2,000	Mr. Ryan	I., 63
Dec. 18th	Greatest distance flown from any point in England into the Continent of Europe on an all-British aeroplane	T. O. M. Sopwith	Br.	Howard-Wright	Br.	E.N.V.	Br.	£4,000	Baron de Forest	I., 70
1911										
May 6th	Race from Brooklands to Brighton	G. Hamel	Br.	Bleriot	Fr.	Gnôme	Fr.	£80	—	I., 93
June 18th-July 7th	The European Circuit	" Beaumont " (Lt. de V. Conneau)	Fr.	Bleriot	Fr.	Gnôme	Fr.	£18,300	Various	I., 98
July 22nd-26th	The Circuit of Britain	"Beaumont" (Lt. de V. Conneau)	Fr.	Bleriot	Fr.	Gnôme	Fr.	£10,000	*Daily Mail*	I., 105

Date	Nature of Contest	Winner	Nat.	Aircraft	Nat.	Engine	Nat.	Prize	Awarded by	Contest described on page
August	Fourteen miles race across Lake Michigan from Chicago, and other events at Chicago	T. O. M. Sopwith	Br.	Bleriot	Fr.	Gnôme	Fr.	15,000 $.	Various	I., 112
1912										
Feb. 14th	Greatest distance flown, non-stop, by an Army officer	Lieut. B. H. Barrington-Kennett	Br.	Nieuport	Fr.	Gnôme	Fr.	£500	Mr. Mortimer Singer	I., 136
April	Ditto, by a Naval officer	Lieut. Longmore, R.N.	Br.	Short	Br.	Gnôme	Fr.	£500	Mr. Mortimer Singer	I., 144
August	The Military Trials	S. F. Cody	Br.	Cody	Br.	Austro-Daimler	Aus	£5,000	British Government	I., 167
September	Dublin to Belfast race	Tie { H. J. D. Astley J. Valentine	Br. Br.	Bleriot Deperdussin	Fr. Fr.	Gnôme Gnôme	Fr. Fr.	} £300	Irish Ae. C.	I., 189
1913										
July 8th	Six out-and-home flights on all-British amphibian, alighting alternately on land and water	H. G. Hawker	Br.	Sopwith Batboat	Br.	Green	Br.	£500	Mr. Mortimer Singer	II., 44
August 25th–27th	Seaplane Circuit of Britain	H. G. Hawker	Br.	Sopwith float seaplane	Br.	Green	Br.	£1,000 (consolation)	*Daily Mail*	II., 53
Nov. 8th	Race from Hendon to Brighton, and back	G. Hamel	Br.	Morane-Saulnier	Fr.	Gnôme	Fr.	£50	Mr. B. Walker	II., 75
Nov. 8th	Ditto, on handicap	P. Verrier	Fr.	M. Farman	Br.	Renault	Fr.	£100	Sussex Motor Yacht Club	II., 75
1914										
June 20th	Race from Hendon to Manchester and back	W. L. Brock	U.S.	Morane-Saulnier	Fr.	Gnôme	Fr.	£650	Anglo-American Oil Co., Ltd.	II., 129
July 11th	Race from Hendon to Paris and back	W. L. Brock	U.S.	Morane-Saulnier	Fr.	Gnôme	Fr.	{ £500 £300	International Correspondence Schools Royal Aero Club	II., 132

APPENDIX C

THE ROLL OF HONOUR

A LIST OF FATAL ACCIDENTS TO BRITISH PILOTS

Pilot	Place of Fatality	Date	Aircraft	Cause of Accident	Accident described on page
		1910			
1. Rolls C.S.	Bournemouth	July 11	French-built Wright biplane	Tail booms broke on pulling out from a short dive	I., 50
2. Grace, Cecil	Straits of Dover	Dec. 22	Short-built Farman biplane	Lost in fog and descended in the North Sea	I., 72
		1911			
3. Benson, Bernard G.	Hendon	May 25	Valkyrie pusher monoplane	Error of judgment by pupil. Stalled in attempting first gliding descent with engine off	I., 96
4. Smith, Vladimir	St. Petersburg	May 27	Russian-built Sommer biplane	Apparently the pilot, who was inexperienced, failed to pull out of a dive in time	I., 96
5. Napier, Gerald	Brooklands	Aug. 1	Bristol biplane	The pilot, who was inexperienced, was caught by a gust in a gliding turn, over-banked, and side-slipped into the ground	I., 110
6. Ridge, Theodore	Farnborough	Aug. 18	de Havilland experimental machine from Army Balloon Factory	The pilot, who was inexperienced, stalled on a gliding turn	I., 110
7. Cammell, R. A.	Hendon	Sept. 17	Valkyrie pusher monoplane (Gnôme)	The pilot, who had no previous experience of this type, overbanked on a gliding turn, and side-slipped into the ground	I., 116
8. Oxley, Hubert	Filey	Dec. 6	Blackburn monoplane	The pilot tore the wings off in trying to pull up sharply from a very fast dive	I., 122
9. Weiss, Robert J.	(Pupil with above)				

Pilot	Place of Fatality	Date	Aircraft	Cause of Accident	Accident described on page
		1912			
10. Gilmour, Graham	Richmond Park	Feb. 17	Martin-Handasyde monoplane (8-cyl. Antoinette)	Exact cause unknown. Probably the aircraft broke in the air as a result of hitting a violent bump. The machine fell vertically 400 ft., and was completely smashed.	I., 136
11. Allen, D. L.	Irish Sea	Apr. 18	Bleriot monoplane (50 h.p. Gnôme)	Lost at Sea	I., 152
12. Fisher, E.V.B.	Brooklands	May 13	Flanders monoplane (60 h.p. Green)	The pilot stalled on a gliding turn at 100 ft., and dived into the ground vertically	I., 156
13. Loraine, E. B.	Salisbury Plain	July 5	Nieuport monoplane (70 h.p. Gnôme)	The pilot attempted a tight turn, side-slipped inwards and dived into the ground from 400 ft.	I., 162
14. Wilson, R. H. V.	(Passenger with above)				
15. Campbell, Lindsay	Brooklands	Aug. 3	Bristol monoplane (50 h.p. Gnôme)	The pilot, who was inexperienced, failed to depress the nose when throttling back to commence a glide. The aircraft stalled at 300 ft., and began a dive from which the pilot recovered, but once more he held the nose up until a second stall and dive took place, and this time there was insufficient height left to enable him to pull out	I., 165
16. Fenwick, R. C.	Salisbury Plain	Aug. 13	Mersey pusher monoplane (45 h.p. Isaacson)	This aircraft was an experimental type, and it is probable that the tail booms were inadequately trussed and consequently flexed, thus causing the machine to dive suddenly to the ground	I., 186
17. Hamilton, Patrick	Graveley	Sept. 6	Deperdussin monoplane (Gnôme)	The machine broke up in the air whilst flying normally at 2,500 feet.	I., 190

Pilot	Place of Fatality	Date	Aircraft	Cause of Accident	Accident described on page
18. Wyness-Stuart	(Passenger with above)	**1912**			
19. Hotchkiss, E.	Oxford	Sept. 10	Bristol monoplane (80 h.p. Gnôme)	The machine broke up in the air owing to the accidental opening of a quick-release fastener during a gliding descent	I., 190
20. Bettington, C. (Passenger with above)					
21. Astley, H. J. D.	Belfast	Sept. 21	Bleriot monoplane (70 h.p. Gnôme	The pilot, who was giving an exhibition flight from a narrow ground, attempted a tight turn in a restricted place at a low height. The machine side-slipped out of the turn into the ground	I., 192
22. Parke, Wilfred	Wembley	Dec. 15	Handley-Page monoplane (50 h.p. Gnôme)	The pilot took off with a failing engine and, finding he could not maintain height, attempted to turn downwind to get back to the aerodrome. He stalled on the turn. His passenger, Mr. A. Hardwick, was also killed	I., 199
23. Petre, Edward	Marske-by-the-Sea	Dec. 24	Martin Handasyde monoplane (65 h.p. Antoinette)	The machine broke up in the air whilst flying normally in a high wind	I., 200
		1913			
24. Macdonald, Leslie F.	Erith	Jan. 13	Vickers tractor biplane (70 h.p. Gnôme)	The pilot, who was very experienced, took off with a failing engine, which let him down in the River Thames. Both he and his passenger, Mr. H. England, were drowned	II., 13
25. England, Geoffrey	Salisbury Plain	March 5	Bristol monoplane (80 h.p. Gnôme)	The machine broke up in the air, several wing-ribs becoming detached from the spars at 600 feet, whilst the machine was gliding	II., 20
26. Berne, E. R.	Eastchurch	April 21	Short tractor biplane (70 h.p. Gnôme)	Paymaster E. R. Berne, R.N., was standing in front of	

Pilot	Place of Fatality	Date	Aircraft	Cause of Accident	Accident described on page
		1913		the machine talking to the pilot when it ran forward, there being no chocks, and the airscrew struck his legs, so that he died two hours later. He was a qualified pilot of the Naval Wing, R.F.C.	
27. Rogers-Harrison, L. C.	Farnborough	April 28	Cody pusher biplane (120 h.p. Austro-Daimler	The aircraft, which had been badly maintained, and was constructed of pieces of older machines, broke up in the air whilst gliding in to land at a height of 500 feet	II., 28
28. Arthur, Desmond L.	Montrose	May 27	B.E.2 tractor biplane (70 h.p. Renault)	The top right-hand wing-tip broke up in the air as a result of faulty repairs to a broken main spar, executed either at the Royal Aircraft Factory, or in the R.F.C.	II., 31
29. Kennedy, Jas. Robt. Branch	Brooklands	June 13	Martin-Handasyde monoplane (120 h.p. Austro Daimler)	The deceased was flying as passenger with Mr. Gordon Bell who stalled low down in a climbing turn, whilst flying dangerously in the course of a stunting exhibition	II., 39
30. Wight, Richard Norton	Shoreham	June 29	Avro tractor biplane (60 h.p. E.N.V.)	The pilot, who was inexperienced, ignored his instructor's warning not to turn with a failing engine. He stalled, and was burned to death	II., 44
31. Hewetson, Alex'der Wm.	Salisbury Plain	July 17	Bristol monoplane (sociable) (50 h.p. Gnôme)	The pilot was a pupil engaged on flying figures of eight as part of the tests for his certificate. He overbanked on a turn and sideslipped into the ground from 100 feet	II., 45

Pilot	Place of Fatality	Date	Aircraft	Cause of Accident	Accident Described on page
		1913			
32. Cody, S. F.	Farnborough	Aug. 7	Cody pusher biplane (100 h.p. Green)	The main front spar of the left lower wing broke in the air whilst the machine was gliding at 200 feet in good weather. The pilot and his passenger, Mr. Evans, were not strapped in, and consequently fell out when the aircraft turned upside down and were killed	II., 52
33. Merrick, Geo. Charlton	Upavon	Oct. 3	Short biplane (70 h.p. Gnôme)	The pilot, who was inexperienced, was making a steep gliding descent, when apparently he slipped out of his seat, having no belt, and fell forward on to the control column, thus causing the machine to bunt on to its back. The pilot fell out and was killed	II., 73
34. Cheeseman E. W.	Kimberley, S. Africa	Oct. 13	Paterson pusher biplane (50 h.p. Gnôme)	No detailed particulars are available, but it seems probable that either the pilot or his pupil stalled the machine at 100 ft. above an aerodrome which was situated at 4,000 ft. above sea level. The passenger escaped unhurt, but the pilot died two days later	II., 74
35. Wildman-Lushington, G. V.	Eastchurch	Dec. 2	Short biplane (Gnôme)	The pilot apparently overbanked on a gliding turn whilst approaching to land, and sideslipped into the ground on to one wing tip. He was crushed by the petrol tank and received injuries from which he died	II., 83

Pilot	Place of Fatality	Date	Aircraft	Cause of Accident	Accident described on page
		1914			
36. Temple, G. Lee	Hendon	Jan. 25	Bleriot monoplane (50 h.p. Gnôme)	Apparently the pilot, who was unwell, fainted in the air and fell forward on to the control column whilst flying level at 150 feet. The machine bunted and landed upside down, the pilot's neck being broken	II., 96
37. Gipps, G. L.	Salisbury Plain	Jan. 26	Bristol monoplane (50 h.p. Gnôme)	The deceased pilot was receiving dual instruction from Mr. Warren Merriam, when a mistake occurred as to who was in control. This resulted in the machine making a flat turn, stalling, and diving into the ground from 50 feet. Mr. Merriam was injured	II., 97
38. Newberry, George	Argentine	Mar. 1	Morane Saulnier monoplane (Le Rhone)	The pilot was starting upon the first attempt to fly over the Andes, when, for some unexplained reason, the machine crashed. The passenger, Lieut. Raston, was seriously injured	II., 98
39. Downer, Cyril Percy	Salisbury Plain	Mar. 10	B.E.2 tractor biplane (70 h.p. Renault)	The pilot was practising gliding turns. It is probable that the elevators jammed down, and that the pilot tugged at the control column until they jerked free, after the machine had dived 1,500 feet. The sudden reversal of the control caused the wings to break up	II., 101
40. Allen, Clement Robert Wedgwood	Salisbury Plain	Mar. 11	B.E. tractor biplane (80 h.p. Gnôme)	The rudder fell off the machine during a gentle turn at a height of 350	II., 101

Pilot	Place of Fatality	Date	Aircraft	Cause of Accident	Accident described on page
		1914		feet. The machine then went into an uncontrollable spin	
41. Burroughs, James Edward Godfrey	(Passenger with above)				
42. Treeby, Hugh Frederic	Salisbury Plain	Mar. 19	Maurice Farman pusher biplane (70 h.p. Renault)	The pilot, who was inexperienced, stalled the machine at 350 feet, when about to commence a glide The machine dived into the ground out of control	II., 102
43. Deane, Eric Norman	Brooklands	April 8	Bristol pusher biplane (50 h.p. Gnôme)	The pilot was not strapped into his seat, and he fell out whilst making a steep gliding turn	II., 110
44. Anderson, E. V.	Farnborough	May 12	Sopwith three-seater tractor biplane (80 h.p. Gnôme)	The machine came into collision with another similar Sopwith, flown by Lieut. C. W. Wilson, at a height of about 500 feet. Both aircraft were wrecked. Capt. Anderson and his passenger, Air Mechanic Carter, were killed instantaneously, and Lieut Wilson was injured	II., 116
45. Empson, John	Northallerton	May 15	B.E.2 tractor biplane (70 h.p. Renault)	The pilot flew into a dense fog and hit a hedge in attempting to make a landing. The machine cartwheeled on to its back, and Lieut. Empson and his passenger, Air Mechanic Geo. Cudmore, were killed instantaneously	II., 117
46. Hamel, Gustav	Straits of Dover	May 23	Morane-Saulnier monoplane (80 h.p. Gnôme)	Lost at sea	II., 120
47. Creswell, T. S.	Calshot	June 4	Short seaplane	Probably the pilot stalled on a turn at a low height, and	II., 125

Pilot	Place of Fatality	Date	Aircraft	Cause of Accident	Accident described on page
		1914		applied full elevator violently in order to pull out of the resultant dive. The left-hand pair of wings collapsed and the machine dived into Southampton Water. Com. Rice, R.N., a passenger in the machine, was also killed	
48. Hordern, L. C.	Gosport	July 20	Henry Farman pusher biplane (80 h.p. Gnôme)	The pilot stalled at 800 feet, and the machine began a left-handed spin, which continued until it hit the ground	II., 137

APPENDIX D

LIST OF PILOTS WHO QUALIFIED FOR R.Ae.C. SPECIAL CERTIFICATES UP TO AND INCLUDING AUGUST 4TH, 1914

Explanatory Note.

Special Certificates were granted by the R.Ae.C. to candidates who passed the following tests :—

" (i). A cross-country flight out and back round a point situated at least fifty miles from the start. The turning point will be selected by the R.Ae.C., and will not be indicated to the candidate until one hour before the starting time selected by the candidate. This flight shall be completed within five hours of the selected starting time.

" (ii). A separate altitude flight of at least 1,000 feet rise, which shall be verified by recording barograph, sealed by the observers prior to the start.

" (iii). To glide from a height of at least 500 feet above the ground to earth, with engine completely cut off, and alight under normal conditions within 100 yards from the starting point. This glide may at the candidate's option, be the conclusion of test (ii)."

Pilot	*Date*	*Aircraft*	*Course flown*
1. Mr. S. F. Cody	Dec. 6th, 1911	Cody biplane	Laffan's Plain to Shrewton, Wilts., and back
2. Mr. James Valentine	Dec. 6th, 1911	Bristol monoplane	Salisbury to Laffan's Plain and back
3. Capt. J. D. B. Fulton, R.F.A.	Dec. 6th, 1911	Bristol biplane	Salisbury to Laffan's Plain and back

Note.—At this stage the rules were amended so as to ensure that in future each candidate should complete tests (ii) and (iii) above before he attempted test (i).

Pilot	*Date*	*Aircraft*	*Course flown*
4. Mr. Geoffrey de Havilland	Jan. 9th, 1912	B.E. biplane	Farnborough to Shrewton and back
5. Lieut. A. G. Fox, R.F.C.	July 16th, 1912	Bristol biplane	Lark Hill to Cheltenham and back
6. Capt. P. Hamilton	July 24th, 1912	Deperdussin monoplane	Lark Hill to Weymouth and back
7. Lieut.-Col. H. R. Cook, R.F.C.	Sept. 3rd, 1912		
8. Mr. Sydney Pickles	July 1st, 1913	Caudron biplane	Hendon to Brighton and back
9. Lieut. R. Cholmondeley, R.F.C.	Sept. 2nd, 1913	H. Farman biplane	Netheravon to Chichester and back

APPENDIX E

AVIATORS' CERTIFICATES ISSUED BY THE ROYAL AERO CLUB

COMPLETE LIST UP TO AND INCLUDING AUGUST 4TH, 1914

Explanatory Notes.

1. *Foreign Subjects*.—The names of the fifty-two foreign subjects who learned to fly in England are set in italics, and their nationality is indicated by symbols in brackets after their names.

2. *Dates*.—The first 452 Certificates bore the date of the committee meeting at which they were issued, and are set out in numerical order below. Many of the pilots who took out certificates in 1910 had actually learned to fly in the previous year, but from 1911 onwards, it may be assumed that each candidate had passed his tests from 7 to 14 days prior to the date on which his certificate was granted. Certificates Nos. 453–864 inclusive, were dated back to the actual date on which the tests were passed, and are set out in chronological, instead of numerical, order.

3. *Machines*.—The machines given in the table are those upon which the tests were passed, and, unless it is otherwise stated, were biplanes. In the case of the earlier certificates, the machines mentioned are not necessarily the machines upon which the candidates had learned to fly originally.

4. *Schools*.—Wherever possible the school of flying at which each pilot was trained is indicated by a symbol as follows :—Ae.S. = Aeronautical Syndicate ; Av. = Avro ; Bea. = Beattie ; Bl. = Bleriot ; Blac. = Blackburn ; Br. = Bristol ; Cau. = Caudron ; C.F.S. = Central Flying School, R.F.C. ; Cod. = Cody ; Dep. = Deperdussin ; Ducq. = Ducrocq ; E.A.C. = Eastbourne Aviation Co. ; Ew. = Ewen ; G.W. = Grahame-White ; Ha. = Hall ; Han. = Hanriot ; H. and B. = Hewlett and Blondeau ; H.P. = Handley-Page ; L.F.S. = Lakes Flying School ; McA. & D. = McArdle and Drexel ; Mel. = Melly ; N.S. = Naval School ; Og. = Ogilvie ; Per. = Percival ; R.F.C. = Royal Flying Corps (Military Wing) ; S.F.S. = Shoreham Flying School ; Sop. = Sopwith ; Sp. = Spencer ; Tem. = Temple ; Vic. = Vickers. Where no indication is given, it may be assumed that the pilot concerned either taught himself to fly, was privately instructed on his own or a friend's machine, or that he learned at a school abroad.

5. *Asterisks*.—The name of each pilot who was killed in a flying accident prior to August 4th, 1914, is marked with an asterisk.

6. *Tests.*—The first four certificates were granted to established pilots before any set tests had been agreed upon. The original and subsequent tests are noted in the table as each change occurred.

No. of Cert.	*Candidate*	*Date granted*	*Machine used for tests*	*Where qualified*
		1910		
1	Mr. J. T. C. Moore Brabazon	Mar. 8,	Short	Shellbeach
2	The Hon. C. S. Rolls*	Mar. 8,	Short-Wright	Shellbeach
3	Mr. A. Rawlinson	Apr. 5,	Henry Farman	Shellbeach
4	Mr. Cecil S. Grace*	Apr. 12,	Short-Wright	Eastchurch

Note.—The following certificates (Nos. 5 to 65 inclusive) were granted upon the candidate having passed the following tests, except those taken abroad, which were granted under the rules of the *Aero Club de France* :—" Three separate flights must be made, each of three miles round a circular course without coming to the ground. These flights need not necessarily be made on the same day. On the completion of each flight the engine must be stopped in the air, and a landing effected within 150 yards of a given spot previously designated by the candidate to the official observers."

No. of Cert.	*Candidate*	*Date granted*	*Machine used for tests*	*Where qualified*
		1910		
5	Mr. G. B. Cockburn	Apr. 26,	Henry Farman	Mourmelon
6	Mr. Claude Grahame-White	Apr. 26,	Bleriot monoplane	Pau
7	Mr. Alec Ogilvie	May 24,	Short-Wright	Camber, near Rye
8	Mr. A. Mortimer-Singer	May 31,	Henry Farman	Mourmelon
9	Mr. S. F. Cody*	June 7,	Cody	Laffan's Plain
10	Lieut. L. D. L. Gibbs	June 7,	Henry Farman	Mourmelon
11	The Hon. Maurice Egerton	June 14,	Short-Wright	Eastchurch
12	Mr. James Radley	June 14,	Bleriot monoplane	Brooklands
13	The Hon. Alan Boyle	June 14,	Avis monoplane	Brooklands
14	*Mr. J. Armstrong Drexel (U.S.A.)*	June 21,	Bleriot monoplane (G.W.)	Beaulieu, Hants
15	Mr. G. C. Colmore	June 21,	Short	Eastchurch
16	Mr. G. A. Barnes	June 21,	Humber monoplane	Brooklands
17	Capt. G. W. P. Dawes	July 26,	Humber monoplane	Wolverhampton
18	Mr. A. V. Roe	July 26,	Roe triplane	Brooklands
19	Mr. A. E. George	Sept. 6,	George and Jobling	Eastchurch
20	Mr. R. Wickham	Sept. 20,	Sommer	Brooklands
21	Mr. F. K. McClean	Sept. 20,	Short	Eastchurch
22	Mr. E. Keith Davies	Oct. 11,	Hanriot monoplane (Han.)	Brooklands
23	*Mons. M. Ducrocq (Fr.)*	Nov. 1	Henry Farman (H. & B.)	Brooklands
24	Mr. J. G. Weir	Nov. 8,	Bleriot monoplane (Bl.)	Hendon
25	Lieut. H. E. Watkins	Nov. 15,	Howard-Wright	Brooklands
26	Mr. C. H. Greswell	Nov. 15,	Grahame-White (G.W.)	Brooklands
27	Capt. J. D. B. Fulton	Nov. 15,	Henry Farman	Salisbury Plain
28	Mr. L. F. Macdonald*	Nov. 15,	Bristol (Br.)	Brooklands
29	Lieut. R. T. Snowden-Smith	Nov. 15,	Henry Farman (H. & B.)	Brooklands
30	Mr. H. Barber	Nov. 22,	Valkyrie monoplane	Hendon
31	Mr. T. O. M. Sopwith	Nov. 22,	Howard-Wright	Brooklands
32	Mr. J. J. Hammond	Nov. 22,	Bristol (Br.)	Salisbury Plain
33	Mr. A. R. Low	Nov. 22,	Bristol (Br.)	Brooklands
34	Mr. Sydney E. Smith	Nov. 22,	Bristol (Br.)	Brooklands
35	Mr. R. C. Fenwick*	Nov. 29,	Planes, Ltd.	Freshfield

No. of Cert.	*Candidate*	*Date granted*	*Machines used for tests*	*Where qualified*
		1910		
36	Capt. A. G. Board	Nov. 29,	Bleriot monoplane (Bl.)	Hendon
37	Capt. H. F. Wood	Nov. 29,	Bristol (Br.)	Brooklands
38	Mr. C. C. Paterson	Dec. 6,	Paterson	Freshfield
39	Mr. B. G. Bouwens	Dec. 31,	Bleriot monoplane (Bl.)	Hendon
40	Lieut. G. B. Hynes	Dec. 31,	Bleriot monoplane (Bl.)	Hendon
41	*Mr. St. Croix Johnstone (U.S.A.)*	Dec. 31,	Bleriot monoplane (Bl.)	Hendon
42	Maj. H. R. Cook	Dec. 31,	Bleriot monoplane (McA. & D.)	Beaulieu, Hants
43	Lieut. B. H. Barrington-Kennett	Dec. 31,	Bleriot monoplane (McA. & D.)	Hendon
44	Mr. P. G. L. Jezzi	Dec. 31,	Jezzi	Eastchurch
45	Lieut. R. A. Cammell	Dec. 31,	Bristol (Br.)	Salisbury Plain
		1911		
46	Mr. O. C. Morison	Jan. 17,	Bleriot monoplane	Brooklands
47	Mr. James Valentine	Jan. 17,	Macfie	Brooklands
48	Mr. H. J. D. Astley*	Jan. 24,	Sommer	Brooklands
49	Mr. Robert Macfie	Jan. 24,	Macfie	Brooklands
50	Mr. C. Howard Pixton	Jan. 24,	Roe (Av.)	Brooklands
51	Mr. H. J. Thomas	Jan. 24,	Bristol (Br.)	Salisbury Plain
52	Mr. E. V. Sassoon	Jan. 24,	Sommer	Brooklands
53	Mr. Geoffrey de Havilland	Feb. 7,	de Havilland	Farnborough
54	Lieut. D. G. Conner	Feb. 7,	Bristol (Br.)	Salisbury Plain
55	*Mr. J. V. Martin* (*U.S.A.*)	Feb. 7,	Henry Farman (G.W.)	Hendon
56	Mr. A. H. Aitken	Feb. 14,	Bleriot monoplane (McA. & D.)	Beaulieu, Hants
57	*Mons. C. L. A. Hubert* (*Fr.*)	Feb. 14,	Henry Farman (G.W.)	Hendon
58	Mr. G. H. Challenger	Feb. 14,	Bristol (Br.)	Salisbury Plain
59	Mr. G. R. S. Darroch	Feb. 14,	Bleriot monoplane (Bl.)	Hendon
60	Mr. Archibald Knight	Feb. 14,	Bristol (Br.)	Brooklands
61	Mr. Collyns P. Pizey	Feb. 14,	Bristol (Br.)	Salisbury Plain
62	*Mons. L. Maron* (*Fr.*)	Feb. 14,	Bristol (Br.)	Salisbury Plain
63	Mr. W. H. Ewen	Feb. 14,	Bleriot monoplane (Bl.)	Hendon
64	Mr. Gustav Hamel*	Feb. 14,	Bleriot monoplane (G.W.)	Hendon
65	*Signor Q. Poggioli* (*It.*)	Feb. 28,	Bleriot monoplane (McA. & D.)	Beaulieu, Hants

Note.—The following certificates (Nos. 66 to 719 inclusive, and No. 727) were granted upon the candidate having passed the following tests :—" *A*. Two distance flights, consisting of at least five kilometres (3 miles, 185 yards), each in a closed circuit, marked out by two posts situated not more than 500 metres (547 yards) apart, the aviator changing his direction after going round each post, so that the circuit shall consist of an uninterrupted series of five figures of eight, and, *B*. One altitude flight, consisting of a minimum height of fifty metres (164 feet), but this must not form part of one of the two flights prescribed above. The method of alighting for each of the three flights shall be with the motor stopped at or before the moment of touching the ground, and the aeroplane must come to rest within a distance of fifty metres (164 feet) from a point indicated previously by the candidate." These tests were applicable to certificates granted by the governing clubs of all nations affiliated to the F.A.I.

No. of Cert.	Candidate	Date granted	Machines used for tests	Where qualified
		1911		
66	Mr. Lewis W. F. Turner	Apr. 4,	Henry Farman (G.W.)	Hendon
67	Mr. W. Ridley Prentice	Apr. 25	Henry Farman (G.W.)	Hendon
68	Mr. E. C. Gordon England	Apr. 25	Bristol (Br.)	Brooklands
69	Mr. H. R. Fleming	Apr. 25,	Bristol (Br.)	Salisbury Plain
70	Mr. C. C. Turner	Apr. 25	Bristol (Br.)	Salisbury Plain
71	Lieut. C. R. Samson, R.N.	Apr. 25,	Short (N.S.)	Eastchurch
72	Lieut. A. M. Longmore, R.N.	Apr. 25,	Short (N.S.)	Eastchurch
73	Lieut. Wilfred Parke, R.N.*	Apr. 25,	Bristol (Br.)	Brooklands
74	Mr. F. Conway Jenkins	May 2,	Avro (Av.)	Brooklands
75	Lieut. R. Gregory, R.N.	May 2,	Short (N.S.)	Eastchurch
76	Lieut. E. L. Gerrard, R.M.L.I.	May 2,	Short (N.S.)	Eastchurch
77	Mr. E. V. B. Fisher*	May 2,	Hanriot monoplane (Han.)	Brooklands
78	Mr. Hubert Oxley*	May 9,	Hanriot monoplane (Han.)	Brooklands
79	Mr. Harold Blackburn	May 9,	Bristol (Br.)	Brooklands
80	Mr. R. C. Kemp	May 9,	Avro (Av.)	Brooklands
81	Mr. R. W. Philpott	May 9,	Bristol (Br.)	Salisbury Plain
82	Mr. W. H. Dolphin	May 9,	Hanriot monoplane (Han.)	Brooklands
83	Lieut. C. H. Marks	May 9,	Henry Farman (H. & B.)	Brooklands
84	Capt. S. D. Massy	May 9,	Bristol (Br.)	Salisbury Plain
85	Mr. F. P. Raynham	May 9,	Avro (Av.)	Brooklands
86	Mr. J. L. Travers	May 16,	Henry Farman (G.W.)	Hendon
87	Mr. Edward Hotchkiss*	May 16,	Bristol (Br.)	Salisbury Plain
88	Capt. T. C. R. Higgins	May 16,	Henry Farman (G.W.)	Hendon
89	Lieut. W. D. Beatty	May 30,	Avro (Av.)	Brooklands
90	Lieut. R. B. Davies, R.N.	May 30,	Henry Farman (G.W.)	Hendon
91	Mr. B. C. Hucks	May 30,	Blackburn monoplane (Blac.)	Filey
92	Lieut. H. R. P. Reynolds	June 6,	Bristol (Br.)	Salisbury Plain
93	Mr. T. H. Sebag-Montefiore	June 13,	Bristol (Br.)	Salisbury Plain
94	Mr. H. R. Busteed	June 13,	Bristol (Br.)	Salisbury Plain
95	Capt. F. H. Sykes	June 20,	Bristol (Br.)	Brooklands
96	Mr. G. Higginbotham	June 27,	Curtiss	Freshfield
97	Mr. H. Stanley-Adams	June 27,	Avro (Av.)	Brooklands
98	Lieut. J. W. Pepper	June 27,	Bristol (Br.)	Salisbury Plain
99	*M. Henri Salmet (Fr.)*	June 27,	Bleriot (Bl.)	Hendon
100	Mr. C. Gordon Bell	July 4,	Hanriot monoplane (Han.)	Brooklands
101	Mr. C. R. Abbott	July 4,	Henry Farman (H. & B.)	Brooklands
102	*Mr. W. M. Hilliard (U.S.A.)*	July 4,	Henry Farman (H. & B.)	Brooklands
103	Mr. W. D. Johnstone	July 4,	Henry Farman (H. & B.)	Brooklands
104	Mr. Gerald Napier*	July 18,	Bristol (Br.)	Brooklands
105	Lieut. T. G. Hetherington	July 18,	Henry Farman (H. & B.)	Brooklands
106	Mr. C. L. Pashley	July 18,	Sommer	Brooklands
107	Mr. H. de Grey Warter	July 18,	Bristol (Br.)	Brooklands
108	Capt. C. R. Brooke-Popham	July 18,	Bristol (Br.)	Brooklands
109	*Mr. H. B. Brown (U.S.A.)*	Aug. 1,	Henry Farman (H. & B.)	Brooklands
110	Mr. E. F. Driver	Aug. 1,	Henry Farman (G.W.)	Hendon
111	Mr. N. S. Percival	Aug. 1,	Billing	Brooklands
112	Mr. W. Oswald Watt	Aug. 1,	Bristol (Br.)	Salisbury Plain
113	Mr. W. Lawrence	Aug. 1,	Bristol (Br.)	Salisbury Plain
114	Mr. G. M. Dyott	Aug. 17,	Bleriot (Bl.)	Hendon
115	Lieut.-Col. C. O. Smeaton	Aug. 17,	Bristol (Br.)	Salisbury Plain
116	*M. Louis Noel (Fr.)*	Aug. 17,	Avro (Av.)	Brooklands
117	Lieut. Spencer D. A. Grey, R.N.	Aug. 17,	Henry Farman (H. & B.)	Brooklands
118	Brig.-Gen. D. Henderson, C.B., D.S.O.	Aug, 17,	Bristol (Br.)	Brooklands
119	Mr. Theodore J. Ridge*	Aug. 17,	Bristol (Br.)	Salisbury Plain
120	*Lieut. C. O. Dahlbeck (Swed.)*	Aug. 29,	Henry Farman (G.W.)	Hendon
121	Lieut. L. V. S. Blacker	Aug. 29,	Bristol (Br.)	Salisbury Plain

No. of Cert.	Candidate	Date granted	Machines used for tests	Where qualified
		1911		
122	Mrs. Hilda B. Hewlett	Aug. 29,	Henry Farman (H. & B.)	Brooklands
123	Mr. W. C. England	Aug. 29,	Henry Farman (G.W.)	Hendon
124	Mr. Herbert Spencer	Aug. 29,	Spencer-Farman	Brooklands
125	Capt. D. Le G. Pitcher	Aug. 29,	Bristol (Br.)	Salisbury Plain
126	Capt. C. G. Hoare	Aug. 29,	Bristol (Br.)	Salisbury Plain
127	Lieut. R. H. C. Hall, R.N.	Aug. 29,	Bristol (Br.)	Brooklands
128	Mr. H. A. Petre	Sept. 12,	Hanriot monoplane (Han.)	Brooklands
129	Mr. W. E. Gibson	Sept. 12,	Bristol (Br.)	Salisbury Plain
130	Mr. E. W. C. Perry	Sept. 12,	Valkyrie monoplane (Ae.S.)	Hendon
131	Mr. E. Harrison	Sept. 12,	Bristol (Br.)	Salisbury Plain
132	Mr. S. P. Cockerell	Sept. 12,	Bristol (Br.)	Salisbury Plain
133	Mr. R. O. Crawshay	Sept. 12,	Bleriot monoplane (Bl.)	Hendon
134	Mr. R. O. Abercrombie	Sept. 12,	Bleriot monoplane (Bl.)	Hendon
135	Lieut. G. J. E. Manisty	Sept. 12,	Hanriot monoplane (Han.)	Brooklands
136	Mr. J. Brereton	Sept. 19,	Bristol (Br.)	Brooklands
137	Mr. A. Hunter	Sept. 19,	Henry Farman (Av.)	Brooklands
138	Mr. A. Dukinfield Jones	Sept. 19,	Bleriot monoplane (Mel.)	Liverpool
139	Mr. E. C. Pashley	Sept. 26,	Sommer	Brooklands
140	Mr. J. L. Longstaffe	Sept. 26,	Henry Farman (H. & B.)	Brooklands
141	Lieut. A. W. Stuart*	Sept. 26,	Bristol (Br.)	Brooklands
142	Capt. F. W. Richey	Oct. 3,	Bristol (Br.)	Brooklands
143	Capt. Steele Hutcheson	Oct. 3,	Bristol (Br.)	Salisbury Plain
144	Lieut. C. L. N. Newall	Oct. 3,	Bristol (Br.)	Salisbury Plain
145	Lieut. E. J. Strover	Oct. 10,	Bristol (Br.)	Salisbury Plain
146	Mr. L. S. Metford	Oct. 17,	Bleriot monoplane (Bl.)	Hendon
147	Mr. W. B. Rhodes-Moorhouse	Oct. 17,	Bleriot monoplane	Huntingdon
148	*Mr. Zee Yee Lee (China)*	Oct. 17,	Bristol (Br.)	Salisbury Plain
149	Lieut. A. F. A. Hooper	Oct. 24,	Bristol (Br.)	Salisbury Plain
150	Lieut. E. G. K. Cross	Oct. 24,	Bristol (Br.)	Salisbury Plain
151	*Mr. F. M. Ballard (U.S.A.)*	Oct. 31,	Spencer (Sp.)	Brooklands
152	Lieut. H. H. Harford	Nov. 7,	Bristol (Br.)	Brooklands
153	Mrs. C. de Beauvoir Stocks	Nov. 7,	Henry Farman (G.W.)	Hendon
154	Capt. E. B. Loraine*	Nov. 7,	Valkyrie monoplane (Ae.S.)	Hendon
155	Mr. O. L. Mellersh	Nov. 14,	Bristol (Br.)	Salisbury Plain
156	Sub.-Lieut. F. E. T. Hewlett, R.N.	Nov. 14,	Henry Farman (H. & B.)	Brooklands
157	Mr. R. B. Slack	Nov. 14,	Bleriot monoplane (Bl.)	Hendon
158	Capt. R. S. M. Harrison	Nov. 14,	Bristol (Br.)	Brooklands
159	Capt. C. R. W. Allen*	Nov. 14,	Bristol (Br.)	Brooklands
160	Lieut. H. A. Williamson, R.N.	Nov. 28,	Bristol (Br.)	Salisbury Plain
161	Mr. R. Smith-Barry	Nov. 28,	Bristol (Br.)	Salisbury Plain
162	Mr. G. B. Dacre	Nov. 28,	Bristol (Br.)	Salisbury Plain
163	Lieut. J. G. Bower, R.N.	Nov. 28,	Bristol (Br.)	Salisbury Plain
164	Mr. J. A Anderson	Nov. 28,	Sommer	Brooklands
165	Maj. R. L. Benwell	Dec. 6,	Bristol (Br.)	Brooklands
166	Capt. R. Gordon, R.M.	Dec. 6,	Bristol (Br.)	Brooklands
167	Mr. J. D. P. Chataway	Dec. 12,	Deperdussin monoplane (Dep.)	Brooklands
168	Mr. C. F. M. Chambers	Dec. 12,	Valkyrie monoplane (Ae.S.)	Hendon
		1912		
169	Lieut. G. T. Porter	Jan. 9,	Bristol (Br.)	Salisbury Plain
170	Lieut. A. E. Borton	Jan. 9,	Bristol (Br.)	Salisbury Plain
171	Mr. B. G. Wood	Jan. 9,	Henry Farman (H. & B.)	Brooklands
172	Mr. S. V. Sippe	Jan. 9,	Avro (Av.)	Brooklands
173	Mr. T. Garne	Jan. 16,	Bristol (Br.)	Brooklands
174	Lieut. N. G. Gill	Jan. 16,	Deperdussin monoplane (Dep.)	Brooklands

No. of Cert.	Candidate	Date granted	Machines used for tests	Where qualified
		1912		
175	Mr. F. B. Fowler	Jan. 16,	Bleriot monoplane (E.A.C.)	Eastbourne
176	Lieut. A. G. Fox	Jan. 30,	Bristol (Br.)	Salisbury Plain
177	Lieut. E. M. Murray	Jan. 30,	Bristol (Br.)	Salisbury Plain
178	*Signor G. Sabelli (It.)*	Jan. 30,	Deperdussin monoplane (Dep.)	Brooklands
179	Mr. F. Warren Merriam	Feb. 6,	Bristol (Br.)	Brooklands
180	Mr. W. Bendall	Feb. 6,	Bristol (Br.)	Salisbury Plain
181	Eng.-Lieut. C. R. J. Randall, R.N.	Feb. 13,	Short (N.S.)	Eastchurch
182	Capt. T. Weeding	Feb. 13,	Bristol (Br.)	Brooklands
183	Mr. D. L. Allen*	Feb. 20,	Bleriot monoplane (Bl.)	Hendon
184	Mr. S. Parr	Feb. 20,	Bleriot monoplane (Bl.)	Hendon
185	Lieut. B. R. W. Beor	Feb. 20,	Bristol (Br.)	Salisbury Plain
186	*M. Marcel Desoutter (Fr.)*	Feb. 27,	Bleriot monoplane (Bl.)	Hendon
187	Lieut. S. C. Winfield-Smith	Feb. 27,	Bristol (Br.)	Brooklands
188	Lieut. C. T. Carfrae	Feb. 27,	Bristol (Br.)	Brooklands
189	Mr. H. D. Cutler	Mar. 5,	Short (N.S.)	Eastchurch
190	Mr. V. Barrington-Kennett	Mar. 5,	Short (N.S.)	Eastchurch
191	Lieut. C. G. W. Head, R.N.	Mar. 5,	Bristol (Br.)	Salisbury Plain
192	Lieut. C. A. H. Longcroft	Mar. 5,	Bristol (Br.)	Brooklands
193	Mr. C. W. Meredith	Mar. 5,	Short (N.S.)	Eastchurch
194	Capt. Patrick Hamilton*	Mar. 12,	Deperdussin monoplane (Dep.)	Brooklands
195	Lieut. C. J. L'Estrange Malone, R.N.	Mar. 12,	Short (N.S.)	Eastchurch
196	Capt. G. H. Raleigh	Mar. 12,	Bristol (Br.)	Brooklands
197	Mr. R. L. Charteris	Mar. 12,	Deperdussin monoplane (Dep.)	Brooklands
198	*Herr G. Prensiel (Ger.)*	Mar. 19,	Bleriot monoplane (Bl.)	Hendon
199	Mr. W. E. Hart	Mar. 26,	Bristol	Penrith, N.S.W.
200	Capt. F. J. Brodigan	Mar. 26,	Bristol (Br.)	Salisbury Plain
201	Lieut. A. E. B. Ashton	April 16,	Bristol (Br.)	Salisbury Plain
202	Lieut. F. A. P. Williams Freeman, R.N.	April 16,	Bristol (Br.)	Salisbury Plain
203	Com. O. Schwann, R.N.	April, 16	Bristol (Br.)	Salisbury Plain
204	Capt. P. W. L. Broke-Smith	April 16,	Bristol (Br.)	Brooklands
205	Lieut. L. C. Rodgers-Harrison*	April 16,	Bristol (Br.)	Salisbury Plain
206	Sub.-Lieut. C. H. K. Edmonds, R.N.	April 16,	Bristol (Br.)	Salisbury Plain
207	Mr. D. G. Young	April 16,	Burgess-Wright (Sop.)	Brooklands
208	Mr. L. A. Tremlett	April 30,	Bleriot monoplane (Bl.)	Hendon
209	Lieut. J. D. Mackworth	April 30,	Bristol (Br.)	Brooklands
210	Lieut. E. F. Chinnery	April 30,	Deperdussin monoplane (Dep.)	Brooklands
211	Mr. J. R. Duigan	April 30,	Avro (Av.)	Brooklands
212	Lieut. H. C. Fielding	April 30,	Bristol (Br.)	Brooklands
213	Maj. Sir A. Bannerman, Bart.	April 30,	Bristol (Br.)	Brooklands
214	Lieut. A. Hartree	May 14,	Bristol (Br.)	Salisbury Plain
215	Lieut. G. S. Shephard	May 14,	Bristol (Br.)	Brooklands
216	Lieut. D. S. Lewis	May 14,	Bristol (Br.)	Brooklands
217	Capt. Godfrey Paine, R.N.	May 14,	Short (N.S.)	Eastchurch
218	Mr. H. C. Biard	June 4,	Howard-Wright (G.W.)	Hendon
219	Mr. H. P. Nesham	June 4,	Bristol (Br.)	Brooklands
220	Mr. C. L. Campbell*	June 4,	Bristol (Br.)	Salisbury Plain
221	Mr. F. H. Fowler	June 4,	Howard-Wright (G.W.)	Hendon
222	Mr. T. O'B. Hubbard	June 4,	Howard-Wright (G.W.)	Hendon
223	Mr. M. R. N. Jennings	June 4,	Bristol (Br.)	Salisbury Plain
224	*Mons. A. Potet (Fr.)*	June 4,	Bleriot monoplane (Bl.)	Hendon

No. of Cert.	Candidate	Date granted	Machines used for tests	Where qualified
		1912		
225	Mr. R. T. Gates	June 4,	Howard-Wright (G.W.)	Hendon
226	Lieut. D. Percival	June 4,	Bristol (Br.)	Salisbury Plain
227	2nd-Cpl. Frank Ridd	June 4,	Bristol (C.F.S.)	Salisbury Plain
228	Lieut. L. Dawes	June 4,	Bristol (Br.)	Salisbury Plain
229	Lieut. J. N. Fletcher	June 4,	Cody (Cod.)	Laffan's Plain
230	Lieut. B. T. James	June 4,	Howard-Wright (G.W.)	Hendon
231	Mr. Marcus D. Manton	June 4,	Howard-Wright (G.W.)	Hendon
232	St.-Sergt. R. H. V. Wilson*	June 18,	Bristol (C.F.S.)	Salisbury Plain
233	Lieut. D. L. Arthur*	June 18,	Bristol monoplane (Br.)	Brooklands
234	*Lieut. Ercole (It.)*	June 18,	Bristol monoplane (Br.)	Salisbury Plain
235	*Mons. P. Dubois (Fr.)*	June 18,	Deperdussin monoplane (Dep.)	Hendon
236	Capt. J. H. W. Becke	June 18,	Bristol (Br.)	Brooklands
237	Mr. N. S. Roupell	June 18,	Howard-Wright (G.W.)	Hendon
238	Mr. E. H. Morriss	June 18,	Howard-Wright (G.W.)	Hendon
239	Capt. A. D. Carden	June 18,	Dunne	Eastchurch
240	Capt. H. C. Agnew	July 2,	Bristol (Br.)	Brooklands
241	Maj. L. B. Moss	July 2,	Bristol (Br.)	Salisbury Plain
242	Capt. T. I. Webb-Bowen	July 2,	Henry Farman (Sop.)	Brooklands
243	Mr. V. H. N. Wadham	July 16,	Henry Farman (Sop.)	Brooklands
244	Lieut. P. L. W. Herbert	July 16,	Henry Farman (Sop.)	Brooklands
245	2nd-Lieut. A. Christie	July 16,	Bristol (Br.)	Brooklands
246	Lieut. H. I. Bulkeley	July 16,	Bristol (Br.)	Brooklands
247	Lieut. E. V. Anderson*	July 16,	Bristol (Br.)	Brooklands
248	Mr. R. H. Kershaw	July 16,	Howard-Wright (G.W.)	Hendon
249	Lieut. K. R. Shaw	July 16,	Bristol (Br.)	Salisbury Plain
250	Mr. R. A. Lister	July 16,	Bristol (Br.)	Salisbury Plain
251	Mr. H. Sweetman-Powell	July 24,	Burgess-Wright (Sop.)	Brooklands
252	Lieut. H. L. Reilly	July 24,	Deperdussin monoplane (Dep.)	Hendon
253	Air-Mech. W. V. Strugnell	July 24,	Bristol (C.F.S.)	Salisbury Plain
254	Lieut. F. M. Worthington-Wilmer	July 24,	Bristol (Br.)	Brooklands
255	Capt. R. C. W. Alston	July 24,	Henry Farman (Sop.)	Brooklands
256	Lieut. C. A. Bettington*	July 24,	Bristol monoplane (Br.)	Salisbury Plain
257	Capt. C. Darbyshire	July 24,	Vickers monoplane (Vic.)	Brooklands
258	Mr. R. W. R. Gill	July 24,	Deperdussin monoplane (Dep.)	Hendon
259	Mr. E. Petre*	July 24,	Handley.Page monoplane (H.P.)	Fairlop
260	Lieut. F. F. Waldron	July 24,	Bristol (Br.)	Brooklands
261	Mr. H. R. Simms	July 24,	Avro (Av.)	Brooklands
262	Pte. J. Edmonds, R.M.L.I.	July 30,	Short (N.S.)	Eastchurch
263	Mr. Sydney Pickles	July 30,	Bristol (Br.)	Brooklands
264	Maj. J. F. A. Higgins	July 30,	Bristol (Br.)	Brooklands
265	Eng.-Lieut. E. F. Briggs, R.N.	July 30,	Short (N.S.)	Eastchurch
266	Capt. C. P. Nicholas	July 30,	Bristol (Br.)	Brooklands
267	Lieut. K. P. Atkinson	July 30,	Bristol (Br.)	Brooklands
268	Mr. R. G. Holyoake	Aug. 13,	Bristol (Br.)	Brooklands
269	Air-Mech. W. T. J. Mc-Cudden	Aug. 13,	Bristol (C.F.S.)	Salisbury Plain
270	Maj. H. M. Trenchard	Aug. 13,	Henry Farman (Sop.)	Brooklands
271	Lieut. R. Cholmondeley	Aug. 13,	Grahame-White (G.W.)	Hendon
272	Capt. J. M. Salmond	Aug. 13,	Grahame-White (G.W.)	Hendon
273	Capt. A. M. MacDonell	Aug. 13,	Bristol (Br.)	Brooklands
274	Mr. W. S. Hedley	Aug. 13,	Henry Farman (Sop.)	Brooklands
275	*Mr. W. J. Harrison (Fr.)*	Aug. 13,	Deperdussin monoplane (Dep.)	Hendon
276	St.-Sergt. W. Thomas	Sept. 3,	Short (C.F.S.)	Salisbury Plain

No. of Cert.	Candidate	Date granted	Machine used for tests	Where qualified
		1912		
277	Capt. R. H. L. Cordner	Sept. 3,	Bristol (C.F.S.)	Salisbury Plain
278	Mr. R. H. Barnwell	Sept. 3,	Bristol (Br.)	Brooklands
279	Capt. The Hon. C. Brabazon	Sept. 3,	Bristol (Br.)	Brooklands
280	Lieut. P. B. Joubert de la Ferté	Sept. 3,	Bristol (Br.)	Brooklands
281	Maj. E. B. Ashmore, M.V.O.	Sept. 3,	Bristol (Br.)	Brooklands
282	Lieut. C. G. S. Gould	Sept. 3,	Bristol (Br.)	Brooklands
283	Lieut. P. H. L. Playfair	Sept. 3,	Bristol (Br.)	Brooklands
284	Lieut. F. A. Wanklyn	Sept. 3,	Bristol (Br.)	Brooklands
285	*Mr. W. L. Brock (U.S.A.)*	Sept. 3,	Deperdussin monoplane (Dep.)	Hendon
286	Eng.-Art. T. O'Connor, R.N.	Sept. 3,	Short (C.F.S.)	Salisbury Plain
287	*Mons. E. Baumann (Swit.)*	Sept. 3,	Deperdussin monoplane and Caudron (Ew.)	Hendon
288	Lieut. P. Shepherd, R.N.	Sept. 17,	Short (C.F.S.)	Salisbury Plain
289	Mr. I. G. Vaughan-Fowler	Sept. 17,	Wright (Og.)	Eastchurch
290	Lieut. G. Wildman-Lushington, R.M.A.*	Sept. 17,	Short (C.F.S.)	Salisbury Plain
291	Mr. J. L. Hall	Sept. 17,	Bleriot monoplane (Bl.)	Hendon
292	Mr. S. Summerfield	Sept. 17,	Bristol (Br.)	Brooklands
293	Mr. E. W. Cheeseman*	Sept. 17,	Bristol (Br.)	Brooklands
294	Asst.-Pmr. G. S. Trewin, R.N.	Sept. 17,	Bristol (C.F.S.)	Salisbury Plain
295	Mr. E. F. Sutton	Sept. 17,	Caudron (Ew.)	Hendon
296	Lieut. J. W. Seddon, R.N.	Sept. 17,	Short (N.S.)	Eastchurch
297	Mr. H. G. Hawker	Sept. 17,	Henry Farman (Sop.)	Brooklands
298	Lieut. A. C. H. MacLean	Sept. 17,	Bristol (Br.)	Brooklands
299	Capt. C. L. Price	Sept. 17,	Bristol (Br.)	Brooklands
300	Lieut. G. B. Stopford	Sept. 17,	Bristol (Br.)	Brooklands
301	Mr. G. W. England*	Sept. 17,	Bristol monoplane (Br.)	Salisbury Plain
302	Mr. Vivian Hewitt	Oct. 1,	Bleriot monoplane	Rhyll
303	Capt. C. E. Risk, R.M.L.I.	Oct. 1,	Short (C.F.S.)	Salisbury Plain
304	Lieut. I. T. Courtney, R.M.L.I.	Oct. 1,	Short (C.F.S.)	Salisbury Plain
305	Capt. E. L. Ellington	Oct. 1,	Henry Farman (Sop.)	Brooklands
306	Mr. V. Yates	Oct. 1,	Bleriot monoplane (E.A.C.)	Eastbourne
307	Lieut. H. F. Glanville	Oct. 1,	Bristol (Br.)	Brooklands
308	Lieut. L. da C. Penn-Gaskell	Oct. 1,	Bristol (Br.)	Brooklands
309	Capt. H. C. MacDonnell	Oct. 1,	Bristol (Br.)	Brooklands
310	Mr. A. E. Geere	Oct. 1,	Vickers monoplane (Vic.)	Brooklands
311	2nd.-Lieut. D. R. Hanlon	Oct. 1,	Bristol (Br.)	Brooklands
312	Lieut. F. V. Holt	Oct. 1,	Bristol (Br.)	Brooklands
313	Capt. G. R. Miller	Oct. 1,	Bristol (Br.)	Brooklands
314	Mr. A. M. Wynne	Oct. 15,	Grahame-White (G.W.)	Hendon
315	Mr. J. H. James	Oct. 15,	Caudron (Ew.)	Hendon
316	Lieut. G. I. Carmichael	Oct. 15,	Bristol (Br.)	Brooklands
317	1st Air-Mech. V. C. Higginbotham	Oct. 15,	Avro (C.F.S.)	Salisbury Plain
318	2nd.-Lieut. D. L. Allen*	Oct. 15,	Grahame-White (G.W.)	Hendon
319	*Lieut. L. Loultchieff (Bulg.)*	Oct. 15,	Bristol (Br.)	Brooklands
320	Lieut. R. G. H. Murray	Oct. 15,	Bristol (E.A.C.)	Eastbourne
321	Dr. D. E. Stodart	Oct. 15,	Caudron (Ew.)	Hendon
322	Mr. E. Birch	Oct. 15,	Bleriot monoplane (Mel.)	Liverpool
323	Mr. W. L. Hardman	Oct. 15,	Bleriot monoplane (Mel.)	Liverpool
324	*Herr R. Hölscher (Ger.)*	Oct. 15,	Grahame-White (G.W.)	Hendon
325	Mr. E. N. Fuller	Oct. 15,	Grahame-White (G.W.)	Hendon
326	Mr. A. V. Bettington	Oct. 15,	Bristol monoplane (Br.)	Salisbury Plain
327	Capt. R. S. H. Grace	Oct. 15,	Bristol (Br.)	Salisbury Plain
328	Lieut. C. L. Courtney, R.N.	Oct. 15,	Short (N.S.)	Eastchurch
329	Mr. C. W. Wilson	Oct. 15,	Grahame-White (G.W.)	Hendon

No. of Cert.	Candidate	Date granted	Machine used for tests	Where qualified
		1912		
330	Pmr. E. R. Berne, R.N.*	Oct. 15,	Short (N.S.)	Eastchurch
331	Mr. Howard T. Wright	Oct. 15,	Henry Farman (Sop.)	Brooklands
332	Mr. H. W. Hall	Oct. 15,	Bristol monoplane (Br.)	Salisbury Plain
333	Elec. A. Deakin, R.N.	Oct. 15,	Short (N.S.)	Eastchurch
334	Bos'n H. C. Bobbett, R.N.	Oct. 15,	Short (N.S.)	Eastchurch
335	Capt. R. Boger	Oct. 22,	Bristol (Br.)	Brooklands
336	Lieut. A. M. Read	Oct. 22,	Bristol (Br.)	Brooklands
337	Mr. A. Payze	Oct. 22,	Bristol (Br.)	Brooklands
338	Lieut. F. E. Styles	Oct. 22,	Bristol (Br.)	Brooklands
339	Mr. N. S. Spratt	Oct. 22,	Deperdussin monoplane (Dep.)	Hendon
340	Capt. J. A. Chamier	Oct. 22,	Caudron (Ew.)	Hendon
341	2nd-Lieut. G. F. Pretyman	Oct. 22,	Bristol (Br.)	Brooklands
342	Lieut. E. L. Conran	Oct. 22,	Caudron (Ew.)	Hendon
343	Lieut. F. G. Small	Oct. 22,	Grahame-White (G.W.)	Hendon
344	Mr. H. H. James	Oct. 22,	Caudron (Ew.)	Hendon
345	Com. A. M. Yeats-Brown, R.N.	Oct. 22,	Grahame-White (G.W.)	Hendon
346	Capt. J. H. Gibbon	Oct. 29,	Bristol (Br.)	Brooklands
347	Lieut. G. A. Parker	Oct. 29,	Bristol (Br.)	Salisbury Plain
348	Capt. J. L. Lucena	Oct. 29,	Bristol (Br.)	Salisbury Plain
349	Mr. C. E. Foggin	Oct. 29,	Bleriot monoplane (E.A.C.)	Eastbourne
350	*Mons. E. L. Gassler* (*Swit.*)	Oct. 29,	Bleriot monoplane (E.A.C.)	Eastbourne
351	Capt. F. St. G. Tucker	Oct. 29,	Deperdussin monoplane (Dep.)	Hendon
352	Capt. R. Pigot	Oct. 29,	Bristol (Br.)	Brooklands
353	Mr. T. Grave	Oct. 29,	Bristol (Br.)	Brooklands
354	Capt. J. C. Halahan	Oct. 29,	Grahame-White (G.W.)	Hendon
355	Mr. D. C. Ware	Oct. 29,	Deperdussin monoplane (Dep.)	Hendon
356	Capt. O. de L. Williams	Nov. 12,	Bristol (Br.)	Salisbury Plain
357	Capt. H. Musgrave	Nov. 12,	Bristol (Br.)	Salisbury Plain
358	Lieut. the Hon. J. D. Boyle	Nov. 12,	Bristol (Br.)	Brooklands
359	Mr. F. W. Lerwill	Nov. 12,	Bristol (E.A.C.)	Eastbourne
360	Lieut. J. F. A. Trotter	Nov. 12,	Waterhen (L.F.S.)	Windermere
361	Ldg. Seaman H. Russell, R.N.	Nov. 12,	Short (N.S.)	Eastchurch
362	Lieut. R. M. Rodwell	Nov. 12,	Bristol (Br.)	Brooklands
363	Capt. F. G. Kunhardt	Nov. 12,	Bristol (Br.)	Salisbury Plain
364	Maj. A. B. Forman	Nov. 12,	Bristol (Br.)	Brooklands
365	Lieut. R. B. Kitson	Nov. 12,	Bristol (Br.)	Brooklands
366	Lieut. C. G. MacArthur, R.N.	Nov. 26,	Bristol (Br.)	Salisbury Plain
367	*Prince Serge Cantacuzene* (*Roum.*)	Nov. 26,	Bristol monoplane (Br.)	Salisbury Plain
368	Mr. John Alcock	Nov. 26,	Henry Farman (Ducq.)	Brooklands
369	Lieut. A. H. L. Soames	Nov. 26,	Vickers monoplane (Vic.)	Brooklands
370	Midshipman N. F. Wheeler, R.N.†	Dec. 17,	Bristol (Br.)	Salisbury Plain
371	*Mons. P. Gratien* (*Fr.*)	Dec. 17,	Bleriot monoplane (Bl.)	Hendon
372	P.O. J. C. Andrews, R.N.	Dec. 17,	Avro (C.F.S.)	Salisbury Plain
373	Capt. J. N. S. Stott	Dec. 17,	Vickers monoplane (Vic.)	Brooklands
374	Shipwright R. W. Edwards, R.N.	Dec. 17,	Short (N.S.)	Eastchurch
375	2nd.-Lieut. W. C. K. Birch	Dec. 17,	Grahame-White (G.W.)	Hendon

†Actually qualified on September 9th, 1911, when under age

No. of Cert.	Candidate	Date granted	Machine used for tests	Where qualified
		1912		
376	Mr. V. P. Taylor	Dec. 17,	Bristol (Br.)	Salisbury Plain
377	Lieut. R. Mills	Dec. 17,	Bristol (Br.)	Brooklands
378	Lieut. E. R. L. Corballis	Dec. 17,	Vickers (Vic.)	Brooklands
379	Lieut. R. V. Pollok	Dec. 17,	Vickers (Vic.)	Brooklands
380	Eng.-Art. F. Susans, R.N.	Dec. 17,	Short (N.S.)	Eastchurch
381	Ldg. Seaman G. Prickett, R.N.	Dec. 17,	Short (C.F.S.)	Salisbury Plain
382	Sub.-Lieut. G. W. W. Hooper, R.N.	Dec. 17,	Deperdussin monoplane (Dep.)	Hendon
		1913		
383	*Lieut. G. Negresco (Roum.)*	Jan. 7,	Bristol monoplane (Br.)	Salisbury Plain
384	Mr. W. Featherstone	Jan. 7,	Bristol monoplane (Br.)	Brooklands
385	Lieut. E. Todd	Jan. 7,	Bristol monoplane (Br.)	Brooklands
386	Lieut. G. W. Mapplebeck	Jan. 7,	Deperdussin monoplane (Dep.)	Hendon
387	Lieut. J. Empson*	Jan. 7,	Bristol (Br.)	Brooklands
388	Lieut. A. Ewing, R.N.	Jan. 7,	Bristol (Br.)	Brooklands
389	Capt. D. W. Powell	Jan. 7,	Bristol (Br.)	Brooklands
390	Mr. G. N. Humphreys	Jan. 7,	Caudron (Per.)	Brooklands
391	Lieut. A. B. Thompson	Jan. 7,	Bristol (Br.)	Brooklands
392	Lieut. L. W. B. Rees	Jan. 7,	Bristol (Br.)	Brooklands
393	Eng.-Art. S. T. Freeman, R.N.	Jan. 21,	Short (N.S.)	Eastchurch
394	Ldg. Seaman B. J. W. Brady R.N.	Jan. 21,	Short (C.F.S.)	Salisbury Plain
395	Ldg. Seaman A. J. Bateman, R.N.	Jan. 21,	Avro (C.F.S.)	Salisbury Plain
396	Sub.-Lieut. A. W. Bigsworth R.N.R.	Jan. 21,	Bristol (Br.)	Salisbury Plain
397	Lieut. F. W. Bowhill, R.N.R.	Jan. 21,	Bristol (Br.)	Salisbury Plain
398	Lieut. A. C. G. Brown, R.N.	Jan. 21,	Bristol (E.A.C.)	Eastbourne
399	Lieut. A. Shekelton	Jan. 21,	Bristol (Br.)	Brooklands
400	Capt. G. B. Richards	Jan. 21,	Bristol (Br.)	Brooklands
401	Mr. H. E. W. Macandrew	Jan. 21,	Henry Farman (Ducq.)	Brooklands
402	Asst.-Pmr. J. H. Lidderdale, R.N.	Jan. 21,	Maurice Farman (C.F.S.)	Salisbury Plain
403	Sub.-Lieut. R. L. G. Marix, R.N.R.	Jan. 21,	Bristol (Br.)	Salisbury Plain
404	Lieut. H. D. Vernon, R.N.	Jan. 21,	Bristol (Br.)	Salisbury Plain
405	Sub.-Lieut. H. A. Littleton, R.N.V.R.	Jan. 21,	Bristol (Br.)	Salisbury Plain
406	Mr. A. L. Russell	Jan. 21,	Caudron (Ew.)	Hendon
407	Mr. E. R. Whitehouse	Jan. 21,	Deperdussin monoplane (Dep.)	Hendon
408	Lieut. J. T. Babington, R.N.	Jan. 21,	Short (N.S.)	Eastchurch
409	Mr. H. A. Buss	Feb. 4,	Blackburn monoplane (Blac.)	Hendon
410	Mr. M. F. Glew	Feb. 4,	Blackburn monoplane (Blac.)	Hendon
411	Mr. H. Scott	Feb. 4,	Deperdussin monoplane (Dep.)	Hendon
412	Air-Mech. R. Collis	Feb. 4,	M. Farman (C.F.S.)	Salisbury Plain
413	Mr. C. Nevile	Feb. 4,	Bristol (Br.)	Brooklands
414	Capt. E G. R. Lithgow	Feb. 4,	Short (C.F.S.)	Salisbury Plain
415	Asst.-Pmr. E. B. Parker, R.N.	Feb. 18,	Short (N.S.)	Eastchurch
416	Lieut. M. W. Noel	Feb. 18,	Caudron (Ew.)	Hendon
417	2nd. Lieu.t. R. M. Vaughan	Feb. 18,	Bristol (Br.)	Salisbury Plain

No. of Cert.	Candidate	Date granted	Machine used for tests	Where qualified
		1913		
418	Mr. H. T. G. Lane	Feb. 18,	Bristol (Br.)	Brooklands
419	Mr. F. F. R. Minchin	Feb. 18,	Bristol (E.A.C.)	Eastbourne
420	Mr. J. Crawford-Kehrmann	Feb. 18,	Bristol (Br.)	Brooklands
421	Capt. W. G. H. Salmond	Feb. 18,	M. Farman (C.F.S.)	Salisbury Plain
422	Lieut. R. P. Ross, R.N.	Feb. 18,	M. Farman (C.F.S.)	Salisbury Plain
423	Lieut. J. R. B. Kennedy, R.N.*	Feb. 18,	M. Farman (C.F.S.)	Salisbury Plain
424	Mr. G. L. Temple	Feb. 18,	Caudron (Ew.)	Hendon
425	Lieut. D. A. Oliver, R.N.	Feb. 18,	Short (C.F.S.)	Salisbury Plain
426	Lieut. T. S. Creswell, R.N.*	Feb. 18,	Short (N.S.)	Eastchurch
427	Lieut. L. L. Maclean	Feb. 18,	Bristol (Br.)	Brooklands
428	*Mons. J. Teulade-Cabanes (Fr.)*	Feb. 18,	Bleriot monoplane (Bl.)	Hendon
429	Lieut. R. G. D. Small	Feb. 18,	Grahame-White (G.W.)	Hendon
430	Mr. J. B. Hall	Feb. 18,	Bristol (Br.)	Brooklands
431	Lieut. C. F. Lee	Feb. 18,	Bristol (Br.)	Brooklands
432	Mr. P. M. Muller	Feb. 18,	H. Farman (Ducq.)	Brooklands
433	Mr. W. P. Hodgson	Feb. 18,	Deperdussin monoplane (Dep.)	Hendon
434	2nd.-Lieut. R. A. Archer	Mar. 4,	Bristol (Br.)	Brooklands
435	2nd.-Lieut. L. G. Hawker	Mar. 4,	Deperdussin monoplane (Dep.)	Hendon
436	2nd.-Lieut. D. J. McMullen	Mar. 4,	Caudron (Ew.)	Hendon
437	Lieut. C. E. H. Rathbone, R.M.L.I.	Mar. 4,	Avro (C.F.S.)	Salisbury Plain
438	Sergt. W. G. Stafford	Mar. 18,	M. Farman (C.F.S.)	Salisbury Plain
439	Sergt. E. J. Street	Mar. 18,	M. Farman (C.F.S.)	Salisbury Plain
440	Lieut. L. C. Hordern*	Mar. 18,	Deperdussin monoplane (Dep.)	Hendon
441	2nd.-Lieut. C. G. G. Bayly	Mar. 18,	Caudron (Ew.)	Hendon
442	Mr. E. H. Lawford	Mar. 18,	Caudron (Ew.)	Hendon
443	Sergt. H. R. Vagg	Mar. 18,	Short (C.F.S.)	Salisbury Plain
444	Sergt. J. Kemper	April 1,	M. Farman (C.F.S.)	Salisbury Plain
445	1st.-Cl. Air Mech. J. C. McNamara	April 1,	M. Farman (C.F.S.)	Salisbury Plain
446	Ldg. Seaman P. E. Bateman, R.N.	April 1,	M. Farman (C.F.S.)	Salisbury Plain
447	Lieut. R. Fitzmaurice, R.N.	April 1,	Short (C.F.S.)	Salisbury Plain
448	Lieut. W. F. R. Dobie	April 1,	Bristol (Br.)	Brooklands
449	Lieut. N. Usborne	April 1,	Caudron (Ew.)	Hendon
450	Lieut. G. Blatherwick, R.N.	April 1,	Bristol (Br.)	Brooklands
451	Lieut. W. Picton-Warlow	April 1,	Bristol (Br.)	Brooklands
452	Mr. A. B. A. Thomson	April 1,	Bristol (E.A.C.)	Eastbourne

Note.—From this date the Certificates were dated back to the date on which the candidate had actually passed his tests, and hence forward they will be set out in chronological order.

		Date qualified		
453	Eng.-Art. H. Hackney, R.N.	Mar. 31,	Bristol (N.S.)	Eastchurch
454	Capt. G. W. Vivian, R.N.	Mar. 31,	Short (C.F.S.)	Upavon
455	Ldg. Seaman G. R. Ashton, R.N.	April 11,	Short (C.F.S.)	Upavon
456	Sergt. H. C. Wright	April 11,	Short (C.F.S.)	Upavon
457	Lieut. T. W. Mulcahy-Morgan	April 12,	Bristol (Br.)	Brooklands
458	Mr. J. H. A. Landon	April 12,	Bristol (Br.)	Brooklands
463	2nd.-Lieut. W. R. Reid	April 12,	Bristol (Br.)	Salisbury Plain
459	Mr. J. H. G. Torr	April 17,	Caudron (Ew.)	Hendon

No. of Cert.	Candidate	Date qualified	Machine used for tests	Where qualified
		1913		
460	Sub.-Lieut. R. E. C. Peirse, R.N.V.R.	April 22,	Bristol (Br.)	Brooklands
461	2nd.-Lieut. V. Waterfall	April 22,	Vickers (Vic.)	Brooklands
462	Mr. R. N. Wight*	April 22,	Vickers (Vic.)	Brooklands
464	Sergt. H. V. Robbins	April 22,	M. Farman (C.F.S.)	Upavon
465	Shipwright D. Shaw, R.N.	April 23,	Short (N.S.)	Eastchurch
466	Mr. H. C. Tower	April 23,	Bristol (Br.)	Salisbury Plain
467	Sergt. W. R. Bruce	April 23,	M. Farman (R.F.C.)	Salisbury Plain
468	Com. F. R. Scarlett, R.N.	April 24,	M. Farman (C.F.S.)	Upavon
469	Lieut. F. J. L. Cogan	April 30,	Bristol (Br.)	Brooklands
470	2nd.-Lieut. R. Marshall	April 30,	Bristol (Br.)	Salisbury Plain
471	2nd.-Lieut. M. R. Chidson	April 30,	Bristol (Br.)	Salisbury Plain
472	2nd.-Lieut. C. G. Hosking	April 30,	Bristol (Br.)	Brooklands
473	Mr. H. Stewart	April 30,	Caudron (Ew.)	Hendon
474	Mr. T. A. Rainey	May 2,	Bristol (E.A.C.)	Eastbourne
475	Sergt. J. Mead	May 2,	M. Farman (R.F.C.)	Montrose
476	Mr. L. H. Strain	May 2,	Bristol (Br.)	Brooklands
477	Mr. F. G. Andreae	May 5,	Vickers (Vic.)	Brooklands
478	Maj. N. J. G. Cameron	May 6,	Vickers (Vic.)	Brooklands
479	Lieut. U. J. D. Bourke	May 9,	Deperdussin monoplane (Dep.)	Hendon
480	Mr. J. G. Barron	May 10,	Deperdussin monoplane (Dep.)	Hendon
481	Lieut. F. G. Brodribb, R.N.	May 13,	Bristol (Br.)	Salisbury Plain
482	Mr. R. A. King	May 16,	H. Farman (Mel.)	Liverpool
483	Lieut. W. G. S. Mitchell	May 17,	Vickers (Vic.)	Brooklands
484	Maj. G. C. Merrick*	May 17,	Bristol (Br.)	Brooklands
485	*Mons. R. L. Desoutter (Fr.)*	May 19,	Bleriot monoplane (Bl.)	Hendon
486	Lieut. G. E. G. McClellan	May 20,	Bristol (Br.)	Brooklands
487	*Señor M. Zubiaga (Sp.)*	May 22,	Caudron (Ew.)	Hendon
488	*Signor T. H. Bayetto (It.)*	May 22,	Bleriot monoplane (Bl.)	Hendon
489	Shipwright C. V. Lacey, R.N	May 23,	Bristol (N.S.)	Eastchurch
490	St.-Surgn. H. V. Wells, R.N.	May 24,	Bristol (N.S.)	Eastchurch
491	Mr. R. O. Paterson	May 24,	Vickers (Vic.)	Brooklands
492	Lieut. P. A. Broder	May 26,	Bristol (Br.)	Brooklands
493	*Mons. P. Gandillon (Swit.)*	May 26,	Bleriot monoplane (Bl.)	Hendon
494	Lieut. W. C. Hicks, R.N.	May 27,	Caudron (Ew.)	Hendon
495	Lieut. G. Adams	May 29,	Short (C.F.S.)	Upavon
496	2nd.-Lieut. A. A. A. Knight	May 29,	Vickers (Vic.)	Brooklands
497	Capt. F. S. Wilson	May 29,	Bristol (Br.)	Brooklands
500	Asst. Pmr. C. R. F. Noyes, R.N.	May 29,	Bristol (N.S.)	Eastchurch
501	Lieut. H. D. Harvey-Kelly	May 30,	M. Farman (C.F.S.)	Upavon
498	Lieut. A. G. Power	June 2,	Grahame-White (G.W.)	Hendon
499	Lieut. M. W. Duncan	June 2,	Bristol (Br.)	Brooklands
502	Shipwright G. T. H. Pack, R.N.	June 2,	Short (C.F.S.)	Upavon
503	Lieut. A. B. Gaskell, R.N.	June 2,	M. Farman (C.F.S.)	Upavon
504	Mr. R. H. Carr	June 2,	Grahame-White (G.W.)	Hendon
505	Lieut. W. G. Sitwell, R.N.	June 3,	M. Farman (C.F.S.)	Upavon
506	Mr. F. W. Goodden	June 3,	Caudron (Ew.)	Hendon
507	Mr. F. Hudson	June 3,	Deperdussin monoplane (Dep.)	Hendon
508	Capt. G. M. Griffith	June 3,	Bristol (Br.)	Salisbury Plain
509	Capt. H. Fawcett, R.M.L.I.	June 3,	M. Farman (C.F.S.)	Upavon
510	Mr. E. B. Bauman	June 3,	Deperdussin monoplane (Dep.)	Hendon
511	*Mons. J. R. de Laplane (Fr.)*	June 12,	Bristol (Br.)	Salisbury Plain
512	Sub.-Lieut. D. C. S. Evill, R.N.	June 13,	Grahame-White (G.W.)	Hendon

No. of Cert.	Candidate	Date qualified	Machine used for tests	Where qualified
		1913		
513	Mr. G. L. Gipps*	June 13,	Bristol (Br.)	Salisbury Plain
514	Mr. F. P. Adams	June 13,	Bristol (Br.)	Salisbury Plain
515	Mr. Wm. Birchenough	June 13,	Grahame-White (G.W.)	Hendon
516	Lieut. R. Burns	June 13,	Bristol (Br.)	Salisbury Plain
517	2nd.-Lieut. C. F. Beevor	June 13,	Vickers (Vic.)	Brooklands
518	Lieut. E. O. Priestley, R.N.	June 14,	Bristol (Br.)	Salisbury Plain
519	Sergt.-Maj. A. Fletcher	June 16,	M. Farman (R.F.C.)	Montrose
520	Sergt.-Maj. A. H. Measures	June 16,	M. Farman (R.F.C.)	Montrose
521	Lieut. G. H. V. Hathorn, R.M.L.I.	June 16,	Short (C.F.S.)	Upavon
522	Sergt. C. Mullen	June 16,	M. Farman (R.F.C.)	Montrose
523	2nd.-Lieut. R. C. H. Bewes	June 17,	Caudron (Ew.)	Hendon
524	Sergt. C. E. Jarvis	June 17,	Avro (C.F.S.)	Upavon
525	Maj. W. Sefton Brancker	June 18,	Vickers (Vic.)	Brooklands
526	Mr. E. Prosser	June 18,	Caudron (Ew.)	Hendon
527	2nd.-Lieut. M. Noott	June 20,	Bristol (Br.)	Brooklands
528	*Capt. A. Popovici (Roum.)*	June 21,	Bristol monoplane (Br.)	Salisbury Plain
533	Lieut. A. W. S. Agar, R.N.	June 25,	Short (C.F.S.)	Upavon
529	Lieut. C. E. Maude, R.N.	June 26,	Avro (C.F.S.)	Upavon
530	Capt. H. H. Shott, D.S.O.	June 30,	Bristol (Br.)	Brooklands
531	2nd.-Lieut. A. V. Newton	June 30,	Bristol (Br.)	Brooklands
532	Lieut.-Col. A. B. Hamilton	June 30,	Bristol (Br.)	Salisbury Plain
534	Lieut. A. J. Miley, R.N.	July 1,	Bristol (Br.)	Salisbury Plain
535	2nd.-Lieut. R. F. Morkill	July 1,	E.A.C. (E.A.C.)	Eastbourne
536	Lieut. E. Osmond, R.N.	July 1,	Bristol (Br.)	Salisbury Plain
537	Mr. W. T. Warren	July 1,	Caudron (Ew.)	Hendon
538	1st Cl. Air-Mech. H. V. Jerrard	July 2,	B.E. (R.F.C.)	Netheravon
539	Capt. A. C. Barnby, R.M.L.I.	July 2,	Bristol (Br.)	Salisbury Plain
540	Lieut. R. E. Orton	July 2,	Bristol (Br.)	Salisbury Plain
541	1st Cl. Air-Mech. F. Pratt	July 3,	Bristol (R.F.C.)	Salisbury Plain
558	Mr. W. S. Roberts	July 3,	Bristol (E.A.C.)	Eastbourne
542	*Lieut. C. Beroniade (Roum.)*	July 4,	Bristol monoplane (Br.)	Salisbury Plain
543	*Lieut. A. Pascanu (Roum.)*	July 4,	Bristol monoplane (Br.)	Salisbury Plain
544	Mr. T. W. Elsdon	July 8,	Vickers (Vic.)	Brooklands
545	Mr. G. E. Harris	July 8,	Bristol (Br.)	Brooklands
546	Sir A. H. M. Sinclair, Bt.	July 8,	Grahame-White (G.W.)	Hendon
547	2nd.-Lieut. A. E. Morgan	July 8,	Bristol (Br.)	Brooklands
548	Lieut. A. C. Boddam-Whetham	July 8,	Grahame-White (G.W.)	Hendon
549	Sergt. E. E. Porter	July 9,	M. Farman (C.F.S.)	Upavon
550	Lieut. M. J. Ambler	July 10,	Caudron (Tem.)	Hendon
551	Lieut. H. Le M. Brock	July 10,	Deperdussin monoplane (Dep.)	Hendon
552	Mr. W. M. F. Pendlebury	July 11,	Bristol (Br.)	Brooklands
553	2nd.-Lieut. J. H. M. Stevenson	July 11,	Bristol (Br.)	Salisbury Plain
554	Shipwright C. B. Snow, R.N.	July 12,	Short (N.S.)	Eastchurch
559	1st Cl. Air-Mech. C. Gallie	July 12,	M. Farman (C.F.S.)	Upavon
555	Mr. H. Bradford	July 14,	Short (N.S.)	Eastchurch
556	Mr. H. P. G. Leigh	July 14,	Short (N.S.)	Eastchurch
557	Mr. G. A. J. Blundell	July 14,	Short (N.S.)	Eastchurch
560	*Herr H. Rolshoven (Ger.)*	July 14,	Avro (Av.)	Shoreham
561	Col. N. M. Smyth, V.C.	July 16,	Deperdussin monoplane (Dep.)	Hendon
562	Lieut. G. S. Low	July 16,	Bristol (Br.)	Brooklands
563	Mr. R. Grey	July 16,	Bristol (Br.)	Brooklands
564	Mr. E. T. Newton-Clare	July 17,	Vickers (Vic.)	Brooklands
572	Able Seaman G. Savill, R.N.	July 18,	M. Farman (C.F.S.)	Upavon
565	Mr. B. H. E. Howard	July 19,	Bristol (Br.)	Brooklands

No. of Cert.	Candidate	Date qualified	Machine used for tests	Where qualified
		1913		
566	Sub.-Lieut. I. H. W. S. Dalrymple-Clark, R.N.R.	July 19,	Caudron (Ew.)	Hendon
567	Lieut. B. F. Moore	July 21,	Grahame-White (G.W.)	Hendon
571	*Mons. M. Osipenko (Rus.)*	July 21,	Grahame-White (G.W.)	Hendon
568	Mr. R. R. Skene	July 21,	Bristol (Br.)	Brooklands
569	Lieut. A. C. H. A. Eales	July 21,	Grahame-White (G.W.)	Hendon
570	Capt. B. C. Fairfax	July 26,	Vickers (Vic.)	Brooklands
573	Sergt. W. J. Waddington	July 28,	Short (C.F.S.)	Upavon
578	Mr. S. J. V. Fill	Aug. 3,	E.A.C. (E.A.C.)	Eastbourne
574	Mr. E. L. M. Leveson-Gower	Aug. 4,	Bleriot monoplane (Bl.)	Hendon
575	Mr. L. A. Strange	Aug. 5,	Caudron (Ew.)	Hendon
579	1st Cl. Air-Mech. W. Smith	Aug. 5,	M. Farman (C.F.S.)	Upavon
580	1st Cl. Air-Mech. F. Dismore	Aug. 5,	Short (C.F.S.)	Upavon
581	Mr. F. M. T. Reilly	Aug. 5,	Bleriot monoplane (Bl.)	Hendon
582	Eng.-Art. P. H. McCartan, R.N.	Aug. 6,	M. Farman (C.F.S.)	Upavon
576	*Mons. M. Leverrier (Fr.)*	Aug. 7,	Caudron (Tem.)	Hendon
583	Sergt.-Maj. A. Levick	Aug. 8,	Short (C.F.S.)	Upavon
577	*Herr L. H. Jagenburg (Ger.)*	Aug. 9,	Caudron (Ew.)	Hendon
584	Mr. R. E. C. Penny	Aug. 9,	Caudron (Tem.)	Hendon
585	2nd.-Lieut. J. F. Mead	Aug. 11,	Bristol (Br.)	Brooklands
586	Shipwright W. Cole, R.N.	Aug. 13,	Short (N.S.)	Eastchurch
587	Capt. H. C. Jackson	Aug. 13,	Bristol (Br.)	Brooklands
588	Mr. Hereward de Havilland	Aug. 13,	Caudron (Ew.)	Hendon
589	Lieut. N. C. G. Cameron	Aug. 13,	Bristol (Br.)	Brooklands
590	Surg. F. G. Hitch, R.N.	Aug. 14,	Bristol (Br.)	Salisbury Plain
591	Mr. D. W. Clappen	Aug. 15,	Bleriot monoplane (Bl.)	Hendon
592	Lieut. C. C. Darley	Aug. 15,	Bristol (Br.)	Brooklands
593	*Mr. Gordon T. K. Wong (Ch.)*	Aug. 15,	Bristol (Br.)	Brooklands
594	Eng.-Art. W. F. Shaw, R.N.	Aug. 15,	Avro (Av.)	Shoreham
627	Lieut. R. J. Bone, R.N.	Aug. 16,	E.A.C. (E.A.C.)	Eastbourne
595	Capt. L. P. Evans	Aug. 20,	Bristol (Br.)	Brooklands
596	Mr. R. C. Powell	Aug. 20,	Bristol (Br.)	Brooklands
597	Lieut. R. E. Lewis	Aug. 20,	Bristol (Br.)	Brooklands
598	Mr. H. Webb	Aug. 20,	Vickers (Vic.)	Brooklands
599	Capt. C. F. Murphy	Aug. 20,	Bristol (Br.)	Salisbury Plain
601	P.O. J. C. Hendry, R.N.	Aug. 20,	Bristol (N.S.)	Eastchurch
600	2nd.-Lieut. O. G. W. G. Lywood	Aug. 21,	Bristol (Br.)	Salisbury Plain
602	2nd.-Lieut. B. M. B. Bateman	Aug. 26,	Bristol (Br.)	Salisbury Plain
603	Lieut. W. R. Crocker, R.N.	Aug. 28,	Short (N.S.)	Eastchurch
604	Sergt. F. E. Bishop, R.M.A.	Aug. 28,	Short (N.S.)	Eastchurch
605	Lieut. Lord George Wellesley	Aug. 28,	Bristol (Br.)	Salisbury Plain
606	Lieut. S. W. Smith	Aug. 29,	Vickers (Vic.)	Brooklands
607	2nd.-Lieut. Lord Ed. Grosvenor	Aug. 29,	Bristol (Br.)	Brooklands
608	Capt. C. P. Downer*	Aug. 29,	Vickers (Vic.)	Brooklands
609	Capt. L. E. O. Charlton	Aug. 29,	Bristol (Br.)	Brooklands
610	Mr. J. C. Joubert de la Ferté	Aug. 29,	Vickers (Vic.)	Brooklands
611	Arm. Mate R. Harper, R.N.	Aug. 29,	Short (N.S.)	Eastchurch
612	Capt. B. D. Fisher	Aug. 30,	Bristol (Br.)	Salisbury Plain
613	The Hon. F. W. L. Vernon	Aug. 30,	Bristol (Br.)	Salisbury Plain
614	Mr. J. J. Bland	Aug. 30,	Waterhen (L.F.S.)	Windermere
615	2nd.-Lieut. H. B. Strong	Sept. 3,	Bristol (Br.)	Brooklands
616	Mr. J. W. W. Slack	Sept. 8,	Wright (Bea.)	Hendon
617	Mr. V. G. Blackburn	Sept. 10,	Bristol (Br.)	Brooklands
618	Mr. W. H. S. Garnett	Sept. 10,	Bristol monoplane (Br.)	Salisbury Plain
619	2nd.-Lieut. L. Playfair	Sept. 11,	E.A.C. (E.A.C.)	Eastbourne
620	Lieut. N. M. Jenkins	Sept. 11,	Bristol (Br.)	Salisbury Plain

No. of Cert.	Candidate	Date qualified	Machine used for tests	Where qualified
		1913		
621	Lieut. H. J. A. Roche	Sept. 12,	Bristol (Br.)	Brooklands
622	Capt. A. J. Ellis	Sept. 12,	Vickers (Vic.)	Brooklands
623	Lieut. J. A. Cunningham	Sept. 12,	Bristol (Br.)	Brooklands
628	Carptr. W.O. L. R. Staddon, R.N.	Sept. 12,	Short (N.S.)	Eastchurch
624	Mr. C. Le de S. W. Roberts	Sept. 12,	Vickers (Vic.)	Brooklands
625	Mr. F. K. Haskins, R.N.	Sept. 13,	Vickers (Vic.)	Brooklands
626	Mr. C. Layzell-Apps	Sept. 13,	Vickers (Vic.)	Brooklands
629	Mr. F. G. Bevis	Sept. 13,	E.A.C. (E.A.C.)	Eastbourne
630	Eng.-Lieut. G. W. S. Aldwell R.N.	Sept. 15,	Short (N.S.)	Eastchurch
631	Eng.-Art. A. E. Case, R.N.	Sept. 17,	M. Farman (C.F.S.)	Upavon
632	Mr. N. Pemberton Billing	Sept. 17,	H. Farman	Brooklands
633	Mr. W. Watts	Sept. 17,	Caudron (Ew.)	Hendon
634	Mr. E. J. Addis	Sept. 17,	Vickers (Vic.)	Brooklands
635	Capt. F. A. Ferguson	Sept. 22,	Bristol (Br.)	Salisbury Plain
636	P.O. F. J. Hooper, R.N.	Sept. 22,	Short (N.S.)	Eastchurch
637	Eng.-Art. V. Rees, R.N.	Sept. 27,	Short (N.S.)	Eastchurch
638	Capt. G. H. Cox	Sept. 27,	Bleriot monoplane (Bl.)	Hendon
639	Mr. F. B. Halford	Oct. 2,	Bristol (Br.)	Brooklands
640	Eng.-Art. W. Badley, R.N.	Oct. 3,	Short (N.S.)	Eastchurch
641	Sir B. B. M. Leighton, Bt.	Oct. 3,	Grahame-White (G.W.)	Hendon
642	Capt. M. S. Keogh, R.N.	Oct. 4,	Short (N.S.)	Eastchurch
643	Mr. I. B. Hart-Davies	Oct. 6,	Grahame-White (G.W.)	Hendon
644	Capt. G. Henderson	Oct. 7,	Bristol (Br.)	Brooklands
645	Lieut. R. M. Boger	Oct. 8,	Bristol (Br.)	Brooklands
646	Mr. C. Draper	Oct. 9,	Grahame-White (G.W.)	Hendon
647	Lieut. E. T. R. Chambers, R.N.	Oct. 9,	M. Farman (C.F.S.)	Upavon
648	Lieut. G. L. E. Sherlock	Oct. 9,	Vickers (Vic.)	Brooklands
649	Lieut. C. B. Spence	Oct. 13,	Bristol (Br.)	Brooklands
650	*Herr Willy Voight (Ger.)*	Oct. 15,	Bristol (Br.)	Salisbury Plain
651	Lieut. E. R. C. Nanson, R.N.R.	Oct. 15,	M. Farman (C.F.S.)	Upavon
652	Capt. H. C. Jenings	Oct. 16,	Caudron (Ew.)	Hendon
653	Capt. T. C. Mudie	Oct. 16,	Bristol (Br.)	Brooklands
654	Eng.-Lieut. C. D. Breese, R.N.	Oct. 16,	M. Farman (C.F.S.)	Upavon
666	Lieut. C. H. Collett, R.M.A.	Oct. 21,	Avro (C.F.S.)	Upavon
683	Lieut. R. H. Walley, R.N.R.	Oct. 21,	M. Farman (C.F.S.)	Upavon
655	Mr. L. C. Kidd	Oct. 22,	Grahame-White (G.W.)	Hendon
667	Capt. C. F. Kilner, R.M.L.I.	Oct. 22,	B.E. (C.F.S.)	Upavon
656	Asst. Pmr. V. H. Coles R.N.R.	Oct. 22,	Vickers (Vic.)	Brooklands
668	Or.-Tel. R. M. Stirling, R.N.	Oct. 22,	Bristol (N.S.)	Eastchurch
657	Capt. G. C. B. Buckland	Oct. 22,	Bristol (Br.)	Salisbury Plain
658	Mr. J. W. H. Scotland	Oct. 23,	Caudron (Ha.)	Hendon
659	Maj. G. Kinsman	Oct. 24,	Vickers (Vic.)	Brooklands
660	Mr. R. K. Pierson	Oct. 24,	Vickers (Vic.)	Brooklands
661	Mr. M. B. Blake	Oct. 24,	Grahame-White (G.W.)	Hendon
662	Lieut. A. Gallaher	Oct. 24,	Bristol (Br.)	Salisbury Plain
663	Lieut. K. F. W. Dunn	Oct. 24,	Bristol (Br.)	Salisbury Plain
669	W.O. W. F. Floyd, R.N.	Oct. 24,	Bristol (N.S.)	Eastchurch
664	Lieut. C. H. Oxlade, R.N.R.	Oct. 25,	E.A.C. (E.A.C.)	Eastbourne
665	Capt. C. G. Billing, R.N.	Oct. 27,	Caudron (Ew.)	Hendon
670	2nd.-Lieut. R. W. G. Hinds	Oct. 31,	Bristol (Br.)	Brooklands
671	Lieut. W. F. MacNeece	Oct. 31,	Bristol (Br.)	Brooklands
672	P.O. J. F. Grady, R.N.	Nov. 1,	M. Farman (C.F.S.)	Upavon

No. of Cert.	Candidate	Date qualified	Machine used for tests	Where qualified
	1913			
673	1st Cl. Air-Mech. W. H. Butt	Nov. 1,	M. Farman (C.F.S.)	Upavon
674	1st Cl. Air-Mech. E. E. Copper	Nov. 1,	M. Farman (C.F.S.)	Upavon
675	E. R. A. H. Nelson, R.N.	Nov. 1,	Bristol (N.S.)	Eastchurch
676	Lieut. de C. W. P. Ireland, R.N.	Nov. 1,	Bristol (N.S.)	Eastchurch
684	Ch. Arm. C. H. Whitlock, R.N.	Nov. 1,	Bristol (N.S.)	Eastchurch
677	Sergt. D. Patterson	Nov. 4,	Short (C.F.S.)	Upavon
678	2nd.-Lieut. G. J. Malcolm	Nov. 5,	Vickers (Vic.)	Brooklands
679	Capt. T. H. C. Frankland	Nov. 5,	Vickers (Vic.)	Brooklands
680	2nd.-Lieut. S. H. Batty-Smith	Nov. 5,	Vickers (Vic.)	Brooklands
681	Sub.-Lieut. J. D. Harvey, R.N.	Nov. 6,	Bristol (Br.)	Brooklands
685	Sergt. F. Farrer	Nov. 7,	M. Farman (C.F.S.)	Upavon
682	2nd.-Lieut. M. W. Huish	Nov. 8,	Bristol (Br.)	Salisbury Plain
727	Com. M. Cumming, R.N.	Nov. 10,	M. Farman	Etampes
686	Lieut. the Hon. H. L. Pelham	Nov. 11,	Vickers (Vic.)	Brooklands
687	Lieut. H. F. Treeby*	Nov. 16,	Bristol (Br.)	Brooklands
688	2nd.-Lieut. W. R. E. Harrison	Nov. 21,	Bristol (Br.)	Salisbury Plain
689	Mr. H. S. N. Courtney	Nov. 22,	Bristol (Br.)	Salisbury Plain
706	Mr. W. H. Elliott	Nov. 22,	Avro (S.F.S.)	Shoreham
690	Lieut. R. J. F. Barton	Nov. 24,	Vickers (Vic.)	Brooklands
691	Sergt. J. McCrae	Nov. 24,	Short (C.F.S.)	Upavon
692	Shipwright H. H. Scott, R.N	Nov. 24,	M. Farman (C.F.S.)	Upavon
693	Capt. D. H. Macdonnel, D.S.O.	Nov. 25,	Vickers (Vic.)	Brooklands
694	Lieut. A. C. E. Marsh	Nov. 26,	Bristol (Br.)	Salisbury Plain
695	Lieut. C. Y. McDonald	Nov. 27,	Bristol (Br.)	Brooklands
696	2nd.-Lieut. G. H. Broadhurst	Nov. 29,	Bristol (Br.)	Brooklands
697	Mr. O. B. Howell	Nov. 29,	Vickers (Vic.)	Brooklands
698	Mr. J. M. R. Cripps	Dec. 2,	Grahame-White (G.W.)	Hendon
699	*Mr. R. G. U. von Segebaden (Swed.)*	Dec. 7,	Grahame-White (G.W.)	Hendon
700	Capt. M. G. Lee	Dec. 8,	Vickers (Vic.)	Brooklands
701	Sergt. D. Mitchell	Dec. 11,	M. Farman (C.F.S.)	Upavon
702	Capt. B. H. L. Hay	Dec. 11,	Bristol (Br.)	Salisbury Plain
703	Mr. H. R. Johnson	Dec. 11,	Caudron (Ew.)	Hendon
704	Mr. N. Howarth	Dec. 11,	Grahame-White (G.W.)	Hendon
707	Sergt. J. R. Gardiner	Dec. 11,	Short (C.F.S.)	Upavon
705	2nd.-Lieut. T. L. S. Holbrow	Dec. 13,	Caudron (Ew.)	Hendon
708	Mr. I. C. Macdonell	Dec. 17,	Bristol (Br.)	Brooklands
709	Mr. R. G. Duff	Dec. 18,	Vickers (Vic.)	Brooklands
710	Mr. J. L. Finney	Dec. 19,	Bristol (Br.)	Brooklands
711	Capt. H. C. T. Dowding	Dec. 20,	Vickers (Vic.)	Brooklands
712	Sergt. F. G. Bateman	Dec. 20,	M. Farman (R.F.C.)	Netheravon
713	Lieut. C. E. R. Bridson	Dec. 20,	Bristol (Br.)	Brooklands
714	Sub.-Lieut. G. R. Bromet, R.N.	Dec. 22,	Bristol (Br.)	Brooklands
715	Lieut. R. E. B. Hunt	Dec. 22,	E.A.C. (E.A.C.)	Eastbourne
716	Lieut. E. D. M. Robertson, R.N.	Dec. 22,	Bristol (Br.)	Brooklands
717	Mr. A. D. Badgery	Dec. 22,	Caudron (Ew.)	Hendon
718	Lieut. R. C. Halahan, R.N.	Dec. 24,	Bristol (Br.)	Salisbury Plain
719	Mr. C. F. Webb	Dec. 31,	Grahame-White (G.W.)	Hendon

Note.—At this stage the tests were altered by increasing the altitude to be attained by candidates to 100 metres (328 feet), and by stipulating that a descent and landing must be made from that height with the motor cut off.

No. of Cer.	Candidate	Date qualified	Machine used for tests	Where qualified
		1914		
720	Mr. R. J. Lillywhite	Jan. 1,	Grahame-White (G.W.)	Hendon
721	Sub.-Lieut. F. G. Saunders, R.N.V.R.	Jan. 1,	Bristol (Br.)	Brooklands
722	Mr. H. B. Martindale	Jan. 1,	Vickers (Vic.)	Brooklands
723	Mr. E. J. Fulton	Jan. 3,	Vickers (Vic.)	Brooklands
724	Lieut. H. E. M. Watkins, R.N.R.	Jan. 15,	Bristol (Br.)	Brooklands
725	Sub.-Lieut. J. R. W. Smyth-Pigott	Jan. 15,	Bristol (Br.)	Brooklands
726	Lieut. J. T. Call, R.N.	Jan. 15,	Bristol (Br.)	Brooklands
728	Mr. F. G. Dunn	Jan. 23,	Bleriot monoplane (Bl.)	Hendon
729	Mr. H. A. Cooper	Jan. 27,	Caudron (Ew.)	Hendon
730	Lieut. M. H. Monckton	Jan. 28,	Vickers (Vic.)	Brooklands
731	Mr. E. F. Norris	Jan. 28,	Grahame-White (G.W.)	Hendon
732	*Mr. F. A. Björklund (Swed.)*	Feb. 3,	Grahame-White (G.W.)	Hendon
733	Lieut. F. H. Pritchard	Feb. 10,	Vickers (Vic.)	Brooklands
734	Capt. A. B. Burdett	Feb. 10,	Bleriot monoplane (Bl.)	Hendon
735	Lieut. D. S. K. Crosbie	Feb. 16,	Vickers (Vic.)	Brooklands
736	Lieut. F. B. Binnie	Feb. 16,	Bristol (Br.)	Brooklands
737	Mr. R. P. Creagh	Feb. 16,	Vickers (Vic.)	Brooklands
738	Mr. J. P. Clark	Feb. 16,	Grahame-White (G.W.)	Hendon
739	Sub.-Lieut. H. A. Busk, R.N.R.	Feb. 17,	M. Farman (C.F.S.)	Upavon
740	Lieut. C. E. Robinson, R.M.L.I.	Feb. 19,	M. Farman (C.F.S.)	Upavon
746	2nd.-Lieut. W. W. A. Burn	Feb. 24,	M. Farman (C.F.S.)	Upavon
741	Lieut. H. M. Fraser, R.N.	Feb. 25,	Bristol (Br.)	Brooklands
742	Mr. W. J. Stutt	Feb. 25,	Bristol (Br.)	Salisbury Plain
743	Capt. A. Ross-Hume	Feb. 25,	Vickers (Vic.)	Brooklands
744	2nd.-Lieut. J. L. Jackson	Feb. 26,	Vickers (Vic.)	Brooklands
745	Sub.-Lieut. J. C. Spencer-Warwick, R.N.V.R.	Feb. 26,	Vickers (Vic.)	Brooklands
747	Ldg. Seaman F. Barnshaw, R.N.	Feb. 26,	M. Farman (C.F.S.)	Upavon
748	1st Cl. Air-Mech. T. Warren	Feb. 26,	M. Farman (C.F.S.)	Upavon
749	Mr. A. E. Barrs	Mar. 7,	Grahame-Wnite (G.W.)	Hendon
750	Mr. D. G. Murray	Mar. 11,	Caudron (Ew.)	Hendon
751	Lieut. H. A. Edridge-Green	Mar. 23,	Grahame-White (G.W.)	Hendon
752	Mr. J. B. Graham	Mar. 23,	Grahame-White (G.W.)	Hendon
753	Mr. C. F. Lan-Davis	Mar. 24,	Avro (Av.)	Brooklands
754	Lieut. V. S. E. Lindop	Mar. 24,	Grahame-White (G.W.)	Hendon
755	Lieut. W. G. Mansergh	Mar. 25,	Vickers (Vic.)	Brooklands
756	Lieut. A. S. Barratt	Mar. 26,	Bristol (Br.)	Salisbury Plain
757	Sergt. C. A. Hobby	Mar. 27,	M. Farman (C.F.S.)	Upavon
758	Capt. E. A. H. Fell	Mar. 27,	Bristol (Br.)	Salisbury Plain
759	Ldg. Seaman S. T. Clemens, R.N.	April 2,	M. Farman (C.F.S.)	Upavon
760	Mr. J. B. Price	April 3,	Caudron (Ew.)	Hendon
761	Lieut. A. K. D. George	April 3,	Bristol (Br.)	Salisbury Plain
762	2nd.-Lieut. J. B. Bolitho	April 15,	Bristol (Br.)	Salisbury Plain
763	*Prince Leon Sapieha (Austria)*	April 15,	Grahame-White (G.W.)	Hendon
764	2nd.-Lieut. J. B. Harman	April 15,	Bristol (Br.)	Salisbury Plain

No. Cert.	Candidate	Date qualified	Machine used for tests	Where qualified
		1914		
765	Mr. O. Lancaster	April 15,	Waterhen (L.F.S.)	Windermere
766	*Comte Jacques de Fitz-James (Fr.)*	April 16,	Vickers (Vic.)	Brooklands
767	Mr. E. V. S. Wilberforce	April 16,	Vickers (Vic.)	Brooklands
768	Mr. M. Dawson	April 16,	Vickers (Vic.)	Brooklands
769	Mr. G. Carruthers	April 21,	Caudron (Ew.)	Hendon
770	Mr. G. C. Gold	April 21,	Bleriot monoplane (Bl.)	Hendon
771	Lieut. P. S. Myburgh	April 21,	Bristol (Br.)	Salisbury Plain
772	Lieut. R. H. Verney	April 22,	Caudron (Ew.)	Hendon
773	Lieut. W. H. D. Acland	April 22,	Vickers (Vic.)	Brooklands
774	Mr. W. Rowland Ding	April 27,	Wright (Bea.)	Hendon
775	Air-Mech. A. J. Locker	April 28,	Bristol (Br.)	Salisbury Plain
776	Mr. E. Parker	April 29,	Grahame-White (G.W.)	Hendon
777	Lieut. W. A. Underhill	May 10,	Vickers (Vic.)	Brooklands
778	Mr. R. J. Mac G. Hurst	May 10,	Vickers (Vic.)	Brooklands
779	2nd.-Lieut. C. E. C. Rabagliati	May 11,	Bristol (Br.)	Brooklands
780	*Mr. F. Curtis (U.S.A.)*	May 11,	Caudron (Cau.)	Hendon
781	2nd.-Lieut. J. A. Liddell	May 14,	Vickers (Vic.)	Brooklands
782	Mr. R. M. M. Murray	May 14,	Vickers (Vic.)	Brooklands
783	Mr. M. G. Smiles	May 14,	Grahame-White (G.W.)	Hendon
784	Mr. V. Mahl	May 14,	Sopwith (Sop.)	Brooklands
785	Mr. B. H. Piercy	May 18,	Grahame-White (G.W.)	Hendon
786	Mr. B. F. Hale	May 18,	Farman (S.F.S.)	Shoreham
787	Maj. E. H. Phillips	May 19,	Vickers (Vic.)	Brooklands
788	Capt. A. G. Moore	May 19,	Grahame-White (G.W.)	Hendon
789	Lieut. N. Wood-Smith	May 20,	Vickers (Vic.)	Brooklands
790	Lieut. J. B. T. Leighton	May 20,	Vickers (Vic.)	Brooklands
793	Cpl. A. C. Robins	May 21,	M. Farman (R.F.C.)	Netheravon
791	Lieut. G. D. Mills	May 22,	Bristol (Br.)	Brooklands
792	*Mons. R. E. Lagrange (Bel.)*	May 22,	Bristol (Br.)	Brooklands
794	Lieut. I. M. Bonham-Carter	May 25,	M. Farman (C.F.S.)	Upavon
795	Mr. L. Parker	May 28,	Bristol (Br.)	Brooklands
796	Mr. P. H. Maskell	May 28,	Farman (S.F.S.)	Shoreham
797	Lieut. G. C. Carpenter	May 29,	Grahame-White (G.W.)	Hendon
798	Lieut. J. Collins	May 29,	Vickers (Vic.)	Brooklands
799	Mr. H. Racine-Jacques	May 29,	Bristol (Br.)	Brooklands
800	Mr. T. S. Duncan	May 30,	Vickers (Vic.)	Brooklands
801	Mr. R. P. Cannon	May 30,	Farman (S.F.S.)	Shoreham
802	Mid. D. S. Don, R.N.	June 2,	Bristol (Br.)	Brooklands
803	Lieut. K. R. Van der Spuy	June 2,	M. Farman (C.F.S.)	Upavon
804	Sub.-Lieut. L. Tomkinson, R.N.	June 2,	M. Farman (C.F.S.)	Upavon
805	Mr. A. Maskell	June 2,	Farman (S.F.S.)	Shoreham
806	Mr. G. E. Cowley	June 3,	Grahame-White (G.W.)	Hendon
807	Mr. G. J. Lusted	June 3,	Farman (S.F.S.)	Shoreham
808	*Herr C. Weber (Hung.)*	June 5,	Grahame-White (G.W.)	Hendon
809	Mr. R. H. Steinbach	June 6,	Vickers (Vic.)	Brooklands
810	Mr. J. P. Wilson	June 8,	Vickers (Vic.)	Brooklands
811	Lieut. J. E. Tennent	June 9,	Vickers (Vic.)	Brooklands
832	Lieut. E. C. Emmett	June 9,	M. Farman (C.F.S.)	Upavon
812	Mr. G. H. Eastwood	June 9,	Bristol (Br.)	Brooklands
813	Mr. J. Lankester Parker	June 18,	Vickers (Vic.)	Brooklands
814	Mr. R. Chambers	June 18,	Bristol (Br.)	Brooklands
815	Mr. L. Gresley	June 19,	Bristol (Br.)	Brooklands
816	Lieut. B. E. Smythies	June 19,	Bristol (Br.)	Brooklands
817	Lieut. F. H. Eberti	June 24,	Vickers (Vic.)	Brooklands
818	Mid. G. C. L. Dalley, R.N.	June 24,	Wright (Bea.)	Hendon
819	Lieut. L. F. Richard	June 24,	Bristol (Br.)	Brooklands
820	Lieut. C. Nugent	June 24,	Bristol (Br.)	Brooklands

No. of Cert.	Candidate	Date qualified	Machine used for tests	Where qualified
		1914		
821	Capt. H. E. C. Walcot	June 24,	Bristol (Br.)	Brooklands
822	Lieut. G. S. Creed	June 24,	M. Farman (C.F.S.)	Upavon
823	Lieut. B. H. Turner	June 24,	M. Farman (C.F.S.)	Upavon
824	Sub.-Lieut. H. G. Wanklyn, R.N.R.	June 24,	M. Farman (C.F.S.)	Upavon
825	Mr. J. G. Miller	June 26,	Vickers (Vic.)	Brooklands
826	Mr. R. S. McGregor	June 26,	Caudron (Cau.)	Hendon
827	Capt. G. P. Wallace	June 29,	B.E. (C.F.S.)	Upavon
828	Lieut. G. L. Farie	June 30,	M. Farman (C.F.S.)	Upavon
829	Mr. D. Gwynne	June 30,	E.A.C. (E.A.C.)	Eastbourne
838	1st. Cl. Air-Mech. W. B. Power	July 1,	M. Farman (C.F.S.)	Upavon
830	Mr. W. H. Charlesworth	July 1,	Bristol (Br.)	Brooklands
831	Mr. J. E. B. Thornely	July 5,	E.A.C. (E.A.C.)	Eastbourne
833	Sub.-Lieut. F. Barr, R.N.R.	July 9,	M. Farman (C.F.S.)	Upavon
834	Capt. J. F. A. Kane	July 9,	Vickers (Vic.)	Brooklands
835	Mr. W. H. Treloar	July 9,	Bristol (Br.)	Brooklands
836	Mr. C. C. Godwin	July 9,	Bristol (Br.)	Brooklands
837	Mr. W. D. South	July 9,	Bleriot monoplane (Bl.)	Brooklands
839	Mtr.-Mariner A. W. Clemson, R.N.R.	July 14,	Vickers (Vic.)	Brooklands
840	Lieut. A. St. J. M. Warrand	July 14,	Vickers (Vic.)	Brooklands
841	Mr. T. F. Rutledge	July 14,	Bristol (Br.)	Brooklands
842	R. Adml. M. E. F. Kerr, R.N.	July 14,	Sopwith	Eleusis
843	Mr. P. D. Robinson	July 16,	Grahame-White (G.W.)	Hendon
844	1st. Cl. Stoker H. J. Lloyd, R.N.	July 17,	M. Farman (C.F.S.)	Upavon
845	Mr. W. C. Adamson	July 17,	Bristol (Br.)	Brooklands
846	*Mr. S. MacGordon (U.S.A.)*	July 17,	Sopwith (Sop.)	Brooklands
847	Mr. J. S. B. Winter	July 18,	Grahame-White (G.W.)	Hendon
848	Mr. H. P. Lowe	July 20,	Grahame-White (G.W.)	Hendon
849	Mr. A. G. Shepherd	July 21,	Grahame-White (G.W.)	Hendon
850	1st. Cl. Air-Mech. W. P. Parker	July 21,	M. Farman (C.F.S.)	Upavon
855	Air-Mech. V. C. Judge	July 21,	M. Farman (C.F.S.)	Upavon
851	Lieut. T. R. Wells	July 21,	Vickers (Vic.)	Brooklands
852	Lieut. A. G. Gillman	July 21,	Vickers (Vic.)	Brooklands
853	Capt. H. T. Lumsden	July 22,	Vickers (Vic.)	Brooklands
854	Mr. T. Hinshelwood	July 27,	Vickers (Vic.)	Brooklands
856	Mr. F. A. Arcier	July 28,	Caudron (Ha.)	Hendon
857	Lieut. G. A. K. Lawrence	July 28,	Bristol (Br.)	Brooklands
858	Lieut. E. R. Coles	July 28,	Bristol (Br.)	Brooklands
864	Sergt. F. James	July 28,	M. Farman (C.F.S.)	Upavon
859	Mr. A. T. Crick	July 29,	Bleriot monoplane (Bl.)	Brooklands
860	Lieut. J. D. G. Sanders	July 30,	Bristol (Br.)	Brooklands
861	Fl.-Sergt. H. McGrane	July 30,	M. Farman (C.F.S.)	Upavon
862	Sergt.-Maj. F. H. Unwin	Aug. 3,	M. Farman (R.F.C.)	Netheravon
863	Sergt. A. R. May	Aug. 4,	M. Farman (R.F.C.)	Netheravon

APPENDIX F

LIST OF BRITISH SUBJECTS WHO QUALIFIED FOR AVIATORS' CERTIFICATES IN FRANCE, UP TO AND INCLUDING AUGUST 4TH, 1914

Explanatory Note.—It should be borne in mind that several of the names on this list will also be found in the list of those who took out English certificates. Those pilots who were subsequently killed in flying accidents prior to Aug. 4th, 1914, are indicated by asterisks.

No. of certif. issued by Ae. C. de F.	*Pilot*	*Make of aeroplane on which tests were passed*	*Date of Certif.*	*Date on which Certif. sanctioned by R. Ae. C.*
5	Mr. Henry Farman	Henry Farman	Jan. 7, 1909	
6	Mr. Maurice Farman	Maurice Farman	Nov. 18, 1909	
9	Mr. Hubert Latham (Anglo Fr.)	Antoinette monoplane	Aug. 17, 1909	
23	The Hon. C. S. Rolls*	Wright	Jan. 6, 1910	
24	Mr. Mortimer Singer	Henry Farman	Jan. 6, 1910	
30	Mr. C. Grahame-White	Henry Farman	Jan. 4, 1910	
40	Mr. J. T. C. Moore-Brabazon	Voisin	May 8, 1910	
71	Capt. Bertram Dickson	Henry Farman	April 19, 1910	
72	Mr. W. D. McArdle	Bleriot monoplane	April 19, 1910	
75	Mr. Graham Gilmour*	Bleriot monoplane	April 19, 1910	
82	Lieut. L. D. L. Gibbs, R.F.A.	Henry Farman	July 10, 1910	
126	Mr. R. Loraine	Henry Farman	July 21, 1910	
151	Mr. Somers-Somerset	Bleriot monoplane	Aug. 1, 1910	
212	Mr. H. Melly	Bleriot monoplane	Aug. 9, 1910	
213	Mr. H. Harding	J.A.P. monoplane	Aug. 9, 1910	
214	Mr. E. Archer	Bleriot monoplane	Aug. 9, 1910	
231	Mr. W. Vladimir Smith*	Sommer	Sept. 19, 1910	
259	Mr. C. R. Esterre	Antoinette monoplane	Oct. 4, 1910	
260	Capt. C. J. Burke	Henry Farman	Oct. 4, 1910	
272	Mr. E. Paul	Bleriot monoplane	Oct. 19, 1910	
357	Mr. M. Weston	Henry Farman	Feb. 3, 1911	
358	Mr. G. Hamel*	Morane monoplane	Feb. 3, 1911	
404	Mr. G. E. J. Woodward	Henry Farman	March 3, 1911	
548	Lieut. J. C. Porte, R.N.	Deperdussin monoplane	July 28, 1911	
	Mr. D. Corbett-Wilson	Bleriot monoplane		Jan. 16, 1912
	Mr. James Grant			Mar. 12, 1912
	Mr. E. Scholefield			April 16, 1912
	Mrs. W. Buller			April 30, 1912
	Lieut. Barry Martyn			Sept. 17, 1912
	Mr. Ernest F. Unwin			Nov. 26, 1912
	Mr. C. H. Voss			Nov. 26, 1912
	Mr. C. Mellor			Dec. 17, 1912
	Mr. W. M. Macneill			Jan. 21, 1913
1213	Lieut. J. E. G. Burroughs*			Jan. 21, 1913
	Mr. H. C. Fuller			Jan. 21, 1913

No. of certif. issued by Ae.C. de F.	Pilot	Make of aeroplane on which tests were passed	Date of Certif.	Date on which Certif. sanctioned by R.Ae.C.
	Lieut. E. G. Harvey			Jan. 21, 1913
	Mr. E. Masterman			Jan. 21, 1913
	Lieut. F. L. M. Boothby, R.N.			Mar. 18, 1913
	Maj. E. M. Maitland			April 1, 1913
	Mr. C. Reynolds			April 1, 1913
	Mr. G. Leith			May 27, 1913
	Mr. F. Leith			May 27, 1913
	Lieut. A. Loftus Bryan			May 27, 1913
	Lieut. B. C. M. Western			July 1, 1913
	Lieut. W. R. Freeman			July 15, 1913
	Mr. S. Douglas			July 15, 1913
	Mr. A. Ford			July 29, 1913
	Capt. O. M. Conran			Aug. 13, 1913
	Lord John Carbery			Sept. 2, 1913
	Mr. H. L. Woodcock			Sept. 16, 1913
	Mr. G. Cruikshank			Oct. 28, 1913
	Mr. J. W. Madeley			Oct. 28, 1913
	Mr. R. Grey			Oct. 28, 1913
	Mr. M. H. Lockwood			Nov. 25, 1913
	Mr. H. A. F. Yates			Nov. 25, 1913
1568	Com. M. Cumming, R.N.	Maurice Farman	Dec. 5, 1913	
	Mr. W. Mansfield			Jan. 20, 1914
	Mr. L. Fry			Jan. 20, 1914
	Mr. B. D. Ash	Maurice Farman	Jan. 24, 1914	
	Mr. T. E. Hearn	Bleriot monoplane	Feb. 10, 1914	
	Mr. V. W. Eyre	Bleriot monoplane	Feb. 26, 1914	
	Mr. C. Ricou	Maurice Farman	April 10, 1914	
	Capt. J. E. Pearce	Maurice Farman	April 21, 1914	
	Mr. J. M. Landry	Bleriot monoplane	May 30, 1914	
1711	Capt. J. R. C. Heathcote	Maurice Farman	June 10, 1914	
1900	Mr. C. M. Smith	Maurice Farman	June 13, 1914	

APPENDIX G

LIST OF BRITISH SUBJECTS WHO QUALIFIED FOR AVIATORS' CERTIFICATES IN THE UNITED STATES OF AMERICA, UP TO AND INCLUDING AUGUST 4TH, 1914

Pilot	*Make of aeroplane on which tests were passed*	*Date of Certif.*	*Date on which Certif. sanctioned by R.Ae.C.*
Mr. Wm. Hoff			Feb. 27, 1912
Mr. W. M. Stark			April 30, 1912
Mr. M. M. Singh			July 2, 1914
Mr. R. B. Russell			July 16, 1912
Mr. A. C. Beech			Sept. 17, 1912
Mr. P. H. Reid (Can.)			Nov. 12, 1912
Capt. E. C. Bass			Sept. 16, 1913
Mr. H. S. Keating			Sept. 30, 1913
Mr. L. E. Brown			Oct. 14, 1913
Mr. H. J. Webster			April 7, 1914
Mr. T. M. R. Ross	Curtiss	April 13, 1914	

APPENDIX H

GLOSSARY OF TECHNICAL TERMS

Note.—These explanations are not necessarily the correct scientific definitions of the various words, but merely define the sense in which the terms are used in this book.

Aerobatics.—Evolutions voluntarily performed in an aeroplane other than those required for normal flying.

Aerobat.—A pilot who performs aerobatics.

Ailerons.—Movable flaps, usually hinged to the wing tips, used for balancing an aeroplane about her longitudinal axis, i.e., for maintaining lateral balance in the air.

Airframe.—That part of an aeroplane distinct from the engine and its accessories.

Airscrew.—A screw with helical blades designed to rotate in the air. In this book used to denote a tractor screw, driven by an engine.

Airspeed.—The speed of an aeroplane through the air. This may differ materially from its speed in relation to the ground. See Ground Speed.

Altimeter.—An aneroid barometer graduated to indicate height.

Amphibian.—An aeroplane capable of alighting on and taking off from either land or water.

Anemometer.—An instrument for measuring the velocity of the wind.

Bank.—The angle between the lateral axis of an aeroplane and the horizontal. *Verb:* To tilt an aeroplane on its side when turning, or side slipping.

b.h.p.—Brake horse power. The actual power output of an engine as recorded by a special testing apparatus. The b.h.p. of an engine frequently differs from the *rated* horse power.

Boss.—The central portion of an airscrew or propeller.

Boxkite.—A term used to denote an old-fashioned pusher biplane.

Bump.—A local eddy in the air which may cause a sharp disturbance of steady flight.

Bunt.—A difficult aerobatic manœuvre in which the pilot dives his aeroplane until it passes beyond the vertical and emerges on its back, flying in the opposite direction. It is the exact reverse of the first half of a loop.

Cabane.—A pyramid of struts to the apex of which the bracing wires of a monoplane's wings were attached. A *cabane* usually straddled the fuselage just in front of the pilot's cockpit.

Camber.—The convexity of the section of an aerofoil, e.g., the curve of the top surface of a wing.

Ceiling (i) *of an aeroplane.*—The limit of height to which the aeroplane will climb.

(ii) *of clouds.*—The height of the bottom of a cloud-layer above the earth's surface.

Chocks.—Blocks placed in front of the wheels of an aeroplane on the ground to prevent it from moving when the engine is started.

Chord.—The extreme width of an aeroplane's wing, measured from the leading to the trailing edge.

Cloche.—See Control Column.

Cockpit.—A portion of a fuselage or *nacelle* designed to accommodate one of the occupants of the aeroplane.

Control Column.—The lever, or pillar and wheel, by which the elevator and aileron controls are operated.

Cowling.—The metal covering over an engine.

Dihedral angle.—The planes of most aeroplanes are set at a dihedral angle in such a way that they are inclined upwards towards the tips.

Dope.—A type of varnish applied to the surfaces of an aeroplane which has the effect of taughtening the fabric.

Drift.—A sideways or crabwise movement of an aeroplane over the ground, caused by a wind moving across the aeroplane's line of flight.

Elevator.—The horizontal control surface by which the upward or downward inclination of an aeroplane is controlled.

Empennage.—See Tail Unit.

Fabric.—Linen used to form the outer covering of an aeroplane's frame-work.

Fairing.—A piece, usually of metal, added to any structure for the sole purpose of reducing its head resistance. *Verb:* to fair,—to add such a piece.

Fin.—A vertical surface set in front of the rudder by which the yawing of an aeroplane in flight is automatically prevented.

Flatten out (*Verb.*)—To change the path of flight from a glide or dive to a path parallel to the ground.

Flying boat.—An aeroplane of which the fuselage is designed, and constructed to form a boat which will support it on the water. *Cf.* Seaplane.

Fuselage.—The main structure or body of an aeroplane to which the main planes and tail unit are attached, and in which the crew sit. A pusher aeroplane usually has a *nacelle* instead of a fuselage.

Gap.—The distance between one plane and the next immediately above or below it.

Glide (*Verb.*)—An aeroplane is said to glide when it descends at a gentle angle with engine off.

Ground Speed.—The speed of an aeroplane in flight, relative to the ground. This may differ materially from the speed of the aeroplane through the air. See Airspeed.

Helicopter.—An aircraft which obtains its lift by the action of power-driven revolving screws or fans instead of by the reaction of fixed planes or wings. *Cf.* Ornithopter.

Joystick.—See Control Column.

Kathedral Angle.—The reverse of Dihedral Angle.

Leading Edge.—The front edge of an aeroplane's wing.

Longeron.—A main longitudinal member of a fuselage or *nacelle*. In a pusher biplane or monoplane the longerons supporting the tail were called tail booms.

Loop.—A complete revolution about the lateral axis of an aeroplane.

Monocoque.—An adjective applied to a fuselage having a smooth, rounded surface externally.

Nacelle.—A term applied to bodies enclosing crew, and/or engines when mounted on or between the planes of an aeroplane. If a *nacelle* extends backwards as far as the tail of the aeroplane, it is called a fuselage.

Ornithopter.—An aircraft designed to obtain its lift by the action of power-driven flapping wings, instead of by the reaction of fixed planes or wings. *Cf.* Helicopter.

Pancake (*Verb.*)—To stall an aeroplane when landing at too great a height above the ground, thus causing it to drop heavily and almost vertically.

Pitot tube.—A tube exposed to the air in which an aeroplane is moving by means of which the aeroplane's speed through the air is determined.

Pusher.—An adjective used to describe an aeroplane which derives its motive force from a propeller situated *behind* the main supporting surfaces or wings. *Cf.* Tractor.

Roll.—A complete revolution about the longitudinal axis of an aeroplane.

Rudder.—A movable vertical surface by which the yawing of an aeroplane is controlled by the pilot. *Cf.* Fin.

Rudderbar.—A bar, swivelling about its centre, by which the pilot operates the rudder with his feet.

Seaplane.—An aeroplane adapted for alighting or rising from water by the substitution of floats for wheels. *Cf.* Flying boat.

Sideslip.—A simple manœuvre useful for losing height. The aeroplane is tilted on its side and permitted to slide downwards, forwards, and sideways, under control. A sideslip may occur unintentionally if too much bank be applied on a turn. *Cf.* Skid.

Skid.—(i) A sideways and outwards motion of an aeroplane, occasioned by insufficient bank on a turn. If an aeroplane be allowed to skid too far it will stall. *Cf.* Sideslip.

(ii) A wooden member, resembling a hockey stick in shape,

set athwart the axle of the undercarriage in such a way that the curved end protrudes forwards and upwards, and thus prevents the aeroplane from nosing over on landing, in the event of the collapse of a wheel or tyre.

Slipstream.—The stream of air that is thrust backwards by a moving airscrew or propeller.

Span.—The overall width of an aeroplane.

Spin.—A dive during which the aeroplane is rotating about the direction of motion of its centre of gravity. Most aeroplanes will fall naturally in a spin as the result of a stall and they remain stalled so long as they are spinning.

Spiral.—A banked continuous gliding turn with engine off. Must be distinguished from a spin. In a spiral the aeroplane has flying speed, but throughout a spin it is stalled.

Stagger.—When the top wing of a biplane is set in advance of the bottom wing the planes are said to be staggered.

Stall (*Verb.*)—An aeroplane is said to stall when its air speed drops below that necessary to support it in the air. This causes the controls to become ineffective until flying speed has been regained.

Stalling Speed.—The air speed at which an aeroplane loses flying speed and stalls. This varies with different types of aeroplane, some of which will fly slower than others.

Stick.—See Control Column.

Strut.—A wooden or metal member forming a rigid connection between two parts of an aeroplane, e.g., interplane struts connecting the upper and lower wings of a biplane.

Stunts.—See Aerobatics.

Tail boom.—One of the main longitudinal members connecting the tail unit of a pusher aeroplane with the main wings. *Cf.* Longerons.

Tail unit.—The combination of stabilizing and controlling surfaces situated at the rear of an aeroplane. Normally it comprises tail plane, elevators, rudder and fin. Sometimes called an *empennage.*

Tailplane.—A fixed horizontal surface which maintains the longitudinal stability of the aeroplane.

Tail Skid.—A device, so arranged as to slide along the ground, upon which the tail of an aeroplane rests when the machine is on the ground.

Take-off (*Verb.*)—To cause an aeroplane to leave the ground in flight.

Taxi (*Verb.*)—An aeroplane is said to taxi when it moves along the ground under its own power.

Torque.—The resistance of an airscrew or propeller to rotation.

Tractor.—An adjective used to describe an aeroplane which derives its motive force from an airscrew situated in front of the main supporting surfaces or wings. *Cf.* Pusher.

Trailing Edge.—The after, or back, edge of an aeroplane's wing.

Undercarriage.—The part of an aeroplane which supports it on the ground and absorbs the shock of landing.

Vol Plané.—Early term for a glide.

Vol piqué.—Early term for a steep glide, or dive.

Warp.—An expression used to indicate a method of maintaining lateral control of an aeroplane by bending the flexible trailing edges of the wings upwards or downwards by means of wires, thus simulating the action of ailerons. *Cf.* Ailerons.

Yaw (*Verb.*)—An aeroplane is said to yaw when the fore and aft axis turns to left or right out of the line of flight.

Zoom.—An aeroplane is said to zoom when its path of flight is suddenly altered from a glide, dive or level flight into a steep climb.

INDEX A

AIRCRAFT

INDEX B

AERO ENGINES

INDEX C

PILOTS